Sixth Workshop on Arabic Natural Language Processing (WANLP 2021)

Held online due to COVID-19

Kiev, Ukraine
19 April 2021

ISBN: 978-1-7138-2972-0

Printed from e-media with permission by:

Curran Associates, Inc.
57 Morehouse Lane
Red Hook, NY 12571

CURRAN ASSOCIATES INC. proceedings.com

Some format issues inherent in the e-media version may also appear in this print version.

Association for Computational Linguistics
209 N. Eighth Street
Stroudsburg, Pennsylvania 18360

Phone: 1-570-476-8006
Fax: 1-570-476-0860

acl@aclweb.org

Additional copies of this publication are available from:

Curran Associates, Inc.
57 Morehouse Lane
Red Hook, NY 12571 USA
Phone: 845-758-0400
Fax: 845-758-2633
Email: curran@proceedings.com
Web: www.proceedings.com

WANLP 2021

The Sixth Arabic Natural Language Processing Workshop

Proceedings of the Workshop

April 19, 2021
Kyiv, Ukraine (Virtual)

Message from the General Chair

Welcome to The Sixth Arabic Natural Language Processing Workshop (WANLP 2021) held with EACL 2021 online. Over the years, WANLP has developed a growing reputation as a high quality venue for researchers and engineers working on Arabic NLP, where they share and discuss their ongoing work. The first in the WANLP series was held in Doha, Qatar (EMNLP 2014), followed by Beijing, China (ACL 2015), Valencia, Spain (EACL 2017), Florence, Italy (ACL 2019), and last year, online, with COLING 2020.

In this iteration of WANLP, we received 40 main workshop submissions (28 long and 12 short). While the total number of submissions is lower than WANLP 2020, it surpassed our expectations since we were concerned about a big drop due to the continuing COVID-19 pandemic and the temporal closeness to WANLP 2020 (less than six months earlier in December 2020). All papers submitted to the main workshop were reviewed by at least three reviewers each. Out of the 40 submissions, 27 were accepted: 18 long papers, and nine short papers (one as a demo paper). We selected 16 papers for oral presentation, and the rest as posters. We did not distinguish between long and short papers, or between oral and poster presentations in terms of quality.

WANLP 2021 included, for the first time, two shared tasks: The Nuanced Arabic Dialect Identification (NADI) shared task and the Sarcasm and Sentiment Detection in Arabic shared task (ArSarcasm). NADI received submissions from eight teams, seven of which have system descriptions in the proceedings; and ArSarcasm received submissions from 30 unique teams, 17 of which have system descriptions in the proceedings. The shared task system descriptions papers were reviewed by two reviewers each. Two additional shared task overview papers are included in the proceedings. The overview papers and the papers of the shared task winning systems were presented as talks in the workshop.

In addition to the first double shared tasks, WANLP 2021 was the first time our workshop was able to secure sponsorship funding (Thanks Google!) which we used to support student registrations. Also in another first for WANLP, we held parallel sessions for part of the workshop. This was a bittersweet decision: on one hand, we were sad to sacrifice the shared experience of the workshop, but on the other, we were happy to see WANLP growing... one step closer to becoming a small conference!

Finally, we would like to thank everyone who submitted a paper to the workshop, as well as all the members of the Program Committee, who worked hard to provide reviews on a very tight schedule.

Nizar Habash, General Chair, on behalf of the workshop organizers.

Website of the workshop: `http://wanlp2021.arabic-nlp.net/`

Workshop Organizers

General Chair

Nizar Habash, New York University Abu Dhabi, UAE

Program Chairs

Houda Bouamor, Carnegie Mellon University in Qatar
Hazem Hajj, American University of Beirut, Lebanon
Walid Magdy, University of Edinburgh, Scotland
Wajdi Zaghouani, Hamad Bin Khalifa University, Qatar

Publication Chair

Fethi Bougares, University of Le Mans, France
Nadi Tomeh, Université Sorbonne Paris Nord

Publicity Chair

Ibrahim Abu Farha, University of Edinburgh, Scotland
Samia Touileb, University of Oslo, Norway

Ex-General Chairs

Wassim El-Hajj, American University of Beirut, Lebanon
Imed Zitouni, Google, USA

Advisory Committee

Ahmed Ali, Qatar Computing Research Institute, Qatar
Fethi Bougares, Le Mans University, France
Hazem Hajj, American University of Beirut, Lebanon
Hend Alkhalifa, King Saud University, Saudi Arabia
Houda Bouamor, Carnegie Mellon University in Qatar
Imed Zitouni, Google, USA
Kamel Smaili, University of Lorraine, France
Kareem Darwish, Qatar Computing Research Institute, Qatar
Khaled Shaalan, The British University in Dubai, UAE
Khalid Choukri, ELDA, European Language Resource Association, France
Lamia Hadrich Belguith, University of Sfax, Tunisia
Mahmoud El-Haj, Lancaster University, UK
Mona Diab, George Washington University, USA
Muhammad Abdul-Mageed, UBC, Canada
Nadi Tomeh, University Sorbonne Paris Nord, France
Nizar Habash, New York University Abu Dhabi, UAE
Samhaa El-Beltagy, Nile University, Egypt
Wajdi Zaghouani, Hamad Bin Khalifa University, Qatar

Walid Magdy, University of Edinburgh, Scotland
Wassim El-Hajj, American University of Beirut, Lebanon

Program Committee

AbdelRahim Elmadany, UBC, Canada
Abdelmajid Ben-Hamadou, Sfax University, Tunisia
Ahmed Abdelali, Qatar Computing Research Institute, HBKU, Qatar
Ahmed Ali, Qatar Computing Research Institute, HBKU, Qatar
Alexis Nasr, University of Marseille, France
Almoataz B. Al-Said, Cairo University, Egypt
Aloulou Chafik, Univeristé de Sfax, Tunisia
Azzeddine Mazroui, University Mohamed I, Morocco
Bashar Alhafni, New York University Abu Dhabi, UAE
Bassam Haddad, University of Petra, Jordan
Bayan AbuShawar, Al Ain University, UAE
Chiyu Zhang, UBC Canada
El Moatez Billah Nagoudi, The University of British Columbia, Canada
Fethi Bougares, Le Mans University, France
Ganesh Jawahar, The University of British Columbia, Canada
Gilbert Badaro, American University of Beirut, Lebanon
Go Inoue, New York University Abu Dhabi, UAE
Haithem Afli, Cork Institute of Technology, Ireland
Hamada Nayel, Benha University, Egypt
Hamdy Mubarak, Qatar Computing Research Institute, HBKU, Qatar
Hazem Hajj, American University of Beirut, Lebanon
Hend Al-Khalifa, King Saud University, KSA
Houda Bouamor, Carnegie Mellon University in Qatar
Hussein AL-NATSHEH, Mawdoo3 Limited, Jordan
Ibrahim Abu Farha, University of Edinburgh, Scotland
Imed Zitouni, Google, USA
Kamel Smaili, University of Lorraine, France
Kareem Darwish, Qatar Computing Research Institute, HBKU, Qatar
Karim Bouzoubaa, Mohammad V University, Morocco
Karima Meftouh, Badji Mokhtar University, Algeria
Khaled Shaalan, The British University in Dubai, UAE
Khaled Shaban, Qatar University, Qatar
Khalid Choukri, ELDA, European Language Resource Association, France
Lamia Hadrich-Belguith, University of Sfax, Tunisia
Maram Hasanain, Qatar University, Qatar
Mona Diab, George Washington University, USA
Mourad Abbas, CRSTDLA, Algeria
Muhammad Abdul-Mageed, UBC Canada
Mustafa Jarrar, Bir Zeit University, Palestine
Nada Ghneim, Higher Institute for Applied Sciences and Technology, Syria
Nadi Tomeh, Université Sorbonne Paris Nord, France
Nasser Zalmout, Amazon Inc., USA
Nizar Habash, New York University Abu Dhabi, UAE
Nora Al-Twairesh, King Saud University, KSA
Obeida ElJundi, American University of Beirut, Lebanon
Omar Trigui, University of Sousse, Tunisia

Peter Sullivan, The University of British Columbia, Canada
Preslav Nakov, Qatar Computing Research Institute, HBKU, Qatar
Reem Suwaileh, Qatar University, Qatar
Riadh Belkebir, New York University Abu Dhabi, UAE
Sahar Ghannay, LIMSI, France
Salam Khalifa, New York University Abu Dhabi, UAE
Salima Harrat, École Normale Supérieure (Bouzaréah), Algeria
Salima medhaffar, Le Mans University, France
Samhaa R. El-Beltagy, Nile University, Egypt
Samia Touileb, University of Oslo, Norway
Seif Mechti, University of Sfax, Tunisia
Shady Elbassuoni, American University of Beirut, Lebanon
Shammur Absar Chowdhury, Qatar Computing Research Institute, HBKU, Qatar
Taha Zerrouki, University of Bouira, Algeria
Tamer Elsayed, Qatar University, Qatar
Violetta Cavalli-Sforza, Al Akhawayn University, Morocco
Wajdi Zaghouani, Hamad Bin Khalifa University, Qatar
Walid Magdy, University of Edinburgh, Scotland
Wassim El-Hajj, American University of Beirut, Lebanon
Wissam Antoun, American University of Beirut, Lebanon
Younes Samih, Heinrich Heine Universität Düsseldorf, Germany

Table of Contents

QADI: Arabic Dialect Identification in the Wild
Ahmed Abdelali, Hamdy Mubarak, Younes Samih, Sabit Hassan and Kareem Darwish 1

DiaLex: A Benchmark for Evaluating Multidialectal Arabic Word Embeddings
Muhammad Abdul-Mageed, Shady Elbassuoni, Jad Doughman, AbdelRahim Elmadany, El Moatez Billah Nagoudi, Yorgo Zoughby, Ahmad Shaher, Iskander Gaba, Ahmed Helal and Mohammed El-Razzaz 11

Benchmarking Transformer-based Language Models for Arabic Sentiment and Sarcasm Detection
Ibrahim Abu Farha and Walid Magdy 21

What does BERT Learn from Arabic Machine Reading Comprehension Datasets?
Eman Albilali, Nora Altwairesh and Manar Hosny 32

Kawarith: an Arabic Twitter Corpus for Crisis Events
Alaa Alharbi and Mark Lee 42

Arabic Compact Language Modelling for Resource Limited Devices
Zaid Alyafeai and Irfan Ahmad 53

Arabic Emoji Sentiment Lexicon (Arab-ESL): A Comparison between Arabic and European Emoji Sentiment Lexicons
Shatha Ali A. Hakami, Robert Hendley and Phillip Smith 60

ArCOV19-Rumors: Arabic COVID-19 Twitter Dataset for Misinformation Detection
Fatima Haouari, Maram Hasanain, Reem Suwaileh and Tamer Elsayed 72

ArCOV-19: The First Arabic COVID-19 Twitter Dataset with Propagation Networks
Fatima Haouari, Maram Hasanain, Reem Suwaileh and Tamer Elsayed 82

The Interplay of Variant, Size, and Task Type in Arabic Pre-trained Language Models
Go Inoue, Bashar Alhafni, Nurpeiis Baimukan, Houda Bouamor and Nizar Habash 92

Automatic Difficulty Classification of Arabic Sentences
Nouran Khallaf and Serge Sharoff 105

Dynamic Ensembles in Named Entity Recognition for Historical Arabic Texts
Muhammad Majadly and Tomer Sagi 115

Arabic Offensive Language on Twitter: Analysis and Experiments
Hamdy Mubarak, Ammar Rashed, Kareem Darwish, Younes Samih and Ahmed Abdelali 126

Adult Content Detection on Arabic Twitter: Analysis and Experiments
Hamdy Mubarak, Sabit Hassan and Ahmed Abdelali 136

UL2C: Mapping User Locations to Countries on Arabic Twitter
Hamdy Mubarak and Sabit Hassan 145

Let-Mi: An Arabic Levantine Twitter Dataset for Misogynistic Language
Hala Mulki and Bilal Ghanem 154

Empathetic BERT2BERT Conversational Model: Learning Arabic Language Generation with Little Data
Tarek Naous, Wissam Antoun, Reem Mahmoud and Hazem Hajj 164

ALUE: Arabic Language Understanding Evaluation
Haitham Seelawi, Ibraheem Tuffaha, Mahmoud Gzawi, Wael Farhan, Bashar Talafha, Riham Badawi, Zyad Sober, Oday Al-Dweik, Abed Alhakim Freihat and Hussein Al-Natsheh 173

Quranic Verses Semantic Relatedness Using AraBERT
Abdullah Alsaleh, Eric Atwell and Abdulrahman Altahhan 185

AraELECTRA: Pre-Training Text Discriminators for Arabic Language Understanding
Wissam Antoun, Fady Baly and Hazem Hajj 191

AraGPT2: Pre-Trained Transformer for Arabic Language Generation
Wissam Antoun, Fady Baly and Hazem Hajj 196

QuranTree.jl: A Julia Package for Quranic Arabic Corpus
Al-Ahmadgaid Asaad 208

Automatic Romanization of Arabic Bibliographic Records
Fadhl Eryani and Nizar Habash 213

SERAG: Semantic Entity Retrieval from Arabic Knowledge Graphs
Saher Esmeir 219

Introducing A large Tunisian Arabizi Dialectal Dataset for Sentiment Analysis
Chayma Fourati, Hatem Haddad, Abir Messaoudi, Moez BenHajhmida, Aymen Ben Elhaj Mabrouk and Malek Naski 226

AraFacts: The First Large Arabic Dataset of Naturally Occurring Claims
Zien Sheikh Ali, Watheq Mansour, Tamer Elsayed and Abdulaziz Al-Ali 231

Improving Cross-Lingual Transfer for Event Argument Extraction with Language-Universal Sentence Structures
Minh Van Nguyen and Thien Huu Nguyen 237

NADI 2021: The Second Nuanced Arabic Dialect Identification Shared Task
Muhammad Abdul-Mageed, Chiyu Zhang, AbdelRahim Elmadany, Houda Bouamor and Nizar Habash 244

Adapting MARBERT for Improved Arabic Dialect Identification: Submission to the NADI 2021 Shared Task
Badr AlKhamissi, Mohamed Gabr, Muhammad ElNokrashy and Khaled Essam 260

Country-level Arabic Dialect Identification Using Small Datasets with Integrated Machine Learning Techniques and Deep Learning Models
Maha J. Althobaiti 265

BERT-based Multi-Task Model for Country and Province Level MSA and Dialectal Arabic Identification
Abdellah El Mekki, Abdelkader El Mahdaouy, Kabil Essefar, Nabil El Mamoun, Ismail Berrada and Ahmed Khoumsi 271

Country-level Arabic Dialect Identification using RNNs with and without Linguistic Features
Elsayed Issa, Mohammed AlShakhori1, Reda Al-Bahrani and Gus Hahn-Powell 276

Arabic Dialect Identification based on a Weighted Concatenation of TF-IDF Features
Mohamed Lichouri, Mourad Abbas, Khaled Lounnas, Besma Benaziz and Aicha Zitouni 282

Machine Learning-Based Approach for Arabic Dialect Identification
Hamada Nayel, Ahmed Hassan, Mahmoud Sobhi and Ahmed El-Sawy 287

Dialect Identification in Nuanced Arabic Tweets Using Farasa Segmentation and AraBERT
Anshul Wadhawan 291

Overview of the WANLP 2021 Shared Task on Sarcasm and Sentiment Detection in Arabic
Ibrahim Abu Farha, Wajdi Zaghouani and Walid Magdy 296

WANLP 2021 Shared-Task: Towards Irony and Sentiment Detection in Arabic Tweets using Multi-headed-LSTM-CNN-GRU and MaRBERT
Reem Abdel-Salam 306

Sarcasm and Sentiment Detection In Arabic Tweets Using BERT-based Models and Data Augmentation
Abeer Abuzayed and Hend Al-Khalifa 312

Multi-task Learning Using a Combination of Contextualised and Static Word Embeddings for Arabic Sarcasm Detection and Sentiment Analysis
Abdullah I. Alharbi and Mark Lee 318

ArSarcasm Shared Task: An Ensemble BERT Model for SarcasmDetection in Arabic Tweets
Laila Bashmal and Daliyah AlZeer 323

Sarcasm and Sentiment Detection in Arabic: investigating the interest of character-level features
Dhaou Ghoul and Gaël Lejeune 329

Deep Multi-Task Model for Sarcasm Detection and Sentiment Analysis in Arabic Language
Abdelkader El Mahdaouy, Abdellah El Mekki, Kabil Essefar, Nabil El Mamoun, Ismail Berrada and Ahmed Khoumsi 334

A Contextual Word Embedding for Arabic Sarcasm Detection with Random Forests
Hazem Elgabry, Shimaa Attia, Ahmed Abdel-Rahman, Ahmed Abdel-Ate and Sandra Girgis . . 340

SarcasmDet at Sarcasm Detection Task 2021 in Arabic using AraBERT Pretrained Model
Dalya Faraj, Dalya Faraj and Malak Abdullah 345

Sarcasm and Sentiment Detection in Arabic language A Hybrid Approach Combining Embeddings and Rule-based Features
Kamel Gaanoun and Imade Benelallam 351

Combining Context-Free and Contextualized Representations for Arabic Sarcasm Detection and Sentiment Identification
Amey Hengle, Atharva Kshirsagar, Shaily Desai and Manisha Marathe 357

Leveraging Offensive Language for Sarcasm and Sentiment Detection in Arabic
Fatemah Husain and Ozlem Uzuner 364

The IDC System for Sentiment Classification and Sarcasm Detection in Arabic
Abraham Israeli, Yotam Nahum, Shai Fine and Kfir Bar 370

Preprocessing Solutions for Detection of Sarcasm and Sentiment for Arabic
Mohamed Lichouri, Mourad Abbas, Besma Benaziz, Aicha Zitouni and Khaled Lounnas 376

iCompass at Shared Task on Sarcasm and Sentiment Detection in Arabic
Malek Naski, Abir Messaoudi, Hatem Haddad, Moez BenHajhmida, Chayma Fourati and Aymen Ben Elhaj Mabrouk 381

Machine Learning-Based Model for Sentiment and Sarcasm Detection
Hamada Nayel, Eslam Amer, Aya Allam and Hanya Abdallah 386

DeepBlueAI at WANLP-EACL2021 task 2: A Deep Ensemble-based Method for Sarcasm and Sentiment Detection in Arabic
Bingyan Song, Chunguang Pan, Shengguang Wang and Zhipeng Luo 390

AraBERT and Farasa Segmentation Based Approach For Sarcasm and Sentiment Detection in Arabic Tweets
Anshul Wadhawan 395

Workshop Program

Monday April 19, 2021 - Time zone · Central European Time (CET)

09:00–09:10 *Opening Remarks*
Nizar Habash

09:10–10:00 *Keynote Speaker*
Hend Al Khalifa

+ ***Main Workshop***

10:00–11:00 Session 1-a: Social Analytics

Arabic Offensive Language on Twitter: Analysis and Experiments
Hamdy Mubarak, Ammar Rashed, Kareem Darwish, Younes Samih and Ahmed Abdelali

Kawarith: an Arabic Twitter Corpus for Crisis Events
Alaa Alharbi and Mark Lee

Adult Content Detection on Arabic Twitter: Analysis and Experiments
Hamdy Mubarak, Sabit Hassan and Ahmed Abdelali

ArCOV19-Rumors: Arabic COVID-19 Twitter Dataset for Misinformation Detection
Fatima Haouari, Maram Hasanain, Reem Suwaileh and Tamer Elsayed

Monday April 19, 2021 - Time zone · Central European Time (CET) (continued)

10:00–11:00 Session 1-b: NLU/NLG

What does BERT learn from Arabic machine reading comprehension datasets?
Eman Albilali, Nora Altwairesh and Manar Hosny

Automatic Difficulty Classification of Arabic Sentences
Nouran Khallaf and Serge Sharoff

ALUE: Arabic Language Understanding Evaluation
Haitham Seelawi, Ibraheem Tuffaha, Mahmoud Gzawi, Wael Farhan, Bashar Talafha, Riham Badawi, Zyad Sober, Oday Al-Dweik, Abed Alhakim Freihat and Hussein Al-Natsheh

Empathetic BERT2BERT Conversational Model: Learning Arabic Language Generation with Little Data
Tarek Naous, Wissam Antoun, Reem Mahmoud and Hazem Hajj

11:00–11:30 ***Coffee Break***

11:30–12:30 Session 2-a: Information Extraction

Dynamic Ensembles in Named Entity Recognition for Historical Arabic Texts
Muhammad Majadly and Tomer Sagi

Improving Cross-Lingual Transfer for Event Argument Extraction with Language-Universal Sentence Structures
Minh Van Nguyen and Thien Huu Nguyen

SERAG: Semantic Entity Retrieval from Arabic knowledge Graphs
Saher Esmeir

Quranic Verses Semantic Relatedness Using AraBERT
Abdullah Alsaleh, Eric Atwell and Abdulrahman Altahhan

Monday April 19, 2021 - Time zone · Central European Time (CET) (continued)

11:30–12:30 Session 2-b: Arabic Dialects

The Interplay of Variant, Size, and Task Type in Arabic Pre-trained Language Models
Go Inoue, Bashar Alhafni, Nurpeiis Baimukan, Houda Bouamor and Nizar Habash

QADI: Arabic Dialect Identification in the Wild
Ahmed Abdelali, Hamdy Mubarak, Younes Samih, Sabit Hassan and Kareem Darwish

DiaLex: A Benchmark for Evaluating Multidialectal Arabic Word Embeddings
Muhammad Abdul-Mageed, Shady Elbassuoni, Jad Doughman, AbdelRahim Elmadany, El Moatez Billah Nagoudi, Yorgo Zoughby, Ahmad Shaher, Iskander Gaba, Ahmed Helal and Mohammed El-Razzaz

Introducing A large Tunisian Arabizi Dialectal Dataset for Sentiment Analysis
Chayma Fourati, Hatem Haddad, Abir Messaoudi, Moez BenHajhmida, Aymen Ben Elhaj Mabrouk and Malek Naski

12:30–13:30 Session 3: Panel: Arabic NLP and Industry

13:30–15:00 *Lunch Break*

15:00–16:00 Session 4: Shared Tasks

NADI 2021: The Second Nuanced Arabic Dialect Identification Shared Task
Muhammad Abdul-Mageed, Chiyu Zhang, AbdelRahim Elmadany, Houda Bouamor and Nizar Habash

Adapting MARBERT for Improved Arabic Dialect Identification: Submission to the NADI 2021 Shared Task
Badr AlKhamissi, Mohamed Gabr, Muhammad ElNokrashy and Khaled Essam

Overview of the WANLP 2021 Shared Task on Sarcasm and Sentiment Detection in Arabic
Ibrahim Abu Farha, Wajdi Zaghouani and Walid Magdy

Multi-task Learning Using a Combination of Contextualised and Static Word Embeddings for Arabic Sarcasm Detection and Sentiment Analysis
Abdullah I. Alharbi and Mark Lee

Monday April 19, 2021 - Time zone · Central European Time (CET) (continued)

16:00–17:30 Session 5: Poster

16:00–16:30 *Poster Boaster*
Nadi Tomeh and Fethi Bougares

QuranTree.jl: A Julia package for Quranic Arabic Corpus
Al-Ahmadgaid Asaad

Let-Mi: An Arabic Levantine Twitter Dataset for Misogynistic Language
Hala Mulki and Bilal Ghanem

UL2C: Mapping User Locations to Countries on Arabic Twitter
Hamdy Mubarak and Sabit Hassan

Arabic Compact Language Modelling for Resource Limited Devices
Zaid Alyafeai and Irfan Ahmad

AraELECTRA: Pre-Training Text Discriminators for Arabic Language Understanding
Wissam Antoun, Fady Baly and Hazem Hajj

AraGPT2: Pre-Trained Transformer for Arabic Language Generation
Wissam Antoun, Fady Baly and Hazem Hajj

Arabic Emoji Sentiment Lexicon (Arab-ESL): A Comparison between Arabic and European Emoji Sentiment Lexicons
Shatha Ali A. Hakami, Robert Hendley and Phillip Smith

AraFacts: The First Large Arabic Dataset of Naturally Occurring Claims
Zien Sheikh Ali, Watheq Mansour, Tamer Elsayed and Abdulaziz Al-Ali

Automatic Romanization of Arabic Bibliographic Records
Fadhl Eryani and Nizar Habash

Benchmarking Transformer-based Language Models for Arabic Sentiment and Sarcasm Detection
Ibrahim Abu Farha and Walid Magdy

ArCOV-19: The First Arabic COVID-19 Twitter Dataset with Propagation Networks
Fatima Haouari, Maram Hasanain, Reem Suwaileh and Tamer Elsayed

\+ ***NADI Shared Task***

Dialect Identification in Nuanced Arabic Tweets Using Farasa Segmentation and AraBERT
Anshul Wadhawan

Arabic Dialect Identification based on a Weighted Concatenation of TF-IDF Features
Mohamed Lichouri, Mourad Abbas, Khaled Lounnas, Besma Benaziz and Aicha Zitouni

BERT-based Multi-Task Model for Country and Province Level MSA and Dialectal Arabic Identification
Abdellah El Mekki, Abdelkader El Mahdaouy, Kabil Essefar, Nabil El Mamoun, Ismail Berrada and Ahmed Khoumsi

Country-level Arabic Dialect Identification Using Small Datasets with Integrated Machine Learning Techniques and Deep Learning Models
Maha J. Althobaiti

Machine Learning-Based Approach for Arabic Dialect Identification
Hamada Nayel, Ahmed Hassan, Mahmoud Sobhi and Ahmed El-Sawy

Country-level Arabic dialect identification using RNNs with and without linguistic features
Elsayed Issa, Mohammed AlShakhori1, Reda Al-Bahrani and Gus Hahn-Powell

\+ ***ArSarcasm Shared Task***

AraBERT and Farasa Segmentation Based Approach For Sarcasm and Sentiment Detection in Arabic Tweets
Anshul Wadhawan

WANLP 2021 Shared-Task: Towards Irony and Sentiment detection in Arabic tweets using Multi-headed-LSTM-CNN-GRU and MaRBERT
Reem Abdel-Salam

Deep Multi-Task Model for Sarcasm Detection and Sentiment Analysis in Arabic Language
Abdelkader El Mahdaouy, Abdellah El Mekki, Kabil Essefar, Nabil El Mamoun, Ismail Berrada and Ahmed Khoumsi

Monday April 19, 2021 - Time zone · Central European Time (CET) (continued)

DeepBlueAI at WANLP-EACL2021 task 2: A Deep Ensemble-based Method for Sarcasm and Sentiment Detection in Arabic
Bingyan Song, Chunguang Pan, Shengguang Wang and Zhipeng Luo

Leveraging Offensive Language for Sarcasm and Sentiment Detection in Arabic
Fatemah Husain and Ozlem Uzuner

iCompass at Shared Task on Sarcasm and Sentiment Detection in Arabic
Malek Naski, Abir Messaoudi, Hatem Haddad, Moez BenHajhmida, Chayma Fourati and Aymen Ben Elhaj Mabrouk

Preprocessing Solutions for Detection of Sarcasm and Sentiment for Arabic
Mohamed Lichouri, Mourad Abbas, Besma Benaziz, Aicha Zitouni and Khaled Lounnas

ArSarcasm Shared Task: An Ensemble BERT Model for Sarcasm Detection in Arabic Tweets
Laila Bashmal and Daliyah AlZeer

SarcasmDet at Sarcasm Detection Task 2021 in Arabic using AraBERT Pretrained Model
Dalya Faraj, Dalya Faraj and Malak Abdullah

Sarcasm and sentiment detection in Arabic language
A hybrid approach combining embeddings and rule-based features
Kamel Gaanoun and Imade Benelallam

A contextual word embedding for Arabic sarcasm detection with random forests
Hazem Elgabry, Shimaa Attia, Ahmed Abdel-Rahman, Ahmed Abdel-Ate and Sandra Girgis

Sarcasm and Sentiment Detection in Arabic: investigating the interest of character-level features
Dhaou Ghoul and Gaël Lejeune

The IDC System for Sentiment Classification and Sarcasm Detection in Arabic
Abraham Israeli, Yotam Nahum, Shai Fine and Kfir Bar

Machine Learning-Based Model for Sentiment and Sarcasm Detection
Hamada Nayel, Eslam Amer, Aya Allam and Hanya Abdallah

Sarcasm and Sentiment Detection In Arabic Tweets Using BERT-based Models and Data Augmentation
Abeer Abuzayed and Hend Al-Khalifa

Monday April 19, 2021 - Time zone · Central European Time (CET) (continued)

	Combining Context-Free and Contextualized Word Representations for Arabic Sarcasm Detection and Sentiment Identification Amey Hengle, Atharva Kshirsagar, Shaily Desai and Manisha Marathe
17:30–18:00	*Closing Ceremony* Nizar Habash

QADI: Arabic Dialect Identification in the Wild

Ahmed Abdelali, Hamdy Mubarak, Younes Samih, Sabit Hassan and **Kareem Darwish**
Qatar Computing Research Institute
Hamad Bin Khalifa University
Doha, Qatar
{aabdelali,hmubarak,ysamih,sahassan2,kdarwish}@hbku.edu.qa

Abstract

Proper dialect identification is important for a variety of Arabic NLP applications. In this paper, we present a method for rapidly constructing a tweet dataset containing a wide range of country-level Arabic dialects —covering 18 different countries in the Middle East and North Africa region. Our method relies on applying multiple filters to identify users who belong to different countries based on their account descriptions and to eliminate tweets that either write mainly in Modern Standard Arabic or mostly use vulgar language. The resultant dataset contains 540k tweets from 2,525 users who are evenly distributed across 18 Arab countries. Using intrinsic evaluation, we show that the labels of a set of randomly selected tweets are 91.5% accurate. For extrinsic evaluation, we are able to build effective country-level dialect identification on tweets with a macro-averaged F1-score of 60.6% across 18 classes.

1 Introduction

Twitter is one of the most popular social media platforms in the Middle East and North Africa (MENA) region with almost two thirds (63%) of Arab youth indicating that they look first to Facebook and Twitter for news (Radcliffe and Bruni, 2019). The popularity of Twitter in MENA is reflected by approximately 164 million active monthly users, who produce a massive volume of Arabic tweets, many of which are in Dialectal Arabic (DA). Hence, many researchers have been using Twitter as a major data source that is representative of current language usage and linguistic phenomena (Mubarak and Darwish, 2014; Samih et al., 2017; Zaghouani and Charfi, 2018a). Though Arabic is the lingua franca of most of the MENA region, different dialects of Arabic are used in different countries. While some dialects may differ significantly from each other (e.g. Egyptian dialect (EG) and Moroccan Maghrebi dialect (MA)[1]), others, particularly those in close geographic proximity, may be more difficult to tweak apart (e.g. variants of the Levantine dialect such as Syrian (SY) and Lebanese (LB)). Figure 1 highlights the dialectal variations across the Arab world. The figure shows that dialects are a continuum that often transcends geographical regions and borders. Automatically distinguishing between the different dialectal variations is valuable for many downstream applications such as machine translations (Diab et al., 2014), POS tagging (Darwish et al., 2020), geo-locating users, and author profiling (Sadat et al., 2014).

Though there has been prior work on performing Arabic Dialect Identification (ADI), much of the work was conducted on datasets with significant limitations in terms of genre (Bouamor et al., 2018; Zaidan and Callison-Burch, 2011), number of dialects (Abdul-Mageed et al., 2018), or focus (Bouamor et al., 2019; Zaghouani and Charfi, 2018a), where often the focus was on geo-locating and profiling users as opposed to dialect identification. In this work, we expand beyond these efforts by utilizing tweets from across the MENA region to build a large, non-genre specific, fine-grained, and balanced country-level dialectal Arabic dataset that we use to build effective Arabic Dialect Identification.

We rely on two main features to build the dataset. The first feature is the Twitter user profile description, where we identify users who self-declare themselves as belonging to a specific country in different forms such as showing signs of loyalty and pride (e.g. "proud Egyptian"). In the second, we use a classifier that utilizes distant supervision to accurately discriminates between MSA and di-

[1]We use ISO 3166-1 alpha-2 for country codes: https://en.wikipedia.org/wiki/List_of_ISO_3166_country_codes

Proceedings of the Sixth Arabic Natural Language Processing Workshop, pages 1–10
Kyiv, Ukraine (Virtual), April 19, 2021.

alects. In doing so, we can identify users who self-declare their identity, mostly tweet in dialectal Arabic, and only retain dialectal user tweets. Further, we use our newly constructed dataset to build models that can effectively distinguish between 18 country-level Arabic dialects. We didn't consider four Arab countries, namely Mauritania, Somalia, Djibouti, and Comoros, because we were not able to find a sufficient number of Twitter users tweeting in Arabic. This could be due to the limited use of Twitter in these countries, or that users may tweet primarily in other languages. For automated dialect identification, our models use a variety of features, such as character-level and word-level n-gram, static word embeddings, and contextual embeddings (e.g. multilingual BERT (mBERT) and AraBERT), and two classification techniques, namely Support Vector Machines (SVM) classification and fine-tuned Transformer models. The contributions of this work are:

- We introduce a method for constructing a highly accurate Arabic dialectal dataset from Twitter. This method can be completely automated such that it can be used in the future to collect fresh dialectal tweets.
- We build QADI (meaning "judge" in Arabic) dataset,[2]. It is the largest balanced non-genre specific country-level Arabic dialectal tweet dataset. The dataset contains more than 540k tweets covering 18 country-level dialects with an associated test set containing 182 tweets per country on average that was manually labeled by native speakers from 18 Arab countries.
- We provide a list of Twitter accounts from 18 Arab countries (a total of 2,525 accounts with an average of 140 accounts per country) that can be used in author profiling tasks.
- We use the new dataset to build state-of-the-art tweet-level Arabic dialect identification models using a variety of features and classifiers.

2 Related Work

Most efforts in building resources for Arabic dialect identification are limited either in terms of genre, granularity, or the size of the data. Zaidan

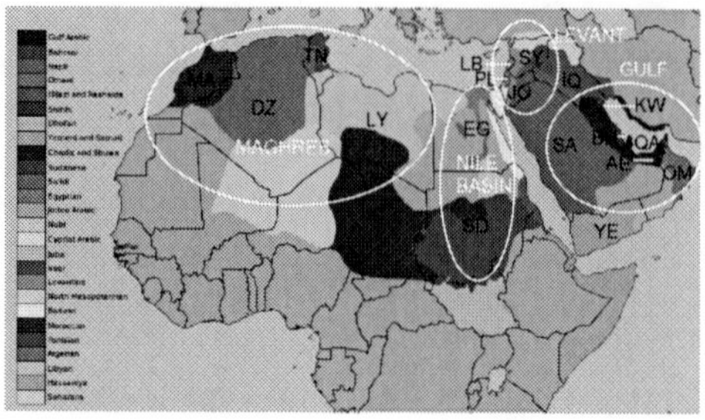

Figure 1: Geographic distribution of Arabic dialects.[3]

and Callison-Burch (2011) curated the Arabic Online Commentary Dataset, a resource of more than 52M-words. They annotated over 108K sentences (41%) of the dataset with one of 5 possible dialects, namely: Maghrebi, Egyptian, Levantine, Gulf, and Iraqi. Similarly, Alshutayri and Atwell (2017), El-Haj et al. (2018), and Alsarsour et al. (2018) annotated collections of texts using the five regions/dialects. Elfardy and Diab (2013) and Darwish et al. (2014) identified whether a sentence is Modern Standard Arabic (MSA) or Egyptian.

In recent years, there have been more efforts to cover more countries with finer granularity. Abdul-Mageed et al. (2018) constructed a dataset that covers 10 countries. Zaghouani and Charfi (2018a) built the "Arap-Tweet" dataset, which includes tweets from 15 countries. They retrieved tweets containing distinct dialectal words and expressions, and then given the users who authored these tweets, they crawled their timelines (Zaghouani and Charfi, 2018b). We approach the problem from a different angle, where we start with self-declared users rather than a pre-defined keywords, which may have limited coverage of dialectal lexical variations. The MADAR (Multi-Arabic Dialect Applications and Resources) project (Bouamor et al., 2018, 2019) produced several resources among which two corpora were used for the shared task on fine-grained dialect identification (Bouamor et al., 2019). The resource includes a lexicon and a 1,000 parallel sentences from the travel domain that were translated into local dialects of 26 Arab cities. Additionally, the project released another set of tweets by searching twitter using a set of 25 seed hashtags corresponding to the 22 states of the Arab League (e.g., #Algeria, #Egypt, #Kuwait, etc.) and relevant hashtags such as: "#ArabWorld", "#ArabLeague", and "#Arab". The approach resulted in a collection of 2,980 profiles. When inspecting the profiles, The majority of the obtained users were from

[2]QADI Dataset, is freely available for research purposes from: http://alt.qcri.org/resources/qadi/

[3]Source: https://en.wikipedia.org/wiki/Varieties_of_Arabic, country codes and regions are added

Saudi Arabia, representing 36% of the total. This was another motivation to curate a more balanced and representative dataset to use for dialect identification. Further, as we show later, this dataset is sub-optimal for tweet-level dialect identification. Abdul-Mageed et al. (2018) built a large tweet collection containing more than 200 million geo-tagged tweets that were collected over 5 years (2013-2018). The resulting collection included tweets from 29 cities from 10 Arab countries, of which 2,500 were manually annotated. The average inter-annotator agreement, Cohen's Kappa (K), was 67%, where the annotators reported not being able to distinguish between dialects from neighboring cities or countries (Abdul-Mageed et al., 2018).

Multiple approaches have been used for dialect ID that exploit a variety of features, such as character or word n-grams (Darwish et al., 2014; Zaidan and Callison-Burch, 2014; Malmasi et al., 2016; Sadat et al., 2014), and techniques such as multiple kernel learning (Ionescu and Popescu, 2016) and distributed representation of dialects (Abdul-Mageed et al., 2018; Zhang and Abdul-Mageed, 2019) to name a few. Zhang and Abdul-Mageed (2019) used semi-supervised learning using multilingual BERT for user-level dialect identification on the MADAR Shared Task. Arabic Tranformers-based approaches (Antoun et al., 2020; Safaya et al., 2020) showed competitive results in NADI (Abdul-Mageed et al., 2020) Shared Task.

3 Data Collection

It is common for users on social networks to disclose social and linguistic information about themselves in their profiles. In Twitter, the user profile provides a header and a short biography. Both fields allow users to freely describe themselves. Surveying Arabic speaking profiles, it is customary to see users declaring their patriotism and national belonging by using their county's flag or explicitly naming the city or country that they are from (e.g. "Kuwait is my home country", "I am a Libyan citizen"). To build our dataset, we obtained a collection of Arabic tweets that was crawled using the Twitter streaming API, where we set the language filter to Arabic ("lang:ar"), during the entirety of March and April, 2018. In all, the collection contains 25M tweets from which we extracted the profile information of all the users who authored these tweets. We applied three filters on user profiles and tweets as we describe in the next subsections.

Country Identification For the first stage, to identify a user's country, we filtered user profiles using a gazetteer that includes:

- All Arab country names written in either Arabic, English, or French,[4] such as المغرب (Almgrb – Morocco), Morocco, and Maroc respectively.
- The names of major cities in these countries in both Arabic and English as specified in Wikipedia,[5] such as القدس (Alqds – Jerusalem) and وهران (whrAn – Oran, Algeria).
- Arabic adjectives specifying all nationalities in both masculine and feminine forms with and without the definite article ال (Al – the) such as عراقي (ErAqy - Iraqi (m.)), عراقية (ErAqyp - Iraqi (f.)), and العراقي (AlErAqy - the Iraqi (m.)).

Arabic Variant Identification The second filter checks if the account mainly tweets in either dialectal Arabic or MSA. Since Arabic users commonly switch between MSA and dialectal Arabic, and we were interested in strictly dialectal tweets, we sought to filter out MSA tweets. There are multiple ways to distinguish between dialectal and MSA text. One such method involves using a list of strictly dialectal words (Darwish et al., 2014). However, constructing such lists across multiple dialects can be challenging. Thus, we opted to train a text classifier using a heuristically labeled tweets. Specifically, given 50 million tweets that we collected between March and September 2018, we assumed that tweets strictly containing the MSA relative pronouns الذي، الذى، التي، التى، الذين ("Al*y, Al*Y, Alty, AltY, Al*yn" - who/that in masculine, feminine, and plural forms) were MSA, and those strictly containing the dialectal relative pronoun اللي، اللى ("Ally, AllY" – who/that) were dialectal. The major advantage of the dialectal relative pronoun اللي is that it is present in most (if not all) Arabic dialects with the same meaning but not in MSA. Table 1 shows some examples of such usage across different dialects. In doing so, we labeled 3.09M tweets as MSA and 3.17M tweets as dialectal. For these tweets, we normalized user mentions to @USER, digits to NUM, emojis to EMOJI, URLs to URL, and the aforementioned relative pronouns to RELATIVE. In doing so, we eliminated Twitter-specific features, which are not

[4]French is widely used in the Maghreb region.

[5]https://en.wikipedia.org/wiki/List_of_countries_by_largest_and_second_largest_cities

linguistic in nature, and eliminated the effect of the relative pronouns we used to construct the dataset.

Dialect	Example/Translation
Egyptian	كنتي كويسه ايه اللي حصل you were good, what happened
Levantine	في ناس منيح اللي ما في متلن it's good that no people like them
Gulf	ابي ابدل المكيف اللي في غرفتي I want to change the AC in my room
Maghrebi	اللي يحبها ما يديرلهاش المشاكل he who loves her, do not troubles her

Table 1: Examples usages of dialectal relative pronoun across dialects.

We set aside 20k MSA and dialectal tweets for testing (10k for each). We trained a fastText classifier (Joulin et al., 2016), which is a deep-learning-based classifier, using character n-grams ranging in length between 3 and 6 grams. We tested on the held-out test set, and the accuracy of distinguishing between MSA and dialectal Arabic was 98%. Using this classifier, we classified the tweets of the users. We retained users, where at least 50% of their tweets were dialectal.

Appropriateness Identification The third filter removed users who were mostly tweeting vulgar, sexually explicit, or pornographic tweets. To filter out these users, we used the obscene word list generated by Mubarak et al. (2017), which contains 288 words and 127 hashtags. We removed users if more than 50% of their tweets contained vulgar words. Removing the tweets of such users was motivated by the fact that their tweets contain strong genre specific signals, which may adversely affect the generalization of dialect identification.

Normalization Tweets often contain tokens that are specific to the Twitter platform such as hashtags and user mentions. To improve generalization of the trained models (hopefully beyond tweets), we split hashtags into their semantic constituents (Bansal et al., 2015; Declerck and Lendvai, 2015) and replaced user mentions and URLs with "@USER" and "URL" respectively.

Constructing the Dataset After applying the three aforementioned filters, we ended up with 2,525 users from 18 countries (140 users per country on average), who authored 540k tweets (30k per country on average) with a total of 8.8M words. Table 2 provides per country breakdown of the dataset.

Data Validation To assess the quality of our new data set, we resorted to manual assessment, where we manually labeled a random sample of 200 tweets from the tweets of each country. Though some expressions may be unique to a dialect of a particular country (e.g. إزيك (<zyk – how are you (Egyptian)), other expressions may be used in dialects from different countries (e.g. لا باس (lA bAs – no problem or good (Algerian (DZ), Moroccan (MA), and Tunisian (TN))). Thus, the instruction we gave to the annotators was: "Is this tweet consistent with the dialect spoken in your country?" The labeling of the tweets from each country was done by native speakers from that country. The average accuracy across countries was 91.5%. For some countries where additional annotators were available, namely Egypt, Algeria, Saudi Arabia, and Syria, we asked a second annotator to also label the tweets. For these countries, the average inter-annotator agreement using Cohen's Kappa (K) was 87%. These four countries cover the major dialect groups.

Figure 2 shows the accuracy per country for all annotators. Of the 200 tweets per country, those that were judged as correctly labeled were removed from the dataset, and we used them as a test set. In all, we had 3,303 test tweets (with 183 tweets on average for each of the 18 countries). Table 2 lists the number of test tweets per country. We are releasing the test set as a benchmark for dialect identification [6]. Additionally, the release will include the training set tweet IDs that can be hydrated in observance of Twitter's data sharing policy.

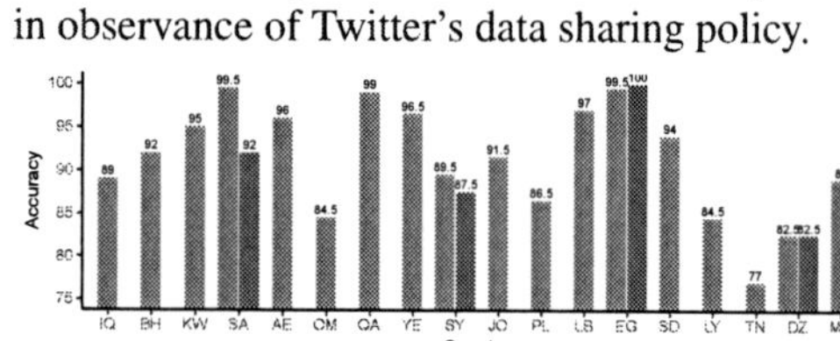

Figure 2: Annotation accuracy per country. Second annotators are colored in "Red".

The manually rejected tweets that the annotators classified as not from their dialects were mostly cases where the users interacted with or responded to users from different countries. In such cases, users tend to code-switch or adopt to other users' dialects. For example, a user identified as Tunisian tweeted انا عموما بحب الظلمة اوي (Ana EmwmA bHb AlZlmp Awy – I generally like darkness a lot).

[6]The data set can be downloaded from: `http://hidden-for-blind-review/`

Country	IQ	BH	KW	SA	AE	OM	QA	YE	SY
Users	142	169	160	149	172	176	139	138	139
Training Tweets (k)	18.4	28.3	49.9	35.4	27.8	24.8	36.7	11.6	18.3
Test tweets	178	184	190	199	192	169	198	193	194
Country	JO	PL	LB	EG	SD	LY	TN	DZ	MA
Users	146	145	141	150	139	149	68	130	73
Training Tweets (k)	34.1	48.6	38.4	67.8	16.3	40.9	12.9	17.6	12.8
Test tweets	180	173	194	200	188	169	154	170	178

Table 2: The number of users and tweets per country in our tweet corpus.

The annotator correctly tagged this as not Tunisian (TN), as it is clearly Egyptian (EG). In this example, the Tunisian user was conversing with a person from Egypt or the Levant. In another example, the tweet هسه جاي تقول أحبك؟ (hsh jAy tqwl >Hbk – just now you come to say I love you), the annotator labeled the tweet as not Yemeni (YE), mostly because of the typically Iraqi word "هسه" (hsh – just now). In this case, we found that the tweet was quoting a popular Iraqi song.

4 Corpus Statistics and Analysis

Upon constructing the dataset, we attempted to explore its characteristics. First, we extracted features that are distinctive for each dialect. To do so, we computed the so-called valence score for each word in each dialect (Conover et al., 2011). The score helps determine the distinctiveness of a given word in a specific dialect in reference to other dialects. Given $N(t, D_i)$, which is the frequency of the term t in Dialect D_i, valence is computed as follows:

$$V(t)_i = 2\frac{\frac{N(t,D_i)}{N(D_i)}}{\sum_n \frac{N(t,D_n)}{N(D_n)}} - 1 \quad (1)$$

Where $N(D_i)$ is the total number of occurrences of all words in dialect D_i. Figure 3 lists the words with highest valence scores per country. Though the majority of the top words were in fact distinctive dialectal words (typically function words), there were three other prominent categories of words that were not. The first was names of locations inside these countries, which implies that geographic locations in a user's Twitter timeline can be a strong features in identifying the country of the user. The second had words that appear in multiple dialects, which is expected given the overlap between dialects from different countries. The third category included MSA words. Though we intentionally excluded all tweets that were identified as MSA, the appearance of such words was expected given the large overlap between MSA and dialects and the frequent context switching between MSA and dialects in user tweets.

Next, we computed the similarity between dialects to ascertain if similarities are consistent with reports in prior literature by visualizing the similarity between different country-level dialects. For such, we constructed a list of the top 10k words with the highest valence scores across all dialects. The resulting list can be viewed as a vector of 19 valence values for each word corresponding to the valence of 18 different country-level dialects in addition to MSA. For MSA data, we used the 3.09M MSA tweets that we used earlier to train the MSA/dialect classifier. Then given the word vectors, we applied SHC bottom-up hierarchical agglomerative clustering (Li and Huang, 2009). The algorithm treats each dialect as a singleton cluster at the outset and then successively merges (or agglomerates) clusters until all clusters have been merged into a single cluster that contains all dialects. Figure 4 shows the results of hierarchical clustering. The figure reflects the similarity and the geographical proximity of various dialects. At higher levels, dialects are grouped per region, where we can identify the major dialectal groups, namely Gulf, Maghrebi, Egyptian, and Levantine. This is aligned with geographical distribution of the dialects as well as the findings of prior work (Salameh et al., 2018).

5 Experimental Setup

Given our new dataset, we conducted a battery of experiments on the dataset to build effective country-level Arabic dialect identification. We experimented with several tweet representation and classification models. For tweet representations, we used: surface features, namely words and character n-grams, static embeddings, and deep contextual embeddings, namely AraBERT and mBERT. For classification, we used two different classifiers,

Figure 3: Highest valence words for each country.

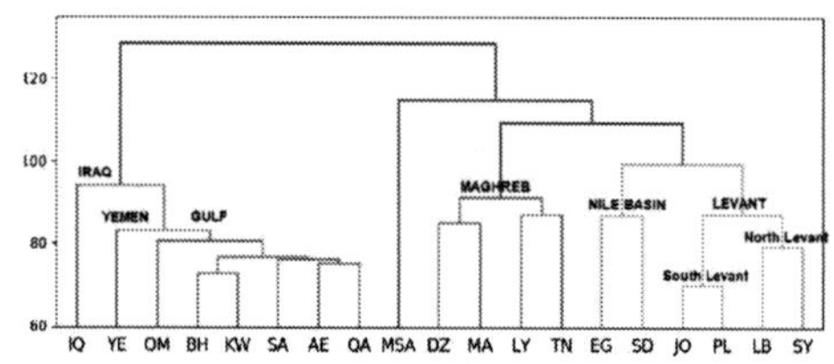

Figure 4: Clustering of Arabic Dialects using valence scores on top 10k words.

namely an SVM classifier and a fine-tuned Transformer model. For comparison, we conducted the same experiments on MADAR dataset. In the following subsections, we present tweet representations and classification models.

5.1 Representations

Surface Features: We used two different surface-level features, namely word and character n-grams. Specifically, we represented tweets using: i) character n-grams, where we used 2 to 6-grams (C{2-6}); ii) word n-grams, where we used unigrams (W{1}) and unigrams to 6-grams (W{1-6}); and iii) a combination of word and character n-grams. For our dataset and MADAR , we normalized URLs, numbers, and user mentions to URL, NUM, and MENTION respectively. We used tf-idf weighting for character and word n-grams.

Static Embeddings: We used **Mazajak** word-level skip-gram embeddings (Abu Farha and Magdy, 2019) that were trained on 250M Arabic tweets with 300-dimensional vectors.

Deep Contextualized Embeddings: We also experimented with two pre-trained contextualized embeddings with fine-tuning for down-stream tasks, namely $\text{BERT}_{\text{base-multilingual}}$ (mBERT) and AraBERT (Antoun et al., 2020). Recently, deep contextualized language models such as BERT (Bidirectional Encoder Representations from Transformers) (Devlin et al., 2019), UMLFIT (Howard and Ruder, 2018), and OpenAI GPT (Radford et al., 2018), to name but a few, have achieved ground-breaking results in many NLP classification and language understanding tasks.

Both mBERT and AraBERT are pre-trained on identical architectures, namely an encoder with 12 Transformer blocks, hidden size of 768, and 12 self-attention heads. However, they differ in one major way. While mBERT is pre-trained on Wikipedia text for 104 languages,AraBERT is trained on a large Arabic news corpus containing 8.5M articles composed of roughly 2.5B tokens. For consistency with mBERT, we used AraBERT with BP. Following Devlin et al. (2019), the classification consists of introducing a dense layer over the final hidden state h corresponding to first token of the sequence, [CLS], adding a softmax activation on top of BERT to predict the probability of the l label: $p(l|h) = softmax(Wh)$, where W is the task-specific weight matrix. We set the learning rate to 2e-5, batch size to 8, max sequence length to 128, and the number fine-tuning epochs to 6. During fine-tuning, all mBERT or AraBERT parameters together with W are optimized end-to-end to maximize the log-probability of the correct labels.

5.2 Classification Models

For classification, we used an SVM classifier and fine-tuned mBERT and AraBERT. We utilized the SVM classifier when using surface features and static pre-trained Mazajak embeddings. We used the Scikit Learn libsvm implementations of the SVM classifier with a linear kernel. When using

Classifier	Training Set QADI	MADAR
MultiLangBERT	58.9	25.3
AraBERT	**60.6**	29.0
Mazajak	39.8	24.6
$SVM_{C\{2-6\}}$	57.3	25.6
$SVM_{W\{1\}}$	50.8	23.7
$SVM_{W\{1-6\}}$	51.8	20.6
$SVM_{C\{2-6\},W\{1-6\}}$	57.6	26.4

Table 3: Classification results for QADI and MADAR sets using the various models

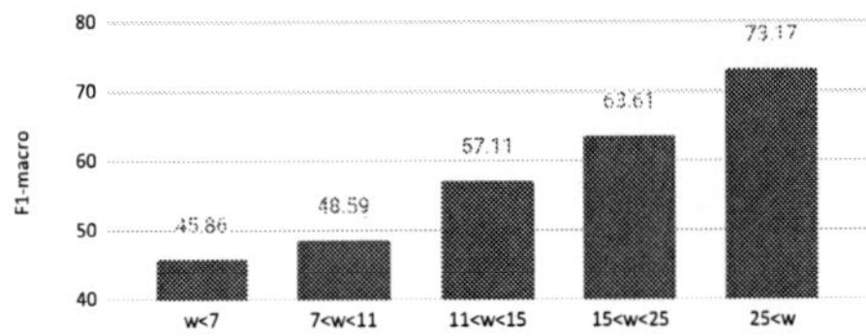

Figure 5: Macro-averaged F1-score given tweet length using AraBERT.

contextualized embeddings, we fine-tuned mBERT or AraBERT by adding a fully-connected dense layer followed by a softmax classifier, minimizing the binary cross-entropy loss function for the training data. We used the PyTorch[7] implementation by HuggingFace[8].

5.3 Experiments and Results

As stated earlier, we ran a number of country-level dialect ID experiments on our new dataset and on MADAR dataset for comparison. The details of the training and test splits for the dataset as as follows:
QADI Dataset: Table 2 provides the statistics of the training and test parts of QADI dataset. Given that manual verification was done at tweet-level, all the experiments on QADI dataset were done at tweet level. In all, the dataset contains 540k training tweets and 3,303 test tweets.
MADAR Dataset: MADAR task 2 dataset was designed for user-level classification, where each user is assigned a country label. The dataset is split into train/dev/test splits that contain 2,180, 300, and 500 users respectively, with approximately 100 sample tweets per users. For our experiments, we merged the training and development splits. Since we were performing tweet-level classification, we assigned the user label to all their tweets, and proceeded to perform tweet-level training and testing. We normalized tweets in the same manner applied on QADI dataset .

Results Table 3 reports on the macro-averaged F1-score results of training and testing using QADI and MADAR datasets. As QADI results show, using contextual embeddings yielded the best results with AraBERT results edging mBERT results. Using an SVM classifier that is trained using either character n-grams only (C{2-6}) or a combination of character and word n-grams (C{2-6},W{1-6}) was slightly lower than using contextual embeddings. Using an SVM classifier is computationally more efficient than using contextual embeddings. Further, character n-grams performed better than using word n-grams, with the combination of both character and word n-grams performing slightly better than using character n-grams alone. Using Mazajak embeddings led to significantly lower results. Further, when inspecting the best classification results (AraBERT), we noted that the length of the tweets impacted the classification results. The longer a tweet, the more accurate the prediction was. Figure 5 shows the accuracy of the classifier for various tweet lengths. This is expected given that longer tweets potentially contain more clues for the classifier. Training using MADAR led to significantly lower results compared to training using QADI . This likely stems from a mismatch between the problem at hand (tweet-level dialect ID) and the purpose for which MADAR was constructed (user-level dialect/country ID). Further, belonging to a country does not guarantee that a user will always tweet in the dialect of that country. Often users from different countries use MSA (or even other languages). We speculated that many of the tweets in the MADAR data are actually MSA, because the tweets were collected without taking into account whether they were actually dialectal or not. To test this hypothesis, we used our aforementioned MSA/dialectal classifier. When we classified the MADAR tweets, the classifier tagged 29% of the tweets as dialectal and the rest as MSA (71%), confirming our hypothesis. Since the vast majority of the tweets were MSA, training on the MADAR dataset led to significantly lower tweet-level dialect classification results. Since QADI filters out MSA tweets, it doesn't have the same issue.

Error Analysis We inspected tweets from the QADI test set that were misclassified by AraBERT (our best system). Generally, the most prominent reason for incorrect classification could be attributed to the fluidity of geolinguistic distinctions between Arabic dialects. To some degree,

[7] `https://pytorch.org/`

[8] `https://github.com/huggingface/transformers`

geographical proximity is associated with dialectal closeness, making it difficult for classifiers to distinguish between the dialects at hand. Note that these dialects share a plethora of linguistic features to warrant their subsumability under the same dialect. As shown in Figure 6, the dialects from the Gulf region (OM, BH, KW, SA, AE, and QA) show the largest confusion due to their similarity. For example, the tweet, دخلت البرنامج سويت حساب.. والرقم ما يدخل وكلمتكم كم مره شوفو لي حل (I logged into the program, created an account, and the number is not accepted ... Find me a solution), could be plausibly attributed to any of the Gulf dialects.

	IQ	YE	OM	BH	KW	SA	AE	QA	DZ	MA	LY	TN	EG	SD	JO	PL	LB	SY
IQ	116	1	6	6	11	8	6	4	3	0	3	0	1	1	6	5	0	1
YE	6	59	13	8	13	18	7	13	3	0	12	0	12	4	4	11	5	5
OM	1	3	107	12	4	13	8	4	2	0	2	0	1	2	3	3	3	1
BH	1	3	7	82	31	13	12	17	0	1	3	0	2	1	3	5	2	1
KW	3	1	4	14	121	12	7	10	1	1	4	1	4	0	3	2	2	0
SA	0	3	8	8	17	125	8	17	0	1	2	0	1	0	5	3	0	1
AE	2	3	16	10	17	13	90	16	1	0	7	0	3	2	4	2	3	3
QA	1	4	7	11	18	13	14	116	0	1	1	1	2	0	2	4	2	1
DZ	2	1	2	1	4	5	2	3	103	8	17	8	3	0	3	3	4	1
MA	0	0	0	2	3	3	1	0	19	124	8	1	7	1	1	4	3	1
LY	2	2	2	3	2	1	0	5	1	1	132	0	9	1	0	5	1	2
TN	0	1	3	1	2	2	0	2	10	2	16	98	7	0	3	5	2	0
EG	1	1	2	0	2	1	0	0	1	0	5	0	178	1	1	6	1	0
SD	3	1	5	0	4	2	2	5	2	2	5	0	19	129	0	5	2	2
JO	2	0	9	4	11	6	2	8	1	0	2	0	5	1	70	45	9	5
PL	0	2	3	3	3	4	2	0	2	0	2	0	8	1	25	103	10	5
LB	2	0	1	2	3	0	1	1	1	0	2	1	1	0	7	8	152	12
SY	1	1	3	2	1	5	3	4	2	0	3	0	4	1	19	19	33	93

Figure 6: Confusion matrix for the test set. The bulk of the mis-classification happens within the region (marked with thick border). Outliers are marked in red where the classification is beyond the region.

Similarly, the second greatest confusion is among dialects from the Levant region (JO, PL, LB, and SY), where we found a considerable amount of mix-up between LB and SY. The tweet, لا الانسان بفكر حالو الوحيد يلي بيفهم . . تأكد انه حمار (When the human thinks that he is the only one who understands ... be sure that he is a donkey), can be equally valid for both dialects. Similar to the results observed for both the Gulf and Levant regions, the Maghrebi dialects (MA, DZ, LY, TN) exhibit a similar pattern. MA and DZ account for considerable confusion. For instance, the tweet الله يبارك فيك خويا!! (God bless you, brother!!), could be used in both dialects. As for the Nile Basin dialects, Egyptian (EG) and Sudanese (SD) could also be confused with one another. The tweet, التويته دي معدلة فوتوشوب (This tweet is modified in Photoshop), is equally valid in both dialects. This is normal since SD is similar to central and southern Sa'idi Egyptian Arabic.[9] Interestingly, we found that about 2% of the misclassified tweets were outliers that were classified outside of their region (highlighted in red in Figure 6). The main reasons for incorrect classification, beyond the region, is due to the fact that many of them contain quotes from popular songs and poems or in few cases they have MSA words. As this YE tweet, وإنت عارف مكانتك ومتأكد منها من غير مايعيشك شعور مرات إنت العمر ومرات ما أعرفك ... (And you know your status, and you are certain about it without making you feel...), misclassified as LY. This tweet despite being manually labelled as YE, it could fit in either country.

6 Conclusion

In this paper, we presented a method for building a country-level dialectal tweet corpus. The construction of the corpus relied on a cascade of filters, where user accounts were filtered on keywords indicating country, and tweets were filtered to remove users who predominantly tweet in MSA or vulgar language. We built a large corpus containing 540k tweets from 2,525 Twitter accounts that cover 18 Arab countries. Based on a manual inspection of a random sample of tweets from the corpus, the estimated accuracy of country-level dialectal tags was 91.5%. We also showed that the resultant corpus can be effective in training a country-level dialect classifier for tweets that achieves a macro-averaged F1-score of 60.6% across 18 different classes. We compared to training on a publicly available dataset, namely MADAR dataset, and MADAR results were significantly lower.

Based on our error analysis, we discovered that a large source of errors was due to the naturally occurring overlap between dialects from neighboring countries and to code switching between different dialects. While overlap between dialects is potentially an intractable problem, detecting code switching between dialects is a future direction that can further help filter training data and identify tweets that may include multiple dialects simultaneously. For future work, we plan to investigate code switching and examine the efficacy of extending our dataset to perform user-level geotagging. Though identifying a user's country may depend on multiple signals, accurate dialect identification is likely a strong signal that can aid classification.

[9] https://en.wikipedia.org/wiki/Egyptian_Arabic

References

Muhammad Abdul-Mageed, Hassan Alhuzali, and Mohamed Elaraby. 2018. You tweet what you speak: A city-level dataset of Arabic dialects. In *Proceedings of the Language Resources and Evaluation Conference (LREC)*, Miyazaki, Japan.

Muhammad Abdul-Mageed, Chiyu Zhang, Houda Bouamor, and Nizar Habash. 2020. NADI 2020: The first nuanced Arabic dialect identification shared task. In *Proceedings of the Fifth Arabic Natural Language Processing Workshop*, pages 97–110, Barcelona, Spain (Online). Association for Computational Linguistics.

Ibrahim Abu Farha and Walid Magdy. 2019. Mazajak: An online Arabic sentiment analyser. In *Proceedings of the Fourth Arabic Natural Language Processing Workshop*, pages 192–198, Florence, Italy. Association for Computational Linguistics.

Israa Alsarsour, Esraa Mohamed, Reem Suwaileh, and Tamer Elsayed. 2018. DART: A Large Dataset of Dialectal Arabic Tweets. In *Proceedings of the Eleventh International Conference on Language Resources and Evaluation (LREC 2018)*, Miyazaki, Japan. European Language Resources Association (ELRA).

Areej Alshutayri and Erik Atwell. 2017. Exploring twitter as a source of an arabic dialect corpus. *International Journal of Computational Linguistics (IJCL)*, 8(2):37–44. This is an open access article under the terms of the Creative Commons Attribution License (CC-BY).

Wissam Antoun, Fady Baly, and Hazem Hajj. 2020. Arabert: Transformer-based model for arabic language understanding. In *Proceedings of The 4th Workshop on Open-Source Arabic Corpora and Processing Tools*, pages 9–15.

Piyush Bansal, Romil Bansal, and Vasudeva Varma. 2015. Towards deep semantic analysis of hashtags. In *European conference on information retrieval*, pages 453–464. Springer.

Houda Bouamor, Nizar Habash, Mohammad Salameh, Wajdi Zaghouani, Owen Rambow, Dana Abdulrahim, Ossama Obeid, Salam Khalifa, Fadhl Eryani, Alexander Erdmann, and Kemal Oflazer. 2018. The MADAR Arabic Dialect Corpus and Lexicon. In *Proceedings of the Language Resources and Evaluation Conference (LREC)*, Miyazaki, Japan.

Houda Bouamor, Sabit Hassan, and Nizar Habash. 2019. The MADAR shared task on Arabic fine-grained dialect identification. In *Proceedings of the Fourth Arabic Natural Language Processing Workshop*, pages 199–207, Florence, Italy. Association for Computational Linguistics.

Michael Conover, Jacob Ratkiewicz, Matthew R Francisco, Bruno Gonçalves, Filippo Menczer, and Alessandro Flammini. 2011. Political polarization on twitter. *ICWSM*, 133:89–96.

Kareem Darwish, Mohammed Attia, Hamdy Mubarak, Younes Samih, Ahmed Abdelali, Lluís Màrquez, Mohamed Eldesouki, and Laura Kallmeyer. 2020. Effective multi dialectal arabic pos tagging. *Natural Language Engineering*, 1(1):18.

Kareem Darwish, Hassan Sajjad, and Hamdy Mubarak. 2014. Verifiably Effective Arabic Dialect Identification. In *Proceedings of the Conference on Empirical Methods in Natural Language Processing (EMNLP)*, Doha, Qatar.

Thierry Declerck and Piroska Lendvai. 2015. Processing and normalizing hashtags. In *Proceedings of the International Conference Recent Advances in Natural Language Processing*, pages 104–109.

Jacob Devlin, Ming-Wei Chang, Kenton Lee, and Kristina Toutanova. 2019. BERT: Pre-training of deep bidirectional transformers for language understanding. In *Proceedings of the 2019 Conference of the North American Chapter of the Association for Computational Linguistics: Human Language Technologies, Volume 1 (Long and Short Papers)*, pages 4171–4186, Minneapolis, Minnesota. Association for Computational Linguistics.

Mona T Diab, Mohamed Al-Badrashiny, Maryam Aminian, Mohammed Attia, Heba Elfardy, Nizar Habash, Abdelati Hawwari, Wael Salloum, Pradeep Dasigi, and Ramy Eskander. 2014. Tharwa: A Large Scale Dialectal Arabic-Standard Arabic-English Lexicon. In *Proceedings of the Language Resources and Evaluation Conference (LREC)*, pages 3782–3789, Reykjavik, Iceland.

Mahmoud El-Haj, Paul Rayson, and Mariam Aboelezz. 2018. Arabic dialect identification in the context of bivalency and code-switching. In *Proceedings of the Eleventh International Conference on Language Resources and Evaluation (LREC-2018)*, Miyazaki, Japan. European Languages Resources Association (ELRA).

Heba Elfardy and Mona Diab. 2013. Sentence Level Dialect Identification in Arabic. In *Proceedings of the Conference of the Association for Computational Linguistics (ACL)*, Sofia, Bulgaria.

Jeremy Howard and Sebastian Ruder. 2018. Universal language model fine-tuning for text classification. In *Proceedings of the 56th Annual Meeting of the Association for Computational Linguistics (Volume 1: Long Papers)*, Melbourne, Australia. Association for Computational Linguistics.

Radu Tudor Ionescu and Marius Popescu. 2016. UnibucKernel: An approach for Arabic dialect identification based on multiple string kernels. In *Proceedings of the Third Workshop on NLP for Similar Languages, Varieties and Dialects (VarDial3)*, pages 135–144, Osaka, Japan. The COLING 2016 Organizing Committee.

Armand Joulin, Edouard Grave, Piotr Bojanowski, and Tomas Mikolov. 2016. Bag of tricks for efficient text classification. *arXiv preprint arXiv:1607.01759*.

X. Li and J. Huang. 2009. Shc: A spectral algorithm for hierarchical clustering. In *2009 International Conference on Multimedia Information Networking and Security*, volume 2, pages 197–200.

Shervin Malmasi, Marcos Zampieri, Nikola Ljubešić, Preslav Nakov, Ahmed Ali, and Jörg Tiedemann. 2016. Discriminating between similar languages and Arabic dialect identification: A report on the third DSL shared task. In *Proceedings of the Third Workshop on NLP for Similar Languages, Varieties and Dialects (VarDial3)*, pages 1–14, Osaka, Japan. The COLING 2016 Organizing Committee.

Hamdy Mubarak and Kareem Darwish. 2014. Using twitter to collect a multi-dialectal corpus of arabic. In *Proceedings of the EMNLP 2014 Workshop on Arabic Natural Language Processing (ANLP)*, pages 1–7.

Hamdy Mubarak, Kareem Darwish, and Walid Magdy. 2017. Abusive language detection on arabic social media. In *Proceedings of the First Workshop on Abusive Language Online*, pages 52–56.

Damian Radcliffe and Payton Bruni. 2019. *State of Social Media Middle East: 2018*. University of Oregon Libraries.

Alec Radford, Karthik Narasimhan, Tim Salimans, and Ilya Sutskever. 2018. Improving language understanding by generative pre-training. *URL https://s3-us-west-2. amazonaws. com/openai-assets/researchcovers/languageunsupervised/language understanding paper. pdf*.

Fatiha Sadat, Farnazeh Kazemi, and Atefeh Farzindar. 2014. Automatic Identification of Arabic Dialects in Social Media. In *Proceedings of the Workshop on Natural Language Processing for Social Media (SocialNLP)*, pages 22–27, Dublin, Ireland.

Ali Safaya, Moutasem Abdullatif, and Deniz Yuret. 2020. Kuisail at semeval-2020 task 12: Bert-cnn for offensive speech identification in social media.

Mohammad Salameh, Houda Bouamor, and Nizar Habash. 2018. Fine-grained Arabic dialect identification. In *Proceedings of the 27th International Conference on Computational Linguistics*, pages 1332–1344, Santa Fe, New Mexico, USA. Association for Computational Linguistics.

Younes Samih, Mohamed Eldesouki, Mohammed Attia, Kareem Darwish, Ahmed Abdelali, Hamdy Mubarak, and Laura Kallmeyer. 2017. Learning from relatives: Unified dialectal Arabic segmentation. In *Proceedings of the 21st Conference on Computational Natural Language Learning (CoNLL 2017)*, pages 432–441, Vancouver, Canada. Association for Computational Linguistics.

Wajdi Zaghouani and Anis Charfi. 2018a. Araptweet: A large multi-dialect twitter corpus for gender, age and language variety identification. *CoRR*, abs/1808.07674.

Wajdi Zaghouani and Anis Charfi. 2018b. Guidelines and annotation framework for arabic author profiling.

Omar F Zaidan and Chris Callison-Burch. 2011. The Arabic Online Commentary Dataset: an Annotated Dataset of Informal Arabic With High Dialectal Content. In *Proceedings of the Conference of the Association for Computational Linguistics (ACL)*, pages 37–41.

Omar F Zaidan and Chris Callison-Burch. 2014. Arabic dialect identification. *Computational Linguistics*, 40(1):171–202.

Chiyu Zhang and Muhammad Abdul-Mageed. 2019. No army, no navy: Bert semi-supervised learning of arabic dialects. pages 279–284.

DiaLex:
A Benchmark for Evaluating Multidialectal Arabic Word Embeddings

Muhammad Abdul-Mageed[1] **Shady Elbassuoni**[2] **Jad Doughman**[2]
AbdelRahim Elmadany[1] **El Moatez Billah Nagoudi**[1] **Yorgo Zoughby**[2]
Ahmad Shaher[1] **Iskander Gaba**[2] **Ahmed Helal**[3] **Mohammed El-Razzaz**[4]

[1]Natural Language Processing Lab, The University of British Columbia, Vancouver, Canada
[2]American University of Beirut, Beirut, Lebanon
[3] Concordia University, Montreal, Canada
[4] Arab Academy for Science and Technology, Cairo, Egypt
[1]{muhammad.mageed,moatez.nagoudi,a.elmadany,ahmad-shaher}@ubc.ca
[2]{sd58,jad17,ytz00,amh90,img02}@aub.edu.lb
[3]amh90@mail.aub.edu [4]mohammed.elrzzaz@gmail.com

Abstract

Word embeddings are a core component of modern natural language processing systems, making the ability to thoroughly evaluate them a vital task. We describe DiaLex, a benchmark for intrinsic evaluation of dialectal Arabic word embeddings. DiaLex covers five important Arabic dialects: Algerian, Egyptian, Lebanese, Syrian, and Tunisian. Across these dialects, DiaLex provides a testbank for six syntactic and semantic relations, namely *male to female*, *singular to dual*, *singular to plural*, *antonym*, *comparative*, and *genitive to past tense*. DiaLex thus consists of a collection of word pairs representing each of the six relations in each of the five dialects. To demonstrate the utility of DiaLex, we use it to evaluate a set of existing and new Arabic word embeddings that we developed. Beyond evaluation of word embeddings, DiaLex supports efforts to integrate dialects into the Arabic language curriculum. It can be easily translated into Modern Standard Arabic and English, which can be useful for evaluating word translation. Our benchmark, evaluation code, and new word embedding models will be publicly available. [1]

1 Introduction

Word embeddings are the backbone of modern natural language processing (NLP) systems. They encode semantic and syntactic relations between words by representing them in a low-dimensional space. Many techniques have been proposed to learn such embeddings (Pennington et al., 2014; Mikolov et al., 2013a; Mnih and Kavukcuoglu, 2013) from large text corpora. As of today, a large number of such embeddings are available in many languages including Arabic. Due to their importance, it is vital to be able to evaluate word embeddings, and various methods have been proposed for evaluating them. These methods can be broadly categorized into *intrinsic* evaluation methods and *extrinsic* evaluation ones. For extrinsic evaluation, word embeddings are assessed based on performance in downstream applications. For intrinsic evaluation, they are assessed based on how well they capture syntactic and semantic relations between words.

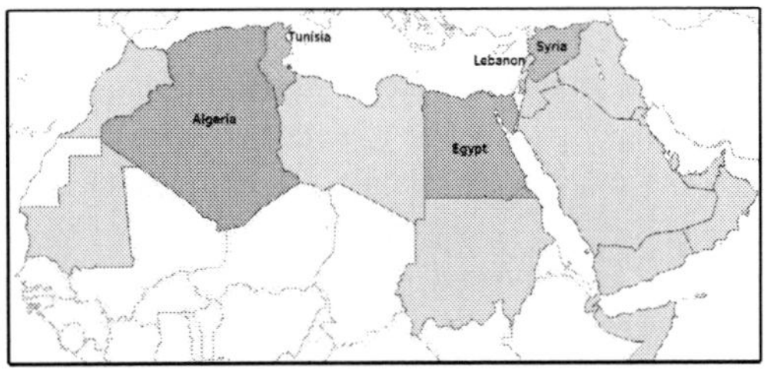

Figure 1: A map of the five Arab countries covered by DiaLex. The five countries cover different regions in the Arab world: two in the western region (Algeria and Tunisia), one in the middle (Egypt), and two in the eastern region (Lebanon and Syria).

Although there exists a benchmark for evaluating modern standard Arabic (MSA) word embeddings (Elrazzaz et al., 2017), no such resource that we know of exists for Arabic dialects. This makes it difficult to measure progress on Arabic dialect processing. In this paper, our goal is to facilitate intrinsic evaluation of dialectal Arabic word embeddings. To this end, we build a new benchmark spanning five different Arabic dialects, from Eastern, Middle, and Western Arab World. Namely, our benchmark covers Algerian (ALG), Egyptian (EGY), Lebanese (LEB), Syr-

[1]https://github.com/UBC-NLP/dialex.

Proceedings of the Sixth Arabic Natural Language Processing Workshop, pages 11–20
Kyiv, Ukraine (Virtual), April 19, 2021.

ian (SYR), and Tunisian (TUN). Figure 1 shows a map of the five Arab countries covered by DiaLex. For each one of these dialects, DiaLex consists of a set of word pairs that are syntactically or semantically related by one of six different relations: *Male to Female, Singular to Plural, Singular to Dual, Antonym, Comparative*, and *Genitive to Past Tense*. Overall, DiaLex consists of over $3,000$ word pairs in those five dialects, evenly distributed. To the best of our knowledge, DiaLex is the first benchmark that can be used to assess the quality of Arabic word embeddings in the five dialects it covers.

To be able to use DiaLex to evaluate Arabic word embeddings, we generate a set of word analogy questions from the word pairs in DiaLex. A word analogy question is generated from two word pairs from a given relation. These questions have recently become the standard in intrinsic evaluation of word embeddings (Mikolov et al., 2013a; Gao et al., 2014; Schnabel et al., 2015). To demonstrate the usefulness of DiaLex in evaluating Arabic word embeddings, we use it to evaluate a set of existing and new Arabic word embeddings. We conclude that both available and newly-developed word embedding models have moderate-to-serious coverage issues and are not sufficiently representative of the respective dialects under study. ***In addition to the benchmark of word pairs, our newly-developed dialectal Arabic word embeddings will also be publicly available.***[2]

Beyond evaluation of word embeddings, we envision DiaLex as a basis for creating multidialectal Arabic resources that can facilitate study of the semantics and syntax of Arabic dialects, for example for pedagogical applications (Mubarak et al., 2020). More broadly, we hope DiaLex will contribute to efforts for integrating dialects in the Arabic language curriculum (Al-Batal, 2017). DiaLex can also be used to complement a growing interest in contextual word embeddings (Peters et al., 2018) and self-supervised language models (Devlin et al., 2019), including in Arabic (Antoun et al., 2020; Abdul-Mageed et al., 2020a; Lan et al., 2020a). Extensions of DiaLex can also be valuable for NLP, for example, DiaLex can be easily translated into MSA, other Arabic dialects, English, or other languages. This extension can enable evaluation of word-level translation systems, including in cross-lingual settings (Aldarmaki et al., 2018; Aldarmaki and Diab, 2019). Our resources can also be used in comparisons against contextual embeddings (Peters et al., 2018) and embeddings acquired from language models such as BERT (Devlin et al., 2019). For example, it can be used in evaluation settings with Arabic language models such as AraBert (Antoun et al., 2020), GigaBERT (Lan et al., 2020b), and the recently developed ARBERT and MARBERT (Abdul-Mageed et al., 2020a). More generally, our efforts are motivated by the fact that the study of Arabic dialects and computational Arabic dialect processing is a nascent area with several existing gaps to fill (Bouamor et al., 2019; Abbes et al., 2020; Abdul-Mageed et al., 2020b, 2021, 2020c).

The rest of the paper is organized as follows. In Section 2, we describe how DiaLex was constructed. Section 3 offers our methodical generation of a testbank for evaluating word embeddings. In Section 4, we provide a case study for evaluating various word embedding models, some of which are newly developed by us. Section 5 is about related work. Section 6 is where we conclude and present future directions.

2 Benchmark Construction

DiaLex consists of a set of word pairs in five different Arabic dialects and for six different semantic and syntactic relations, namely Male to Female, Singular to Plural, Singular to Dual, Antonym, Comparative, and Genitive to Past Tense. We chose only this set of relations as they are standard in previous literature. In addition, they are comprehensive enough to reflect dialect specificity. A good word embeddings model should thus have close representation of word pairs for each of these relations in the embeddings space.

For each dialect, word pairs were *manually* generated by at least one native speaker of the dialect. Each person independently came up with the word pairs representing a given relation based on their knowledge of the dialect and while trying to include words that are typically representative and unique in that dialect. That is, to the best of our ability, the words were chosen so that they are frequently-used words in the dialect and are not the same as in MSA. One challenge we faced when generating the word pairs was orthographic variation. For example, consider the antonym of the

[2]Our benchmark, evaluation code, and new word embedding models will be available at: `https://github.com/UBC-NLP/dialex`.

Dialect	antonym	compara	genitive-pt	male-fem	sing-pl	sing-dual	all
Algerian	100	100	100	100	102	105	**607**
Egyptian	98	98	998	99	97	98	**588**
Lebanese	98	99	109	96	105	126	**633**
Syrian	98	97	98	101	97	102	**593**
Tunisian	100	100	100	100	102	147	**649**
Total	**494**	**494**	**505**	**496**	**503**	**578**	**3,070**

Table 1: Statistics of DiaLex across different relations. (**Genitive-pt**= genitive-past tense).

word ورا ("behind") in the Egyptian dialect. It can be written as قدام or أودام ("in front of") . We decided to include all variations of the same word in the benchmark. A second challenge was the need to present the relationship using more than one word. For instance, consider Algerian and the relationship dual, the word زوج ("pair") is sometimes used to describe two items of something. So, for instance, for the word ساعة ("hour"), the dual can be either زوج سوايع ("pair of hours") or ساعتين ("two hours"). Again, we opted for including both variants in the benchmark. Overall, for each dialect and each relation, around 100 word pairs were generated. Table 1 shows the statistics of DiaLex's word pairs lists and Table 2 shows some example word pairs in DiaLex and their English and MSA translations. Overall, DiaLex consists of a total of $3,070$ word pairs distributed evenly among the dialects and the relations.

3 Testbank for Evaluating Word Embeddings and Evaluation Metric

Given the word pair lists in DiaLex, we generate a testbank consisting of 260,827 tuples. Each tuple consists of two word pairs (a, b) and (c, d) from the same relation and the same dialect. For each of our five dialects and for each of our six relations, we generate a tuple by combining two different word pairs from the same relation in the same dialect. Once tuples have been generated, they can be used as word analogy questions to evaluate different word embeddings as defined by Mikolov et al. (Mikolov et al., 2013a). A word analogy question for a tuple consisting of two word pairs (a, b) and (c, d) can be formulated as follows: "a to b is like c to ?". Each such question will then be answered by calculating a target vector $t = b - a + c$. We then calculate the cosine similarity between the target vector t and the vector representation of each word w in a given word embeddings V. Finally, we retrieve the most similar word w to t, i.e., $argmax_{w \in V \& w \notin \{a,b,c\}} \frac{w \cdot t}{||w|| ||t||}$. If $w = d$ (i.e., the same word) then we assume that the word embeddings V has answered the question correctly.

Moreover, we extend the traditional word analogy task by taking into consideration if the correct answer is among the top K, with $K \in \{5, 10\}$, closest words in the embedding space to the target vector t, which allows us to more leniently evaluate the embeddings. This is particularly important in the case of Arabic since many forms of the same word exist, usually with additional prefixes or suffixes such as the equivalent of the article "the" or possessive determiners such as "her", "his", or "their". For example, consider one question which asks راجل to ست is like أمير to " ?", i.e., "man" to "woman" is like "prince" to "?", with the answer being "أميرة" or "princess". Now, if we rely only on the top-1 word and it happens to be "للأميرة" which means "for the princess" in English, the question would be considered to be answered wrongly. To relax this, and ensure that different forms of the same word will not result in a mismatch, we use the top-5 and top-10 words for evaluation rather than just the top-1.

Note that we consider a question to be answered wrongly if at least one of the words in the question are not present in the word embeddings. That is, we take into consideration the coverage of the embeddings as well (Gao et al., 2014).

Finally, we report the number of questions that were answered correctly over the total numbers of questions available. That is, assume the number of questions for a given dialect and a given relation is n, and assume that a given embeddings model M correctly answered m out of those n questions as explained above. Then, the accuracy of the model

Dialect	male-fem	sing-pl	sing-dual
Algerian	سردوك - دجاجة	كسكروط - زوج كسكروطات	بليغة - زوج بليغات
MSA	ديك - دجاجة	شطيرة - شطيرتان	نعلان - نعل
Eng.	rooster - chicken	sandwich - two sandwiches	shoe - pair of shoes
Egyptian	عسول - عسولة	أوضة - إوض	ودن - ودنين
MSA	لطيف - لطيفة	غرفة - غرف	أذن - أذنين
Eng.	nice (m) - nice (f)	room - rooms	ear - two ears
Lebanese	رجال - مرا	إداحة - اداديح	ملئعة - ملئعتين
MSA	رجل - إمرأة	ولاعة - ولاعات	ملعقة - ملعقتين
Eng.	man - woman	lighter - lighters	spoon - two spoons
Syrian	جردون - فارة	كاتو - كاتويات	زنار - زنارين
MSA	جرذ - فأرة	كعكة - كعكات	حزام - حزامين
Eng.	mouse (m) - mouse (f)	cake - cakes	belt - belts
Tunisian	تحفون - تحفونة	علوش - علالش	ريدو - زوز ريدووات
MSA	وسيم - جميلة	خروف - خرفان	ستار - ستاران
Eng.	handsome - beautiful	sheep (sing) - sheep (pl)	curtain - two curtains

Dialect	antonym	comparative	genitive-past tense
Algerian	قاوي - ضعيف	قرعاج - قرعاج أكثر	حوّس - تحواس
MSA	قوي - ضعيف	فضولي - أكثر فضولا	تنزه - نزهة
Eng.	strong - weak	nosy - nosier	promenade - promenaded
Egyptian	ورا - أودام	وحش - أوحش	عيط - عياط
MSA	خلف - أمام	سئ - أسوأ	بكي - بكاء
Eng.	back - front	bad - worse	cried - crying
Lebanese	مرتاح - مزعوج	جكل - اجكل	فات - فوتة
MSA	مرتاح - منزعج	وسيم - أوسم	دخل - دخول
Eng.	restful - restless	handsome - more handsome	entered - entering
Syrian	دفش - خبط	فهمان - افهم	بحبش - بحبشة
MSA	دفع - اصطدم	ذكي - أذكي	فتش - تفتيش
Eng.	push - bump into	smart - smarter	inspect - inspection
Tunisian	منحوس - مزهار	ميزر - ميزر أكثر	صرفق - تصرفيق
MSA	منكود - محظوظ	فقير - أفقر	صفع - صفع
Eng.	unlucky - lucky	poor - poorer	slap - slapping

Table 2: Example DiaLex word pairs in every dialect across the various relations. For each pair, we also provide MSA and English translations.

M will be $\frac{m}{n}$.

4 Evaluation of Arabic Word Embeddings Using DiaLex

In this section, we demonstrate how DiaLex can be used to evaluate word embeddings across the different dialects it covers. Particularly, we evaluate two large word embeddings models based on Word2Vec (Mikolov et al., 2013b) released by Zahran et al. (2015). One model is based on skip grams (Zah_SG) and the other is a continuous bag-of-words (Zah_CBOW). Both of these models have a vocabulary size of $626,3435$ words. We also create four CBOW Word2Vec models, all of which have 300 word vector embedding dimensions, as we describe next.

4.1 Newly-Developed Word Embedding Models

The following are our four newly-developed dialectal Arabic word embedding models:

Twitter-1B. Our first model was trained using a one billion in-house Arabic tweet collection. All tweets were crawled by putting a bounding box crawler around the whole Arab world. Since this collection is large, we only performed *light* preprocessing on it. This involved removing hashtags, URLs, and reducing consecutive repetitions of the same character into only 2. We then trained a CBOW Word2Vec model using the Python library gensim. We set the minimum word frequency at 100 and a window size of 5 words. This model has a vocabulary size of $929,803$ words.

Twitter-250K-MC50. This model uses the same data as Twitter-1B, yet with stricter preprocessing. Namely, we normalize usually orthographically confused Arabic characters by converting *Alif maksura* to *Ya*, reducing all *hamzated Alif* to plain *Alif*, and removing all non-Arabic characters. We then only keep tweets with length ≥ 5 words. This gives us a total of $223,387,189$ tweets (and hence the name *Twitter-250K*). We then use the same parameters as the 1B model, but we set the minimum count to 50 words (again, hence the name Twitter-250K-MC50 where MC50 meaning minimum count of 50). We acquire a model with a vocabulary size of $536,846$ words.

Twitter-250K-MC100. This model is identical with the Twitter-250K-MC50 model, but uses a minimum count of 100 words when training Word2Vec. This model has a vocabulary size of $202,690$ words.

Dialect	Model	K=1	K=5	K=10
ALG	Zah_SG	1.79	6.16	7.96
	Zah_CBOW	3.40	8.51	10.78
	Ours-1B	1.32	3.60	5.53
	Ours-MC-50	3.02	8.25	10.90
	Ours-Seeds	**3.88**	9.19	11.51
	Ours-MC-100	3.87	**11.33**	**15.03**
EGY	Zah_SG	1.90	5.93	8.17
	Zah_CBOW	2.06	6.75	8.98
	Ours-1B	2.09	5.86	8.65
	Ours-MC-50	**4.68**	**11.59**	15.67
	Ours-Seeds	3.21	8.19	11.63
	Ours-MC-100	4.33	11.49	**15.97**
SYR	Zah_SG	1.53	4.14	5.20
	Zah_CBOW	1.86	4.76	6.15
	Ours-1B	1.23	4.036	6.85
	Ours-MC-50	2.49	6.50	8.66
	Ours-Seeds	2.54	5.88	8.02
	Ours-MC-100	**3.14**	**9.39**	**12.97**
LEB	Zah_SG	5.14	10.97	13.69
	Zah_CBOW	6.72	12.88	15.51
	Ours-1B	2.29	5.71	7.70
	Ours-MC-50	3.97	9.71	13.83
	Ours-Seeds	3.96	8.77	11.66
	Ours-MC-100	**5.29**	**12.90**	**17.87**
TUN	Zahran_SG	1.38	6.06	8.26
	Zah_CBOW	2.63	8.19	10.77
	Ours-1B	2.53	5.54	8.47
	Ours-MC-50	3.81	8.07	12.20
	Ours-Seeds	**3.80**	**9.08**	**12.49**
	Ours-MC-100	2.49	7.68	12.14

Table 3: Evaluation of six word embedding models using our benchmark across the five dialects. In most cases, our Twitter-250K-MC100 (Ours-MC-100) achieves the best performance.

Twitter-Seeds. We use all unigram entries in our benchmark to crawl Twitter, using the search API. In order to avoid overfitting to our benchmark, we randomly sample only 400 words from it for this process. This gives us about $\sim 3M$ tweets. We then crawl up to $3,200$ tweets from the timelines of all $\sim 300K$ users who have posted the initially collected $3M$ tweets. The resulting collection is at $214,161,138$ tweets after strict cleaning and removal of all tweets of length < 5 words. To train an embedding model on this dataset, we use the same Word2Vec parameters as with Twitter-250K-MC50 (i.e., with a minimum count of 50 words). This model has a vocabulary size of $773,311$ words.

4.2 Model Evaluation

We evaluate the two models from Zahran et al. (2015) and our four models described above using DiaLex. Table 3 shows average evaluation re-

Dialect	Relation	K=1	K=5	K=10
ALG	sing-dual	None	None	None
	sing-pl	17.39	38.51	47.20
	gen-pt	0.00	2.52	2.52
	antonym	0.83	5.19	7.91
	comp	None	None	None
	male-fem	10.00	35.00	35.00
	total acc	3.87	11.33	15.03
EGY	sing-dual	13.89	27.78	36.11
	sing-pl	27.62	54.29	60.95
	gen-pt	3.40	8.85	13.55
	antonym	3.02	9.51	13.71
	comp	None	None	None
	male-fem	5.00	15.00	20.00
	total acc	4.33	11.49	15.97
SYR	sing-dual	0.00	0.00	0.00
	sing-pl	7.00	30.00	43.00
	gen-pt	0.46	3.72	4.80
	antonym	0.40	2.81	4.81
	comp	3.83	10.71	14.49
	male-fem	6.89	16.70	23.17
	total acc	3.14	9.39	12.97
LEB	sing-dual	0.00	2.04	6.12
	sing-pl	20.99	41.67	50.31
	gen-pt	1.66	4.92	8.36
	antonym	0.43	5.18	9.31
	comp	13.14	26.72	33.62
	male-fem	5.56	13.89	22.22
	total acc	5.29	12.90	17.87
TUN	sing-dual	0.00	0.00	0.00
	sing-pl	11.44	23.20	30.39
	gen-pt	0.00	4.94	11.11
	antonym	0.41	4.00	7.67
	comp	None	None	None
	male-fem	0.00	0.00	0.00
	total acc	2.48	7.68	12.14

Table 4: Evaluation across all relations for our Twitter-MC-100 model. Values shown as "None" are for relationships where the model did not include any of the word pairs in the question tuples in the model vocabulary. Zeros mean the model includes the words in its vocabulary but no correct answers were returned in the top-K.

sults across the different word relationships. For top-1 performance, one or another of our models scores best. For top-5 results, our Twitter-250K-MC100 (Ours-MC-100) acquires best performance for most dialects. Exceptions are EGY and TUN dialects. Ours-MC-100 also performs best on all but TUN dialect. These results show the necessity of developing dialectal resources for the various varieties and that a model trained on large MSA data such as that of Zahran et al. (2015) is quite sub-optimal.

Table 4 shows per-relation results evaluation of the Twitter-250K-MC100 model. We show all-relations results only for this model for space limitations, and we choose this model since it tends to perform well compared to other models. As Table 4 shows, the model works best on the LEB dialect (17.87 accuracy for top-10) and worst on TUN (12.14 accuracy for top-10). The table also shows that the sing-plural relationship is the one most challenging for the model. Clearly, the dual feature either involves (1) bigrams (in which case these unigram models do not work and hence the "None" values) or (2) different ways of expressing the same meaning of duality. For example, in the LEB pair كوريدور-كوريدورين "corridor-two corridors", duality can be expressed also by the phrase كوريدور ٢, using the digit "2" instead of the dual suffix ين in كوريدورين. Overall, these results suggest that even our developed models are neither sufficiently powerful nor large enough (even with large vocabularies close to 1M words) to cover all the dialects. We also observe that models need to see enough contexts (words > 50 minimum count) to scale well. This calls for the development of more robust models with wider coverage and more frequent contexts. Our Twitter collection of 5M words can be used towards that goal, but we opted for not exploiting it for building a word embeddings model since this would be considered overfitting to our benchmark.

5 Related Work

5.1 Arabic Word Embeddings

The number of available Arabic word embeddings is increasing rapidly. Some of these are strictly trained using textual corpora written in MSA, while others were trained using dialectal data. We review the most popular embedding models we are aware of here.

Zahran et al. (2015) built three models for Arabic word embeddings (CBOW, SKIP-G, and GloVe). To train these models, they used a large collection of MSA texts totaling $\sim$ 5.8B words. The sources used include Arabic Wikipedia, Arabic Gigaword (Parker et al., 2009), Open Source Arabic Corpora (OSAC) (Saad and Ashour, 2010), OPUS (Tiedemann, 2012), MultiUN (Chen and Eisele, 2012), and a few others. Soliman et al. (2017) proposed *AraVec* a set of Arabic word embedding models. It consist of six word embedding models built on top of three different Arabic content domains; Wikipedia Arabic, World Wide Web pages, and Tweets with more than 3.3 billion word. Both CBOW and SKIP-Gram architecture are investigated in this work.

Abdul-Mageed et al. (2018) build an SKIP-G model using $\sim$ 234M tweets, with vector dimensions at 300. The authors, however, do not exploit their model in downstream tasks. Abu Farha and Magdy (2019) built two word embeddings models (CBOW and SKIP-Gram) exploiting 250M tweets. The authors used the models in the context of training the sentiment analysis system *Mazajak*. The dimensions of each embedding vector in the Mazajak models are at 300.

More recently, El-Haj (2020) developed *Habibi*, a Multi Dialect Multi-National Arabic Song Lyrics Corpus which comprises more than $30,000$ Arabic song lyrics from 18 Arab countries and six Arabic dialects for singers. *Habibi* contains $500,000$ sentences (song verses) with more than 3.5 million words. Moreover, the authors provided a 300 dimension CBOW word embeddings of the corpus. Doughman et al. (2020) built a set of word embeddings learnt from three large Lebanese news archives, which collectively consist of $609,386$ scanned newspaper images and spanning a total of 151 years, ranging from 1933 till 2011. To train the word embeddings, Optical Character Recognition (OCR) was employed to transcribe the scanned news archives, and various archive-level as well as decade-level word embeddings were trained. In addition, models were also built using a mixture of Arabic and English data. For example, Lachraf et al. (2019) presented *AraEngVec* an Arabic-English cross-lingual word embedding models. To train their bilingual models, they used a large dataset with more than 93 million pairs of Arabic-English parallel sentences (with more than 1.8 billion words) mainly extracted from the Open Parallel Corpus Project (OPUS) (Tiedemann, 2012). In order to train the models, they have chosen CBOW and SKIP-Gram as an architecture. Indeed, they propose three methods for pre-processing the opus dataset: parallel sentences, word-level alignment and random shuffling. Both extrinsic and intrinsic evaluations for the different *AraEngVec* model variants. The extrinsic evaluation assesses the performance of models on the Arabic-English Cross-Language Semantic Textual Similarity (CL-STS) task (Nagoudi et al., 2018), while the intrinsic evaluation is based on the Word Translation (WT) task.

Some works have also investigated the utility of using morphological knowledge to enhance word embeddings. For example, Erdmann and Habash (2018) demonstrated that out-of-context rule-based knowledge of morphological structure can complement what word embeddings can learn about morphology from words' in-context behaviors. They quantified the value of leveraging subword information when learning embeddings and the further value of noise reduction techniques targeting the sparsity caused by complex morphology such as in the Arabic language case.

El-Kishky et al. (2019) tackled the problem of root extraction from words in the Semitic language family. They proposed a constrained sequence-to-sequence root extraction method. Furthermore, they demonstrated how one can leverage the root information alongside a simple slot-based morphological decomposition to improve upon word embedding representations as evaluated through word similarity, word analogy, and language modeling tasks. In this paper, we have demonstrated the effectiveness of our benchmark DiaLex in the evaluation of a chosen set of these available word embedding models and compared them to newly-developed ones by us as we explain in the next section.

5.2 Word Embeddings Evaluation

There is a wealth of research on evaluating unsupervised word embeddings, which can be broadly divided into intrinsic and extrinsic evaluations. Intrinsic evaluations mostly rely on word analogy questions and measure the similarity of words in the low-dimensional embedding space (Mikolov et al., 2013a; Gao et al., 2014; Schnabel et al., 2015). Extrinsic evaluations assess the quality of the embeddings as features in models for other tasks, such as semantic role labeling and part-of-speech tagging (Collobert et al., 2011), or noun-phrase chunking and sentiment analysis (Schnabel et al., 2015). However, all of these tasks and benchmarks are built for English and thus cannot be used to assess the quality of Arabic word embeddings, which is the main focus here.

To the best of our knowledge, only a handful of recent studies attempted evaluating Arabic word embeddings. Zahran et al. (2015) translated the English benchmark in (Mikolov et al., 2013a) and used it to evaluate different embedding techniques when applied on a large Arabic corpus. However, as the authors themselves point out, translating an English benchmark is not the best strategy to evaluate Arabic embeddings. Zahran et al. (2015) also consider extrinsic evaluation on two NLP tasks, namely query expansion for Information Retrieval and short answer grading.

Dahou et al. (2016) used the analogy questions from Zahran et al. (2015) after correcting some Arabic spelling mistakes resulting from the translation and after adding new analogy questions to make up for the inadequacy of the English questions for the Arabic language. They also performed an extrinsic evaluation using sentiment analysis. Finally, Al-Rfou et al. (2013) generated word embeddings for 100 different languages, including Arabic, and evaluated the embeddings using part-of-speech tagging, however the evaluation was done only for a handful of European languages. Elrazzaz et al. (2017) built a benchmark in MSA that can be utilized to perform intrinsic evaluation of different word embeddings using word analogy questions. They then used the constructed benchmark to evaluate various Arabic word embeddings. They also performed extrinsic evaluation of these word embeddings using two NLP tasks, namely Document Classification and Named Entity Recognition.

Salama et al. (2018) investigated enhancing Arabic word embeddings by incorporating morphological annotations to the embeddings model. They tuned the generated word vectors to their lemma forms using linear compositionality to generate lemma-based embeddings. To assess the effectiveness of their model, they used the benchmark built by Elrazzaz et al. (2017). Taylor and Brychcín (2018b) demonstrated several ways to use morphological Arabic word analogies to examine the representation of complex words in semantic vector spaces. They presented a set of morphological relations, each of which can be used to generate many word analogies.

El Bazi and Laachfoubi (2017) investigated the effect of stemming on Arabic word representations. They applied various stemmers on different word representations approaches, and conducted an extrinsic evaluation to assess the quality of these word vectors by evaluating their impact on the Named Entity Recognition task for Arabic. Taylor and Brychcín (2018a) provided a corpus of Arabic analogies focused on the morphological constructs which can participate in verb, noun and prepositional phrases. They conducted an examination of ten different semantic spaces to see which of them is most appropriate for this set of analogies, and they illustrated the use of the corpus to examine phrase-building. Barhoumi et al. (2020) proposed intrinsic and extrinsic methods to evaluate word embeddings for the specific task of Arabic sentiment analysis. For intrinsic evaluation, they proposed a new method that assesses what they define as the "sentiment stability" in the embedding space. For extrinsic evaluation, they relied on the performance of the word embeddings to be evaluated for the task of sentiment analysis. They also trained various word embeddings using different types of corpora (polar and non-polar) and evaluated them using their proposed methods. To the best of our knowledge, our proposed benchmark is the first benchmark developed in various Arabic dialects and that can be used to perform intrinsic evaluation of Arabic word embedding with respect to those dialects.

6 Conclusion

We described DiaLex, a benchmark for evaluating dialectal Arabic word embeddings. DiaLex comes in five major Arabic dialects, namely Algerian, Egyptian, Lebanese, Syrian, and Tunisian. Across these dialects, DiaLex offers a testbank of word pairs for six syntactic and semantic relations, namely *male to female*, *singular to dual*, *singular to plural*, *antonym*, *comparative*, and *genitive to past tense*. To demonstrate the utility of DiaLex, we used it to evaluate a set of available and newly-developed Arabic word embedding models. Our evaluations are intended to showcase the utility of our new benchmark. DiaLex as well as the newly-developed word embeddings will be publicly available.

DiaLex can be used to support integration of dialects in the Arabic language curriculum, and for the study of the syntax and semantics of Arabic dialects. It can also complement evaluations of contextual word embeddings. In the future, we plan to use DiaLex to for more extensive evaluation of all publicly-available Arabic word embedding models. We will also train a dialectal Arabic word embeddings model with a larger dataset and evaluate it using DiaLex. Finally, we will translate DiaLex into MSA and English to facilitate use of the resource for evaluating word translation.

References

Ines Abbes, Wajdi Zaghouani, Omaima El-Hardlo, and Faten Ashour. 2020. Daict: A dialectal Arabic irony corpus extracted from twitter. In *Proceedings of The 12th Language Resources and Evaluation Conference*, pages 6265–6271.

Muhammad Abdul-Mageed, Hassan Alhuzali, and Mohamed Elaraby. 2018. You tweet what you speak: A city-level dataset of arabic dialects. In *LREC*, pages 3653–3659.

Muhammad Abdul-Mageed, AbdelRahim Elmadany, and El Moatez Billah Nagoudi. 2020a. ARBERT & MARBERT: Deep bidirectional transformers for Arabic. *arXiv preprint arXiv:2101.01785*.

Muhammad Abdul-Mageed, Chiyu Zhang, Houda Bouamor, and Nizar Habash. 2020b. Nadi 2020: The first nuanced arabic dialect identification shared task. In *Proceedings of the Fifth Arabic Natural Language Processing Workshop*, pages 97–110.

Muhammad Abdul-Mageed, Chiyu Zhang, Abdel-Rahim Elmadany, Houda Bouamor, and Nizar Habash. 2021. NADI 2021: The Second Nuanced Arabic Dialect Identification Shared Task. In *Proceedings of the Sixth Arabic Natural Language Processing Workshop (WANLP 2021)*.

Muhammad Abdul-Mageed, Chiyu Zhang, Abdel-Rahim Elmadany, and Lyle Ungar. 2020c. Micro-dialect identification in diaglossic and code-switched environments. In *Proceedings of the 2020 Conference on Empirical Methods in Natural Language Processing (EMNLP)*, pages 5855–5876.

Ibrahim Abu Farha and Walid Magdy. 2019. Mazajak: An online Arabic sentiment analyser. In *Proceedings of the Fourth Arabic Natural Language Processing Workshop*, pages 192–198, Florence, Italy. Association for Computational Linguistics.

Mahmoud Al-Batal. 2017. *Arabic as one language: Integrating dialect in the Arabic language curriculum*. Georgetown University Press.

Rami Al-Rfou, Bryan Perozzi, and Steven Skiena. 2013. Polyglot: Distributed word representations for multilingual nlp. *arXiv preprint arXiv:1307.1662*.

Hanan Aldarmaki and Mona Diab. 2019. Context-aware cross-lingual mapping. *arXiv preprint arXiv:1903.03243*.

Hanan Aldarmaki, Mahesh Mohan, and Mona Diab. 2018. Unsupervised word mapping using structural similarities in monolingual embeddings. *Transactions of the Association for Computational Linguistics*, 6:185–196.

Wissam Antoun, Fady Baly, and Hazem˙ Hajj. 2020. Arabert: Transformer-based model for Arabic language understanding. *arXiv preprint arXiv:2003.00104*.

Amira Barhoumi, Nathalie Camelin, Chafik Aloulou, Yannick Estève, and Lamia Hadrich Belguith. 2020. Toward qualitative evaluation of embeddings for arabic sentiment analysis. In *Proceedings of The 12th Language Resources and Evaluation Conference*, pages 4955–4963.

Houda Bouamor, Sabit Hassan, and Nizar Habash. 2019. The madar shared task on arabic fine-grained dialect identification. In *Proceedings of the Fourth Arabic Natural Language Processing Workshop (WANLP19), Florence, Italy*.

Yu Chen and Andreas Eisele. 2012. Multiun v2: Un documents with multilingual alignments. In *LREC*, pages 2500–2504.

Ronan Collobert, Jason Weston, Léon Bottou, Michael Karlen, Koray Kavukcuoglu, and Pavel Kuksa. 2011. Natural language processing (almost) from scratch. *The Journal of Machine Learning Research*, 12:2493–2537.

Abdelghani Dahou, Shengwu Xiong, Junwei Zhou, Mohamed Houcine Haddoud, and Pengfei Duan. 2016. Word embeddings and convolutional neural network for arabic sentiment classification. In *International Conference on Computational Linguistics*, pages 2418–2427.

Jacob Devlin, Ming-Wei Chang, Kenton Lee, and Kristina Toutanova. 2019. Bert: Pre-training of deep bidirectional transformers for language understanding. In *Proceedings of the 2019 Conference of the North American Chapter of the Association for Computational Linguistics: Human Language Technologies, Volume 1 (Long and Short Papers)*, pages 4171–4186.

Jad Doughman, Fatima Abu Salem, and Shady Elbassuoni. 2020. Time-aware word embeddings for three lebanese news archives. In *Proceedings of The 12th Language Resources and Evaluation Conference*, pages 4717–4725.

Ismail El Bazi and Nabil Laachfoubi. 2017. Is stemming beneficial for learning better arabic word representations? In *First International Conference on Real Time Intelligent Systems*, pages 508–517. Springer.

Mahmoud El-Haj. 2020. Habibi - a multi dialect multi national Arabic song lyrics corpus. In *Proceedings of The 12th Language Resources and Evaluation Conference*, pages 1318–1326, Marseille, France. European Language Resources Association.

Ahmed El-Kishky, Xingyu Fu, Aseel Addawood, Nahil Sobh, Clare Voss, and Jiawei Han. 2019. Constrained sequence-to-sequence semitic root extraction for enriching word embeddings. In *Proceedings of the Fourth Arabic Natural Language Processing Workshop*, pages 88–96.

Mohammed Elrazzaz, Shady Elbassuoni, Khaled Shaban, and Chadi Helwe. 2017. Methodical evaluation of arabic word embeddings. In *Proceedings of the 55th Annual Meeting of the Association for Computational Linguistics (Volume 2: Short Papers)*, pages 454–458.

Alexander Erdmann and Nizar Habash. 2018. Complementary strategies for low resourced morphological modeling. In *Proceedings of the Fifteenth Workshop on Computational Research in Phonetics, Phonology, and Morphology*, pages 54–65.

Bin Gao, Jiang Bian, and Tie-Yan Liu. 2014. Wordrep: A benchmark for research on learning word representations. *arXiv preprint arXiv:1407.1640.*

Raki Lachraf, El Moatez Billah Nagoudi, Youcef Ayachi, Ahmed Abdelali, and Didier Schwab. 2019. ArbEngVec : Arabic-English cross-lingual word embedding model. In *Proceedings of the Fourth Arabic Natural Language Processing Workshop*, pages 40–48, Florence, Italy. Association for Computational Linguistics.

Wuwei Lan, Yang Chen, Wei Xu, and Alan Ritter. 2020a. An empirical study of pre-trained transformers for arabic information extraction. In *Proceedings of the 2020 Conference on Empirical Methods in Natural Language Processing (EMNLP)*, pages 4727–4734.

Wuwei Lan, Yang Chen, Wei Xu, and Alan Ritter. 2020b. Gigabert: Zero-shot transfer learning from english to arabic. In *Proceedings of The 2020 Conference on Empirical Methods on Natural Language Processing (EMNLP)*.

Tomas Mikolov, Kai Chen, Greg Corrado, and Jeffrey Dean. 2013a. Efficient estimation of word representations in vector space. *arXiv preprint arXiv:1301.3781.*

Tomas Mikolov, Ilya Sutskever, Kai Chen, Greg S Corrado, and Jeff Dean. 2013b. Distributed representations of words and phrases and their compositionality. In *Advances in neural information processing systems*, pages 3111–3119.

Andriy Mnih and Koray Kavukcuoglu. 2013. Learning word embeddings efficiently with noise-contrastive estimation. In *Advances in Neural Information Processing Systems*, pages 2265–2273.

Hamdy Mubarak, Shimaa Amer, Ahmed Abdelali, and Kareem Darwish. 2020. Arabic curriculum analysis. In *Proceedings of the 28th International Conference on Computational Linguistics: System Demonstrations*, pages 80–86.

El Moatez Billah Nagoudi, Jérémy Ferrero, Didier Schwab, and Hadda Cherroun. 2018. Word embedding-based approaches for measuring semantic similarity of arabic-english sentences. In *Arabic Language Processing: From Theory to Practice*, pages 19–33, Cham. Springer International Publishing.

Robert Parker, David Graff, Ke Chen, Junbo Kong, and Kazuaki Maeda. 2009. Arabic gigaword.

Jeffrey Pennington, Richard Socher, and Christopher Manning. 2014. Glove: Global Vectors for Word Representation. In *Proceedings of the 2014 Conference on Empirical Methods in Natural Language Processing (EMNLP)*, pages 1532–1543, Doha, Qatar. Association for Computational Linguistics.

Matthew Peters, Mark Neumann, Mohit Iyyer, Matt Gardner, Christopher Clark, Kenton Lee, and Luke Zettlemoyer. 2018. Deep contextualized word representations. In *Proceedings of the 2018 Conference of the North American Chapter of the Association for Computational Linguistics: Human Language Technologies, Volume 1 (Long Papers)*, volume 1, pages 2227–2237.

Motaz K Saad and Wesam Ashour. 2010. Osac: Open source arabic corpora. In *6th ArchEng Int. Symposiums, EEECS*, volume 10.

Rana Aref Salama, Abdou Youssef, and Aly Fahmy. 2018. Morphological word embedding for arabic. *Procedia computer science*, 142:83–93.

Tobias Schnabel, Igor Labutov, David M Mimno, and Thorsten Joachims. 2015. Evaluation methods for unsupervised word embeddings. In *EMNLP*, pages 298–307.

Abu Bakr Soliman, Kareem Eissa, and Samhaa R El-Beltagy. 2017. Aravec: A set of arabic word embedding models for use in arabic nlp. *Procedia Computer Science*, 117:256–265.

Stephen Taylor and Tomáš Brychcín. 2018a. Arabic word analogies and semantics of simple phrases. In *2018 2nd International Conference on Natural Language and Speech Processing (ICNLSP)*, pages 1–6. IEEE.

Stephen Taylor and Tomáš Brychcín. 2018b. The representation of some phrases in arabic word semantic vector spaces. *Open Computer Science*, 8(1):182–193.

Jörg Tiedemann. 2012. Parallel data, tools and interfaces in opus. In *LREC*, volume 2012, pages 2214–2218.

Mohamed A Zahran, Ahmed Magooda, Ashraf Y Mahgoub, Hazem Raafat, Mohsen Rashwan, and Amir Atyia. 2015. Word representations in vector space and their applications for arabic. In *International Conference on Intelligent Text Processing and Computational Linguistics*, pages 430–443. Springer.

Benchmarking Transformer-based Language Models for Arabic Sentiment and Sarcasm Detection

Ibrahim Abu Farha[1] and Walid Magdy[1,2]
[1]School of Informatics, The University of Edinburgh, Edinburgh, United Kingdom
[2]The Alan Turing Institute, London, United Kingdom
i.abufarha@ed.ac.uk, wmagdy@inf.ed.ac.uk

Abstract

The introduction of transformer-based language models has been a revolutionary step for natural language processing (NLP) research. These models, such as BERT, GPT and ELECTRA, led to state-of-the-art performance in many NLP tasks. Most of these models were initially developed for English and other languages followed later. Recently, several Arabic-specific models started emerging. However, there are limited direct comparisons between these models. In this paper, we evaluate the performance of 24 of these models on Arabic sentiment and sarcasm detection. Our results show that the models achieving the best performance are those that are trained on only Arabic data, including dialectal Arabic, and use a larger number of parameters, such as the recently released MARBERT. However, we noticed that AraELECTRA is one of the top performing models while being much more efficient in its computational cost. Finally, the experiments on AraGPT2 variants showed low performance compared to BERT models, which indicates that it might not be suitable for classification tasks.

1 Introduction

In recent years, the development of contextualised language representations led to a revolution in the natural language process (NLP) field. Early work on representing language started with pre-trained word representations such as Word2Vec (Mikolov et al., 2013), GloVe (Pennington et al., 2014) and fastText (Bojanowski et al., 2017). However, these word representations were static and did not rely on the context, in which they appear. Other works tried to address this issue with contextualised word representations such as ELMo (Peters et al., 2018). Howard and Ruder (2018) proposed ULMFiT, which is a method for transfer-learning that can be applied to any task in NLP. The introduction of BERT (Devlin et al., 2019) revolutionised the research on NLP. BERT is based on complicated neural network models, namely transformers. The utilisation of BERT led to achieving state-of-the-art results on many NLP tasks such as sentence completion, question answering and sentiment analysis. The advantage of BERT and similar models is that they are pre-trained on large amounts of data, which the model utilises to learn a representation of the language. Following BERT, many other transformer-based language models were released such as ELECTRA (Clark et al., 2020), GPT-1/2/3 (Radford et al., 2019; Brown et al., 2020) and T5 (Raffel et al., 2020). These models tried to improve the performance of BERT through some slight modifications on the training objective such as RoBERTa (Liu et al., 2019). Or completely changing the training methodology such as ELECTRA (Clark et al., 2020). These models were mostly specific for English with the exception of some multilingual ones such as the multilingual BERT (mBERT) (Devlin et al., 2019). Researchers on other languages followed the trend and released other language-specific models such as CamamBERT (Martin et al., 2020) for French, PhoBERT (Nguyen and Tuan Nguyen, 2020) for Vienamese, FinBERT (Virtanen et al., 2019) for Finnish, BERTje (de Vries et al., 2019) for Dutch and others.

AraBERT (Antoun et al., 2020) was the first Arabic-specific transformer-based language model. The introduction of AraBERT helped improving the performance in many Arabic NLP tasks. Recently, a large set of transformer-based Arabic language models has been released. These include BERT based models such as the new large version of AraBERT (Antoun et al., 2020), QARiB (Chowdhury et al., 2020), ARBERT/MARBERT (Abdul-Mageed et al., 2020). Also, Arabic variants of other models were released such as AraGPT2

Proceedings of the Sixth Arabic Natural Language Processing Workshop, pages 21–31
Kyiv, Ukraine (Virtual), April 19, 2021.

(Antoun et al., 2021b), AraELECTRA (Antoun et al., 2021a) and Arabic ALBERT (KUIS-AI-Lab). These models vary in their architectures, sizes and the nature of their training data. While most of these models were trained on modern standard Arabic (MSA) data; some of them, such as MARBERT, included dialectal Arabic in their training data.

Most of these models were evaluated on a small set of Arabic NLP tasks and without any direct comparison with other models. Thus, there is no clear measure of the effectiveness of one of these models on a specific task compared to the others. Hence, in this paper, we aim to provide a comparative study of the performance of all of the recently introduced Arabic language models for the well-studied Arabic sentiment analysis (SA) task and the emerging Arabic sarcasm detection task.

In this paper, we provide a rigorous comparison of the effectiveness of 24 recently-released Arabic language models. These models were evaluated for the tasks of Arabic sentiment analysis and sarcasm detection. We test these models on the newly released ArSarcasm-v2 dataset (Abu Farha et al., 2021), which was released along with the shared task on Arabic sarcasm detection. The experiments show the following: First, the models trained on dialectal Arabic are the most effective to handle the tasks under study, where the best model MARBERT achieved an F_{PN} of 0.724 on the SA task and F1-sarcastic of 0.584 on the sarcasm detection task. Second, language-specific models achieve higher results than the multilingual ones. Third, the training procedure of ELECTRA is better than the other models, as AraELECTRA (Antoun et al., 2021a) achieved results close to larger models while being smaller and more efficient. Fourth, AraGPT2 is not suited for classifications tasks as it performed worse than all the other models.

2 Related Work

2.1 Arabic Language Models

The introduction of Bidirectional Encoder Representation from Transformers (BERT) (Devlin et al., 2019) led to a revolution in the NLP world. Since then, many other models have been released such as ELECTRA (Clark et al., 2020), GPT-1/2/3 (Radford et al., 2019; Brown et al., 2020) and RoBERTa (Liu et al., 2019). Those models helped achieving state-of-the-art results on different tasks such as sentiment analysis, named entity recognition (NER), sentence completion and others. However, those models were trained mostly on English data while others included data from other languages such as the multilingual BERT (Devlin et al., 2019). Recently, Arabic NLP researchers started training Arabic variants of these models such as the works of (Antoun et al., 2020, 2021a; Chowdhury et al., 2020; Abdul-Mageed et al., 2020). AraBERT (v0.1/v1) (Antoun et al., 2020) was built using the same architecture as BERT-base (Devlin et al., 2019). AraBERT was trained using a combination of different Arabic news corpora. The authors utilised Farasa (Abdelali et al., 2016) for the preprocessing and segmentation, then they trained a SentencePiece tokenizer (Kudo, 2018) on the segmented text with a vocabulary of 60K subword tokens. Recently, the authors released AraBERT (v0.2/v2), which was trained on a larger dataset of 77GB of text. The authors trained two variants of AraBERT based on BERT-base and BERT-large architectures. AraBERT was evaluated on three tasks: named entity recognition (NER), question answering and sentiment analysis. In another work, the authors released AraELECTRA (Antoun et al., 2021a), which is trained using the same architecture and procedure used to train the original ELECTRA model(Clark et al., 2020). AraELECTRA was trained using the same preprocessing used with AraBERT(v2) and using the same data. AraELCTRA was tested only for question answering task, where it achieved state-of-the-art results on multiple datasets. In (Antoun et al., 2021b), the authors released AraGPT2, which is based on the original GPT2 (Radford et al., 2019) architecture, this model was also trained on the same data used for AraELECTRA and AraBERT(v2). Since GPT2 is trained using causal language modelling objective, the authors did not test the model on any datasets and relied on the perplexity reported during training.

In (Lan et al., 2020a), the authors pre-trained a customised bilingual BERT, GigaBERT, that is designed specifically for Arabic NLP and English-to-Arabic zero-shot transfer learning. The training data was around 13M news articles collected from different sources. They also augmented their data with code-switched samples to improve the cross-lingual performance. GigaBERT was evaluated on multiple NLP tasks such as: NER, part of speech (POS) tagging, relation extraction and argument role labelling. In (Abdul-Mageed et al., 2020), the authors proposed two new Arabic specific BERT models, ARBERT and MARBERT. For ARBERT, they used BERT-base architecture and 61GB of text as training data. The training data for ARBERT is mostly in modern standard Arabic (MSA) with a small portion in Egyptian dialect. For MARBERT, the authors aimed to improve the model's ability to handle dialectal Arabic. They enriched their training data through adding a set of randomly sampled 1B Arabic tweets. The final training dataset was around 128GB of text, 50% of which are tweets. Abdul-Mageed et al. (2020) provide an extensive evaluation of their models on many tasks such as sentiment analysis, dialect identification, NER, and others. In (Chowdhury et al., 2020), the authors introduced a new Arabic BERT (QARiB). In their work, the authors tried to improve the performance of the model through diversifying the training data. In their experiments, they show that a BERT model trained on a mixture of formal and informal data has much better generalization power compared to BERT models that are trained on formal text only. QARiB was evaluated only on a text categorization task.

From the previous summary, it is noticeable that there is a lack of direct comparison between these new language models. This, in turn, raises the question about the effectiveness of each of them against the others. In this work, we offer a direct comparison between all the new Arabic language models on two classifications tasks, sentiment analysis and sarcasm detection.

2.2 Arabic Sentiment and Sarcasm Classification

Arabic sentiment analysis (SA) has been under the researchers' radar for a while. Early work on Arabic SA such as (Abdul-Mageed et al., 2011; Abbasi et al., 2008), focused on modern standard Arabic (MSA). Later, attention started moving towards dialects such as the work of (Mourad and Darwish, 2013), where the authors introduced an expandable Arabic sentiment lexicon along with a corpus of tweets. Other works aimed to create datasets such as the works of (Kiritchenko et al., 2016; Rosenthal et al., 2017; Elmadany et al., 2018). Regarding sentiment analysis systems, there were many attempts such as the works of (El-Beltagy et al., 2017; Al-Smadi et al., 2019; Abdulla et al., 2013; Alayba et al., 2018; Abu Farha and Magdy, 2019). Abu Farha and Magdy (2021) provide a thorough comparative analysis of the available SA approaches. In their work, they compared a large variety of models on three benchmark datasets. Their analysis shows that deep learning models combined with word embeddings achieve much better performance compared to classical machine learning models, such as SVMs. However, their experiments show that the utilisation of transformer-based language models achieves better results than deep learning models. They show that a fine-tuned AraBERT (Antoun et al., 2020) model outperforms all existing classical and deep learning models on all the three benchmark datasets they examined (Abu Farha and Magdy, 2021). AraBERT achieved F_{PN} scores of 0.69 and 0.92 on SemEval-2017 (Rosenthal et al., 2017) and ArSAS (Elmadany et al., 2018) datasets respectively. Abdul-Mageed et al. (2020) tested their new language models on many SA datasets such as SemEval-2017, ArSAS and ArSarcasm (Abu Farha and Magdy, 2020) datasets. The best model (MARBERT) achieved F_{PN} scores of 0.710, 0.930, and 0.715 on the three datasets respectively.

Unlike Arabic SA, the work on Arabic sarcasm is scarce and limited to a few attempts. The earliest work on Arabic sarcasm/irony is (Karoui et al., 2017), where the authors created a dataset of Arabic tweets, which they collected using a set of political keywords. They filtered sarcastic content using distant supervision, where they used the Arabic equivalent of #sarcasm. The dataset contains 5,479 tweets, 1,733 of which are sarcastic/ironic. In their work, the authors utilised various features to experiment with their data. These features include punctuation marks, emoticons, quotations, opposition words, sentiment features, shifters features and contextual clues. They experimented with various classifiers such as SVM, Naive Bayes, Logistic Regression, Linear Regression. Random Forest was the best model, where it achieved an F1-score of 0.73. The authors of (Ghanem et al., 2019) organised a shared task competition for Arabic irony detection. They collected their data using distant supervision and used similar Arabic hashtags to the ones in (Karoui et al., 2017). In addition, they manually annotated a subset of tweets, which were sampled from ironic and non-ironic sets. The first place was (Khalifa and Hussein, 2019), where they achieved an F1-score of 0.85. In their work, they utilised a set of features that include word n-grams, topic modelling features, sentiment features, statistical features and word embeddings. They experimented with multiple classifiers such as BiLSTM,

Random Forest, XGBoost.

Abbes et al. (2020) created a corpus of ironic tweets, namely DAICT, which contains around 5,000 sarcastic/ironic tweets. In (Abu Farha and Magdy, 2020), the authors proposed ArSarcasm dataset for sarcasm detection, which contains 10,547 tweets, 1,682 of which are sarcastic. They created their data through the reannotation of previous Twitter sentiment dataset. In their work, they provided a baseline model, which was based on a BiLSTM and achieved an F1-score of 0.46 on the sarcastic class. Recently, Abdul-Mageed et al. (2020) created a set of BERT-based models and tested them on the ArSarcasm dataset, where the best model (MARBERT) achieved a macro F1 of 0.76. Those results are not directly comparable with the baseline in (Abu Farha and Magdy, 2020), as their official metric is F1-score over the sarcastic class.

A new version of ArSarcasm dataset was released, namely ArSarcasm-v2 (Abu Farha et al., 2021). This dataset is an extension of the original ArSarcasm dataset (Abu Farha and Magdy, 2020), where the authors annotated an additional 5,000 tweets and provided a new train/test split. In this work, we compare the performance of all existing Arabic transformer-based LMs on the sentiment and sarcasm detection tasks of the ArSarcasm-v2 dataset to have a comprehensive report of their performance on such tasks.

3 Experimental Setup

3.1 Dataset

In the experiments, we use ArSarcasm-v2 dataset which was released along with the WANLP 2021 shared task on sarcasm and sentiment detection in Arabic (Abu Farha et al., 2021). ArSarcasm-v2 is an extension of the original ArSarcasm dataset (Abu Farha and Magdy, 2020). The authors extended the dataset through annotating more data for sarcasm, sentiment and dialect. The authors collected the new data through random sampling from Twitter. To ensure the presence of sarcastic tweets, the authors utilised portions of DAICT corpus (Abbes et al., 2020), which contains around 5,000 tweets, most of which are sarcastic. To ensure annotation consistency, the authors re-annotated the portions from DAICT along with the newly collected tweets. The authors used Appen[1] crowd-sourcing platform for the annotation. Each tweet was annotated for sarcasm, sentiment and dialect. The final dataset consists of 15,548 tweets divided into 12,548 training tweets and 3,000 testing tweets. Table 1 provides the detailed statistics of the dataset.

[1] https://appen.com

3.2 Models

This section goes over the models used in the experiments. Each of these models has been fine-tuned for sentiment classification and sarcasm detection. The fine-tuning is done through adding a fully connected layer on top of the pre-trained model. After that, each model is fine-tuned for the specific task. In this work, we compare the following models:

- **Bi-LSTM**: a baseline model based on a BiLSTM combined with Mazajak word embeddings (Abu Farha and Magdy, 2019).

- **mBERT**: multilingual BERT provided by (Devlin et al., 2019). This model is based on BERT-base architecture and was trained on data from the Wikipedia dumps of 104 languages.

- **GigaBERT**: provided by (Lan et al., 2020a). The model was trained on a large set of Arabic news articles. The training data was augmented with English translations to improve cross lingual performance.

- **XLM-RoBERTa (XLM-R)**: multilingual extension of the original RoBERTa model Liu et al. (2020) provided by (Conneau et al., 2020). We use two variants of this model, XLM-R-base and XLM-R-large .

- **AraBERT**: Arabic-specific BERT provided by (Antoun et al., 2020). We use all the versions of AraBERT (v0.1/1/0.2/2). AraBERT (v0.2/2) models are trained on more data compared to AraBERT (v0.1/1). We experiment with all the variants of these models (base and large) and the models with and without Farasa (Abdelali et al., 2016) presegmentation. AraBERT (v0.1/1) was trained on 23GB of text while AraBERT (v0.2/2) was trained on 77GB of text.

- **AraELECTRA**: Arabic-specific ELECTRA provided by (Antoun et al., 2021a). ELECTRA contains two modules, a generator and a discriminator. Usually, the discriminator is taken and fine-tuned for downstream tasks. In

Set	Sarcasm		Sentiment			Total
	Sarcastic	Non-sarcastic	Positive	Negative	Neutral	
Training	2,168	10,380	2,180	4,621	5,747	12,548
Testing	821	2,179	575	1,677	748	3,000
Total	2,989	12,559	2,577	6,298	6,495	15,548

Table 1: Statistics of training and testing datasets, showing the number of examples for both sarcasm detection and sentiment analysis tasks.

this work, we experiment with both the generator and the discriminator. AraELECTRA was trained on the same 77GB of text used for AraBERT.

- **Arabic BERT**: provided by (Safaya et al., 2020). The model was trained on 95GB of text from the Arabic version of the unshuffled OSCAR corpus (Ortiz Suárez et al., 2020) and the Arabic Wikipedia. The model is available in two variants based on the number of parameters (base and large).
- **Arabic ALBERT**: provided by (KUIS-AI-Lab). An Arabic version of ALBERT (Lan et al., 2020b). This model was trained on data from the Arabic version of the unshuffled OSCAR corpus (Ortiz Suárez et al., 2020) and the Arabic Wikipedia. There are three variants of this model based on the number of parameters (base, large, xlarge).
- **ARBERT/MARBERT**: provided by (Abdul-Mageed et al., 2020). These models are based on the BERT-base and trained on a set of books and news articles. ARBERT was trained on 66GB of text only from news articles. MARBERT was trained on a larger dataset (128 GB), 50% of which is tweets. The variation in MARBERT's training data gives it the ability to better handle the variations in dialectal Arabic, which is very useful to the tasks in this paper.
- **QARiB**: provided by (Chowdhury et al., 2020). This model was trained on various sources of data including news articles and tweets.
- **AraGPT2**: Arabic-specific GPT2 provided by (Antoun et al., 2021b). AraGPT2 is a stacked transformer-decoder model trained using the causal language modelling objective. The model was trained on 77GB of Arabic text (same as AraELECTRA and AraBERT). AraGPT2 comes in four variants: AraGPT2-base, AraGPT2-medium, AraGPT2-large and AraGPT2-mega. We experiment with the base, medium and large variants.

A summary of details about these models and their variants is shown in Table 3.

3.3 Hyper-parameters and evaluation

In the experiments [2], we relied on the implementation provided by HuggingFace's Transformers library (Wolf et al., 2019). We used the provided *AutoModelForSequenceClassification* which matches each model to the proper implementation. We trained the models for 5 epochs with a learning rate of $5e{-}6$. The maximum sequence length was set to 128 tokens. For AraBERT experiments, we used the provided pipeline, which uses Farasa (Abdelali et al., 2016) segmentation for some models. For the BiLSTM model, we used 128 hidden units, Rectified Linear Unit (*ReLU*), and *Adam* (Kingma and Ba, 2015) optimiser with a learning rate of 0.0001.

For evaluation, we used the official metrics used in the WANLP 2021 shared task on sarcasm and sentiment detection in Arabic (Abu Farha et al., 2021). For the sarcasm detection task, F1-score of the sarcastic class is the main metric. For sentiment analysis, the macro average of the F1-scores of the positive and negative classes (F_{PN}) is the main metric. This metric, F_{PN}, has been adopted as the standard metric for sentiment classification in SemEval tasks (Rosenthal et al., 2017).

4 Results

4.1 Models Effectiveness for Sentiment and Sarcasm Detection

Table 2 shows the results achieved by all the models on the dataset for both sentiment analysis and sarcasm detection tasks. The first five rows include

[2] All the experiments in this work were conducted on a server machine with a 32 core CPU, 512GB RAM and a Quadro RTX 6000 GPU (24GB GPU Memory).

Model	Sentiment Analysis			Sarcasm Detection		
	Recall	Accuracy	F_{PN}	Precision	Recall	F1-sarcastic
BiLSTM	0.623	0.671	0.691	0.728	0.653	0.483
mBERT	0.570	0.624	0.625	0.683	0.622	0.425
GigaBERT	0.625	0.662	0.673	0.717	0.676	0.527
XLM-R-base	0.605	0.643	0.661	0.700	0.670	0.518
XLM-R-large	0.641	0.678	0.699	0.709	0.691	0.551
AraBERT-base (v01)	0.630	0.670	0.691	0.723	0.699	0.565
AraBERT-base (v1)	0.638	0.677	0.696	0.723	0.679	0.532
AraBERT-base (v02)	0.654	0.686	0.709	0.723	0.694	0.556
AraBERT-base (v2)	0.651	0.690	0.711	0.732	0.676	0.525
AraBERT-large (v02)	0.659	0.695	0.718	0.728	0.709	0.579
AraBERT-large (v2)	0.660	**0.700**	**0.724**	0.713	0.707	0.575
AraELECTRA (discriminator)	0.649	0.687	0.709	0.731	0.708	0.578
AraELECTRA (generator)	0.604	0.648	0.663	0.675	0.691	0.527
Arabic BERT-base	0.627	0.668	0.687	0.724	0.670	0.516
Arabic BERT-large	0.648	0.678	0.699	0.720	0.694	0.556
Arabic ALBERT-base	0.600	0.653	0.663	0.706	0.693	0.555
Arabic ALBERT-large	0.603	0.657	0.669	0.701	0.674	0.523
Arabic ALBERT-xlarge	0.623	0.674	0.691	0.705	0.678	0.530
MARBERT	**0.664**	0.693	**0.724**	0.714	**0.714**	**0.584**
ARBERT	0.642	0.673	0.695	0.729	0.709	0.578
QARiB	0.661	0.688	0.720	**0.734**	0.690	0.551
AraGPT2-base	0.594	0.647	0.662	0.717	0.673	0.522
AraGPT2-medium	0.602	0.649	0.666	0.697	0.673	0.522
AraGPT2-large	0.562	0.612	0.629	0.681	0.671	0.521

Table 2: Results achieved by all models on sentiment analysis and sarcasm detection tasks.

the BiLSTM baseline along with the multilingual BERT models. The rest of the table contains the results achieved by Arabic-specific language models. As can be seen in Table 2, most models, including the BiLSTM baseline, are achieving good results on the sentiment analysis task. On the sarcasm detection task, which is more challenging, the use of Arabic-specific language models provides a large boost in performance. The overall best model is MARBERT, which is a BERT model trained 128GB of textual data, 50% of which is dialectal Arabic. MARBERT achieved an F_{PN} score of 0.724 on the sentiment analysis task and an F1-score (sarcastic class) of 0.584. AraBERT-large (v2) achieved similar performance on SA, while slightly falling behind on the sarcasm detection task.

From Table 2, it is noticeable that larger models tend to achieve higher results, which is due to their larger representational power. The large variants of AraBERT are achieving higher than the other smaller models. Additionally, the nature of the training data has a significant effect on the performance. Models such as MARBERT and QARiB were trained on a mixture of MSA and dialectal Arabic. It is noticeable that the performance of these models is better than other similar or even larger models such as Arabic BERT-large and Arabic ALBERT-large. Nevertheless, it is also noticeable the applied prepossessing has an effect where similar models achieve different results. For example, AraBERT-base and Arabic BERT are based on the same architecture and trained on similar data, but AraBERT achieves higher results. The preprocessing used for AraBERT includes the removal of non-Arabic words, while Arabic BERT data has some inline non-Arabic words. Additionally, it is clear that the training methodology is an important factor in a model's performance. Models trained with masked language modelling (MLM), BERT variants, or replaced token detection (RTD), ELECTRA, are better for classification tasks. AraGPT2 is trained using causal language modelling objective, which is quite useful for sentence completion and language generation tasks, but it seems that it is not as effective for classification tasks. Finally, it is clear that monolingual models achieve higher scores than the multilingual ones such as mBERT, XLM-R, and GigaBERT.

4.2 Models Computational Cost

The development of transformer-based language models embarked the war to develop larger and larger models with billions of parameters. This raised the question of the computational cost, the

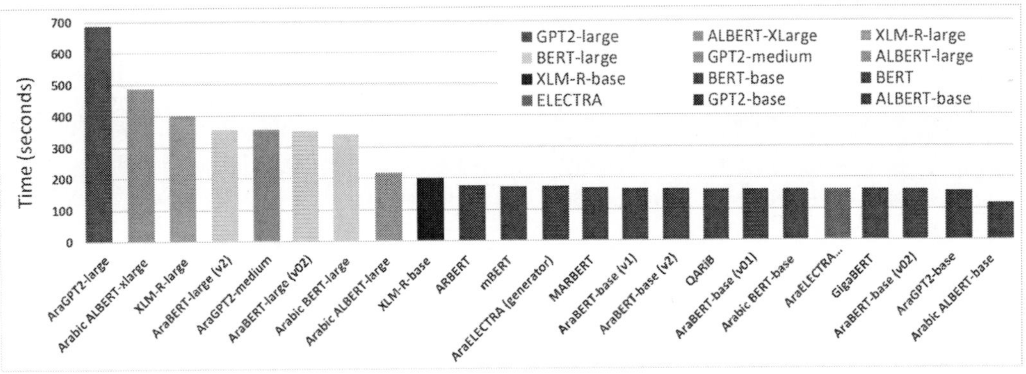

Figure 1: Time (in seconds) needed to fine-tune each model for one epoch for the sarcasm detection task.

accessibility of such models and the time needed to train and fine tune them. The largest model we experimented with is AraGPT2-Mega, which we were not able to fine-tune on the aforementioned machine due to lack of memory. Figure 1 shows the time needed to fine-tune each of the models for one epoch with the same batch size. From the figure, it is noticeable that the time is monotonically increasing with the number of parameters within the model. AraGPT2-large (792M parameters) is the slowest while the fastest is Arabic ALBERT-base.

When considering both the time and performance, AraELECTRA is one of the fastest and lightest models to fine-tune, yet it achieves results closer to other larger models. Thus, it could be the choice when dealing with limited resources. In our experiments, AraELECTRA achieved results closer to larger models (AraBERT-large), while it consumes half the space in the memory and can be fine-tuned much faster.

5 Summary of Findings

From the experimentation of the existing transformer-based LMs on Arabic sentiment and sarcasm detection, we can learn the following:

- Existing Arabic specific models are better than multilingual ones. In the experiments, Arabic-specific models achieved higher results than their multilingual equivalents. Larger multilingual models achieve similar scores to smaller monolinguals.
- Large models (based on the number of parameters) achieve better results than small ones, when trained on similar data. This is due to the larger representational power.
- Models that included social media text in the training data, achieve better results on these tasks, which also contain dialectal Arabic. Enriching the training data with social media data would increase the model's ability to handle dialectal Arabic, which is crucial for many NLP tasks.
- ELECTRA is more efficient while still being effective. The training procedure of ELECTRA produces better representation than other models. AraELECTRA achieved similar results to AraBERT that has double the number of parameters.
- For classification tasks, BERT is better than GPT2. BERT is trained using masked language modelling (MLM) objective, while GPT2 is trained using causal language modelling. Since all the variants of AraGPT2 achieved lower scores compared to other models, we can conclude that the representation learnt by BERT/ELECTRA is better suited for classification.

Table 3 summarises all our findings on these models, including their details, performance, architecture, number of parameters, training data size and source.

We hope that this benchmark study would guide future research in Arabic sentiment and sarcasm detection, and generally in Arabic NLP tasks including the creation of new language resources.

6 Conclusion and Future Work

In this paper, we provided a comprehensive benchmark to the 24 existing transformed-based language models that support Arabic on two NLP

Model	Text nature	Lang	Text size	Variant	Number of parameters	Time $mm{:}ss$	Sentiment F_{PN}	Sarcasm $F1$
mBERT	W	multi	N/A	-	110M	2:51	0.625	0.425
GigaBERT	W, N, OC, CS	Ar-En	N/A	-	125M	2:40	0.673	0.527
XLM-R	CC	multi	N/A	base	270M	3:17	0.661	0.518
				large	550M	6:41	0.699	0.551
AraBERT-v1	W, N, OC	Ar	23GB	base (v01)	136M	2:40	0.691	0.565
				base (v1)*	136M	2:43	0.696	0.532
AraBERT-v2	W, N, OC	Ar	77GB	base (v02)	136M	2:39	0.709	0.556
				base (v2)*	136M	2:43	0.711	0.525
				large (v02)	371M	5:51	0.718	0.579
				large (v2)*	371M	5:57	0.724	0.575
AraELECTRA	W, N, OC	Ar	77GB	discriminator	135M	2:40	0.709	0.578
				generator	60M	2:51	0.663	0.527
Arabic BERT	W, OC	Ar	95GB	base	110M	2:40	0.687	0.516
				large	340M	5:41	0.699	0.556
Arabic ALBERT	W, OC	Ar	N/A	base	N/A	1:56	0.663	0.555
				large		3:37	0.669	0.523
				xlarge		8:06	0.691	0.53
MARBERT	W, N, OC, B, T	Ar	128GB	-	163M	2:47	0.724	0.584
ARBERT	W, N, OC, B		61GB	-	163M	2:55	0.695	0.578
QARiB	N, T, S		N/A	-	N/A	2:41	0.72	0.551
AraGPT2	W, N, OC	Ar	77GB	base	135M	2:34	0.662	0.522
				medium	370M	5:55	0.666	0.522
				large	792M	11:27	0.629	0.521

Table 3: Summary of the results achieved by each model on the sarcasm detection and sentiment analysis tasks. The table includes details about the model variant, architecture, training data size, training data nature, number of parameters, time needed to fine-tune for one epoch (batch size=4). In text nature types are : tweets (T), Wikipedia (W), news (N), OSCAR corpus (OC), Common Crawl (CC), subtitles (S), and books (B). (CS) stands for code-switching, and (*) indicates that Farasa segmentation is applied to the text. Finally, (N/A) indicates that information is not available.

tasks, sentiment analysis and sarcasm detection. The experiments showed that including social media data in the training would improve the performance on the tasks under study. Also, language-specific models tend to perform better than the multilingual ones. Additionally, the experiments showed that the training procedure has a major effect on a model's performance, where GPT2 variants performed poorly compared to other models. Also, the experiments showed that ELECTRA-based models learn better representation than other similar size models, where AraELECTRA was on par with AraBERT with double the number of parameters.

For future work, one of the immediate studies that is essential for Arabic NLP researchers is to extend a more comprehensive benchmark study on the effectiveness of these model on other Arabic NLP tasks, including other classification tasks, text generation, and information extraction tasks. Such work would be an excellent guide for researchers in the field and will provide insights on the required efforts for improving these language models on different NLP tasks.

7 Acknowledgement

This work was partially supported by the Defence and Security Programme at the Alan Turing Institute, funded by the UK Government.

References

Ahmed Abbasi, Hsinchun Chen, and Arab Salem. 2008. Sentiment analysis in multiple languages: Feature selection for opinion classification in web forums. *ACM Transactions on Information Systems (TOIS)*, 26(3):1–34.

Ines Abbes, Wajdi Zaghouani, Omaima El-Hardlo, and Faten Ashour. 2020. DAICT: A dialectal Arabic irony corpus extracted from Twitter. In *Proceedings of the 12th Language Resources and Evaluation Conference*, pages 6265–6271, Marseille, France. European Language Resources Association.

Ahmed Abdelali, Kareem Darwish, Nadir Durrani, and Hamdy Mubarak. 2016. Farasa: A fast and furious segmenter for Arabic. In *Proceedings of the 2016 Conference of the North American Chapter of the Association for Computational Linguistics: Demonstrations*, pages 11–16, San Diego, California. Association for Computational Linguistics.

Muhammad Abdul-Mageed, Mona T. Diab, and Mohammed Korayem. 2011. Subjectivity and sentiment analysis of modern standard arabic. In *Proceedings of the 49th Annual Meeting of the Association for Computational Linguistics: Human Language Technologies: Short Papers - Volume 2*, HLT '11, pages 587–591, Stroudsburg, PA, USA. Association for Computational Linguistics.

Muhammad Abdul-Mageed, AbdelRahim Elmadany, and El Moatez Billah Nagoudi. 2020. Arbert & marbert: Deep bidirectional transformers for arabic. *arXiv preprint arXiv:2101.01785*.

N. A. Abdulla, N. A. Ahmed, M. A. Shehab, and M. Al-Ayyoub. 2013. Arabic sentiment analysis: Lexicon-based and corpus-based. In *2013 IEEE Jordan Conference on Applied Electrical Engineering and Computing Technologies (AEECT)*, pages 1–6.

Ibrahim Abu Farha and Walid Magdy. 2019. Mazajak: An online Arabic sentiment analyser. In *Proceedings of the Fourth Arabic Natural Language Processing Workshop*, pages 192–198, Florence, Italy. Association for Computational Linguistics.

Ibrahim Abu Farha and Walid Magdy. 2020. From Arabic sentiment analysis to sarcasm detection: The ArSarcasm dataset. In *Proceedings of the 4th Workshop on Open-Source Arabic Corpora and Processing Tools, with a Shared Task on Offensive Language Detection*, pages 32–39, Marseille, France. European Language Resource Association.

Ibrahim Abu Farha and Walid Magdy. 2021. A comparative study of effective approaches for arabic sentiment analysis. *Information Processing Management*, 58(2):102438.

Ibrahim Abu Farha, Wajdi Zaghouani, and Walid Magdy. 2021. Overview of the wanlp 2021 shared task on sarcasm and sentiment detection in arabic. In *Proceedings of the Sixth Arabic Natural Language Processing Workshop*.

Mohammad Al-Smadi, Bashar Talafha, Mahmoud Al-Ayyoub, and Yaser Jararweh. 2019. Using long short-term memory deep neural networks for aspect-based sentiment analysis of Arabic reviews. *International Journal of Machine Learning and Cybernetics*, 10(8):2163–2175.

Abdulaziz M. Alayba, Vasile Palade, Matthew England, and Rahat Iqbal. 2018. A combined cnn and lstm model for arabic sentiment analysis. In *Machine Learning and Knowledge Extraction*, pages 179–191, Cham. Springer International Publishing.

Wissam Antoun, Fady Baly, and Hazem Hajj. 2020. AraBERT: Transformer-based model for Arabic language understanding. In *Proceedings of the 4th Workshop on Open-Source Arabic Corpora and Processing Tools, with a Shared Task on Offensive Language Detection*, pages 9–15, Marseille, France. European Language Resource Association.

Wissam Antoun, Fady Baly, and Hazem Hajj. 2021a. Araelectra: Pre-training text discriminators for arabic language understanding. In *Proceedings of the Sixth Arabic Natural Language Processing Workshop*.

Wissam Antoun, Fady Baly, and Hazem Hajj. 2021b. Aragpt2: Pre-trained transformer for arabic language generation. In *Proceedings of the Sixth Arabic Natural Language Processing Workshop*.

Piotr Bojanowski, Edouard Grave, Armand Joulin, and Tomas Mikolov. 2017. Enriching word vectors with subword information. *Transactions of the Association for Computational Linguistics*, 5:135–146.

Tom B Brown, Benjamin Mann, Nick Ryder, Melanie Subbiah, Jared Kaplan, Prafulla Dhariwal, Arvind Neelakantan, Pranav Shyam, Girish Sastry, Amanda Askell, et al. 2020. Language models are few-shot learners. *arXiv preprint arXiv:2005.14165*.

Shammur Absar Chowdhury, Ahmed Abdelali, Kareem Darwish, Jung Soon-Gyo, Joni Salminen, and Bernard J. Jansen. 2020. Improving Arabic text categorization using transformer training diversification. In *Proceedings of the Fifth Arabic Natural Language Processing Workshop*, pages 226–236, Barcelona, Spain (Online). Association for Computational Linguistics.

Kevin Clark, Minh-Thang Luong, Quoc V. Le, and Christopher D. Manning. 2020. ELECTRA: Pre-training text encoders as discriminators rather than generators. In *ICLR*.

Alexis Conneau, Kartikay Khandelwal, Naman Goyal, Vishrav Chaudhary, Guillaume Wenzek, Francisco Guzmán, Edouard Grave, Myle Ott, Luke Zettlemoyer, and Veselin Stoyanov. 2020. Unsupervised cross-lingual representation learning at scale. In *Proceedings of the 58th Annual Meeting of the Association for Computational Linguistics*, pages 8440–8451, Online. Association for Computational Linguistics.

Jacob Devlin, Ming-Wei Chang, Kenton Lee, and Kristina Toutanova. 2019. BERT: Pre-training of deep bidirectional transformers for language understanding. In *Proceedings of the 2019 Conference of the North American Chapter of the Association for Computational Linguistics: Human Language Technologies*, pages 4171–4186, Minneapolis, Minnesota. Association for Computational Linguistics.

Samhaa R. El-Beltagy, Mona El Kalamawy, and Abu Bakr Soliman. 2017. NileTMRG at SemEval-

2017 task 4: Arabic sentiment analysis. In *Proceedings of the 11th International Workshop on Semantic Evaluation (SemEval-2017)*, pages 790–795, Vancouver, Canada. Association for Computational Linguistics.

AbdelRahim A Elmadany, Hamdy Mubarak, and Walid Magdy. 2018. Arsas: An arabic speech-act and sentiment corpus of tweets. In *OSACT 3: The 3rd Workshop on Open-Source Arabic Corpora and Processing Tools*, page 20.

Bilal Ghanem, Jihen Karoui, Farah Benamara, Véronique Moriceau, and Paolo Rosso. 2019. Idat at fire2019: Overview of the track on irony detection in arabic tweets. In *Proceedings of the 11th Forum for Information Retrieval Evaluation*, pages 10–13.

Jeremy Howard and Sebastian Ruder. 2018. Universal language model fine-tuning for text classification. In *Proceedings of the 56th Annual Meeting of the Association for Computational Linguistics*, pages 328–339, Melbourne, Australia. Association for Computational Linguistics.

Jihen Karoui, Farah Banamara Zitoune, and Veronique Moriceau. 2017. Soukhria: Towards an irony detection system for arabic in social media. *Procedia Computer Science*, 117:161–168.

M. Khalifa and Noura Hussein. 2019. Ensemble learning for irony detection in arabic tweets. In *FIRE*.

Diederik P. Kingma and Jimmy Ba. 2015. Adam: A method for stochastic optimization. In *3rd International Conference on Learning Representations*, pages 1–15.

Svetlana Kiritchenko, Saif Mohammad, and Mohammad Salameh. 2016. Semeval-2016 task 7: Determining sentiment intensity of english and arabic phrases. In *Proceedings of the 10th international workshop on semantic evaluation (SEMEVAL-2016)*, pages 42–51.

Taku Kudo. 2018. Subword regularization: Improving neural network translation models with multiple subword candidates. In *Proceedings of the 56th Annual Meeting of the Association for Computational Linguistics*, pages 66–75, Melbourne, Australia. Association for Computational Linguistics.

KUIS-AI-Lab. Arabic-albert.

Wuwei Lan, Yang Chen, Wei Xu, and Alan Ritter. 2020a. Gigabert: Zero-shot transfer learning from english to arabic. In *Proceedings of The 2020 Conference on Empirical Methods on Natural Language Processing (EMNLP)*.

Zhenzhong Lan, Mingda Chen, Sebastian Goodman, Kevin Gimpel, Piyush Sharma, and Radu Soricut. 2020b. Albert: A lite bert for self-supervised learning of language representations. In *International Conference on Learning Representations*.

Yinhan Liu, Myle Ott, Naman Goyal, Jingfei Du, Mandar Joshi, Danqi Chen, Omer Levy, Mike Lewis, Luke Zettlemoyer, and Veselin Stoyanov. 2019. Roberta: A robustly optimized bert pretraining approach. *arXiv preprint arXiv:1907.11692*.

Yinhan Liu, Myle Ott, Naman Goyal, Jingfei Du, Mandar Joshi, Danqi Chen, Omer Levy, Mike Lewis, Luke Zettlemoyer, and Veselin Stoyanov. 2020. Ro{bert}a: A robustly optimized {bert} pretraining approach.

Louis Martin, Benjamin Muller, Pedro Javier Ortiz Suárez, Yoann Dupont, Laurent Romary, Éric de la Clergerie, Djamé Seddah, and Benoît Sagot. 2020. CamemBERT: a tasty French language model. In *Proceedings of the 58th Annual Meeting of the Association for Computational Linguistics*, pages 7203–7219, Online. Association for Computational Linguistics.

Tomas Mikolov, Kai Chen, Greg Corrado, and Jeffrey Dean. 2013. Efficient estimation of word representations in vector space. In *1st International Conference on Learning Representations*, pages 1–12.

Ahmed Mourad and Kareem Darwish. 2013. Subjectivity and sentiment analysis of modern standard arabic and arabic microblogs. In *Proceedings of the 4th workshop on computational approaches to subjectivity, sentiment and social media analysis*, pages 55–64.

Dat Quoc Nguyen and Anh Tuan Nguyen. 2020. PhoBERT: Pre-trained language models for Vietnamese. In *Findings of the Association for Computational Linguistics: EMNLP 2020*, pages 1037–1042, Online. Association for Computational Linguistics.

Pedro Javier Ortiz Suárez, Laurent Romary, and Benoît Sagot. 2020. A monolingual approach to contextualized word embeddings for mid-resource languages. In *Proceedings of the 58th Annual Meeting of the Association for Computational Linguistics*, pages 1703–1714, Online. Association for Computational Linguistics.

Jeffrey Pennington, Richard Socher, and Christopher Manning. 2014. Glove: Global vectors for word representation. In *Proceedings of the 2014 Conference on Empirical Methods in Natural Language Processing*, pages 1532–1543, Doha, Qatar. Association for Computational Linguistics.

Matthew Peters, Mark Neumann, Mohit Iyyer, Matt Gardner, Christopher Clark, Kenton Lee, and Luke Zettlemoyer. 2018. Deep contextualized word representations. In *Proceedings of the 2018 Conference of the North American Chapter of the Association for Computational Linguistics: Human Language Technologies*, pages 2227–2237, New Orleans, Louisiana. Association for Computational Linguistics.

Alec Radford, Karthik Narasimhan, Tim Salimans, and Ilya Sutskever. Improving language understanding by generative pre-training.

Alec Radford, Jeff Wu, Rewon Child, David Luan, Dario Amodei, and Ilya Sutskever. 2019. Language models are unsupervised multitask learners.

Colin Raffel, Noam Shazeer, Adam Roberts, Katherine Lee, Sharan Narang, Michael Matena, Yanqi Zhou, Wei Li, and Peter J. Liu. 2020. Exploring the limits of transfer learning with a unified text-to-text transformer. *Journal of Machine Learning Research*, 21(140):1–67.

Sara Rosenthal, Noura Farra, and Preslav Nakov. 2017. SemEval-2017 task 4: Sentiment analysis in twitter. In *Proceedings of the 11th International Workshop on Semantic Evaluation (SemEval-2017)*, pages 502–518, Vancouver, Canada. Association for Computational Linguistics.

Ali Safaya, Moutasem Abdullatif, and Deniz Yuret. 2020. KUISAIL at SemEval-2020 task 12: BERT-CNN for offensive speech identification in social media. In *Proceedings of the Fourteenth Workshop on Semantic Evaluation*, pages 2054–2059, Barcelona (online). International Committee for Computational Linguistics.

Antti Virtanen, Jenna Kanerva, Rami Ilo, Jouni Luoma, Juhani Luotolahti, Tapio Salakoski, Filip Ginter, and Sampo Pyysalo. 2019. Multilingual is not enough: Bert for finnish. *arXiv preprint arXiv:1912.07076*.

Wietse de Vries, Andreas van Cranenburgh, Arianna Bisazza, Tommaso Caselli, Gertjan van Noord, and Malvina Nissim. 2019. Bertje: A dutch bert model. *arXiv preprint arXiv:1912.09582*.

Thomas Wolf, Lysandre Debut, Victor Sanh, Julien Chaumond, Clement Delangue, Anthony Moi, Pierric Cistac, Tim Rault, R'emi Louf, Morgan Funtowicz, and Jamie Brew. 2019. Huggingface's transformers: State-of-the-art natural language processing. *ArXiv*, abs/1910.03771.

What does BERT learn from Arabic machine reading comprehension datasets?

Eman Albilali, Nora Al-Twairesh and Manar Hosny
College of Computer and Information Sciences
King Saud University, KSA
{ealbilali, twairesh, mifawzi}@ksu.edu.sa

Abstract

In machine reading comprehension tasks, a model must extract an answer from the available context given a question and a passage. Recently, transformer-based pre-trained language models have achieved state-of-the-art performance in several natural language processing tasks. However, it is unclear whether such performance reflects true language understanding. In this paper, we propose adversarial examples to probe an Arabic pre-trained language model (AraBERT), leading to a significant performance drop over four Arabic machine reading comprehension datasets. We present a layer-wise analysis for the transformer's hidden states to offer insights into how AraBERT reasons to derive an answer. The experiments indicate that AraBERT relies on superficial cues and keyword matching rather than text understanding. Furthermore, hidden state visualization demonstrates that prediction errors can be recognized from vector representations in earlier layers.

1 Introduction

The rise of pre-trained Language Models (LM), including ELMo (Peters et al., 2018), BERT (Devlin et al., 2019), GPT (Radford et al., 2019), and RoBERTa (Liu et al., 2019), has shifted the field of Natural Language Processing (NLP) from training complex neural models from scratch to fine-tuning on downstream tasks. These contextual embeddings are generated by training on a general language model task, such that these vectors encode the structure and meaning of each word in the context. This approach has replaced the effort needed to tailor complex neural models with a simple fine-tuning using a relatively small amount of data for a specific task. As the use of LMs is growing in various NLP tasks, it is important to understand how they achieve high performance. This understanding can be used to leverage their strengths, identify their vulnerabilities, and rectify their weaknesses.

Morphologically Rich Languages (MRL) are languages in which significant information is expressed morphologically via word variation, such as in Arabic, Hebrew, and Turkish, rather than syntactically, as in English (Habash, 2010). The diversity of word forms requires machine learning models to cope with the extreme data sparseness that follows from the complex word structure, which further complicates automatic semantic identification. Furthermore, as each word can appear in multiple forms, some are unseen in the annotated data, which amplifies the Out-of-Vocabulary (OOV) problem.

Recently, a considerable number of research studies have sought to analyze different LMs in the context of the English language, while other languages have received limited attention. Most studies, including (Hewitt and Manning, 2019), (Tenney et al., 2019a), and (Tenney et al., 2019b), use black-box external probes to assess model robustness and to identify its weaknesses. The present study follows this direction and proposes adversarial examples as external probes to investigate what underpins the reported performance of Arabic pre-trained LMs.

This paper focuses on the task of Arabic Machine Reading Comprehension (MRC), which requires the model to extract a span from the text as the answer, given a question and a passage. Our approach involves probing the fine-tuned AraBERT (version 0.1) (Antoun et al., 2020a) model by appending distractors containing keywords to examples in the test set and, in turn, evaluating model robustness. The goal is to mislead the model into making incorrect predictions by adding uninterpretable information to the passage, noting that humans can still easily find the correct answer. To the best of our knowledge, no previous research study

Proceedings of the Sixth Arabic Natural Language Processing Workshop, pages 32–41
Kyiv, Ukraine (Virtual), April 19, 2021.

Source: TyDI QA dataset

Context: **تشيلسي بريمن إعارته دي حيث سيتي 2012 عام إشراكه البلجيكي في لمانشستر ثم انضم في 11 متى نادر كان جينك تم إلى دي نادي وفاز انضم – مسيرته بلقب حيث المباريات المحترفين فيردر تمت ، الإنجليزي الانجليزي؟ كيفن بروين دوري في ، إلى لاعباً بدأ عادياً2010 .**
بدأ دي بروين مسيرته في جينك، حيث كان لاعباً عادياً وفاز بلقب دوري المحترفين البلجيكي 2010–11. في عام 2012، انضم إلى نادي تشيلسي الإنجليزي، حيث تم إشراكه في المباريات بشكل نادر ثم تمت إعارته إلى فيردر بريمن. وقع مع فولفسبورج مقابل 18 مليون جنيه استرليني في عام 2014، وفي عام 2015 حصل على لقب أفضل لاعب في السنة في ألمانيا.[11] في وقت لاحق من ذلك العام، انضم إلى مانشستر سيتي مقابل 54 مليون جنيه استرليني.

Question: متى انضم اللاعب كيفن دي بروين لمانشستر سيتي الانجليزي؟

Answer: 2015.

Figure 1: An instance from the TyDI QA MRC dataset with a distractor sentence (presented in bold) appended to the beginning of the passage.

analyzes the Arabic pre-trained LM fine-tuned on MRC task.

Figure 1 shows an example of a distractor sentence appended to the passage. We construct an unreadable distractor by concatenating a variation of keywords from the question, answer, and a random sentence from the passage, and shuffling the word order in the input. Our experimental results show a significant performance drop, implying that AraBERT (version 0.1) relies on statistical cues and keyword matching and, moreover, can be distracted easily when irrelevant information is added to the passage.

Although the task of Arabic MRC has gained popularity in the research community, the question of what information must be captured by a model to achieve high performance remains unclear. We extend our analysis on adversarial examples by examining the hidden state vectors between encoder layers. At this end, we visualize vector transformations in each layer of the transformer for correctly-predicted and falsely-predicted answers. This visualization exposes incorrect predictions in the earlier layers and reveals the part of the context that the model regards as supporting facts.

We summarize the main contributions of this research as follows:

- We conduct a deep analysis of the state of the art Arabic LM (namely, AraBERT (Antoun et al., 2020a)) on Arabic MRC datasets.
- We construct adversarial examples for Arabic MRC that fool the model and undermine its performance substantially.
- We visualize and analyze the hidden state vectors in each layer of the transformer model for Arabic MRC.

The rest of the paper is organized as follows: Section 2 reviews the related work. Section 3 discusses the methodology to construct adversarial examples and visualizes the transformer's hidden state vectors. We conduct several experiments and discuss our findings in section 4. Finally, we conclude the paper in section 5.

2 Related Work

The interpretability and probing of models for NLP tasks fall into three areas: probing tasks to understand linguistic properties captured by the model; adversarial examples to understand the flaws and weaknesses of the model; and assessing dataset quality by conducting partial training and constructing challenging sets (Belinkov and Glass, 2019). We discuss the first two directions as they are the focus of our work.

Probing tasks The most common approach used to understand the linguistic properties captured by a model is to investigate its hidden states by designing probing tasks. The authors in (Tenney et al., 2019b) designed a novel edge probing task to measure the effectiveness of a pre-trained model in capturing linguistic information, which involved probing core NLP tasks encompassing diverse syntactic and semantic phenomena. In (Tenney et al., 2019a), the authors discovered that BERT follows a classical NLP pipeline in an interpretable and localizable way. The authors in (van Aken et al., 2019) applied a set of general and QA-specific probing tasks to discover information in each representation layer. An attention-based probing classifier was proposed by (Clark et al., 2019) to demonstrate syntactic information and coreference captured by BERT's attention. Through structural probes, (Hewitt and Manning, 2019) suggested that syntactic information can be recovered from BERT token representations.

As multiple probing studies report that BERT possesses syntactic, semantic, and world knowledge information, (Tenney et al., 2019a) emphasized that the absence of linguistic patterns in a probing classifier cannot lead one to conclude that the information is not there, nor can the presence of such information reveal how it is used. Furthermore, it is worth questioning the extent to which a probing classifier can be complex such that the recovered information is extracted from the original model rather than the probing classifier (Rogers et al., 2020). To rectify these issues,

(Elazar et al., 2020) proposed amnesic probing, which involves removing certain information from the model (e.g., part-of-speech tags) and evaluating the performance change.

Adversarial examples Adversarial examples have gained immense popularity in the NLP field, particularly as a way to understand model failures. Most research studies have focused on constructing black-box attacks due to the nature of the text (Belinkov and Glass, 2019). First, the discrete nature of the input complicates the task of measuring the distance between the original and the adversarial example. Second, it is difficult to formulate minimizing the distance as an optimization problem for a discrete input. In (Jia and Liang, 2017), it was shown that appending a distractor sentence to the passage in an MRC task lowers the performance for state-of-the-art models. The authors in (Alzantot et al., 2018) proposed a black-box genetic algorithm to construct semantically and syntactically similar examples, the aim being to fool sentiment analysis and textual entailment models. The performance of BERT dropped when evaluated on unreadable adversarial examples, which were generated by appending keywords to candidate answers in multiple-choice reading comprehension datasets (Si et al., 2019). Recently, model-in-the-loop adversarial annotation, which has been investigated by (Wallace et al., 2019), (Nie et al., 2020), and (Kaushik et al., 2020), is a new direction that has been applied to annotate challenging datasets using an adversarial model to retrieve hard examples. The annotators are allowed to interact with the adversary during the annotation process, and they can use model feedback to inform the generation process.

Only one study, that of (Alshemali and Kalita, 2019), has investigated adversarial examples in the Arabic language. Specifically, noun-adjective agreement in Arabic was violated in order to construct a perturbed input text. This attack fooled a word-level Bidirectional Long Short-term Memory (BiLSTM) model and a word-level Convolutional Neural Network (CNN) model, and it successfully reduced model performance when evaluated on a sentiment analysis task.

Transformer models Our analysis focuses on AraBERT (version 0.1) (Antoun et al., 2020a), an Arabic pre-trained language model based on the BERT-BASE architecture (Devlin et al., 2019). BERT is a stack of transformer encoder layers with multiple self-attention heads (Vaswani et al., 2017). In (Antoun et al., 2020a), the authors trained the BERT-BASE architecture on manually-scraped Arabic news websites, the public-words Arabic corpus, and the Open Source International Arabic News Corpus (OSIAN). Since then, several Arabic transformer models have been proposed. Safaya et al. (2020) introduced an Arabic BERT, a pre-trained BERT-BASE on Arabic Wikipedia dump and the Arabic version of OSCAR (Ortiz Suárez et al., 2020). In ARBERT and MARBERT, (Abdul-Mageed et al., 2020) pre-trained BERT model on Modern Standard Arabic (MSA) and dialects. Antoun et al. (2020b) generated AraGPT2 trained from scratch on large Arabic corpora following the architecture and training procedure of GPT2 (Radford et al., 2019).

To the best of our knowledge, no research study has been undertaken to analyze recent Arabic pre-trained language models. Arabic adversarial examples were constructed for sentiment analysis task (Alshemali and Kalita, 2019), but no previous study has examined adversarial examples for Arabic MRC.

3 Methodology

We focus our analysis on AraBERT (version 0.1) fine-tuned on the task of Arabic MRC using four different Arabic MRC datasets. We propose two approaches to investigate the model's failures and to study the transformation of hidden vectors in each layer. First, we construct an unreadable perturbed sentence and append it to the context to generate adversarial examples. Following this, we qualitatively analyze the vector transformations by examining their position in vector space.

3.1 Adversarial Examples

This subsection introduces the method for constructing adversarial examples. We first fine-tune AraBERT (version 0.1) on the original training set and, in turn, evaluate it on the perturbed set. To generate an adversarial example, we append an unreadable perturbed sentence to the passage. To obtain the distractor sentence, we concatenate different parts from the example, as shown in Figure 2. We generate an ungrammatical sentence by randomly shuffling the sentence and changing the word order in the input. Note that we only shuffle the distractor sentence and leave the answer unchanged, as

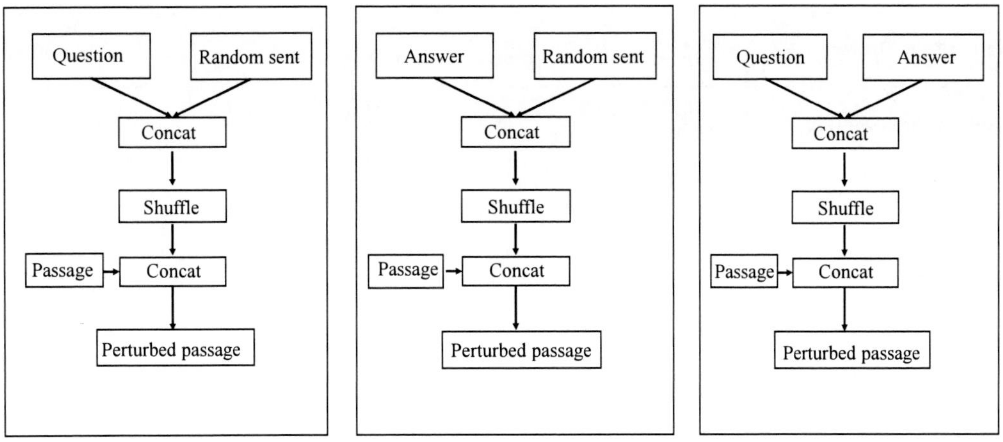

(a) Question-Sent-Shuffled (b) Answer-Sent-Shuffled (c) Question-Answer-Shuffled

Figure 2: Procedure for constructing adversarial examples for MRC.

well as the other sentences. For this reason, the example's answer remains the same.

We construct three variants for the adversarial attack based on the information appended to the distractor. *Q-Sent-Shuffled* attack is constructed by concatenating the question and a random sentence from the passage that does not contain the answer. In *Answer-Sent-Shuffled* attack, the distractor is formed by mixing the answer and random sentence words. Even if the answer appears twice in the context, the model should extract the answer from the relevant context rather than from the unreadable text. The shuffled question and answer are appended to the text in *Q-Answer-Shuffled* attack.

To ensure that the distractor is ungrammatical and difficult to interpret, we reshuffle the sequence based on the shuffle degree as follows:

$$ShuffleDegree = \frac{MinimumEditDistance}{SequenceLength}$$

The Minimum Edit Distance (MED) is calculated between the original sequence and the shuffled sequence. The original sequence is re-shuffled until the shuffle degree exceeds a threshold value (in this case, 0.65). The main trigger, here, is that certain words from the question appear in the passage with other random sentences. Ideally, if the pre-trained LM understands the text and does not rely on keyword matching, it will not be fooled by the distractor sentence.

3.2 Visualization of Transformed Tokens

BERT's architecture is based on a stacked transformer that allows the vector transformation to be traced for each token traversing from the bottom to the top layers. Following (van Aken et al., 2019), we use this characteristic and analyze the vector transformation for correctly-predicted and falsely-predicted answers.

To analyze vector transformation for the Arabic pre-trained LM fine-tuned on an MRC task, we randomly select correct and incorrect answer samples from the respective test sets. We extract the vector representation for each token in the sequence from each layer and remove padding. We consider the distance between vectors in the vector space as an indication of the semantic relation. The BERT-BASE model uses hidden vectors with a dimension of 768, and we need to visualize the relation between vectors within a 2-dimensional (2D) space. Accordingly, we apply Principal Component Analysis (PCA) to reduce the vector dimensions into 2D in each layer.

4 Experiments and Analysis

4.1 Datasets

In this paper, we analyze four Arabic MRC datasets. We briefly introduce each one in the following subsections.

	AR TyDI QA dev	AR XQuAD	AR MLQA	Arabic WikiReading	Average
AraBERTv0.1	68.94	25.88	23.73	63.01	-
Q-Sent-Shuffled	48.47 -29.7%	**13.89** **-46.33%**	**12.66** **-46.65%**	**53.07** **-15.1%**	-34.45%
Answer-Sent-Shuffled	50.97 -26.07%	22.98 -11.21%	20.00 -15.72%	58.37 -6.62%	-14.9%
Q-Answer-Shuffled	**44.08** **-36.06%**	18.74 -27.59%	19.48 -17.91	-	-27.19%
Average drop	-30.61%	-28.38%	-26.76%	-10.86%	-25.51%

Table 1: EM scores for fine-tuned AraBERT (version 0.1) on the original and perturbed test sets with adversarial examples. Italicized numbers represent the percentage of performance drop relative to the original performance. Bold performance values indicate the most effective method to distract the model for each dataset.

TyDI QA is a multi-lingual dataset covering 11 topological diverse languages (Clark et al., 2020). The dataset was collected by annotators who were presented with a short prompt from Wikipedia and asked to write a question inspired by the prompt. The Wikipedia article that best matched the question using Google search was returned as the context. After that, the annotator selected the passage containing the answer, if any, along with the minimal span containing the answer. This dataset evaluates three tasks: passage selection, minimal answer selection, and gold passage. We are interested in the gold passage task; to extract the answer from a passage rather than from a long text to facilitate the comparison with other datasets.

XQuAD is a cross-lingual MRC dataset composed of 240 paragraphs and 1,190 question-answer pairs translated from SQuADv1.1 by professional translators into 10 languages, one of which is Arabic (Artetxe et al., 2020).

MLQA is a multilingual QA dataset comprising 7 languages (Lewis et al., 2020). Question-answer pairs were collected by crowd-workers in the English language, after which they were translated into the target languages by professional translators.

Arabic WikiReading[1] The dataset was automatically constructed under a distant supervision strategy using the Wikidata statement property as a query and the statement value as the ground truth answer. Arabic articles were collected from *arwikiExtracts*[2] by parsing an Arabic *20190920* Wikipedia dump, using the *WikiExtractor*[3] tool to strip away images, tables, info-boxes, and figures. The first paragraph of each article, which captures the essential information of an article, was extracted and paragraphs with fewer than 300 characters were discarded. Arabic Wikidata dump was extracted from the *20190909.JSON* dump using the *Wikidata-filter*[4] tool. All statements with the same item and property were consolidated into a single (item, property, answer) triple. Query-answer pairs were then matched with the relevant paragraph by replacing each Wikidata item in the (item, property, answer) triples with the appropriate Wikipedia curated paragraph, knowing the title of the Wikipedia article that matches the item in the collected triples, and discarding any item not linked to Wikipedia articles to form approximately 98,000 MRC instances.

4.2 Experimental Setup

We base our training code on the PyTorch implementation of Hugging Face transformers[5]. We use AraBERT (version 0.1) (Antoun et al., 2020a), a BERT BASE model (Devlin et al., 2019) pre-trained on an Arabic corpus with 12 layers, 12 self-attention heads, and a total of 110 million parameters. We fine-tune AraBERT (version 0.1) on Arabic MRC datasets. Precisely, we train on the Arabic TyDI QA gold passage (Clark et al., 2020) training set, and we evaluate on the original development set and the perturbed variants, as the test

[1]https://github.com/esulaiman/Arabic-WikiReading-and-KaifLematha-datasets

[2]https://github.com/motazsaad/arwikiExtracts

[3]https://github.com/attardi/wikiextractor

[4]https://github.com/xwhan/wikidata-filter

[5]https://huggingface.co/transformers/

	AR TyDI QA dev	AR XQuAD	AR MLQA	Arabic WikiReading	Average
AraBERTv0.1	81.70	41.04	39.64	68.27	-
Q-Sent-Shuffled	**62.90** **-23.01%**	**22.36** **-45.52%**	**21.61** **-45.48%**	**58.08** **-13.66%**	-31.92%
Answer-Sent-Shuffled	67.18 -17.77%	37.49 -8.66%	35.38 -10.75%	66.81 -0.68%	-9.47%
Q-Answer-Shuffled	68.84 -15.74%	40.12 -2.24	43.66 +10.14	-	-2.6%
Average drop	-18.84%	-18.87%	-15.36%	-7.17%	-14.66%

Table 2: F1 scores for fine-tuned AraBERT (version 0.1) on the original and perturbed test sets with adversarial examples. Italicized numbers represent the percentage of performance drop relative to the original performance. Bold performance values indicate the most effective method to distract the model for each dataset.

set is not publicly available. We further evaluate the model on the original Arabic XQuAD (Artetxe et al., 2020) and Arabic MLQA (Lewis et al., 2020) test sets and their perturbed variants. Additionally, we train on the Arabic WikiReading training set and evaluate using the test set and the constructed adversarial examples. Each training run is performed over 3 epochs with a batch size equals 8, and we follow (Mozannar et al., 2019) by adopting a learning rate of 3e-5. The maximum sequence length chosen is 512. Tokens exceeding this length are truncated, while the input sequence is padded to reach the maximum sequence length.

4.3 Results and Discussion

The performance results are reported in Tables 1 and 2. Table 1 shows the EM score for the AraBERT (version 0.1) model tested on the original MRC datasets and the attacked variants with adversarial examples discussed in Section 3. Note that the question and the ground-truth answers are unchanged. AraBERT (version 0.1) achieves F1 scores of 81.70 and 68.27 when tested on Ar-TyDI QA and Arabic WikiReading, respectively, while Ar-XQuAD and Ar-MLQA perform poorly with 41.04 and 39.64 F1 score, respectively. When evaluating using the adversarial examples, the performance drops by around 45% for Ar-XQuAD and Ar-MLQA, and by 23% for TyDI QA for the question-random sentence attack. This indicates that AraBERT (version 0.1) was fooled by the adversarial sentence inserted into the passage, which was unreadable even for humans. This implies that the BERT model relies heavily on statistical cues and keyword matching rather than an understanding of the text. This result is consistent with English LM studies (Si et al., 2019), suggesting that BERT is not robust against adversarial attacks.

Generally, the inclusion of question words into the perturbed sentence causes the greatest reduction in F1 score over all the datasets. Similarly, when the question words appear in the distractor sentence, the EM score decreases substantially across all the datasets. Adversarial attacks targeted at the Arabic WikiReading dataset yield the lowest performance decrease compared to other MRC datasets. This may be due to the nature of the question, which consists of a small number of tokens compared to other MRC datasets.

Token Transformation Analysis Figure 3 shows the vector representation for the question and the passage tokens reduced into 2D using PCA. Vector transformation from the bottom to the top layers suggests that the model follows several phases to answer the question. Figure 3a indicates that earlier layers in AraBERT (version 0.1) group tokens with similar subjects into clusters, simulating an embedding layer in the neural network architecture.

In the middle layers (layer 5 in the figure), we observe that some tokens remain grouped based on topical similarity (sorp, qrAn and Ayp), سورة، قرآن و آية while other tokens transform to represent the relation between entities given the input context. For instance, the model identifies that the tokens are (mrym and Alkhf) مريم و الكهف related to each other as *sorp* سورة rather than as pronouns and these tokens were observed close to each other in the vector space. The task-specific function of matching the question with the support-

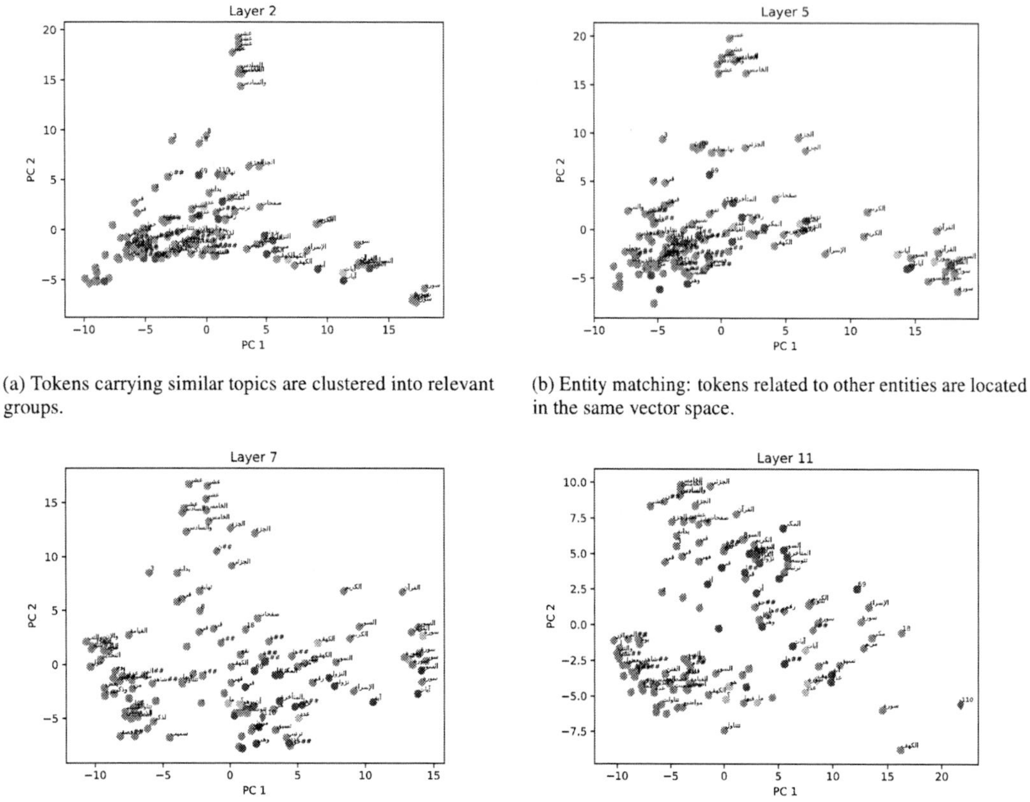

(a) Tokens carrying similar topics are clustered into relevant groups.

(b) Entity matching: tokens related to other entities are located in the same vector space.

(c) Supporting fact matching: question tokens are matched to the relevant sentence from the context.

(d) Answer extraction: the answer is separated from other tokens.

Figure 3: Vector visualization for the question-context tokens from different AraBERT (version 0.1) layers after applying PCA dimensionality reduction. Red diamond represents the answer token, dark cyan dots indicate supporting fact tokens, turquoise dots are question tokens, and gray dots show other tokens in the sequence.

ing facts appears at layer 7. Question tokens are transformed to the same vector space as the context tokens related to the answer. Finally, in the last layer, the model dissolves most of the previous clusters and distinguishes the possible answer from other tokens, while irrelevant tokens form a separate cluster, as depicted in Figure 3d.

Adversarial Examples Analysis We visualize the vector transformation for an incorrectly predicted answer in a perturbed example from the TyDi QA development set depicted in figure 1. The example was generated by concatenating a shuffled question and random sentence to the passage. We further compare it to the original example before adding the perturbed sentence, thereby investigating the effect of the attack on model understanding. Figures 4a and 4b represent the vector space for the question and context tokens in layer 7. As discussed earlier, the question tokens are transformed in the middle layers to group with supporting facts from the context. Figures 4a and 4b show that the question tokens are far from the supporting fact tokens (illustrated with green dots), while tokens from the perturbed sentence in Figure 4b cover the same vector space as the question tokens. This suggests the importance of supporting fact extraction in layer 7. In particular, when the model was unable to extract the supporting fact from the context, it was fooled, and question tokens were matched with the perturbed sentence containing words from the question. As a result, the answer *2012* was selected from the perturbed sentence rather than the correct answer *2015*.

Although the model predicted *2015* as the correct answer in Figure 4c, the vector visualizations indicate that the other candidate answers *2014,*

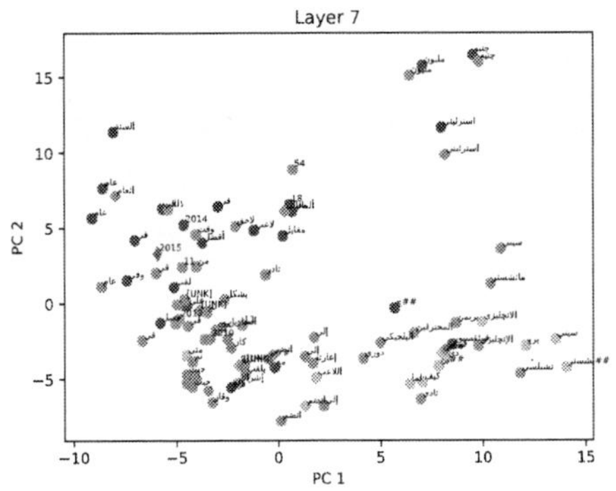

(a) Question tokens are not matched with the supporting fact and located far away in the vector space.

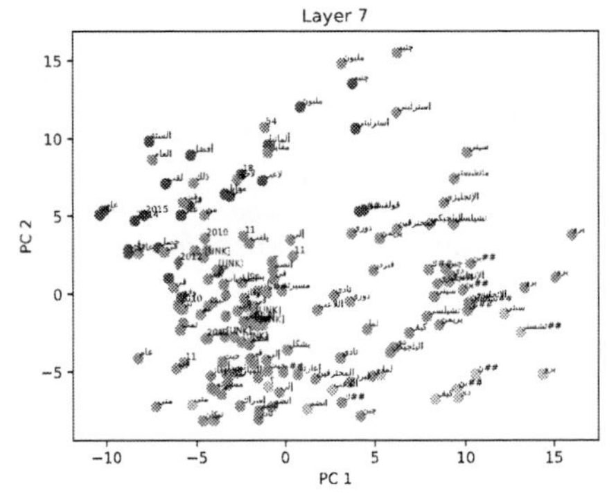

(b) Question tokens are far from supporting facts and matched with perturbed sentence tokens.

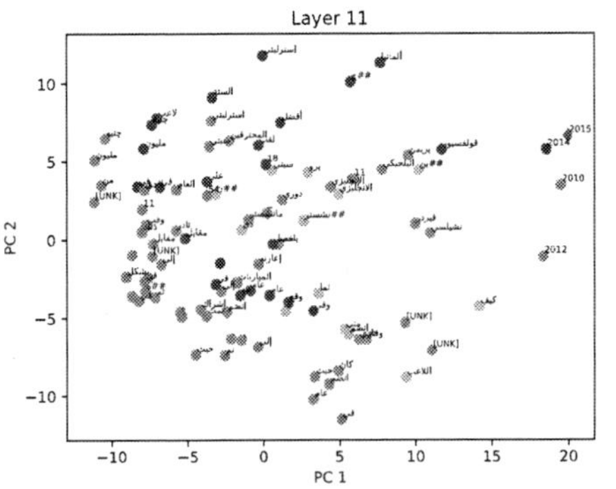

(c) The answer (2015) is extracted as the answer, while other candidate answers appeared in the same vector space.

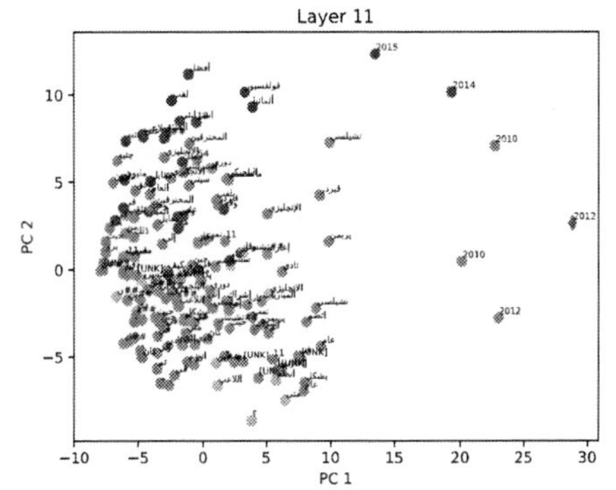

(d) A token (2012) from the perturbed sentence is extracted as the answer.

Figure 4: Vector visualization for the question-context tokens from different AraBERT layers after applying PCA dimensionality reduction. Red diamond represents the answer token, dark cyan dots indicate supporting fact tokens, turquoise dots are question tokens, and gray dots show other tokens in the sequence.

2010, and 2012 cover the same vector space as the correct answer, and the other tokens are spread over the vector space rather than forming a homogeneous group. However, the model predicted the answer *110* in Figure 3d with high confidence since that other tokens were separated from the answer and formed groups far away from the answer.

5 Conclusion

This paper analyzed hidden state transformations through layers and adversarial examples to explore what an Arabic pre-trained LM learns from MRC datasets. We proposed a simple yet effective method to construct adversarial examples that fool AraBERT, which resulted in a substantial performance drop. Our analysis suggests that pre-trained LMs achieve competitive performance simply by relying on superficial cues such as lexical overlap or entity type matching.

Qualitative analysis of the hidden states of transformers indicated that uninterpretable information can be used to understand the reasons that underpin model failure and weaknesses. We demonstrated that locating the correct supporting fact for MRC earlier in the middle layers contributes to correct predictions. Our finding suggests that different layers solve different problems. We suggest examining part of the network or connecting non-adjacent layers based on the downstream task at hand.

It would be worthwhile for future work to analyze the degree to which different tokenization methods (input representations) assist in the learning of better morphology and the modeling of infrequent words in Arabic pre-trained LMs. Furthermore, we are interested in extending our adversarial examples to cover other Arabic pre-trained LMs and constructing unanswerable questions.

References

Muhammad Abdul-Mageed, AbdelRahim Elmadany, and El Moatez Billah Nagoudi. 2020. Arbert & marbert: Deep bidirectional transformers for arabic. *arXiv preprint arXiv:2101.01785*.

Betty van Aken, Benjamin Winter, Alexander Löser, and Felix A. Gers. 2019. How does bert answer questions? a layer-wise analysis of transformer representations. In *Proceedings of the 28th ACM International Conference on Information and Knowledge Management*, CIKM '19, page 1823–1832, New York, NY, USA. Association for Computing Machinery.

Basemah Alshemali and Jugal Kalita. 2019. Adversarial examples in arabic. In *2019 International Conference on Computational Science and Computational Intelligence (CSCI)*, pages 371–376. IEEE.

Moustafa Alzantot, Yash Sharma, Ahmed Elgohary, Bo-Jhang Ho, Mani Srivastava, and Kai-Wei Chang. 2018. Generating natural language adversarial examples. In *Proceedings of the 2018 Conference on Empirical Methods in Natural Language Processing*, pages 2890–2896, Brussels, Belgium. Association for Computational Linguistics.

Wissam Antoun, Fady Baly, and Hazem Hajj. 2020a. AraBERT: Transformer-based model for Arabic language understanding. In *Proceedings of the 4th Workshop on Open-Source Arabic Corpora and Processing Tools, with a Shared Task on Offensive Language Detection*, pages 9–15, Marseille, France. European Language Resource Association.

Wissam Antoun, Fady Baly, and Hazem Hajj. 2020b. Aragpt2: Pre-trained transformer for arabic language generation.

Mikel Artetxe, Sebastian Ruder, and Dani Yogatama. 2020. On the cross-lingual transferability of monolingual representations. In *Proceedings of the 58th Annual Meeting of the Association for Computational Linguistics*, pages 4623–4637, Online. Association for Computational Linguistics.

Yonatan Belinkov and James Glass. 2019. Analysis methods in neural language processing: A survey. *Transactions of the Association for Computational Linguistics*, 7:49–72.

Jonathan H. Clark, Eunsol Choi, Michael Collins, Dan Garrette, Tom Kwiatkowski, Vitaly Nikolaev, and Jennimaria Palomaki. 2020. TyDi QA: A benchmark for information-seeking question answering in typologically diverse languages. *Transactions of the Association for Computational Linguistics*, 8:454–470.

Kevin Clark, Urvashi Khandelwal, Omer Levy, and Christopher D. Manning. 2019. What does BERT look at? an analysis of BERT's attention. In *Proceedings of the 2019 ACL Workshop BlackboxNLP: Analyzing and Interpreting Neural Networks for NLP*, pages 276–286, Florence, Italy. Association for Computational Linguistics.

Jacob Devlin, Ming-Wei Chang, Kenton Lee, and Kristina Toutanova. 2019. BERT: Pre-training of deep bidirectional transformers for language understanding. In *Proceedings of the 2019 Conference of the North American Chapter of the Association for Computational Linguistics: Human Language Technologies, Volume 1 (Long and Short Papers)*, pages 4171–4186, Minneapolis, Minnesota. Association for Computational Linguistics.

Yanai Elazar, Shauli Ravfogel, Alon Jacovi, and Yoav Goldberg. 2020. When bert forgets how to pos: Amnesic probing of linguistic properties and mlm predictions. *arXiv preprint arXiv:2006.00995*.

Nizar Y Habash. 2010. Introduction to arabic natural language processing. *Synthesis Lectures on Human Language Technologies*, 3(1):1–187.

John Hewitt and Christopher D. Manning. 2019. A structural probe for finding syntax in word representations. In *Proceedings of the 2019 Conference of the North American Chapter of the Association for Computational Linguistics: Human Language Technologies, Volume 1 (Long and Short Papers)*, pages 4129–4138, Minneapolis, Minnesota. Association for Computational Linguistics.

Robin Jia and Percy Liang. 2017. Adversarial examples for evaluating reading comprehension systems. In *Proceedings of the 2017 Conference on Empirical Methods in Natural Language Processing*, pages 2021–2031, Copenhagen, Denmark. Association for Computational Linguistics.

Divyansh Kaushik, Eduard Hovy, and Zachary C Lipton. 2020. Learning the difference that makes a difference with counterfactually-augmented data. *International Conference on Learning Representations (ICLR)*.

Patrick Lewis, Barlas Oguz, Ruty Rinott, Sebastian Riedel, and Holger Schwenk. 2020. MLQA: Evaluating cross-lingual extractive question answering. In *Proceedings of the 58th Annual Meeting of the Association for Computational Linguistics*, pages 7315–7330, Online. Association for Computational Linguistics.

Yinhan Liu, Myle Ott, Naman Goyal, Jingfei Du, Mandar Joshi, Danqi Chen, Omer Levy, Mike Lewis, Luke Zettlemoyer, and Veselin Stoyanov. 2019. Roberta: A robustly optimized bert pretraining approach. *arXiv preprint arXiv:1907.11692*.

Hussein Mozannar, Elie Maamary, Karl El Hajal, and Hazem Hajj. 2019. Neural Arabic question answering. In *Proceedings of the Fourth Arabic Natural Language Processing Workshop*, pages 108–118,

Florence, Italy. Association for Computational Linguistics.

Yixin Nie, Adina Williams, Emily Dinan, Mohit Bansal, Jason Weston, and Douwe Kiela. 2020. Adversarial NLI: A new benchmark for natural language understanding. In *Proceedings of the 58th Annual Meeting of the Association for Computational Linguistics*, pages 4885–4901, Online. Association for Computational Linguistics.

Pedro Javier Ortiz Suárez, Laurent Romary, and Benoît Sagot. 2020. A monolingual approach to contextualized word embeddings for mid-resource languages. In *Proceedings of the 58th Annual Meeting of the Association for Computational Linguistics*, pages 1703–1714, Online. Association for Computational Linguistics.

Matthew Peters, Mark Neumann, Mohit Iyyer, Matt Gardner, Christopher Clark, Kenton Lee, and Luke Zettlemoyer. 2018. Deep contextualized word representations. In *Proceedings of the 2018 Conference of the North American Chapter of the Association for Computational Linguistics: Human Language Technologies, Volume 1 (Long Papers)*, pages 2227–2237, New Orleans, Louisiana. Association for Computational Linguistics.

Alec Radford, Jeff Wu, Rewon Child, David Luan, Dario Amodei, and Ilya Sutskever. 2019. Language models are unsupervised multitask learners.

Anna Rogers, Olga Kovaleva, and Anna Rumshisky. 2020. A primer in bertology: What we know about how bert works. *Transactions of the Association for Computational Linguistics*, 8:842–866.

Ali Safaya, Moutasem Abdullatif, and Deniz Yuret. 2020. KUISAIL at SemEval-2020 task 12: BERT-CNN for offensive speech identification in social media. In *Proceedings of the Fourteenth Workshop on Semantic Evaluation*, pages 2054–2059, Barcelona (online). International Committee for Computational Linguistics.

Chenglei Si, Shuohang Wang, Min-Yen Kan, and Jing Jiang. 2019. What does bert learn from multiple-choice reading comprehension datasets? *arXiv preprint arXiv:1910.12391*.

Ian Tenney, Dipanjan Das, and Ellie Pavlick. 2019a. BERT rediscovers the classical NLP pipeline. In *Proceedings of the 57th Annual Meeting of the Association for Computational Linguistics*, pages 4593–4601, Florence, Italy. Association for Computational Linguistics.

Ian Tenney, Patrick Xia, Berlin Chen, Alex Wang, Adam Poliak, R. Thomas McCoy, Najoung Kim, Benjamin Van Durme, Samuel R. Bowman, Dipanjan Das, and Ellie Pavlick. 2019b. What do you learn from context? probing for sentence structure in contextualized word representations. In *International Conference on Learning Representations*.

Ashish Vaswani, Noam Shazeer, Niki Parmar, Jakob Uszkoreit, Llion Jones, Aidan N Gomez, ukasz Kaiser, and Illia Polosukhin. 2017. Attention is all you need. In *Advances in Neural Information Processing Systems*, volume 30, pages 5998–6008. Curran Associates, Inc.

Eric Wallace, Shi Feng, Nikhil Kandpal, Matt Gardner, and Sameer Singh. 2019. Universal adversarial triggers for attacking and analyzing NLP. In *Empirical Methods in Natural Language Processing*.

Kawārith: an Arabic Twitter Corpus for Crisis Events

Alaa Alharbi[1,2] **Mark Lee**[1]
[1]School of Computer Science, University of Birmingham, Birmingham, UK
[2]College of Computer Science and Engineering, Taibah University, Medina, KSA
{axa1314,m.g.lee}@cs.bham.ac.uk
alaharbi@taibahu.edu.sa

Abstract

Social media (SM) platforms such as Twitter provide large quantities of real-time data that can be leveraged during mass emergencies. Developing tools to support crisis-affected communities requires available datasets, which often do not exist for low resource languages. This paper introduces Kawārith[1] a multi-dialect Arabic Twitter corpus for crisis events, comprising more than a million Arabic tweets collected during 22 crises that occurred between 2018 and 2020 and involved several types of hazard. Exploration of this content revealed the most discussed topics and information types, and the paper presents a labelled dataset from seven emergency events that serves as a gold standard for several tasks in crisis informatics research. Using annotated data from the same event, a BERT model is fine-tuned to classify tweets into different categories in the multi-label setting. Results show that BERT-based models yield good performance on this task even with small amounts of task-specific training data.

1 Introduction

Recent studies have revealed the significant role of Twitter during emergency events (Imran et al., 2013a; Olteanu et al., 2015; Imran et al., 2016). In particular, Twitter messages have been shown to contain valuable and timely crisis-related information that serves to enhance situational awareness and supports humanitarian response efforts. Accessible datasets enable crisis informatics researchers to leverage this valuable user-generated data.

The present study focuses on crisis-related Arabic Twitter content. Alshaabi et al. (2020) reported that Arabic is one of the most used languages on Twitter. Nevertheless, this content has attracted relatively little research attention. Arabic dialects, which differ in their morphology, phonology and syntax, have limited resources. The lack of sufficient resources makes developing natural language processing (NLP) tools utilising Arabic SM messages more challenging. To the best of our knowledge, there is no accessible Arabic Twitter corpus of multi-crisis events. For that reason, we assembled a large-scale crisis-related corpus[2] of more than a million tweets from 22 Middle East crises involving different hazard types. Using NLP techniques, our detailed analysis of the corpus identified the main information types shared on Twitter, and we used these to label a subset of the data. The dataset can facilitate information extraction from SM to support situational awareness and enable decision-makers to respond effectively during mass emergencies. The paper makes a number of contributions to the existing literature.

- Creation and publication of a large-scale crisis-related Arabic Twitter corpus.
- Analysis of the corpus content, including the main information categories of conversations posted during a range of crisis events.
- Compilation of 405 domain-independent multi-dialect Arabic stop words[3].
- Manually annotated Arabic Twitter dataset of more than 12k messages from seven different crises.

The remainder of the paper is organised as follows. Section 2 outlines relevant related work. Section 3 describes how data were collected from the Twitter platform to create Kawārith. Section 4 provides a detailed description and analysis of the corpus. Section 5 discusses the annotation scheme, and section 6 presents the results of fine-tuning a BERT language model to automatically classify the la-

[1]This is the Romanised form of the Arabic word كوارث, meaning crises.

[2]The corpus is available at https://github.com/alaa-a-a/kawarith.

[3]The stop word list is available at https://github.com/alaa-a-a/multi-dialect-arabic-stop-words.

Proceedings of the Sixth Arabic Natural Language Processing Workshop, pages 42–52
Kyiv, Ukraine (Virtual), April 19, 2021.

belled dataset. The paper concludes in Section 7.

2 Related Work

In the publicly available Twitter crisis-related corpora in the crisis informatics literature, supervised approaches have been used to extract messages of interest from human-labelled datasets, including actionable information that enhances situational awareness. In the present context, accessible unlabelled corpora have been used for a range of purposes, including key topic extraction, social analytics and public sentiment assessment during emergency events.

Imran et al. (2013a,b) shared two annotated datasets labelled for two tasks: identifying informative messages that contribute to situational awareness and assigning these to information categories such as *cautions* and *donations*. The first set, ISCRAM2013, comprises 3617 tweets about the Joplin tornado, and the second includes 2987 tweets collected during Hurricane Sandy in 2012. Cobo et al. (2015) collected and published ~$2K$ Spanish Tweets from the Chilean earthquake in 2010, which were human-labelled as *relevant* or *irrelevant* to the crisis. Cresci et al. (2015) created the SoSItalyT4 dataset, comprising ~$5.6K$ Italian tweets collected during four natural disasters in Italy between 2009 and 2014, which were annotated for the purposes of damage assessment as *damage*, *no damage* or *irrelevant*.

One of the largest labelled and publicly accessible crisis datasets is CrisisLex, which incorporates two collections: CrisisLexT6 (Olteanu et al., 2014) and CrisisLexT26 (Olteanu et al., 2015). CrisisLexT6 includes $60K$ English tweets from six crisis events during 2012 and 2013. The messages were annotated by relatedness to the event in question (*related* vs. *not related*). CrisisLexT26 contains tweets collected during 26 crises that also occurred in 2012 and 2013. About $28K$ posts were annotated in terms of informativeness (*informative* vs. *uninformative*), information type and information source, and most of the subsequent research followed the proposed taxonomies. Imran et al. (2016) released CrisisNLP, a corpus of ~$52K$ annotated tweets collected during 19 crisis events between 2013 and 2015. The tweets were manually labelled by information type by paid workers and volunteers. For the purpose of coordinating humanitarian response efforts, different annotation schemes (labels) were used for different event types. Most messages in CrisisLex and CrisisNLP were written in English but they also include posts written in other languages such as Italian, Spanish and French, and both datasets have been widely used in the Twitter crisis detection literature.

Alam et al. (2018a) created CrisisMMD, a multimodal dataset of ~$16K$ English tweets with attached images collected in 2017 from seven natural disasters. Entries were labelled according to three dimensions: informativeness, information categories and damage severity. TREC-IS[4] (McCreadie et al., 2020) provided crisis-related Twitter datasets from 48 past emergency events, which were manually labelled by information types and priority levels. Alharbi and Lee (2019) shared a dataset of $4K$ Arabic tweets that refer to four high-risk floods in three Middle Eastern countries during October and November 2018, annotated by relatedness and information type. Hamoui et al. (2020) presented FloDusTA data, comprises ~$9k$ tweets from floods, dust storms, and traffic accident events that occurred in Saudi Arabia. The messages were labeled by event type and time of occurrence (*historical*, *immediate*, *future* or *irrelevant*). To identify different types of eyewitness report during crises, Zahra et al. (2020) published a labelled dataset of ~$14K$ English tweets gathered during four natural disasters. Kozlowski et al. (2020) built a dataset of ~$13K$ French tweets collected from different ecological crises, labelled for *relatedness*, *urgency* and *intention to act* as information types that reflect categories in other studies.

Several large published Twitter crisis corpora that provide no human labels can only be reused by reassembling the data from tweet IDs. Unlike small datasets, Twitter's Developer Policy did not allow the distribution of tweets for large-scale datasets (Zubiaga, 2018). Examples include $6M$ geo-tagged tweet IDs from Hurricane Sandy (Wang et al., 2015), ~$7M$ English tweets from Hurricane Harvey (Phillips, 2017) and $35M$ tweet IDs related to Hurricanes Irma and Harvey. Alam et al. (2018b) also published a Twitter corpus of more than $8M$ message IDs collected in 2017 from Hurricanes Irma, Harvey and Maria. More recently, research interest has focused increasingly on the COVID-19 pandemic, and several crisis informatics studies have released large-scale Twitter datasets. While some of these are limited to a single language like English (Lamsal, 2020; Gupta et al., 2020) or Ara-

[4] http://dcs.gla.ac.uk/~richardm/TREC_IS/

bic (Alqurashi et al., 2020; Haouari et al., 2020; Addawood, 2020), others have created multi-lingual datasets (Chen et al., 2020; Banda et al., 2020; Qazi et al., 2020; Singh et al., 2020; Alshaabi et al., 2021). Liu et al. (2020) created EPIC, an epidemic corpus consisting of $\sim 20M$ tweets related to various diseases.

To contribute to this body of research, the present study introduces a large-scale Arabic Twitter corpus and a subset of tweets from seven crises, manually labelled in terms of their content. In contrast to previous presented work, we consider a multi-label annotation scheme, which is described in detail below.

3 Crisis Events and Data Collection

The Kawārith corpus comprises Arabic tweets from 22 crisis events that occurred between October 2018 and September 2020. Kawarith focuses on high- to medium-risk events that are most likely to trigger substantial Twitter activity and encompasses a wide range of hazard types, including floods, shootings, bombing, wildfires, pandemics, sandstorms and explosions. Table 1 lists these crises by date; flood events occurring in the same area are referenced by country and year of occurrence. As these crises occurred in diverse Arabic-speaking regions, the corpus should include tweets written in different dialects. Previous studies have revealed that Arabic dialects are strongly present in SM, although many messages—especially those sent from news and organisation accounts—are written in Modern Standard Arabic (MSA).

Using the Twitter search API [5], these data were collected iteratively. During each crisis, we began by using trending crisis-related hashtags or keywords as query terms. If no relevant trends were found during this initial phase of data collection, we used the API to search Twitter using a logical AND combination of the terms *hazard type* and *crisis location*. Additionally, as an alternative search term, we linked the two terms in hashtag form, as we observed that people tended to use crisis-related hashtags like #سيول_الكويت "#Kuwait_floods" and #جائحة_كورونا "#corona_pandemic" for the Kuwait floods and COVID-19 crises, respectively. This first step led us to crawl an initial set of tweets, which was manually inspected to identify any new hashtags that related strongly to the event. The dataset was then expanded by tracking these hashtags, and this step was repeated until no new relevant hashtags could be found. Finally, we updated our query to include all manually selected keywords linked by logical OR to extract crisis messages in the next timeframe. Concurrently, we updated the query with any new relevant keywords emerging as trends on Twitter. Keywords could be in the form of observed hashtags, phrases or single words. We adopted a cautious approach to keyword selection, often using event-specific (discriminative) terms rather than hazard descriptors such as أمطار غزيرة "heavy rain" or يغرق "drowns" to reduce false positives—especially for flood events, which usually occurred simultaneously. Terms such as country name hashtags were generally disregarded, especially if the event had little impact on that country. The decision to use such terms as search queries was generally based on recently retrieved tweets; a candidate term was added to the query if it retrieved event-relevant messages. Importantly, as we favoured precision rather than recall, many relevant tweets were likely to be missed. However, we are satisfied that our data captured the key aspects of the crises. In the case of COVID-19, we tracked only nine keywords referring to the crisis by name because the event has triggered many other topics (such as conspiracy theories) that were not immediately relevant to our purposes. As our study focused on building an Arabic dataset, data collection was confined to tweets that Twitter tagged as Arabic, and this language parameter necessarily excluded tweets in other languages. In Lebanon, for instance, people also tweeted in Arabizi (Romanised Arabic), English and other languages, which may account for the relatively small volume of Arabic data crawled for those events despite their severity and relevance.

Data gathering continued from the first day of a crisis until the end, which we chose to define as the point at which it no longer triggered conversations on Twitter and related keywords no longer appeared in the Twitter trending list for that geographical area. We treated long-term crises like the COVID-19 as exceptions to this rule. In the case of COVID-19, data collection was delayed until near the peak of the epidemic in the Middle East. In other words, the goal was to obtain representative rather than comprehensive samples. Lists of the query terms and collection dates have been included in the published data. In total, we

[5] https://developer.twitter.com/en/docs/tweets/search/api-reference/get-search-tweets

year	crisis name	country	start date	# tweets	# unique authors	# tweets by verified users
2018	Jordan floods	Jordan	25/10/18	8493	5376	452
2018	Kuwait floods-18	Kuwait	04/11/18	34315	20285	637
2018	Qurayyat floods	Saudi Arabia	10/11/18	9731	6781	176
2018	Hafr Albatin floods-18	Saudi Arabia	14/11/18	6069	4218	105
2018	Leeth floods	Saudi Arabia	23/11/18	9596	6170	99
2019	Khartoum massacre	Sudan	03/06/19	12305	6811	50
2019	Cairo bombing	Egypt	04/08/19	2018	1320	182
2019	Lebanon wildfires	Lebanon	13/10/19	8585	5907	100
2019	Egypt floods	Egypt	21/10/19	10938	4138	51
2019	Hafr Albatin floods-19	Saudi Arabia	25/10/19	14546	8398	120
2019	Karbala massacre	Iraq	28/10/19	11961	6593	328
2019	Dubai floods	United Emirates	10/11/19	2480	1983	75
2019	Coronavirus disease	Worldwide	01/12/19	775169	345381	16295
2019	Lebanon floods	Lebanon	09/12/19	8415	5272	148
2019	Kuwait floods-19	Kuwait	15/12/19	25491	15566	312
2020	Dragon storms	Egypt	12/03/20	92014	49037	1479
2020	Aden floods	Yemen	21/04/20	37019	10638	147
2020	Oman floods	Oman	30/05/20	80673	25240	755
2020	Ta'if floods	Saudi Arabia	24/07/20	25424	13524	69
2020	Beirut explosion	Lebanon	04/08/20	307795	158427	7584
2020	Syria wildfires	Syria	03/09/20	22632	15162	167
2020	Sudan floods	Sudan	04/09/20	153126	96257	815
Total				1658795	812484	30146

Table 1: List of crises sorted by date, with tweets and users statistics

collected $1,658,795$ unique tweets from 22 emergency events. Apart from COVID-19, which was global, the crises occurred in eleven different countries[6] (see Table 1).

4 Data Description

4.1 Tweet-related & User-related Statistics

The Twitter search API supports search of tweets published in the previous seven days. As tweets matching different queries within the same time-frame might be captured on multiple occasions during our iterative collection process, we removed repetitive messages (ID-based duplicates) from the corpus and retained only tweets with unique IDs. Table 1 shows the number of unique tweets and unique authors for each crisis, along with the number of tweets published by verified accounts. In total, only $\sim$1.8% of messages were sent by such accounts, indicating that few crisis-related tweets were generated by public interest accounts (e.g. media, government) which are typically verified. We found a strong Pearson correlation of 0.76 between tweets posted by verified users and those that included URLs. The Cairo bombing returned the largest percentages of both (9.02% and 24.43%, respectively). This suggests that many of the tweets related to this event were published by authentic news accounts rather than by the general public, who might have little to share about an instantaneous and focalised event of this kind. On average, only 7.9% of the corpus tweets include URLs. Overall, the corpus includes $40,175$ unique links, excluding links pointing to other posts in quote tweets.

[6]Dragon storms have affected several countries, but we focused our collection on the Egyptian Twitter content.

4.2 Tweet Content Analysis

4.2.1 Content Redundancy

To explore the amount of duplicated content in the corpus, two tweets were considered duplicates if they exhibited a matching sequence of tokens (words or emojis). To identify duplicate content, we first cleaned the tweet text by removing RT, URL, user name, punctuation and special characters. This pre-processing also removed diacritics and elongation. This process revealed that more than half of the tweets in the corpus were duplicates, most of which were retweets. Other identical messages included shared news, emergency updates and instructions. We anticipated that this content was received and copied from different sources. We also expected that posts expressing emotional support would include similar common prayers and condolence phrases. In addition, we noticed that many nearly identical tweets were spam that included similar text (tokens), with shared shortened links referring to the same URL or to URLs with similar content. Spammers habitually exploit

crisis name	# new messages	# retweets	# messages with unique text	% duplicates
Jordan floods	2379	6114	2383	71.94%
Kuwait floods-18	5504	28811	6139	82.11%
Qurayyat floods	903	8828	885	90.91%
Hafr Albatin floods-18	734	5335	786	87.05%
Leeth floods	1898	7698	1945	79.73%
Khartoum massacre	974	11331	1296	89.47%
Cairo bombing	747	1271	711	64.77%
Lebanon wildfires	1353	7232	3122	63.63%
Egypt floods	2207	8731	2384	78.20%
Hafr Albatin floods-19	1475	13071	2023	86.09%
Karbala massacre	2147	9814	1880	84.28%
Dubai floods	416	2064	383	84.56%
Coronavirus disease	189697	585472	250980	67.62%
Lebanon floods	2899	5516	3275	61.08%
Kuwait floods-19	5947	19544	6984	72.60%
Dragon storms	23125	68889	21815	76.29%
Aden floods	6640	30379	6274	83.05%
Oman floods	15843	64830	18224	77.41%
Ta'if floods	3910	21514	4612	81.86%
Beirut explosion	54956	252839	63408	79.40%
Syria wildfires	6459	16173	6160	72.78%
Sudan floods	45702	107424	23577	84.60%

Table 2: Kawārith content redundancy statistics

trending hashtags to advertise and spread malicious content. A duplicate could be a new message. Non-duplicates are messages with unique text, whether new or retweeted. Table 2 shows the percentage of duplicates in Kawārith by crisis, along with the number of new messages and retweets.

4.2.2 Prevalent Topics

To inspect keywords and prevalent topics in the corpus at event level, we employed word cloud and probabilistic topic models. Prior to topic identification, we performed two main steps. First, we removed noise by eliminating URLs, user names, punctuation, emojis and stop words. We also omitted hashtags from the vocabulary, as these were used as query terms and therefore occurred with greater frequency. The second step involved four types of letter normalisation: different forms of alef أ ،إ ،آ were normalised to ا , alef maqsora ى to ya ي , wāw mahmoza ؤ to wāw و and ta marbouta ة to ha ه . Stop words were removed from the vocabulary because of their high frequency of occurrence without adding meaningful content to the domain in question. For this purpose, we employed Arabic stop words from NLTK toolkit (Bird, 2006) and Alrefaie's repository[7], which contain 243 and 750 such words from MSA and classical Arabic, respectively. We found that many of the dialectal stop words in our corpus are not used in MSA, as Arabic-speaking people also tweet in their own dialects, and to the best of our knowledge there is no available domain-independent multi-dialect Arabic stop word list. To identify such words, samples of tweets were collected from the countries in our list and the dialectal stop words were manually identified from the most frequent words in each sample.

Using the Mo3jam dictionary[8], we added synonyms in other dialects, taking account of spelling variations. For example, the word لسع (lsς[9]) "not yet", which blends لساعته "to this moment" or حتى هذه الساعة "until this moment" (Aldrsoni, 2012), also takes the form لساته (lsAth). Arabic speakers tend to adopt a phonological system of spelling when writing non-MSA words, and the former could also be written as لسه (lsh), لسا (lsA) or لسى (lsý). We also included common misspellings of frequently occurring words such as أصلن (ÂSln) "ever" for the word أصلاً (ÂSlA). It is important to note that as we disregarded diacritics, homographic stop words that share spellings with commonly used non-stop words were discarded. For instance, to avoid filtering out the word دُوَل which translates as 'countries', we removed the word دُول (dwl) which means 'these/those' in Egyptian and Higazi dialects. Our final list contained 405 multi-dialect Arabic stop words. Adding these words to the NLTK and Alrefaie's

[7] https://github.com/mohataher/arabic-stop-words

[8] https://en.mo3jam.com/

[9] We used Habash-Soudi-Buckwalter transliteration scheme (Habash et al., 2007)

lists, 1177 (1098 after letter normalisation) words were identified as stop words to be filtered out before identifying keywords and underlying topics.

Most frequent words

To gain insights of the most frequent unigrams and bigrams, we used word clouds to visualise the text corpus for each crisis. Figure 1 shows word clouds of the top 200 words associated with 6 crises. In general, the diagrams show that the most frequently occurring terms are location names. For many events, terms related to emotional support and prayers show a high rate of occurrence. A closer look reveals that most of the top 200 terms are hazard descriptors; for example, common terms for flood events include الدفاع المدني "civil defense", الأمطار "rains", البنية التحتية "infrastructure", as well as victim names and many weather-related terms. In the case of COVID-19, prevalent terms include وزارة الصحة "Ministry of Health", الإجراءات الاحترازية "prevention measures", إصابة جديدة "new case" and الصحة العالمية "WHO". Human-induced crises share many common event-independent terms such as دماء "bloods" مستشفيات ,"hospitals" and مصابين "injured people", along with crisis-specific terms. Unlike other crises, events like the Khartoum massacre generated words related to internet blockage. Following duplicate filtration, visualisation revealed further hazard-related words, confirming that a single topic may dominate the dataset. Retweeted messages or content duplicates are not necessarily relevant to the crisis, as spam messages associated with crisis-related hashtags sometimes attract a large number of shares, and word clouds may include irrelevant terms (e.g. advertisements). For instance, phrases about invoking blessings upon the prophet Mohammed populate the Dragon storm diagram because the event occurred on Friday. This confirms the importance of removing duplicates and irrelevant posts from crisis data in pursuit of meaningful insights. Figure 2 shows words frequently associated with the Khartoum massacre and Dragon storms before and after duplicate removal. Observation suggests that one crisis can be discussed using data from another; for example #لبنان_ينتفض (which relates to the Lebanese protests) is the second most frequent hashtag in the Lebanese floods data. For that reason, it is useful to identify messages in terms of crisis type following data collection.

Figure 1: Word clouds showing the top 200 words from Kawārith for 6 selected crises

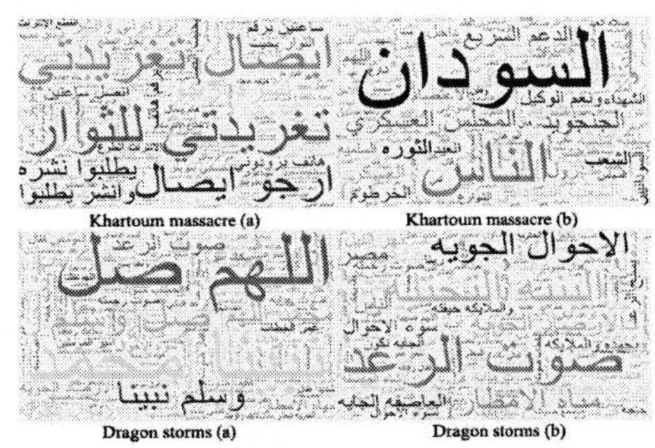

Figure 2: Word clouds for two crises: (a) for all data and (b) after duplicate removal

LDA Topics and Content Categorisation

We investigated the main topics discussed during crises using the Latent Dirichlet Allocation (LDA) modelling technique (Blei, 2012). LDA is a probabilistic topic model commonly used to disclose hidden topics in unstructured data. In this study, we used c_v coherence measure as an indicator to identify the optimum number of topics per event. To assign interpretations to topics, we manually analysed examples of tweets containing the top topic words to explore their meanings in context. Use of the selected dialectal stop words improved c_v scores by 37% on average. Analysis of example tweets yielded the following findings.

- Most of the broad information types used to coordinate response efforts as reported in previous work (Olteanu et al., 2015; Imran et al., 2016) appear in our corpus, varying in frequency across events. For covid19, in-domain fine-grained topics were identified, including disease spread, COVID-19 symptoms, treatment, volunteering, prevention measures, cautions, other relevant events, prayers, opinions and personal messages.

- Many of the relevant tweets represent public opinion. Other on-topic tweets describe relevant events and consequences such as authority resignations.
- A tweet can communicate different information types; for example, the message below includes warning updates about affected individuals and weather conditions:

> #الاردن #عاجل. وفاة طفلة بسبب السيول الجارفة اليوم الجمعة وفقدان عدد من الاشخاص في عدة مناطق. وتشهد الاردن ومناطق واسعة من #السعودية موجة من الأمطار الغزيرة وتشكلا للسيول. ويتوقع اشتداد الحالة الجوية هذا المساء وغدا السبت. #سيول_الاردن #وسم #غدق #طقس
>
> "#Jordan #Breaking. A child has died in flash flooding this Friday and several people are missing in many areas. Jordan and wide regions of Saudi are witnessing heavy rainfall leading to floods. Severe weather conditions are expected this evening and tomorrow. #Jordan_flood #wasm #Ghadag #weather"

In this study, we employed a multi-label annotation scheme to categorise messages as different information types based on manual interpretation of prevalent topics and in light of earlier taxonomies. Unlike previous work taxonomies, we did not consider 'other useful information' class since usefulness is a subjective concept depending on the person who receives the information. Instead, we introduced 'other crisis updates' as a *"catchall"* category for other information that vary across crises such as flood level and wind. We observed that such updates were usually mentioned as *caution*. Hence, we merged these two categories together. As a few messages related to donation and volunteering in most cases, we merged this category with affected individuals, as these were usually mentioned together. We also tagged opinions, supplications and prayers. These may not be of use to humanitarian responders or contribute to situational awareness but can be used for other purposes, including opinion mining and measurement of event impact. Table 3 shows some example tweets from each category. In the case of COVID-19, a tweet was classified as either relevant or irrelevant to the event[10]. The following section describes the manual labelling process.

[10]To comply with Twitter's policies, we explicitly avoided coding data about users' health.

5 Manual Annotation and Inter-rater Reliability

Parts of our corpus were manually labelled to facilitate automatic identification of information categories by machine learning algorithms and to assess the frequency of the different message types posted on Twitter during emergencies. Seven crises were selected for annotation: the Jordan floods, Kuwait floods-18, Hafr Albatin floods-19, the Cairo bombing, the Dragon storms, the Beirut explosion and COVID-19. We focused on flood events as frequent occurrences in the Middle East.

To construct the labelled dataset, we considered only tweets with unique texts. We excluded duplicate messages as identified in section 4.2.1 to avoid labelling messages with the same content. We did not consider propagating labels to duplicate tweets after labelling the unique messages to avoid experimental bias in classification. Including duplicates in the dataset results in an overestimated performance if there is an overlap between test and training data (Alam et al., 2020). We also removed tweets containing less than 4 tokens as these are too short to convey any meaningful message. When calculating a tweet's length, we split the hashtags. As noted earlier, user mentions and URLs were not considered proper tokens. Each hyperlink was replaced with the Arabic word رابط to inform coders of a link referring to a website, image or video. Annotators were not required to visit the hyperlinks, as tweets were judged only on their text content. We sampled a different number of tweets for annotation from each event, ensuring that samples were taken from different timeframes. About 70–85% of flood events data were considered, along with all unique examples from the Cairo bombing (which contains only 711 distinct tweets). In the case of Dragon storms and Beirut explosion, about 1050 posts were sampled from each crisis. Regarding COVID-19, we considered 2005 tweets.

The data was annotated by volunteers. All annotators were native Arabic speakers. Each example was judged by two annotators, who were provided with annotation instructions and a news or Wikipedia article summarising the crisis. To begin, coders were trained using a short quiz with examples from each category and explanations of the correct answers. To further ensure reliability, annotators were tested on 30 examples from one event, and only those scoring 70% were allowed to proceed. The judgments were provided by 21

Label	Tweet
Affected individuals & help	عشرة عناصر من اطفاء بيروت مفتودين. "Ten members of Beirut firefighters are missing." قسم الطوارئ في مستشفى اوتيل ديو يستغيث ويطلب للتبرع بالدم. "The Emergency Department at the Hôtel-Dieu hospital calls for help and appeals for blood donations. "
Infrastructure & utilities damage	قطع المياه عن محافظة القاهرة بالكامل لسوء الأحوال الجوية ـ بوابة الشروق. "Water is cut off in Cairo governorate due to bad weather - Al Shorouk Gate."
Caution, preparations & other crisis updates	الارصاد تحذر امطار وسيول وانخفاض في درجات الحرارة ورمال واتربة. وتعطيل للدراسة الخميس بسبب الاحوال الجوية. "The Meteorological Department warns of rains, floods, temperature drop, sand and dust. And schools are closing on Thursday due to weather conditions."
Emotional support, prayers & supplications	اللهم احفظ مصر وأهلها. "May Allah save Egypt and its people."
Opinions & criticism	الاستقالات لا تكفي، وانما المطلوب محاسبة ومحاكمة كل مسئول مهمل. "Resignations are not enough, what is required is accountability and trial for every negligent official. "
Irrelevant	في أعماقنا رعد وبرق وعواصف وأمطار لا تشير إليها الأرصاد الجوية. "Deep inside us are thunder, lightning, storms and rain that have never been detected by weather forecast."

Table 3: Labels with example tweets

Label	Jordan floods	Kuwait floods-18	Hafr Albatin floods-19	Cairo bombing	Dragon storms	Beirut explosion
Affected individuals & help	331	414	83	138	70	186
Infrastructure & utilities damage	39	271	100	17	105	64
Caution, preparations & other crisis updates	268	980	475	214	252	170
Emotional support, prayers & supplications	709	816	202	222	120	277
Opinions & criticism	604	1355	189	181	221	198
Irrelevant	118	399	637	6	309	177
Total number of labelled examples	2000	4100	1615	706	1010	1010

Table 4: Distribution of labels: Flood crises, Cairo bombing, Dragon storms and Beirut explosion

Label	COVID-19
Relevant	1782
Irrelevant	223
Total number of labelled examples	2005

Table 5: Distribution of labels: COVID-19

trusted coders. (The annotation instructions have been included with the published datasets.) Average inter-rater agreement for the seven events as measured by Krippendorff's alpha was about 0.7, indicating substantial agreement and clear instructions. If two annotators disagreed, the message was judged by a third person; if coder 3 did not agree with coder 1 or 2, majority voting was applied to select the label agreed by at least two coders. A tweet was discarded if all three annotators completely disagree with each other. In total, we obtained $12,446$ labelled examples. Tables 4 and 5 show the distribution of categories and the total number of labelled tweets for the seven events. The dataset is imbalanced, and the distribution of information types varies across events. On average, only 4.4% of dataset instances have more than one label. Most relevant messages conveyed emotional support, opinions, cautions and crisis updates. Among COVID-19 tweets, we observed that the largest category of relevant messages relates to disease spread. The non-negligible percentage of irrelevant tweets (15% of the dataset) highlights the need for a classification step following data collection to filter out irrelevant posts.

6 Tweets Classification

To benchmark the dataset, we fine-tuned the Arabic Bidirectional Encoder Representation from Transformer (AraBERT) base model (Antoun et al., 2020). For reproducibility, we split the data into stratified train and test sets (80% and 20%, respectively). We fine-tuned a BERT model for each event using its training data by adding a linear classification layer on top of the BERT model, preceded by a dropout layer of a probability (0.2) to prevent the model from over-fitting. The learning rate of Adam optimizer was set to $5e$-5 and the loss function to binary cross-entropy. We set the maximum sequence length to 60 tokens as the longest tweet in Kawārith has 60 words. All models were trained for 5 epochs, which was empirically chosen. We experimented with batch sizes of 8 and 32. Each experiment was repeated three times with random seeds of $\{a, b, c\}$ because different seeds can yield considerably different results (Dodge et al., 2020).

Event	Acc.		Mac. f1		Mic. f1		HL	
	batch=8	batch=32	batch=8	batch=32	batch=8	batch=32	batch=8	batch=32
Jordan floods	82.8	85.8	72	75.6	83.65	86.59	0.055	0.045
Kuwait floods-18	81.38	81.99	79.51	80.3	82.3	83	0.06	0.057
Hafr Albatin floods-19	82.7	82.93	79.52	79.55	83.38	83.92	0.057	0.054
Cairo bombing	85.3	83.84	70.42	57.33	86.74	84.98	0.048	0.053
Dragon storms	78.7	78.81	77.33	78.73	79.84	81.01	0.071	0.066
Beirut explosion	76.37	76.17	72.91	73.45	76.77	78.06	0.079	0.073
COVID-19	94.1	93.5	82.95	81.9	-	-	-	-

Table 6: The accuracy, f1 scores and Hamming loss of the AraBERT model on the test set for each crisis

Text was pre-processed by removing noise as described in section 4.2.2. Evaluation was based on accuracy, known as Hamming score for the multi-label setting (Godbole and Sarawagi, 2004), macro f1, micro f1 and Hamming loss (HL) measures. The HL captures the fraction of labels that are incorrectly predicted. The binary COVID-19 data was evaluated using the accuracy and macro f1. The average scores of the three runs for each experiment are displayed in Table 6.

Results show that BERT achieved good accuracy and micro-f1 scores despite the relatively small training data used to fine-tune the models. Obtaining low HL scores indicates that a few labels were incorrectly predicted. While achieving a high macro-f1 is challenging with a skewed class distribution, BERT achieved macro-f1 scores higher than 70% in almost all cases without handling the data imbalance problem. Investigating different data augmentation techniques to improve the models' performance is left for future work. Generally, we found that fine-tuning in batches of 32 yields small gains in performance. In the case of the Cairo bombing, batch size of 8 achieved better results in all random runs, which we relate to the small number of training data (only 565 examples). When repeating the experiments for the other events using less than (randomly selected) 600 training examples, we found that it is more effective to fine-tune the models in batches of 8 instead of 32, which resulted in improvements in most cases.

Looking at the classification errors of the best models, we found that the models' mispredictions are not associated with a specific information category, and error types vary across events. We observed that many of the irrelevant tweets (especially from flood crises) were mistakenly classified as opinions. Most of these misclassified irrelevant tweets are ambiguous messages that express negative opinions about some topics that could be related to the crisis in some way. It is important to note that the two main annotators disagreed on most of such ambiguous posts. For many events, the models confused some messages from 'opinions & criticism' class with other classes. Classifying COVID-19 data obtained high accuracy and f1 scores. Performing such binary classification to filter out spam and other irrelevant posts prior to message categorisation could alleviate errors of classifying them as opinions. For future work, we will explore the BERT's performance when classifying cross-event data.

7 Conclusion

This paper introduced Kawārith, an Arabic Twitter corpus for 22 crises. We also reported a preliminary analysis of tweet content and provided a gold-standard multi-label dataset comprising $12k$ unique tweets. We believe this corpus can be leveraged for several tasks, including crisis detection and crisis type classification. Assigning messages to categories in order to identify informative posts can enhance situational awareness and assist emergency responders in organising effective relief efforts. The labelled dataset can also be utilised to gauge public opinion and sentiment during crises.

References

Aseel Addawood. 2020. Coronavirus: Public arabic twitter dataset.

Firoj Alam, Ferda Ofli, and Muhammad Imran. 2018a. Crisismmd: Multimodal twitter datasets from natural disasters. In *Twelfth International AAAI Conference on Web and Social Media.*

Firoj Alam, Ferda Ofli, Muhammad Imran, and Michael Aupetit. 2018b. A twitter tale of three hurricanes: Harvey, irma, and maria. *arXiv preprint arXiv:1805.05144.*

Firoj Alam, Hassan Sajjad, Muhammad Imran, and Ferda Ofli. 2020. Standardizing and benchmarking crisis-related social media datasets for humanitarian information processing. *arXiv preprint arXiv:2004.06774.*

Sulaiman Aldrsoni. 2012. معجم اللهجات المحكية *[Dictionary of Spoken Dialects]*. King Fahd National Library, Riyadh, KSA.

Alaa Alharbi and Mark Lee. 2019. Crisis detection from Arabic tweets. In *Proceedings of the 3rd Workshop on Arabic Corpus Linguistics*, pages 72–79, Cardiff, United Kingdom. Association for Computational Linguistics.

Sarah Alqurashi, Ahmad Alhindi, and Eisa Alanazi. 2020. Large arabic twitter dataset on covid-19. *arXiv preprint arXiv:2004.04315*.

Thayer Alshaabi, Michael V Arnold, Joshua R Minot, Jane Lydia Adams, David Rushing Dewhurst, Andrew J Reagan, Roby Muhamad, Christopher M Danforth, and Peter Sheridan Dodds. 2021. How the world's collective attention is being paid to a pandemic: Covid-19 related n-gram time series for 24 languages on twitter. *Plos one*, 16(1):e0244476.

Thayer Alshaabi, David R Dewhurst, Joshua R Minot, Michael V Arnold, Jane L Adams, Christopher M Danforth, and Peter Sheridan Dodds. 2020. The growing echo chamber of social media: Measuring temporal and social contagion dynamics for over 150 languages on twitter for 2009–2020. *arXiv preprint arXiv:2003.03667*.

Wissam Antoun, Fady Baly, and Hazem Hajj. 2020. Arabert: Transformer-based model for arabic language understanding. *arXiv preprint arXiv:2003.00104*.

Juan M Banda, Ramya Tekumalla, Guanyu Wang, Jingyuan Yu, Tuo Liu, Yuning Ding, and Gerardo Chowell. 2020. A large-scale covid-19 twitter chatter dataset for open scientific research–an international collaboration. *arXiv preprint arXiv:2004.03688*.

Steven Bird. 2006. NLTK: The Natural Language Toolkit. In *Proceedings of the COLING/ACL 2006 Interactive Presentation Sessions*, pages 69–72, Sydney, Australia. Association for Computational Linguistics.

David M Blei. 2012. Probabilistic topic models. *Communications of the ACM*, 55(4):77–84.

Emily Chen, Kristina Lerman, and Emilio Ferrara. 2020. Covid-19: The first public coronavirus twitter dataset. *arXiv preprint arXiv:2003.07372*.

Alfredo Cobo, Denis Parra, and Jaime Navón. 2015. Identifying relevant messages in a twitter-based citizen channel for natural disaster situations. In *Proceedings of the 24th International Conference on World Wide Web*, pages 1189–1194.

Stefano Cresci, Maurizio Tesconi, Andrea Cimino, and Felice Dell'Orletta. 2015. A linguistically-driven approach to cross-event damage assessment of natural disasters from social media messages. In *Proceedings of the 24th International Conference on World Wide Web*, pages 1195–1200.

Jesse Dodge, Gabriel Ilharco, Roy Schwartz, Ali Farhadi, Hannaneh Hajishirzi, and Noah Smith. 2020. Fine-tuning pretrained language models: Weight initializations, data orders, and early stopping. *arXiv preprint arXiv:2002.06305*.

Shantanu Godbole and Sunita Sarawagi. 2004. Discriminative methods for multi-labeled classification. In *Pacific-Asia conference on knowledge discovery and data mining*, pages 22–30. Springer.

Raj Kumar Gupta, Ajay Vishwanath, and Yinping Yang. 2020. Covid-19 twitter dataset with latent topics, sentiments and emotions attributes. *arXiv preprint arXiv:2007.06954*.

Nizar Habash, Abdelhadi Soudi, and Timothy Buckwalter. 2007. On arabic transliteration. In *Arabic computational morphology*, pages 15–22. Springer.

Btool Hamoui, Mourad Mars, and Khaled Almotairi. 2020. FloDusTA: Saudi tweets dataset for flood, dust storm, and traffic accident events. In *Proceedings of the 12th Language Resources and Evaluation Conference*, pages 1391–1396, Marseille, France. European Language Resources Association.

Fatima Haouari, Maram Hasanain, Reem Suwaileh, and Tamer Elsayed. 2020. Arcov-19: The first arabic covid-19 twitter dataset with propagation networks. *arXiv preprint arXiv:2004.05861*.

Muhammad Imran, Shady Elbassuoni, Carlos Castillo, Fernando Diaz, and Patrick Meier. 2013a. Extracting information nuggets from disaster-related messages in social media. In *Iscram*.

Muhammad Imran, Shady Elbassuoni, Carlos Castillo, Fernando Diaz, and Patrick Meier. 2013b. Practical extraction of disaster-relevant information from social media. In *Proceedings of the 22nd International Conference on World Wide Web*, pages 1021–1024.

Muhammad Imran, Prasenjit Mitra, and Carlos Castillo. 2016. Twitter as a lifeline: Human-annotated twitter corpora for nlp of crisis-related messages. *arXiv preprint arXiv:1605.05894*.

Diego Kozlowski, Elisa Lannelongue, Frédéric Saudemont, Farah Benamara, Alda Mari, Véronique Moriceau, and Abdelmoumene Boumadane. 2020. A three-level classification of french tweets in ecological crises. *Information Processing & Management*, 57(5):102284.

Rabindra Lamsal. 2020. Corona virus (covid-19) tweets dataset. ieee dataport.

Junhua Liu, Trisha Singhal, Lucienne Blessing, Kristin L Wood, and Kwan Hui Lim. 2020. Epic: An epidemics corpus of over 20 million relevant tweets. *arXiv preprint arXiv:2006.08369*.

Richard McCreadie, Cody Buntain, and Ian Soboroff. 2020. Incident streams 2019: Actionable insights and how to find them. In *Proceedings of the International ISCRAM Conference*.

Alexandra Olteanu, Carlos Castillo, Fernando Diaz, and Sarah Vieweg. 2014. Crisislex: A lexicon for collecting and filtering microblogged communications in crises. In *Eighth international AAAI conference on weblogs and social media.*

Alexandra Olteanu, Sarah Vieweg, and Carlos Castillo. 2015. What to expect when the unexpected happens: Social media communications across crises. In *Proceedings of the 18th ACM conference on computer supported cooperative work & social computing*, pages 994–1009. ACM.

Mark Edward Phillips. 2017. Hurricane harvey twitter dataset.

Umair Qazi, Muhammad Imran, and Ferda Ofli. 2020. Geocov19: a dataset of hundreds of millions of multilingual covid-19 tweets with location information. *SIGSPATIAL Special*, 12(1):6–15.

Lisa Singh, Shweta Bansal, Leticia Bode, Ceren Budak, Guangqing Chi, Kornraphop Kawintiranon, Colton Padden, Rebecca Vanarsdall, Emily Vraga, and Yanchen Wang. 2020. A first look at covid-19 information and misinformation sharing on twitter. *arXiv preprint arXiv:2003.13907.*

Haoyu Wang, Eduard Hovy, and Mark Dredze. 2015. The hurricane sandy twitter corpus. In *Workshops at the twenty-ninth AAAI conference on artificial intelligence.*

Kiran Zahra, Muhammad Imran, and Frank O Ostermann. 2020. Automatic identification of eyewitness messages on twitter during disasters. *Information processing & management*, 57(1):102107.

Arkaitz Zubiaga. 2018. A longitudinal assessment of the persistence of twitter datasets. *Journal of the Association for Information Science and Technology*, 69(8):974–984.

Arabic Compact Language Modelling for Resource Limited Devices

Zaid Alyafeai
KFUPM, Dhahran, Saudi Arabia
g201080740@kfupm.edu.sa

Irfan Ahmad
KFUPM, Dhahran, Saudi Arabia
irfan.ahmad@kfupm.edu.sa

Abstract

Natural language modelling has gained a lot of interest recently. The current state-of-the-art results are achieved by first training a very large language model and then fine-tuning it on multiple tasks. However, there is little work on smaller more compact language models for resource-limited devices or applications. Not to mention, how to efficiently train such models for a low-resource language like Arabic. In this paper, we investigate how such models can be trained in a compact way for Arabic. We also show how distillation and quantization can be applied to create even smaller models. Our experiments show that our largest model which is 2x smaller than the baseline can achieve better results on multiple tasks with 2x less data for pretraining.

1 Introduction

Language Modelling refers to the process of designing a model that can mimic language understanding in humans. The trained models can then be fine-tuned on multiple tasks by using them as feature extractors by adding extra layers at thend of such models. This is a difficult task since, language understanding and comprehension require huge amounts of data. Recently, advances in machine learning and particularly deep learning is proving significant in different tasks like text classification, sentiment analysis, question answering, summarization and language inference using transformer-based architectures (Devlin et al., 2018). This approach requires training a deep architecture that models the language using unsupervised techniques on unlabelled data. The outcome of this method is a large model that has a huge memory footprint. This limits the deployment of such models on resource-limited devices because of memory constraints. Furthermore, the model needs to be retrained to make it useful for other more interesting tasks. Recently, a lot of approaches have emerged in making these deep architectures more practical using methods like distillation (Sun et al., 2020) and quantization (Zafrir et al., 2019). Unfortunately, most of the work that is available in the literature targets English language because of the availability of data and research development tools. In this work we train a compact Arabic language model that can be fine-tuned on different tasks. Moreover, we make the model efficient for embedded devices with relatively a small loss in accuracy.

The paper is organized as follows: In section 2, we revise the literature for related work. In section 3, we describe our methodology where we discuss the pretraining dataset, the tasks used for evaluation and our training procedure for the teacher and student models. Finally, we summarize the experiments and discuss the results.

2 Related Work

Deep architectures like GPT (Radford et al., 2018), BERT (Devlin et al., 2018) and T5 (Raffel et al., 2019) require a huge amount of data and computation. Moreover, such language models are very large and cannot be deployed on embedded devices due to memory constraints. Recently, many approaches have been applied in order to make such models smaller and more practical. Mainly, the literature focuses on two main approaches which are quantization and distillation.

Quantization is defined as reducing the memory footprint by mapping parameters to low dimensional spaces. For instance, we can map `float32` to `int16`. This is usually done at the deployment phase where the model is already trained. Many studies have been published that adopt this approach. Zafrir et al. applied this approach to BERT in order to create a quantized 8 bit model (Q8bert) (Zafrir et al., 2019). More recently, a more

Proceedings of the Sixth Arabic Natural Language Processing Workshop, pages 53–59
Kyiv, Ukraine (Virtual), April 19, 2021.

advanced approach called Hessian-based ultra low precision quantization has been applied to BERT (Q-BERT) (Shen et al., 2020). In another work, the authors designed an architecture called GOBO that targets quantizing attention-based models for language understanding (Zadeh and Moshovos, 2020).

On the other hand, another approach is called distillation which mimics the task of a teacher and student for training smaller language models (Alkhulaifi et al., 2020). These methods have been developed in computer vision but they were recently extended to language modelling. The teacher model, usually a large model, is a pretrained model that can be used to distil the knowledge to a smaller model called the student model. The student model is a much smaller architecture. The distillation process has been applied in many fields in machine learning and takes many forms like teacher-student optimization (Yang et al., 2019), teacher assistant (Mirzadeh et al., 2019), contrastive representation distillation (Tian et al., 2019) and patient knowledge distillation (Sun et al., 2019). Other approaches make the process task-agnostic like the work by Sun et al. in their architecture called mobileBERT (Sun et al., 2020).

From the research perspective, Arabic language modelling is under-represented in the literature let alone implementing compression techniques. Noticeably, there were a few main attempts to adapt deep models for Arabic like Hulmuna (ElJundi et al., 2019) which retrains ELMo (Peters et al., 2018) for Arabic and fine-tunes it on different tasks. Moreover, we have AraBERT which retrains BERT for Arabic (Antoun et al., 2020). More recently, other larger variants have been introduced namely ARBERT and MARBERT (Abdul-Mageed et al., 2020). These models are comparatively very large and are trained with a huge amount of data usually larger than 20 GB of text and the models are typically more than 100 million parameters in size. Arabic poses its own challenges when considered for natural language processing tasks. Arabic is a morphologically rich language where words can take different representations by connecting different prefixes, infixes and suffixes. Hence words need better representations in order to tackle the out-of-vocabulary problem (Gerz et al., 2018) by applying different preprocessing approaches. For instance, segmentation slightly achieves a better performance compared to direct tokenization (Antoun et al., 2020). Not to mention applying preprocessing to deal the linguistic parts like diacritics, normalization, cleaning, mixed foreign characters, etc.

In this work we consider applying distillation and quantization on Arabic language models for resource-limited devices. Up to our knowledge, there is no previous work that applies compression directly on Arabic. There are some related work that applies distillation on a cross-lingual level (Cui et al., 2017) but it is evident from the literature that monolingual models are more powerful (Antoun et al., 2020), (Martin et al., 2019).

3 Experimentation

In this section we explain in details our approach that we take for training compact language models for Arabic. First we train a large teacher model in an unsupervised fashion on a large corpus. Then we distil the knowledge from the teacher model to the student model and evaluate it by fine-tuning on different tasks. Finally, we use quantization as a final step for reducing the memory footprint of our distilled student models. For the comparison we use the first version of AraBERT as the baseline for evaluating our models.

3.1 Pretraining Dateset

We collected a wide variety of datasets in order to cover as many tasks as possible. We used four different datasets for pretraining. Mainly, we collected 10 GB from the 1.5 billion words corpus (El-Khair, 2016), 1.5 GB from wikipedia, 1 GB books from Alshamila (shamela, 2005) and around 500 MB from Twitter. We clean all the datasets by removing diacritics and applying normalization (mapping different forms of a character to a single character). We then converted the dataset to `tfrecords` for faster training. In Table 1, we present the total number of tokens for each dataset. We use the WordPiece algorithm (Devlin et al., 2018) for tokenization with a fixed sequence length of 512. We fixed the max sequence length to 512 with max predictions per sequence as 20. The masked tokens probability is set to 15 % with a duplication factor of size 5.

3.2 Tasks

We evaluate the models on a variety of datasets and tasks from the literature. Some datasets are not split by the authors so we split them randomly into training and testing sets. In all the experiments we

Table 1: Number of tokens in each dataset. B:billions and M:millions.

Dataset	Number of Tokens
Billion Words Corpus	1.3 B
Wikipedia	148 M
Alshamila	112 M
Twitter	68 M

use the same split to test the models.

1. **Hard**: Named the Arabic Reviews Dataset (Elnagar et al., 2018), The dataset consists of 93,700 reviews in total where we have 46,850 reviews for each positive and negative sentiments.

2. **ASTD**: called the Arabic Sentiment Tweets Dataset which contains 10,000 tweets written in both MSA and Egyptian dialect (Nabil et al., 2015). We used the balanced dataset on binary sentiment classification.

3. **ArSenTD-Lev**: The Arabic Sentiment Twitter Dataset for Levantine dialect (ArSenTD-LEV) (Baly et al., 2018) contains 4,000 tweets written in Arabic and equally collected from Lebanon, Jordan, Syria. and Palestine.

4. **LABR**: The Large-scale Arabic Book Reviews dataset (Aly and Atiya, 2013). It contains over 63,000 book reviews that were collected from the website Goodreads during the month of March 2013. Each book review comes with the rating (1 to 5) and the text of the review. The ratings 1 and 2 are considered negative while 4 and 5 are considered positive.

5. **AJGT**: The Arabic Jordanian General Tweets dataset (Alomari et al., 2017) consists of 1,800 tweets written in Jordanian dialect and modern standard Arabic (MSA). The tweets were manually annotated as either positive or negative to be used for sentiment analysis tasks.

6. **TEAD**: A large-scale dataset of tweets gathered in 2017. The dataset was annotated using emojis and sentiment lexicons. We only use a small subset of the dataset that contains 2000 positive and 2000 negative labels.

7. **ARCD**: The Arabic Reading Comprehension Dataset (ARCD) is composed of 1,395 questions annotated by crowd workers on Wikipedia articles (Mozannar et al., 2019). The authors also published a translated version of the English SQuAD called the Arabic-SQuAD. The question answering tasks are usually reported using F1 score and exact match (EM) score in literature.

8. **PADT** treebank is based on the Prague Arabic Dependency Treebank (PADT) (Zeman, 2015). We use this dataset for the part-of-speech tagging (PoS) tasks. The treebank is composed of 7,664 sentences (282,384 tokens) and its domain is mainly news. The results are reported using precision, recall and F1.

3.3 Pretraining Models

We train the teacher and student models on TPUv3-8 which distributes the batch size over 8 nodes. Furthermore, TensorFlow 1.15 is used as the main library for training all the models. For the pretraining we use Google Cloud and for fine-tuning we use Google Colab notebooks.

3.3.1 Teacher Model

We follow the same approach as in (Sun et al., 2020) where the teacher model has the same depth as $\text{BERT}_{\text{LARGE}}$, i.e., 24 blocks each one containing a multi-head attention and feed-forward network with a normalization layer after each one. However, in order to reduce the number of parameters, a linear transformation is applied to modify the input and the output size to 512 (i.e., bottleneck). The linear transformations are applied after the embeddings and after the end of the fully connected layers of each block. The output size of each layer in each block is named inner block-neck size and it was set to 1024 in the original architecture. However, we train with smaller inner block-neck of size 256 instead of 1024 in order to reduce the model size. Also we train different models with vocabulary sizes of 30K and 50K with hidden sizes 512 and 256, respectively. The number of layers is 24 and the number of attention heads is 4. We use the lamb optimizer (You et al., 2019) with a learning rate 0.0015. We train the model for around 2 million steps with a batch size of 256.

3.3.2 Student Model

For the student model we train two types of models: the first one has 4 feed-forward layers and the smaller model has 1 per each block. The number of layers and attention heads is the same as the teacher model. The model is first trained using knowledge transfer as a combination of attention transfer and feature map transfer. Attention transfer $\mathcal{L}_{AT}$ maps the attention weights from the teacher model to the student model. While the feature map transfer $\mathcal{L}_{FMT}$ maps the weights from each block in the teacher to each block in the student. We train each model for 500K steps for attention transfer and 2 million steps for pretraining distillation. The pre-training distillation objective is defined as combination of BERT training objectives and knowledge distillation objectives

$$\mathcal{L}_{PD} = \alpha\mathcal{L}_{MLM} + (1-\alpha)\mathcal{L}_{KD} + \mathcal{L}_{NSP}$$

Masked language model (**MLM**) is the objective for predicting the masked word in the corpus. Next sentence prediction (**NSP**) optimizes the probability of predicting next sentence. Knowledge distillation (**KD**) is a mixture of training on current corpus and teacher labels. Similar to the teacher model, We use the lamb optimizer, a learning rate 0.0015 and batch size 256. In Table 2, we summarize the hyper-parameters for training during the distillation process. The beta and gamma distillation factors measure the difference between the mean and the variances between the teacher and student models. The hidden distillation factor is used for weighted layer wise distillation and the distillation ground truth parameter is used for the mixed label training.

Table 2: Hyper-parameters for training the student models.

Parameter	Value
Beta distillation factor	500
Gamma distillation factor	5
Hidden distillation factor	100
Distillation ground truth	0.5

4 Evaluation

We use fine-tuning on down-stream tasks as the main approach for evaluating our models. In all of our experiments, we follow the same procedure for the teacher and the student models. Note that in order to make the comparison fair to AraBERT, we don't do any preprocessing to our datasets. This is in order to avoid any bias towards our models. This might cause our models to preform worse than expected because some characters in the datasets might cause unknown tokens to show up. Mainly, we train for 5 epochs and we use a learning rate of 3×10^{-5} for the text classification and question answering tasks while we use a learning rate of 2×10^{-3} for the PoS tagging task. In Figure 1, we compare inverted-block BERT for Arabic (IBERTA) for two different vocabulary sizes. To make the comparison fair, we decrease the hidden size to 256 for the model with vocabulary size 50K. We see as the number of iterations increases, the accuracy increases for both models. However, the model with vocabulary size 50K achieve better results across the different iterations compared to the vocabulary size 30K. This is due to the fact that Arabic is morphologically rich language with a huge and sparse vocabulary. We use the model with the vocabulary size 50K as the teacher model and we refer to it as (IBERTA).

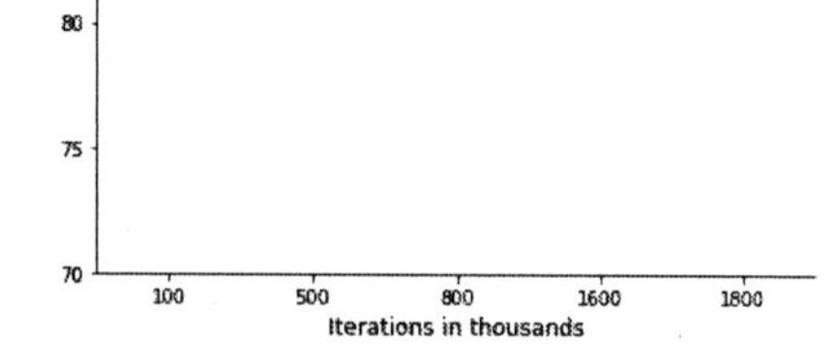

Figure 1: Comparison between the teacher models when fine-tuned in the AJGT task.

In Table 3, we compare IBERTA to AraBERT for different datasets and tasks. We can notice that our teacher model achieves better results on most of the text classification tasks. In tasks that require more token information like question answering

Table 3: Comparing IBERTA with 50K vocabulary size, MBERTA, MBERTA II and AraBERT for multiple tasks.

Dataset	Metric	IBERTA	AraBERT	MBERTA	MBERTA II
AJGT	Accuracy	**93.3**	89.7	90.8	89.1
HARD	Accuracy	**95.7**	95.4	95.5	95.4
ArSenTD	Accuracy	**55.8**	55.3	55.1	53.6
LABR	Accuracy	87.5	**89.3**	86.7	87.6
TEAD	Accuracy	**68.5**	65.4	66.9	66.6
ASTD	Accuracy	**86.2**	84.6	83.6	81.8
PADT	Precision	**85.2**	84.4	85.2	82.4
	Recall	78.1	**83.0**	79.0	79.9
	F1	78.8	**83.8**	80.5	80.9
ARCD	Exact Match	26.1	**29.6**	21.5	21.1
	F1	58.4	**62.2**	49.9	51.3

and PoS tagging, our models perform worse. We believe that our model fails in token-based tasks because AraBERT was trained on a much larger dataset and has larger vocabulary size; more by around 14K tokens compared to our vocabulary size. Note that we only consider AraBERT without any pre-segmentation. On the right side of Table 3, we show the results for the distilled student models. The larger model (MBERTA) uses 4 feed-forward networks while the smaller model (MBERTA II) uses only 1. We notice that it achieves comparable results for Hard, ArsenTD and LABR. It also shows better results in terms of precision for the PoS tagging task. However, it achieves much worse results on question answering task. We believe that the reason behind that is the complexity of the task and the quality of the dataset which has some automatically created translations. In Table 4, we compare all the models in terms of the number of parameters, on-disk space and quantized models. We observe that our teacher model is around half of the size of AraBERT but achieves comparable results. We also notice that we can reduce the model size further by applying quantization using the `tflite` library. This has a big impact especially for resource limited devices. The models can be compressed into even smaller sizes depending on the memory/storage constraints. Of course, further compression will lead to some deterioration in accuracy and other performance measures.

5 Conclusion

In this paper we trained compact Arabic language models through pretraining, distillation and quantization. We showed that such compact language models can achieve comparable results to state-of-the-art models even though they have significantly a fewer number of parameters and while trained on smaller datasets. We benchmark the models on six different classification datasets, one part-of-speech tagging dataset and one question answering dataset. We believe such smaller models can be very practical because they enable deploying such models on resource-limited devices like mobile phones and embedded devices. Moreover, we showed that using smaller datasets with smaller vocabulary, we can achieve reasonable results compared to other models in the literature. This shows that carefully curated datasets with high diversity even if smaller can get some good results. We believe that we can achieve better results by applying some hyper-parameter tuning through approaches like grid search. It is also interesting to look at how the parameters of mobileBERT distillation affect the training process and if changing some of them from the original model can achieve better results for Arabic. Also, a closer look at the distillation process can give us some estimate about the bias towards a certain linguistic phenomenon (Hooker et al., 2020).

Table 4: Memory consumption and size on disk for the fine-tuned and quantized models. M:millions, MB:Megabyte, GB:Gigabyte.

	AraBERT	IBERTA	MBERTA	MBERTA II
Base model number of parameters	135.2 M	66.7 M	23.7 M	**14.2 M**
Fine-tuned model's size on disk	1.6 GB	763 MB	272 MB	**163 MB**
Fine-tuned quantized model's size on disk	516 MB	255 MB	91 MB	**55 MB**

Acknowledgements

We would like to thank Zhiqing Sun (author of mobileBERT paper) for his suggestions and insights to train the models for Arabic. Also, we would like to thank Paige Bailey and Zak Stone for providing the TPU access as part of the TensorFlow Research Cloud (TFRC) program to train our models.

References

Abdul-Mageed, M., Elmadany, A., and Nagoudi, E. M. B. (2020). Arbert & marbert: Deep bidirectional transformers for arabic. *arXiv preprint arXiv:2101.01785*.

Abid, A., Ali, W., Farooq, M. S., Farooq, U., Sabir, N., and Abid, K. (2020). Semi-automatic classification and duplicate detection from human loss news corpus. *IEEE Access*.

Alkhulaifi, A., Alsahli, F., and Ahmad, I. (2020). Knowledge distillation in deep learning and its applications. *arXiv preprint arXiv:2007.09029*.

Alomari, K. M., ElSherif, H. M., and Shaalan, K. (2017). Arabic tweets sentimental analysis using machine learning. In *International Conference on Industrial, Engineering and Other Applications of Applied Intelligent Systems*, pages 602–610. Springer.

Aly, M. and Atiya, A. (2013). Labr: A large scale arabic book reviews dataset. In *Proceedings of the 51st Annual Meeting of the Association for Computational Linguistics (Volume 2: Short Papers)*, pages 494–498.

Antoun, W., Baly, F., and Hajj, H. (2020). Arabert: Transformer-based model for arabic language understanding. *arXiv preprint arXiv:2003.00104*.

Baly, R., Khaddaj, A., Hajj, H., El-Hajj, W., and Bashir Shaban, K. (2018). Arsentd-lev: A multi-topic corpus for target-based sentiment analysis in arabic levantine tweets. *OSACT3*.

Cui, J., Kingsbury, B., Ramabhadran, B., Saon, G., Sercu, T., Audhkhasi, K., Sethy, A., Nussbaum-Thom, M., and Rosenberg, A. (2017). Knowledge distillation across ensembles of multilingual models for low-resource languages. In *2017 IEEE International Conference on Acoustics, Speech and Signal Processing (ICASSP)*, pages 4825–4829. IEEE.

Devlin, J. et al. (2018). Bert: Pre-training of deep bidirectional transformers for language understanding. preprint, arXiv.

El-Khair, I. A. (2016). 1.5 billion words arabic corpus. *arXiv preprint arXiv:1611.04033*.

ElJundi, O., Antoun, W., El Droubi, N., Hajj, H., El-Hajj, W., and Shaban, K. (2019). hulmona: The universal language model in arabic. In *Proceedings of the Fourth Arabic Natural Language Processing Workshop*, pages 68–77.

Elnagar, A., Khalifa, Y. S., and Einea, A. (2018). Hotel arabic-reviews dataset construction for sentiment analysis applications. In *Intelligent Natural Language Processing: Trends and Applications*, pages 35–52. Springer.

Gerz, D., Vulić, I., Ponti, E., Naradowsky, J., Reichart, R., and Korhonen, A. (2018). Language modeling for morphologically rich languages: Character-aware modeling for word-level prediction. *Transactions of the Association for Computational Linguistics*, 6:451–465.

Hooker, S., Moorosi, N., Clark, G., Bengio, S., and Denton, E. (2020). Characterising bias in compressed models. *arXiv preprint arXiv:2010.03058*.

Kudo, T. and Richardson, J. (2018). Sentencepiece: A simple and language independent subword tokenizer and detokenizer for neural text processing. *arXiv preprint arXiv:1808.06226*.

Martin, L., Muller, B., Suárez, P. J. O., Dupont, Y., Romary, L., de la Clergerie, É. V., Seddah, D., and Sagot, B. (2019). Camembert: a tasty french language model. *arXiv preprint arXiv:1911.03894*.

Mirzadeh, S.-I., Farajtabar, M., Li, A., Levine, N., Matsukawa, A., and Ghasemzadeh, H. (2019). Improved knowledge distillation via teacher assistant. *arXiv preprint arXiv:1902.03393*.

Mozannar, H., Hajal, K. E., Maamary, E., and Hajj, H. (2019). Neural arabic question answering. *arXiv preprint arXiv:1906.05394*.

Nabil, M., Aly, M., and Atiya, A. (2015). Astd: Arabic sentiment tweets dataset. In *Proceedings of the 2015 conference on empirical methods in natural language processing*, pages 2515–2519.

Peters, M. E., Neumann, M., Iyyer, M., Gardner, M., Clark, C., Lee, K., and Zettlemoyer, L. (2018). Deep contextualized word representations. *arXiv preprint arXiv:1802.05365*.

Radford, A. et al. (2018). *Improving language understanding by generative pre-training*. URL understanding paper. pdf.

Raffel, C. et al. (2019). Exploring the limits of transfer learning with a unified text-to-text transformer. preprint, arXiv.

shamela (2005). shamela.

Shen, S., Dong, Z., Ye, J., Ma, L., Yao, Z., Gholami, A., Mahoney, M. W., and Keutzer, K. (2020). Q-bert: Hessian based ultra low precision quantization of bert. In *AAAI*, pages 8815–8821.

Sun, S., Cheng, Y., Gan, Z., and Liu, J. (2019). Patient knowledge distillation for bert model compression. *arXiv preprint arXiv:1908.09355*.

Sun, Z., Yu, H., Song, X., Liu, R., Yang, Y., and Zhou, D. (2020). Mobilebert: a compact task-agnostic bert for resource-limited devices. *arXiv preprint arXiv:2004.02984*.

Tian, Y., Krishnan, D., and Isola, P. (2019). Contrastive representation distillation. *arXiv preprint arXiv:1910.10699*.

Yang, C., Xie, L., Su, C., and Yuille, A. L. (2019). Snapshot distillation: Teacher-student optimization in one generation. In *Proceedings of the IEEE Conference on Computer Vision and Pattern Recognition*, pages 2859–2868.

You, Y., Li, J., Reddi, S., Hseu, J., Kumar, S., Bhojanapalli, S., Song, X., Demmel, J., Keutzer, K., and Hsieh, C.-J. (2019). Large batch optimization for deep learning: Training bert in 76 minutes. *arXiv preprint arXiv:1904.00962*.

Zadeh, A. H. and Moshovos, A. (2020). Gobo: Quantizing attention-based nlp models for low latency and energy efficient inference. *arXiv preprint arXiv:2005.03842*.

Zafrir, O., Boudoukh, G., Izsak, P., and Wasserblat, M. (2019). Q8bert: Quantized 8bit bert. *arXiv preprint arXiv:1910.06188*.

Zeman, D. (2015). Universal dependencies. `https://github.com/UniversalDependencies/UD_Arabic-PADT`.

Arabic Emoji Sentiment Lexicon (Arab-ESL): A Comparison between Arabic and European Emoji Sentiment Lexicons

Shatha Ali A. Hakami
University of Birmingham &
Jazan University
United Kingdom / Saudi Arabia
sahakami@jazanu.edu.sa

Robert Hendley
University of Birmingham,
School of Computer Science
United Kingdom
r.j.hendley@cs.bham.ac.uk

Phillip Smith
University of Birmingham
School of Computer Science
United Kingdom
p.smith.7@cs.bham.ac.uk

Abstract

Emoji (the popular digital pictograms) are sometimes seen as a new kind of artificial and universally usable and consistent writing code. In spite of their assumed universality, there is some evidence that the sense of an emoji, specifically in regard to sentiment, may change from language to language and culture to culture. This paper investigates whether contextual emoji sentiment analysis is consistent across Arabic and European languages. To conduct this investigation, we, first, created the Arabic emoji sentiment lexicon (Arab-ESL). Then, we exploited an existing European emoji sentiment lexicon to compare the sentiment conveyed in each of the two families of language and culture (Arabic and European). The results show that the pairwise correlation between the two lexicons is consistent for emoji that represent, for instance, hearts, facial expressions, and body language. However, for a subset of emoji (those that represent objects, nature, symbols, and some human activities), there are large differences in the sentiment conveyed. More interestingly, an extremely high level of inconsistency has been shown with food emoji.

1 Introduction

Textual digital communication has become habitual these days among Internet users. However, it has been argued that in such communication, the vital nonverbal cues are missing, which can potentially lead to ambiguity and misunderstanding (Kiesler et al., 1984). To address this issue, users tend to employ many surrogates, including non-standard punctuation, emoticons, and emoji.

Evans (2017) defined emoji as a form of developed punctuation (the way of encoding nonverbal prosody cues in writing systems) that supplements written language to facilitate the writers articulating their emotions in text-based communication. Practically, emoji are actual icons in Unicode Transformation Format (UTF) that are a successor to emoticons (i.e., ASCII character based) with more sophisticated rendering. These icons can represent facial expressions, body language, food, animals, places, and natural objects like flowers and trees. It has been observed that including emoticons, as well as emoji, in text not only helps the receivers to infer some contextual information, but it also eases understanding of the expressed sentiment (Dresner and Herring, 2010; Skovholt et al., 2014).

Sentiment analysis, is the computational study of people's opinions, sentiments, emotions, and attitudes. It is one of the most active research areas in natural language processing (NLP) and is also extensively studied in data mining, web mining, and text mining (Ambady et al., 2000; Chen Yuet Wei, 2012). Usually, it is a one dimensional measure from negative to positive and often it is quantized to just three values: negative, neutral or positive. Sentiment analysis has become an important tool in classifying and interpreting text.

As digital language is increasingly used across platforms (Ai et al., 2017; Danesi, 2016), emoji are studied as an integral aspect of sentiment analysis in various research domains. This includes marketing (Ge and Gretzel, 2018), law (Goldman, 2018), healthcare (Willoughby and Liu, 2018), food-related (Vidal et al., 2016) and addictive-substances-related contents (Tran et al., 2018).

The basis of many sentiment analysis approaches is the sentiment lexicon, with words and phrases classified as conveying positive or negative sentiments. Several general-purpose word-based and phrase-based lexicons of subjectivity and sentiment have been constructed. Emoji, likewise, can and should be viewed as an integral feature in the sentiment analysis process. However, most sentiment-analysis research has focused on emoji in languages other than Arabic and, consequently, most of the resources developed (such as emoji sentiment lexicons and emoji-specific corpora) are non-Arabic. Thus, an analysis of Arabic emoji sentiment us-

Proceedings of the Sixth Arabic Natural Language Processing Workshop, pages 60–71
Kyiv, Ukraine (Virtual), April 19, 2021.

age, provided as a result of this study, would be a valuable resource for research in Arabic language analysis.

In this work, we seek to investigate the differences in sentiment interpretation of emoji expressed in informal texts between two cultures (Arabic and European), through the following:

- **Constructing** an Arabic sentiment lexicon of 1034 emoji, extracted from 144,196 tweets in existing Arabic datasets. The lexicon is made available for open-access for research use[1].
- **Comparing** the sentiment conveyed by a subset of emoji in the Arabic lexicon with the corresponding ones in a standard European emoji lexicon.

The rest of this paper is organized as follows. Section 2 reviews related work upon which we build; Section 3 presents the study's design; Section 4 presents the results analysis and discussion. Finally, in Section 5 we draw conclusions from this work along with highlighting its limitations as well as some recommendations for future work.

2 Related Work

The usage patterns of emoji have been studied from several viewpoints such as relationships with specific topics (Zhao et al., 2018), seasons (Barbieri et al., 2018b), countries and regions (Ljubešić and Fišer, 2016) as well as languages (Cohn et al., 2018). Here, we review some of the existing research that analyses emoji across cultures, and as sentiment features.

2.1 Emoji Across Cultures

Emoji usage can be understood as "visible acts of meaning" (Miller et al., 2017). Visible acts of meaning, as defined by Bavelas and Chovil (2000), are analogically encoded symbols that are sensitive to a sender-receiver relationship, and that are fully integrated with the accompanying words. This involves the sender-receiver cultural background as an aspect that might affect emoji-text sentiment analysis.

For example, Gao and VanderLaan (2020) presented a study suggesting that Eastern and Western cultures are different in their use of mouth versus eye cues when interpreting emotions. According to the study, the norm in Western cultures is to display the overt emotion while in Eastern cultures, the norm is to present more subtle emotion. Westerners interpret facial emotional expressions through the mouth region. Conversely, Eastern cultures focus more on the eyes. The researchers also found that such differences extend to written and paralinguistic signals such as emoji and, consequently, this has implications for digital communication.

From another perspective, Guntuku et al. (2019) compared emoji use across cultures in terms of frequency, context, and topic associations. This includes potential mapping of emoji use differences with previously identified cultural differences in users' expression about diverse concepts such as death, money, emotions and family. They also investigated the relative correspondence of validated psycho-linguistic categories with Ekman's emotions (Ekman, 1992). The study considered two Eastern countries (China and Japan) and three Western countries (USA, UK and Canada). Their analysis revealed recognizable normative and culture specific patterns. Also, it revealed the ways in which emoji can be used for cross-cultural communication. For example, the emoji categories of emotion 'Anger' (e.g., 😒, 😠, 😤, 😡) in the study was tied to the basic emotions of anger which had been found by Ekman (1992) to be universally expressed and recognized facially across cultures. By contrast, the study showed that the emoji for rice bowl (🍚) and ramen (🍜) dominated the East, while meat-related emoji (e.g., 🍗, 🍖) are the majority in the West, meaning that such emoji seemingly are cultural-specific.

There are few studies of the use of emoji in Arabic culture. An Arabic socio-linguistic investigation on the use of emoji was applied to Omani, WhatsApp textual contents by Al Rashdi (2018). This work performed a qualitative analysis of selected texts with emoji using theories and methods of interactional sociolinguistics. The results of the work demonstrated that Arab users (mainly Omanis) utilize emoji not only as indicators of their emotions, but also as what Gumperz (1982) calls "contextualization cues". In line with Gumperz's theory, the study showed that emoji use in Arabic culture is as indicators of celebration, other message approvals, or a signal of task fulfillment. Also, Arabs use emoji as a response to thanks/compliment expressions; linking devices, and openings/closings of conversations.

[1] https://github.com/ShathaHakami/Arabic-Emoji-Sentiment-Lexicon-Version-1.0

Another recent investigation of the phenomenon of emoji as a sentiment indicator within Arabic text was done by Hakami et al. (2020). In this work, the researchers undertook an empirical sentiment analysis along with a "Coding and Counting" approach (Herring et al., 2004). They concluded that an emoji in Arabic context, and perhaps in other cultural contexts as well, can be a true sentiment indicator, a multi-sentiment indicator, an ambiguous sentiment indicator, or a No-sentiment indicator.

2.2 Emoji as Sentiment Features

Many researchers have dedicated their efforts to exploiting emoji as a textual feature for sentiment analysis. One of the key elements of the use of emoji in sentiment analysis is the emoji sentiment lexicon. These have been constructed for different languages. Emoji Sentiment Ranking (ESR) is the first emoji sentiment lexicon with 751 emoji (Kralj Novak et al., 2015). The lexicon was constructed from over 70,000 tweets in 13 European languages, including English, Spanish, Polish, Russian, a union of tweets in Serbian, Croatian and Bosnian; Hungarian, German, Swedish, Slovak, Slovenian, Portuguese, Bulgarian and Albanian. This corpus was annotated for sentiment by 83 human annotators, each of whom was a native speaker of at least one of the languages. The sentiment of the emoji was computed from the sentiment of the tweets in which they occur and reflects the actual use of emoji in a context. The researchers of the work observed no significant differences in the emoji sentiment rankings between the 13 languages. Consequently, they considered the constructed lexicon a generic European language-independent resource for automated sentiment analysis. We use this lexicon for our investigation, and we refer to as European Emoji Sentiment Lexicon (Euro-ESL).

The number of emoji included in the European lexicon is smaller than that of the current set of emoji. Expanding the lexicon manually requires time and effort to reconstruct the labeled dataset. This encouraged Kimura and Katsurai (2017) to present a simple and efficient method for automatically constructing an emoji sentiment lexicon with arbitrary sentiment categories. The method extracted sentiment words from WordNet-Affect (Strapparava et al., 2004) and calculates the co-occurrence frequency between the sentiment words and each emoji. Based on the ratio of the number of occurrences of each emoji among the sentiment categories, each emoji is assigned a multidimensional vector whose elements indicate the strength of the corresponding sentiment. In experiments conducted on a collection of tweets, they were able to show a high correlation between the European lexicon and their lexicon for three sentiment categories.

Compared to other languages, even less research has been done on emoji for sentiment in the Arabic language. Nonetheless, some significant recent work does exist. One of the earliest works on analysing Arabic emoji usage for emotional content was done by Hussien et al. (2016). This study addressed the problem of emotion detection in Arabic tweets using emoji. The aim of the work was to show that training a sentiment classifier on an automatically annotated tweet (using emoji) provides more accurate results than training the same classifier on a manually annotated tweet.

Other work aims at exploring the impact of combining emoji based features with various forms of textual features on the sentiment classification of dialectical Arabic tweets (Al-Azani and El-Alfy, 2018a). The study concluded that simpler models can be constructed with much better results when emoji are merged with a Word2vec embedding model and the selection of the most relevant subset of features as input to the classifier. Different work by the same researchers adopted the Euro-ESL lexicon, mentioned earlier, to evaluate emoji as nonverbal features for sentiment analysis in Arabic texts (Al-Azani and El-Alfy, 2018b). Several machine learning algorithms were evaluated on the suggested features. The experimental results demonstrated that emoji-based features alone can be a very effective means for detecting sentiment polarity.

Similarly, Abdellaoui and Zrigui (2018) used ten subjective emoji (from the Euro-ESL) along with the Arabic word sentiment lexicon Ar-SeLn (Badaro et al., 2014) to construct and annotate a large-scale dataset for Arabic sentiment analysis. Their process used a dataset of 6 million Arabic tweets with a vocabulary of 602,721 distinct entities. They named their dataset TEAD and released a subset of it for public use.

The most recent Arabic study for emotion analysis of textual content with emoji has been done by Hussien et al. (2019). The study proposed a distant supervised learning approach where the training sentences are automatically annotated based on the

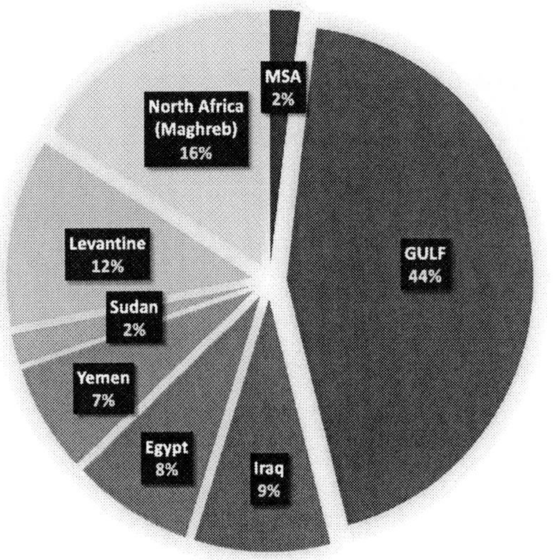

Figure 1: A regional-based distribution of the Arabic dialects in the collected dataset. This distribution includes the modern standard Arabic (MSA).

emoji they contain. The study's authors experimentally showed that training classifiers on cheap, large and possibly erroneous data annotated using their approach leads to more accurate results compared with training the same classifiers on the more expensive, much smaller and error-free manually annotated training data.

3 Study Design

Kralj Novak et al. (2015) conducted a study, which considered context-sensitivity when analyzing the sentiment of emoji and texts, described above (i.e., in subsection 2.2). We followed their approach, with some additional steps, to construct our Arabic emoji sentiment lexicon (Arab-ESL) as follows:

3.1 Data Collection

Before we collected our data, some criteria were defined. Our consideration was on data that is from a social media platform, written in the Arabic language, multi-dialect, multi-aspect and, more importantly, containing emoji. With such criteria, collecting, cleaning and preparing a great deal of raw data for sentiment annotation in a short time is impossible. Therefore, we targeted 14 different public datasets of Arabic social media (all are tweets from the Twitter platform). These contain 144,196 tweets that meet our criteria. This data collection procedure resulted in a dataset that is diverse in its Arabic dialects. They are from all of the Arabic regions: Levantine (Syria, Lebanon, Jordan, and Palestine), Iraq, Gulf (Saudi Arabia, Kuwait, Qatar, Bahrain, UAE, and Oman), Yemen, Egypt, Sudan, and Maghrib (Libya, Algeria, Tunisia, and Morocco). CAMeL Tools (Obeid et al., 2020) were used to detect and classify these dialects in our dataset based on their Arabic regions as illustrated in Figure 1.

Some of the targeted datasets were constructed for sentiment classification tasks or other related tasks, such as hate speech detection. Therefore, these datasets have been manually annotated with sentiment labels, emotional labels, or other related labels like *hate* and *offensive*. For some other datasets (i.e., ATSAD (Train & Test), Arabic Twitter Data for Sentiment, and TEAD), they were available for public use with automatically predicted sentiment labels. This meant that we had to re-annotate these datasets with sentiment labels after testing their reliability. The details of this procedure are explained in the following subsection. Table 1 summarises all the details of the considered tweets from the targeted datasets.

3.2 Data Preparation

We applied our data preparations based on the work in (El-Beltagy et al., 2017). For general preparation, we removed URLs, all non-emoji symbols (including #, @, and emoticons), punctuation marks, numbers and repeated letters. For Arabic text specific preparation, we unified the letters that appear in different forms, and removed diacritics and unknown characters (e.g., Quranic symbols).

In addition, we normalized all the Emoji ZWJ sequences into their base emoji. An emoji ZWJ sequence is a combination of multiple emoji which display as a single emoji on supporting platforms. These sequences are joined with a Zero Width Joiner (ZWJ) character, which is an invisible Unicode character that joins two or more other characters together in sequence to create a new emoji. For example, the *Woman with Veil: Medium Skin Tone* emoji (🧕🏽) is a ZWJ sequence combining *Person With Veil* (🧕), *Medium Skin Tone* (🏽), *Zero Width Joiner* (invisible) and *Female Sign* (♀). For such cases, we considered the base emoji only, which is the *Person With Veil* (🧕).

In general, this initial data preparation procedure aimed to normalise the data into a coherent form so that it can be handled easily for sentiment analysis by both human and machine.

Dataset Name / Sentiment Annotation Process	Dataset Reference	# of Tweets Containing Emoji
ATSAD (Train & Test) / (Re-annotated) Automatic	(Abu Kwaik et al., 2020)	77,211
Arabic Twitter Data for Sentiment / (Re-annotated) Automatic	(Fathi, 2019)	42,832
TEAD / (Re-annotated) Automatic	(Abdellaoui and Zrigui, 2018)	11,950
ArSAS / Manual	(Elmadany AbdelRahim and Magdy, 2018)	4,266
ATSAD (Gold) / Manual	(Abu Kwaik et al., 2020)	3,775
SS2030 / Manual	(Alyami and Olatunji, 2020)	1,061
SemEval-2018 (Task1 & Task2) / Manual	(Mohammad et al., 2018) (Barbieri et al., 2018a)	594
ArSenTD-Lev / Manual	(Baly et al., 2019)	389
SemEval-2017 (Task4) / Manual	(Rosenthal et al., 2017)	263
Syria Tweets / Manual	(Salameh et al., 2015)	64
L-HSAB / Manual	(Mulki et al., 2019)	23
Arabic Floods Detection / (Re-annotated) Manual	(Alharbi and Lee, 2019)	768
DART / (Re-annotated) Manual	(Alsarsour et al., 2018)	470
ArSAS / (Re-annotated) Manual	(Elmadany AbdelRahim and Magdy, 2018)	285
Arabic-Tweets-vs-Dialects / (Re-annotated) Manual	(Abdelaal, 2018)	129
L-HSAB / (Re-annotated) Manual	(Mulki et al., 2019)	42
	Total	**144,196**

Table 1: Summary of the datasets used.

3.3 Manual Sentiment Annotation

As mentioned above, most of the targeted datasets (10 out of 13 datasets) were previously manually annotated with inconsistent labels. Therefore, unifying the annotation labels was necessary, and applied as follows.

Syria Tweets, SemEval-2017 (Task4), ArSenTD-Lev, ArSAS, SS2030, and ATSAD (Gold) datasets were constructed for a sentiment analysis task. In this case, we only unified their labels to be *negative*, *neutral*, or *positive*. The ArSAS dataset had a group of tweets labelled as *Mixed* which we kept for later manual re-annotation with sentiments.

On the other hand, labels in SemEval-2018 and L-HSAB datasets were not explicitly for sentiment. The L-HSAB dataset is intended to be for an offensive/hate-speech detection task. In this dataset, we replaced the labels *Abusive* and *Hate* with the label *negative*. However, we kept the tweets that were labeled as *Normal* for later manual re-annotation with sentiment. In SemEval-2018, the labels were for the emotions rather than sentiments. Thus, the negative labels (i.e., *Anger*, *Fear*, and *Sadness*) were replaced by the label *negative*; and the positive label (i.e., *Joy*) was replaced by the word *positive*.

Finally, the DART, Arabic-Tweets-vs-Dialects and Arabic Floods Detection datasets were created for natural language processing tasks other than sentiment analysis. The DART and Arabic-Tweets-vs-Dialects datasets were for an Arabic-dialects specification task while the Arabic Floods Detection dataset was for a disaster detection task. Along with the tweets in the ArSAS dataset that were labelled as *Mixed* and in the L-HSAB that were labelled as *Normal*; we formed a collection of tweets including Arabic Floods Detection, DART and Arabic-Tweets-vs-Dialects datasets to be manually re-annotated with sentiment. This annotation was done, independently, by four native Arabic speaking annotators, two males and two females. Table 1 specifies the number of tweets from each dataset that have been re-annotated.

3.4 Machine Sentiment Annotation

Sentiment annotation by a machine needs some preprocessing steps. In our case, besides the dataset preparation mentioned above, the following steps were applied.

First, all of the emoji in the collected dataset were extracted, and all of their official Unicode English names were found. We used the Python library *emoji*. Then, the emoji's English names were translated into the Arabic language in two steps: using the *Google Translate* API for Python, follwoed by manual Arabic-English translation checking by a linguist. Lastly, each emoji symbol within a text was replaced with its Arabic name. This was to ensure that the machine will not neglect any token (i.e., Arabic word) in the provided textual context and that it will classify its sentiment appropriately.

For automatic annotation of our Arabic textual dataset with sentiment, two recently released Arabic machine sentiment annotators were tested: Mazajak and CAMeL Tools.

Mazajak (Abu Farha and Magdy, 2019) is the first online Arabic sentiment analyser, it is based on a deep learning model built on a convolutional neural network (CNN) followed by a long short-term memory (LSTM). It achieves state-of-the-art results on many Arabic dialect datasets including SemEval 2017 and ASTD. This analyser provides different functionalities for Arabic sentiment analysis including two modes for raw text processing: the batch mode and the online API. We used the API mode.

CAMeL Tools (Obeid et al., 2020), on the other hand, is a collection of open-source tools for Arabic NLP in Python. It provides utilities for many NLP tasks, including dialect identification and sentiment analysis. The sentiment analyser in this system was built using large pre-trained language models (i.e., HuggingFace's Transformers, mBERT, and AraBERT); and various Arabic dialectic datasets for fine-tuning and evaluation.

3.5 Validity and Reliability Tests for Sentiment Annotations

Regarding human annotation, we assumed that all of the tweets extracted from the already-existing datasets were reliably annotated. However, as described in subsection 3.3 above, it was necessary to re-annotate a subset of that data that was not labeled with sentiment. For that, we used the majority-voting approach between four human annotators (two males, and two females) as the procedure for this labelling reliability assurance. Two annotators, at least, had to be in agreement on one sentiment label for a tweet. In cases where two annotators disagreed on a specific sentiment, the annotation from a third annotator was considered to determine the decision.

To test the reliability of the machine annotation, we first sampled a random set of tweets which were already manually annotated. Then we used the accuracy metric between the manual and the automatic annotations in two ways. The first accuracy test was conducted between the labels from the manually annotated tweets and the labels of the same tweets annotated by Mazajak. The test resulted in an $accuracy = 0.71$. The second test was between the labels of the same manually annotated tweets and their sentiment annotation results from CAMeL Tools. This test resulted in an $accuracy = 0.74$. Although the two tests results are close, CAMeL Tools out-performed Mazajak by 0.03. Therefore, we used the sentiment labels assigned by CAMeL Tools.

3.6 Arabic Emoji Sentiment Lexicon (Arab-ESL) Construction

We applied the Emoji Sentiment Ranking (ESR) model, that was proposed for Euro-ESL by (Kralj Novak et al., 2015), to construct an Arabic emoji sentiment lexicon (Arab-ESL) using our prepared data. In this model, the sentiment of the emoji was computed from the sentiment of texts labelled by human annotators. Sentiment labels take one of three values: negative, neutral and positive. Each sentiment label, c, is a discrete three-valued variable:

$$c \in \{-1, 0, +1\}$$

This variable represents the order of the sentiment values and the distances between them. An emoji could occur in several tweets each of which are labelled with sentiment. A discrete distribution:

$$N(c), \sum N(c) = N, c \in \{-1, 0, +1\}$$

captures the sentiment distribution for the set of relevant tweets. N denotes the number of all the occurrences of the object in the tweets, and $N(c)$ are the occurrences in tweets with the sentiment label c. We considered the multiple occurrence of

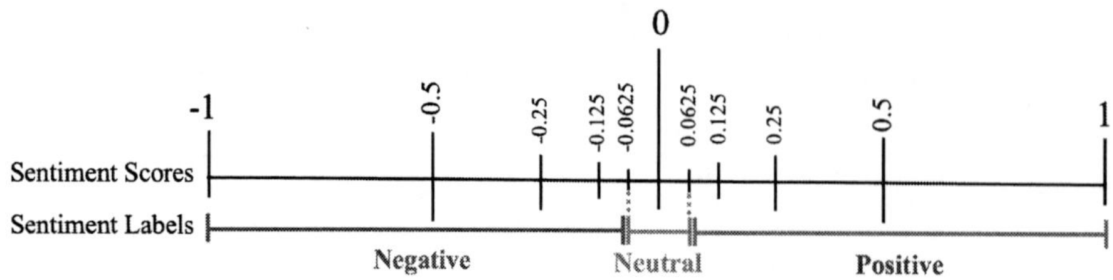

Figure 2: A scale for determine sentiment labels from sentiment scores.

Emoji	Emoji Name	Emoji Class	Occurrence (N)	Sentiment Score ($\overline{S}$)	Sentiment Label (L)
😂	Tears of Joy	Facial Expression	25,908	0.272426	positive
💔	Broken Heart	Heart	18,564	-0.934066	negative
❤️	Red Heart	Heart	15,876	0.560658	positive
😭	Loudly Crying Face	Facial Expression	12,318	-0.677789	negative
😍	Smiling Face with Heart-Eyes	Facial Expression	6,815	0.869552	positive
🌹	Rose	Nature	6,173	0.766402	positive
🙂	Slightly Smiling Face	Facial Expression	5,717	0.226692	positive
💕	Two Hearts	Heart	5,573	0.487888	positive
😅	Grinning Face with Sweat	Facial Expression	5,499	0.533552	positive
💙	Blue Heart	Heart	5,444	0.616091	positive

Table 2: The top ten emoji in the Arabic Emoji Sentiment Lexicon (Arab-ESL).

an emoji in a single tweet. From the above we formed a discrete probability distribution:

$$(p_-, p_0, p_+), \sum_c P(c) = 1$$

The components of the distribution (i.e., p_-, p_0, and p_+) denote the negativity, neutrality, and positivity of the emoji, respectively. Then, we estimated the probabilities from relative frequencies:

$$P(c) = \frac{N(c)}{N}$$

This estimation gives a good approximation for large samples. However, we used the Laplace estimate (Good, 1965) when $N \leq 900$, as it is recommended when estimating the probability of small samples.

Then, the sentiment score $\overline{S}$ of the emoji was computed as the mean of the distribution:

$$\overline{S} = (-1 \,.\, P(-)) + (0 \,.\, P(0)) + (+1 \,.\, P(+))$$

Furthermore, finding sentiment labels of emoji in both lexicons helps test the agreement between the two, which we will explain later. Therefore, three scaled-groups of sentiment scores have been classified under three sentiment labels L. Figure 2 demonstrates the scale that we have used to determine the thresholds in the sentiment scores when determining the sentiment labels in our lexicon. Emoji with sentiment score i, where -1 $\leq i <$ -0.0625, was classified as negative. On the other hand, emoji with sentiment score i, where 1 $\geq i >$ 0.0625, was classified as positive. Lastly, an emoji was classified as neutral when its sentiment score i was in the range where -0.0625 $\leq i \leq$ 0.0625. Part of the resulting emoji sentiment lexicon (10 out of 1034 emoji) is shown in Table 2.

3.7 Correlation and Agreement Tests between Euro-ESL and Arab-ESL

Because of the richness and diversity of the emoji, it is difficult to hypothesize, a priori, how specific emoji may differ between cultures. Therefore, we aim to make this investigation depend on the sentiment scores' correlation rather than causality. For that, a correlation measurement between the Euro-ESL and the Arab-ESL was utilized. The metric was the Pearson correlation coefficient and the focus was on the sentiment scores of 479 common emoji in the two lexicons.

Emoji Category	# of Emoji	Pearson	p-value	Cohen's κ
Object	106	0.414	0.101	0.1092
Nature	87	0.391	0.000	0.1430
Facial Expression	79	0.747	0.269	0.4379
Symbol	79	0.275	0.254	0.0581
Food	46	-0.159	0.289	0.0160
Body Language	38	0.583	0.000	0.2438
Human Activity	19	0.275	0.254	-0.0556
Heart	16	0.834	0.584	1.0000

Table 3: Correlation and agreement tests results of the common emoji in Arab-ESL and Euro-ESL under eight different categories. The green color indicates the highest correlation/agreement and the red color the lowest.

Heart Emoji		Arab-ESL		Euro-ESL	
Emoji	**Name**	**Score**	**Label**	**Score**	**Label**
💔	Broken Heart	-0.934066	negative	-0.120846	negative
❤️	Red Heart	0.560658	positive	0.746087	positive
💕	Two Hearts	0.487888	positive	0.632917	positive
💘	Heart with Arrow	0.240646	positive	0.683417	positive
💖	Sparkling Heart	0.862897	positive	0.713381	positive

Table 4: Example heart emoji sentiment scores and labels in both Arab-ESL and Euro-ESL.

Specifically, we, first, extracted the common emoji between the two lexicons, where their frequency N is greater than or equal to 5. This resulted in 479 emoji in total. Then, we sorted the emoji in the Arab-ESL based on their frequency N in descending order. Accordingly, we sorted the corresponding emoji in the Euro-ESL based on their order in the Arab-ESL.This sorting process eased testing the correlation of the same emoji in the two lexicons. Moreover, we applied this test on eight emoji categories, independently, using the correlation measure in each. The emoji categories are: *Facial Expressions*, *Body Language*, *Human Activity*, *Hearts*, *Nature*, *Food*, *Object* and *Symbol*. Also, we disregarded two categories, *Place* (with seven emoji) and *Flag* (with two emoji), due to the small numbers of emoji. The test's results for each emoji category are tabulated in Table 3.

Agreement between the labels refers to the degree of concordance between the two sets of labels. The statistical Cohen's Kappa agreement tests (McHugh, 2012) was used to assess the variability of emoji sentiment labels in Euro-ESL and Arab-ESL. Again, we applied this agreement test on the eight emoji categories that were mentioned in the correlation testing process. The results of this agreement test under each emoji category are shown in Table 3.

4 Results Analysis and Discussion

Here, we analyze our data patterns from an abductive perspective (Haig, 2018) to form preliminary cultural emoji sentiment theories between European and Arabic languages. As is shown in Table 3, across the two lexicons, the Pearson correlation for *Heart* and *Facial Expression* emoji categories are 0.834, and 0.747, respectively. Likewise, the sentiment labels agreement tests for the *Heart* and *Facial Expression emoji* are the highest (i.e., almost perfect for *Heart* and moderate for *Facial Expression*) among other emoji categories. This indicates a strong consistency and detects a normal pattern in these types of emoji that are common across the two cultures.

Indeed, many sociological theories, proposing the universality of basic emotions (Ekman, 1992), point out the tendency of emotional emoji to show high levels of similarity even between distinct cultures, like West and East (Guntuku et al., 2019). Thus, emoji categories of *Facial Expression*, *Heart*, and *Body Language* would be expected to be more convergent compared to other categories. Table 4 exemplifies such matches between the two cultures for sentiment scores and labels, for heart emoji.

On the other hand, the lowest correlations in emoji sentiment between the two lexicons occur in the *Food* (-0.159), *Symbol* (0.275), and *Human*

Food Emoji		Arab-ESL		Euro-ESL	
Emoji	**Name**	**Score**	**Label**	**Score**	**Label**
🎂	Birthday Cake	0.733333	positive	0.612745	positive
🍯	Honey Pot	0.212766	positive	0.045455	neutral
🍥	Fish Cake with Swirl	0.575758	positive	-0.593750	negative
🍺	Beer Mug	-0.206897	negative	0.492537	positive
🍼	Baby Bottle	-0.058824	neutral	0.454545	positive

Table 5: Example food emoji sentiment scores and labels in both Arab-ESL and Euro-ESL.

Activities (0.275) categories. Sentiment label agreement tests showed similar results with the same emoji categories. Also, the Cohen's Kappa agreement coefficient resulted in κ = 0.0160 for *Food* emoji, κ = 0.0581 for *Symbol* emoji, and κ=-0.0556 for *Human Activity* emoji.

In fact, this is not surprising. Cultures are often instantiated in cuisines representing identities, religions, and dietary preferences (Van Gelder, 2014; Jallad, 2008; Van den Berghe, 1984). Besides, symbols are often representative figurative characters of many specific cultural values (Aaker et al., 2001). Moreover, many human activities such as praying, working, or playing are affected by culture (Smith et al., 2013). As an example, Table 5 illustrates the differences in emoji sentiment scores and labels under the *Food* category between Arab-ESL and Euro-ESL.

5 Conclusion, Limitations and Future Work

Investigating emoji sentiment indications between cultures is one of the primary applications of an emoji sentiment lexicon. In this work, we exploited most of the existing Arabic resources (covering all Arabic dialects) to contribute an Arabic emoji sentiment lexicon (Arab-ESL). As an application of the constructed lexicon, we compared the Arab-ESL with the already-existing similar European one. The results shows that cultures might share similar emoji sentiment indications. This occurs with emoji that represent common human behaviours, such as facial expressions, and body language, or basic emotions such as love and sadness. However, there are other emoji where their sentiments might be affected by a cultural-specific aspect, such as food, symbols, and human activities. These conclusions can be drawn from the results of employing two statistical methods: correlation coefficient and agreement coefficient.

We are aware that there are variations, both geographically and *within* a specific culture (e,g., Arabic or European) that makes it very difficult to completely rely on the results of such an investigation. However, we intend in the future to make the resulting emoji sentiment lexicon more fine grain for further, focused and detailed analytical studies of emoji within the Arabic language.

Another limitation is that the sentiment dimensions are more than just a one dimensional-scale (i.e., negative to positive), and that this should be explored in the future. The emoji's eloquence allows them to be assigned more fine-grained sentiment labels like very negative and slightly negative, or more detailed emotional labels like anger, happiness, and sadness. In the future, this might help for an additional structuring of the emoji that can be obtained from correlations between their sentiments or emotions. For example, deriving different forms of facial expressions expressing happiness.

Also, the tests on sentiment classification were only based on simple statistics of sentiment scores of emoji in texts. Future work can combine emoji sentiment scores within Arabic semantics for more advanced sentiment analysis. Besides, an emoji's textual context is crucial in determining the role of the emoji as a modifier of the meaning. More investigation should be applied with Arabic content.

Finally, considering the promise of emoji in NLP application tasks, studies should discover the contribution of emoji in multi-modal and cross-lingual sentiment analysis along with transfer learning and deep learning tasks. Moreover, it will be interesting to observe how the use of emoji by Arabic users is growing, and whether their textual communication is increasingly being replaced by this pictorial language. Also, the correlation between sentiment and meaning of emoji evolves over time. It might be important to explore the change in the meaning of controversial emoji, and how they are affected by the corresponding social processes.

References

Jennifer Lynn Aaker, Veronica Benet-Martinez, and Jordi Garolera. 2001. Consumption symbols as carriers of culture: A study of japanese and spanish brand personality constucts. *Journal of personality and social psychology*, 81(3):492.

Ahmad Abdelaal. 2018. Arabic-Tweets-vs-Dialects. https://www.kaggle.com/ahmed9914/arabic-tweets-vs-dialects. Online; accessed 24 October 2020.

Houssem Abdellaoui and Mounir Zrigui. 2018. Using Tweets and Emojis to Build TEAD: an Arabic Dataset for Sentiment Analysis. *Computación y Sistemas*, 22:777 – 786.

Ibrahim Abu Farha and Walid Magdy. 2019. Mazajak: An online Arabic sentiment analyser. In *Proceedings of the Fourth Arabic Natural Language Processing Workshop*, pages 192–198, Florence, Italy. Association for Computational Linguistics.

Kathrein Abu Kwaik, Stergios Chatzikyriakidis, Simon Dobnik, Motaz Saad, and Richard Johansson. 2020. An Arabic tweets sentiment analysis dataset (ATSAD) using distant supervision and self training. In *Proceedings of the 4th Workshop on Open-Source Arabic Corpora and Processing Tools, with a Shared Task on Offensive Language Detection*, pages 1–8, Marseille, France. European Language Resource Association.

Wei Ai, Xuan Lu, Xuanzhe Liu, Ning Wang, Gang Huang, and Qiaozhu Mei. 2017. Untangling emoji popularity through semantic embeddings. In *Proceedings of the International AAAI Conference on Web and Social Media*, volume 11.

Sadam Al-Azani and El-Sayed M El-Alfy. 2018a. Combining emojis with arabic textual features for sentiment classification. In *2018 9th International Conference on Information and Communication Systems (ICICS)*, pages 139–144. IEEE.

Sadam Al-Azani and El-Sayed M El-Alfy. 2018b. Emoji-based sentiment analysis of arabic microblogs using machine learning. In *2018 21st Saudi Computer Society National Computer Conference (NCC)*, pages 1–6. IEEE.

Fathiya Al Rashdi. 2018. Functions of emojis in whatsapp interaction among omanis. *Discourse, Context & Media*, 26:117–126.

Alaa Alharbi and Mark Lee. 2019. Crisis detection from arabic tweets. In *Proceedings of the 3rd Workshop on Arabic Corpus Linguistics*, pages 72–79.

Israa Alsarsour, Esraa Mohamed, Reem Suwaileh, and Tamer Elsayed. 2018. DART: A large dataset of dialectal Arabic tweets. In *Proceedings of the Eleventh International Conference on Language Resources and Evaluation (LREC 2018)*, Miyazaki, Japan. European Language Resources Association (ELRA).

Sarah N. Alyami and Sunday O. Olatunji. 2020. Application of support vector machine for arabic sentiment classification using twitter-based dataset. *Journal of Information & Knowledge Management*, 19(01):2040018.

Nalini Ambady, Frank J Bernieri, and Jennifer A Richeson. 2000. Toward a histology of social behavior: Judgmental accuracy from thin slices of the behavioral stream. In *Advances in experimental social psychology*, volume 32, pages 201–271. Elsevier.

Gilbert Badaro, Ramy Baly, Hazem Hajj, Nizar Habash, and Wassim El-Hajj. 2014. A large scale arabic sentiment lexicon for arabic opinion mining. In *Proceedings of the EMNLP 2014 workshop on arabic natural language processing (ANLP)*, pages 165–173.

Ramy Baly, Alaa Khaddaj, Hazem M. Hajj, Wassim El-Hajj, and Khaled Bashir Shaban. 2019. Arsentd-lev: A multi-topic corpus for target-based sentiment analysis in arabic levantine tweets. *CoRR*, abs/1906.01830.

Francesco Barbieri, Jose Camacho-Collados, Francesco Ronzano, Luis Espinosa-Anke, Miguel Ballesteros, Valerio Basile, Viviana Patti, and Horacio Saggion. 2018a. SemEval 2018 task 2: Multilingual emoji prediction. In *Proceedings of The 12th International Workshop on Semantic Evaluation*, pages 24–33, New Orleans, Louisiana. Association for Computational Linguistics.

Francesco Barbieri, Luis Marujo, Pradeep Karuturi, William Brendel, and Horacio Saggion. 2018b. Exploring emoji usage and prediction through a temporal variation lens. *arXiv preprint arXiv:1805.00731*.

Janet Beavin Bavelas and Nicole Chovil. 2000. Visible acts of meaning: An integrated message model of language in face-to-face dialogue. *Journal of Language and social Psychology*, 19(2):163–194.

Pierre L Van den Berghe. 1984. Ethnic cuisine: Culture in nature. *Ethnic and Racial Studies*, 7(3):387–397.

Amanda Chen Yuet Wei. 2012. *Emoticons and the nonverbal communication: With reference to Facebook*. Ph.D. thesis, Christ University.

Neil Cohn, Tim Roijackers, Robin Schaap, and Jan Engelen. 2018. Are emoji a poor substitute for words? sentence processing with emoji substitutions. In *CogSci*.

Marcel Danesi. 2016. *The semiotics of emoji: The rise of visual language in the age of the internet*. Bloomsbury Publishing.

Eli Dresner and Susan C Herring. 2010. Functions of the nonverbal in cmc: Emoticons and illocutionary force. *Communication theory*, 20(3):249–268.

Paul Ekman. 1992. An argument for basic emotions. *Cognition & emotion*, 6(3-4):169–200.

Samhaa R El-Beltagy, Mona El Kalamawy, and Abu Bakr Soliman. 2017. Niletmrg at semeval-2017 task 4: Arabic sentiment analysis. *arXiv preprint arXiv:1710.08458*.

Hamdy Mubarak Elmadany AbdelRahim and Walid Magdy. 2018. Arsas: An arabic speech-act and sentiment corpus of tweets. In *Proceedings of the Eleventh International Conference on Language Resources and Evaluation (LREC 2018)*, Paris, France. European Language Resources Association (ELRA).

Vyvyan Evans. 2017. *The emoji code: The linguistics behind smiley faces and scaredy cats*. Picador USA.

Mohammed Fathi. 2019. Arabic Twitter Data for Sentiment. https://www.kaggle.com/muhammedfathi/arabic-twitter-data-for-sentiment. Online; accessed 24 October 2020.

Boting Gao and Doug P VanderLaan. 2020. Cultural influences on perceptions of emotions depicted in emojis. *Cyberpsychology, Behavior, and Social Networking*, 23(8):567–570.

Jing Ge and Ulrike Gretzel. 2018. Emoji rhetoric: a social media influencer perspective. *Journal of Marketing Management*, 34(15-16):1272–1295.

Eric Goldman. 2018. Emojis and the law. *Wash. L. Rev.*, 93:1227.

Irving John Good. 1965. The estimation of probabilities: An essay on modern bayesian methods, vol. 30.

John J Gumperz. 1982. *Discourse strategies*. 1. Cambridge University Press.

Sharath Chandra Guntuku, Mingyang Li, Louis Tay, and Lyle H Ungar. 2019. Studying cultural differences in emoji usage across the east and the west. In *Proceedings of the International AAAI Conference on Web and Social Media*, volume 13, pages 226–235.

Brian D Haig. 2018. An abductive theory of scientific method. In *Method matters in psychology*, pages 35–64. Springer.

Shatha Hakami, Robert Hendley, and Phillip Smith. 2020. Emoji as sentiment indicators: An investigative case study in arabic text. In *The Sixth International Conference on Human and Social Analytics*, pages 26–32. IARIA.

Susan C Herring, S Barab, R Kling, and J Gray. 2004. An approach to researching online behavior. *Designing for virtual communities in the service of learning*, 338:338–376.

Wegdan Hussien, Mahmoud Al-Ayyoub, Yahya Tashtoush, and Mohammed Al-Kabi. 2019. On the use of emojis to train emotion classifiers. *arXiv preprint arXiv:1902.08906*.

Wegdan A Hussien, Yahya M Tashtoush, Mahmoud Al-Ayyoub, and Mohammed N Al-Kabi. 2016. Are emoticons good enough to train emotion classifiers of arabic tweets? In *2016 7th International Conference on Computer Science and Information Technology (CSIT)*, pages 1–6. IEEE.

Nader Al Jallad. 2008. The concepts of al-halal and al-haram in the arab-muslim culture: a translational and lexicographical study. *Language design: journal of theoretical and experimental linguistics*, 10:077–86.

Sara Kiesler, Jane Siegel, and Timothy W McGuire. 1984. Social psychological aspects of computer-mediated communication. *American psychologist*, 39(10):1123.

Mayu Kimura and Marie Katsurai. 2017. Automatic construction of an emoji sentiment lexicon. In *Proceedings of the 2017 ieee/acm international conference on advances in social networks analysis and mining 2017*, pages 1033–1036.

Petra Kralj Novak, Jasmina Smailović, Borut Sluban, and Igor Mozetič. 2015. Sentiment of emojis. *PloS one*, 10(12):e0144296.

Nikola Ljubešić and Darja Fišer. 2016. A global analysis of emoji usage. In *Proceedings of the 10th Web as Corpus Workshop*, pages 82–89.

Mary L McHugh. 2012. Interrater reliability: the kappa statistic. *Biochemia medica: Biochemia medica*, 22(3):276–282.

Hannah Miller, Daniel Kluver, Jacob Thebault-Spieker, Loren Terveen, and Brent Hecht. 2017. Understanding emoji ambiguity in context: The role of text in emoji-related miscommunication. In *Proceedings of the International AAAI Conference on Web and Social Media*, volume 11.

Saif Mohammad, Felipe Bravo-Marquez, Mohammad Salameh, and Svetlana Kiritchenko. 2018. SemEval-2018 task 1: Affect in tweets. In *Proceedings of The 12th International Workshop on Semantic Evaluation*, pages 1–17, New Orleans, Louisiana. Association for Computational Linguistics.

Hala Mulki, Hatem Haddad, Chedi Bechikh Ali, and Halima Alshabani. 2019. L-HSAB: A Levantine Twitter dataset for hate speech and abusive language. In *Proceedings of the Third Workshop on Abusive Language Online*, pages 111–118, Florence, Italy. Association for Computational Linguistics.

Ossama Obeid, Nasser Zalmout, Salam Khalifa, Dima Taji, Mai Oudah, Bashar Alhafni, Go Inoue, Fadhl Eryani, Alexander Erdmann, and Nizar Habash. 2020. Camel tools: An open source python toolkit for arabic natural language processing. In *Proceedings of the 12th language resources and evaluation conference*, pages 7022–7032.

Sara Rosenthal, Noura Farra, and Preslav Nakov. 2017. SemEval-2017 task 4: Sentiment analysis in Twitter. In *Proceedings of the 11th International Workshop on Semantic Evaluation (SemEval-2017)*, pages 502–518, Vancouver, Canada. Association for Computational Linguistics.

Mohammad Salameh, Saif Mohammad, and Svetlana Kiritchenko. 2015. Sentiment after translation: A case-study on Arabic social media posts. In *Proceedings of the 2015 Conference of the North American Chapter of the Association for Computational Linguistics: Human Language Technologies*, pages 767–777, Denver, Colorado. Association for Computational Linguistics.

Karianne Skovholt, Anette Grønning, and Anne Kankaanranta. 2014. The communicative functions of emoticons in workplace e-mails::-. *Journal of Computer-Mediated Communication*, 19(4):780–797.

Peter B Smith, Ronald Fischer, Vivian L Vignoles, and Michael Harris Bond. 2013. *Understanding social psychology across cultures: Engaging with others in a changing world*. Sage.

Carlo Strapparava, Alessandro Valitutti, et al. 2004. Wordnet affect: an affective extension of wordnet. In *Lrec*, volume 4, page 40. Citeseer.

Tuan Tran, Dong Nguyeny, Anh Nguyeny, and Erik Golenz. 2018. Sentiment analysis of emoji-based reactions on marijuana-related topical posts on facebook. In *IEEE International Conference on Communications (ICC)*.

Geert Jan Van Gelder. 2014. *Of Dishes and Discourse: Classical Arabic Literary Representations of Food*. Routledge.

Leticia Vidal, Gastón Ares, and Sara R Jaeger. 2016. Use of emoticon and emoji in tweets for food-related emotional expression. *Food Quality and Preference*, 49:119–128.

Jessica Fitts Willoughby and Shuang Liu. 2018. Do pictures help tell the story? an experimental test of narrative and emojis in a health text message intervention. *Computers in Human Behavior*, 79:75–82.

Peijun Zhao, Jia Jia, Yongsheng An, Jie Liang, Lexing Xie, and Jiebo Luo. 2018. Analyzing and predicting emoji usages in social media. In *Companion Proceedings of the The Web Conference 2018*, pages 327–334.

ArCOV19-*Rumors*: Arabic COVID-19 Twitter Dataset for Misinformation Detection

Fatima Haouari, Maram Hasanain, Reem Suwaileh, Tamer Elsayed
Computer Science and Engineering Department, Qatar University
{200159617, maram.hasanain, rs081123, telsayed}@qu.edu.qa

Abstract

In this paper we introduce ArCOV19-*Rumors*, an Arabic COVID-19 Twitter dataset for misinformation detection composed of tweets containing claims from 27th January till the end of April 2020. We collected 138 verified claims, mostly from popular fact-checking websites, and identified 9.4K relevant tweets to those claims. Tweets were manually-annotated by veracity to support research on misinformation detection, which is one of the major problems faced during a pandemic. ArCOV19-*Rumors* supports two levels of misinformation detection over Twitter: verifying free-text claims (called *claim-level verification*) and verifying claims expressed in tweets (called *tweet-level verification*). Our dataset covers, in addition to health, claims related to other topical categories that were influenced by COVID-19, namely, social, politics, sports, entertainment, and religious. Moreover, we present benchmarking results for tweet-level verification on the dataset. We experimented with SOTA models of versatile approaches that either exploit content, user profiles features, temporal features and propagation structure of the conversational threads for tweet verification.

1 Introduction

In addition to being a medium for the spread and consumption of news, Twitter has been shown to capture the dynamics of real-world events including the spread of diseases such as the seasonal influenza (Kagashe et al., 2017) or more severe epidemics like Ebola (Roy et al., 2020). Since the first reported case of the Novel Coronavirus (COVID-19) in China, in November 2019, the COVID-19 topic has drawn the interest of many Arab users over Twitter. Their interest, reflected in the Arabic content on the platform, has reached a peak after two months when the first case was reported in the United Arab Emirates late in January 2020. This ongoing pandemic has, unsurprisingly, spiked discussions on Twitter covering a wide range of topics such as general information about the disease, preventive measures, procedures and newly-enforced decisions by governments, up-to-date statistics of the spread in the world, and even the change in our daily habits and work styles. With the great importance and spread of COVID-19 information, misinformation and fake news have infected the Twitter stream. An early study quantifying COVID-19 medical misinformation on Twitter found that 25% of collected tweets contained misinformation (Kouzy et al., 2020). During COVID-19 pandemic, we observed that misinformation stretched beyond spreading fake and potentially-harmful medical information, to information that can have adverse negative political effects (example: *"In light of the unresponsiveness of Yemeni government to requests of evacuation from Yemeni students in Wuhan, Sultan of Oman orders their evacuation."*) and economical effects too (example: *"Kuwaitis boycott AlMarai Saudi dairy company after reports on Coronavirus infected employees."*). Combating the spread of such claims and verifying them becomes essential during this sensitive time.

In this work, we aim to facilitate research on misinformation detection on social media during this complex and historical period of our time by introducing a manually-annotated Arabic dataset, **ArCOV19-*Rumors***, that covers tweets spreading COVID-19 related claims. To construct ArCOV19-*Rumors*, we start from an existing COVID-19 Arabic dataset (Haouari et al., 2021), ArCOV-19, that is the first Arabic COVID-19 Twitter dataset with propagation networks. Our proposed ArCOV19-*Rumors* includes a set of 138 COVID-19 verified claims and 9.4K corresponding relevant tweets that were *manually-annotated* to support both *claim-level* and *tweet-level* verification tasks. Claim-level verification is defined as follows: *given a short*

Proceedings of the Sixth Arabic Natural Language Processing Workshop, pages 72–81
Kyiv, Ukraine (Virtual), April 19, 2021.

Dataset	# Tweets	# Annotated	Labels	Multi-task	Conversations	Manual Annot.
Elhadad et al. (2020a)	220K	220K	misleading, real	-	-	-
Alsudias and Rayson (2020)	1M	2K	false, true, unrelated	-	-	✓
Mubarak and Hassan (2020)	30M	8K	rumor, info, advice, ...	-	-	✓
Alqurashi et al. (2021)	4.5M	8.8K	misinformation, other	-	-	✓
ArCOV19-*Rumors*	1M	9.4K	false, true, other	✓	✓	✓

Table 1: Comparison between ArCOV19-*Rumors* and existing Arabic COVID-19 datasets for verification over tweets.

free-text claim (in 1 or 2 sentences) and its corresponding relevant tweets, predict whether the claim is true or false. Tweet-level verification is defined as follows: *given a tweet containing a claim, detect whether it is true or false.*

To our knowledge, ArCOV19-*Rumors* is the only Arabic dataset made available to support both claim-level and tweet-level verification tasks in Twitter given the propagation networks of the tweets in general and on COVID-19 in particular. Some related Twitter datasets were recently released by Alqurashi et al. (2021), Mubarak and Hassan (2020), Alsudias and Rayson (2020), and Elhadad et al. (2020a). None of these datasets has the propagation networks of the tweets, and they either support the tweet verification task (Elhadad et al., 2020a; Alsudias and Rayson, 2020), misinformation detection (Alqurashi et al., 2021) or multi-class categorization including rumors as one category (Mubarak and Hassan, 2020). Differently from ArCOV19-*Rumors*, Elhadad et al. (2020a) used an automatic approach to annotate tweets, while Alsudias and Rayson (2020) only cover COVID-19 health-oriented claims. Starting from some health misinformation reported by the Ministry of Health in Saudi Arabia and the World Health Organization (WHO), Alqurashi et al. (2021) annotated COVID-19 tweets as misinformation or not. Differently, our dataset covers in addition to health, other types of claims that were influenced by COVID-19, namely, social, politics, sports, entertainment, and religious. Table 1 demonstrates the differences between ArCOV19-*Rumors* and the aforementioned datasets.

The contribution of this paper is three-fold:

- We construct and release[1] the first Arabic dataset for misinformation detection over Twitter, covering both claim and tweet verification tasks. It contains 138 COVID-19 verified claims that scale to 9.4K labeled relevant tweets along with their propagation networks.
- We suggest and motivate several research tasks that can be addressed using our *labeled* dataset for misinformation detection.
- We present benchmark results on tweet-level verification using SOTA models that either exploit content, user profiles, or the temporal features and the propagation structure of the conversational threads. Results offer baselines for future research on the problem.

[1] `https://gitlab.com/bigirqu/ArCOV-19/-/tree/master/ArCOV19-Rumors`

The remainder of the paper is organized as follows. We present studies related to COVID-19 misinformation analysis and datasets in Section 2. The construction of ArCOV19-*Rumors* is presented in Section 3. Several use cases supported by our dataset are discussed in Section 4. Our benchmarks and their performances are presented in Section 5. We detail the released components of the dataset in Section 6, and conclude in Section 7.

2 Related Work

The negative effects and spread of misinformation about COVID-19, triggered efforts to understand this phenomenon. Many studies analyzed misinformation spreading on Twitter related to COVID-19 (Shahi et al., 2020; Cinelli et al., 2020; Gallotti et al., 2020; Kouzy et al., 2020; Singh et al., 2020). Singh et al. (2020) analyzed the spread of five health misinformation over time. Shahi et al. (2020) analyzed false and partially false tweets that have been previously fact-checked by a fact-checking platform. Kouzy et al. (2020) focused only on health misinformation and analyzed tweets negating health information by trusted sources (e.g., WHO). Cui and Lee (2020) and Hossain et al. (2020) published an English dataset for claim verification, and tweet verification respectively, while Dharawat et al. (2020) released a Twitter dataset for health risk assessment of COVID-19-related English tweets.

In this work, we extend an existing raw *Arabic* COVID-19 Twitter dataset, ArCOV-19 (Haouari et al., 2021), to include manually-annotated tweets to support both claim and tweet verification. To our knowledge, there is no work that released a large manually-annotated Arabic dataset for misinformation detection on COVID-19 at both claim and tweet levels. The closest work to ours is that done by Elhadad et al. (2020a) and Alsudias and Rayson (2020). However, neither have the propagation networks of the annotated tweets, and they both solely support the tweet verification task. Moreover, ArCOV19-*Rumors* has the largest number of *manually* annotated tweets.

Claim verification is a widely studied problem in general. Several non-COVID-19 datasets exist for claim verification (e.g., (Gorrell et al., 2019)), however, they either support English language (Zubiaga et al., 2016; Derczynski et al., 2017; Gorrell et al., 2019; Ma et al., 2017) or Chinese language (Ma et al., 2017). Among these studies, some only focused on tweet-level verification (Ma et al., 2017; Liu and Wu, 2018; Bian et al., 2020; Khoo et al., 2020) while others addressed claim-level verification (Vosoughi et al., 2017; Dang et al., 2019).

There are few initiatives targeting Arabic online content, but they support rumors detection (i.e., rumor or non-rumor) (Alzanin and Azmi, 2019; Alkhair et al., 2019), tweet verification without propagation networks (Elhadad et al., 2020a; Alsudias and Rayson, 2020), misinformation detection (Alqurashi et al., 2021), or tweet credibility (El Ballouli et al., 2017). Another notable work is a shared task by CLEF CheckThat! Lab for claim verification (Elsayed et al., 2019; Barrón-Cedeño et al., 2020; Barrón-Cedeno et al., 2020). To the best of our knowledge, this is the first Arabic dataset that supports both claim and tweet verification on social media using the propagation networks.

3 Methodology

We extended ArCOV-19, an Arabic Twitter dataset about COVID-19 (Haouari et al., 2021), by annotating a subset of the tweets to support research on misinformation detection, which is one of the major problems faced during a pandemic. We aim to support two classes of the misinformation detection problem (with variants) over Twitter: verifying free-text claims (called *claim-level verification*) and verifying claims expressed in tweets (called *tweet-level verification*), covering two common use cases. To that end, we need to collect COVID-19 *verified* claims, then, for each claim, we need to find, in ArCOV-19, corresponding *relevant* tweets, and finally, among the relevant tweets, identify those that are either expressing the claim or negating it (to easily *propagate* the veracity of the claims to the tweets). This section details how that pipeline was implemented (Sections 3.1-3.6).

3.1 Collecting COVID-19 Verified Claims

We manually collected a set of verified COVID-related claims from two popular Arabic fact-checking platforms: Fatabyyano[2] and Misbar.[3] We identified 113 false claims and 18 true claims during the period of ArCOV19-*Rumors*. To improve balance between false and true claims, we collect an additional 31 true claims from these sources:

1. **Authoritative Health Organizations**: We retrieved, from ArCOV-19, all tweets from Twitter accounts of the World Health Organization (WHO), ministries of public health in Arab countries, UNESCO, and UNICEF. Then, we manually extracted a set of true claims from the retrieved tweets.

2. **English Fact-checking Platforms**: We collected (and translated to Arabic) a few true claims from English Fact-checking platforms: PolitiFact,[4] Snopes,[5] and FullFact.[6]

That yielded a total of 162 claims, 113 false and 49 true, that are potentially suitable for our purpose.

3.2 Finding Relevant Tweets

For each claim, we manually constructed and refined a set of search queries in order to retrieve potentially-relevant tweets from ArCOV-19 using Boolean search. To help identify the queries and maximize our coverage, we considered keywords that appeared in the social media posts, expressing the claim, provided as examples by the fact-checking platforms, and we also interactively search in Twitter to find the best possible keywords that can retrieve relevant tweets to the claim. We then used the queries to search ArCOV-19. An example is the true claim "Trump suggests injecting disinfectants as a treatment for COVID-19".[7]

[2]https://fatabyyano.net
[3]https://misbar.com/
[4]https://www.politifact.com/
[5]https://www.snopes.com/
[6]https://fullfact.org/
[7]https://tinyurl.com/y4btakuw

We noticed that the claim and also the tweet given as an example by Misbar fact-checking platform are using two different Arabic words that reflect "disinfectants", namely *mutaharat* (*disinfectants* in English) and *mueaqamat* (*sterilizers* in English), so we used both in combination with either *Trump* or *US president* as search queries.

For each claim, we manually filtered the retrieved tweets to discard the non-relevant ones. This is conducted by one author of this paper. Examples of tweets that were considered relevant are tweets expressing or negating the claim, tweets having multiple claims including the target claim, tweets expressing advice, questions, or personal opinions about the claim, or even sarcastic tweets about it. Overall, more than half of the retrieved tweets were non-relevant, yielding 14,472 tweets relevant to the collected claims.

3.3 Filtering Claims

After identifying the relevant tweets, we excluded some claims for different reasons. We excluded claims with less than two relevant tweets due to extremely-insufficient content. We also excluded the ones (especially health-related claims) for which the veracity changed within the period of the dataset (e.g., "*Pets do not catch COVID-19*"), or those for which there are still no clear evidence with or against the claim (e.g., "*Bats are the source of COVID-19*"). Moreover, we discarded the claims that are not very specific, i.e., too general (e.g., "*Many Arab countries took security measures against those who refuse to quarantine*"). We eventually kept 95 false and 43 true claims, a total of 138 claims. Those claims have a total of 9,414 relevant tweets. The final set of claims is diverse and claims fall under different categories, as the misinformation propagating in Twitter during COVID-19 pandemic was not restricted to health. In fact, only 45 of them were health-related. The rest are distributed over social (38), political (22), religious (18), entertainment (9), and sports (6) topical categories.

3.4 Annotating Relevant Tweets

After collecting relevant tweets for each claim, it was time to identify tweets expressing or negating the claim, so that we can *propagate* the label of the claim to them. For each claim, one of the authors of this paper labelled all of its relevant tweets by stance using the following three categories:[8]

- "Expressing same claim" if the main (focused) claim in the tweet is restating, expressing, or rephrasing the target claim. This tweet then receives the *same* veracity of the target claim; thus inheriting its label (whether *true* or *false*).
- "Negating the claim" if the main (focused) claim in the tweet is negating or denying the target claim. The veracity of this tweet is then the *opposite* of the veracity of the target claim, i.e., it is labeled as *true* if the target claim is *false*, and vice-versa.
- "Other" if the tweet cannot be labelled as one of the two earlier cases, e.g., expressing opinion or giving advice regarding the claim.

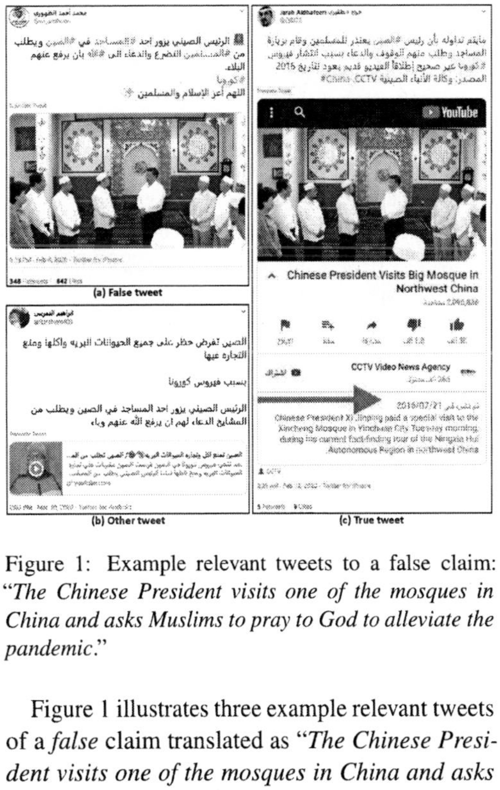

Figure 1: Example relevant tweets to a false claim: "*The Chinese President visits one of the mosques in China and asks Muslims to pray to God to alleviate the pandemic.*"

Figure 1 illustrates three example relevant tweets of a *false* claim translated as "*The Chinese President visits one of the mosques in China and asks Muslims to pray to God to alleviate the pandemic*", which is literally stated in the tweet shown in Figure 1(a), thus it is *false*. On the contrary, the tweet illustrated in Figure 1(c) is denying the claim, and thus is *true*. It is translated as "*What is being circulated about the Chinese President, apologizing to*

[8] Full annotation guidelines: https://gitlab.com/bigirqu/ArCOV-19/-/blob/master/ArCOV19-Rumors/annotations_guidelines.md

Muslims and visits the mosques and asking them to pray because of the spread of the #Corona virus, is totally incorrect. The video is old and dated back to 2016. Source: the Chinese news agency CCTV". Finally, the tweet illustrated in Figure 1(b) is labelled as "*other*" due to expressing multiple claims. It is translated as "*China bans eating all wild animals and their trade due to Corona Virus. The Chinese President visits a mosque in China and asks the scholars to pray to alleviate the pandemic*".

It is worth mentioning that expressing or negating the claim can be over an external link in the tweet, stated in an image, or said in a video, rather than in the text of the tweet. This was considered while annotating tweets. Providing such tweets in ArCOV19-*Rumors* allows the development of multi-modal systems, that can use signals in text, images, or videos, to make verification decisions.

3.5 Data Quality

As mentioned earlier, our dataset was annotated by a single annotator to reduce annotation time and because the annotator was well-experienced with the task. To measure annotation quality, we randomly selected 10% of the relevant tweets, and asked a second annotator to label them. We found that the agreement ratio between annotators is 0.87 and 0.80 for relevance and stance respectively. Due to subjectivity of the stance labelling task specifically (and since the annotator was also asked to consider images, videos, links, etc. in annotation which might lead to further subjectivity), we believe the agreement level is acceptable.

3.6 Collecting Propagation Networks

We also collected the propagation networks (i.e., retweets and conversational threads) for each relevant tweet. The propagation networks for tweets that contain misinformation are essential to study its spreading behaviour and can constitute evidential signals for verification. Figure 2 shows some replies to the false tweet presented in Figure 1(a). We notice that some replies have a clear stance against the claim. Moreover, one reply presents evidence that the claim in the original tweet is false. In addition to the replies, exploiting profiles of propagators can play a significant role in verifying the tweet (Liu and Wu, 2018).

Figure 2: Evidence from replies (with translation) against the false tweet in Fig. 1(a).

Table 2: Statistics of Claims in ArCOV19-*Rumors* (RPs=Replies, RTs=Retweets).

	Claims Subset		Tweet Vf. Subset	
Total tweets	9,414		3,584	
False Tweets	1,753	(18.6%)	1,753	(48.9%)
True Tweets	1,831	(19.4%)	1,831	(51.1%)
Other Tweets	5,830	(61.9%)	0	
Average tweets / claim	68		26	
Tweets with RPs	3,161	(33.6%)	1,222	(34.1%)
Tweets with RTs	3,810	(40.5%)	1,629	(45.5%)
Tweets with RPs & RTs	2,006	(21.3%)	772	(21.5%)
Average RPs / tweet	33		31	
Average RTs per / tweet	16		19	

4 Immediate Use Cases

Table 2 presents a statistical summary of the labeled tweets in ArCOV19-*Rumors*. We define two subsets of tweets. The first is denoted as **Claims Subset**, which includes all relevant tweets of the claims (labeled as *true*, *false*, or *other*). This is of high interest since all tweets relevant to a specific claim can be used in verifying it. The other is denoted as **Tweet Verification Subset**, which only includes the relevant tweets that are either *expressing* or *denying* the original claims, excluding the ones labeled as *other*. This is also of high interest since each of those tweets is subject to verification.

The table indicates that, out of 9.4k labelled relevant tweets, about 3.6k of them are either true or false (constituting the tweet verification subset); each is considered a separate tweet-level verification query. We notice that the distribution of *true* vs. *false* tweets is balanced, making it a good resource for training verification systems. We also notice that a good portion of both subsets have retweets and replies, indicating potentially-useful propagation networks. Accordingly and based on the two subsets, our labeled data can support three different misinformation detection tasks.

4.1 Claim-level Verification

This task is defined as follows: *given a claim and all corresponding relevant tweets (with their propagation networks), detect the veracity of the claim, i.e., whether the claim is true or false.* There are some initiatives to support Arabic claim verification. However, in one of the most prominent ones (CheckThat! lab at CLEF-2019), a pre-defined set of Web page was used in verification (Elsayed et al., 2019) while in ArCOV19-*Rumors* we focus on Twitter.

4.2 Tweet-level Verification

This task is defined as follows: *given a tweet (with its propagation networks), detect its veracity, i.e., whether the tweet is true or false.* Addressing this task in Arabic has never been studied. Existing studies for Arabic tweet verification mainly rely on the source tweet content only (Elhadad et al., 2020b; Alsudias and Rayson, 2020), or, additionally, the potentially-relevant Web pages (Barrón-Cedeño et al., 2020; Barrón-Cedeno et al., 2020).

ArCOV19-*Rumors* supports another variant of this task. This variant makes also available (to the verification system) the tweets that are relevant to its target claim but were posted *earlier* (with their propagation networks) allowing for early claim verification. To our knowledge, there is no study that addressed this problem. This is an interesting problem for several reasons. First, with the lack of any propagation networks for a target tweet, a verification system can still exploit networks of earlier relevant tweets to verify the tweet. Second, as time is critical to debunk fake claims, exploiting relevant tweets posted earlier allows verifying the tweet as soon as it is posted, without waiting for its propagation networks. Third, even if the target tweet has propagation networks, relevant tweets might provide more evidence, hence improving verification accuracy.

4.3 Claim Retrieval

This task is defined as follows: *given a tweet that expresses a claim (i.e., a tweet in the tweet verification subset), find all tweets that are expressing the same claim.* To our knowledge, this task is under-studied; an exception is the work done by Shaar et al. (2020) and the task proposed by Barrón-Cedeño et al. (2020) in CLEF CheckThat! 2020 lab; [9] however, they focus more on claims than tweets and they release English-only datasets to support this task. Solving this problem helps in applications like finding previously-verified tweets, or clustering tweets expressing the same claim, to avoid re-verification.

5 Experiments and Evaluation

In this section, we present *benchmarking results* using SOTA models on the *tweet-level* verification task to facilitate future research. We experimented with variant models that either exploit content only, user profile features, temporal features, or propagation structure of the conversational threads for tweet verification. We present our preprocessing approach in Section 5.1, the SOTA models used for benchmarking in Section 5.2, and finally a discussion of the results in Section 5.3.

5.1 Preprocessing

In all experiments, we used our **tweets with RPs** subset, since some of the SOTA methods we experiment with depend on replies of tweets to be verified (*target tweets* hereafter). In ArCOV19-*Rumors*, some of the target tweets were replies to previous tweets. In our experiments, we considered the direct and indirect replies that were posted *only after* the target tweet. We also eliminated target tweets that have no textual replies, i.e., containing only emojis, non Arabic content, images, or videos. We ended up with 1,108 tweets, 597 True and 511 False, with 16 replies on average. We split our data by target tweets over 5 folds, ensuring there is no overlap of claims across folds (i.e., no overlap between tweets of the same claim).[10]

We processed the tweets and the replies by removing non-Arabic letters, URLs, handles, special characters, and diacritics.

5.2 Verification Models

We experimented with two SOTA models that exploit the propagation networks for tweet verification. Moreover, due to proven effectiveness of BERT-based classifiers in versatile text classification tasks, we elect to develop a simple and effective BERT-based classifier that we fine-tune for the

[9] `https://sites.google.com/view/clef2020-checkthat/`

[10] Folds used in our experiments: `https://gitlab.com/bigirqu/ArCOV-19/-/tree/master/ArCOV19-Rumors/baselines_folds`

task. In this BERT-based classification architecture, we experimented with two Arabic pre-trained BERT models, namely, AraBERT and MARBERT. Further details on the models are presented below.

1. Bi-GCN Bian et al. (2020): a bidirectional Graph Convolutional Networks model that leverages Graph Convolutional Networks to verify tweets given the target tweet and replies content, in addition to the replies tree structure. The model was called bidirectional for its ability to capture the bottom-up and top-down replies tree for each tweet. We used the authors implementation and setup[11] in our experiments. Each tweet/reply was represented using a vector of 5K content features, which are the most frequent 5K words in the dataset excluding stop words.

2. PPC-RNN+CNN Liu and Wu (2018): a multivariate time series model that exploits user profiles to verify tweets. Each time step involves a single user represented by a vector of user features. A user can be the author of the target tweet or a reply to it. The user vectors were sorted by posting time starting from the target tweet to capture the temporal features. In the original paper, the model uses a fixed number of time steps. In our experiments, we find the average number of replies per target tweet is 16, thus, we set the time steps to 17 taking into account the target tweet. We implemented this model using Keras[12] following the same setup presented in the original paper.

3. AraBERT Baly et al. (2020): a pretrained BERT model on a large-scale Arabic corpus of news articles. We fine-tuned the model to classify the tweets as True or False *given the target tweet content only*. We used the fine-tuning implementation with the same hyper-parameters setup shared by the model developers,[13] using AraBERTv1, which is based on pre-segmentation using Farasa segmenter,[14] and we set the max sequence length to 128. The model was fine-tuned with a batch size of 16 for 8 epochs, with a learning rate of 10^{-5}.

[11]https://github.com/TianBian95/BiGCN

[12]https://keras.io/

[13]https://colab.research.google.com/drive/1P9iQHtUH5KUbTVtp8B4-AopZzEEPE01w?usp=sharing

[14]https://farasa.qcri.org/

Table 3: Tweet-level verification results.

Model	Class	Acc	P	R	F1	macro-F1
Majority	-	0.533	0.266	0.500	-	0.343
Bi-GCN	F	0.669	0.731	0.526	0.580	0.649
	T		0.662	0.830	0.718	
RNN+CNN	F	0.682	0.631	0.783	0.688	0.673
	T		0.749	0.600	0.657	
AraBERT	F	0.730	0.733	0.671	0.691	0.713
	T		0.719	0.763	0.735	
MARBERT	F	0.757	0.763	0.692	0.717	0.740
	T		0.743	0.788	0.762	

4. MARBERT Abdul-Mageed et al. (2020): a pretrained BERT model on a large Twitter dataset. We selected this model since in our task, we are solely working with Twitter data and thus, a pretrained model from the same domain might be more suitable. We fine-tuned the model for a classification task given the same input as AraBERT. We used the authors' code[15] and setup to fine-tune the model. The model was fine-tuned with a batch size of 32 for 5 epochs, with a learning rate of $2 * 10^{-6}$. Similar to AraBERT, the max sequence length was set to 128.

5.3 Results and Discussion

Table 3 presents the performance of the four models, in addition to a simple majority baseline. For each model, we report the overall accuracy, and also F1, precision, and recall for each class. Starting from the same set of 5 folds, we trained each model 5 times, each with a random seed, and we report the average over those runs then over folds.[16]

Results show that all models significantly outperform the majority baseline. Moreover, the pre-trained BERT models are superior to the other models, despite the fact that they leverage the reply tree in addition to the target tweet. More specifically, MARBERT exhibits better performance than AraBERT, indicating the effectiveness of matching the pre-training domain with the testing one, and achieving 0.74 macro-averaged F1.

The results also demonstrate that the models are better in detecting True claims than False claims, with an exception of the PPC-RNN+CNN model.

[15]https://colab.research.google.com/drive/1M01s7EPUildwqIDh6HNfJ5y826XvcgGX?usp=sharing

[16]It is worth noting that since we set the hyper-parameters values as reported by original papers, better performance might be achieved if hyper-parameters are tuned on our dataset.

This can be attributed to the fact that the average number of replies for False tweets is 12 vs. 19 for True tweets. We note that, in case the time steps are actually less than 17 (the average indicated earlier), the model *randomly* fills the missing time steps with user features from other repliers to the target tweet. Such limitation in the model might lead to added noise and thus a poor performance with False tweets.

Moreover, the Bi-GCN model is language-dependent, and since we are working with Arabic data, we may need to test preprocessing the data with different techniques, such as considering stemming the content or replacing the top 5000 words features with content embeddings instead.

6 Data Release

In summary, we release the following resources as ArCOV19-*Rumors* dataset, taking into consideration Twitter content redistribution policy:[17]

- **Verified Claims**: 138 verified claims, each labeled as true or false.
- **Claims Subset**: IDs of the tweets relevant to the verified claims, each labeled as true, false, or other.
- **Propagation Networks of the Claims Subsets**: which includes for each tweet in the claim subset:
  - **Retweets**: IDs of the full retweet set.
  - **Conversational Threads**: tweet IDs of the full reply thread (including direct and indirect replies).
- **Annotation guidelines:** guidelines used to annotate the relevant tweets.
- **Baselines folds:** tweet IDs for folds used to train our baselines.

Along with the dataset, we plan to provide some pointers to publicly-available crawlers that users can easily use to crawl the tweets given their IDs.

7 Conclusion

In this paper, we presented ArCOV19-*Rumors*, which is an Arabic Twitter dataset that supports both claim-level and tweet-level verification tasks given the propagation networks. We released 138 verified claims associated with 9.4K relevant tweets. Our dataset covers, in addition to health, other types of claims that were influenced by COVID-19, namely, social, politics, sports, entertainment, and religious. To facilitate future research, we presented benchmarking performance results of some SOTA models on the tweet verification task.

[17]https://developer.twitter.com/en/developer-terms/agreement-and-policy

Acknowledgments

The work of Tamer Elsayed and Maram Hasanain was made possible by NPRP grant# NPRP 11S-1204-170060 from the Qatar National Research Fund (a member of Qatar Foundation). The work of Reem Suwaileh was supported by GSRA grant# GSRA5-1-0527-18082 from the Qatar National Research Fund and the work of Fatima Haouari was supported by GSRA grant# GSRA6-1-0611-19074 from the Qatar National Research Fund. The statements made herein are solely the responsibility of the authors.

References

Muhammad Abdul-Mageed, AbdelRahim Elmadany, and El Moatez Billah Nagoudi. 2020. Arbert & marbert: Deep bidirectional transformers for arabic. *arXiv preprint arXiv:2101.01785.*

Maysoon Alkhair, Karima Meftouh, Kamel Smaïli, and Nouha Othman. 2019. An arabic corpus of fake news: Collection, analysis and classification. In *International Conference on Arabic Language Processing*, pages 292–302. Springer.

Sarah Alqurashi, Btool Hamoui, Abdulaziz Alashaikh, Ahmad Alhindi, and Eisa Alanazi. 2021. Eating garlic prevents covid-19 infection: Detecting misinformation on the arabic content of twitter. *arXiv preprint arXiv:2101.05626.*

Lama Alsudias and Paul Rayson. 2020. COVID-19 and Arabic Twitter: How can Arab world governments and public health organizations learn from social media? In *Proceedings of the 1st Workshop on NLP for COVID-19 at ACL 2020.* Association for Computational Linguistics.

Samah M Alzanin and Aqil M Azmi. 2019. Rumor detection in arabic tweets using semi-supervised and unsupervised expectation–maximization. *Knowledge-Based Systems*, 185:104945.

Fady Baly, Hazem Hajj, et al. 2020. Arabert: Transformer-based model for arabic language understanding. In *Proceedings of the 4th Workshop on Open-Source Arabic Corpora and Processing Tools, with a Shared Task on Offensive Language Detection*, pages 9–15.

Alberto Barrón-Cedeño, Tamer Elsayed, Preslav Nakov, Giovanni Da San Martino, Maram Hasanain,

Reem Suwaileh, and Fatima Haouari. 2020. Checkthat! at clef 2020: Enabling the automatic identification and verification of claims in social media. In *European Conference on Information Retrieval*, pages 499–507. Springer.

Alberto Barrón-Cedeno, Tamer Elsayed, Preslav Nakov, Giovanni Da San Martino, Maram Hasanain, Reem Suwaileh, Fatima Haouari, Nikolay Babulkov, Bayan Hamdan, Alex Nikolov, et al. 2020. Overview of checkthat! 2020: Automatic identification and verification of claims in social media. In *International Conference of the Cross-Language Evaluation Forum for European Languages*, pages 215–236. Springer.

Tian Bian, Xi Xiao, Tingyang Xu, Peilin Zhao, Wenbing Huang, Yu Rong, and Junzhou Huang. 2020. Rumor detection on social media with bi-directional graph convolutional networks. In *Proceedings of the AAAI Conference on Artificial Intelligence*, pages 549–556.

Matteo Cinelli, Walter Quattrociocchi, Alessandro Galeazzi, Carlo Michele Valensise, Emanuele Brugnoli, Ana Lucia Schmidt, Paola Zola, Fabiana Zollo, and Antonio Scala. 2020. The covid-19 social media infodemic. *arXiv preprint arXiv:2003.05004*.

Limeng Cui and Dongwon Lee. 2020. Coaid: Covid-19 healthcare misinformation dataset. *arXiv preprint arXiv:2006.00885*.

Anh Dang, Abidalrahman Moh'd, Aminul Islam, and Evangelos Milios. 2019. Early detection of rumor veracity in social media. In *Proceedings of the 52nd Hawaii International Conference on System Sciences*.

Leon Derczynski, Kalina Bontcheva, Maria Liakata, Rob Procter, Geraldine Wong Sak Hoi, and Arkaitz Zubiaga. 2017. SemEval-2017 task 8: RumourEval: Determining rumour veracity and support for rumours. In *Proceedings of the 11th International Workshop on Semantic Evaluation (SemEval-2017)*. Association for Computational Linguistics.

Arkin Dharawat, Ismini Lourentzou, Alex Morales, and ChengXiang Zhai. 2020. Drink bleach or do what now? covid-hera: A dataset for risk-informed health decision making in the presence of covid19 misinformation. *arXiv preprint arXiv:2010.08743*.

Rim El Ballouli, Wassim El-Hajj, Ahmad Ghandour, Shady Elbassuoni, Hazem Hajj, and Khaled Shaban. 2017. Cat: Credibility analysis of arabic content on twitter. In *Proceedings of the Third Arabic Natural Language Processing Workshop*, pages 62–71.

Mohamed K Elhadad, Kin Fun Li, and Fayez Gebali. 2020a. Covid-19-fakes: a twitter (arabic/english) dataset for detecting misleading information on covid-19. In *International Conference on Intelligent Networking and Collaborative Systems*, pages 256–268. Springer.

Mohamed K Elhadad, Kin Fun Li, and Fayez Gebali. 2020b. An ensemble deep learning technique to detect covid-19 misleading information. In *International Conference on Network-Based Information Systems*, pages 163–175.

Tamer Elsayed, Preslav Nakov, Alberto Barrón-Cedeño, Maram Hasanain, Reem Suwaileh, Giovanni Da San Martino, and Pepa Atanasova. 2019. Overview of the clef-2019 checkthat! lab: Automatic identification and verification of claims. In *International Conference of the Cross-Language Evaluation Forum for European Languages*, pages 301–321. Springer.

Riccardo Gallotti, Francesco Valle, Nicola Castaldo, Pierluigi Sacco, and Manlio De Domenico. 2020. Assessing the risks of" infodemics" in response to covid-19 epidemics. *arXiv preprint arXiv:2004.03997*.

Genevieve Gorrell, Elena Kochkina, Maria Liakata, Ahmet Aker, Arkaitz Zubiaga, Kalina Bontcheva, and Leon Derczynski. 2019. Semeval-2019 task 7: Rumoureval, determining rumour veracity and support for rumours. In *Proceedings of the 13th International Workshop on Semantic Evaluation*, pages 845–854.

Fatima Haouari, Maram Hasanain, Reem Suwaileh, and Tamer Elsayed. 2021. Arcov-19: The first arabic covid-19 twitter dataset with propagation networks. In *Proceedings of the Sixth Arabic Natural Language Processing Workshop*, WANLP 2021.

Tamanna Hossain, Robert L. Logan IV, Arjuna Ugarte, Yoshitomo Matsubara, Sean Young, and Sameer Singh. 2020. COVIDLies: Detecting COVID-19 misinformation on social media. In *Proceedings of the 1st Workshop on NLP for COVID-19 (Part 2) at EMNLP 2020*.

Ireneus Kagashe, Zhijun Yan, and Imran Suheryani. 2017. Enhancing seasonal influenza surveillance: topic analysis of widely used medicinal drugs using twitter data. *Journal of medical Internet research*, 19(9):e315.

Ling Min Serena Khoo, Hai Leong Chieu, Zhong Qian, and Jing Jiang. 2020. Interpretable rumor detection in microblogs by attending to user interactions. *arXiv preprint arXiv:2001.10667*.

Ramez Kouzy, Joseph Abi Jaoude, Afif Kraitem, Molly B El Alam, Basil Karam, Elio Adib, Jabra Zarka, Cindy Traboulsi, Elie W Akl, and Khalil Baddour. 2020. Coronavirus goes viral: quantifying the covid-19 misinformation epidemic on twitter. *Cureus*, 12(3).

Yang Liu and Yi-Fang Brook Wu. 2018. Early detection of fake news on social media through propagation path classification with recurrent and convolutional networks. In *Thirty-Second AAAI Conference on Artificial Intelligence*.

Jing Ma, Wei Gao, and Kam-Fai Wong. 2017. Detect rumors in microblog posts using propagation structure via kernel learning. In *Proceedings of the 55th Annual Meeting of the Association for Computational Linguistics (Volume 1: Long Papers)*, pages 708–717.

Hamdy Mubarak and Sabit Hassan. 2020. Arcorona: Analyzing arabic tweets in the early days of coronavirus (covid-19) pandemic. *arXiv preprint arXiv:2012.01462*.

Melissa Roy, Nicolas Moreau, Cécile Rousseau, Arnaud Mercier, Andrew Wilson, and Laëtitia Atlani-Duault. 2020. Ebola and localized blame on social media: analysis of twitter and facebook conversations during the 2014–2015 ebola epidemic. *Culture, Medicine, and Psychiatry*, 44(1):56–79.

Shaden Shaar, Giovanni Da San Martino, Nikolay Babulkov, and Preslav Nakov. 2020. That is a known lie: Detecting previously fact-checked claims. *arXiv preprint arXiv:2005.06058*.

Gautam Kishore Shahi, Anne Dirkson, and Tim A Majchrzak. 2020. An exploratory study of covid-19 misinformation on twitter. *arXiv preprint arXiv:2005.05710*.

Lisa Singh, Shweta Bansal, Leticia Bode, Ceren Budak, Guangqing Chi, Kornraphop Kawintiranon, Colton Padden, Rebecca Vanarsdall, Emily Vraga, and Yanchen Wang. 2020. A first look at covid-19 information and misinformation sharing on twitter. *arXiv preprint arXiv:2003.13907*.

Soroush Vosoughi, Mostafa 'Neo' Mohsenvand, and Deb Roy. 2017. Rumor gauge: Predicting the veracity of rumors on twitter. *ACM Transactions on Knowledge Discovery from Data (TKDD)*, 11(4):1–36.

Arkaitz Zubiaga, Maria Liakata, Rob Procter, Geraldine Wong Sak Hoi, and Peter Tolmie. 2016. Analysing how people orient to and spread rumours in social media by looking at conversational threads. *PloS one*, 11(3).

ArCOV-19: The First Arabic COVID-19 Twitter Dataset with Propagation Networks

Fatima Haouari, Maram Hasanain, Reem Suwaileh, Tamer Elsayed
Computer Science and Engineering Department, Qatar University
{200159617, maram.hasanain, rs081123, telsayed}@qu.edu.qa

Abstract

In this paper, we present ArCOV-19, an Arabic COVID-19 Twitter dataset that spans one year, covering the period from 27th of January 2020 till 31st of January 2021. ArCOV-19 is the *first* publicly-available Arabic Twitter dataset covering COVID-19 pandemic that includes about 2.7M tweets alongside the *propagation networks* of the most-popular subset of them (i.e., most-retweeted and -liked). The propagation networks include both retweets and conversational threads (i.e., threads of replies). ArCOV-19 is designed to enable research under several domains including natural language processing, information retrieval, and social computing. Preliminary analysis shows that ArCOV-19 captures rising discussions associated with the first reported cases of the disease as they appeared in the Arab world. In addition to the source tweets and propagation networks, we also release the search queries and language-independent crawler used to collect the tweets to encourage the curation of similar datasets.

1 Introduction

Twitter streams hundreds of millions of tweets daily. In addition to being a medium for the spread and consumption of news, it has been shown to capture the dynamics of real-world events including the spread of diseases such as the seasonal influenza (Kagashe et al., 2017) or more severe epidemics like Zika (Vijaykumar et al., 2018), Ebola (Roy et al., 2020), and H1N1 (McNeill et al., 2016). Moreover, collective conversations on Twitter about an event can have a great influence on the event's outcomes, e.g., US 2016 presidential elections (Grover et al., 2019). Analyzing tweets about an event, as it evolves, offers a great opportunity to understanding its structure and characteristics, informing decisions based on its development, and anticipating its outcomes as represented in Twitter and, more importantly, in the real world.

Since the first reported case of Novel Coronavirus (COVID-19) in China, in November 2019, the COVID-19 topic has drawn the interest of many Arab users over Twitter. Their interest, reflected in the Arabic content on the platform, has reached a peak after two months when the first case was reported in the United Arab Emirates late in January 2020. This ongoing pandemic has, unsurprisingly, spiked discussions on Twitter covering a wide range of topics such as general information about the disease, preventive measures, procedures and newly-enforced decisions by governments, up-to-date statistics of the spread in the world, and even the change in our daily habits and work styles.

In this work, we aim to support future research on social media during this historical period of our time by curating an Arabic dataset (ArCOV-19) that exclusively covers tweets about COVID-19. We limit the dataset to Arabic since it is among the most dominant languages in Twitter (Alshaabi et al., 2020a), yet under-studied in general.

ArCOV-19 is the *first* Arabic Twitter dataset designed to capture tweets discussing COVID-19 starting from January 27th 2020 till end of January 2021[1], constituting about 2.7M tweets, alongside the propagation networks of the most-popular subset of them. To our knowledge, there is no publicly-available Arabic Twitter dataset for COVID-19 that includes the propagation networks of a good subset of its tweets. Some existing efforts have already started to curate COVID-19 datasets including Arabic tweets, but Arabic is severely under-represented (e.g., (Chen et al., 2020a; Singh et al., 2020)) or represented by a random sample that is not specifically focused on COVID-19 (e.g., (Alshaabi et al., 2020b)), or the dataset is limited in the period it covers and does not include the propagation networks (e.g., (Alqurashi et al., 2020)).

[1] The dataset will be continuously augmented with new tweets over the coming months.

Proceedings of the Sixth Arabic Natural Language Processing Workshop, pages 82–91
Kyiv, Ukraine (Virtual), April 19, 2021.

The contribution of this paper is three-fold:

- We release ArCOV-19,[2] the first Arabic Twitter dataset about COVID-19 that comprises about 2.7M tweets collected via Twitter search API. It covers a full year allowing for capturing discussions on the topic since it started to be popular in the Arab world. In addition to the tweets, ArCOV-19 includes propagation networks of the most popular subset, search queries, and documented implementation of our language-independent tweets crawler.
- We present a preliminary analysis on ArCOV-19, which reveals insights from the dataset concerning temporal, geographical, and topical aspects.
- We suggest several use cases to enable research on Arabic tweets in different research areas including, but not limited to, emergency management, misinformation detection, and social analytics.

The reminder of the paper is organized as follows. We present the crawling process followed to acquire ArCOV-19 in Section 3. We then thoroughly discuss the analysis that we conducted on the dataset in Section 4. We suggest some use cases to enable research on Arabic tweets in Section 5. We finally conclude in Section 6.

2 Related Work

Social media platforms and Twitter specifically showed to be an indispensable medium for sharing information and discussions about the COVID-19 pandemic since December 2019. A considerable body of raw social media datasets were released to facilitate analyzing these discussions including Twitter datasets (Banda et al., 2020; Lopez et al., 2020; Chen et al., 2020b; Qazi et al., 2020; Gao et al., 2020; Alqurashi et al., 2020; Dashtian and Murthy, 2021), Instagram (Zarei et al., 2020), or the Chinese social media platform Weibo (Hu et al., 2020; Gao et al., 2020).

Banda et al. (2020) released a multilingual dataset that includes over 800M tweets, the data is collected since 1st of January 2020 using Twitter streaming API. Dashtian and Murthy (2021), collected multilingual tweets posted between March and July 2020. The most dominant languages covered by their dataset are English and Spanish constituting 65% and 12% of the tweets respectively. Chen et al. (2020b) are continously collecting tweets since 21st of January 2020, where at the time of writing, around 66% and 11% of the tweets are in English and Spanish respectively. Another multilingual ongoing collection is released by Lopez et al. (2020). Qazi et al. (2020) enriched their large-scale multilingual Twitter dataset with geolocation information.

The only raw Arabic Twitter dataset available is the one released by Alqurashi et al. (2020), however it covers the period from 1st of January to 15th April 2020 only. Moreover, it does not include the propagation networks of tweets.

Compared to existing datasets, we release an only-Arabic collection of tweets, where we exclude retweets to avoid having copies of the same tweet. Moreover, we also release the most-popular subset of them (i.e., most-retweeted and -liked and spam free tweets). Furthermore, we collect the propagation networks including both retweets and conversational threads (i.e., threads of replies) for the most-popular subset.

3 Data Collection

ArCOV-19 includes two major components: the **source tweets** (i.e., tweets collected via Twitter search API every day) and the **propagation networks** (i.e., retweets and conversational threads of a subset of the source tweets). In this section, we present how we collected each in Sections 3.1, and 3.2 respectively, and summarize the released data in Section 3.3.

3.1 Tweets Collection

To collect the source tweets, we used our tweet crawler[3] that uses Twitter *search* API[4]. The crawler takes a set of manually-crafted queries, comprising a target topic, as input. At the end of each day, the crawler issues a search request for each of those queries. Queries can be keywords (e.g., "Corona"), phrases (e.g., "the killing virus"), or hashtags (e.g., "#the_new_coronavirus"). Twitter returns a maximum of 3,200 tweets per query. We customized the search requests to return only *Arabic* tweets,[5] and to exclude all retweets to avoid having copies

[2] `https://gitlab.com/bigirqu/ArCOV-19/`

[3] `https://gitlab.com/bigirqu/ArCOV-19/-/tree/master/code/crawler`

[4] `https://developer.twitter.com/en/docs/tweets/search/api-reference/get-search-tweets`

[5] Language of tweets to return is a configurable parameter.

of the same tweet. Additionally, duplicate tweets (returned by different queries) are removed in each day. Finally, tweets are sorted chronologically.

We started collecting our data since 27th of January 2020 using a set of queries that we manually-updated based on our daily tracking of trending keywords and hashtags. For example, starting from 16th of December 2020, we extended our queries to cover tweets related to COVID-19 vaccines as that sub-topic was gaining interest on Arabic social media. The full list of queries used in each day is released alongside our dataset. We denote all collected tweets as ***source tweets***.

Due to technical reasons, we missed collecting tweets for a few days. Since Twitter search API limits the search results to the past 7 days, we missed the old tweets. To overcome that, we used GetOldTweets3[6] python library to download the search results using the same trending keywords and hashtags we selected around those days.

3.2 Propagation Networks Collection

In addition to the source tweets, we also collected the ***propagation networks*** (i.e., retweets and conversational threads) of the top 1000 most popular (i.e., top-retweeted & -liked) tweets each day. To our knowledge, this is the *first* Arabic tweet dataset to include such propagation networks.

Before getting the most popular tweets on any day, we started from source tweets collected in that day and applied a qualification pipeline. We first excluded tweets containing any inappropriate word (using a list of inappropriate words we constructed). Next, tweets with more than two URLs or four hashtags, or shorter than four tokens (all are potentially spam) were dropped. Additionally, duplicate tweets that have exact textual content are also dropped to avoid redundancy; only the most popular of them (according to our scoring criterion below) is kept. Qualified tweets are then scored by popularity defined by the sum of the tweet's retweet and favorite counts. We finally sort the qualified tweets by their scores and select the most popular 1,000 tweets. We denote the set of all such tweets over all days as the **top subset**.

For those 1K top tweets per day, we then collected all retweets and conversational threads (i.e., direct and indirect replies).[7] We collected the retweets using Pickaw,[8] a platform for organizing contests on social media, and the replies using PHEME (Zubiaga et al., 2016) Twitter conversation collection script.[9]

3.3 Data Release

In summary, we release the following resources as ArCOV-19 dataset, taking into consideration Twitter content redistribution policy:[10]

- **Source Tweets**: IDs of the tweets crawled in each day.
- **Search Queries**: the list of search queries, including keywords, phrases, and hashtags, used in each period to collect our source tweets.
- **Top Subset**: IDs of the top 1,000 most popular tweets for each day.
- **Propagation Networks**: the propagation networks for the top subset which include for each tweet in the top subset:
  - **Retweets**: IDs of the full retweet set.
  - **Conversational Threads**: tweet IDs of the full reply thread (including direct and indirect replies).

Along with the dataset, we provide some pointers to publicly-available crawlers that users can easily use to crawl the tweets given their IDs.

4 ArCOV-19 in Numbers

In this section, we present a statistical summary and conduct an analysis on ArCOV-19 to shed some light on its major characteristics.

4.1 Tweets and Users Distribution

Table 1 presents an overall summary of the tweets and users statistics in ArCOV-19. It indicates that the total number of source tweets in the dataset is about 2.7M posted by over 690k unique users. We note that 18.66% of the tweets were posted by verified users (who constitute only 0.81% of the unique users). This is a relatively large percentage, showing that a good portion of the source tweets are popular. The average numbers of followers, friends, and statuses of users are also relatively large, showing that users observed in ArCOV-19 are also popular (and possibly more influential).

[6] https://github.com/Mottl/GetOldTweets3

[7] At the time of writing, we have collected the replies for tweets until end of April 2020 and we are still collecting the rest; we will make all available in the near future.

[8] https://pickaw.com/en/twrench-becomes-pickaw

[9] https://github.com/azubiaga/pheme-twitter-conversation-collection

[10] https://developer.twitter.com/en/developer-terms/agreement-and-policy

The table also indicates that 25.40% of the tweets include URLs. We anticipate that this is due to the extensive spreading of news (linked from tweets) during this period. The numbers of tweets that are geotagged and geolocated are also indicated in the table; however, we defer the discussion of such types of tweets to Section 4.3.

Figure 1 illustrates the monthly distribution of tweets in ArCOV-19. The volume of tweets drastically increased in March when the virus started to spread in several Arab countries. Then, tweets number started to decrease monthly. We speculate this is due to the fact that the topic was not heavily discussed as in the first days. In December, we expanded our queries list to include hashtags and keyword related to more current sub-topics such as vaccines and the new variant of the virus, which resulted in an increase in the volume of tweets.

Figure 2 presents the top 25 tweeting users in ArCOV-19. We notice that several of them are news sources, and 20 are verified Twitter accounts.

Tweets Statistics		
Source Tweets	2,675,049	
Geotagged	2,078	(0.08%)
Geolocated	60,873	(2.28%)
Posted by verified users	499,351	(18.66%)
Include URL	679,482	(25.40%)
Include Media	973,952	(36.41%)
Top Subset	370,132	(13.84%)
Retweets of Top Subset	7,925,821	
Replies of Top Subset	1,476,950	
Users Statistics		
Unique	690,339	
Verified	5,575	(0.81%)
Average followers count	4,630	
Average friends count	918	
Average statuses count	9,054	

Table 1: Tweets and users statistics of ArCOV-19. Stats for replies are for tweets until end of April 2020.

4.2 Tweets Content & Topics

It is important to demonstrate that the tweets in ArCOV-19 constitute a good representative sample of the Arabic tweets posted during the target period on COVID-19, and that they cover the prevalent topics discussed over Twitter during that period. To help examine this hypothesis, we analyzed the textual content of the tweets; in particular, we identified the most-frequent words, hashtags, and Arab

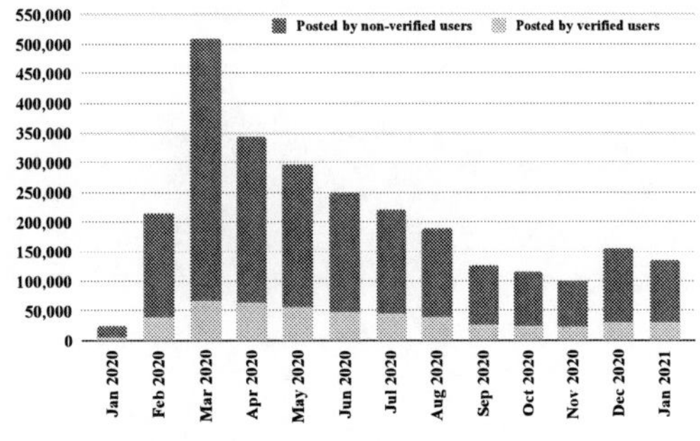

Figure 1: Monthly distribution of source tweets of ArCOV-19.

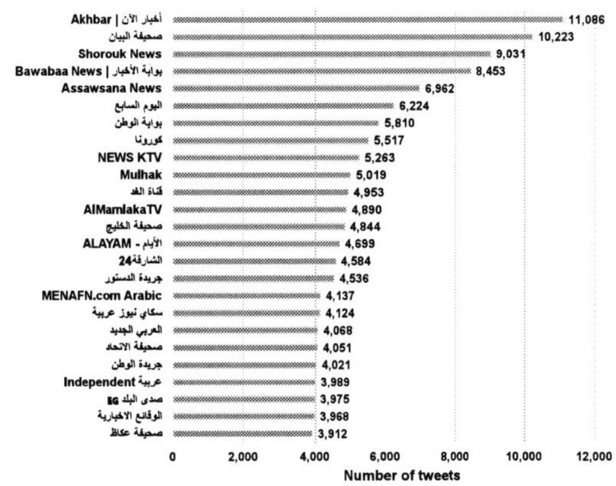

Figure 2: Number of tweets posted by the top 25 tweeters in ArCOV-19 for the period of 27th Jan 2020 to 31st Jan 2021.

country names for the tweets posted in the period of 27th Jan to 31st Mar 2020. We focus on this critical period since the virus started to spread in the Arab world during that time. We then tracked their frequency over time. Figure 3 shows the time series (over days) of the three types of keywords.[11]

The 10 most-frequent words shown in Figure 3(a) indicate two different types of words: those that are directly related to COVID-19 (e.g., "health") and those that are not but related to prayers and supplications (e.g., "Allah/God")). It is interesting to see the word "Allah" is very frequent early on when the news about the virus started to spread (probably over discussions around whether the pandemic is a punishment from God or not, we believe), then declines over time only to become frequent again when the virus started to widely spread in the Arab world.

[11]When identifying the most frequent words and hashtags, we excluded the ones we used in our search queries since they are expected to be very frequent by definition.

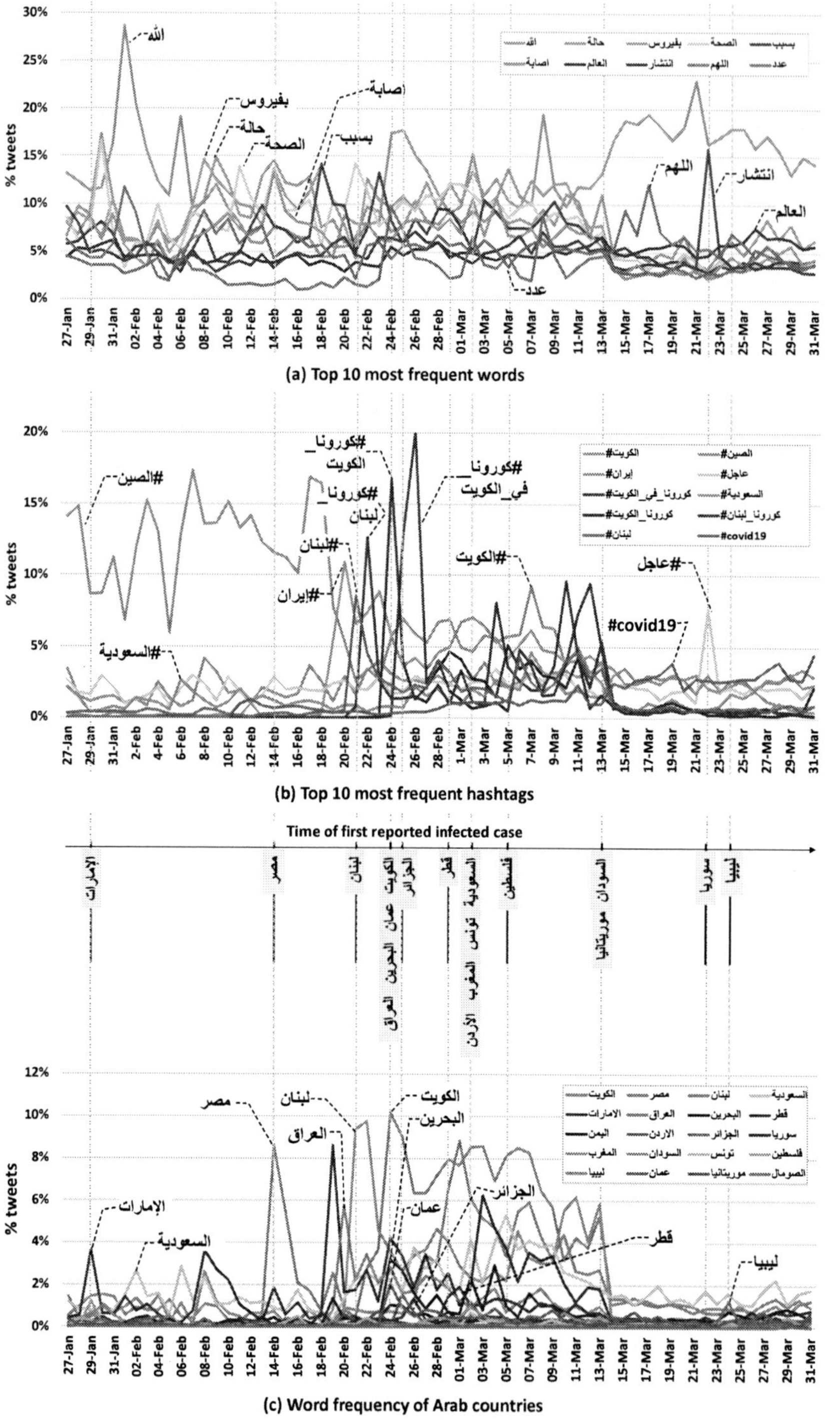

Figure 3: Time series of the frequency (in percentage of tweets) of top general keywords, hashtags, and Arab country words for the period of 27th Jan to 31st Mar. The time of first reported cases in Arab countries is also indicated and aligned with the time series.

Figure 3(b) demonstrates how "#China" hashtag was the most trending one from 27 of January until 20 of February, as COVID-19 was prevalent only in China and still not widely spread (at that time) in other countries. We can see how it started to be less trending as the number of cases started to decline in China by that date.[12] On the other hand, when COVID-19 started to spread in the Arab world, other hashtags started to become viral. Furthermore, Figure 3(b) shows that frequency spikes of "#Iran", "#Lebanon", and "#Kuwait" exactly match the confirmation dates of first reported cases in Iran,[13] Lebanon,[14] and Kuwait,[15] respectively.

To further analyze trending topics, Figure 3 features the timeline of the first reported cases in the Arab countries and aligns them with the time series throughout the figure. Aligning the timeline with the series in Figure 3(c) reveals a significant match between the frequency peaks of several country names and the corresponding dates of first reported cases in those countries, most notably in UAE, Egypt, Lebanon, Kuwait, Oman, Bahrain, Algeria, and Libya.

Figure 3 also demonstrates the power of ArCOV-19 in capturing further controversial and trending topics. Table 2 shows a timeline covering dates of specific topics of discussion trending on social media around times of peaks in tweeting frequency in Figure 3(c).

Country	Date	Topic	Related News
UAE	Feb 19	Yemeni Foreign Affairs Minister thanks UAE for evacuating Yemeni students from China	http://tiny.cc/71qtmz
Iraq	Feb 20	Iraq announces closure of borders with Iran	http://tiny.cc/yzrtmz
Egypt	Mar 2	Egyptian health minister announces a visit to China	http://tiny.cc/7iqtmz
	Mar 7	Kuwait bans travels with Egypt including entry of Egyptian residents	http://tiny.cc/lqstmz
KSA	Mar 4-5	Closure of The Grand Mosque in Mecca	http://tiny.cc/iqrtmz

Table 2: Examples of trending topics in social media matched by spikes in tweeting frequency in ArCOV-19

We further explore the topics discussed in

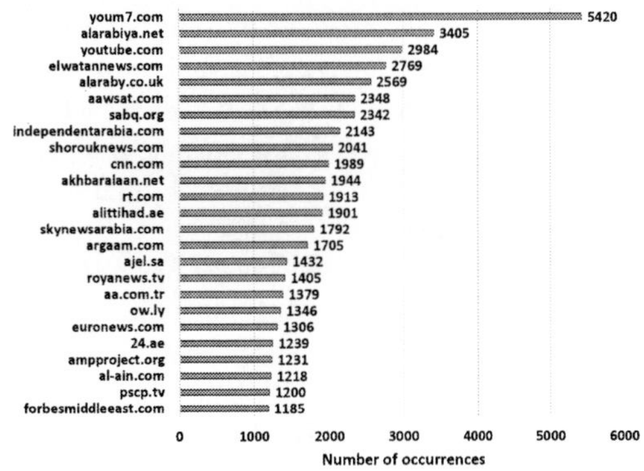

Figure 4: Most frequently-linked domains in the top tweets subset for the period of 27th Jan 2020 to 31st Jan 2021.

ArCOV-19 by considering the domains of URLs shared in the tweets. We focused on the top tweets subset of ArCOV-19 (constructed as detailed in Section 3.2) and identified the URLs posted in those tweets. We then expanded them (since Twitter URLs are shortened) and dropped URLs of images and videos uploaded to Twitter, to focus only on URLs referring to external sources. We extracted 110,220 URLs from 2,617 unique domains. Figure 4 shows that URLs from news websites are dominantly the most-commonly shared. We observe that these news websites mainly originate from three Arab countries, namely, Egypt, Saudi Arabia, and United Arab Emirates. Interestingly, videos from YouTube are among the most commonly shared media. Coupled with the fact that 36% of the tweets in ArCOV-19 include embedded images and videos (Table 1), we believe this enables ArCOV-19 to be a potential dataset to further support the evaluation of multi-modal retrieval and classification systems.

4.3 Geographic Distribution of Tweets

Although Twitter provides automatic geo-reference functionally, few users (solely around 1-3% (Murdock, 2011; Jurgens et al., 2015)) opt to enable it due to privacy and safety reasons. Alternatively, to have an insight about the geographical distribution and diversity of the tweets in our dataset, we examined the *place* and *coordinates* attributes of the Tweet object.[16] We note that the *place* attribute is an optional attribute that allows the user to select a

[12] https://tinyurl.com/rfj5khn

[13] https://tinyurl.com/yykgwbox

[14] https://tinyurl.com/yxkg78g5

[15] https://tinyurl.com/y4nlgz5h

[16] https://developer.twitter.com/en/docs/tweets/data-dictionary/overview/geo-objects

location from a list provided by Twitter (therefore, the location might not necessarily show the actual location from where the tweet is posted), whereas the *coordinates* attribute represents the geographic location of the tweet as reported by the user or client application.

Table 1 shows that ArCOV-19 has 60,873 geolocated tweets (i.e., having values in the *place* attribute) and 2,078 geotagged tweets (i.e., having values in the *coordinates* attribute). Those tweets were posted by 24,072 and 256 unique users respectively. The geolocated tweets constitute about 2.28% of the total source tweets, which is consistent with previous studies (Huang and Carley, 2019).

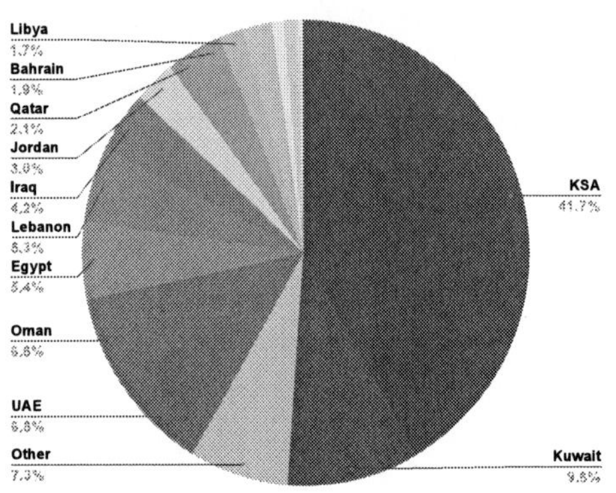

Figure 5: Distribution of geolocated tweets for the period of 27th Jan 2020 to 31st Jan 2021.

The geolocated tweets were indeed posted by users from 102 countries from around the globe. We found that 92.75% of them were posted from the Arab world. The largest contribution of the geolocated content (about 41.7%) comes from Saudi Arabia; this is somewhat expected as Saudi users represent the highest number of active Twitter users in the Arab world.[17] Surprisingly, Kuwait comes second with 9.6% of the geolocated content. We believe the rationale is that it was among the first countries that reported COVID-19 cases in the Middle East. Since then, Kuwait started a series of strict precautions such as a wide lock-down in many vital facilities until the government had imposed a nationwide curfew. We think, after the curfew, the people become more active on Twitter as a platform to break news and discuss developments of the virus. Additionally, we used related phrases and hashtags to "*Kuwait*", "*Lebanon*", and "*UAE*"

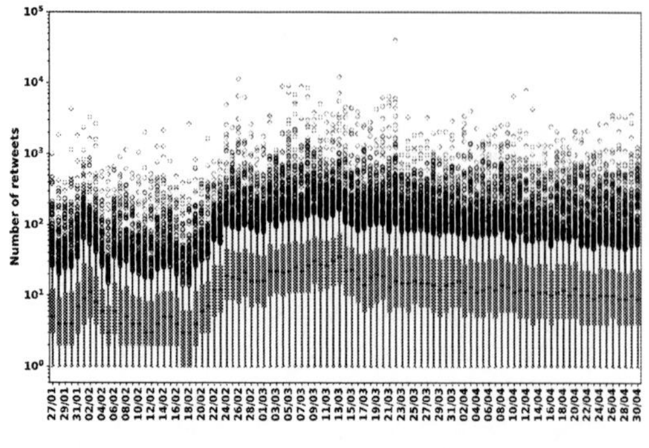

Figure 6: Distribution of retweets per day for the top subset for the period of 27th Jan 2020 to 30th April 2020.

among the tracking keywords in the period between 22 of February and 13 of March. Furthermore, it is not surprising to see the countries that have a few cases have the smallest portions of contribution to the content. Others have small audience userbases on Twitter (e.g., Tunisia).

4.4 Propagation Networks

As discussed earlier, we collected the propagation networks of the top subset. Overall, the number of retweets is 7,925,821 for the entire subset, and the number of replies is 1,476,950 [18].

At the time of collecting the retweets, we were not able to get the retweets of some of the tweets either because they were deleted or they were posted from private accounts. For those collected successfully, Figure 6 illustrates the distribution of retweets per day using boxplots. It shows that the average (and median) number of retweets follows a similar pattern to what was shown in Figure 1 (notice that the Y-axis here is in log scale). We also notice that a good number of tweets got more than 100 retweets; some of them got even larger numbers reaching about 10k retweets or more, showing highly propagated content. As shown in Figure 7, we applied a similar analysis to the replies per day, and found similar patterns to the retweets.

5 Enabling Research

With the spread of Novel Coronavirus in several Arab countries and the subsequent procedural measures taken by the local governments, it continued to dominate discussions over social media (and

[17] https://tinyurl.com/jmkttt3

[18] The stats are for the replies for data until end of April 2020 and we are still collecting the rest; we will make all available in the near future.

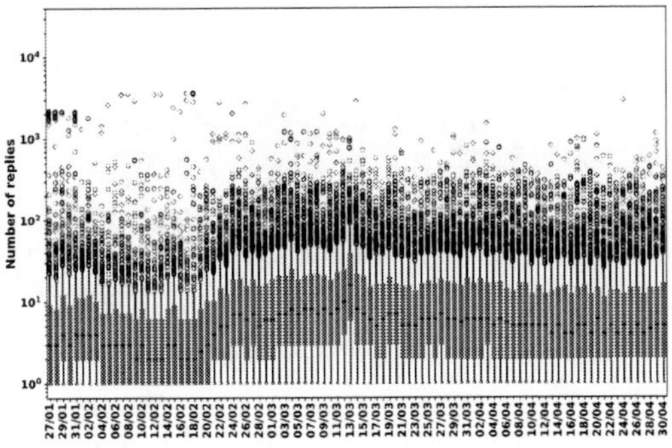

Figure 7: Distribution of replies per day for the top subset for the period of 27th Jan 2020 to 30th April 2020.

Twitter in particular) to the time of this writing. To enable research on different tasks on Arabic Tweets, we make ArCOV-19 publicly-available for the research community. Having quantified the topical, geographical, and community representativeness of ArCOV-19, we envision that it is suitable for diverse natural language processing, information retrieval, and computational social science research tasks including, but not limited to, emergency management, misinformation detection, and social analytics, as we discuss below. Furthermore, we provide propagation networks of daily highly popular subset (the most popular 1K) to ensure the quality of tweets. This sample is drawn after filtering out potential low-quality tweets (e.g., spam) and content duplicates. We anticipate the top subset and the network to support these tasks on the popular Arabic tweets that we assume have the most effect on shaping public opinion and understanding.

Emergency Management: As COVID-19 is an international pandemic, national and international health organizations need to analyze the effects of the outbreak. We believe ArCOV-19 can support several tasks in that domain, such as filtering of informative content, events and sub-events detection, summarization, identification of eyewitnesses, geolocation, and studying information and situational awareness propagation, to name a few.

Social Analytics: In addition to sharing reports and awareness during the outbreak, people tend to discuss their opinions (e.g., stance towards the situation and its consequences) and express their emotions (e.g., big changes in lifestyle, social distancing, loss of their beloved ones, etc.). Therefore, analyzing the tweets to detect sentiment, stance, hate speech, and generally, offensive language, among other aspects, is of interest to many stakeholders.

Misinformation Detection: With the sheer amount of information shared about COVID-19, many rumors are disseminated and getting high attention from the community, which causes a fast propagation of misinformation. This hinders the efforts of the health and governmental organizations on fighting the pandemic as such rumors spread panic and may lead to undesirable consequences (e.g., increase of cases and mortality rate, or lack of supplies due to hoarding). ArCOV-19 supports studying information/claims propagation, claims check-worthiness detection and verification tasks on the most popular tweets. Furthermore, the retweet networks and conversational threads provide a valuable resource for early detection of fake news and identification of malicious rumor-spreading accounts. To further facilitate work in this domain of problems, we recently constructed ArCOV19-*Rumors*, an annotated dataset on top of ArCOV-19 to support claim and tweet verification (Haouari et al., 2021).

6 Conclusion

In this paper, we presented ArCOV-19, the first Arabic Twitter dataset about the Novel Coronavirus (COVID-19) that includes propagation networks of a large subset of tweets. We release all source tweets, top subset, search queries, and the propagation networks. Preliminary analysis showed that ArCOV-19 captured spikes in tweeting frequency for country-specific tweets that are consistent with the first reported cases of COVID-19 in several Arab countries. We also found dominance of news agencies among top tweeting users and among most shared URLs. ArCOV-19 enables research under many domains including natural language processing, information retrieval, and social computing. We plan to continue collecting tweets for the foreseeable future and the dataset will be continuously updated with newly collected tweets and propagation networks.

Acknowledgments

The work of Tamer Elsayed and Maram Hasanain was made possible by NPRP grant# NPRP 11S-1204-170060 from the Qatar National Research Fund (a member of Qatar Foundation). The work of Reem Suwaileh was supported by GSRA grant# GSRA5-1-0527-18082 from the Qatar National Research Fund and the work of Fatima Haouari was supported by GSRA grant# GSRA6-1-0611-19074 from the Qatar National Research Fund. The statements made herein are solely the responsibility of the authors.

References

Sarah Alqurashi, Ahmad Alhindi, and Eisa Alanazi. 2020. Large Arabic Twitter Dataset on COVID-19. *arXiv preprint arXiv:2004.04315*.

Thayer Alshaabi, David R Dewhurst, Joshua R Minot, Michael V Arnold, Jane L Adams, Christopher M Danforth, and Peter Sheridan Dodds. 2020a. The growing echo chamber of social media: Measuring temporal and social contagion dynamics for over 150 languages on twitter for 2009–2020. *arXiv preprint arXiv:2003.03667*.

Thayer Alshaabi, JR Minot, MV Arnold, Jane Lydia Adams, David Rushing Dewhurst, Andrew J Reagan, Roby Muhamad, Christopher M Danforth, and Peter Sheridan Dodds. 2020b. How the world's collective attention is being paid to a pandemic: Covid-19 related 1-gram time series for 24 languages on twitter. *arXiv preprint arXiv:2003.12614*.

Juan M Banda, Ramya Tekumalla, Guanyu Wang, Jingyuan Yu, Tuo Liu, Yuning Ding, and Gerardo Chowell. 2020. A large-scale covid-19 twitter chatter dataset for open scientific research–an international collaboration. *arXiv preprint arXiv:2004.03688*.

Emily Chen, Kristina Lerman, and Emilio Ferrara. 2020a. Covid-19: The first public coronavirus twitter dataset. *arXiv preprint arXiv:2003.07372*.

Emily Chen, Kristina Lerman, and Emilio Ferrara. 2020b. Tracking social media discourse about the covid-19 pandemic: Development of a public coronavirus twitter data set. *JMIR Public Health and Surveillance*, 6(2):e19273.

Hassan Dashtian and Dhiraj Murthy. 2021. Cml-covid: A large-scale covid-19 twitter dataset with latent topics, sentiment and location information. *arXiv preprint arXiv:2101.12202*.

Zhiwei Gao, Shuntaro Yada, Shoko Wakamiya, and Eiji Aramaki. 2020. Naist covid: Multilingual covid-19 twitter and weibo dataset. *arXiv preprint arXiv:2004.08145*.

Purva Grover, Arpan Kumar Kar, Yogesh K. Dwivedi, and Marijn Janssen. 2019. Polarization and acculturation in us election 2016 outcomes – can twitter analytics predict changes in voting preferences. *Technological Forecasting and Social Change*, 145:438 – 460.

Fatima Haouari, Maram Hasanain, Reem Suwaileh, and Tamer Elsayed. 2021. Arcov19-rumors: Arabic covid-19 twitter dataset for misinformation detection. In *Proceedings of the Sixth Arabic Natural Language Processing Workshop*, WANLP 2021.

Yong Hu, He-Yan Huang, Anfan Chen, and Xian-Ling Mao. 2020. Weibo-cov: A large-scale covid-19 social media dataset from weibo. In *Proceedings of the 1st Workshop on NLP for COVID-19 (Part 2) at EMNLP 2020*.

Binxuan Huang and Kathleen M Carley. 2019. A large-scale empirical study of geotagging behavior on Twitter. In *Proceedings of the 2019 IEEE/ACM International Conference on Advances in Social Networks Analysis and Mining*, pages 365–373.

David Jurgens, Tyler Finethy, James McCorriston, Yi Tian Xu, and Derek Ruths. 2015. Geolocation prediction in twitter using social networks: A critical analysis and review of current practice. In *Proceedings of the Ninth International AAAI Conference on Web and Social Media*.

Ireneus Kagashe, Zhijun Yan, and Imran Suheryani. 2017. Enhancing seasonal influenza surveillance: topic analysis of widely used medicinal drugs using twitter data. *Journal of medical Internet research*, 19(9):e315.

Christian E Lopez, Malolan Vasu, and Caleb Gallemore. 2020. Understanding the perception of covid-19 policies by mining a multilanguage twitter dataset. *arXiv preprint arXiv:2003.10359*.

Andrew McNeill, Peter R. Harris, and Pam Briggs. 2016. Twitter influence on uk vaccination and antiviral uptake during the 2009 h1n1 pandemic. *Frontiers in Public Health*, 4:26.

Vanessa Murdock. 2011. Your mileage may vary: On the limits of social media. *SIGSPATIAL Special*, 3(2):62–66.

Umair Qazi, Muhammad Imran, and Ferda Ofli. 2020. Geocov19: a dataset of hundreds of millions of multilingual covid-19 tweets with location information. *SIGSPATIAL Special*, 12(1):6–15.

Melissa Roy, Nicolas Moreau, Cécile Rousseau, Arnaud Mercier, Andrew Wilson, and Laëtitia Atlani-Duault. 2020. Ebola and localized blame on social media: Analysis of twitter and facebook conversations during the 2014–2015 ebola epidemic. *Culture, Medicine, and Psychiatry*, 44(1):56–79.

Lisa Singh, Shweta Bansal, Leticia Bode, Ceren Budak, Guangqing Chi, Kornraphop Kawintiranon, Colton Padden, Rebecca Vanarsdall, Emily Vraga, and Yanchen Wang. 2020. A first look at covid-19 information and misinformation sharing on twitter. *arXiv preprint arXiv:2003.13907*.

Santosh Vijaykumar, Glen Nowak, Itai Himelboim, and Yan Jin. 2018. Virtual zika transmission after the first us case: who said what and how it spread on twitter. *American journal of infection control*, 46(5):549–557.

Koosha Zarei, Reza Farahbakhsh, Noel Crespi, and Gareth Tyson. 2020. A first instagram dataset on covid-19. *arXiv preprint arXiv:2004.12226*.

Arkaitz Zubiaga, Maria Liakata, Rob Procter, Geraldine Wong Sak Hoi, and Peter Tolmie. 2016. Analysing how people orient to and spread rumours in social media by looking at conversational threads. *PloS one*, 11(3).

The Interplay of Variant, Size, and Task Type in Arabic Pre-trained Language Models

Go Inoue, Bashar Alhafni, Nurpeiis Baimukan, Houda Bouamor,[†] Nizar Habash
Computational Approaches to Modeling Language (CAMeL) Lab
New York University Abu Dhabi
[†]Carnegie Mellon University in Qatar
{go.inoue,alhafni,nurpeiis,nizar.habash}@nyu.edu
hbouamor@qatar.cmu.edu

Abstract

In this paper, we explore the effects of language variants, data sizes, and fine-tuning task types in Arabic pre-trained language models. To do so, we build three pre-trained language models across three variants of Arabic: Modern Standard Arabic (MSA), dialectal Arabic, and classical Arabic, in addition to a fourth language model which is pre-trained on a mix of the three. We also examine the importance of pre-training data size by building additional models that are pre-trained on a scaled-down set of the MSA variant. We compare our different models to each other, as well as to eight publicly available models by fine-tuning them on five NLP tasks spanning 12 datasets. Our results suggest that the variant proximity of pre-training data to fine-tuning data is more important than the pre-training data size. We exploit this insight in defining an optimized system selection model for the studied tasks.

1 Introduction

Pre-trained language models such as BERT (Devlin et al., 2019) and RoBERTa (Liu et al., 2019b) have shown significant success in a wide range of natural language processing (NLP) tasks in various languages. Arabic has benefited from extensive efforts in building dedicated pre-trained language models, achieving state-of-the-art results in a number of NLP tasks, across both Modern Standard Arabic (MSA) and Dialectal Arabic (DA) (Antoun et al., 2020; Abdul-Mageed et al., 2020a).

However, it is hard to compare these models to understand what contributes to their performances because of their different design decisions and hyperparameters, such as data size, language variant, tokenization, vocabulary size, number of training steps, and so forth. Practically, one may empirically choose the best performing pre-trained model by fine-tuning it on a particular task; however, it is still unclear why a particular model is performing better than another and what design choices are contributing to its performance.

To answer this question, we pre-trained various language models as part of a controlled experiment where we vary pre-training data sizes and language variants while keeping other hyperparameters constant throughout pre-training. We started by scaling down MSA pre-training data size to measure its impact on performance in fine-tuning tasks. We then pre-trained three different variants of Arabic: MSA, DA, and classical Arabic (CA), as well as a mix of these three variants.

We evaluate our models along with eight other recent Arabic pre-trained models across five different tasks covering all the language variants we study, namely, named entity recognition (NER), part-of-speech (POS) tagging, sentiment analysis, dialect identification, and poetry classification, spanning 12 datasets.

Our contributions can be summarized as follows:

- We create and release eight Arabic pre-trained models, which we name CAMeLBERT, with different design decisions, including one (CAMeLBERT-Mix) that is trained on the largest dataset to date.[1]
- We investigate the interplay of data size, language variant, and fine-tuning task type through controlled experimentation. Our results show that variant proximity of pre-training data and task data is more important than pre-training data size.
- We exploit this insight in defining an optimized system selection model.

[1]Our pre-trained models are available at https://huggingface.co/CAMeL-Lab, and the fine-tuning code and models are available at https://github.com/CAMeL-Lab/CAMeLBERT.

Proceedings of the Sixth Arabic Natural Language Processing Workshop, pages 92–104
Kyiv, Ukraine (Virtual), April 19, 2021.

Ref	Model	Variants	Size	#Word	Tokens	Vocab	#Steps
	BERT (Devlin et al., 2019)	-	-	3.3B	WP	30k	1M
X_1	mBERT (Devlin et al., 2019)	MSA	-	-	WP	120k	-
X_2	AraBERTv0.1 (Antoun et al., 2020)	MSA	24GB	-	SP	60k	1.25M
X_3	AraBERTv0.2 (Antoun et al., 2020)	MSA	77GB	8.6B	WP	60k	3M
X_4	ArabicBERT (Safaya et al., 2020)	MSA	95GB	8.2B	WP	32k	4M
X_5	Multi-dialect-Arabic-BERT (Talafha et al., 2020)	MSA/DA	-	-	WP	32k	-
X_6	GigaBERTv4 (Lan et al., 2020)	MSA	-	10.4B	WP	50k	1.48M
X_7	MARBERT (Abdul-Mageed et al., 2020a)	MSA/DA	128GB	15.6B	WP	100K	17M
X_8	ARBERT (Abdul-Mageed et al., 2020a)	MSA	61GB	6.5B	WP	100K	8M
	CAMeLBERT-MSA	MSA	107GB	12.6B	WP	30k	1M
	CAMeLBERT-DA	DA	54GB	5.8B	WP	30k	1M
	CAMeLBERT-CA	CA	6GB	847M	WP	30k	1M
	CAMeLBERT-Mix	MSA/DA/CA	167GB	17.3B	WP	30k	1M

Table 1: Configurations of existing models and CAMeLBERT models. Ref is a model identifier used in Table 5. WP is WordPiece and SP is SentencePiece.

2 Related Work

There have been several research efforts on Arabic pre-trained models achieving state-of-the-art results in a number of Arabic NLP tasks. One of the earliest efforts includes AraBERT (Antoun et al., 2020), where they pre-trained a monolingual BERT model using 24GB of Arabic text in the news domain. Safaya et al. (2020) pre-trained ArabicBERT using 95GB of text mainly from the Arabic portion of the OSCAR corpus. Based on ArabicBERT, Talafha et al. (2020) further pre-trained their model using 10 million tweets, which included dialectal data. Lan et al. (2020) released several English-Arabic bilingual models dubbed GigaBERTs, where they studied the effectiveness of cross-lingual transfer learning and code-switched pre-training using Wikipedia, Gigaword, and the OSCAR corpus. Most recently, Abdul-Mageed et al. (2020a) developed two models, ARBERT and MARBERT, pre-trained on a large collection of datasets in MSA and DA. They reported new state-of-the-art results on the majority of the datasets in their fine-tuning benchmark.

Moreover, there have been various studies explaining why pre-trained language models perform well on downstream tasks either in monolingual (Hewitt and Manning, 2019; Jawahar et al., 2019; Liu et al., 2019a; Tenney et al., 2019a,b) or multilingual settings (Wu and Dredze, 2019; Chi et al., 2020; Kulmizev et al., 2020; Vulić et al., 2020). Most of these efforts leveraged probing techniques to explore the linguistic knowledge that is captured by pre-trained language models such as morphosyntactic and semantic knowledge. More recently, there have been additional efforts investigating the effects of pre-training data size and tokenization on the performance of pre-trained language models. Zhang et al. (2020) showed that pre-training RoBERTa requires 10M to 100M words to learn representations that reliably encode most syntactic and semantic features. However, a much larger quantity of data is needed for the model to perform well on typical downstream NLU tasks. Rust et al. (2020) empirically compared multilingual pre-trained language models to their monolingual counterparts on a set of nine typologically diverse languages. They showed that while the pre-training data size is an important factor, the designated tokenizer of each monolingual model plays an equally important role in the downstream performance.

In this work, we primarily focus on understanding the behavior of pre-trained models against variables such as data sizes and language variants. We compare against eight existing models. We find that AraBERTv02 (X_3) is the best on average and it wins or ties for a win in six out of 12 subtasks. Our CAMeLBERT-Star model is second overall on average, and it wins or ties for a win in five out of 12 subtasks. Interestingly, these systems are complementary in their performance and between the two, they win or tie for a win in ten out of 12 subtasks.

3 Pre-training CAMeLBERT

We describe the datasets and the procedure we use to pre-train our models. We use the original implementation released by Google for pre-training.[2]

3.1 Data

MSA Training Data For MSA, we use the Arabic Gigaword Fifth Edition (Parker et al., 2011), Abu El-Khair Corpus (El-Khair, 2016), OSIAN corpus (Zeroual et al., 2019), Arabic Wikipedia,[3] and the unshuffled version of the Arabic OSCAR corpus (Ortiz Suárez et al., 2020).

DA Training Data For DA, we collect a range of dialectal corpora: LDC97T19-CALLHOME Transcripts (Gadalla et al., 1997); LDC2002T38-CALLHOME Supplement Transcripts (Linguistic Data Consortium, 2002); LDC2005S08-Babylon Levantine Arabic Transcripts (BBN Technologies, 2005); LDC2005S14-CTS Levantine Arabic Transcripts (Maamouri et al., 2005); LDC2006T07-Levantine Arabic Transcripts (Maamouri et al., 2006); LDC2006T15-Gulf Arabic Transcripts (Appen Pty Ltd, 2006a); LDC2006T16-Iraqi Arabic Transcripts (Appen Pty Ltd, 2006b); LDC2007T01-Levantine Arabic Transcripts (Appen Pty Ltd, 2007); LDC2007T04-Fisher Levantine Arabic Transcripts (Maamouri et al., 2007); Arabic Online Commentary Dataset (AOC) (Zaidan and Callison-Burch, 2011); LDC2012T09-English/Arabic Parallel text (Raytheon BBN Technologies et al., 2012); Arabic Multi Dialect Text Corpora (Almeman and Lee, 2013); A Multidialectal Parallel Corpus of Arabic (Bouamor et al., 2014); Multi-Dialect, Multi-Genre Corpus of Informal Written Arabic (Cotterell and Callison-Burch, 2014); YouDACC (Salama et al., 2014); PADIC (Meftouh et al., 2015); Curras (Jarrar et al., 2016); WERd (Ali et al., 2017); LDC2017T07-BOLT Egyptian SMS (Chen et al., 2017); Shami (Abu Kwaik et al., 2018); SUAR (Al-Twairesh et al., 2018); Arap-Tweet (Zaghouani and Charfi, 2018); Gumar (Khalifa et al., 2018); MADAR (Bouamor et al., 2018); Habibi (El-Haj, 2020); NADI (Abdul-Mageed et al., 2020b); and QADI (Abdelali et al., 2020).

CA Training Data For CA, we use the OpenITI corpus (v1.2) (Nigst et al., 2020).

[2] https://github.com/google-research/bert

[3] https://archive.org/details/arwiki-20190201

3.2 Pre-processing

After extracting the raw text from each corpus, we apply the following pre-processing. We first remove invalid characters and normalize white spaces using the utilities provided by the original BERT implementation. We also remove lines without any Arabic characters. We then remove diacritics and kashida using CAMeL Tools (Obeid et al., 2020). Finally, we split each line into sentences with a heuristic-based sentence segmenter.

3.3 Preparing Data for BERT Pre-training

We follow the original English BERT model's hyperparameters for pre-training. We train a WordPiece (Schuster and Nakajima, 2012) tokenizer on the entire dataset (167 GB text) with a vocabulary size of 30,000 using Hugging Face's tokenizers.[4] We do not lowercase letters nor strip accents. We use whole word masking and a duplicate factor of 10. We set maximum predictions per sequence to 20 for the datasets with a maximum sequence length of 128 tokens and 80 for the datasets with a maximum sequence length of 512 tokens.

3.4 Pre-training Procedure

We use a Google Cloud TPU (v3-8) for model pre-training. We use a learning rate of 1e-4 with a warmup over the first 10,000 steps. We pre-trained our models with a batch size of 1,024 sequences with a maximum sequence length of 128 tokens for the first 900,000 steps. We then continued pre-training with a batch size of 256 sequences with a maximum sequence length of 512 tokens for another 100,000 steps. In total, we pre-trained our models for one million steps. Pre-training one model took approximately 4.5 days.

4 Fine-tuning Tasks

We evaluate our pre-trained language models on five NLP tasks: NER, POS tagging, sentiment analysis, dialect identification, and poetry classification. Specifically, we fine-tune and evaluate the models using 12 datasets (corresponding to 12 subtasks). We used Hugging Face's transformers (Wolf et al., 2020) to fine-tune our CAMeLBERT models.[5] The fine-tuning was done by adding a fully connected linear layer to the last hidden state.

[4] https://github.com/huggingface/tokenizers

[5] We used transformers v3.1.0 along with PyTorch v1.5.1

Task	Dataset/Subtask	#Label	#Train	#Test	Unit	Variant	%MSA
NER	ANERcorp (Benajiba et al., 2007)	9	125,102	25,008	Token	MSA	83.6
POS	PATB (MSA) (Maamouri et al., 2004)	32	503,015	63,172	Token	MSA	85.1
	ARZTB (EGY) (Maamouri et al., 2012)	33	133,751	20,464	Token	DA	21.5
	Gumar (GLF) (Khalifa et al., 2018)	35	162,031	20,100	Token	DA	30.0
SA	ASTD (Nabil et al., 2015)	3	23,327	663	Sent	MSA	56.9
	ArSAS (Elmadany et al., 2018)	3	23,327	3,705	Sent	MSA	60.5
	SemEval (Rosenthal et al., 2017)	3	23,327	6,100	Sent	MSA	77.7
DID	MADAR-26 (Salameh et al., 2018)	26	41,600	5,200	Sent	DA	14.1
	MADAR-6 (Salameh et al., 2018)	6	54,000	12,000	Sent	DA	17.2
	MADAR-Twitter-5 (Bouamor et al., 2019)	21	39,836	9,116	Grp	MSA	92.3
	NADI (Abdul-Mageed et al., 2020b)	21	21,000	5,000	Sent	DA	38.3
Poetry	APCD (Yousef et al., 2019)	23	1,391,541	173,963	Sent	CA	71.3

Table 2: Statistics of our fine-tuning datasets. Unit refers to a unit we use to calculate the number of examples in Train and Test. For MADAR-Twitter-5, we use a group of five tweets as a unit (Grp). A language variant is determined based on dataset design and the estimated proportion of MSA sentences in the dataset.

Tasks and Variants We selected the fine-tuning datasets and subtasks to represent multiple variants of Arabic by design. For some of the datasets, the variant is readily known. However, other datasets contain a lot of social media text where the dominant variant of Arabic is unknown. Therefore, we estimate the proportion of MSA sentences in each dataset by identifying whether the text is MSA or DA using the Corpus 6 dialect identification model in Salameh et al. (2018) as implemented in CAMeL Tools (Obeid et al., 2020). This technique does not model CA. Of course, none of the datasets was purely MSA or DA; however, based on known dataset variants, we observe that having about 40% or fewer MSA labels strongly suggests that the dataset is dialectal (or a strong dialectal mix).

Table 2 presents the number of labels, size, unit, variant, and MSA percentage for the datasets used in the subtasks.

4.1 Named Entity Recognition

Dataset We fine-tuned our models on the publicly available Arabic NER Dataset ANERcorp (~150K words) (Benajiba et al., 2007) which is in MSA and we followed the splits defined by Obeid et al. (2020). We also kept the same IOB (inside, outside, beginning) tagging format defined in the dataset covering four classes: Location (LOC), Miscellaneous (MISC), Organization (ORG), and Person (PERS).

Experimental Setup During fine-tuning, we used the representation of the first sub-token as an input to the linear layer. All models were fine-tuned on a single GPU for 3 epochs with a learning rate of 5e-5, batch size of 32, and a maximum sequence length of 512. Since ANERcorp does not have a dev set, we used the last checkpoint after the fine-tuning is done to report results on the test set using the F_1 score.

4.2 Part-of-Speech Tagging

Dataset We fine-tuned our models on three different POS tagging datasets: (1) the Penn Arabic Treebank (PATB) (Maamouri et al., 2004) which is in MSA and includes 32 POS tags; (2) the Egyptian Arabic Treebank (ARZATB) (Maamouri et al., 2012) which is in Egyptian (EGY) and includes 33 POS tags; and (3) the GUMAR corpus (Khalifa et al., 2018) which is in Gulf (GLF) and includes 35 POS tags.

Experimental Setup Similar to NER, we used the representation of the first sub-token as an input to the linear layer. Our models were fine-tuned on a single GPU for 10 epochs with a learning rate of 5e-5, batch size of 32, and a maximum sequence length of 512. We used the same hyperparameters for the fine-tuning across the three POS tagging datasets. After the fine-tuning, we used the best checkpoints based on the dev sets to report results on the test sets using the F_1 score.

4.3 Sentiment Analysis

Dataset We used a combination of sentiment analysis datasets to fine-tune our models. The datasets are: (1) the Arabic Speech-Act and Sentiment Corpus of Tweets (ArSAS) (Elmadany et al., 2018); (2) the Arabic Sentiment Tweets Dataset (ASTD) (Nabil et al., 2015); (3) SemEval-2017 task 4-A benchmark dataset (Rosenthal et al., 2017); and (4) the Multi-Topic Corpus for Target-based Sentiment Analysis in Arabic Levantine Tweets (ArSenTD-Lev) (Baly et al., 2019). We combined and preprocessed the datasets in a similar way to what was done by Abu Farha and Magdy (2019) and Obeid et al. (2020). That is, we removed diacritics, URLs, and Twitter usernames from all the tweets.

Experimental Setup Our models were fine-tuned on ArSenTD-Lev and the train splits from SemEval, ASTD, and ArSAS (23,327 tweets) on a single GPU for 3 epochs with a learning rate of 3e-5, batch size of 32, and a maximum sequence length of 128. After the fine-tuning, we used the best checkpoint based on a single dev set from SemEval, ASTD, and ArSAS to report results on the test sets. We used the F_1^{PN} score which was defined in the SemEval-2017 task 4-A; F_1^{PN} is the macro F_1 score over the positive and negative classes only while neglecting the neutral class.

4.4 Dialect Identification

Dataset We fine-tuned our models on four different dialect identification datasets: (1) MADAR Corpus 26 which includes 26 labels; (2) MADAR Corpus 6 which includes six labels; (3) MADAR Twitter Corpus (Bouamor et al., 2018; Salameh et al., 2018; Bouamor et al., 2019) which includes 21 labels; and (4) NADI Country-level (Abdul-Mageed et al., 2020b) which includes 21 labels. The datasets were preprocessed by removing diacritics, URLs, and Twitter usernames while maintaining the same train, dev, and test splits for each dataset. Moreover, we collated the tweets belonging to a particular user in the MADAR Twitter Corpus in groups of 5 before feeding them to the model. We refer to this preprocessed version as MADAR-Twitter-5 to avoid confusion with the publicly available original MADAR Twitter Corpus.

Experimental Setup Our models were fine-tuned for 10 epochs with a learning rate of 3e-5, batch size of 32, and a maximum sequence length of 128. After the fine-tuning, we used the best checkpoints based on the dev sets to report results on the test sets using the F_1 score. Moreover, for the MADAR-Twitter-5 evaluation, we took a voting approach. That is, each user in the dev and test sets is assigned to the most frequent predicted country label. In case of a tie, we always pick the most frequent predicted country label based on the training set.

4.5 Poetry Meter Classification

Dataset We used the Arabic Poem Comprehensive Dataset (APCD) (Yousef et al., 2019), which is mostly in CA, to fine-tune our models to identify the meters of Arabic poems. The dataset contains around 1.8M poems and covers 23 meters. We preprocessed the dataset by removing diacritics from the poems and separated the halves of each verse by using the `[SEP]` token. We applied an 80/10/10 random split to create train, dev, and test sets respectively.

Experimental Setup We fine-tuned our models on a single GPU for 3 epochs with a learning rate of 3e-5, batch size of 32, and a maximum sequence length of 128. After the fine-tuning, we used the best checkpoint based on the dev set to report results on the test set using the F_1 score.

5 Evaluation Results and Discussion

We first present an experiment where we investigate the effect of pre-training data size. We then report on CAMeLBERT models pre-trained on MSA, DA, and CA data, in addition to a model that is pre-trained on a mixture of these variants. We then provide a comparison against publicly available models.

5.1 Models with Different Data Sizes

To investigate the effect of pre-training data size on fine-tuning tasks, we pre-train MSA models in a controlled setting where we scale down the MSA pre-training size by a factor of two while keeping all other hyperparameters constant. We pre-train four CAMeLBERT models on MSA data as follows: MSA-1/2 (54GB, 6.3B words), MSA-1/4 (27GB, 3.1B words), MSA-1/8 (14GB, 1.5B words), and MSA-1/16 (6GB, 636M words). In Table 3, we show the results on our fine-tuning subtasks.

We observe that the full MSA model is on average the highest performing system by a slight margin, and it wins or ties for a win in seven out of 12 subtasks. It is also the best model on average in the MSA and DA subtasks. However, we note that

Task	Subtask	Variant	%Performance MSA (107GB)	MSA-1/2 (53GB)	MSA-1/4 (27GB)	MSA-1/8 (14GB)	MSA-1/16 (6GB)	Max-Min
NER	ANERcorp	MSA	**82.4**	82.3	82.0	82.3	80.5	1.9
POS	PATB (MSA)	MSA	**97.4**	**97.4**	**97.4**	**97.4**	**97.4**	0.1
	ARZTB (EGY)	DA	**90.8**	90.3	90.5	90.5	90.4	0.5
	Gumar (GLF)	DA	**97.1**	97.0	97.0	**97.1**	97.0	0.1
SA	ASTD	MSA	**76.9**	76.0	76.8	76.7	75.3	1.6
	ArSAS	MSA	**93.0**	92.6	92.5	92.5	92.3	0.8
	SemEval	MSA	72.1	70.7	**72.8**	71.6	71.2	2.0
DID	MADAR-26	DA	62.6	62.0	**62.8**	62.0	62.2	0.8
	MADAR-6	DA	91.9	91.8	**92.2**	92.1	92.0	0.4
	MADAR-Twitter-5	MSA	77.6	**78.5**	77.3	77.7	76.2	2.3
	NADI	DA	**24.9**	24.6	24.6	**24.9**	23.8	1.1
Poetry	APCD	CA	79.7	79.9	**80.0**	79.7	79.8	0.3
Variant-wise-average		MSA	**83.2**	82.9	83.1	83.0	82.1	1.1
		DA	**73.5**	73.1	73.4	73.3	73.1	0.4
		CA	79.7	79.9	**80.0**	79.7	79.8	0.3
Macro-average			**78.9**	78.6	78.8	78.7	78.2	0.7

Table 3: Performance of CAMeLBERT models trained on MSA datasets with different sizes. We use F_1 score as a metric for all tasks. Max-Min refers to the difference in performance among the models for each dataset. Variant-wise-average refers to average over a group of tasks in the same language variant. The best results among the models are in bold.

the MSA-1/4 wins or ties for a win in five subtasks and performs best in the CA subtask, even though it was pre-trained on a quarter of the full MSA data.

We also observe that different subtasks have different patterns. For some subtasks, plateauing in performance happens rather early. For instance, the performance on PATB (MSA) does not change even if we increase the size. Similarly, the difference in performance on Gumar (GLF) is very small (0.1%). For other subtasks, the improvement is not consistent with the size, particularly in SemEval. When we calculate the correlation between the performance and the pre-training data size, we note that ArSAS has a strong positive correlation of 0.96, however, MADAR-6 has a negative correlation of -0.62. In fact, the average of the correlation of each of the 12 experiments is 0.37, which is not a strong pattern correlating size with performance. These observations suggest that the size of pre-training data has limited and inconsistent effect on the fine-tuning performance. This is consistent with Micheli et al. (2020), where they concluded that pre-training data size does not show a strong monotonic relationship with fine-tuning performance in their controlled experiments on French corpora.

5.2 Models with Different Language Variants

Next, we explore the relationship between language variants in pre-training and fine-tuning datasets.

5.2.1 MSA, DA, and CA

Task Type Difference We compare the behavior of three models pre-trained on MSA, DA, and CA data. From Table 4, we observe that the difference in performance (Max-Min) among CAMeLBERT's MSA, DA, and CA models is 4.9% on average, ranging from 0.7% to 16.2%. To study trends by task type, we compute the average performance difference across the subtasks for each task. NER is the most sensitive to the pre-trained model variant (16.2%), followed by sentiment analysis (8.2%), dialect identification (3.8%), poetry classification (1.3%), and POS tagging (1.3%). This indicates the importance of optimal pairing of pre-trained models and fine-tuning tasks.

On average the CAMeLBERT-MSA model performs best, and is the winner in 10 out of 12 subtasks. The following are the two exceptions: (a) the CAMeLBERT-DA model performs best in the highly dialectal MADAR-6 subtask; and (b) the CAMeLBERT-CA model outperforms other models in the poetry classification task, which is

Task	Dataset	Variant	%Performance Star	Mix	MSA	DA	CA	Max-Min	%OOV Mix	MSA	DA	CA
NER	ANERcorp	MSA	**82.4**	80.2	**82.4**	74.2	66.2	16.2	0.2	0.2	1.4	4.2
POS	PATB (MSA)	MSA	**97.4**	97.3	**97.4**	96.5	96.6	1.0	0.2	0.2	0.9	3.0
	ARZTB (EGY)	DA	90.1	90.1	**90.8**	89.4	88.6	2.2	0.6	0.8	1.0	7.3
	Gumar (GLF)	DA	**97.3**	**97.3**	97.1	97.0	96.5	0.7	0.2	0.8	0.3	5.4
SA	ASTD	MSA	**76.9**	76.3	**76.9**	74.6	69.4	7.5	0.9	1.1	1.2	5.3
	ArSAS	MSA	**93.0**	92.7	**93.0**	91.8	89.4	3.6	1.3	1.5	1.8	7.4
	SemEval	MSA	**72.1**	69.0	**72.1**	68.4	58.5	13.6	1.9	2.1	2.4	6.6
DID	MADAR-26	DA	**62.9**	**62.9**	62.6	61.8	61.9	0.8	0.4	0.8	0.8	7.5
	MADAR-6	DA	**92.5**	**92.5**	91.9	92.2	91.5	0.7	0.1	1.1	0.2	8.1
	MADAR-Twitter-5	MSA	**77.6**	75.7	**77.6**	74.2	71.4	6.2	2.4	2.6	3.0	6.7
	NADI	DA	24.7	24.7	**24.9**	20.1	17.3	7.6	1.6	2.0	2.4	8.1
Poetry	APCD	CA	**80.9**	79.8	79.7	79.6	**80.9**	1.3	0.4	1.1	2.7	0.9
Variant-wise-average		MSA	**83.2**	81.9	**83.2**	79.9	75.3	8.0	1.2	1.3	1.8	5.5
		DA	**73.5**	**73.5**	**73.5**	72.1	71.1	2.3	0.6	1.1	0.9	7.3
		CA	**80.9**	79.8	79.7	79.6	**80.9**	1.3	0.4	1.1	2.7	0.9
Macro-average			**79.0**	78.2	78.9	76.6	74.0	4.9	0.9	1.2	1.5	5.9

Table 4: Performance of CAMeLBERT models trained on MSA, DA, CA, and their Mix data. Star refers to a way of choosing CAMeLBERT models based on the language variant of the fine-tuning dataset. We use F_1 score as a metric for all tasks. Max-Min refers to the difference in performance among CAMeLBERT's MSA, DA, and CA models only. Variant-wise-average refers to average over a group of tasks in the same language variant. The best results among CAMeLBERT's MSA, DA, and CA models are underlined. The best results among CAMeLBERT's MSA, DA, CA, Mix, and Star are in bold. The OOV rate for each dataset is calculated based on the data used for pre-training each model. We underline the lowest OOV value per dataset.

in classical Arabic. These two exceptions suggest that performance in fine-tuning tasks may be associated with the variant proximity of the pre-training data to fine-tuning data; although we also acknowledge that CAMeLBERT-MSA's data is two times the size of CAMeLBERT-DA's, and 18 times the size of CAMeLBERT-CA's, which may give CAMeLBERT-MSA an advantage.

OOV Effect To further investigate the effect of variant proximity on performance, we compute the word out-of-vocabulary (OOV) rate of all fine-tuning test sets against the pre-training data, as a way to estimate their similarity.[6] Note that CAMeLBERT-Mix, where we concatenate MSA, DA, and CA pre-training data, has the lowest OOV rate by design. In Table 4, we show the OOV rates for each dataset.

In all the cases except Gumar (11 out of 12), we obtain the best performance where the model has the lowest OOV rate. To better understand the relationship between fine-tuning performance and OOV rates, we assessed the correlation between model performance and OOV rates for each dataset. We found a strong negative correlation of -0.82 on average. Interestingly, the CAMeLBERT-CA model which was pre-trained only on 6 GB of data outperforms other models that are pre-trained on significantly larger data in the poetry classification task. It is also worth mentioning that the CAMeLBERT-CA model has the lowest OOV rate on the poetry dataset (0.9%), while having access to approximately 18 times less data compared to the CAMeLBERT-MSA model (6GB vs 107GB). This again suggests that the variant proximity of pre-training data to fine-tuning data is more important than the size of pre-training data.

5.2.2 Mix of MSA, DA, and CA

To further study the interplay of language variants and pre-training data size, we pre-trained a model (CAMeLBERT-Mix) on the concatenation of the MSA, DA, and CA datasets. This is the largest dataset used to pre-train an Arabic language model to date. As shown in Table 4, the CAMeLBERT-Mix model improves over other models in three cases, all of which are dialectal, suggesting that the

[6]We use a simple token as a unit, where we segment text with white space and punctuation.

Task	Dataset	Variant	Star	Mix	MSA	DA	CA	X_1	X_2	X_3	X_4	X_5	X_6	X_7	X_8
			%Performance												
NER	ANERcorp	MSA	82.4	80.2	82.4	74.2	66.2	76.7	82.4	82.0	80.3	77.3	82.0	79.3	**83.6**
POS	PATB (MSA)	MSA	**97.4**	97.3	**97.4**	96.5	96.6	96.5	97.2	97.3	97.2	96.8	**97.4**	96.8	**97.4**
	ARZTB (EGY)	DA	90.1	90.1	90.8	89.4	88.6	88.1	89.9	**91.2**	89.8	90.1	90.6	90.3	90.5
	Gumar (GLF)	DA	**97.3**	**97.3**	97.1	97.0	96.5	96.3	97.0	**97.3**	96.9	96.7	97.1	97.0	97.0
SA	ASTD	MSA	76.9	76.3	76.9	74.6	69.4	64.5	74.2	**78.1**	69.5	71.7	72.0	77.6	72.0
	ArSAS	MSA	93.0	92.7	93.0	91.8	89.4	88.4	91.5	**93.3**	89.4	90.8	90.8	92.3	90.8
	SemEval	MSA	72.1	69.0	72.1	68.4	58.5	57.5	69.5	**72.7**	66.8	67.2	66.7	69.7	69.8
DID	MADAR-26	DA	**62.9**	**62.9**	62.6	61.8	61.9	60.4	61.9	62.2	59.6	59.6	59.5	61.9	59.3
	MADAR-6	DA	**92.5**	**92.5**	91.9	92.2	91.5	90.8	91.9	92.3	90.6	90.8	90.4	91.1	90.4
	MADAR-Twitter-5	MSA	77.6	75.7	77.6	74.2	71.4	71.8	**79.0**	**79.0**	77.0	76.5	74.4	77.2	74.9
	NADI	DA	24.7	24.7	24.9	20.1	17.3	16.7	21.1	24.5	23.5	25.4	20.5	**26.1**	24.2
Poetry	APCD	CA	**80.9**	79.8	79.7	79.6	**80.9**	78.8	79.6	79.9	75.1	73.6	74.5	74.2	74.9
Variant-wise-average		MSA	83.2	81.9	83.2	79.9	75.3	75.9	82.3	**83.7**	80.0	80.1	80.6	82.2	81.4
		DA	**73.5**	**73.5**	**73.5**	72.1	71.1	70.5	72.4	**73.5**	72.1	72.5	71.6	73.3	72.3
		CA	**80.9**	79.8	79.7	79.6	**80.9**	78.8	79.6	79.9	75.1	73.6	74.5	74.2	74.9
Macro-average			79.0	78.2	78.9	76.6	74.0	73.9	77.9	**79.1**	76.3	76.4	76.3	77.8	77.1

Table 5: Performance of CAMeLBERT models and other existing models. We use F_1 score as a metric for all the tasks. Star refers to a way of choosing CAMeLBERT models based on the language variant of the fine-tuning dataset. $X_1, \cdots, X_8$ corresponds to the models in Table 1. Variant-wise-average refers to average over a group of tasks in the same language variant. The best results among the models are in bold.

CAMeLBERT-Mix model does better in some dialectal context. However, we do not see an increase in performance in other cases when compared with the best performing model, although the size of the pre-training data and the variety of the data are increased. This suggests that having a wide language variety in pre-training data can be beneficial for DA subtasks, whereas variant proximity of pre-training data to fine-tuning data is important MSA and CA subtasks.

5.2.3 Selecting an Optimal Model

Taking these insights into consideration, one cannot help but consider the exciting possibility of a system-selection ensembling approach that can help users make decisions with reasonable expectations using what they know of their specific tasks. We outline here such a setup: the user has access to three versions of the models: CAMeLBERT's CA, MSA, and Mix. If the task data is known a priori to be CA, then we select the CAMeLBERT-CA model; if the task data is known to be MSA, we select the CAMeLBERT-MSA model; otherwise, we use the CAMeLBERT-Mix model (for dialects, i.e.). We report on this model in Table 4 and 5 as CAMeLBERT-Star.

It is noteworthy that this model is not the same as oracularly selecting the best performer among our four models (MSA, DA, CA, and Mix). In fact, it is lower in performance than such oracular system as the CAMeLBERT-MSA model performs better than CAMeLBERT-Mix model in ARZTB and NADI. We do not claim here that this is a foolproof method; however, it is an interesting candidate for *common wisdom* of the kind we are hoping to develop through this effort.

5.3 Comparison with Existing Models

Table 5 compares our work with other existing models. We do not use models that require morphological pre-tokenization to allow direct comparison, and also because existing tokenization systems are mostly focused on MSA or EGY (Pasha et al., 2014; Abdelali et al., 2016; Obeid et al., 2020).

We are aware that design decisions such as vocabulary size and number of training steps are not the same across these eight existing pre-trained models, which might be a contributing factor to their varying performances. We plan to investigate the effects of such decisions in future work.

Task Performance Complementarity The best model on average is AraBERTv02 (X_3); it wins or ties for a win in six out of 12 subtasks (four MSA and two DA). Our CAMeLBERT-Star is second overall on average, and it wins or ties for a win in five out of 12 subtasks (three DA, one MSA, one CA). Interestingly, the two systems are complementary in their performance and between the two they win or tie for a win in 10 out of 12 subtasks. The two remaining subtasks are uniquely won by MARBERT (X_7) (NADI, DA), and ARBERT (X_8) (ANERcorp, MSA). In practice, such complementarity can be exploited by system developers to achieve higher overall performance.

Size and Performance Considering the data size and performance of the other pre-trained models (X_1 to X_8), we observe a similar trend to our CAMeLBERT models. AraBERTv02 (X_3) is the best on average, with only 77GB of pre-training data. AraBERTv01 (X_2) is the smallest (24GB); however, on average it outperforms other models pre-trained on much larger datasets, such as MARBERT (X_7, 128GB), and ArabicBERT (X_4, 95GB). This confirms that pre-training data size may not be an important factor to fine-tuning performance, as we showed in Section 5.1.

Variant Proximity and Performance When we examine the proximity in terms of language variants of the pre-training data and the fine-tuning data across the eight existing pre-trained models, we observe the following. First, the monolingual MSA models (X_2, X_3, X_4, X_8) are better performers than the mixed models (X_5, X_7) on average (77.6% and 77.1%, respectively).[7] Second, the monolingual MSA models perform better than the mixed models in MSA subtasks on average (81.9% and 81.1%, respectively), while the mixed models perform better than the MSA models in DA subtasks on average (72.9% and 72.6%, respectively).[8] This result is consistent with our analysis of the CAMeLBERT-Mix and the CAMeLBERT-MSA models in Section 5.2, where we found that the CAMeLBERT-Mix model is the best choice for DA subtasks, whereas the CAMeLBERT-MSA model is the best in MSA subtasks.

On MARBERT and ARBERT In another study that compared models pre-trained on MSA alone or a mix of MSA and DA data, Abdul-Mageed et al. (2020a) reported that MARBERT (X_7, pre-trained on MSA-DA mix) is more powerful than ARBERT (X_8, pre-trained on MSA). In our study, we do replicate their specific relative performance in terms of macro-average in our experiments (77.8% for MARBERT and 77.1% for ARBERT). It is not clear why MARBERT and ARBERT do not exhibit similar trends as observed in the analysis of our own CAMeLBERT models and other existing models. This may be attributed to numerous factors such as the degree of MSA-DA mixture, genre, and the pre-training procedure details. It is also worth noting that the data used to pre-train our CAMeLBERT-MSA model is a subset of the data used to pre-train our CAMeLBERT-Mix model, whereas the pre-training data for MARBERT and ARBERT are derived from different data sources.

[7]The average over macro-average performances.

[8]The average over variant-wise-average performances.

6 Conclusion and Future Work

In this paper, we investigated the interplay of size, language variant, and fine-tuning task type in Arabic pre-trained language models using carefully controlled experiments on a number of Arabic NLP tasks. Our results show that pre-training data and subtask data variant proximity is more important than pre-training data size. We confirm these results on existing models. We exploit this insight in defining an optimized system selection model for the studied tasks. We make all of our created models and fine-tuning code publicly available.

In future work, we plan to explore other design decisions that may contribute to the fine-tuning performance, including vocabulary size, tokenization techniques, and additional data mixtures. We also plan to utilize CAMeLBERT models in a number of other Arabic NLP tasks, and integrate them in the open-source toolkit, CAMeL Tools (Obeid et al., 2020).

Acknowledgment

This research was supported with Cloud TPUs from Google's TensorFlow Research Cloud (TFRC). This work was also carried out on the High Performance Computing resources at New York University Abu Dhabi. The first and second authors were supported by the New York University Abu Dhabi Global PhD Student Fellowship program. We thank Salam Khalifa, and Ossama Obeid for helpful discussions. We also thank the anonymous reviewers for their valuable comments.

References

Ahmed Abdelali, Kareem Darwish, Nadir Durrani, and Hamdy Mubarak. 2016. Farasa: A fast and furious segmenter for Arabic. In *Proceedings of the Conference of the North American Chapter of the Association for Computational Linguistics (NAACL)*, pages 11–16, San Diego, California.

Ahmed Abdelali, Hamdy Mubarak, Younes Samih, Sabit Hassan, and Kareem Darwish. 2020. Arabic dialect identification in the wild.

Muhammad Abdul-Mageed, AbdelRahim Elmadany, and El Moatez Billah Nagoudi. 2020a. ARBERT & MARBERT: Deep bidirectional transformers for Arabic.

Muhammad Abdul-Mageed, Chiyu Zhang, Houda Bouamor, and Nizar Habash. 2020b. NADI 2020: The First Nuanced Arabic Dialect Identification Shared Task. In *Proceedings of the Fifth Arabic Natural Language Processing Workshop (WANLP 2020)*, Barcelona, Spain.

Ibrahim Abu Farha and Walid Magdy. 2019. Mazajak: An online Arabic sentiment analyser. In *Proceedings of the Fourth Arabic Natural Language Processing Workshop*, pages 192–198, Florence, Italy. Association for Computational Linguistics.

Kathrein Abu Kwaik, Motaz Saad, Stergios Chatzikyriakidis, and Simon Dobnik. 2018. Shami: A corpus of Levantine Arabic dialects. In *Proceedings of the Eleventh International Conference on Language Resources and Evaluation (LREC 2018)*, Miyazaki, Japan. European Language Resources Association (ELRA).

Nora Al-Twairesh, Rawan Al-Matham, Nora Madi, Nada Almugren, Al-Hanouf Al-Aljmi, Shahad Alshalan, Raghad Alshalan, Nafla Alrumayyan, Shams Al-Manea, Sumayah Bawazeer, Nourah Al-Mutlaq, Nada Almanea, Waad Bin Huwaymil, Dalal Alqusair, Reem Alotaibi, Suha Al-Senaydi, and Abeer Alfutamani. 2018. SUAR: Towards building a corpus for the Saudi dialect. In *Proceedings of the International Conference on Arabic Computational Linguistics (ACLing)*.

Ahmed Ali, Preslav Nakov, Peter Bell, and Steve Renals. 2017. WERD: using social text spelling variants for evaluating dialectal speech recognition. In *2017 IEEE Automatic Speech Recognition and Understanding Workshop, ASRU 2017, Okinawa, Japan, December 16-20, 2017*, pages 141–148. IEEE.

Khalid Almeman and Mark Lee. 2013. Automatic building of Arabic multi dialect text corpora by bootstrapping dialect words. In *Proceedings of the International Conference on Communications, Signal Processing, and their Applications (ICCSPA)*, pages 1–6.

Wissam Antoun, Fady Baly, and Hazem Hajj. 2020. AraBERT: Transformer-based model for Arabic language understanding. In *Proceedings of the 4th Workshop on Open-Source Arabic Corpora and Processing Tools, with a Shared Task on Offensive Language Detection*, pages 9–15, Marseille, France. European Language Resource Association.

Appen Pty Ltd. 2006a. Gulf Arabic Conversational Telephone Speech, Transcripts LDC2006T15.

Appen Pty Ltd. 2006b. Iraqi Arabic Conversational Telephone Speech, Transcripts LDC2006T16.

Appen Pty Ltd. 2007. Levantine Arabic Conversational Telephone Speech, Transcripts LDC2007T01.

Ramy Baly, Alaa Khaddaj, Hazem Hajj, Wassim El-Hajj, and Khaled Bashir Shaban. 2019. ArSentD-LEV: A multi-topic corpus for target-based sentiment analysis in Arabic Levantine tweets.

BBN Technologies. 2005. BBN/AUB DARPA Babylon Levantine Arabic Speech and Transcripts LDC2005S08.

Yassine Benajiba, Paolo Rosso, and José Miguel Benedí Ruiz. 2007. ANERsys: An Arabic Named Entity Recognition System Based on Maximum Entropy. In *Computational Linguistics and Intelligent Text Processing*, pages 143–153, Berlin, Heidelberg. Springer Berlin Heidelberg.

Houda Bouamor, Nizar Habash, and Kemal Oflazer. 2014. A multidialectal parallel corpus of Arabic. In *Proceedings of the Language Resources and Evaluation Conference (LREC)*, Reykjavik, Iceland.

Houda Bouamor, Nizar Habash, Mohammad Salameh, Wajdi Zaghouani, Owen Rambow, Dana Abdulrahim, Ossama Obeid, Salam Khalifa, Fadhl Eryani, Alexander Erdmann, and Kemal Oflazer. 2018. The MADAR Arabic Dialect Corpus and Lexicon. In *Proceedings of the Language Resources and Evaluation Conference (LREC)*, Miyazaki, Japan.

Houda Bouamor, Sabit Hassan, and Nizar Habash. 2019. The MADAR shared task on Arabic fine-grained dialect identification. In *Proceedings of the Fourth Arabic Natural Language Processing Workshop*, pages 199–207, Florence, Italy. Association for Computational Linguistics.

Song Chen, Dana Fore, Stephanie Strassel, Haejoong Lee, and Jonathan Wright. 2017. BOLT Egyptian Arabic SMS/Chat and Transliteration LDC2017T07.

Ethan A. Chi, John Hewitt, and Christopher D. Manning. 2020. Finding universal grammatical relations in multilingual BERT. In *Proceedings of the 58th Annual Meeting of the Association for Computational Linguistics*, pages 5564–5577, Online. Association for Computational Linguistics.

Ryan Cotterell and Chris Callison-Burch. 2014. A Multi-Dialect, Multi-Genre Corpus of Informal Written Arabic. In *Proceedings of the Language Resources and Evaluation Conference (LREC)*, pages 241–245, Reykjavik, Iceland.

Jacob Devlin, Ming-Wei Chang, Kenton Lee, and Kristina Toutanova. 2019. BERT: Pre-training of deep bidirectional transformers for language understanding. In *Proceedings of the 2019 Conference of the North American Chapter of the Association for Computational Linguistics: Human Language Technologies, Volume 1 (Long and Short Papers)*, pages 4171–4186, Minneapolis, Minnesota. Association for Computational Linguistics.

Mahmoud El-Haj. 2020. Habibi - a multi dialect multi national Arabic song lyrics corpus. In *Proceedings of The 12th Language Resources and Evaluation Conference*, pages 1318–1326, Marseille, France. European Language Resources Association.

Ibrahim Abu El-Khair. 2016. 1.5 billion words Arabic corpus. *CoRR*, abs/1611.04033.

AbdelRahim Elmadany, Hamdy Mubarak, and Walid Magdy. 2018. ArSAS: An Arabic speech-act and sentiment corpus of tweets. In *Proceedings of the Eleventh International Conference on Language Resources and Evaluation (LREC 2018)*, Paris, France. European Language Resources Association (ELRA).

Hassan Gadalla, Hanaa Kilany, Howaida Arram, Ashraf Yacoub, Alaa El-Habashi, Amr Shalaby, Krisjanis Karins, Everett Rowson, Robert MacIntyre, Paul Kingsbury, David Graff, and Cynthia McLemore. 1997. CALLHOME Egyptian Arabic transcripts LDC97T19. Web Download. Philadelphia: Linguistic Data Consortium.

John Hewitt and Christopher D. Manning. 2019. A structural probe for finding syntax in word representations. In *Proceedings of the 2019 Conference of the North American Chapter of the Association for Computational Linguistics: Human Language Technologies, Volume 1 (Long and Short Papers)*, pages 4129–4138, Minneapolis, Minnesota. Association for Computational Linguistics.

Mustafa Jarrar, Nizar Habash, Faeq Alrimawi, Diyam Akra, and Nasser Zalmout. 2016. Curras: an annotated corpus for the Palestinian Arabic dialect. *Language Resources and Evaluation*, pages 1–31.

Ganesh Jawahar, Benoît Sagot, and Djamé Seddah. 2019. What does BERT learn about the structure of language? In *Proceedings of the 57th Annual Meeting of the Association for Computational Linguistics*, pages 3651–3657, Florence, Italy. Association for Computational Linguistics.

Salam Khalifa, Nizar Habash, Fadhl Eryani, Ossama Obeid, Dana Abdulrahim, and Meera Al Kaabi. 2018. A morphologically annotated corpus of Emirati Arabic. In *Proceedings of the Eleventh International Conference on Language Resources and Evaluation (LREC 2018)*, Miyazaki, Japan. European Language Resources Association (ELRA).

Artur Kulmizev, Vinit Ravishankar, Mostafa Abdou, and Joakim Nivre. 2020. Do neural language models show preferences for syntactic formalisms? In *Proceedings of the 58th Annual Meeting of the Association for Computational Linguistics*, pages 4077–4091, Online. Association for Computational Linguistics.

Wuwei Lan, Yang Chen, Wei Xu, and Alan Ritter. 2020. An empirical study of pre-trained transformers for Arabic information extraction. In *Proceedings of the 2020 Conference on Empirical Methods in Natural Language Processing (EMNLP)*, pages 4727–4734, Online. Association for Computational Linguistics.

Linguistic Data Consortium. 2002. CALLHOME Egyptian Arabic Transcripts Supplement LDC2002T38.

Nelson F. Liu, Matt Gardner, Yonatan Belinkov, Matthew E. Peters, and Noah A. Smith. 2019a. Linguistic knowledge and transferability of contextual representations. In *Proceedings of the 2019 Conference of the North American Chapter of the Association for Computational Linguistics: Human Language Technologies, Volume 1 (Long and Short Papers)*, pages 1073–1094, Minneapolis, Minnesota. Association for Computational Linguistics.

Yinhan Liu, Myle Ott, Naman Goyal, Jingfei Du, Mandar Joshi, Danqi Chen, Omer Levy, Mike Lewis, Luke Zettlemoyer, and Veselin Stoyanov. 2019b. RoBERTa: A robustly optimized BERT pretraining approach.

Mohamed Maamouri, Ann Bies, Tim Buckwalter, and Wigdan Mekki. 2004. The Penn Arabic Treebank: Building a Large-Scale Annotated Arabic Corpus. In *Proceedings of the International Conference on Arabic Language Resources and Tools*, pages 102–109, Cairo, Egypt.

Mohamed Maamouri, Ann Bies, Seth Kulick, Dalila Tabessi, and Sondos Krouna. 2012. Egyptian Arabic Treebank DF Parts 1-8 V2.0 - LDC catalog numbers LDC2012E93, LDC2012E98, LDC2012E89, LDC2012E99, LDC2012E107, LDC2012E125, LDC2013E12, LDC2013E21.

Mohamed Maamouri, Tim Buckwalter, David Graff, and Hubert Jin. 2006. Levantine Arabic QT Training Data Set 5, Transcripts LDC2006T07.

Mohamed Maamouri, Tim Buckwalter, David Graff, and Hubert Jin. 2007. Fisher Levantine Arabic Conversational Telephone Speech, Transcripts LDC2007T04.

Mohamed Maamouri, Tim Buckwalter, and Hubert Jin. 2005. Levantine Arabic QT Training Data Set 4 (Speech + Transcripts) LDC2005S14.

Karima Meftouh, Salima Harrat, Salma Jamoussi, Mourad Abbas, and Kamel Smaili. 2015. Machine translation experiments on PADIC: A parallel Arabic dialect corpus. In *Proceedings of the Pacific Asia Conference on Language, Information and Computation*.

Vincent Micheli, Martin d'Hoffschmidt, and François Fleuret. 2020. On the importance of pre-training data volume for compact language models. In *Proceedings of the 2020 Conference on Empirical Methods in Natural Language Processing (EMNLP)*, pages 7853–7858, Online. Association for Computational Linguistics.

Mahmoud Nabil, Mohamed Aly, and Amir Atiya. 2015. ASTD: Arabic sentiment tweets dataset. In *Proceedings of the 2015 Conference on Empirical Methods in Natural Language Processing*, pages 2515–2519, Lisbon, Portugal. Association for Computational Linguistics.

Lorenz Nigst, Maxim Romanov, Sarah Bowen Savant, Masoumeh Seydi, and Peter Verkinderen. 2020. OpenITI: a Machine-Readable Corpus of Islamicate Texts.

Ossama Obeid, Nasser Zalmout, Salam Khalifa, Dima Taji, Mai Oudah, Bashar Alhafni, Go Inoue, Fadhl Eryani, Alexander Erdmann, and Nizar Habash. 2020. CAMeL tools: An open source python toolkit for Arabic natural language processing. In *Proceedings of the 12th Language Resources and Evaluation Conference*, pages 7022–7032, Marseille, France. European Language Resources Association.

Pedro Javier Ortiz Suárez, Laurent Romary, and Benoît Sagot. 2020. A monolingual approach to contextualized word embeddings for mid-resource languages. In *Proceedings of the 58th Annual Meeting of the Association for Computational Linguistics*, pages 1703–1714, Online. Association for Computational Linguistics.

Robert Parker, David Graff, Ke Chen, Junbo Kong, and Kazuaki Maeda. 2011. Arabic Gigaword Fifth Edition. LDC catalog number No. LDC2011T11, ISBN 1-58563-595-2.

Arfath Pasha, Mohamed Al-Badrashiny, Mona Diab, Ahmed El Kholy, Ramy Eskander, Nizar Habash, Manoj Pooleery, Owen Rambow, and Ryan Roth. 2014. MADAMIRA: A fast, comprehensive tool for morphological analysis and disambiguation of Arabic. In *Proceedings of the Language Resources and Evaluation Conference (LREC)*, pages 1094–1101, Reykjavik, Iceland.

Raytheon BBN Technologies, Linguistic Data Consortium, and Sakhr Software. 2012. Arabic-Dialect/English Parallel Text LDC2012T09.

Sara Rosenthal, Noura Farra, and Preslav Nakov. 2017. Semeval-2017 task 4: Sentiment analysis in twitter. In *Proceedings of the International Workshop on Semantic Evaluation (SemEval)*, pages 501–516, Vancouver, Canada.

Phillip Rust, Jonas Pfeiffer, Ivan Vulić, Sebastian Ruder, and Iryna Gurevych. 2020. How good is your tokenizer? on the monolingual performance of multilingual language models.

Ali Safaya, Moutasem Abdullatif, and Deniz Yuret. 2020. KUISAIL at SemEval-2020 task 12: BERT-CNN for offensive speech identification in social media. In *Proceedings of the Fourteenth Workshop on Semantic Evaluation*, pages 2054–2059, Barcelona (online). International Committee for Computational Linguistics.

Ahmed Salama, Houda Bouamor, Behrang Mohit, and Kemal Oflazer. 2014. YouDACC: the Youtube Dialectal Arabic Comment Corpus. In *Proceedings of the Language Resources and Evaluation Conference (LREC)*, pages 1246–1251, Reykjavik, Iceland.

Mohammad Salameh, Houda Bouamor, and Nizar Habash. 2018. Fine-grained Arabic dialect identification. In *Proceedings of the 27th International Conference on Computational Linguistics*, pages 1332–1344, Santa Fe, New Mexico, USA. Association for Computational Linguistics.

Mike Schuster and Kaisuke Nakajima. 2012. Japanese and Korean voice search. In *International Conference on Acoustics, Speech and Signal Processing*, pages 5149–5152.

Bashar Talafha, Mohammad Ali, Muhy Eddin Za'ter, Haitham Seelawi, Ibraheem Tuffaha, Mostafa Samir, Wael Farhan, and Hussein Al-Natsheh. 2020. Multi-dialect Arabic BERT for country-level dialect identification. In *Proceedings of the Fifth Arabic Natural Language Processing Workshop*, pages 111–118, Barcelona, Spain (Online). Association for Computational Linguistics.

Ian Tenney, Dipanjan Das, and Ellie Pavlick. 2019a. BERT rediscovers the classical NLP pipeline. In *Proceedings of the 57th Annual Meeting of the Association for Computational Linguistics*, pages 4593–4601, Florence, Italy. Association for Computational Linguistics.

Ian Tenney, Patrick Xia, Berlin Chen, Alex Wang, Adam Poliak, R Thomas McCoy, Najoung Kim, Benjamin Van Durme, Sam Bowman, Dipanjan Das, and Ellie Pavlick. 2019b. What do you learn from context? probing for sentence structure in contextualized word representations. In *International Conference on Learning Representations*.

Ivan Vulić, Edoardo Maria Ponti, Robert Litschko, Goran Glavaš, and Anna Korhonen. 2020. Probing pretrained language models for lexical semantics. In *Proceedings of the 2020 Conference on Empirical Methods in Natural Language Processing (EMNLP)*, pages 7222–7240, Online. Association for Computational Linguistics.

Thomas Wolf, Lysandre Debut, Victor Sanh, Julien Chaumond, Clement Delangue, Anthony Moi, Pierric Cistac, Tim Rault, Rémi Louf, Morgan Funtowicz, Joe Davison, Sam Shleifer, Patrick von Platen, Clara Ma, Yacine Jernite, Julien Plu, Canwen Xu, Teven Le Scao, Sylvain Gugger, Mariama Drame, Quentin Lhoest, and Alexander M. Rush. 2020. Huggingface's transformers: State-of-the-art natural language processing.

Shijie Wu and Mark Dredze. 2019. Beto, bentz, becas: The surprising cross-lingual effectiveness of BERT. In *Proceedings of the 2019 Conference on Empirical Methods in Natural Language Processing and the 9th International Joint Conference on Natural Language Processing (EMNLP-IJCNLP)*, pages 833–844, Hong Kong, China. Association for Computational Linguistics.

Waleed A. Yousef, Omar M. Ibrahime, Taha M. Madbouly, and Moustafa A. Mahmoud. 2019. Learning meters of Arabic and English poems with recurrent neural networks: a step forward for language understanding and synthesis.

Wajdi Zaghouani and Anis Charfi. 2018. ArapTweet: A Large Multi-Dialect Twitter Corpus for Gender, Age and Language Variety Identification. In *Proceedings of the Language Resources and Evaluation Conference (LREC)*, Miyazaki, Japan.

Omar F Zaidan and Chris Callison-Burch. 2011. The Arabic Online Commentary Dataset: an Annotated Dataset of Informal Arabic With High Dialectal Content. In *Proceedings of the Conference of the Association for Computational Linguistics (ACL)*, pages 37–41.

Imad Zeroual, Dirk Goldhahn, Thomas Eckart, and Abdelhak Lakhouaja. 2019. OSIAN: Open source international Arabic news corpus - preparation and integration into the CLARIN-infrastructure. In *Proceedings of the Fourth Arabic Natural Language Processing Workshop*, pages 175–182, Florence, Italy. Association for Computational Linguistics.

Yian Zhang, Alex Warstadt, Haau-Sing Li, and Samuel R. Bowman. 2020. When do you need billions of words of pretraining data?

Automatic Difficulty Classification of Arabic Sentences

Nouran Khallaf, Serge Sharoff
School of Languages, University of Leeds
Leeds, LS2 9JT, United Kingdom
mlnak,s.sharoff@leeds.ac.uk

Abstract

In this paper, we present a Modern Standard Arabic (MSA) Sentence difficulty classifier, which predicts the difficulty of sentences for language learners using either the CEFR proficiency levels or the binary classification as simple or complex. We compare the use of sentence embeddings of different kinds (fastText, mBERT , XLM-R and Arabic-BERT), as well as traditional language features such as POS tags, dependency trees, readability scores and frequency lists for language learners. Our best results have been achieved using finedtuned Arabic-BERT. The accuracy of our 3-way CEFR classification is F-1 of 0.80 and 0.75 for Arabic-Bert and XLM-R classification respectively and 0.71 Spearman correlation for regression. Our binary difficulty classifier reaches F-1 0.94 and F-1 0.98 for sentence-pair semantic similarity classifier.

1 Introduction

In the last century, measuring *text readability (TR)* has been undertaken in education, psychology, and linguistics. There appears to be some agreement that TR is the quality of a given text to be easy to comprehend by its readers in adequate time with reasonable effort (Cavalli-Sforza et al., 2018). Research to date has tended to focus on assigning readability levels to whole text rather than to individual sentences, despite the fact that any text is composed of a number of sentences, which vary in their difficulty (Schumacher et al., 2016). Assigning readability levels for a text is a challenging task and it is even more challenging on the sentence level as much less information is available. Also, the sentence difficulty is influenced by many parameters, such as, genre or topics, as well grammatical structures, which need to be combined in a single classifier. Difficulty assessment at the sentence level is a more challenging task in comparison to the better researched text level task, but the availability of a readability sentence classifier for Arabic is vital, since this is a prerequisite for research on *automatic text simplification* (ATS), i.e. the process of reducing text-linguistic complexity, while maintaining its meaning (Saggion, 2017).

We focus here on experiments aimed at measuring to what extent a sentence is understandable by a reader, such as a learner of Arabic as a foreign language, and at exploring different methods for readability assessment. The main aim of this paper lies in developing and testing different sentence representation methodologies, which range from using linguistic knowledge via feature-based machine learning to modern neural methods.

In summary, the contributions of this paper are:

1. We compiled a novel dataset for training on the sentence level;
2. We developed a range of linguistic features, including POS, syntax and frequency information;
3. We evaluated a range of different sentence embedding approaches, such as fastText, BERT and XLM-R, and compared them to the linguistic features;
4. We cast the readability assessment as a regression problem as well as a classification problem;
5. Our model is the first sentence difficulty system available for Arabic.

2 Corpora and Tools

2.1 Dataset One: Sentence-level annotation

This dataset was used for Arabic sentence difficulty classification. We started building our own dataset by compiling a corpus from three available source classified for readability on the document level along with a large Arabic corpus obtained by Web crawling.

Proceedings of the Sixth Arabic Natural Language Processing Workshop, pages 105–114
Kyiv, Ukraine (Virtual), April 19, 2021.

The first corpus source is the reading section of the **Gloss**[1] Corpus developed by the Defense Language Institute (DLI). It has been treated as a gold standard and used in the most recent studies on document level predictions (Forsyth, 2014; Saddiki et al., 2015; Nassiri et al., 2018a,b). Texts in Gloss have been annotated on a six level scale of the Inter-Agency Language Roundtable (IL), which has been matched to the CEFR levels according to the schema introduced by (Tschirner et al., 2015). Gloss is divided according to the four competence areas (lexical, structural, socio-cultural and discursive) and ten different genres (culture, economy, politics, environment, geography, military, politics, science, security, society, and technology).

The second corpus source is the **ALC** , which consists of Arabic written text produced by learners of Arabic in Saudi Arabia collected by (Alfaifi and Atwell, 2013). Each text file is annotated with a proficiency level of the student. We mapped these student proficiency levels to CEFR levels.

Our third corpus source comes from textbook **"Al-Kitaab fii TaAallum al-Arabiyya"** (Brustad et al., 2015) which was compiled from texts and sentences from parts one and two of the third edition but only texts from part three third edition. This book is widely used to teaching Arabic as a second language. These texts were originally classified according to the American Council on the Teaching of Foreign Languages (ACTFL) guidelines which we mapped to CEFR levels.

As these corpora have been annotated on the document level and not on the sentence level, we assigned each sentence to the document level in which it appears, by using several filtering heuristics, such as sentence length and containment, as well as via re-annotation through machine learning, see the dataset cleaning procedure below.

A counterpart corpus of texts not produced for language learners in mind is provided by I-AR, 75,630 Arabic web pages collected by wide crawling (Sharoff, 2006). A random snapshot of 8627 sentences longer than 15 words was used to extend the limitations of C-level sentences coming from corpora for language learners.

Table 1 shows distribution of the number of used sentences and tokens per each Common European Framework of language proficiency Reference [CEFR] Level. In principle we have data for 5-way (A1, A2, B1, etc), 3-way (A, B or C) and binary (A+B vs C) classification tasks, but here in this presentation, we focus on the 3-way and binary (simple vs complex) classification tasks.

[1] https://gloss.dliflc.edu/

CEFR	**Old**		**New**	
	S	T	S	T
A	8661	187225	9030	195343
B	5532	126805	5083	117825
C	8627	287275	8627	287275
Total	22820	601305	22740	600443

Table 1: (S)sentences and (T)tokens available per each CEFR Level in the two versions of the corpus

Dataset cleaning: In our initial experiments we noticed unreliable sentence-level assignments in the training corpus. Therefore, we decided to improve the quality of the training corpus by an error analysis strategy introduced by Di Bari et al. (2014), which is based on detecting agreement between classifiers belonging to different Machine Learning paradigms. The cases when the majority of the classifiers agreed on predicting a label while the gold standard was different were inspected manually by a specialist in teaching Arabic. In our Dataset cleaning experiment we used the following classifiers: SVM (with the rbf kernel), Random Forest, KNeighbors, Softmax and XgBoost using linguistic features discussed in Section 3, trained them via cross-validation and compared their majority vote to the gold standard.

We modified the error classification tags introduced by Di Bari et al. (2014) as follows:

Wrong if the classifiers have wrongly labelled the data, and the gold standard is correct.

Modify if the classifiers are correct and we need to modify the gold standard.

Ambiguous if we consider both either label is possible based on different perspectives.

False is an added label which represent the disagreement between the gold standard and the classifiers, when neither is correct.

For each sentence, five different predictions are assigned. Compared to the gold standard CEFR-label, the classifiers agreed in predicting 10204 instances. Then what we need to consider is when all classifiers agree on the predicted label and it contradicts with the gold standard's one. In that matter, the classifiers agreed on 1943 sentence classification. We manually investigated random sentences and assigned the error classification tags. We found that the main classification confusion was in Level B instances. The analysis results as in Table 4 show the distribution of categories where each error type occurred. In the end, 380 instances had to be assigned to lower level (usually from B to A).

2.2 Dataset Two: Simplification examples

A set of simple/complex parallel sentences has been compiled from the internationally acclaimed Arabic novel **"Saaq al-Bambuu"** (Al-Sanousi, 2013) which has an authorized simplified version for students of Arabic as a second language (Familiar, 2016). We assume that a successful classifier should be able to detect sentences in the original text that require simplification. Dataset Two consists of 2980 parallel sentences Table 2.

Level	Sentence	Token
Simple A+B	2980	34447
Complex C	2980	46521
Total	5690	80968

Table 2: Number of Sentences and Tokens available per each CEFR Level in Dataset two

3 Features and extraction methods

We work with following groups of features in Table 3: Part of speech tagging features (POS-features); Syntactic structure features (Syntactic-features); CEFR-level lexical features; Sentence embeddings.

3.1 Linguistic features

While the sentence-level classification task is novel, we borrowed some features from previous studies of text-level readability (Forsyth, 2014; Saddiki et al., 2015; Nassiri et al., 2018a,b). We decided to exclude the sentence length from the feature set, as this creates an artificial skew in understanding what is difficult: more difficult writing styles are often associated with longer sentences, but it is not the sentence length which makes them difficult. Specifically, many long Arabic sentences contain shorter ones, which are connected by conjunctions such as ' /wa /= and'. According to the experience of language teachers such sentences do not present problems for the learners.

3.1.1 The POS-features

[Table 3 features (1-21)], these features represent the distribution of different word categories in the sentence, and the morpho-syntactic features of these words. According to Knowles and Don (2004), Arabic lemmatization, unlike that of English, is an essential process for analysing Arabic text, because it is a methodology for dictionary construction. Therefore, we used the Lemma/Type ratio instead of Word/Type ratio. Adding features represents the different verb types (Verb pseudo, Passive verbs, Perfective verbs, Imperfective verbs and 3rdperson). As conjunction is one of the important features in representing sentence complexity in Arabic (Forsyth, 2014), we used the annotated discourse connectors introduced by Alsaif (2012) by splitting this list into 23 simple connectors and 56 complex connectors referring to non-discourse connectors and discourse connectors respectively. For POS-features extraction we used MADAMIRA a robust Arabic morphological analyser and part of speech tagger (Pasha et al., 2014).

3.1.2 Syntactic features

Features (22-27) from Table 3 provide some information about the sentences structures and number of phrases as well as phases types. These features are derived from a dependency grammar analysis. Because dependency grammar is based on word-word relations, it assumes that the structure of a sentence consists of lexical items that are attached to each other by binary asymmetrical relations, which is known as dependency relations. These relations will be more representative for this task. We used CamelParser (Shahrour et al., 2016) a system for Arabic syntactic dependency analysis together with contextually disambiguated morphological features which rely on the MADAMIRA morphological analysis for more robust results.

3.1.3 CEFR-level lexical features

Features (28-34) from Table 3 are used to assign each word in the sentence with an appropriate CEFR level. For this, we created a new Arabic word list consisting of 8834 unique lemmas labelled with CEFR levels. This list was a combination of three frequency lists, 1) Buckwalter and Parkinson 5000 frequency word list based on

POS_Features			
1	TTR of word forms	**12**	Numeric_Adj_Tokens
2	Morphemes_word	**13**	Comparative_Adj_Tokens
3	TTR of Lemma	**14**	Conjunction _Tokens
4	Nouns_Tokens	**15**	Conjunction _Subordination _Tokens
5	Verbs_Tokens	**16**	Proper noun_Tokens
6	Adj_Tokens	**17**	Pronoun_Tokens
7	Verb_pseudo_Tokens	**18**	Punc_Tokens
8	Passive verbs_Tokens	**19**	Simple_Connector_Tokens
9	Perfective verbs _Tokens	**20**	Complex_ Connector _Tokens
10	Imperfective verbs _Tokens	**21**	All_Sent_ Connector _Tokens
11	3rdperson_verb_Verbs		
Syntactic Features			
22	Incidence of subjects	**25**	Incidence of coordination
23	Incidence of objects	**26**	Average phrases/sentence
24	Incidence of modifier/root	**27**	Average phrases depth
CEFR Word Features			
28	Incidence of Level A1	**32**	Incidence of Level C1
29	Incidence of Level A2	**33**	Incidence of Level C2
30	Incidence of Level B1	**34**	Word entropy with respect to CEFR
31	Incidence of Level B2		
35	**Sentence Embeddings Features**		

Table 3: The Feature set. (all measures are for the rate of tokens on the sentence levels)

30-million-word corpus of academic/non-academic and written/spoken texts (Buckwalter and Parkinson, 2014) KELLY's list which is produced from the Kelly project (Kilgarriff et al., 2014), which directly mapped a frequency word list to the CEFR levels using numerous corpora and languages, 3) lists presented at the beginning of each chapter in 'Al-Kitaab' (Brustad et al., 2015). Merging the lists and aligning them with the Madamira lemmatiser led to our new wide-coverage Arabic frequency list, which can be used to predict difficulty as Entropy of the probability distribution of each label in a sentence. The current list shows some consistency with the English profile list in terms of the percentage of words allocated to each CEFR level.

3.2 Sentence embeddings

In addition to the 34 traditional features we can represent sentences as embedding vectors using different neural models as following:

fastText A straightforward way to create sentence representations is to take a weighted average of word embeddings (WE) of each word, for example, using fastText vectors. This embedding was trained on Common Crawl and Wikipedia using fastText [2] tool. Using the Arabic ar.300.bin file in which each word in WE is represented by the 1D vector mapped of 300 attributes (Grave et al., 2018). We had to normalize the sentence vectors to have the same length with respect to dimensions. For this, we calculated tf-idf weights of each word in the corpus to use them as weights:

$$s = w_1 w_2 \ldots . w_n$$

$$Embed.[s] = \frac{1}{n} \sum_i tfidf[w_i] * Embed.[w_i] \quad (1)$$

Universal sentence encoder (Yang et al., 2019) This model requires modeling the meaning of word sequences rather than just individual words. Also it was generated mainly to be used on the sentence level which after sentence tokenization, it encodes sentence to a 512-dimensional vector. We used here the large version[3].

Multilingual BERT (Devlin et al., 2018) Pretrained transformers models proved their ability to learn successful representations of language inspired by the transformer model presented in

[2] https://fasttext.cc/docs/en/crawl-vectors.html

[3] https://tfhub.dev/google/universal-sentence-encoder-multilingual/1

(Vaswani et al., 2017) — who introduced using attention instead to incorporate context information into sequence representation. BERT. Here, we used the last layer produced by BERT transformers while padding the sentences to the maximum length of 128 tokens.

XLM-R (Conneau et al., 2019) This is another multilingual BERT-like model, which is different from mBERT by being trained on Common Crawl (instead of Wikipedias) with slightly different parameters. We used the same setup for classification as in the case of mBERT, while also testing a different setup of combining its output with linguistic features and using it as a joined vector of features for traditional ML classification.

Arabic BERT We trained two available BERT-like pre-trained Arabic transformer models available at Hugging face transformers (AraBERT[4] and Arabic-BERT[5]).

Both models contain both Modern Standard Arabic (MSA) and Dialectal Arabic (DA). The pre-training data used for the AraBERT model consist of 70 million sentences (Antoun et al., 2020). Arabic-BERT trained on both filtered Arabic Common Crawl and a recent dump of Arabic Wikipedia contain approximately 8.2 Billion words(Safaya et al., 2020).

4 Experiments

CEFR language proficiency levels can be presented as labels or as a continuous scale. The former is solved as a classification task with macro-averaged F-1 as the main measure for accuracy. The latter is solved as a regression task (Vajjala and Loo, 2014). At first we decided to work with the three main levels (A,B,and C) because it was quite difficult to determine the boundary between the inner sub levels as in the boundary between B1 and B2.Yet, the other binary classification is either Simple (A+B) or Complex (C). Here there is a problem for evaluation, since the gold standard labels are represented as integers 1, 2, 3 (for the A, B and C levels respectively), which leads to a large number of ties. Out of the standard correlation measures, Kendall's tau-b is designed to handle ties, so in addition to Pearson's ρ this is our measure for regression (Maurice and Dickinson, 1990).

[4]https://huggingface.co/aubmindlab/bert-base-arabert

[5]https://huggingface.co/asafaya/

Classification models	**P**	**R**	**F-1**
Features			
KNeighbors	0.51	0.55	0.52
Naive bayes	0.68	0.65	0.65
Decision Tree	0.75	0.77	0.74
Random Forest	0.59	0.75	0.66
XgBoost	0.74	0.77	0.74
Softmax	0.74	0.77	0.74
SVM, Linear	0.75	0.77	0.74
SVM, rbf kernel	**0.75**	**0.77**	**0.75**
Neural			
FastText	0.57	0.59	0.58
UCS	0.52	0.53	0.52
mBERT	0.53	0.54	0.53
ArabicBERT	**0.78**	**0.80**	**0.80**
AraBERT	0.73	0.73	0.73
XLM-R	0.56	0.70	0.61

Table 4: 3-way classification using weighted macro-averaged precision, recall and F-1, Dataset One Using all features versus neural models.

4.1 Readability as a Classification Problem

Table 4 presents the results of classification using updated version of dataset one after application of the error analysis. Applying different ML approaches with 10-fold cross-validation on the 3-way multi-class classification. The classification results as presented in Table 4 divided into two categories: 1) [Linguistics] adding XLM-R vectors to the original set of linguistics features and train with 1058 features [1024 XLM-R dimensions + 34 linguistics features]; 2) [Neural] represents the sentence only by sentence embeddings with neural models.

On the one hand, using linguistic features along with sentence embedding vectors, SVM with rbf kernel classifier provides the best F-1 with 0.75 on the updated corpus version. The SVM classifier is slightly better than both Xgboost and Softmax in precision and they have roughly the same recall value. On the other hand, comparing sentence embeddings of different kinds such as: XLM-R, mBERT, FasText and UCS along with AraBERT and Arabic-BERT.his indicated that Arabic-BERT is a clear winner with F-1 0.80. Since the architecture for building for all BERT-like models are very similar, we suspect that the more Arabic varied corpus (Common Crawl and Wikipedia for Arabic-BERT vs Common Crawl XML-R vs Wikipedia for BERT, AraBert and UCS) used to train the Arabic-

BERT model is responsible for its better performance

The confusion matrix in Table 5 shows a clear separation between the lower and higher level of proficiency. The majority of errors are between neighbouring levels and the number of errors decreases when we move away from the true class. The most problematic level was B which has a tendency to be classified as CEFR Level A.

Predicted	A	B	C
A	7485	1021	156
B	4506	1112	0
C	0	0	8627

Table 5: Confusion Matrix of SVM (rbf) on 3-way classification with XLM-R.

4.2 Readability as a Regression Problem

Regression allows us to make ranked predictions along the discrete CEFR levels thus assessing which text is more difficult than the other. The training just as in the previous experiment with applying different ML approaches with 10-fold cross-validation. The results for regression can be rated using mean absolute error (MAE) from the gold standard and the correlation coefficients, Pearson, Spearman and Kendall's tau. The results are listed in Table 6. As with classification, error analysis leads to improved results across all methods. The best MAE rate of 0.34 shows that sentence difficulty prediction is quite close to the gold labels. As mentioned before, our model has a very large number of ties for the gold labels (which can only take three values), so the preferred evaluation measure for regression is Kendall's tau-b. The best models are RF and SVR on the XLM-R features.

Model	Pearson	Spearman	Kendall
Decision Tree 2T	0.82	0.62	0.44
Decision Tree 5T	**0.83**	0.64	0.47
Random Forest	**0.82**	0.70	**0.54**
Xgboost	0.78	0.56	0.37
Linear	0.74	0.67	0.49
MLP	0.81	0.68	0.49
SVR,rbf kernel	0.78	0.69	0.52
SVR, Linear	0.8	**0.71**	**0.54**

Table 6: Regression using all features and XLM-R for sentences

4.3 Feature Selection

Interpreting feature importance and effectiveness is a way for a better understanding of the classification ML model's logic. This process provides ranking the features by assigning a score for each feature represents its contribution in the target label prediction. These scores provide insights into data representation and model performance. Working with these features ranking can improve the model efficiency and effectiveness by focusing only on the important variables and ignore the irrelevant or noisy features. For this purpose, we applied the Recursive Feature Elimination (RFE) a wrapper method for feature selection approach on the basis of SVM classifier. RFE works with recursively removing some features and testing the remain features to select the best feature set affecting the classifier decisions. The results of using RFE approach testing the SVM classifier as represented in Table 7 showing the best ten features contributes to the prediction model. Sentence embedding using XLM-R appeared at the top of the list conveying that it is the most useful feature for sentence difficulty scoring. Followed by the CEFR word frequency features with four features in different positions (Label A1, Label B2, Label C2, and Entropy). The third most effective features are that of the syntactic-set representing more in-depth into the sentence's syntactic knowledge.

35	**Sentence embedding**
26	**Average phrases/sentence**
31	**Incidence of Level B2**
27	Average phrases depth
28	**Incidence of Level A1**
24	Incidence of modifier/root
23	Incidence of objects
22	Incidence of subjects
32	Incidence of Level C1
34	Words CEFR levels entropy

Table 7: List of ten most effective features using REF approach based on SVM classifier

4.4 Ablation

Going further, we performed feature ablation experiments by excluding certain sets of features. We applied SVM rbf classifier on the full dataset while excluding one of the four main group of features blocks POS, Syntactic-features, CEFR-level lexical features, sentence embedding, along with using only the sentence embeddings (XLM-R since this was shown in comparison of embeddings below). This shows that the sentence embeddings significantly contribute to the classification results Table 8), in spite of the efforts to create hand-crafted features. Nevertheless, the linguistic features are useful in interpreting the results of purely neural classification. This results prove that the transformer models provide a rich representation for the sentences covering linguistic features.

According to the primary results from the feature selection and the ablation experiments, which proved the use of sentence embedding alone could fulfill the task without extensive use of linguistics features. These results encouraged us to continue experimentation with applying only the sentence embedding feature to reduce the number of features which consequently decreases the data analysis and training time.

Feature set	**P**	**R**	**F-1**
Exclude XLM-R	0.49	0.63	0.55
Exclude POS	0.55	0.71	0.62
Exclude Syntactic	0.57	0.69	0.59
Exclude CEFR	0.55	0.71	0.62
Only XLM-R	0.75	0.77	**0.75**

Table 8: SVM Classification ablation experiment on 3-way classification

4.5 Testing on Dataset Two

For the binary classification, the classifier reached F-1 of 0.94 and 0.98 for Arabic-BERT and SVM XML-R respectively. However, when testing the binary classifiers trained from DataSet One on Dataset Two the accuracy drops considerably, see Table 9.

As the confusion matrix in Table 10 shows, both classifiers performed better in identifying the complex instances rather than simple ones, so the F1 measure drops. However, the initial results on dataset two shows that XLM-R classifier performed better than Arabic-BERT, we still consider Arabic-BERT classifiers [both 3-way and binary] as best classifier so far. Our interpretation for these confusions is because of the fictional nature of Dataset Two. First, the fiction is well represented in the training data for the A+B levels in Dataset One, while the C level (Snapshot corpus) contains texts of many different types from the internet, so that the classifiers could not handle the mismatch in genres. The other possible reason is that what is considered as complex sentences which are worth simplification according to developers of Dataset Two does not really seem to be complex as to be only suitable for the C-level students. More research is needed to identify the difference between the two datasets.

	Arabic-BERT	**XLM-R**
P	0.60	0.56
R	0.50	0.53
F-1	0.53	0.54

Table 9: Fine-tuned Arabic-BERT versus SVM XLM-R Classifier's performance on Dataset two

	ArabicBert		**XLM-R**	
Predicted	**A**	**C**	**A**	**C**
A	19	2961	138	2842
C	46	2934	223	2757

Table 10: Confusion Matrix with binary classifier Arabic-BERT versus XLM-R on Dataset Two.

4.6 Dataset Two Sentence Similarity

For the purpose of this experiment we needed to include non-simplified sentence to the Dataset two. So that, we duplicated the 2980 complex sentences without simplification aligned with the exact sentence without modification and labeled them with 0 indicating not paraphrased/simplified. Resulting in a Dataset consist of 2980 sentences with right simplification labeled as 1 and other 2980 non-simplified with label 0, in a total of 5960 sentence. The two models trained on this similarity task (AraBert and Arabic-Bert) achieve the F-1 measure of 0.98, leading to the ability to detect sentences which need simplification according to the Dataset Two standard.

5 Related Work on Arabic

The last two decades have seen enormous efforts (especially for the English language) to develop readability measurement ranging from the traditional readability formulae to ML algorithms. English language researchers have introduced more than 200 readability formulae (DuBay, 2004) as well as hundreds of models (Schwarm and Ostendorf, 2005). In contrast, less research has addressed Arabic language issues and their challenges for robust readability formulae.

Some attempts to formulate statistical formulae

for the Arabic language reflected traditional English formulae such as the Flesch–Kincaid Grade. The simplest formulae included the average word length, the average sentence and other surface features. According to Cavalli-Sforza et al. (2018) these simple formulae are Dawood formula (1977), Al-Heeti formula (1984), and the formula presented by Daud et al. (2013) based on a corpus. The more sophisticated formulae represent the syllables and more insights the Arabic sentences, such as AARI Base by Al Tamimi et al. (2014) and OSMAN by El-Haj and Rayson (2016).

Other studies were conducted to measure text readability by targeting either first or second language learners for Arabic language modelled using different ML algorithms. Most of these studies used the previously traditional features along with varying lists of part of speech features (POS) representing the words in each document as in studies by (Al-Khalifa and Al-Ajlan, 2010; Forsyth, 2014; Saddiki et al., 2015; Nassiri et al., 2018a). Forsyth (2014) used the word frequency dictionary by Buckwalter and Parkinson (2014) to classify the words' level against this dictionary frequencies. The dictionary was used later by Nassiri et al. (2018b) along with 133 POS features to achieve an accuracy of 100% with 3-classes. The 'Al-Kitaab' textbook has a word list introduced at the beginning of each chapter in the book. These lists were used by Cavalli-Sforza et al. (2014) for comparing the words appeared in a text against this list and labelling them by (target, known, unknown). Saddiki et al. (2018), highlight adding new syntactic features to their features targeting more in-depth analysis. They used two different datasets for both first and second Arabic language learning. This yielded an accuracy of 94.8%, 72.4% for first language learners and second language learners respectively.

6 Conclusions

We present the first attempt to build a methodology for Arabic difficulty classification on the **sentence** level. We have found that while linguistic features, such as POS tags, syntax or frequency lists are useful for prediction, Deep Learning is the most important contribution to performance, but the traditional features can help in interpreting the black box of Deep Learning alone. For this specific task and for the Arabic language, fine-tuned Arabic-BERT offers better performance than other sentence embedding methods. Also, application of the classifiers trained on one dataset to a very different evaluation corpus shows that the classifiers learn some important properties of what is difficult in Arabic, but the transfer is more successful for the feature-based models than for the BERT-based ones.

In the end, our best classifier is reasonably reliable in detecting complex sentences; however, it is less successful in separating between the lower learner levels. Still the binary classifier provides the functionality for filtering out really difficult sentences, not suitable for the learners. If we are thinking of Arabic learners especially in higher education, we are expecting learners to graduate with a BA degree in the case of Arabic as a complex language with confidence in reading B2 texts, which implies that the tool for separating A+B vs C level texts is really useful for undergraduate teaching.

Through our tool providing computational assessment of difficulty, we will be able: i) to select the appropriate texts for students; ii) to access ever-larger volumes of information to find educational material of the right difficulty online; iii) to explore curriculum-based assessment to find what is most effective in finding gaps in a curriculum that can be filled according to students' needs.

Our future work involves building a parallel simple/complex Arabic corpus for sentence simplification. The corpus will be classified on the basis of how difficult the sentences are in a Common Crawl snapshot of Arabic web pages. Using the text difficulty classifier, we can split the corpus into two groups for complex and simple sentences. We also consider the semantic similarity detection on **"Saaq al-Bambuu"** as a benchmark, which could be used in the corpus compilation. In this study we only performed some ablation analysis, but because BERT-like models are more useful as the classifiers, we want to investigate their performance via probing for linguistic features following the BERTology framework (Rogers et al., 2020; Sharoff, 2021). We also want to explore the link between the difficulty assessment on the document vs sentences levels (Dell'Orletta et al., 2014).

7 Acknowledgments

This research is a part of PhD project funded by Newton-Mosharafa Fund. All experiments presented in this paper were performed using Advanced Research Computing (ARC) facilities provided by Leeds University.

References

Hend S Al-Khalifa and Amani A Al-Ajlan. 2010. Automatic readability measurements of the arabic text: An exploratory study. *Arabian Journal for Science and Engineering*, 35(2 C):103–124.

Saud Al-Sanousi. 2013. *Saaq al-Bambuu*. Arab Scientific Publishers Inc., Lebanon.

Abdel Karim Al Tamimi, Manar Jaradat, Nuha Al-Jarrah, and Sahar Ghanem. 2014. Aari: automatic arabic readability index. *Int. Arab J. Inf. Technol.*, 11(4):370–378.

A. Alfaifi and Eric S Atwell. 2013. Arabic learner corpus v1: A new resource for arabic language research. In *In proceedings of the Second Workshop on Arabic Corpus Linguistics (WACL-2)*. Leeds.

Amal Alsaif. 2012. *Human and automatic annotation of discourse relations for Arabic*. University of Leeds.

Wissam Antoun, Fady Baly, and Hazem Hajj. 2020. Arabert: Transformer-based model for arabic language understanding. *arXiv preprint arXiv:2003.00104*.

K Brustad, M Al-Batal, and A Al-Tonsi. 2015. *Al-Kitaab fii Tacallum al-cArabiyya. A Textbook for Beginning Arabic: Part One Third Edition*. Georgetown University Press.

Tim Buckwalter and Dilworth Parkinson. 2014. *A frequency dictionary of Arabic: Core vocabulary for learners*. Routledge.

Violetta Cavalli-Sforza, Mariam El Mezouar, and Hind Saddiki. 2014. Matching an arabic text to a learners' curriculum. In *Proc. 5th Int. Conf. on Arabic Language Processing (CITALA), Oujda, Morocco*, pages 79–88.

Violetta Cavalli-Sforza, Hind Saddiki, and Naoual Nassiri. 2018. Arabic readability research: Current state and future directions. *Procedia computer science*, 142:38–49.

Alexis Conneau, Kartikay Khandelwal, Naman Goyal, Vishrav Chaudhary, Guillaume Wenzek, Francisco Guzmán, Edouard Grave, Myle Ott, Luke Zettlemoyer, and Veselin Stoyanov. 2019. Unsupervised cross-lingual representation learning at scale. *arXiv preprint arXiv:1911.02116*.

Nuraihan Mat Daud, Haslina Hassan, and Normaziah Abdul Aziz. 2013. A corpus-based readability formula for estimate of arabic texts reading difficulty. *World Applied Sciences Journal*, 21:168–173.

Felice Dell'Orletta, Simonetta Montemagni, and Giulia Venturi. 2014. Assessing document and sentence readability in less resourced languages and across textual genres. *ITL-International Journal of Applied Linguistics*, 165(2):163–193.

Jacob Devlin, Ming-Wei Chang, Kenton Lee, and Kristina Toutanova. 2018. Bert: Pre-training of deep bidirectional transformers for language understanding. *arXiv preprint arXiv:1810.04805*.

Marilena Di Bari, Serge Sharoff, and Martin Thomas. 2014. Multiple views as aid to linguistic annotation error analysis. In *Proceedings of LAW VIII-The 8th Linguistic Annotation Workshop*, pages 82–86.

William H DuBay. 2004. The principles of readability. *Online Submission*.

Mahmoud El-Haj and Paul Rayson. 2016. Osman—a novel arabic readability metric. In *Proceedings of the Tenth International Conference on Language Resources and Evaluation (LREC'16)*, pages 250–255.

Laila Familiar. 2016. *Saud al-Sanousi's Saaq al-Bambuu: The Authorized Abridged Edition for Students of Arabic*. Georgetown University Press.

Jonathan Neil Forsyth. 2014. *Automatic readability prediction for modern standard Arabic*. Ph.D. thesis, Brigham Young University. Department of Linguistics and English Language.

Edouard Grave, Piotr Bojanowski, Prakhar Gupta, Armand Joulin, and Tomas Mikolov. 2018. Learning word vectors for 157 languages. *Proceedings of the Eleventh International Conference on Language Resources and Evaluation (LREC 2018) [Online]*.

Adam Kilgarriff, Frieda Charalabopoulou, Maria Gavrilidou, Janne Bondi Johannessen, Saussan Khalil, Sofie Johansson Kokkinakis, Robert Lew, Serge Sharoff, Ravikiran Vadlapudi, and Elena Volodina. 2014. Corpus-based vocabulary lists for language learners for nine languages. *Language resources and evaluation*, 48(1):121–163.

Gerry Knowles and Zuraidah Mohd Don. 2004. The notion of a "lemma": Headwords, roots and lexical sets. *International Journal of Corpus Linguistics*, 9(1):69–81.

Kendall Maurice and Gibbons Jean Dickinson. 1990. Rank correlation methods. *London: Edward Arnold*.

Naoual Nassiri, Abdelhak Lakhouaja, and Violetta Cavalli-Sforza. 2018a. Arabic readability assessment for foreign language learners. In *International Conference on Applications of Natural Language to Information Systems*, pages 480–488. Springer.

Naoual Nassiri, Abdelhak Lakhouaja, and Violetta Cavalli-Sforza. 2018b. Modern standard arabic readability prediction. In *International Conference on Arabic Language Processing*, pages 120–133. Springer.

Arfath Pasha, Mohamed Al-Badrashiny, Mona T Diab, Ahmed El Kholy, Ramy Eskander, Nizar Habash, Manoj Pooleery, Owen Rambow, and Ryan Roth. 2014. Madamira: A fast, comprehensive tool for morphological analysis and disambiguation of arabic. In *Lrec*, volume 14, pages 1094–1101.

Anna Rogers, Olga Kovaleva, and Anna Rumshisky. 2020. A primer in BERTology: What we know about how BERT works. *Transactions of the Association for Computational Linguistics*, 8:842–866.

Hind Saddiki, Karim Bouzoubaa, and Violetta Cavalli-Sforza. 2015. Text readability for arabic as a foreign language. In *2015 IEEE/ACS 12th International Conference of Computer Systems and Applications (AICCSA)*, pages 1–8. IEEE.

Hind Saddiki, Nizar Habash, Violetta Cavalli-Sforza, and Muhamed Al Khalil. 2018. Feature optimization for predicting readability of arabic l1 and l2. In *Proceedings of the 5th Workshop on Natural Language Processing Techniques for Educational Applications*, pages 20–29.

Ali Safaya, Moutasem Abdullatif, and Deniz Yuret. 2020. Kuisail at semeval-2020 task 12: Bert-cnn for offensive speech identification in social media. In *Proceedings of the Fourteenth Workshop on Semantic Evaluation*, pages 2054–2059.

Horacio Saggion. 2017. Automatic text simplification. *Synthesis Lectures on Human Language Technologies*, 10(1):1–137.

Elliot Schumacher, Maxine Eskenazi, Gwen Frishkoff, and Kevyn Collins-Thompson. 2016. Predicting the relative difficulty of single sentences with and without surrounding context. *arXiv preprint arXiv:1606.08425*.

Sarah Schwarm and Mari Ostendorf. 2005. Reading level assessment using support vector machines and statistical language models. In *Proceedings of the 43rd Annual Meeting of the Association for Computational Linguistics (ACL'05)*, pages 523–530, Ann Arbor, Michigan. Association for Computational Linguistics.

Anas Shahrour, Salam Khalifa, Dima Taji, and Nizar Habash. 2016. Camelparser: A system for arabic syntactic analysis and morphological disambiguation. In *Proceedings of COLING 2016, the 26th International Conference on Computational Linguistics: System Demonstrations*, pages 228–232.

Serge Sharoff. 2006. Open-source corpora: using the net to fish for linguistic data. *International Journal of Corpus Linguistics*, 11(4):435–462.

Serge Sharoff. 2021. Genre annotation for the web: text-external and text-internal perspectives. *Register studies*, 3.

E Tschirner, O Bärenfänger, and K Wisniewski. 2015. Assessing evidence of validity of the actfl cefr listening and reading proficiency tests (lpt and rpt) using a standard-setting approach. *Technical Report 2015-EU-PUB-2*.

Sowmya Vajjala and Kaidi Loo. 2014. Automatic cefr level prediction for estonian learner text. In *Proceedings of the third workshop on NLP for computer-assisted language learning*, pages 113–127.

Ashish Vaswani, Noam Shazeer, Niki Parmar, Jakob Uszkoreit, Llion Jones, Aidan N Gomez, ukasz Kaiser, and Illia Polosukhin. 2017. Attention is all you need. In *Advances in neural information processing systems*, pages 5998–6008.

Yinfei Yang, Daniel Cer, Amin Ahmad, Mandy Guo, Jax Law, Noah Constant, Gustavo Hernandez Abrego, Steve Yuan, Chris Tar, Yun-Hsuan Sung, et al. 2019. Multilingual universal sentence encoder for semantic retrieval. *arXiv preprint arXiv:1907.04307*.

Dynamic Ensembles in Named Entity Recognition for Historical Arabic Texts

Muhammad Majadly
Department of Computer Science
University of Haifa
Haifa, Israel
mu.ib.mj@gmail.com

Tomer Sagi
Department of Information Systems
University of Haifa
Haifa, Israel
tsagi@is.haifa.ac.il

Abstract

The use of Named Entity Recognition (NER) over archaic Arabic texts is steadily increasing. However, most tools have been either developed for modern English or trained over English language documents and are limited over historical Arabic text. Even Arabic NER tools are often trained on modern web-sourced text, making their fit for a historical task questionable. To mitigate historic Arabic NER resource scarcity, we propose a dynamic ensemble model utilizing several learners. The dynamic aspect is achieved by utilizing predictors and features over NER algorithm results that identify which have performed better on a specific task in real-time. We evaluate our approach against state-of-the-art Arabic NER and static ensemble methods over a novel historical Arabic NER task we have created. Our results show that our approach improves upon the state-of-the-art and reaches a 0.8 F-score on this challenging task.

1 Introduction

Digitized historical literature is an essential resource in facilitating historical and social research. Information extraction, the task of automatically extracting structured information from digitized documents, has emerged as a method to scale the analysis of texts and allow the integration of information from different sources (e.g., (Ehrmann et al., 2020), (Ren et al., 2017)). One of the cardinal tasks in information extraction is NER, extracting entities from text and categorizing them into predefined categories. Numerous NER algorithms have been suggested, from rule-based approaches (Mesfar, 2007) to machine learning (ML) approaches e.g., (Zhou and Su, 2002). However, an overwhelming majority of the algorithms have been developed over modern English text. Rule-based approaches designed using modern English grammatical rules are irrelevant to Arabic (Shaalan, 2014). ML approaches rely on large modern English corpora sourced from international news outlets and social media. Training these tools to extract named entities from historical texts written in ancient Arabic requires large amounts of tagged text in the same language and preferably the same dialect, which are sorely missing.

In this work, we explore two avenues to mitigate the weakness of existing Arabic NER tools over historical Arabic texts (Shaalan, 2014). First, we utilize an approach named *dynamic prediction*, that was used in adjacent fields such as schema matching (Sagi and Gal, 2013), business process matching (Weidlich et al., 2013), and pattern recognition (Ko et al., 2008). In dynamic prediction, the results of different techniques are combined according to each result's (or component of the result) predicted quality. Here, we build an ensemble learning model based on dynamic prediction for NER algorithms. To alleviate the lack of resources in Arabic historical NER, we have created a novel dataset – the Bedaya Corpus and examine how training ML-based NER tools on historic Arabic impacts their performance instead of training them over modern Arabic text.

The contribution of this paper can, therefore, be summarized as follows. 1) We introduce a dynamic ensemble model for NER over historical Arabic texts. 2) We present Bedaya corpus, an Arabic historical dataset. 3) We perform a detailed empirical evaluation of our approach over baseline and state-of-the-art methods. We now provide background and preliminary definitions of NER and ensemble-learning in Section 2 and present related work in Section 3. In Section 4 we present our predictors and ensemble learning technique. In Section 5, we present the datasets. In Section 6, we report the results of our empirical evaluation, concluding our work in Section 7.

Proceedings of the Sixth Arabic Natural Language Processing Workshop, pages 115–125
Kyiv, Ukraine (Virtual), April 19, 2021.

2 Background

2.1 NER

Named Entity Recognition (NER) seeks to locate and classify named entities mentioned in unstructured text into categories such as person names, organizations, locations, events, and others. For example, the output for the sentence *"Romeo and Juliet meet in Verona."* is as follows.

> **[Romeo]**(Person) and **[Juliet]**(Person) meet in **[Verona]**(Location).

Some NER algorithms provide a *confidence value* (usually over $[0, 1]$) associated with each mapping. Others provide a set of confidence values for each token, one for each possible class. There are two broad approaches to constructing NER algorithms. *Rule based approaches*, rely on rules and patterns manually created in order to capture terms from input documents. For example, Mikheev et al. (Mikheev et al., 1999) suggest the following rule:

> **[Xxxx]** (sequence of capitalized words) + 'is' + 'a' + **[JJ*]** (sequence of zero or more adjectives) + **[REL]** (relative). then **[Xxxx]** is (Person), e.g., "**[John White]** is a beloved brother".

Rule-based systems achieve high precision but require a significant time investment to develop. Moreover, transferring rules from one language to another or between domains is very challenging (Jiang et al., 2016).

In *machine-learning (ML)-based approaches*, an algorithm containing rules or some other internal representation is learned from training examples (Mansouri et al., 2008). This approach can be further categorized into supervised, unsupervised, semi-supervised. Supervised approaches rely on manually tagged examples. Unsupervised approaches attempt to divide the tokens into similar groups, hopefully grouping the same class's entities. Semi-supervised approaches use a small number of tagged examples to guide the otherwise unsupervised process. Several features are used in ML-based approaches, such as part of speech, capitalized words, special marks (punctuation, numbers, dates, and titles), and word length. Recent NER systems rely on (deep) neural-networks over sequences of words (Li et al., 2020). Gazetteers, or entity dictionaries, are an essential resource for NER that support entity tagging (Zamin and Oxley, 2011) by allowing to look up words and phrases that are commonly used as named entities (e.g., (Shaalan and Raza, 2009), (Sajadi and Minaei, 2017)).

NER over Arabic text has proved much more challenging than other languages due to the complexity of Arabic morphology, absence of capital letters, and the lack of resources on which to train ML-based tools (Shaalan, 2014). For example, while performance on CONLL 2000, a common NER task in English has reached an F1-score of 97.3% (Liu et al., 2019), the best performance on a modern Arabic corpus ANERcorp only achieves an F1-score of 89.9% (Balla and Delany, 2020). Arabic texts can be categorized into classical Arabic, Modern Standard Arabic (MSA), and Arabic dialects (Shaalan, 2014). Historical Islamic literature is written in classical Arabic (Habash, 2010). According to (Hetzron, 1997), MSA differs from classical Arabic in vocabulary, syntax and styles. moreover they present 9 common morphonology changes that happened upon the time that lead for MSA from classical Arabic, thus changes leads to changes in syntax and words meanings. Researchers must consider these differences when using modern datasets and NER tools to build NER tools for historical Arabic texts.

2.2 Ensemble Learning

Ensemble learning algorithms (Definition 2.1) aim to combine the outputs of several base-algorithms (e.g., classifiers) to get better predictive performance. Ensemble methods have been demonstrated to provide superior predictive performance versus single algorithms on a variety of problems. The potential for performance improvement is higher when the algorithms' performance is diverse, such that different algorithms succeed and fail on different tasks (Oza and Russell, 2001).

Definition 2.1 (NER ensemble learning algorithm). Let $D \subseteq \mathcal{D}$ be a set of training documents and let $f_m : T_D \rightarrow C$ be the expected mapping between each token in this set and a class (supervised labels). Let $\mathcal{F}$ be the set of all possible NER algorithms and let $F \subset \mathcal{F}$ be the set of base NER algorithms. Let M_D be the set of all such possible mappings for D and let $m_F \subset M_D$ be the set of NER algorithm results returned by F over D. A *NER ensemble learning algorithm* is a function $f : 2^{\mathcal{D}} \times M_D \times 2^{M_D} \rightarrow \mathcal{F}$. Given a specific training set D, an expected mapping f_m, a set of NER algorithms F, and a set of NER algorithm results m_F, f outputs a NER algorithm.

Different ensemble learning approaches have been attempted. In voting based approaches, each classifier votes for a class, and the class with the most votes is chosen (Dietterich, 2000). Linear approaches assign a weight to each classifier, and the class with the highest combined score is then chosen. Several ensemble methods are based on heuristics. *Bagging* (Breiman, 1996) algorithms train each model in the ensemble using a randomly drawn subset of the training set. In contrast, *Boosting* (Schapire, 1990) algorithms gradually build the model by training each new model instance to highlight the cases that previous models misclassified.

However, the above mentioned approaches are trained once, and their combined algorithm remains static, regardless of base classifiers' results. This static approach can lead to unexpected results. For example, a reliable classifier utilizes a word's capitalization as a major signal. In a long sentence that is, for some reason, capitalized throughout (perhaps for emphasis), this classifier may decide that all tokens belong to one long, named entity. The result would appear wrong to human eyes but will be taken heavily into account due to the classifier's static high importance in the ensemble. In section 4.2, we present our dynamic approach.

3 Related work

Speck and Ngomo 2014 explore the use of NER ensemble learning in English, combining four NER algorithms using 15 different ensemble learning algorithms. They evaluate these methods over five different English language datasets and show that ensembles can reduce the error rate by an average of 40%. However, all of the ensemble learning methods evaluated were static methods. In this work, we employ predictors to assess the quality of NER results dynamically.

For Arabic NER, Abdallah et al. 2012 integrate an ML-based approach with a rule-based one. They train a decision tree model to combine the results, achieving an F1-score of 87.8%. (Sajadi and Minaei, 2017) learn a static ensemble for named entity recognition over classical Arabic text and rely on the Adaboost algorithm, an implementation of the multi-class boosting method. Using their novel NOORcorp (5) historic Arabic corpus, the system was evaluated over its ability to recognize three classes: location, person, organization. Ekbal and Bandyopadhyay 2010 propose a NER for Arabic based on Support Vector Machines (SVM) (Hearst et al., 1998) used to classify feature vectors for every word.

Recent NER systems rely on (deep) neural-networks over sequences of words. These systems infer features from raw sentences by using several layers of components allowing to represent higher levels of abstraction over the word sequence (see survey (Li et al., 2020)). The current state of the art are NER systems based on the contextual word embedding approach (Peters et al., 2018) and especially systems which employ BERT (Devlin et al., 2018), a novel pre-trained deeply bidirectional, unsupervised language representation, that takes into account the context for each occurrence of a given word. Al-Smadi et al., 2020 propose an Arabic NER system using a six-layer deep neural network model based on the transfer learning architectures among deep neural networks (Yosinski et al., 2014), (Devlin et al., 2018). The system achieves an overall F1-score of 90% Compared with their baseline BI-LSTM-CRF model which reached an overall F1-score of 73%. Their work is trained and tested over MSA, they used WikiFANE-Gold (Alotaibi and Lee, 2014) as a dataset that builds over the Arabic version of Wikipedia. While our work focus on historical text, and emphasizes (see 6.4) the non improving NER over historical Arabic text using MSA.

Dynamic prediction has been previously proposed for schema matching (Sagi and Gal, 2013) and pattern matching (Ko et al., 2008). To the best of our knowledge, it has not been used to combine NER algorithms, as proposed here.

4 Employing Predictors for Dynamic Ensemble Building

Static ensemble methods rely on the base NER algorithms' results to generate a NER algorithm that combines their results such that on every document set, the results of the base NER algorithms are combined in the same way. Predictors have been explored for schema matching (Sagi and Gal, 2013) and pattern recognition (Ko et al., 2008) as a method for fine-tuning the ensemble creation method to the task at hand. Predictors assess the result of each base algorithm on the task and provide a score. The ensemble model can use this score to determine whether or not the algorithm has succeeded in this specific occasion to identify the correct class. Formally:

Definition 4.1 (Predictor). Let D be a set of documents and let $\{T_D | \forall t \in T_D : t \in d \wedge d \in D\}$ be the set of tokens contained in these documents. Let C be a set of classes, and let $f : T_D \rightarrow C \times \mathbb{R}$ be a NER algorithm result assigning a real number and a class to each token. Let $\mathcal{N}$ be the set of all possible such NER algorithm results and let $n \in \mathbb{D}$ be some natural non-zero number, then a *predictor* is a function $f : \mathcal{N} \rightarrow \mathbb{R}^n$.

Thus, a predictor assesses the quality of the algorithm's outputs without knowing the expected results. Predictors are defined over different result cardinalities. *Dataset-level* predictors output a single number for the entire dataset. *Sentence-level* predictors output one number for each sentence, and *token-level* predictors output a number for each token. Furthermore, as mentioned in Section 2, a NER algorithm result may include a confidence score for each token for each of the possible classes. In this case the NER algorithm result (and predictor input) is a function $f : T_D \rightarrow (C \times \mathbb{R})^{|C|}$. Here, we propose the following predictors.

4.1 Predictors

Token-level Predictors Our token-level predictors are calculated over the NER algorithm's confidence rates for each token and class. Thus, an algorithm tasked with classifying tokens into four classes will report four confidence values for each token, representing the confidence in its prediction for every class. The first predictor is *max confidence rate token* (MCT), which takes the value of the maximum confidence rate per token. Usually, this is the reported confidence for the chosen class. This predictor indicates how confident the NER tool is in its outcome, which leads it to prefer NER tools with higher confidence rates. The second predictor is the *Difference confidence Rate Token* (DCT), which measures the difference between the token's maximal confidence and second-best confidence rate, another indication of how confident the NER tool is in its outcome.

Sentence-level Predictors We explore two approaches to constructing sentence-level predictors. The first two predictors rely on the confidence rate information as in the token-level predictors. The latter two rely on counting results. *Binary distance* (BD) measures the sum of distances between the reported confidence value and the closest binary value. BD indicates the number of confident tokens in a sentence. A higher value for confident tokens leads to a lower value of BD. For each token's sentence, the confidence value is rounded towards the closest binary value, and the difference is taken and summed. For example, in Figure 1, given the confidence values from two NER's output, the lower BD indicates a confident NER. This predictor's rationale is that good NER results are those in which the NER algorithm is confident and either marks a token as belonging to the class or not. Half-hearted values are penalized. Following a similar rationale, *difference confidence rate sentence* DCS is the sum of differences between the highest and second-highest confidence rate for every token in the sentence. Like DCT, DCS indicates the NER tool's confidence in its outcome. The second group of *sentence-level* predictors utilizes a counting representation of the sentence over the number of named entities in general or the number of named entities from a specific class. With these predictors, the ensemble model can prefer a NER Tool with good performance for recognizing a type of Named Entity or can ignore others that are bad at recognizing this type. *Sentence number of named entities* (SNN) counts the number of tokens marked as belonging to named entities in the sentence normalized over the sentence's length. We similarly define three additional predictors: *sentence number of persons* (SNP), *sentence number of organizations* (SNO), and *sentence Number of Locations* (SNL). Each predictor counts the number of tokens from their respective class. Finally, SLD measures the proportion of tokens associated with the most prevalent class in the sentence from all tokens in the sentence. Table 1 contains examples for predictor calculation over the sentence *"Sherlock Holmes lives on Baker Street"*.

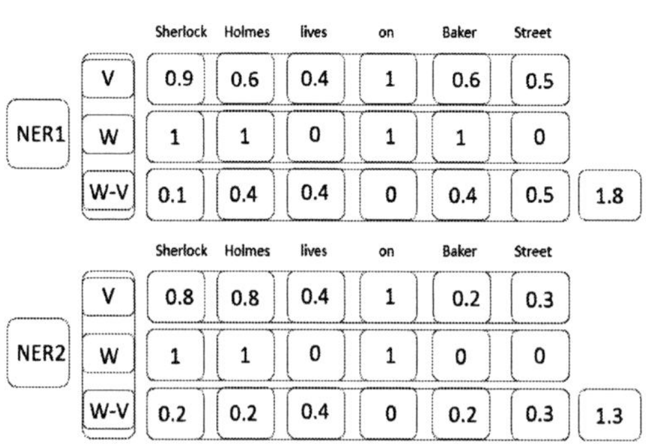

Figure 1: BD-sentence example.

Predictor Name	Example
MCT	If the confidence rate for *'Sherlock'* is 0.9 for *Person* class and 0.7, 0.8, and 0.3 for *Location*, *Organization*, and *Other* classes respectively, its MCT will be 0.9.
DCT	If the confidence rate for *'Sherlock'* is 0.9 for *Person* class and 0.7, 0.8, and 0.3 for *Location*, *Organization* and *Other* classes respectively, its DCT will be 0.9 - 0.8 = 0.1.
BD	In figure 1 we describe two NER tools NER_1 and NER_2. NER_2 is judged superior by BD since it is very confident for three tokens and only uncertain for two versus NER_1 that is only confident for two tokens.
DCS	If the confidence rate for every token in the sentence (six in our example) is 0.9 for the *Person* class and 0.7, 0.5, and 0.3 for the *Location*, *Organization*, and *Other* classes respectively. DSC for this sentence will be $\sum_{n=1}^{6}(0.9 - 0.7)$.
SNN	If NER_1 recognizes just *Sherlock* and *Holmes* as *Person* (or another NE) the predictor score will be 2 for this NER tool.
SNP, SNO, SNL	If NER_1 recognizes just *Sherlock* and *Holmes* as *Person* (or another NE) the predictor score will be 2 for *Person*, and zero for *Organization* and *Location*.
SLD	If NER_1 recognizes *Sherlock*, *Holmes* as *Person*, and *Baker* as *Location* (or another named entity) the predictor score will be 2/3.

Table 1: Predictor examples.

4.2 A Dynamic Ensemble Model (DEM) for NER Algorithms

Figure 2 shows the workflow of our technique. After training NER base algorithms over the training data, predictors are calculated over the results. Both the predictor value and the raw NER algorithm results serve as inputs for the ensemble-learning model, aiming to learn an ensemble method. When the learned method is employed at test/usage, the dataset is first fed into the NER tools to get the NER results, then the predictors are calculated, and the learned ensemble method combines both to give a class label for each token.

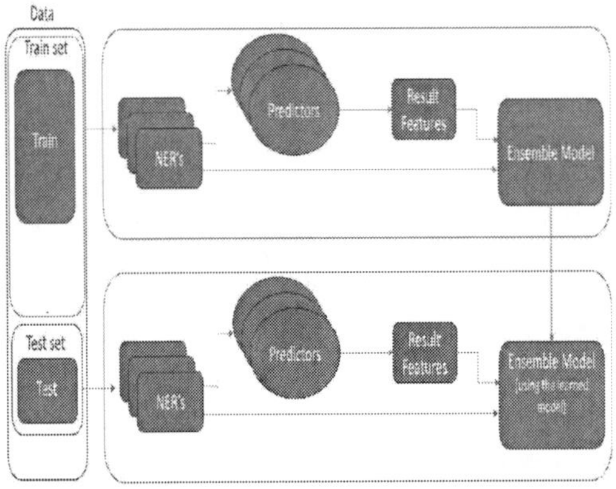

Figure 2: Workflow of the proposed approach.

5 Datasets

There is an apparent lack of Arabic corpora (Abouenour et al., 2010). Moreover, few of these corpora have been made freely and publicly available for research purposes (Bies et al., 2012). while others are available but under licenses (Mostefa et al., 2009) Thus, researchers often rely on private corpora, which precludes reproducing previous work and comparing its performance over a consistent benchmark.

In this work we use three corpora, NoorCorp (Sajadi and Minaei, 2017) based on a different historical book circa 800 AD, ANERcorp (Benajiba et al., 2007), a modern corpus which has become a standard in Arabic NER works. ANERcorp is based upon web-documents written in modern Arabic collected from 316 articles from newspapers such as bbc[1] and aljazeera[2]. Table 2 compares the corpora's token counts and class distributions. The datasets are tagged into four classes, *Person*, *Organization*, *Location*, and *Other*. The latter is assigned to tokens that do not belong to the first three classes. The third corpus is a historic one contributed in this work.

[1] https://www.bbc.com/arabic
[2] https://www.aljazeera.net/

Bedaya corpus

The scarcity of public Historic NER datasets has led us to create a new corpus. The *Bedaya* corpus[3], is based on Ibn Kathir's historical Arabic opus Al-Bidāya wa-al-Nihāya (The Beginning and The End). Kathir's ten volumes contain an extensive description of the world's history from its creation and are widely used in Islamic studies. The dataset is taken continuously from the 7th part of the book. It contains 20,500 tokens with 5,664 different tokens. Named entities were annotated manually by one of the authors and verified by an Arabic language expert that reviewed 50% of the dataset with a 99.998% inter-rater agreement.

Over a 80-20% training-test partition (Sajadi and Minaei, 2017) over NOORCorp dataset reached approximately 97% F1-score. In our evaluation of the NOORCorp dataset, we challenge our tools with a harder task, which is to train over one dataset and to be tested on a different one. [4] Thus, we ensure the generality of our algorithm and obtain enough space for ensemble algorithms improving.

Class	Noor	Bedaya	ANER
Loc.	1,320 (1.2%)	328 (1.6%)	6,426 (4.8%)
Pers.	15,873 (14%)	2,840 (14%)	5,036 (3.4%)
Org.	1,932 (1.7%)	336 (1.6%)	3,402 (2.3%)
O	93,055 (83%)	17,016 (83%)	133,768 (90%)
All	112,180	20,520	148,632
Voc size	19,319	5,664	33,208

Table 2: Dataset Token Counts and Class Distribution.

6 Experiments

We now present a series of empirical evaluations examining the following questions. Which predictors are the most correlated with our desired quality measures (§ 6.2)? Does our dynamic ensemble approach outperform the baseline approaches of using a single NER algorithm and using static ensemble learning (§ 6.3)? What is the performance impact of training NER algorithms over modern Arabic text versus historic Arabic for a historic Arabic NER task (§ 6.4)? We begin by introducing the experimental setup.

6.1 Setup

6.1.1 Ensemble Algorithm

We employ C4.5 (Quinlan, 2014) as our ensemble learning algorithm. C4.5 generates a decision tree, a learned classifier that uses a tree-like graph or model of decisions and possible outcomes. Each internal node represents an "examination" on an attribute, each branch represents the outcome of the *examination*, and each leaf node represents a class label. The paths from the root to the leaves represent classification rules. Our DEM approach utilizes the J48 implementation of C4.5 in Weka (Hall et al., 2009).

6.1.2 NER Tools

The following are the NER algorithms used in this work. **Pattern** is a rule-based tool. The tool uses pattern comparison with a small lexicon containing the 50 most prevalent words for every named entity-tag in the historical Arabic dataset NoorCourp. Additionally, the tool employs six rules related to the Arabic language and historic Arabic specifications taken from (Sajadi and Minaei, 2017) and (Shaalan and Raza, 2009) with some minor changes. Table 3 presents the rules we use.

The rest of the tools utilize an ML approach. **CRF** uses the conditional random field technique (Lafferty et al., 2001), a discriminative model for sequence labeling. It models the dependency between each sample and the entire input sequence. CRF uses the following extracted features: Part of speech (Stanford POS tagger (Manning et al., 2014)), special flag marks (is punctuation?, is a number?), words, word parts (last three, two, one letter), word length, and nearby words features. **LSTM-CRF** (Huang et al., 2015) combines a bidirectional long short-term memory neural network (Hochreiter and Schmidhuber, 1997) with CRF. Long short-term memory (LSTM) is an artificial recurrent neural network (Rumelhart et al., 1986). Unlike standard feedforward neural networks, LSTM has feedback connections and can process entire sequences of data. **Polyglot** (Al-Rfou et al., 2015) is a multilingual, semi-supervised ML-based NER that uses word embedding. Word embeddings are representations of words acquired by using vast amounts of raw text. These representations capture information about words' syntactic functionality and semantics. Polyglot embeddings

[3]available at `https://github.com/muhammad-majadly/Bedaya-dataset`

[4]It should be noted, that in preliminary work we were able to reproduce these same results over an 80-20 split of NOORCorp using both static and dynamic ensembles.

Rule Name	Rule Format
Person Rule 1	word1[noun] + (son of) + word2[noun] then word1 and word2 is a person.
Person Rule 2	(equivalent words to Mr./MRs) + word[noun] word is a person.
King Rule	king [or equal words like 'Khalifa'] + word[noun] word is a person.
Location Rule	word1[pers] + (from/born) + word2[noun] then word2 is a Location.
Organization Rule	word1[first word of tribes' names] + word2[noun] then word1 and word2 is an organization.
Same NER Rule	word1[NE=x] + (and/like) + word2[noun] then word2 is x.

Table 3: Pattern-NER rules.

are trained on Wikipedia, the text consists of the most frequent 100K words for each language, and the word representation consists of 64 dimensions. The polyglot model learns a simple three-layer neural network using the word embedding representation for classification, taking as features the embeddings for the words in a nearby interval of text around each word.

The last three algorithms (**SVM**, **LR**, and **DT**) use three different machine learning classifiers over the same feature space: part of speech tags, and word length. SVM (Chang and Lin, 2011) works by finding a hyperplane in N-dimensional space (N number of features) that distinctly classifies the data points. Logistic Regression (LR) (Hosmer Jr et al., 2013) uses a logistic function to model a binary dependent variable. Decision Tree (DT) (Quinlan, 1986) is a decision support tool that uses a tree-like graph or model of decisions and their possible consequences, including chance event outcomes. To ensure diversity in our ensemble approach, we chose these non-sequence ML-based algorithms that consider token-level information together with the sequence-based algorithms CRF, LSTM-CRF, and Polyglot. The classifiers use the following extracted features: Part Of Speech tags, the word itself, words, and word length.

6.1.3 NER Diversity

Ensemble methods have been demonstrated to provide superior predictive performance versus single algorithms on a variety of problems. The potential for performance improvement is higher when the algorithms' performance is diverse, such that different algorithms succeed and fail on different tasks (Oza and Russell, 2001). To ensure diversity, we choose both rule-based and machine learning algorithms, and within the latter group, a diverse set of principles and models. Empirical diversity was measured over this task by using the Pearson product-moment correlation coefficient (PPMCC) (Steel et al., 1960) between each pair of NER algorithms results over the Bedaya dataset. An absolute value of 1.0 indicates a perfect correlation, and 0.0 indicates no correlation at all. CRF is positively correlated with LSTM-CRF at 0.7 and less correlated with POLYGLOT at 0.38. Polyglot is highly correlated with LR with 0.7. DT with LR and SVM with LSTM-CRF are very correlated at 0.84. Pattern and LR have a 0.78 correlation between them. The most correlated tools are SVM NER and DT with 0.96.

6.1.4 Measures

We measure NER performance using the commonly employed precision, recall, and F1-score. *Precision* is the portion of correctly classified tokens (true positives) among the tokens classified as belonging to a named entity by the NER system (predicted positive). In contrast, *recall* is the fraction of true positives predicted by the NER system among the total number of tokens belonging to named entities in the dataset (actual positive). *F1-score* is the harmonic mean of precision and recall.

Oracle We use the concept of an oracle (Ko et al., 2008) to measure the upper limit for the ensemble of classifiers' performance. An oracle is the union of true positive results of all classifiers. If one classifier can correctly classify a given input, then an ensemble of classifiers that can classify this input will not be better than the oracle.

Definition 6.1 (Oracle). Let T be a token and let C be the set of classes where $c \in C$ is the expected class of token T and let $O \in C$ be the class for tokens labeled as a non named entity. The *oracle* over NER tools $[N_1, ..., N_n]$ is defined as follows.

$$Oracle(T) = \begin{cases} c & \exists i \in [1, .., n] | N_i(T) = c \\ \mathcal{O} & \text{else} \end{cases}$$

The oracle's performance over Bedaya dataset is **94%** Precision, **75%** Recall, and F1-score **83%**.

6.2 Evaluating Predictors

To assess the quality of a predictor, we use the correlation between the predictor value and the result's eventual quality. In our case, we measure it using PPMCC and Point Biserial Correlation (PBC) (Tate, 1954). PPMCC can be used between two continuous variables to assess their linear relationship. PBC is used to measure the correlation between a binary (is entity?) and continuous variable (prediction). We split our dataset (Bedaya) into sentences for sentence-level predictors, run all base NER algorithms over each sentence, and compare the predictor value over each sentence to precision and recall calculated on it using PPMCC. For token-level predictors (DCT and MCT), we use PBC with true/false token predictions. Correlation measurement is done on two levels, for all the tools together and for each tool individually. Predictors correlated with all the tools are more general and make the system more effective. On the other hand, predictors correlated with one tool can give helpful information to the ensemble model about a specific tool. Table 4 summarizes correlation results for predictors with all the tools reporting their correlation over 10,000 tokens and 500 sentences using seven different NER tools with quality measures precision and recall. The best-correlated sentence-level predictor is DCS, and the best token-level predictor is MCT. A cross-correlational analysis revealed that BD is correlated strongly with DCS, SNN is strongly correlated with SNP, and DCT is correlated with MCT. Other predictor pairs are weakly correlated.

	Pearson		**Biserial**	
Predictor	Precision	Recall	R_{pb}	p_{value}
BD	-0.181	-0.233		
DCS	**0.182**	**0.255**		
SNN	0.121	0.147		
SNP	0.096	0.120		
SNO	0.110	0.120		
SNL	0.040	0.070		
SLD	0.020	-0.014		
DCT			0.42	< 0.001
MCT			0.40	< 0.001

Table 4: Correlation results for our proposed predictors. Pearson Correlation with Precision and Recall, and Biserial Correlation with true/false token prediction.

Type	**Precision**	**Recall**	**F1**
CRF	90.0%	68.0%	77.4%
LSTMCRF	81.3%	64.6%	73.0%
SVM	86.3%	66.0%	74.8%
LR	88.3%	50.0%	63.8%
DT	85.0%	65.3%	75.2%
Pattern	84.0%	30.0%	42.0%
PolyGlot	59.0%	39.0%	47.0%
DEM	**90.8%**	**71.0%**	**79.8%**
Oracle	**94.0%**	**75.0%**	**83.0%**

Table 5: Performance of DEM vs. single NER Tools.

6.3 Evaluating DEM

When applying NER algorithms over Bedaya (Table 5) with NoorCorp (Table 5) as a train dataset, somewhat surprisingly, classic CRF achieves the best score while the state-of-the-art ML-model LSTM-CRF NER is only the fourth-best tool. Using DEM results in an ensemble that outperforms CRF by three percentage points on recall and 2.4 percentage points on F1-score. In table 6 DEM is compared with the following static ensemble methods: C4.5(Quinlan, 2014), Adaboost (M1)(Freund and Schapire, 1996) and bagging (BG) (Breiman, 1996) with RandomForest (Breiman, 2001), REPTree, and C4.5 as the base classifiers. The rest of the static ensemble methods are Logistic Model Trees (LMT) (Landwehr et al., 2005), Sequential Minimal Optimization (SMO) (Hastie and Tibshirani, 1998), and Naive Bayes (NB) (John and Langley, 1995). As we chose the C4.5 algorithm as our dynamic ensemble method, we can see the impact of utilizing C4.5 with predictors versus using it without predictors by comparing the other eight static models' results. It seems that in this setup and over this task, DEM can improve both the recall and the resulting F1-score by approximately three percentage points compared with the best static method's performance. When comparing to the Oracle, one can see that DEM manages to close half of the distance between the best performing NER and the Oracle in terms of F1-score. In contrast, the next best ensemble method only manages to close a quarter of this distance.

Type	Precision	Recall	F1
NB	86.50%	67.90%	76.10%
SMO	91.00%	68.20%	78.00%
LMT	91.00%	68.30%	78.00%
BG (REPTree)	91.00%	68.20%	78.00%
BG (randomForest)	91.10%	68.40%	78.14%
BG (C4.5)	91.08%	68.34%	78.09%
C4.5	91.10%	68.30%	78.07%
M1(c4.5))	91.10%	68.30%	78.07%
DEM	**90.80%**	**71.00%**	**79.80%**
Oracle	**94.00%**	**75.00%**	**83.00%**

Table 6: Performance of DEM vs. Static Models.

6.4 Modern Text Versus Historical Text

Of the seven NER algorithms we evaluate, five are ML-based. Here, we evaluate their performance when trained on modern and historical datasets. Figure 3 shows the algorithms' performance when tested over the Bedaya dataset and trained over two different datasets: ANER (Benajiba et al., 2007) a modern corpus, NoorCorp (Sajadi and Minaei, 2017) a historical corpus, and over both. The results demonstrate the importance of historic Arabic datasets as algorithms trained on historic data achieve better performance than when trained upon modern data. When trained over a mix of historical and modern data, didn't lead to improvement, thus relatively poor performance highlights the need to find better ways to transfer learning from modern to historical texts. Table 7 shows some outputs of tokens from Bedaya dataset by CRF-NER tool (the best tool in our ensemble model) when it trained over modern and historic text.

7 Conclusion and Future Work

We have proposed a dynamic ensemble model for NER and demonstrated its efficacy over a historical Arabic task. We have shown that training ML-based NER algorithms over modern Arabic text negatively impacts their performance over historical text, even when the training is combined with historical sources. This result highlights the need for more tagged historical datasets, such as the Bedaya corpus contributed by this work. In future work, we intend to enhance the dynamic ensemble model by exploring additional predictors and alternative ensemble learning methods. We further intend to explore different ways to utilize modern Arabic corpora in historical text analysis tasks.

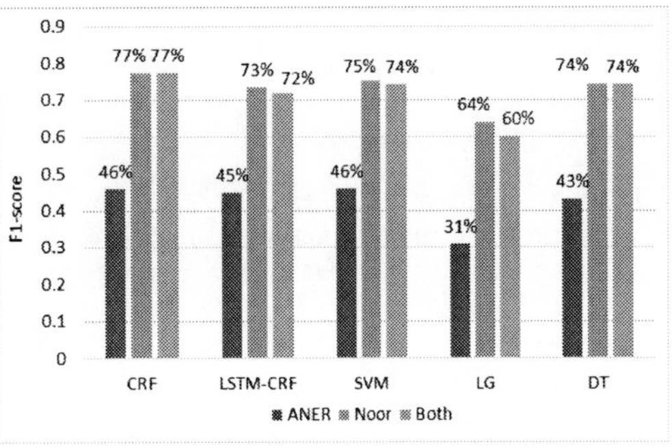

Figure 3: Comparative results of NER trained over modern (ANER) and historic (NoorCorp) data.

Token	CRF (MSA)	CRF (Historic)	Class
'talha'	O	PERS	PERS
'mnaf'	O	PERS	PERS
'almgazi'	O	LOC	LOC
'alhodybya'	O	LOC	LOC
'alshabha'	O	ORG	ORG
'bniAMR'	O	ORG	ORG

Table 7: Output Examples for CRF-NER when trained over modern and historical text.

References

Sherief Abdallah, Khaled Shaalan, and Muhammad Shoaib. 2012. Integrating rule-based system with classification for Arabic named entity recognition. In *International Conference on Intelligent Text Processing and Computational Linguistics (CICLing '12)*, pages 311–322. Springer.

Lahsen Abouenour, Karim Bouzoubaa, and Paolo Rosso. 2010. Using the yago ontology as a resource for the enrichment of Named Entities in Arabic WordNet. In *Proceedings of The Seventh International Conference on Language Resources and Evaluation (LREC 2010) Workshop on Language Resources and Human Language Technology for Semitic Languages*, pages 27–31.

Rami Al-Rfou, Vivek Kulkarni, Bryan Perozzi, and Steven Skiena. 2015. Polyglot-ner: Massive multilingual named entity recognition. In *Proceedings of the society of industrial applied mathematics (SIAM '15) International Conference on Data Mining*, pages 586–594. SIAM.

Mohammad Al-Smadi, Saad Al-Zboon, Yaser Jararweh, and Patrick Juola. 2020. Transfer learning for arabic named entity recognition with deep neural networks. *IEEE Access*, 8:37736–37745.

Fahd Alotaibi and Mark Lee. 2014. A hybrid approach to features representation for fine-grained arabic named entity recognition. In *Proceedings of COLING 2014, the 25th International Conference on Computational Linguistics: Technical Papers*, pages 984–995.

Husameldin AMN Balla and Sarah Jane Delany. 2020. Exploration of approaches to arabic named entity recognition.

Yassine Benajiba, Paolo Rosso, and José Miguel Benedíruiz. 2007. Anersys: An Arabic named entity recognition system based on maximum entropy. In *International Conference on Intelligent Text Processing and Computational Linguistics (CICLing '07)*, pages 143–153. Springer.

Ann Bies, Denise DiPersio, and Mohamed Maamouri. 2012. *Linguistic resources for Arabic machine translation*. John Benjamins, Amsterdam, The Netherlands.

Leo Breiman. 1996. Bagging predictors. *Machine learning*, 24(2):123–140.

Leo Breiman. 2001. Random forests. *Machine learning*, 45(1):5–32.

Chih-Chung Chang and Chih-Jen Lin. 2011. Libsvm: A library for support vector machines. *ACM transactions on intelligent systems and technology (TIST '11)*, 2(3):1–27.

Jacob Devlin, Ming-Wei Chang, Kenton Lee, and Kristina Toutanova. 2018. Bert: Pre-training of deep bidirectional transformers for language understanding. *arXiv preprint arXiv:1810.04805*.

Thomas G. Dietterich. 2000. Ensemble methods in machine learning. In *Proceedings of the First International Workshop on Multiple Classifier Systems*, (MCS '00), page 1–15, Berlin, Heidelberg. Springer-Verlag.

Maud Ehrmann, Matteo Romanello, Alex Flückiger, and Simon Clematide. 2020. Extended overview of clef hipe 2020: named entity processing on historical newspapers. In *CLEF 2020 Working Notes. Conference and Labs of the Evaluation Forum*, volume 2696. CEUR.

Asif Ekbal and Sivaji Bandyopadhyay. 2010. Named entity recognition using support vector machine: A language independent approach. *International Journal of Electrical, Computer, and Systems Engineering*, 4(2):155–170.

Yoav Freund and Robert E. Schapire. 1996. Experiments with a new boosting algorithm. In *Proceedings of the Thirteenth International Conference on International Conference on Machine Learning*, ICML'96, page 148–156, San Francisco, CA, USA. Morgan Kaufmann Publishers Inc.

Nizar Y Habash. 2010. Introduction to Arabic natural language processing. *Synthesis Lectures on Human Language Technologies*, 3(1):1–187.

Mark Hall, Eibe Frank, Geoffrey Holmes, Bernhard Pfahringer, Peter Reutemann, and Ian H Witten. 2009. The weka data mining software: an update. *ACM SIGKDD explorations newsletter*, 11(1):10–18.

Trevor Hastie and Robert Tibshirani. 1998. Classification by pairwise coupling. In *Proceedings of the 1997 Conference on Advances in Neural Information Processing Systems 10*, (NIPS '97), page 507–513, Cambridge, MA, USA. MIT Press.

Marti A. Hearst, Susan T Dumais, Edgar Osuna, John Platt, and Bernhard Scholkopf. 1998. Support vector machines. *IEEE Intelligent Systems and their applications*, 13(4):18–28.

Robert Hetzron. 1997. *The Semitic Languages*. Taylor & Francis.

Sepp Hochreiter and Jürgen Schmidhuber. 1997. Long short-term memory. *Neural computation*, 9(8):1735–1780.

David W Hosmer Jr, Stanley Lemeshow, and Rodney X Sturdivant. 2013. *Applied logistic regression*, volume 398. John Wiley & Sons.

Zhiheng Huang, Wei Xu, and Kai Yu. 2015. Bidirectional lstm-crf models for sequence tagging. *arXiv preprint arXiv:1508.01991*.

Ridong Jiang, Rafael E Banchs, and Haizhou Li. 2016. Evaluating and combining name entity recognition systems. In *Proceedings of the Sixth Named Entity Workshop*, pages 21–27. Association for Computational Linguistics (ACL '16).

George H. John and Pat Langley. 1995. Estimating continuous distributions in bayesian classifiers. In *Proceedings of the Eleventh Conference on Uncertainty in Artificial Intelligence*, (UAI '95), page 338–345, San Francisco, CA, USA. Morgan Kaufmann Publishers Inc.

Albert HR Ko, Robert Sabourin, and Alceu Souza Britto Jr. 2008. From dynamic classifier selection to dynamic ensemble selection. *Pattern recognition*, 41(5):1718–1731.

John D. Lafferty, Andrew McCallum, and Fernando C. N. Pereira. 2001. Conditional random fields: Probabilistic models for segmenting and labeling sequence data. In *Proceedings of the Eighteenth International Conference on Machine Learning*, ICML '01, page 282–289, San Francisco, CA, USA. Morgan Kaufmann Publishers Inc.

Niels Landwehr, Mark Hall, and Eibe Frank. 2005. Logistic model trees. *Machine learning*, 59(1-2):161–205.

Jing Li, Aixin Sun, Jianglei Han, and Chenliang Li. 2020. A survey on deep learning for named entity recognition. *IEEE Transactions on Knowledge and Data Engineering*.

Yijin Liu, Fandong Meng, Jinchao Zhang, Jinan Xu, Yufeng Chen, and Jie Zhou. 2019. Gcdt: A global context enhanced deep transition architecture for sequence labeling. *arXiv preprint arXiv:1906.02437*.

Christopher D Manning, Mihai Surdeanu, John Bauer, Jenny Rose Finkel, Steven Bethard, and David McClosky. 2014. The stanford corenlp natural language processing toolkit. In *Proceedings of 52nd annual meeting of the association for computational linguistics: system demonstrations*, pages 55–60.

Alireza Mansouri, Lilly Suriani Affendey, and Ali Mamat. 2008. Named entity recognition approaches. *International Journal of Computer Science and Network Security IJCSNS*, 8(2):339–344.

Slim Mesfar. 2007. Named entity recognition for Arabic using syntactic grammars. In *International Conference on Application of Natural Language to Information Systems (NLDB '07)*, pages 305–316. Springer.

Andrei Mikheev, Marc Moens, and Claire Grover. 1999. Named entity recognition without gazetteers. In *Ninth Conference of the European Chapter of the Association for Computational Linguistics (EACL '99)*.

Djamel Mostefa, Mariama Laïb, Stéphane Chaudiron, Khalid Choukri, and G Chalendar. 2009. A multilingual named entity corpus for Arabic, English and French. *MEDAR*, 2009:2nd.

Nikunj Chandrakant Oza and Stuart Russell. 2001. *Online ensemble learning*. University of California, Berkeley.

Matthew E Peters, Mark Neumann, Luke Zettlemoyer, and Wen-tau Yih. 2018. Dissecting contextual word embeddings: Architecture and representation. *arXiv preprint arXiv:1808.08949*.

J. Ross Quinlan. 1986. Induction of decision trees. *Machine learning*, 1(1):81–106.

J Ross Quinlan. 2014. *C4. 5: programs for machine learning*. Elsevier.

Xiang Ren, Jiaming Shen, Meng Qu, Xuan Wang, Zeqiu Wu, Qi Zhu, Meng Jiang, Fangbo Tao, Saurabh Sinha, David Liem, et al. 2017. Life-inet: A structured network-based knowledge exploration and analytics system for life sciences. In *Proceedings of ACL 2017, System Demonstrations*, pages 55–60.

David E Rumelhart, Geoffrey E Hinton, and Ronald J Williams. 1986. Learning representations by back-propagating errors. *Nature*, 323(6088):533–536.

Tomer Sagi and Avigdor Gal. 2013. Schema matching prediction with applications to data source discovery and dynamic ensembling. *The VLDB Journal*, 22(5):689–710.

Mohamad Bagher Sajadi and Behrooz Minaei. 2017. Arabic named entity recognition using boosting method. In *2017 Artificial Intelligence and Signal Processing Conference (AISP '17)*, pages 281–288, Shiraz, Iran. IEEE.

Robert E Schapire. 1990. The strength of weak learnability. *Machine learning*, 5(2):197–227.

Khaled Shaalan. 2014. A survey of Arabic named entity recognition and classification. *Computational Linguistics*, 40(2):469–510.

Khaled Shaalan and Hafsa Raza. 2009. Nera: Named entity recognition for Arabic. *Journal of the American Society for Information Science and Technology*, 60(8):1652–1663.

René Speck and Axel-Cyrille Ngonga Ngomo. 2014. Ensemble learning for named entity recognition (iswc '13). In *International semantic web conference*, pages 519–534. Springer.

Robert George Douglas Steel, James Hiram Torrie, et al. 1960. Principles and procedures of statistics.

Robert F Tate. 1954. Correlation between a discrete and a continuous variable. point-biserial correlation. *The Annals of mathematical statistics*, 25(3):603–607.

Matthias Weidlich, Tomer Sagi, Henrik Leopold, Avigdor Gal, and Jan Mendling. 2013. Predicting the quality of process model matching. In *Business Process Management (BPM '13)*, pages 203–210. Springer.

Jason Yosinski, Jeff Clune, Yoshua Bengio, and Hod Lipson. 2014. How transferable are features in deep neural networks? *arXiv preprint arXiv:1411.1792*.

Norshuhani Zamin and Alan Oxley. 2011. Building a corpus-derived gazetteer for named entity recognition. In *International Conference on Software Engineering and Computer Systems*, pages 73–80. Springer.

GuoDong Zhou and Jian Su. 2002. Named entity recognition using an HMM-based chunk tagger. In *proceedings of the 40th Annual Meeting on Association for Computational Linguistics*, pages 473–480. Association for Computational Linguistics.

Arabic Offensive Language on Twitter: Analysis and Experiments

Hamdy Mubarak [1] **Ammar Rashed**[2] **Kareem Darwish**[1]
Younes Samih[1] **Ahmed Abdelali**[1]
[1]Qatar Computing Research Institute, HBKU
[2]Özyeğin University
{hmubarak, kdarwish, ysamih, aabdelali}@hbku.edu.qa
ammar.rasid@ozu.edu.tr

Abstract

Detecting offensive language on Twitter has many applications ranging from detecting/predicting bullying to measuring polarization. In this paper, we focus on building a large Arabic offensive tweet dataset. We introduce a method for building a dataset that is not biased by topic, dialect, or target. We produce the largest Arabic dataset to date with special tags for vulgarity and hate speech. We thoroughly analyze the dataset to determine which topics, dialects, and gender are most associated with offensive tweets and how Arabic speakers use offensive language. Lastly, we conduct many experiments to produce strong results (F1 = 83.2) on the dataset using SOTA techniques.

1 Introduction

Disclaimer: Due to the nature of the paper, some examples herein contain highly offensive language and hate speech. They don't reflect the views of the authors in any way. This work is an attempt to help fight such speech.

Much recent interest has focused on the detection of offensive language and hate speech in online social media. Offensiveness is often associated with undesirable behaviors such as trolling, cyberbullying, online extremism, political polarization, and propaganda. Thus, offensive language detection is instrumental for a variety of application such as: quantifying polarization (Barberá and Sood, 2015; Conover et al., 2011), trolls and propaganda account detection (Darwish et al., 2017), hate crimes likelihood estimation (Waseem and Hovy, 2016); and predicting conflicts (Chadefaux, 2014). In this paper, we describe our methodology for building a large dataset of Arabic offensive tweets. Given that roughly 1-2% of all Arabic tweets are offensive (Mubarak and Darwish, 2019), targeted annotation is essential to efficiently build a large dataset. Since our methodology does not use a seed list of offensive words, it is not biased by topic, target, or dialect. Using our methodology, we tagged a 10,000 Arabic tweet dataset for offensiveness, where offensive tweets account for roughly 19% of the tweets. Further, we labeled tweets as vulgar or hate speech. To date, this is the largest available dataset, which we plan to make publicly available along with annotation guidelines. We use this dataset to characterize Arabic offensive language to ascertain the topics, dialects, and users' gender that are most associated with the use of offensive language. Though we suspect that there are common features that span different languages and cultures, some characteristics of Arabic offensive language are language and culture specific. Thus, we conduct a thorough analysis of how Arab users use offensive language. Next, we use the dataset to train strong Arabic offensive language classifiers using state-of-the-art representations and classification techniques. Specifically, we experiment with static and contextualized embeddings for representation along with a variety of classifiers such as Transformer-based and Support Vector Machine (SVM) classifiers. The contributions of this paper are as follows:

- We built the largest Arabic offensive language dataset to date that is also labeled for vulgar language and hate speech and is not biased by topic or dialect. We describe the methodology for building it along with annotation guidelines.
- We performed thorough analysis to describe the peculiarities of Arabic offensive language.
- We experimented with SOTA classification techniques to provide strong results on detecting offensive language.

Proceedings of the Sixth Arabic Natural Language Processing Workshop, pages 126–135
Kyiv, Ukraine (Virtual), April 19, 2021.

2 Related Work

Many recent papers have focused on the detection of offensive language, including hate speech (Agrawal and Awekar, 2018; Badjatiya et al., 2017; Davidson et al., 2017; Djuric et al., 2015; Kwok and Wang, 2013; Malmasi and Zampieri, 2017; Nobata et al., 2016; Yin et al., 2009). Offensive language can be categorized as: *vulgar*, which include explicit and rude sexual references, *pornographic*, and *hateful*, which includes offensive remarks concerning people's race, religion, country, etc. (Jay and Janschewitz, 2008). Prior works have concentrated on building annotated corpora and training classification models. Concerning corpora, `hatespeechdata.com` attempts to maintain an updated list of hate speech corpora for multiple languages including Arabic and English. Further, SemEval 2019 ran an evaluation task targeted at detecting offensive language, which focused exclusively on English (Zampieri et al., 2019). For SemEval 2020, they extended the task to include other languages including Arabic (Zampieri et al., 2020). As for classification models, most studies used supervised classification at either word level (Kwok and Wang, 2013), character sequence level (Malmasi and Zampieri, 2017), and word embeddings (Djuric et al., 2015). The studies used different classification techniques including Naïve Bayes (Kwok and Wang, 2013), Support Vector Machines (SVM) (Malmasi and Zampieri, 2017), and deep learning (Agrawal and Awekar, 2018; Badjatiya et al., 2017; Nobata et al., 2016) classification. The accuracy of the aforementioned system ranged between 76% and 90%. Earlier work looked at the use of sentiment words as features as well as contextual features (Yin et al., 2009).

The work on Arabic offensive language detection is relatively nascent (Abozinadah, 2017; Alakrot et al., 2018; Albadi et al., 2018; Mubarak et al., 2017; Mubarak and Darwish, 2019). Mubarak et al. (2017) suggested that certain users are more likely to use offensive languages than others, and they used this insight to build a list of offensive Arabic words and to construct a labeled set of 1,100 tweets. Abozinadah (2017) used supervised classification based on a variety of features including user profile features, textual features, and network features. They reported an accuracy of nearly 90%. Alakrot et al. (2018) used supervised classification based on word n-grams to detect offensive language in YouTube comments. They improved classification with stemming and achieved a precision of 88%. Albadi et al. (2018) focused on detecting religious hate speech using a recurrent neural network.

Arabic is a morphologically rich language with a standard variety called Modern Standard Arabic (MSA), which is typically used in formal communication, and many dialectal varieties that differ from MSA in lexical selection, morphology, phonology, and syntactic structures. In MSA, words are typically derived from a set of thousands of roots by fitting a root into a stem template and the resulting stem may accept a variety of prefixes and suffixes. Though word segmentation, which greatly improves word matching, is quite accurate for MSA (Abdelali et al., 2016), with accuracy approaching 99%, dialectal segmentation is not sufficiently reliable, with accuracy ranging between 91-95% for different dialects (Samih et al., 2017). Since dialectal Arabic is ubiquitous in Arabic tweets and many tweets have creative spellings of words, recent work on Arabic offensive language detection used character-level models (Mubarak and Darwish, 2019).

3 Data Collection

3.1 Collecting Arabic Offensive Tweets

Our target is to build a large Arabic offensive language dataset that is representative of its appearance on Twitter and is hopefully not biased to specific dialects, topics, or targets. One of the main challenges is that offensive tweets constitute a very small portion of overall tweets. To quantify their proportion, we took 3 random samples of tweets from different days, with each sample composed of 1,000 tweets, and we found that only 1-2% of them were offensive (including pornographic advertisements). This percentage is consistent with previously reported percentages (Mubarak et al., 2017). Thus, annotating random tweets is grossly inefficient. One way to overcome this problem is to use a seed list of offensive words to filter tweets. However, doing so is problematic, as it would skew the dataset to particular types of offensive language or to specific dialects. Offensiveness is often dialect and country specific.

After inspecting many tweets, we observed that many offensive tweets have the vocative particle يا ("yA" – meaning "O")[1], which is mainly used

[1]Arabic words are provided along with their Buckwalter

in directing the speech to a specific person or group. The ratio of offensive tweets increases to 5% if a tweet contains one vocative particle and to 19% if it has at least two vocative particles. Users often repeat this particle for emphasis, as in: يا أمي يا حنونة ("yA Amy yA Hnwnp" – O my mother, O kind one), which is endearing and non-offensive, and يا كلب يا قذر ("yA klb yA q*r" – "O dog, O dirty one"), which is offensive. We decided to use this pattern to increase our chances of finding offensive tweets. One of the main advantages of the pattern يا ... يا ("yA ... yA") is that it is not associated with any specific topic or genre, and it appears in all Arabic dialects. Though the use of offensive language does not necessitate the appearance of the vocative particle, the particle does not favor any specific offensive expressions and greatly improves our chances of finding offensive tweets. Using Twitter APIs, we collected 660k Arabic tweets having this pattern between April 15 – May 6, 2019. To increase diversity, we sorted the word sequences between the vocative particles and took the most frequent 10,000 unique sequences. For each word sequence, we took a random tweet containing that sequence. Then we annotated those tweets, ending up with 1,915 offensive tweets which represent roughly 19% of all tweets. Each tweet was labeled as: offensive, which could additionally be labeled as vulgar and/or hate speech, or Clean. We describe in greater detail our annotation guidelines, which are compatible with the OffensEval2019 annotation guidelines (Zampieri et al., 2019). For example, if a tweet has insults or threats targeting a group based on their nationality, ethnicity, gender, political affiliation, religious belief, or other common characteristics, this is considered hate speech (Zampieri et al., 2019). It is worth mentioning that we also considered insulting groups based on their sport affiliation as a form of hate speech. Often, being a fan of a particular sporting club is considered a part of the personality that rarely changes over time (similar to religious and political affiliations). Many incidents of violence have occurred among fans of rival clubs.

Although we used a generic pattern that is used across dialects and topics, such may not cover all the stylistic diversity of offensive expressions. However, our approach considerably narrows the search space for offensive tweets, which constitute a small percentage of tweets in general, while being far more generic than using a seed list of offensive words, which may greatly skew the distribution of offensive tweets. For future work, we plan to explore other methods for identifying offensive tweets with greater stylistic diversity.

transliteration and English translation.

3.2 Annotating Tweets

We developed annotation guidelines jointly with an experienced annotator, who is a native Arabic speaker with good knowledge of various Arabic dialects, in accordance to the OffensEval2019 guidelines. Tweets were given one or more of the following four labels: *offensive*, *vulgar*, *hate speech*, or *clean*. Since the *offensive* label covers both vulgar and hate speech and vulgarity and hate speech are not mutually exclusive, a tweet can be just offensive or offensive and vulgar and/or hate speech. The annotation adhered to the following guidelines:

OFFENSIVE (OFF): Offensive tweets contain explicit or implicit insults or attacks against other people, or inappropriate language, such as:
Direct threats or incitement, ex: احرقوا مقرات المعارضة ("AHrqwA mqrAt AlmEArDp" – "burn opposition headquarters") and اقتلوا هذا المنافق ("h*A AlmnAfq yjb qtlh" – "kill this hypocrite").
Insults and expressions of contempt, which include: *Animal analogies*, ex: يا كلب ("yA klb" – "O dog") and كل تبن ("kl tbn" – "eat hay").; *Insult to family*, ex: يا روح أمك ("yA rwH Amk" – "O mother's soul"); *Sexually-related insults*, ex: يا ديوث ("yA dywv" – "O cuckold"); *Damnation*, ex: الله يلعنك ("Allh ylEnk" – "may God curse you"); and *Attacks on morals*, ex: يا كاذب ("yA kA*b" – "O liar").

VULGAR (VLG): Vulgar tweets are offensive tweets that contain profanity, such as mentions of private parts or sexual-related acts or references.

HATE SPEECH (HS): Hate speech tweets are offensive tweets targeting group based on common characteristics such as: *Race*, ex: يا زنجي ("yA znjy" – "O Negro"); *Ethnicity*, ex. الفرس الأنجاس ("Alfrs AlAnjAs" – "Impure Persians"); *Group or party*, ex: أبوك شيوعي ("Abwk $ywEy" – "your father is a communist"); and *Religion*, ex: دينك القذر

("dynk Alq*r" – "your filthy religion").

CLEAN (CLN): Clean tweets do not contain vulgar or offensive language. We noticed that some tweets have some offensive words, but the whole tweet should not be considered as offensive due to the intention of users. This suggests that normal string match without considering contexts may fail in some cases. Examples of such ambiguous cases include: *Humor*, ex: يا عدوة الفرحة هههه ("yA Edwp AlfrHp hhh" – "O enemy of happiness hahaha"); *Advice*, ex: لا تقل لصاحبك يا خنزير ("lA tql lSAHbk yA xnzyr" – "don't say to your friend: You are a pig"); *Condition*, ex: إذا عارضتهم يقولون يا عميل ("A*A EArDthm yqwlwn yA Emyl" – "if you disagree with them, they call you a spy"); *Condemnation*, ex: لماذا نسب بقول: يا بقرة؟ ("lmA*A nsb bqwl: yA bqrp?" – "Why do we insult others by saying: O cow?"); *Self offense*, ex: تعبت من لساني القذر ("tEbt mn lsAny Alq*r" – "I am tired of my dirty tongue"); *Non-human target*, ex: يا بنت المجنونة يا كورة ("yA bnt Almjnwnp yA kwrp" – "O daughter of the crazy one O football"); and *Quotation from a movies or a story*, ex: تاني يا زكي! تاني يا فاشل ("tAny yA zky! tAny yA fA$l" – "again smarty! again O loser"). For ambiguous expressions, the annotator searched Twitter to observe real sample usages.

Table 1 shows the distribution of the annotated tweets. There are 1,915 offensive tweets, including 225 vulgar tweets and 506 hate speech tweets, and 8,085 clean tweets. To validate annotation quality, we asked three additional annotators to annotate two tweet sample sets. The first was a random sample of 100 tweets containing 50 offensive and 50 non-offensive tweets. The Inter-Annotator Agreement (IIA) between the annotators using Fleiss's Kappa coefficient (Fleiss, 1971) was 0.92. The second was general random samples containing 100 tweets each from the dataset, and the IIA with the dataset was: 0.97, 0.96, and 0.97. This high level of agreement gives more confidence in the quality of the annotation. Data can be downloaded from:
`https://alt.qcri.org/resources/OSACT2020-sharedTask-CodaLab-Train-Dev-Test.zip`

	Tweets	Words
Offensive	1,915	38k
– Vulgar	225	4k
– Hate speech	506	13k
Clean	8,085	151k
Total	10,000	193k

Table 1: Distribution of offensive and clean tweets.

3.3 Statistics and User Demographics

Given the annotated tweets, we wanted to ascertain the distribution of: types of offensive language, genres or topics where it is used, the dialects used, and the gender of users using such language. Accordingly, the annotator manually examined and tagged all the offensive tweets.

Topic: Figure 1 shows the distribution of topics associated with offensive tweets. As the figure shows, sports and politics are most dominant for offensive language including vulgar and hate speech.

Dialect: We looked at MSA and four major dialects, namely Egyptian (EGY), Leventine (LEV), Maghrebi (MGR), and Gulf (GLF). Figure 2 shows that 71% of vulgar tweets were written in EGY followed by GLF, which accounted for 13% of vulgar tweets. MSA was not used in any vulgar tweets. As for offensive tweets in general, EGY and GLF were used in 36% and 35% of the offensive tweets respectively. Unlike the case of vulgar language, 15% of the offensive tweets were written in MSA. For hate speech, GLF and EGY were again dominant and MSA constituted 21% of the tweets. This is consistent with findings for other languages, e.g. English and Italian, where vulgarity was more frequently associated with colloquial language (Mattiello, 2005; Maisto et al., 2017).

Gender: Figure 3 shows that the vast majority of offensive tweets, including vulgar and hate speech, were authored by males. Female Twitter users accounted for 14% of offensive tweets in general and 6% and 9% of vulgar and hate speech respectively. Figure 4 shows a detailed categorization of hate speech types, where the top three include insulting groups based on their political ideology, origin, and sport affiliation. Religious hate speech appeared in only 15% of all hate speech tweets.

Next, we analyzed all tweets labeled as offensive to better understand how Arabic speakers use offensive language. Here is a breakdown of usage:

Direct name calling: The most frequent attack is to call a person an animal name, and the most used

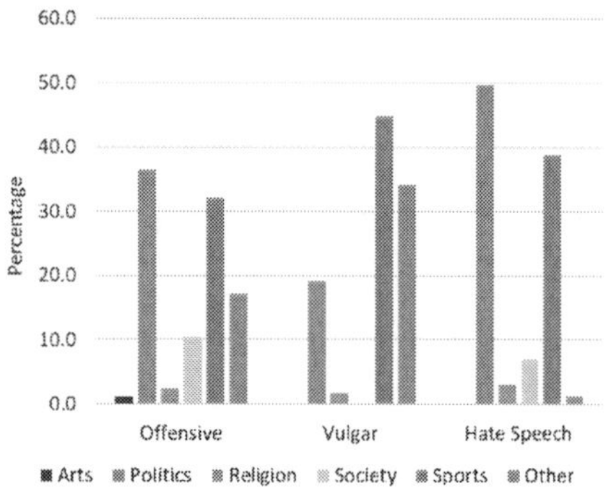

Figure 1: Topic distribution for offensive language and its sub-categories

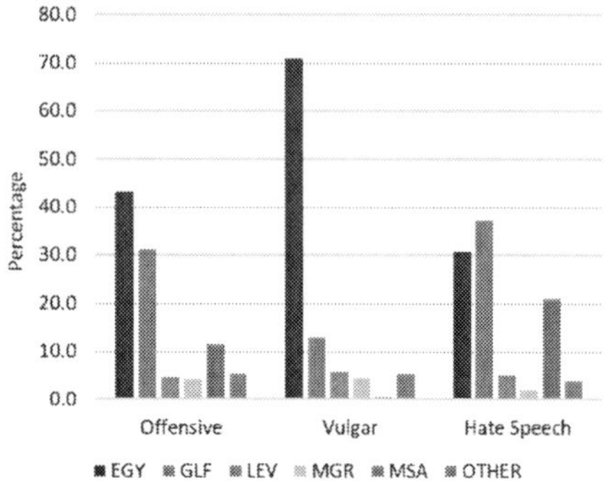

Figure 2: Dialect distribution for offensive language and its sub-categories

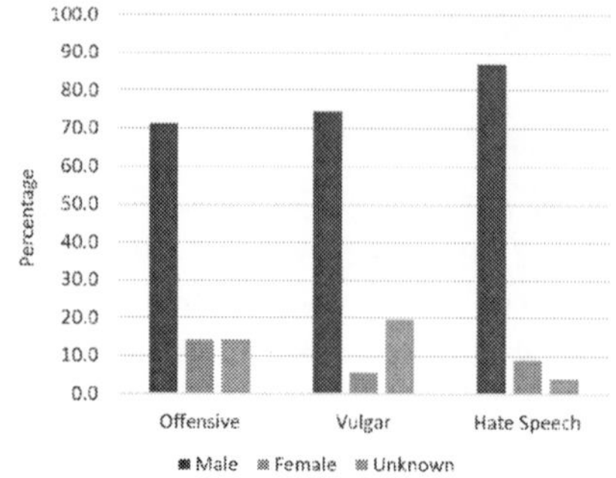

Figure 3: Gender distribution for offensive language and its sub-categories

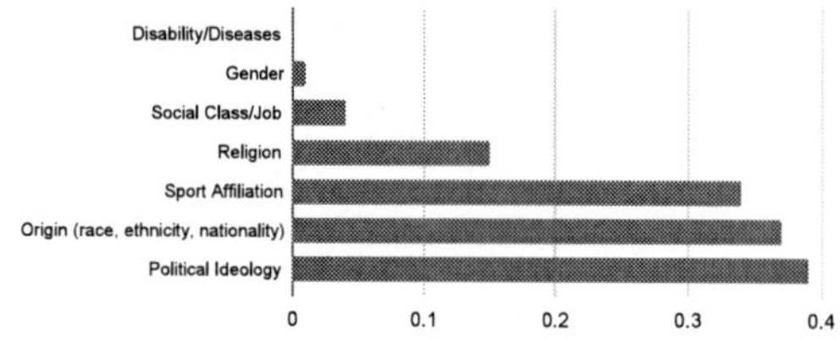

Figure 4: Distribution of Hate Speech Types. Note: A tweet may have more than one type.

Figure 5: Tag cloud for words with top valence score among offensive class, e.g. name calling (animals), curses, insults, etc.

animals were كلب ("klb" – "dog"), حمار ("HmAr" – "donkey"), and بهيم ("bhym" – "beast"). The second most common was insulting mental abilities using words such as غبي ("gby" – "stupid") and عبيط ("EbyT" –"idiot"). Culturally, not all animal names are used as insults. For example, animals such as أسد ("Asd" – "lion"), صقر ("Sqr" – "falcon"), and غزال ("gzAl" – "gazelle") are typically used for praise. For other insults, people use: some *bird* names such as دجاجة ("djAjp" – "chicken"), بومة ("bwmp" – "owl"), and غراب ("grAb" – "crow"); *insects* such as ذبابة ("*bAbp" – "fly"), صرصور ("SrSwr" – "cockroach"), and حشرة ("H$rp" – "insect"); *microorganisms* such as جرثومة ("jrvwmp" – "microbe") and طحالب ("THAlb" – "algae"); *inanimate objects* such as جزمة ("jzmp" – "shoes") and سطل ("sTl" – "bucket") among other usages.

Simile and metaphor: Users use simile and metaphor were they would compare a person to: an *animal* as in زي الثور ("zy Alvwr" – "like a bull"), سمعني نهيقك ("smEny nhyqk" – "let me hear your braying"), and هز ديلك ("hz dylk" – "wag your tail"); a person with *mental or physical disability* such as منغولي ("mngwly" – "Mongolian (Down syndrome)"), معوق ("mEwq" – "disabled"), and قزم ("qzm" – "dwarf"); and to the *opposite gender* such as جيش نوال ("jy$ nwAl" – "Nawal's army

(Nawal is female name)") and نادي زيزي ("nAdy zyzy" – "Zizi's club (Zizi is a female nickname)").
Indirect speech: This includes: *sarcasm* such as أذكى إخواتك ("A*kY AxwAtk" – "smartest one of your siblings") and فيلسوف الحمير ("fylswf AlHmyr" – "the donkeys' philosopher"); *questions* such as ايه كل الغباء ده ("Ayh kl AlgbA dh" – "what is all this stupidity"); and *indirect speech* such as النقاش مع البهايم غير مثمر ("AlnqA$ mE AlbhAym gyr mvmr" – "no use arguing with cattle").
Wishing Evil: This entails wishing death or major harm to befall someone such as ربنا ياخدك ("rbnA yAxdk" – "May God take (kill) you"), الله يلعنك ("Allh ylEnk" – "may God curse you"), and روح في داهية ("rwH fy dAhyp" – equivalent to "go to hell").
Name alteration: One common way to insult others is to change a letter or two in their names to produce new offensive words that rhyme with the original names. Some such examples include changing الجزيرة ("Aljzyrp" – "Aljazeera (channel)") to الخنزيرة ("Alxnzyrp" – "the pig") and خلفان ("xlfAn" – "Khalfan (person name)") to خرفان ("xrfAn" – "crazed").
Societal stratification: Some insults are associated with: certain *jobs* such as بواب ("bwAb" – "doorman") or خادم ("xAdm" – "servant"); and specific *societal components* such بدوي ("bdwy" – "bedouin") and فلاح ("flAH" – "farmer").
Immoral behavior: These insults are associated with negative moral traits or behaviors such as حقير ("Hqyr" – "vile"), خاين ("xAyn" – "traitor"), and منافق ("mnAfq" – "hypocrite").
Sexually related: They include expressions such as خول ("xwl" – "gay"), وسخة ("wsxp" – "prostitute"), and عرص ("ErS" – "pimp").

Figure 5 shows the top words with the highest valance scores for individual words in the offensive tweets. Larger fonts are used to highlight words with highest scores and align as well with the categories mentioned in the breakdown for the offensive languages. We slightly modified the valence score described by (Conover et al., 2011) to magnify its value by multiplying valence with frequency of occurrence.

4 Experiments

We conducted an extensive battery of experiments on the dataset to establish strong Arabic offensive language classification results. Though offensive tweets have finer-grained labels where offensive tweet could also be vulgar and/or hate speech, we conducted coarser-grained classification to determine if a tweet was offensive or not. For classification, we experimented with several tweet representation and classification models. For tweet representations, we used: the count of positive and negative terms, based on a polarity lexicon; static embeddings, namely fastText and Skip-Gram; and deep contextual embeddings, namely $\text{BERT}_{\text{base-multilingual}}$ and AraBERT (Antoun et al., 2020).

4.1 Data Pre-processing

We performed several text pre-processing steps. First, we tokenized the text using the Farasa Arabic NLP toolkit (Abdelali et al., 2016). Second, we removed URLs, numbers, and all tweet specific tokens, namely mentions, retweets, and hashtags as they are not part of the language semantic structure, and therefore, not usable in pre-trained embeddings. Third, we performed basic Arabic letter normalization, namely variants of the letter *alef* to *bare alef*, *ta marbouta* to *ha*, and *alef maqsoura* to *ya*. We also separated words that are commonly incorrectly attached such as ياكلب ("yAklb" – "O dog"), is split to يا كلب ("yA klb"). Lastly, we normalized letter repetitions to allow for a maximum of 2 repeated letters. For example, the token ههههه ("hhhhh" – "hahahahaha") is normalized to هه ("hh"). We also removed Arabic diacritics and word elongations (kashida).

4.2 Representations

Lexical Features Since offensive words typically have a negative polarity, we wanted to test the effectiveness of using a polarity lexicon in detecting offensive tweets. For the lexicon, we used NileULex (El-Beltagy, 2016), which is an Arabic polarity lexicon containing 3,279 MSA and 2,674 Egyptian terms, out of which 4,256 are negative and 1,697 are positive. We used the counts of terms with positive polarity and terms with negative polarity in tweets as features.

Static Embeddings We experimented with various static embeddings that were pre-trained on different corpora with different vector dimensionality. We compared pre-trained embeddings to embeddings that were trained on our dataset. For pre-trained embeddings, we used: **fastText** Egyptian Arabic pre-trained embeddings (Bojanowski et al., 2017) with vector dimensionality of 300; **AraVec** skip-gram embeddings (Mohammad et al., 2017), trained on 66.9M Arabic tweets with 100-dimensional vectors; and **Mazajak** skip-gram embeddings (Abu Farha and Magdy, 2019), trained on 250M Arabic tweets with 300-dimensional vectors. Sentence embeddings were calculated by taking the mean of the embeddings of their tokens. The importance of testing a character level n-gram model like fastText lies in the agglutinative nature of the Arabic language. We trained a new fastText text classification model (Joulin et al., 2017) on our dataset with vectors of 40 dimensions, 0.5 learning rate, $2-10$ character n-grams as features, for 30 epochs. These hyper-parameters were tuned using a 5-fold cross-validated grid-search.

Deep Contextualized Embeddings We also experimented with pre-trained contextualized embeddings with fine-tuning for down-stream tasks. Recently, deep contextualized language models such as BERT (Bidirectional Encoder Representations from Transformers) (Devlin et al., 2019), UMLFIT (Howard and Ruder, 2018), and OpenAI GPT (Radford et al., 2018), have achieved ground-breaking results in many NLP classification and language understanding tasks. In this paper, we fine-tuned $\text{BERT}_{\text{base-multilingual}}$ (or simply BERT) and AraBERT embeddings to classify Arabic offensive language on Twitter as it eliminates the need for feature engineering. Although Robustly Optimized BERT (RoBERTa) embeddings perform better than ($\text{BERT}_{\text{large}}$) on GLUE (Wang et al., 2018), RACE (Lai et al., 2017), and SQuAD (Rajpurkar et al., 2016) tasks, pre-trained multilingual RoBERTa models are not available. BERT is pre-trained on Wikipedia text from 104 languages, and AraBERT is trained on a large Arabic news corpus containing 8.5M articles composed of roughly 2.5B tokens. Both use identical architectures and come with hundreds of millions of parameters. Both contain an encoder with 12 Transformer blocks, hidden size of 768, and 12 self-attention heads. These embedding use BP sub-word segments. Following Devlin et al. (2019), the classification consists of introducing a dense layer over the final hidden state h corresponding to first token of the sequence, [CLS], adding a softmax activation on the top of BERT to predict the probability of the l label: $p(l|h) = softmax(Wh)$, where W is the task-specific weight matrix. During fine-tuning, all BERT/AraBERT parameters together with W are optimized end-to-end to maximize the log-probability of the correct labels.

4.3 Classification Models

We explored different classifiers. When using lexical features and pre-trained static embeddings, we primarily used an SVM classifier with a radial basis function kernel. Only when using the Mazajak embeddings, we experimented with other classifiers such as AdaBoost and Logistic regression. The SVM classifier performed the best on static embeddings, and we picked the Mazajak embeddings because they yielded the best results among all static embeddings. We used the Scikit Learn implementations of all the classifiers such as libsvm for the SVM classifier. We also experimented with fastText, which trained embeddings on our data. When using contextualized embeddings, we fine-tuned BERT and AraBERT by adding a fully-connected dense layer followed by a softmax classifier, minimizing the binary cross-entropy loss function for the training data. For all experiments, we used the PyTorch[2] implementation by HuggingFace[3] as it provides pre-trained weights and vocabularies.

4.4 Evaluation

For all of our experiments, we used 5-fold cross validation with identical folds for all experiments. Table 2 reports on the results of using lexical features, static pre-trained embeddings with an SVM classifier, embeddings trained on our data with fastText classifier, and BERT and AraBERT over a dense layer with softmax activation. As the results show, using fine-tuned AraBERT yielded the best results overall, followed closely by Mazajak/SVM, with large improvements in precision over using BERT. The success of AraBERT was surprising given that it was not trained on social media text. Perhaps, pre-training a Transformer model on social media text may improve results further. We suspect that the Mazajak/SVM combination performed better than BERT due to the fact that the Mazajak embeddings, though static, were trained

[2] `https://pytorch.org/`

[3] `https://github.com/huggingface/transformers`

on in-domain data, as opposed to BERT. For completeness, we compared 7 other classifiers with SVM using Mazajak embeddings. As results in Table 3 show, using SVM yielded the best results.

Model/classifier	Prec.	Recall	F1
Lexical Features			
SVM	68.5	35.3	46.6
Pre-trained static embeddings			
fastText/SVM	76.7	43.5	55.5
AraVec/SVM	85.5	69.2	76.4
Mazajak/SVM	**88.6**	72.4	79.7
Embeddings trained on our data			
fastText/fastText	82.1	68.1	74.4
Contextualized embeddings			
$\text{BERT}_{\text{base-multilingual}}$	78.3	74.0	76.0
AraBERT	84.6	**82.4**	**83.2**

Table 2: Classification performance with different features and models.

Model	Prec.	Recall	F1
Decision Tree	51.2	53.8	52.4
Random Forest	82.4	42.4	56.0
Gaussian NB	44.9	**86.0**	59.0
Perceptron	75.6	67.7	66.8
AdaBoost	74.3	67.0	70.4
Gradient Boosting	84.2	63.0	72.1
Logistic Regression	84.7	69.5	76.3
SVM	**88.6**	72.4	**79.7**

Table 3: Performance of different classification models on Mazajak embeddings.

4.5 Error Analysis

We inspected the tweets of one fold that were misclassified by the Mazajak/SVM model (36 false positives/121 false negatives) to determine the most common errors. They were as follows:

Four false positive types:

- **Gloating:** ex. يا هبيدة ("yA hbydp" - "O you delusional") referring to fans of rival sports team for thinking they could win.
- **Quoting:** ex. لما حد يسب ويقول يا كلب ("lmA Hd ysb wyqwl yA klb" – "when someone swears and says: O dog").
- **Idioms:** ex. يا فاطر رمضان يا خاسر دينك ("yA fATr rmDAn yA xAsr dynk" – "o you who does not fast Ramadan, you have lost your faith"), which is a colloquial idiom.
- **Implicit Sarcasm:** ex. يا خاين انت عايز تشكك في حب الشعب للريس 😂😂 ("yA xAyn Ant EAwz t$kk fy Hb Al$Eb llrys" – "O traitor, (you) want to question people's love for the president 😂😂") where the author is mocking the president's popularity.

Two false negative types:

- **Mixture of offensiveness and admiration:** ex. calling a girl a puppy يا كلبوبة ("yA klbwbp" – "O puppy") in a flirtatious manner.
- **Implicit offensiveness:** ex. calling for cure while implying sanity: وتشفي حكام بلدك من المرض ("wt$fy HkAm bldk mn AlmrD" – "and cure rulers of your country from illness").

5 Conclusion and Future Work

In this paper we presented a systematic method for building an Arabic offensive language tweet dataset that does not favor specific dialects, topics, or genres. We developed detailed guidelines for tagging the tweets as clean or offensive, including special tags for vulgar tweets and hate speech. We tagged 10,000 tweets, which we plan to release publicly and would constitute the largest available Arabic offensive language dataset. We characterized the offensive tweets in the dataset to determine the topics that illicit such language, the dialects that are most often used, the common modes of offensiveness, and the gender distribution of their authors. We performed this breakdown for offensive tweets in general and for vulgar and hate speech tweets separately. We believe that this is the first detailed analysis of its kind. Lastly, we conducted a large battery of experiments on the dataset, using cross-validation, to establish a strong system for Arabic offensive language detection. We showed that using an Arabic specific BERT model (AraBERT) and static embeddings trained on tweets produced competitive results on the dataset.

For future work, we plan to pursue several directions. First, we want explore target specific offensive language, where attacks against an entity or a group may employ certain expressions that are only offensive within the context of that target and completely innocuous otherwise. Second, we plan to examine the effectiveness of cross dialectal and cross lingual learning of offensive language.

References

Ahmed Abdelali, Kareem Darwish, Nadir Durrani, and Hamdy Mubarak. 2016. Farasa: A fast and furious segmenter for arabic. In *Proceedings of the 2016 conference of the North American chapter of the association for computational linguistics: Demonstrations*, pages 11–16.

Ehab Abozinadah. 2017. *Detecting Abusive Arabic Language Twitter Accounts Using a Multidimensional Analysis Model*. Ph.D. thesis, George Mason University.

Ibrahim Abu Farha and Walid Magdy. 2019. Mazajak: An online Arabic sentiment analyser. In *Proceedings of the Fourth Arabic Natural Language Processing Workshop*, pages 192–198, Florence, Italy. Association for Computational Linguistics.

Sweta Agrawal and Amit Awekar. 2018. Deep learning for detecting cyberbullying across multiple social media platforms. In *European Conference on Information Retrieval*, pages 141–153. Springer.

Azalden Alakrot, Liam Murray, and Nikola S Nikolov. 2018. Towards accurate detection of offensive language in online communication in arabic. *Procedia computer science*, 142:315–320.

Nuha Albadi, Maram Kurdi, and Shivakant Mishra. 2018. Are they our brothers? analysis and detection of religious hate speech in the arabic twittersphere. In *2018 IEEE/ACM International Conference on Advances in Social Networks Analysis and Mining (ASONAM)*, pages 69–76. IEEE.

Wissam Antoun, Fady Baly, and Hazem Hajj. 2020. Arabert: Transformer-based model for arabic language understanding. In *Proceedings of the 4th Workshop on Open-Source Arabic Corpora and Processing Tools, with a Shared Task on Offensive Language Detection*, pages 9–15.

Pinkesh Badjatiya, Shashank Gupta, Manish Gupta, and Vasudeva Varma. 2017. Deep learning for hate speech detection in tweets. In *Proceedings of the 26th International Conference on World Wide Web Companion*, pages 759–760. International World Wide Web Conferences Steering Committee.

Pablo Barberá and Gaurav Sood. 2015. Follow your ideology: Measuring media ideology on social networks. In *Annual Meeting of the European Political Science Association, Vienna, Austria. Retrieved from http://www. gsood. com/research/papers/mediabias. pdf.*

Piotr Bojanowski, Edouard Grave, Armand Joulin, and Tomas Mikolov. 2017. Enriching word vectors with subword information. *Transactions of the Association for Computational Linguistics*, 5:135–146.

Thomas Chadefaux. 2014. Early warning signals for war in the news. *Journal of Peace Research*, 51(1):5–18.

Michael Conover, Jacob Ratkiewicz, Matthew R Francisco, Bruno Gonçalves, Filippo Menczer, and Alessandro Flammini. 2011. Political polarization on twitter. *ICWSM*, 133:89–96.

Kareem Darwish, Dimitar Alexandrov, Preslav Nakov, and Yelena Mejova. 2017. Seminar users in the arabic twitter sphere. In *International Conference on Social Informatics*, pages 91–108. Springer.

Thomas Davidson, Dana Warmsley, Michael Macy, and Ingmar Weber. 2017. Automated hate speech detection and the problem of offensive language. In *Eleventh International Conference on Web and Social Media (ICWSM)*, pages 512–515.

Jacob Devlin, Ming-Wei Chang, Kenton Lee, and Kristina Toutanova. 2019. BERT: Pre-training of deep bidirectional transformers for language understanding. In *Proceedings of the 2019 Conference of the North American Chapter of the Association for Computational Linguistics: Human Language Technologies, Volume 1 (Long and Short Papers)*, pages 4171–4186, Minneapolis, Minnesota. Association for Computational Linguistics.

Nemanja Djuric, Jing Zhou, Robin Morris, Mihajlo Grbovic, Vladan Radosavljevic, and Narayan Bhamidipati. 2015. Hate speech detection with comment embeddings. In *Proceedings of the 24th international conference on world wide web*, pages 29–30. ACM.

Samhaa R. El-Beltagy. 2016. NileULex: A phrase and word level sentiment lexicon for Egyptian and modern standard Arabic. In *Proceedings of the Tenth International Conference on Language Resources and Evaluation (LREC'16)*, pages 2900–2905, Portorož, Slovenia. European Language Resources Association (ELRA).

Joseph L Fleiss. 1971. Measuring nominal scale agreement among many raters. *Psychological bulletin*, 76(5):378.

Jeremy Howard and Sebastian Ruder. 2018. Universal language model fine-tuning for text classification. In *Proceedings of the 56th Annual Meeting of the Association for Computational Linguistics (Volume 1: Long Papers)*, Melbourne, Australia. Association for Computational Linguistics.

Timothy Jay and Kristin Janschewitz. 2008. The pragmatics of swearing. *Journal of Politeness Research. Language, Behaviour, Culture*, 4(2):267–288.

Armand Joulin, Edouard Grave, Piotr Bojanowski, and Tomas Mikolov. 2017. Bag of tricks for efficient text classification. In *Proceedings of the 15th Conference of the European Chapter of the Association for Computational Linguistics: Volume 2, Short Papers*, pages 427–431. Association for Computational Linguistics.

Irene Kwok and Yuzhou Wang. 2013. Locate the hate: Detecting tweets against blacks. In *Twenty-seventh AAAI conference on artificial intelligence*.

Guokun Lai, Qizhe Xie, Hanxiao Liu, Yiming Yang, and Eduard Hovy. 2017. Race: Large-scale reading comprehension dataset from examinations.

Alessandro Maisto, Serena Pelosi, Simonetta Vietri, Pierluigi Vitale, and Via Giovanni Paolo II. 2017. Mining offensive language on social media. *CLiC-it 2017 11-12 December 2017, Rome*, page 252.

Shervin Malmasi and Marcos Zampieri. 2017. Detecting hate speech in social media. *arXiv preprint arXiv:1712.06427*.

Elisa Mattiello. 2005. The pervasiveness of slang in standard and non-standard english. *Mots Palabras Words*, 5:7–41.

Abu Bakr Mohammad, Kareem Eissa, and Samhaa El-Beltagy. 2017. Aravec: A set of arabic word embedding models for use in arabic nlp. *Procedia Computer Science*, 117:256–265.

Hamdy Mubarak and Kareem Darwish. 2019. Arabic offensive language classification on twitter. In *International Conference on Social Informatics*, pages 269–276. Springer.

Hamdy Mubarak, Kareem Darwish, and Walid Magdy. 2017. Abusive language detection on arabic social media. In *Proceedings of the First Workshop on Abusive Language Online*, pages 52–56.

Chikashi Nobata, Joel Tetreault, Achint Thomas, Yashar Mehdad, and Yi Chang. 2016. Abusive language detection in online user content. In *Proceedings of the 25th international conference on world wide web*, pages 145–153. International World Wide Web Conferences Steering Committee.

Alec Radford, Karthik Narasimhan, Tim Salimans, and Ilya Sutskever. 2018. Improving language understanding by generative pre-training. *URL https://s3-us-west-2. amazonaws. com/openai-assets/researchcovers/languageunsupervised/language understanding paper. pdf*.

Pranav Rajpurkar, Jian Zhang, Konstantin Lopyrev, and Percy Liang. 2016. Squad: 100,000+ questions for machine comprehension of text.

Younes Samih, Mohamed Eldesouki, Mohammed Attia, Kareem Darwish, Ahmed Abdelali, Hamdy Mubarak, and Laura Kallmeyer. 2017. Learning from relatives: unified dialectal arabic segmentation. In *Proceedings of the 21st Conference on Computational Natural Language Learning (CoNLL 2017)*, pages 432–441.

Alex Wang, Amanpreet Singh, Julian Michael, Felix Hill, Omer Levy, and Samuel R. Bowman. 2018. Glue: A multi-task benchmark and analysis platform for natural language understanding.

Zeerak Waseem and Dirk Hovy. 2016. Hateful symbols or hateful people? predictive features for hate speech detection on twitter. In *Proceedings of the NAACL student research workshop*, pages 88–93.

Dawei Yin, Zhenzhen Xue, Liangjie Hong, Brian D Davison, April Kontostathis, and Lynne Edwards. 2009. Detection of harassment on web 2.0. *Proceedings of the Content Analysis in the WEB*, 2:1–7.

Marcos Zampieri, Shervin Malmasi, Preslav Nakov, Sara Rosenthal, Noura Farra, and Ritesh Kumar. 2019. Semeval-2019 task 6: Identifying and categorizing offensive language in social media (offenseval). *arXiv preprint arXiv:1903.08983*.

Marcos Zampieri, Preslav Nakov, Sara Rosenthal, Pepa Atanasova, Georgi Karadzhov, Hamdy Mubarak, Leon Derczynski, Zeses Pitenis, and Çağrı Çöltekin. 2020. Semeval-2020 task 12: Multilingual offensive language identification in social media (offenseval 2020). *arXiv preprint arXiv:2006.07235*.

Adult Content Detection on Arabic Twitter: Analysis and Experiments

Hamdy Mubarak, Sabit Hassan and **Ahmed Abdelali**
Qatar Computing Research Institute
Doha, Qatar
{hmubarak,sahassan2,aabdelali}@hbku.edu.qa

Abstract

With Twitter being one of the most popular social media platforms in the Arab region, it is not surprising to find accounts that post adult content in Arabic tweets; despite the fact that these platforms dissuade users from such content. In this paper, we present a dataset of Twitter accounts that post adult content. We perform an in-depth analysis of the nature of this data and contrast it with normal tweet content. Additionally, we present extensive experiments with traditional machine learning models, deep neural networks and contextual embeddings to identify such accounts. We show that from user information alone, we can identify such accounts with F1 score of 94.7% (macro average). With the addition of only one tweet as input, the F1 score rises to 96.8%.

1 Introduction

Disclaimer: Due to the nature of this research, we provide examples that contain adult language. We follow academic norms to present them in an appropriate form, however the discretion of the reader is cautioned.

In recent years, Twitter has become one of the most popular social media platforms in the Arab region (Abdelali et al., 2020). On average, Arab users post more than 27 million tweets per day (Alshehri et al., 2018). Such popularity has also spawned a number of spammers who exploit the popularity to post malicious content. Such malicious content may contain pornographic references or advertisement. We refer to such content as adult content. Adult content may have deliberating effects on many, particularly among those of younger age groups. Users who fall for the pornographic advertisements are at risk of losing money and sensitive information to the spammers. Due to the massive amount of user-generated content on Twitter, it is impossible to detect such accounts manually and this calls for automatic detection —the focus of this paper.

Twitter's policy prohibits users from posting adult content[1]. However, the methods deployed for detecting spams such as adult content are mostly expanded from English and are not very effective for detecting accounts who post adult content in other languages as such as the case of Arabic (Abozinadah et al., 2015). Traditional methods such as filtering by list of words are not effective since spammers use smart ways such as intentional spelling mistakes to evade such filtering (Alshehri et al., 2018).

Despite the dire need of eliminating adult content from Arabic social media, there has been a very few notable works (Alshehri et al., 2018; Abozinadah et al., 2015; Abozinadah and Jones, 2017) in the field. In contrast to the existing work (Alshehri et al., 2018; Abozinadah et al., 2015; Abozinadah and Jones, 2017) that rely on extracting collection of tweets from each account to classify whether they post adult content, we present a dataset and several models aimed at classifying accounts based on minimal information. By minimal information, we mean user information such as username, user description or just one random tweet from each account. In our study, we focus on using textual features to detect adult content and we leave multimedia (e.g. images) and social network features for future work.

Our dataset consists of 6k manually annotated Twitter accounts who post adult content and 44k ordinary Twitter accounts in addition to a tweet from each account (a total of 50k accounts and tweets). We perform extensive analysis of the data to identify characteristics of these accounts. Lastly, we experiment extensively with traditional machine learning models such as Support Vector

[1] https://help.twitter.com/en/rules-and-policies/media-policy

Proceedings of the Sixth Arabic Natural Language Processing Workshop, pages 136–144
Kyiv, Ukraine (Virtual), April 19, 2021.

Machines (SVM) and Multinomial Naive Bayes (MNB), Deep Learning models such as FastText and Contextual Embedding models (BERT). We analyze contribution of each information available (username, user description, or single tweet) to the performance of the models.

Since accounts that post adult-content want to attract others, their usernames and user descriptions are often catchy and contain references that are indicators of them posting adult content. We demonstrate that with just username and user description, we can detect these accounts with macro-averaged F1 score of 94.7%. With addition of single tweet as available information, we achieve macro-averaged F1 score of 96.8%. Detecting accounts who post adult content with minimal information (e.g. from username or description) will allow such accounts to be detected early and possible warning messages can be sent to users to protect them from potential harm or inappropriateness.

The contribution of this work can be summed as: 1) Providing the largest dataset of Twitter accounts that is manually annotated for adult content detection in Arabic, and we make it available for researchers. 2) Exploring the dataset to learn silent features used in the domain as well as features related to users and their profiles. We show that user information can be used for early detection of adult accounts even before tweeting, and when they are combined with tweet text, results are improved. 3) Evaluating a number of machine learning and deep neural approaches for classification of adult content.

The paper is structured as follows: In section 2, we discuss related work in the field. In section 3, we describe the data collection method and present analysis of the data. In section 4, we present our experimental setups and results. In section 5, we examine features learned by our best model and perform error analysis that provides insight on how to improve the data and models in the future. Lastly, in section 6, we present conclusions of our work.

2 Related Work

Despite the fact that many social media platforms enforce rules and conditions about the content shared on their platforms, malicious users attempt to circumvent these rules and guidelines. Researchers have attempted different approaches for exposing malignant content. Spam detection in particular has gained a lot interest among researchers (e.g., (Po-Ching Lin and Po-Min Huang, 2013; Yang et al., 2013; Herzallah et al., 2018; Grier et al., 2010; Mubarak et al., 2020)). Spam detection is a generalized approach for detecting unsolicited messages. Our focus in this paper is on the more concentrated field of detecting adult-content, which categorically includes pornographic references.

For English language, there is a number of works devoted to adult-content detection in terms of analyzing the social networks or the content itself. Mitchell et al. (Mitchell et al., 2003) study exposure to adult content and its relation to age/gender. Singh et al. (Singh et al., 2016) propose Random Forest classifier to detect pornographic spammers on Twitter. Cheng et al. (Cheng et al., 2015) propose an iterative graph classification technique for detecting Twitter accounts who post adult content. Harish et al. (Yenala et al., 2017) study deep learning based methods for detecting inappropriate content in text.

In Arabic, however, the field of adult-content detection is still relatively unexplored. A related field that has been explored recently in Arabic is abusive/hate-speech detection. There has been a few recent works (Mubarak et al., 2017; Albadi et al., 2018; Hassan et al., 2020a,b) in the areas of offensive and hate-speech detection. However, offensive language and hate-speech have few fundamental differences with adult-content. While offensive language and hate-speech typically consist of profanity and attack on individuals or groups, adult-content may contain profanity but primarily consist of pornographic references. More concentrated work on adult-content detection have been conducted by (Alshehri et al., 2018; Abozinadah et al., 2015; Abozinadah and Jones, 2017). In (Alshehri et al., 2018), a list of hashtags was used to automatically construct dataset of tweets that contain adult content. In (Abozinadah et al., 2015), 500 Twitter accounts were manually annotated for adult-content posts. Both (Abozinadah et al., 2015; Alshehri et al., 2018) use traditional machine learning models such as Support Vector Machine (SVM) or Multinomial Naive Bayes (MNB) for classification. Using statistical features of tweet text for classification was proposed in (Abozinadah and Jones, 2017). Although (Alshehri et al., 2018) perform some analysis of screennames, they do not use them or any other user information for classification. While (Abozinadah et al., 2015) explore number of tweets, followers and following by the accounts, they do not utilize username or user description either. These works rely on collection of tweets from each user for classification.

3 Data Description

We describe the method used to collect the dataset, some statistics and observations about it including most frequent words, emojis and hashtags. We show also the geographical distribution of Adult accounts and some differences between our dataset and previous datasets.

3.1 Data Collection

It is common for users on Twitter to describe themselves by providing a header (username), a short bio (description) and a location in their profiles. We noticed that many Arabic speaking profiles that post adult content declare their location in terms of the country or the city that they are from. They use this information mainly to describe themselves and/or to communicate with other users. This information can be found in username, user location or user description. Alshehri et. al in (Alshehri et al., 2018) reported that it's common for user names to have city or country names (ex: سالب الرياض (bottom from Riyadh)) but in fact this is observed in other profile fields as well. Figure 1 shows sample of profiles for artificial adult accounts where city or country names frequently appear in any of profile fields.

To build a list of country and city names, we obtained all Arabic country names written in either Arabic, English, or French and their major cities from Wikipedia[2], and we added adjectives specifying nationalities in masculine and feminine forms, for example: مصر، بيروت، عراقي، مغربية (Egypt, Beirut, Iraqi (m.), Moroccan (f.)) and so on. We call this list "CountryList".

We used Twitter API to crawl Arabic tweets in March and April 2018 using language filter ("lang:ar"). During this period, we collected 25M tweets from which we identified all users who posted these tweets. We considered only accounts that contain any entry from CountryList in their profile fields. By doing so, we obtained a list of 60k accounts and one random tweet from each user. As an initial classification, we provided the result as obtained from the best system reported by (Mubarak and Darwish, 2019) for detecting vulgar tweets. Then we asked an Arabic native speaker who is familiar with different dialects to judge whether an account can be considered as adult or not based on all available textual information: user profile information, a sample tweet, and the automatic initial classification. Profile pictures or network features (e.g. followers and followees) were not used during annotation and this can be explored in the future. The annotator was allowed to check Twitter accounts in case of ambiguous cases.

Final annotation showed that 6k accounts can be considered as Adult while the rest can be considered as Non-Adult. While the system reported by (Mubarak and Darwish, 2019) achieved F1 = 90 in detecting vulgar language on Egyptian tweets used in communication between users, its performance dropped dramatically due to dialect mismatch and the big differences between vulgar communication and adult content[3].

To conform with Twitter policy that allows sharing up to 50k public tweets and user objects[4], we took all Adult accounts and 44k from the Non-Adult accounts to have a total of 50k accounts and tweets. To verify annotation quality, Two annotators reviewed a random sample of 100 accounts and tweets (50 Adult and 50 Non-Adult), and agreement was 100% and 94% in the Adult and Non-Adult classes respectively. Cohen's kappa (κ) was used to measure the Inter-Annotator Agreement (IAA). The Cohen's κ value was 0.94 ($p\text{-}value$ $<$ 10e-5) which indicates an "Almost Perfect" agreement according to the interpretation of the Kappa value (Landis and Koch, 1977) . Preliminary statistics about the dataset are shown in Table 1, and it can be downloaded from this link: `https://alt.qcri.org/resources/AdultContentDetection.zip`.

3.2 Analysis

In this subsection, we report some observations about length of Adult and Non-Adult tweets, existence of user mentions, URLs and emojis in both classes, distinguishing words, emojis, and hashtags, etc.

Figure 2-(up) shows that Adult tweets are normally shorter than Non-Adult tweets (9 words ver-

[2] `https://en.wikipedia.org/wiki/List_of_countries_by_largest_and_second_largest_cities`

[3] Out of 5,854 accounts classified automatically as vulgar, only 825 accounts are manually classified as adult (14%).

[4] `https://developer.twitter.com/en/developer-terms/policy`

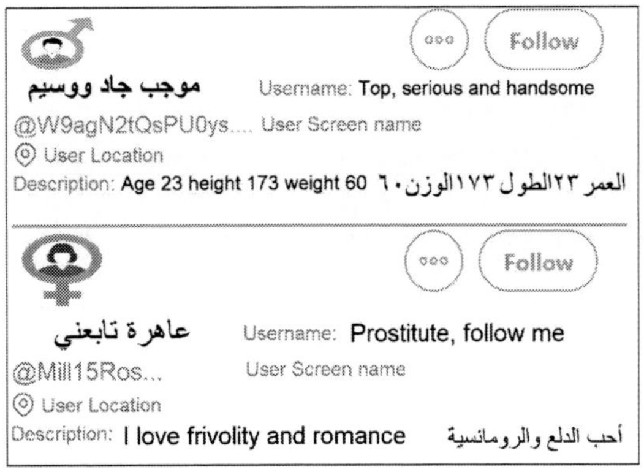

Figure 1: User profile on Twitter for male and female artificial adult accounts

Table 1: Dataset statistics. Tokens and Types (unique Tokens) are calculated for tweet text.

	Tweets (also Accounts)	%	Tokens	Types
Adult	6k	12%	59k	19k
Not Adult	44k	88%	707k	195k
Total	50k		766k	201k

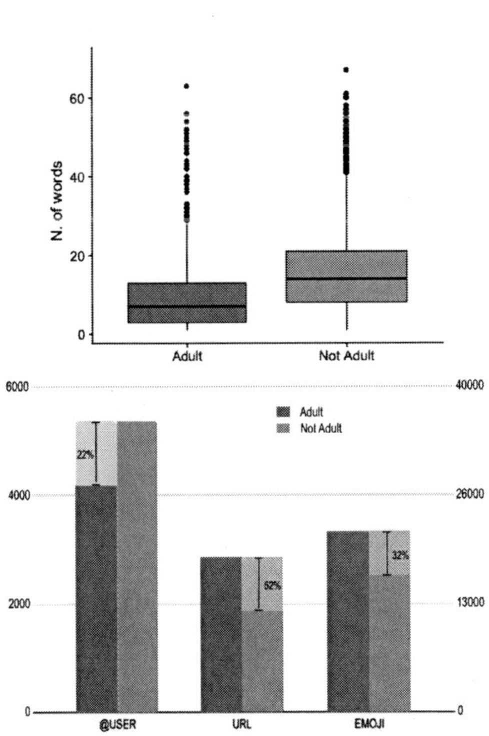

Figure 2: Features comparison between Adult and Non-Adult classes. Boxplot (up) shows the length distributions in both classes. Barplots (down) show the counts for @USER mentions, URLs and emojis per class.

sus 15 words). While Adult tweets tend to have few words to tell users to contact in private or to look at external movies or pictures, Non-Adult tweets normally talk about news, stories or opinions that need more words to describe. This is a significant difference that could highlight the differences in writing style.

This is also confirmed by Figure 2 for the "@USER" mentions. They are less common in the Adult tweets. Typically these tweets are not directed to specific persons but are more an attempt to reach a broad audience. In contrast to Adult tweets, there are a large number of Non-Adult tweets that reference specific @USER either in a response or as a mention. We also observe that, in contrast to Non-Adult tweets, Adult tweets use almost 52% more URLs and 32% more emojis.

Diving further in our analysis, we would like to investigate the different words and emojis that discriminate each class; for such, we will employ the valence score (Conover et al., 2011) in this analysis. The valence score $\vartheta(t)_C$ helps determine the importance of a given word/symbol t in a given class C while considering its presence or absence in other classes. This includes all tokenized words and symbols. Given $freq(t, AD)$ and $freq(t, NA)$ representing the frequency of the term t in Adult and Non-Adult classes respectively, the valence is computed as follows:

Figure 3: Top 10 emojis for Adult class with valence score $\vartheta(.) >= 0.98$.

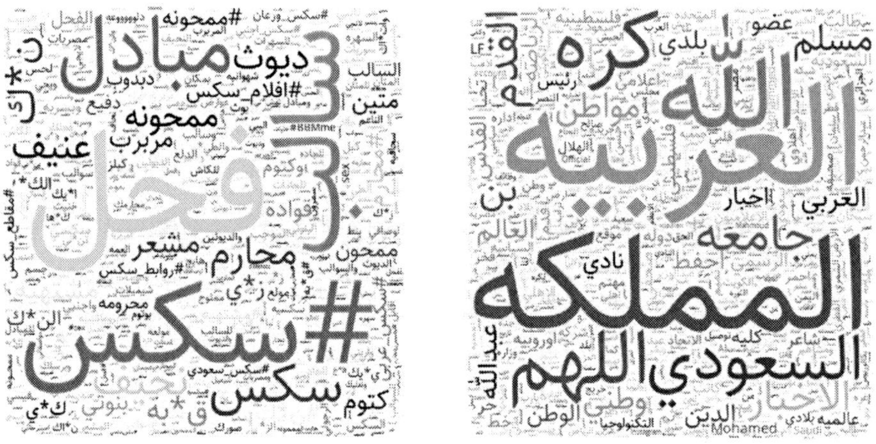

Figure 4: Word cloud for Adult (left) and Non-Adult (right) user information. Most Adult words are related to genitals and sexual actions while most of the Non-Adult words are related to religion, politics, sports, etc.

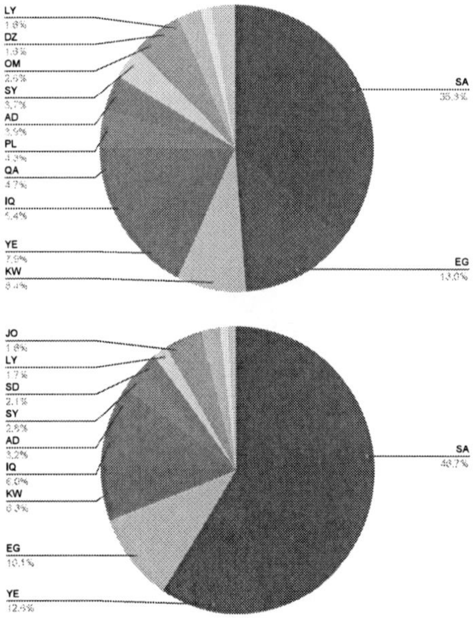

Figure 5: Distribution of the countries for all accounts (up) and for Adult Accounts (down).

$$\vartheta(t)_{AD} = 2\frac{\frac{freq(t,AD)}{N(AD)}}{\frac{freq(t,AD)}{N(AD)} + \frac{freq(t,NA)}{N(NA)}} - 1 \quad (1)$$

Where $N(AD)$ and $(N(NA))$ are the total number of occurrences of all vocabulary in the Adult and Non-Adult classes respectively.

Using Equation 1, we computed the prominence - valence score- for emojis and words in both classes. Figure 3 shows the top most frequent emojis in Adult class, and Figure 4 shows top most frequent words in both classes.

Figure 5 shows the geographical distribution of all accounts in the dataset and Adult accounts as obtained from self-declaration in user profile (user location, username, or user description). We use ISO 3166-1 alpha-2 for country codes[5]. As 36% of all accounts in our dataset are from Saudi Arabia (SA), it was expected also to find the largest number of Adult accounts (2801 accounts, 47% of all Adult accounts) to come from the same country.

[5] `https://en.wikipedia.org/wiki/List_of_ISO_3166_country_codes`

We extracted the hashtags that have a valence score of 1 (appear only in the Adult class). The top 150 hashtags list can be downloaded from the same data link: `https://alt.qcri.org/resources/AdultContentDetection.zip`.

It is worth mentioning that from the 100 seed hashtags used in (Alshehri et al., 2018) to collect adult tweets, we found 37 hashtags that are common between the two lists. We found some noisy hashtags (not necessary to be used in adult tweets) in the seed hashtags from (Alshehri et al., 2018) such as: #طفلة, #عمانيه, #عرب, #زواج, #سكايب (#baby_girl ,#Skype, #marriage, #Arabs, #Omani(f.)), while very strong hashtags such as: #جنس, #ليزبيان (#sex, #lesbian) are missed. We believe that our obtained list of adult hashtags are more accurate and diverse and can be used to extract larger and accurate adult tweets.

4 Experiments

To train classifiers for automatic detection of Adult tweets, we split the data into training set (70%), development set (10%), and a test set (20%).

We experiment extensively with 1) different classifiers, and 2) dataset variants with different degree of information available about accounts. Although we conducted experiments on different preprocessing techniques such as removing diacritics or normalizing Arabic text, we did not notice any significant improvement (between 0.1%-0.2%) in performance. We omit these experiments to make room for more significant results.

4.1 Classifier Description

We conduct our experiments with traditional machine learning classifiers Support Vector Machines (SVM) and Multinomial Naive Bayes (MNB), Deep learning based model FastText (Joulin et al., 2016), and contextual embedding models BERT-Multilingual (Devlin et al., 2019) and AraBERT (Antoun et al., 2020). FastText and MNB were seen to be outperformed by the other three classifiers. For compactness, we only include the top three classifiers along with the baseline model in our discussion and results.

4.1.1 Baseline Model

Our baseline model simply predicts the majority class, Non-Adult, for every instance. Purpose of the baseline model is to simply act as a reference point for the other classifiers we experimented with.

4.1.2 Support Vector Machines (SVM)

To train our SVM models, we use scikit-learn library[6].We transform the input text to character and word n-grams vectors using term frequencies (tf)-inverse document frequencies (idf) vectorizer. We experiment with different ranges of n-grams for character and words. We experiment by training the SVM 1) on only character n-gram vectors, 2) on only word n-gram vectors, and 3) on both character and word n-gram vectors stacked together. We experimented with ranges from [2-2] to [2-6] for character n-grams and from [1-1] to [1-5] for word n-grams. We found that the results did not improve beyond [2-4] for character n-grams and [1-2] for word n-grams. Only the best results are reported in Table 2 and Table 3.

We also experimented with the pre-trained Mazajak word embeddings (skip-gram model trained on 250M tweets) (Abu Farha and Magdy, 2019) as input features for the SVM. Due to its lower performance compared to the n-gram features, we omit these results from the paper.

4.1.3 Multilingual BERT

Deep contextual embedding models such as BERT (Devlin et al., 2019) have been seen to outperform many other models for Natural Language Processing (NLP) tasks. Multilingual BERT is a BERT-based model pre-trained on Wikipedia text of 104 languages that includes Arabic. We fine-tune the model for the task of adult content detection by running it for 4 epochs on the training data with learning rate of 8e-5 using ktrain library (Maiya, 2020).

4.1.4 AraBERT

AraBERT (Antoun et al., 2020) is a BERT-based model specifically trained for Arabic language. The model is pre-trained on Arabic Wikipedia and news articles from various sources. Similar to Multilingual BERT, we fine-tune AraBERT for 4 epochs with learning rate of 8e-5 using ktrain library (Maiya, 2020).

4.2 Dataset Variants

One of our primary goals is to understand how much information is required to detect accounts who post Adult tweets. To achieve this, we examine contribution of different information available about the Twitter accounts. We also evaluate the

[6]https://scikit-learn.org/

Table 2: Performance on user information

model	feats.	screen_name				username				user description			
		P	**R**	**F1**	**mF1**	**P**	**R**	**F1**	**mF1**	**P**	**R**	**F1**	**mF1**
baseline	-	0.0	0.0	0.0	46.7	0.0	0.0	0.0	46.7	0.0	0.0	0.0	46.7
SVM	c[2-4]	53.1	**12.6**	**20.4**	**56.9**	**93.8**	65.3	**77**	**87.1**	94.8	61.6	74.7	85.9
SVM	w[1-2]	0.0	0.0	0.0	46.7	89.0	61.8	72.9	84.9	93.0	58.1	71.5	84.2
SVM	c[2-4], w[1-2]	**81.5**	7.9	14.3	54.1	91.2	**66.2**	76.7	87.0	**94.8**	62.3	75.2	86.2
Multi-BERT	-	0.0	0.0	0.0	46.7	85.6	64.2	73.4	85.1	90.1	**65.8**	76	86.6
Ara-BERT	-	0.0	0.0	0.0	46.7	85.1	65.34	73.9	85.4	92.1	64.8	**76**	**86.6**

Table 3: Performance on tweet and combination of tweet + user information

model	feats.	username+user description				tweet				username+user description+tweet			
		P	**R**	**F1**	**mF1**	**P**	**R**	**F1**	**mF1**	**P**	**R**	**F1**	**mF1**
baseline	-	0.0	0.0	0.0	46.7	0.0	0.0	0.0	46.7	0.0	0.0	0.0	46.7
SVM	c[2-4]	**96.6**	84.7	90.3	94.5	**88.5**	70.9	78.7	88.0	**96.3**	91.7	94.0	96.6
SVM	w[1-2]	92.2	82.5	87.1	92.7	85.5	71.3	77.8	87.5	93.5	90.1	91.8	95.3
SVM	c[2-4], w[1-2]	96.1	85.8	**90.7**	**94.7**	87.4	74.5	**80.4**	**88.9**	95.3	93.0	94.1	96.6
Multi-BERT	-	93.4	86.4	89.8	94.2	83.4	73.8	78.3	87.7	94.4	92.6	93.5	96.3
Ara-BERT	-	91.1	**88.3**	89.7	94.1	82.2	**76.1**	79.1	88.1	94.7	**94.0**	**94.4**	**96.8**

classifier when combinations of these information are made available.

4.2.1 Individual Information

We compare performance of the classifiers when they have access to only i)username, ii) screen_name, iii) user description, or iv) single tweet from an account.

4.2.2 Combination of Information

We give the classifiers access to increasingly more information to evaluate how their performance change. We notice that addition of screen_name does not contribute to any improvement in performance, and thus, it is excluded from our discussion. We discuss change in performance when i) other user information (username and user description) is combined and, ii) the user information is combined with a single tweet from the account. To combine information, we concatenate the strings representing user information and the single tweet.

4.3 Experiment Results

In Table 2 and Table 3, we present results of different models on variants of information available. We report precision (P), recall (R), and F1 for the Adult class on the test set. We also report the macro-averaged F1 (mF1), i.e. average of F1 for the Adult and Non-Adult classes because the data is not balanced. We use mF1 metric for comparison in our discussion. The key findings are listed below.

- Among the different individual user information available (username, screen_name, description), usernames of Twitter accounts carry most importance. From usernames alone, SVMs trained with character n-gram features achieve mF1 score of **87.1**, an increase of **40.4** from baseline (46.7). Screen_name has very little importance as it increases mF1 by only 10.2 from baseline. User description alone results in mF1 score of 86.6 with AraBERT model.
- When username and user description are combined, we get a notable spike in performance —mF1 score of **94.7**, an increase of **48** from baseline. This is achieved by SVM when character and word n-grams are combined.
- From a single tweet, the maximum mF1 score achieved is **88.9**, an increase of **42.2** from baseline. This is also achieved by SVM with character and word n-gram vectors as features.
- When a single tweet is added to username and user description, the maximum mF1 score achieved is **96.8**, an increase of **50.1** from baseline and an increase of **2.1** from user infor-

Table 4: Confusion matrix of AraBERT model

		Predicted	
		Adult	Non-Adult
Reference	Adult	1161	74
	Non-Adult	65	8700

mation alone. This is achieved by AraBERT model and is our best-performing model.

- SVM trained on word n-gram features alone is outperformed by other classifiers in all cases. It's behind by about **2** in mF1 score compared to the best system in each case. This suggests character-level/contextual information are important for detecting adult content.
- SVMs trained on character n-gram, combination of character and word n-gram, MultiBERT and AraBERT are very close to each other. For example, in the case of username+user description+tweet, the maximum difference between their performances is **0.5**.

5 Error Analysis

The confusion matrix of predictions by our best system, AraBERT trained on user information+tweet, is shown in Table 4. We manually analyzed all classification errors and these errors can be summarized as follows:

Non-Adult accounts that are detected as Adult: this occurred 65 times. We found that in 70% of these cases, they were annotated incorrectly in the reference, for example when an account has كاش وجاد (cash and serious) in either user information or tweet text, this account should be marked as Adult as such term is commonly used by Adult accounts. This suggests that automatic classification can be used iteratively to detect possible annotation errors. The rest of the errors were due to the existence of frequently-used words in Adult accounts such as مساج (massage) but these words can be used also by Non-Adult accounts.

Adult accounts that are detected as Non-Adult: this occurred 74 times. Only 7 of these cases were due to errors in the reference annotation while majority of errors were due to: i) using unseen words in the training data (ex: creative spelling of some dialectal adult words); ii) complex cases where combining features in user profiles can intuitively reveal adult accounts to human annotators, e.g. when a screen_name is "K3Eut8i8t3pFMy..." and the user described himself as رومانسي فوق العادة (extraordinary romantic) and the tweet is an invitation to come in private. For classifiers, it maybe difficult to capture such complex intuition.

6 Conclusion

We presented a dataset for detecting Twitter accounts who post adult content in Arabic tweets. We performed extensive analysis of the data to identify characteristics of such accounts. In our experiments, we have shown that Support Vector Machines and contextual embedding models AraBERT and Multilingual BERT can detect these accounts with impressive reliability while having access to minimal information about the accounts. In the future, we aim to explore if similar methods can be adopted to identify accounts who post other variants of undesirable content such as unsolicited advertisement. Also, we plan to experiment tools that detect adult content in multimedia (e.g. in images) and compare performance with our model that depends only on textual information.

References

Ahmed Abdelali, Hamdy Mubarak, Younes Samih, Sabit Hassan, and Kareem Darwish. 2020. Arabic dialect identification in the wild. *arXiv preprint arXiv:2005.06557*.

Ehab Abozinadah, Alex Mbaziira, and James Jr. 2015. Detection of abusive accounts with arabic tweets. volume 1.

Ehab A. Abozinadah and James H. Jones. 2017. A statistical learning approach to detect abusive twitter accounts. In *Proceedings of the International Conference on Compute and Data Analysis*, ICCDA '17, page 6–13, New York, NY, USA. Association for Computing Machinery.

Ibrahim Abu Farha and Walid Magdy. 2019. Mazajak: An online Arabic sentiment analyser. In *Proceedings of the Fourth Arabic Natural Language Processing Workshop*, pages 192–198, Florence, Italy. Association for Computational Linguistics.

N. Albadi, M. Kurdi, and S. Mishra. 2018. Are they our brothers? analysis and detection of religious hate speech in the arabic twittersphere. In *2018 IEEE/ACM International Conference on Advances in Social Networks Analysis and Mining (ASONAM)*, pages 69–76.

Ali Alshehri, El Moatez Billah Nagoudi, Hassan Alhuzali, and Muhammad Abdul-Mageed. 2018. Think before your click: Data and models for adult content in arabic twitter.

Wissam Antoun, Fady Baly, and Hazem M. Hajj. 2020. Arabert: Transformer-based model for arabic language understanding. *ArXiv*, abs/2003.00104.

H. Cheng, X. Xing, X. Liu, and Q. Lv. 2015. Isc: An iterative social based classifier for adult account detection on twitter. *IEEE Transactions on Knowledge and Data Engineering*, 27(4):1045–1056.

Michael Conover, Jacob Ratkiewicz, Matthew R Francisco, Bruno Gonçalves, Filippo Menczer, and Alessandro Flammini. 2011. Political polarization on twitter. *ICWSM*, 133:89–96.

Jacob Devlin, Ming-Wei Chang, Kenton Lee, and Kristina Toutanova. 2019. BERT: Pre-training of deep bidirectional transformers for language understanding. In *Proceedings of the 2019 Conference of the North American Chapter of the Association for Computational Linguistics: Human Language Technologies, Volume 1 (Long and Short Papers)*, pages 4171–4186, Minneapolis, Minnesota. Association for Computational Linguistics.

Chris Grier, Kurt Thomas, Vern Paxson, and Michael Zhang. 2010. @spam: The underground on 140 characters or less. In *Proceedings of the 17th ACM Conference on Computer and Communications Security*, CCS '10, page 27–37, New York, NY, USA. Association for Computing Machinery.

Sabit Hassan, Younes Samih, Hamdy Mubarak, and Ahmed Abdelali. 2020a. ALT at SemEval-2020 task 12: Arabic and English offensive language identification in social media. In *Proceedings of the Fourteenth Workshop on Semantic Evaluation*, pages 1891–1897, Barcelona (online). International Committee for Computational Linguistics.

Sabit Hassan, Younes Samih, Hamdy Mubarak, Ahmed Abdelali, Ammar Rashed, and Shammur Chowdhury. 2020b. Alt submission for osact shared task on offensive language detection. In *Proceedings of the 4th Workshop on Open-Source Arabic Corpora and Processing Tools (LREC 2020)*, page 61–65.

Wafa Herzallah, Hossam Faris, and Omar Adwan. 2018. Feature engineering for detecting spammers on twitter: Modelling and analysis. *Journal of Information Science*, 44(2):230–247.

Armand Joulin, Edouard Grave, Piotr Bojanowski, Matthijs Douze, Hervé Jégou, and Tomas Mikolov. 2016. Fasttext.zip: Compressing text classification models. *CoRR*, abs/1612.03651.

J. Richard Landis and Gary G. Koch. 1977. The measurement of observer agreement for categorical data. *Biometrics*, 33(1):159–174.

Arun S. Maiya. 2020. ktrain: A low-code library for augmented machine learning. *arXiv*, arXiv:2004.10703 [cs.LG].

Kimberly J Mitchell, David Finkelhor, and Janis Wolak. 2003. The exposure of youth to unwanted sexual material on the internet: A national survey of risk, impact, and prevention. *Youth & Society*, 34(3):330–358.

Hamdy Mubarak, Ahmed Abdelali, Sabit Hassan, and Kareem Darwish. 2020. Spam detection on arabic twitter. In *Social Informatics*, pages 237–251, Cham. Springer International Publishing.

Hamdy Mubarak and Kareem Darwish. 2019. Arabic offensive language classification on twitter. In *International Conference on Social Informatics*, pages 269–276. Springer.

Hamdy Mubarak, Kareem Darwish, and Walid Magdy. 2017. Abusive language detection on Arabic social media. In *Proceedings of the First Workshop on Abusive Language Online*, pages 52–56, Vancouver, BC, Canada. Association for Computational Linguistics.

Po-Ching Lin and Po-Min Huang. 2013. A study of effective features for detecting long-surviving twitter spam accounts. In *2013 15th International Conference on Advanced Communications Technology (ICACT)*, pages 841–846.

Monika Singh, Divya Bansal, and Sanjeev Sofat. 2016. Behavioral analysis and classification of spammers distributing pornographic content in social media. *Social Network Analysis and Mining*, 6.

Chao Yang, Robert Harkreader, and Guofei Gu. 2013. Empirical evaluation and new design for fighting evolving twitter spammers. *IEEE Transactions on Information Forensics and Security*, 8(8):1280–1293.

Harish Yenala, Ashish Jhanwar, Manoj Chinnakotla, and Jay Goyal. 2017. Deep learning for detecting inappropriate content in text. *International Journal of Data Science and Analytics*.

UL2C: Mapping User Locations to Countries on Arabic Twitter

Hamdy Mubarak and **Sabit Hassan**
Qatar Computing Research Institute
Doha, Qatar
{hmubarak,sahassan2}@hbku.edu.qa

Abstract

Mapping user locations to countries can be useful for many applications such as dialect identification, author profiling, recommendation systems, etc. Twitter allows users to declare their locations as free text, and these user-declared locations are often noisy and hard to decipher automatically. In this paper, we present the largest manually labeled dataset for mapping user locations on Arabic Twitter to their corresponding countries. We build effective machine learning models that can automate this mapping with significantly better efficiency compared to libraries such as geopy. We also show that our dataset is more effective than data extracted from GeoNames geographical database in this task as the latter covers only locations written in formal ways.

1 Introduction

Twitter is one of the most popular social media platforms in the Arab region. Spoken across more than 20 countries, Arabic is one of the most dominant languages on Twitter. Arabic Twittersphere presents us with an audience of diverse demographics. Identifying countries of the users can help in various NLP tasks such as dialect identification, author profiling, and recommendation systems. Identifying geolocation of Twitter users can also help in event detection (Agarwal et al., 2012) or disaster management (Earle et al., 2012; Carley et al., 2016).

Deducing a Twitter user's location from geotagged tweets is difficult because less than 1% of tweets are geotagged (Cheng et al., 2010; Hecht et al., 2011). Although Twitter provides an option to users to declare their location in their profile, this is often noisy. Users can choose to specify their location at the level of countries, regions, cities or towns. Many of these names are written in informal way and sometimes in mixed languages. Some of these names also contain emojis and special symbols. This makes it difficult to automatically infer the country of many users. This complication often prompts researchers to manually annotate user profiles for their countries. Many works therefore, (e.g., (Bouamor et al., 2019; Charfi et al., 2019)), manually annotate user profiles for their locations. Being expensive, manual annotation often limits size of datasets. This is evident in the datasets by Bouamor et al. (2019) and Charfi et al. (2019) since they both contain around 3K manually annotated users.

Related works for Arabic primarily focus on dialect identification (e.g., (Bouamor et al., 2019; Abdelali et al., 2020; Zaidan and Callison-Burch, 2011), many of which involve manual annotation of dialects for sentences. Our focus in this work significantly differs from dialect identification since our purpose is to provide a dataset that can be used to map Twitter user locations to countries, which in turn, can aid in NLP tasks such as dialect identification or event detection. To our knowledge, there has been very few works for Arabic that map noisy user locations to countries, with work by Mubarak and Darwish (2014) being one of the most notable ones and the closest to our work. Mubarak and Darwish (2014) map the most common 10K locations to Arab countries in order to build a multi-dialectal Arabic corpus. We refer to this dataset as **Top10KLoc**. Our work extends Top10KLoc by increasing unique user locations from most common 10K to random 28K user locations obtained from 160K locations that are self-declared by users[1].

The contributions of this paper are summarized below:

[1]About 2.2K locations from Top10KLoc appear in our dataset.

Proceedings of the Sixth Arabic Natural Language Processing Workshop, pages 145–153
Kyiv, Ukraine (Virtual), April 19, 2021.

- We present **UL2C**; the largest dataset for mapping user locations on Arabic Twitter to countries which contains more than 28K unique locations.
- We perform analysis of the data collected, identifying key characteristics.
- We show that by using machine learning models trained on our dataset, we can achieve significantly better results compared to existing libraries (e.g. geopy package) or resources (e.g. GeoNames or Top10KLoc[2] datasets). Models trained on our dataset achieve macro-average F1 score of 88.1, which outperforms similar models trained on other datasets with at least 26% relative improvement.
- We provide a web interface that users can use to map user locations to countries.

2 Related Work

There has been a number of works that focus on identifying locations of Twitter users. Krishnamurthy et al. (2008) study geographical growth of Twitter using UTC offset data about tweets. Hecht et al. (2011) built Bayesian probability models on tweets to predict countries and state-level locations. They cover four countries (United States, the United Kingdom, Canada, and Australia) and 50 states of United States. Miura et al. (2017) use combination of text, metadata and user network representation with neurual network and utilize attention mechanism to predict geolocation. Rahimi et al. (2018) use combination of text and user network with Graph Convolutional Neural Network to predict user geolocation. Rahimi et al. (2015) note that although user network information can improve results, scaling to large datasets may become an issue. Huang and Carley (2019) build hierarchical neural networks for identifying location of Twitter users. Mahmud et al. (2014) also use hierarchical approach to predict home location of Twitter users. The authors also identify if users are traveling to improve accuracy of location detection.

Despite Arabic being one of the most popular languages on Twitter, there has been very few works aimed at mapping user location in the Arab region to countries. The related field of dialect identification has received significant attention recently. Some works identify country-level dialects of Arabic tweets (e.g., (Abdelali et al., 2020) and some focus on dialects at user-level (Bouamor et al., 2019). While Abdelali et al. (2020) automatically labeled 500K+ tweets for their country-level dialects, Bouamor et al. (2019) manually labeled about 3K users for their countries of origin. Some works targeted region level classification of Arabic dialects. Zaidan and Callison-Burch (2011) collected a 52M word dataset from newspapers and annotated them for dialects of 5 Arab regions, namely, Maghrebi, Egyptian, Levantine, Gulf, and Iraqi. Alshutayri and Atwell (2017) and El-Haj et al. (2018) annotate texts from the five regions. Some other works target city level classification of Arabic dialects. Salameh et al. (2018) present a parallel corpus of dialects of 25 cities and Abdul-Mageed et al. (2018) construct a dataset representing dialects of 29 cities from 10 Arab countries. Charfi et al. (2019) presents a corpus of 5M tweets of about 3K users from 17 different Arab countries.

As discussed earlier, the closest work to ours that targets converting user locations directly to countries is by Mubarak and Darwish (2014). The authors collect 10K top user locations from 92M tweets. To map these locations to countries, the authors first use GeoNames dataset and then manually revise them. Further, the authors show that after filtering out non-dialectal tweets, the countries obtained from the user locations can be strong indicator of dialects for the remaining tweets.

3 Data Collection

We used twarc search API[3] to collect Arabic tweets. During the years 2018, 2019 and 2020, we collected 88M tweets with language filter set to Arabic (lang:ar). From unique users who authored those tweets, we randomly selected 160K unique users for which we obtained 28K unique user locations.

The user locations are information provided by Twitter users, and they can be real locations (e.g., country and city names written in formal, informal ways or nicknames), landmarks, or unreal locations, and can be written in any language. In our data collection, we found that 62% of users pro-

[2] Mubarak and Darwish (2014) didn't build an automatic classifier for mapping locations to countries.

[3] https://github.com/DocNow/twarc

vided non-empty locations. Around 60% of the non-empty locations are written in Arabic and 40% are written in other languages, mainly in English.

4 Data annotation

We used geopy[4] to map user locations to countries. geopy is a Python package that locates the coordinates of addresses, cities, countries, and landmarks across the globe using third-party geocoders and other data sources. It includes geocoder classes for the OpenStreetMap Nominatim, Google Geocoding API (V3), and many other geocoding services. Figure 1 shows the output from geopy for an arbitrary location. In our study, we focus on mapping user locations to countries and we use ISO 3166-1 alpha-2 for country codes[5]. We observed that geopy has difficulties in identifying many locations when they are short, have special characters, or unreal locations in addition to many correct locations. Table 1 shows some examples for these errors.

We used geopy output as an initial mapping of user locations to countries then all unique user locations were revised manually by an Arabic native speaker.

In addition to mapping clear locations to countries, the annotator was asked to consider any clues in user location string that indicate belonging to a specific country. Some common examples and special annotation cases are shown in Table 2.

We randomly selected 500 unique user locations and checked annotation quality. We agreed with the manual annotations in 98% of the cases which indicates that annotation quality is very high.

User locations and their country mapping (UL2C dataset) can be downloaded from this link: `https://alt.qcri.org/resources/UL2C-UserLocationsToCountries.tsv`

4.1 GeoNames Dataset

GeoNames geographical database covers all countries and contains over 11M placenames whereof 4.8M populated places and 13M alternate names. Users can manually edit, correct and add new names using a user friendly interface. Dataset can be downloaded from: `https://www.geonames.org/`.

Figure 2 shows some information about Damascus, the capital of Syria, and its alternate names written in tens of languages as obtained from GeoNames. We extracted Arabic and English names of all places with population of 10K or more[6]. The figure shows also an example of the excluded locations that we anticipate users will not use to describe their locations. We ended up with having a list of 66K English location names (ASCII name field) and a shorter list of 13K Arabic names for some of them.
In the experiments section, we will examine the efficiency of using GeoNames to identify countries of Twitter users.

5 Data Analysis

By assigning countries to unique user locations, we could map locations of $\approx$ 90K users to countries which represent 56% of the 160K users in our dataset. Many of user locations were either empty (38%) or cannot be mapped to a specific country (6%). Distribution of user countries is shown in Figure 3. Although there are 22 Arab countries, in our collection we didn't find locations from two countries, namely Djibouti and Comoros. We observe that users from Saudi Arabia (SA) represent more than half of Arab Twitter users. Around 70% of Twitter users are from Gulf region (countries: SA, KW, OM, AE, QA and BH), 4% of users are from Levant region (JO, PS, LB and SY), 3% of users are from Maghreb region (DZ, LY, MA and TN), and users from other regions (EG, YE and IQ) are in between. It's worth mentioning that country distribution obtained from UL2C and Top10KLoc datasets are very similar which indicates that most probably any random big collection of tweets will have similar country distribution.

From the geographical map of all Twitter users shown in Figure 4, we can see that Arabic tweets come from almost all world countries. The top 5 countries outside the Arab World where Arabic tweets come from are: US (United States), GB (United Kingdom), TR (Turkey), DE (Germany) and FR (France) in order. This can give an estimation about countries that Arabs live in

[4]https://pypi.org/project/geopy/

[5]`https://en.wikipedia.org/wiki/List_of_ISO_3166_country_codes`

[6]We want to exclude river names, mountain names, lakes, etc.

```
from geopy.geocoders import Nominatim
geolocator = Nominatim(user_agent="specify_your_app_name_here")
location = geolocator.geocode("175 5th Avenue NYC")
print(location.raw)

# Output:
{'place_id': 150272128, 'licence': 'Data © OpenStreetMap contributors, ODbL 1.0. https://osm.org/copyright', 'osm_
'boundingbox': ['40.7407597', '40.7413004', '-73.9898715', '-73.9895014'],
'lat': '40.741059199999995', 'lon': '-73.98964162240998',
'display_name': 'Flatiron Building, 5th Avenue, Flatiron District, Manhattan, Manhattan Community Board 5,
'New York County, New York, 10010, United States of America',
'class': 'tourism', 'type': 'attraction', 'importance': 0.6305988542685403,
'icon': 'https://nominatim.openstreetmap.org/images/mapicons/poi_point_of_interest.p.20.png'}
```

Figure 1: geopy example

Location	Translation	geopy Country	Correct Country	Case
ولاية صحار سلطنة عمان	Sohar, Sultanate of Oman	-	OM	Unknown
Al Taif - Ksa	Ta'if city - KSA	SD	SA	Transliteration
الوطن العربي	the Arab World	JO	Unknown	Unspecified location
7th sky		DE	Unknown	Unreal location
cario	Cairo (capital of Egypt)	SA	EG	Letter case
Q8	Abbreviation for Kuwait	IT	KW	Short text, abbrev.
(11 . !)		FR	Unknown	Punctuation, numbers

Table 1: geopy sample errors

Name	Country	Feature class	Latitude	Longitude
Damascus Al-Sham,Al-Shām,An Damaisc,Cham,DAM,Damas,Damasc,Damascus, دمشق...	Syria, Dimashq	capital of a political entity population 1,569,394	N 33° 30' 36''	E 36° 17' 28''
Statue of Liberty Agalma tes eleutherias,Askatasunaren Estatua,Estatua da Liberdade,Estatua d	United States New York	monument elevation 2m	N 40° 41' 21''	W 74° 2' 40''

Figure 2: GeoNames examples: First place is included and second place is excluded from our dataset

outside Arab countries. We notice also that tweets from US are more than those from individual Maghreb countries like DZ and TN.

Figure 5 shows the most common words used in user locations for 4 countries, namely SA (Saudi Arabia), EG (Egypt), SY (Syria) and DZ (Algeria) which represent major regions in the Arab World (Gulf, Levant, Nile Basin and Maghreb regions respectively). We can see country and major city names are written in bigger font in different languages. For example, while majority of names are written in Arabic in SA (Gulf region), they are written in Arabic, English and French in DZ (Maghreb region). Arabic and English names are widely used in EG and SY. This gives an indication about the popularity of language usage across different regions in the Arab World.

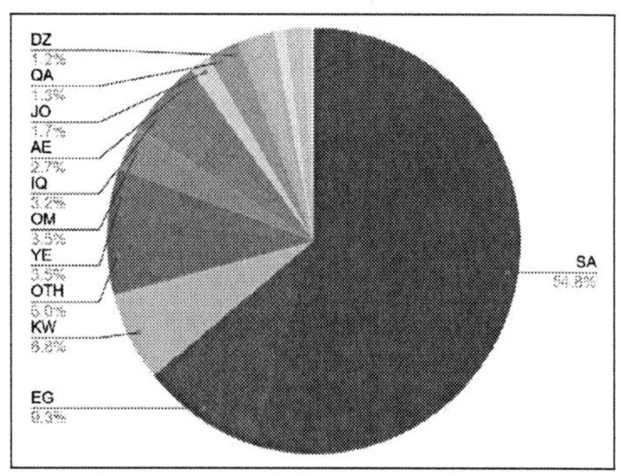

Figure 3: Country distribution of Twitter users

6 Experiments and Results

In this section, we compare effectiveness of mapping user locations to countries with classifiers trained on different datasets, namely, UL2C, Top10KLoc, GeoNames and combination of these datasets. In our experiments, we merge all countries that are outside Arab region to "UNK/OTHER" class, yielding a total of 21 classes (20 Arab countries + Unknown/Other).

6.1 Preprocessing text

In order to reduce noise in user-declared locations, we perform the following preprocessing steps:

Location	Translation	Country	Case
مدينة رسول الله	City of Prophet Mohamed	SA	Common knowledge in Arabic culture
xx@outlook.kw		KW	Website/email domain name
كعبة المضيوم	Kaaba (Destination) of the oppressed	QA	Nickname or informal common name
WhatsApp 00964xx		IQ	Country calling code
لبناني وأفتخر	Lebanese and proud	LB	Nationality
Alhilal_FC	Al Hilal Saudi Football Club	SA	Club fans
دبي - لندن	Dubai-London	AE	Multiple countries (1st is selected)

Table 2: Annotation clues and special cases

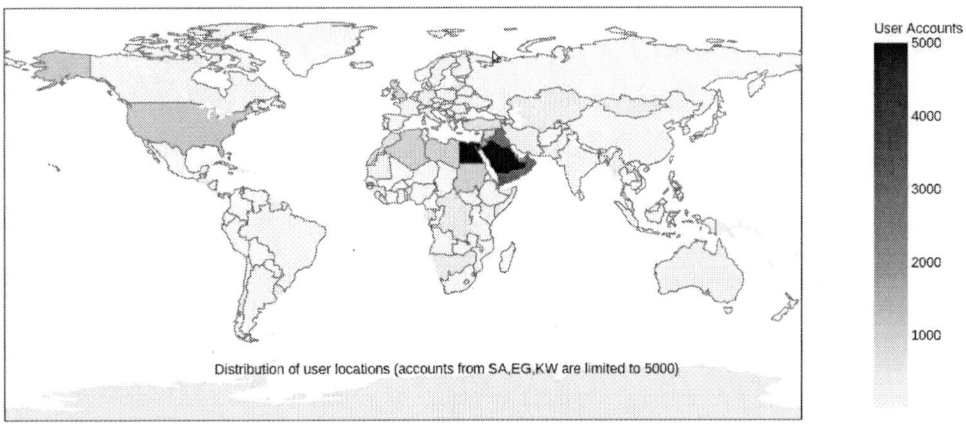

Figure 4: Country map of Twitter users

Figure 5: Top locations in 4 countries: SA, EG, SY and DZ in order

- Remove all Arabic diacritics
- Remove all punctuation marks and emojis
- Convert all Latin letters to lowercase
- Normalize different shapes of Arabic Hamza, final Alif Maqsoura and Taa Marbouta letters to plain Alif, Yaa and Haa letters respectively
- Convert English and Arabic decorated letters (e.g. some Farsi letters) to original letters using the mapping list shared by (Mubarak and Abdelali, 2016).For example, we map “α, β” to “a, B” and “پ ، چ ، گ” to “ب ، ج ، ک” in order.

In summary, a location like “$\alpha\beta$HA1 :) أَبْهَا*, ” is converted to “abha ابها” (city in SA) after decorated letters mapping and applying other normalization steps.

6.2 Features

Word n-gram Since our input text is name of a location and therefore, typically short, we limit range of word n-gram to [1-2]. We use term frequency-inverse term document frequency (tf-idf) for weighting the n-gram vectors.

Character n-gram We experimented with character n-grams ranging from [2-3] to [2-5], beyond which, we did not see any further improvement. Similar to word n-gram, we used tf-idf weighting.

Data	Model	Features	Acc	P	R	F1
-	geopy (baseline)	-	68.1	78.2	65.3	69.2
UL2C	SVM	Word [1-2]	90.1	93.1	81.8	86.7
		Char [2-3]	90.2	93.7	80.6	86.0
		Char [2-4]	91.1	**94.4**	83.1	88.0
		Char [2-5]	**91.2**	94.1	**83.5**	**88.1**
GeoNames	SVM	Word [1-2]	59.9	58.6	44.5	46.6
		Char [2-3]	39.7	56.9	35.0	38.9
		Char [2-4]	47.0	60.4	47.4	48.8
		Char [2-5]	48.7	60.7	49.2	50.1
Top10KLoc	SVM	Word [1-2]	83.2	85.0	62.1	70.5
		Char [2-3]	79.4	85.2	52.7	63.2
		Char [2-4]	80.6	85.2	55.0	65.2
		Char [2-5]	81.2	85.4	56.6	66.5
UL2C + GeoNames	SVM	Word [1-2]	90.2	90.1	84.3	86.7
		Char [2-3]	90.3	90.5	83.2	86.1
		Char [2-4]	91.5	90.2	86.7	87.9
		Char [2-5]	91.6	90.7	86.7	88.2
UL2C + Top10KLoc	SVM	Word [1-2]	90.0	93.7	81.2	86.6
		Char [2-3]	89.4	94.5	78.7	85.2
		Char [2-4]	90.4	**95.0**	81.5	87.3
		Char [2-5]	90.6	**95.0**	81.8	87.5

Table 3: Evaluation of different datasets

6.3 Classification Models

geopy baseline The geopy library acts as our baseline. We call library with Twitter user locations and extract countries they are mapped to by the library.

Support Vector Machines (SVMs) SVMs have traditionally been used for many classification tasks. Even in recent Arabic text classification tasks such as offensive language identification (Hassan et al., 2020b,a), spam detection (Mubarak et al., 2020), adult content detection (Mubarak et al., 2021), and dialect identification (Abdelali et al., 2020), SVMs have shown promising results. We used LibSVM implementation with default parameters by scikit-learn[7] for training.

6.4 Experiment results

geopy baseline Serving as our baseline model, geopy achieves F1 score of 69.2 when evaluated on UL2C dataset.

GeoNames We trained several classifiers on GeoNames dataset and evaluated on our UL2C dataset. The classifiers yielded very poor results initially. We noticed that many of the locations were outside Arab region which likely caused the poor performance (omitted here for conciseness). To address this problem, we rebalanced the dataset to have equal number of locations from within and outside the Arab region. This yielded a total of 8,632 unique instances (4,316 from the Arab region and 4,316 from outside the Arab region). The results are summarized in Table 3. We can see that even after rebalancing the data, with maximum F1 score of 50.1, the classifiers trained on GeoNames are outperformed by all others.

Top10KLoc We trained similar set of classifiers on Top10KLoc dataset and evaluated on our dataset. The models were seen to outperform geopy by a small margin and GeoNames by a large margin with maximum F1 score of 70.5 (see Table 3).

UL2C (Our dataset) We performed 5-fold cross-validation with same set of classifiers on the dataset presented in this paper. The results were seen to improve by a significant margin since the best results were obtained by SVM trained with character [2-5] n-grams, a relative improvement of 26% in F1 score from previous best (70.5) when trained on Top10KLoc.

[7]http://scikit-learn.org/

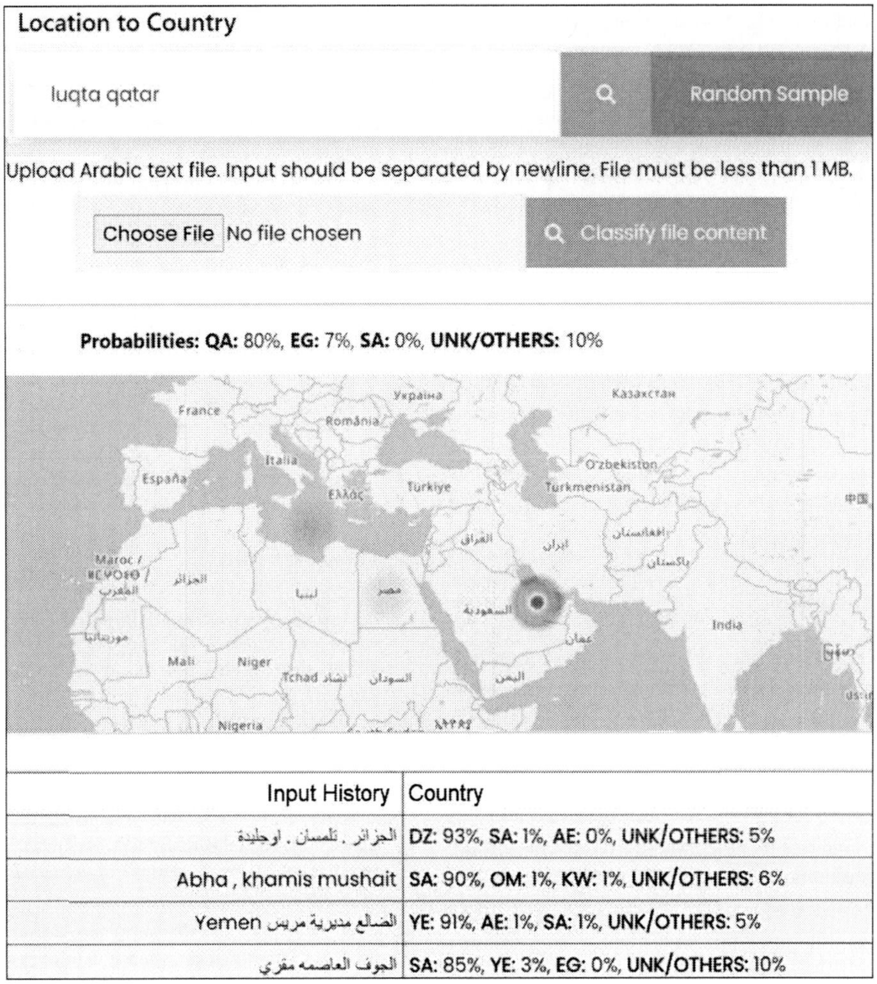

Figure 6: Online interface for mapping user locations to countries (https://asad.qcri.org)

UL2C + GeoNames In this set of experiments, we modified the cross-validation setting by adding GeoNames dataset with each of the 5 folds of our dataset during training. We can see from Table 3 that adding our dataset to GeoNames dataset offsets the lower performance when using GeoNames alone and with F1 score of 88.2, improves the results from using UL2C dataset alone by a small margin.

UL2C + Top10KLoc Lastly, we modified the cross-validation setting by adding Top10KLoc to each of the folds during training. From Table 3, we see a similar trend where the lower performance of using Top10KLoc only is offset by use of UL2C. However, there is no significant improvement when additional data is used compared to when using only UL2C.

7 Interface

We build an interface for users to map user locations to countries. The web interface is added to Arabic Social media Analytics and unDerstanding (ASAD) (Hassan et al., 2021) at `https://asad.qcri.org`. Figure 6 shows sample outputs from the website.

7.1 Design

The user can type user location to be mapped to countries. The user can also test random samples from UL2C dataset to see their mapping. This allows the user to easily understand the functionalities of the interface. The user is then shown probabilities of the location belonging to different countries. To help the users visualize distribution of possible countries related to the location, we display a heatmap of the probabilities. We also allow the user to upload a file consisting user locations. This allows users to map many user locations at the same time. We impose a restriction on file size in order to limit abuse of our system. The user is then able to download a file containing predictions and probabilities of the user locations belonging to different countries.

7.2 Implementation

We use Bootstrap[8] for our responsive frontend design. We use Flask[9], a python-based web development framework, for backend development and javascript for communication between backend and frontend. To visualize the heatmap, we use Leaflet.js[10] and Heatmap.js[11] with OpenStreetMap[12] map server.

8 Conclusion

In this paper, we have presented a large manually annotated and publicly available dataset of Twitter user locations from the Arab region, mapped to their respective countries. We analyzed different characteristics of our data such as country distribution and top locations. We built machine learning models that can use the data to map user locations to countries more effectively compared to existing resources such as geopy Python package or GeoNames geographical database. Lastly, we provide a web interface to access this service easily.

References

Ahmed Abdelali, Hamdy Mubarak, Younes Samih, Sabit Hassan, and Kareem Darwish. 2020. Arabic dialect identification in the wild. *ArXiv*, abs/2005.06557.

Muhammad Abdul-Mageed, Hassan Alhuzali, and Mohamed Elaraby. 2018. You tweet what you speak: A city-level dataset of Arabic dialects. In *Proceedings of the Eleventh International Conference on Language Resources and Evaluation (LREC-2018)*, Miyazaki, Japan. European Languages Resources Association (ELRA).

Puneet Agarwal, R. Vaithiyanathan, Saurabh Sharma, and G. Shroff. 2012. Catching the long-tail: Extracting local news events from twitter. In *ICWSM*.

[8]https://getbootstrap.com/

[9]https://flask.palletsprojects.com/en/1.1.x/

[10]https://leafletjs.com/

[11]https://www.patrick-wied.at/static/heatmapjs/

[12]https://www.openstreetmap.org/

Areej Alshutayri and Erik Atwell. 2017. Exploring twitter as a source of an arabic dialect corpus. *International Journal of Computational Linguistics (IJCL)*, 8(2):37–44. This is an open access article under the terms of the Creative Commons Attribution License (CC-BY).

Houda Bouamor, Sabit Hassan, and Nizar Habash. 2019. The MADAR shared task on Arabic fine-grained dialect identification. In *Proceedings of the Fourth Arabic Natural Language Processing Workshop*, pages 199–207, Florence, Italy. Association for Computational Linguistics.

Kathleen M. Carley, Momin Malik, Peter M. Landwehr, Jürgen Pfeffer, and Michael Kowalchuck. 2016. Crowd sourcing disaster management: The complex nature of twitter usage in padang indonesia. *Safety Science*, 90:48 – 61. Building Community Resilience to Global Hazards: A Sociotechnical Approach.

Anis Charfi, Wajdi Zaghouani, Syed Hassan Mehdi, and Esraa Mohamed. 2019. A fine-grained annotated multi-dialectal Arabic corpus. In *Proceedings of the International Conference on Recent Advances in Natural Language Processing (RANLP 2019)*, pages 198–204, Varna, Bulgaria. INCOMA Ltd.

Zhiyuan Cheng, James Caverlee, and Kyumin Lee. 2010. You are where you tweet: a content-based approach to geo-locating twitter users. In *CIKM '10*.

Paul Earle, Daniel Bowden, and Michelle Guy. 2012. Twitter earthquake detection: Earthquake monitoring in a social world. *Annals of geophysics = Annali di geofisica*, 54.

Mahmoud El-Haj, Paul Rayson, and Mariam Aboelezz. 2018. Arabic dialect identification in the context of bivalency and code-switching. In *Proceedings of the Eleventh International Conference on Language Resources and Evaluation (LREC-2018)*, Miyazaki, Japan. European Languages Resources Association (ELRA).

Sabit Hassan, Hamdy Mubarak, Ahmed Abdelali, and Kareem Darwish. 2021. Asad: Arabic social media analytics and understanding. In *Proceedings of the Software Demonstrations of the 16th Conference of the European Chapter of the Association for Computational Linguistics*.

Sabit Hassan, Younes Samih, Hamdy Mubarak, and Ahmed Abdelali. 2020a. ALT at SemEval-2020 task 12: Arabic and English offensive language identification in social media. In *Proceedings of the Fourteenth Workshop on Semantic Evaluation*, pages 1891–1897, Barcelona (online). International Committee for Computational Linguistics.

Sabit Hassan, Younes Samih, Hamdy Mubarak, Ahmed Abdelali, Ammar Rashed, and Shammur Absar Chowdhury. 2020b. ALT submission for OSACT shared task on offensive language detection. In *Proceedings of the 4th Workshop on Open-Source Arabic Corpora and Processing Tools, with a Shared Task on Offensive Language Detection*, pages 61–65,

Marseille, France. European Language Resource Association.

Brent Hecht, Lichan Hong, Bongwon Suh, and Ed H. Chi. 2011. Tweets from justin bieber's heart: The dynamics of the location field in user profiles. In *Proceedings of the SIGCHI Conference on Human Factors in Computing Systems*, CHI '11, page 237–246, New York, NY, USA. Association for Computing Machinery.

Binxuan Huang and Kathleen Carley. 2019. A hierarchical location prediction neural network for twitter user geolocation. In *Proceedings of the 2019 Conference on Empirical Methods in Natural Language Processing and the 9th International Joint Conference on Natural Language Processing (EMNLP-IJCNLP)*, pages 4732–4742, Hong Kong, China. Association for Computational Linguistics.

Balachander Krishnamurthy, Phillipa Gill, and Martin Arlitt. 2008. A few chirps about twitter. pages 19–24.

Jalal Mahmud, Jeffrey Nichols, and Clemens Drews. 2014. Home location identification of twitter users. *ACM Transactions on Intelligent Systems and Technology*, 5(3):1–21.

Yasuhide Miura, Motoki Taniguchi, Tomoki Taniguchi, and Tomoko Ohkuma. 2017. Unifying text, metadata, and user network representations with a neural network for geolocation prediction. In *Proceedings of the 55th Annual Meeting of the Association for Computational Linguistics (Volume 1: Long Papers)*, pages 1260–1272, Vancouver, Canada. Association for Computational Linguistics.

Hamdy Mubarak and Ahmed Abdelali. 2016. Arabic to english person name transliteration using twitter. In *Proceedings of the Tenth International Conference on Language Resources and Evaluation (LREC'16)*, pages 351–355.

Hamdy Mubarak, Ahmed Abdelali, Sabit Hassan, and Kareem Darwish. 2020. Spam detection on arabic twitter. In *Social Informatics*, pages 237–251, Cham. Springer International Publishing.

Hamdy Mubarak and Kareem Darwish. 2014. Using twitter to collect a multi-dialectal corpus of Arabic. In *Proceedings of the EMNLP 2014 Workshop on Arabic Natural Language Processing (ANLP)*, pages 1–7, Doha, Qatar. Association for Computational Linguistics.

Hamdy Mubarak, Sabit Hassan, and Ahmed Abdelali. 2021. Adult content detection on arabic twitter: Analysis and experiments. In *Proceedings of the Sixth Arabic Natural Language Processing Workshop*.

Afshin Rahimi, Trevor Cohn, and Timothy Baldwin. 2015. Twitter user geolocation using a unified text and network prediction model. In *Proceedings of the 53rd Annual Meeting of the Association for Computational Linguistics and the 7th International Joint Conference on Natural Language Processing (Volume 2: Short Papers)*, pages 630–636, Beijing, China. Association for Computational Linguistics.

Afshin Rahimi, Trevor Cohn, and Timothy Baldwin. 2018. Semi-supervised user geolocation via graph convolutional networks. In *Proceedings of the 56th Annual Meeting of the Association for Computational Linguistics (Volume 1: Long Papers)*, pages 2009–2019, Melbourne, Australia. Association for Computational Linguistics.

Mohammad Salameh, Houda Bouamor, and Nizar Habash. 2018. Fine-grained Arabic dialect identification. In *Proceedings of the 27th International Conference on Computational Linguistics*, pages 1332–1344, Santa Fe, New Mexico, USA. Association for Computational Linguistics.

Omar F. Zaidan and Chris Callison-Burch. 2011. The Arabic online commentary dataset: an annotated dataset of informal Arabic with high dialectal content. In *Proceedings of the 49th Annual Meeting of the Association for Computational Linguistics: Human Language Technologies*, pages 37–41, Portland, Oregon, USA. Association for Computational Linguistics.

Let-Mi: An Arabic Levantine Twitter Dataset for Misogynistic Language

Hala Mulki
The ORSAM Center
for Middle Eastern Studies
Ankara, Turkey
hala.mulki@orsam.org.tr

Bilal Ghanem
University of Alberta
Edmonton, Canada
bilalhgm@gmail.com

Abstract

Online misogyny has become an increasing worry for Arab women who experience gender-based online abuse on a daily basis. Misogyny automatic detection systems can assist in the prohibition of anti-women Arabic toxic content. Developing such systems is hindered by the lack of the Arabic misogyny benchmark datasets. In this paper, we introduce an Arabic Levantine Twitter dataset for Misogynistic language (LeT-Mi) to be the first benchmark dataset for Arabic misogyny. We further provide a detailed review of the dataset creation and annotation phases. The consistency of the annotations for the proposed dataset was emphasized through inter-rater agreement evaluation measures. Moreover, Let-Mi was used as an evaluation dataset through binary/multi-/target classification tasks conducted by several state-of-the-art machine learning systems along with Multi-Task Learning (MTL) configuration. The obtained results indicated that the performances achieved by the used systems are consistent with state-of-the-art results for languages other than Arabic, while employing MTL improved the performance of the misogyny/target classification tasks.

1 Introduction

Social media are the digital tribunes where people can express their thoughts and opinions with the ultimate freedom. However, this freedom comes at a price, especially when it enables spreading abusive language and hate speech against individuals or groups. Misogyny is one type of hate speech that disparages a person or a group having the female gender identity; it is typically defined as hatred of or contempt for women (Nockleby, 2000; Moloney and Love, 2018). According to (Poland, 2016), based on the misogynistic behavior, misogynistic language can be classified into several categories such as discredit, dominance, derailing, sexual harassment, stereotyping and objectification, and threat of violence.

During the last decade, online misogynistic language has been recognized as a universal phenomenon spread across social media platforms such as Facebook and Twitter. Similar to their peers worldwide, women in the Arab region are subjected to several types of online misogyny, through which gender inequality, lower social status, sexual abuse, violence, mistreatment and underestimation are, unfortunately, reinforced and justified. Moreover, in specific contexts, online misogyny may evolve into systematic bullying campaigns, launched on social media to attack and, sometimes, violently threaten women who have a powerful influence over the society; as it is the case with female journalists/reporters (Ferrier and Garud-Patkar, 2018).

The automatic detection of online misogynistic language can facilitate the prohibition of anti-women toxic contents. While many efforts have been spent in this domain for Indo-European languages, the development of Arabic misogyny detection systems is hindered by the lack of the Arabic annotated misogyny resources. Building such resources involves several challenges in terms of data collection and annotation, especially with the drastic lexical variations among the Arabic dialects and the ambiguity introduced by some underrepresented dialects such as the Levantine dialect. Levantine is one of the five major varieties of Arabic dialects. People in Syria, Lebanon, Palestine, and Jordan are considered the native speakers of Levantine with minor differences from one country to another (Sleiman and Menon, 2018).

The 17th October 2019 protests in Lebanon witnessed a heavy use of Twitter especially by the journalists (Aurora, 2019). While covering the protests on the ground, many female journalists were, unfortunately, prone to gender-based abuse receiving misogynistic replies for the tweets they post.

Proceedings of the Sixth Arabic Natural Language Processing Workshop, pages 154–163
Kyiv, Ukraine (Virtual), April 19, 2021.

In this paper, we introduce the first Arabic **Le**vantine **T**witter dataset for **Mi**sogynistic language (LeT-Mi) to be a benchmark dataset for automatic detection of online misogyny written in the Arabic and Levantine dialect[1]. The proposed dataset consists of 6,550 tweets annotated either as neutral (misogynistic-free) or as one of seven misogyny categories: discredit, dominance, cursing/damning, sexual harassment, stereotyping and objectification, derailing, and threat of violence. The credibility and consistency of the annotations was evaluated through using inter-annotator agreement measures: agreement without chance correction(Cohen's Kappa) and overall Inter-annotator agreement (Krippendorff's alpha). In addition, we benchmark SOTA approaches on the dataset to evaluate the effectiveness of current approaches for misogyny detection task in the Arabic language.

2 Related Work

Since no previous Arabic resources were created for misogyny, and given that misogyny language is considered a type of hate speech, we opted to review the non-Arabic misogyny datasets, and the Arabic abusive and hate speech datasets proposed in the literature. We focus on the characteristics of the presented Arabic annotated resources: data source, data size the tackled toxic categories (for non-misogyny datasets), and annotation/collection strategies.

2.1 Misogyny Detection in Non-Arabic Languages

Misogyny detection has been investigated only in a set of languages; precisely in English, Spanish, and Italian. To the best of our knowledge, there are only three datasets in the literature. The work in (Fersini et al., 2018b) proposed the first English and Spanish misogyny detection datasets to organize a shared task on automatic detection of misogyny (AMI). The datasets were collected using three different ways: 1) using seed words like *bi**h*, *w**re*, *c*nt*, etc., to collect tweets; 2) monitoring accounts of potential victims (e.g. well known feminist women); 3) downloading tweets from the history of misogynist Twitter accounts, i.e. accounts that explicitly declared hate against women in their Twitter bio (screen name). After collecting tweets, the authors used CrowdFlower platform [2] to annotate the tweets. The sizes of the final datasets are 3,977 and 4,138 tweets for English and Spanish, respectively. The authors in (Fersini et al., 2018a) organized another shared task on AMI, but with focusing only on English and Italian languages. The authors followed the (Fersini et al., 2018b) approach to build their datasets. The size of the final datasets is 5,000 tweets for each language. Both previous works annotated their datasets for two main sub-tasks: Misogyny Identification (i.e. if the tweet is misogynous or not), and Misogynistic Behaviour and Target Classification (i.e. identifying the type of misogyny and recognition of the targets that can be either a specific user or group of women).

2.2 Arabic Resources for Online Toxicity

According to (Al-Hassan and Al-Dossari, 2019), the toxic contents on social media can be classified into: abusive, obscene, offensive, violent, adult content, terrorism, and religious hate speech. A detailed review of the datasets that covered online toxicity is provided below.

In (Mubarak et al., 2017), two datasets were proposed: a Twitter dataset of 1,100 dialectal tweets and a dataset of 32K inappropriate comments collected from a popular Arabic news site and annotated as obscene, offensive, or clean. The authors in (Alakrota et al., 2018), provided a dataset of 16K Egyptian, Iraqi, and Libyan comments collected from YouTube. The comments were annotated as either offensive, inoffensive, or neutral. The inter-annotator agreement for the whole sample was 71%. The religious hate speech detection was investigated in (Albadi et al., 2018) where a multi-dialectal dataset of 6.6K tweets was introduced. The annotation guidelines included an identification of the religious groups targeted by hate speech. The calculated inter-annotator agreement for differentiating religious hate speech was 81% while this value decreased to 55% when specifying the religious groups targeted by the hate speech. Another type of hate speech was tackled in (Al-Ajlan and Ykhlef, 2018) where the authors presented a Twitter dataset for bullying detection. A dataset of 20K multi-dialectal Arabic tweets was collected and annotated manually with bullying and non-bullying labels. In this study, no annotation evaluation was provided. More recently, a Twitter dataset L-HSAB of 6K tweets was introduced in (Mulki et al., 2019) as a benchmark dataset for automatic detection of

[1]will be made publicly available on Github.

[2]The platform name changed to *Appen*: https://appen.com

Arabic Levantine abusive language and hate speech. The inter-annotator agreement metric denoted by Krippendorff's alpha (α) was 76.5% and indicated consistent annotations.

3 Let-Mi Dataset

Let-Mi can be described as a political dataset as it is composed of tweet replies scraped from the timelines of popular female journalists/reporters during October 17th protests in Lebanon. In the following subsections, we provide a qualitative overview of the proposed dataset, while an annotation evaluation is presented in Section 3.5.

3.1 Data Collection

The proposed dataset was constructed out of Levantine tweets harvested using Twitter API[3]. The collection process relied on scraping tweet replies written at the timelines of several Lebanese female journalists who covered the protests in Lebanon during the period (October 20- November 3, 2019). The accounts of the journalists were selected based on their activity on Twitter and the engagement they get from the people(Aurora, 2019). As a result, we identified seven journalist accounts as resources of the tweet replies, who represent different national news agencies in Lebanon. Initially, we retrieved 77,856 tweets, and then we manually removed the non-Levantine tweets to cope with the paper's goal, which is to provide a Levantine dataset. We also filtered out the non-textual, Arabic-Arabizi mixed tweets, retweets and duplicated instances. In addition, based on regular expressions, we spotted many tweets whose content represents a single hashtag or a sequence of hashtags. We opted to remove these tweets as they were non-informative and were written just to make a hashtag trending. Moreover, to assure that the collected replies are written to target the journalist herself and not a part of side debates among the users within a thread, we removed tweets that mention accounts other than the journalist's. Thus, we ended up with 6,603 direct tweet replies. Table 1 lists the journalist names[4], their news agencies, and the number of tweet replies collected from the timeline of each. In order to prepare the collected tweets for annotation, we normalized them by eliminating Twitter-inherited symbols, digits, and URLs. It should be mentioned that as the hashtags encountered within a tweet can indicate a misogynistic content, we removed the hashtag symbol while retaining the hashtag words.

[3]We used python *Tweepy* library http://www.tweepy.org.

[4]We masked the journalists' names referring to them as J1, J2,... etc.

Journalist	News Agency	#Tweets
J1	LBC	4,677
J2	Freelancer	1,012
J3	MTV	351
J4	LBC	179
J5	LBC	112
J6	Aljadeed	171
J7	OTV	101

Table 1: Journalists and their tweet replies size.

3.2 Annotation Guidelines

The annotation process for Let-Mi dataset requires labeling the tweets as non-misogynistic, i.e. none or as one of seven misogynistic categories: *discredit, derailing, dominance, stereotyping & objectification, sexual harassment, threat of violence*, and *damning*. It should be noted that, besides the standard misogynistic categories that are usually adopted in the misogyny datasets provided for Indo-European languages (Fersini et al., 2018b,a; Anzovino et al., 2018), we added the "*damning*" category which represents a novel misogynistic behavior inspired by the Arabic culture. It can be described as the Arabic version of cursing where people ask God to make a woman ill, handicapped, dead, hurt, etc. Given the difficulty associated with the recognition of misogynistic behaviors (Schmidt and Wiegand, 2017), they were clearly defined through our designed annotation guidelines. This enabled the annotators to have a unified perspective about misogynistic language categories and contributed to improving the inter-annotator agreement scores. Based on the definition of misogynistic behaviors in (Poland, 2016), we designed the annotation guidelines for Let-Mi dataset such that the eight label categories are identified as follows:

- Non-Misogynistic (none): tweets are those instances that do not express any hatred, insulting or verbal abuse towards women.
- Discredit refers to tweets that combine slurring over women with no other larger intention.
- Derailing: used to describe tweets that indicate a justification of women abuse while re-

Label	Example
None	لما بكون الأمر واضح وبتاخدي لمكان آخر بيضرب مصداقيتك When a matter is clear, and you manipulate it, it affects your credibility
Discredit	انت خلقتي حمارة وعشتي جحشة ولح تموتي بغلة You were born as a donkey, and you're living as a colt, and you will die as a mule
Derailing	هيدي معاقه وصار لازم العالم تتمسخر عليها بلكي بتحس عا حاله عميلة الاعلام She is retarded, people must mock her, maybe she realizes what she's done...Media Rat!
Dominance	لو منعرفك زلمه منرد عليك We'd have answered you if you were a man
Stereotyping & Objectification	مش حضرتك لبتقرري هيدا شي انتي فيكي تقرري شو تلبسي وكيف تتمكيجي مش اكتر You're not the one who can decide such a thing, you can just decide what to wear and how to put your makeup
Threat of violence	والله والله العظيم وين بلاقيك بدي اقتلك قواص ذبح حيالله I swear by God that wherever I find you I will shoot you or slay you
Sexual Harassment	و سوف نغتصبك أيضا و معك J1 الواطية We will rape you and rape degenerate J1 as well
Damning	الله يلعنك ويحرقك ويبعتلك سرطان براسك May God curse and burn you and put cancer in your brain

Table 2: Tweet examples of the annotation labels.

jecting male responsibility with an attempt to disrupt the conversation in order to refocus it.

- Dominance: tweets are those that express male superiority or preserve male control over women.
- Stereotyping & objectification: used to annotate tweets that promote a widely held but fixed and oversimplified image/idea of women. This label also refers to tweet instances that describe women's physical appeal and/or provide comparisons to narrow standards.
- Threat of violence: used to annotate tweets that intimidate women to silence them with an intent to assert power over women through threats of violence physically.
- Sexual harassment: used for tweets that describe actions such as sexual advances, requests for sexual favors, and sexual nature harassment.
- Damning: used to annotate tweets that contain prayers to hurt women; most of the prayers are death/illness wishes besides praying God to curse women.

Table 2 lists the relevant examples to each class.

In addition, we provide target annotation for each tweet found to be misogynistic (fall in one of the seven misogynistic categories), therefore we asked the annotators to tag each misogynistic tweet as belonging to one of the following two target categories:

- Active (individual): the text includes offensive tweets purposely sent to a specific target (explicit indication of addressee or mention of the journalist name);
- Passive (generic): it refers to tweets posted to many potential receivers (e.g. groups of women).

3.3 Annotation Process

The annotation task was assigned to three annotators, one male and two females Levantine native speakers. Besides the previous annotation guidelines, and based on the domain and context of the proposed dataset,we made the annotators aware of specific phrases and terms which look normal/neutral while they indicate toxicity. These phrases/terms are either related to the Lebanese culture or developed during the protests in accordance with the incidents. For example, "بلوطة" (*oak*), which represents a tree type is actually derived from a Lebanese idiom and usually used to describe someone as a liar. Also, the word "سحسوح" (*a slap*) has recently emerged and used during the protest incidents to express an act of violence.

Annotation Case	#Tweets
Unanimous agreement	5,529
Majority agreement (2 out of 3)	1,021
Conflicts	53

Table 3: Summary of annotation statistics.

Having all the annotation rules setup, we asked the three annotators to label the 6,603 tweets as either non-misogynistic or one of the seven misogynistic language categories. When exploring the annotations obtained for the whole dataset, we faced three cases:

1. Unanimous agreement: the three annotators annotated a tweet with the same label. This was encountered in 5,529 tweets.
2. Majority agreement: two out of three annotators agreed on a label of a tweet. This was encountered in 1,021 tweets.
3. Conflicts: each annotator annotated a tweet differently. This case was found in 53 tweets.

After excluding the tweets having three conflicted judgments, the final version of Let-Mi composed of 6,550 tweets. A summary of the annotation statistics is presented in Table 3.

3.4 Annotation Results

With the annotation process accomplished, and considering the annotation cases in Table 3, the final label of each tweet was determined. For tweets falling under the unanimous annotation case, the final labels were directly deduced, while for those falling under the majority annotation case, we selected the label that has been agreed upon by two annotators out of three. Consequently, we got 3,388 non-misogynistic tweets and 3,162 misogynistic tweets where the latter were distributed among the seven misogynistic categories. A detailed review of the statistics of Let-Mi final version is provided in Table 4 where Voc. denotes the vocabulary size for each class.

Label	#Tweets	#Words	Voc.
None	3,388	28,610	12,763
Discredit	2,327	16,587	6,817
Stereotyping & objectification	290	2,235	1,426
Damning	256	1,479	868
Threat of violence	175	1,356	971
Derailing	59	497	391
Dominance	38	292	228
Sexual harassment	17	94	87

Table 4: Tweets distribution across Let-Mi classes.

To identify the words commonly used within misogynistic contexts, we investigated the lexical distribution of the dataset words across the misogynistic classes. Therefore, we subjected Let-Mi to further normalization, where we removed stop-words based on a manually built Levantine stop-words list. Later, we identified the five most frequent words and their frequencies in the misogynistic classes as seen in Table 5, where Dist. denotes the word's distribution in a specific class.

Dominance	Dist.	Violence	Dist.
السيد *Al-Sayyid*	3.77%	J1 *J-name*	1.90%
راسك *your head*	3.42%	راسك *your head*	1.17%
اشرف *more honest)*	3.41%	موتي *be dead*	0.66%
صرمايتو *his slippers*	1.37%	الواطية *degenerate*	0.51%
داعس *step on*	1.03%	سحسوح *slap*	0.44%

Table 5: Distribution of top 5 frequent terms in dominance/threat of violence classes.

3.5 Annotation Evaluation

We evaluated the annotations using two inter-annotator agreement measures: Cohen's kappa (McHugh, 2012) and Krippendorff's α (Krippendorff, 2011). For the obtained annotations, we found that pairwise Cohen's Kappa between the two female annotators (F1,F2) was 86.2%, while for the annotator pairs (male, female), the value decreased to 81.6% and 80.8%, respectively. Moreover, the calculated Krippendorff's α was 82.9% which is considered "good" (Krippendorff, 2011) and indicates the consistency of the annotations. Aiming to investigate the disagreement among the annotators, we explored the tweets for which the annotators gave different judgments. A sample of the tweets along with the annotations assigned by the annotators is listed in Table 6 where F and M denote female and male, respectively.

As seen in Table 6, the disagreements spotted among the annotators can be justified by the gender of the annotator where both female annotators had the same judgment for tweets that describe women-related issues (e.g. Botox) besides they were more sensitive to violent threats compared to the male annotator. On the other hand, when it comes to sarcastic tweets, regardless of the gender, the annotators provided different class labels due to the normal difference of sense of humor among them.

Tweet	F1	F2	M1
يلا انزلي انتي جاي عبالك سحسوح مرتب شطة *Come on! Try to be at the protests, it seems that you'd like a perfect slap*	violence	violence	derailing
عقبال القتلة الجاية هههه *Wishing you a next beating hhhh*	violence	derailing	violence
تروح تنقبر وتلتهي بالبوتوكس وموتوكس وتترك السياسة يحرق روحا *She should be taking care of her Botox and abandon politics; Damn her soul!*	stereotyping	stereotyping	damning

Table 6: Disagreements among annotators.

4 Experiments and Evaluation

In this section, we describe our experiments on the Let-Mi data. We evaluate the performance of SOTA models on our dataset. We design our experiments at three levels (tasks):

1. Misogyny identification (Binary): tweets contents are classified into *misogynistic* and *non-misogynistic*. This requires merging the seven categories of misogyny into the misogyny class.

2. Categories classification (Multi-class): tweets are classified into categories: *discredit, dominance, damning, derailing, sexual harassment, stereotyping and objectification, and threat of Violence*, or *non-misogynistic*.

3. Target classification (Multi-class): tweets are classified into either *passive, active*, or *non-misogynistic*.

4.1 Models

To present a diverse evaluation on the Let-Mi dataset, we test various approaches that use different text representations. In the following, we present the used approaches:

1. BOW + TF-IDF: word ngrams model with TF-IDF weighting scheme. We test several classifiers on a validation part, and we select Naive Bayes classifier[5].

2. Frenda et al. (2018) model: we use one of the SOTA systems on misogyny identification task. This model combines character ngrams with several lexicons created by the authors to highlight important cues in the misogynistic tweets. For instance, the *Stereotypes* lexicon contains words related to the stereotypes about women, like cooking, taking care of children, etc. Since this approach was proposed for English and Spanish languages, we used Google Translation API to translate the lexicons to the Arabic language. It is worthy of mentioning that we discard the *Abbreviations* lexicon as it is untranslatable. Following the authors' configurations, and we use an ensemble technique (majority voting) to combine the predictions from three different classifiers (NB, SVM, and LR).

3. LSTM: A Long Short-Term Memory (LSTM) neural network that uses Aravec Arabic word embeddings (Soliman et al., 2017) to represent texts. The output representation of the LSTM is fed to a softmax layer.

4. BERT: is a text representation model that showed leading performance on multiple NLP benchmarks (Devlin et al., 2019). Since BERT was trained for the English language, we used AraBert (Antoun et al., 2020) which is a version trained on Arabic texts. We fed the hidden representation of the special [CLS] token that BERT uses to summarize the full input sentence, to a softmax layer.

4.2 Experimental Setup

Given that Let-Mi dataset is not balanced, especially in the category classification task, we split the dataset into training, validation, and test sets using stratified sampling technique; we take a random 20% of the tweets from each class for the validation and test sets. Discarding the classes' size in the splitting process may affect the minority classes (e.g., sexual harassment). For the preprocessing of the text, we remove all special characters, URLs, users mentions, and hashtags to ensure that the evaluation models are not biased to any Twitter-inherited symbol. Regarding the experiments' metrics, we used accuracy and macro precision, recall, and F1 score.

[5]We tested Logistic Regression (LR), Random Forest (RF), Naive Bayes (NB), and Support Vector Machine (SVM) classifiers

4.3 Results

In Table 7, we present the results of the misogyny identification task. Considering the F1 metric, the best result of this task is achieved using the BERT model, performing better than the rest of the models. We can see that (Frenda et al., 2018) model performs slightly better than the BOW and the LSTM models. The results show that the LSTM-based model has the lowest performance.

Model	Acc.	Prec.	Rec.	F1
Majority class	0.52	0.26	0.50	0.34
BOW + TF-IDF	0.84	0.84	0.84	0.84
Frenda et al. (2018) model	0.85	0.86	0.85	0.85
LSTM	0.82	0.82	0.82	0.82
BERT	0.88	0.89	0.88	**0.88**

Table 7: Results of the misogyny identification task.

Regarding the category classification task, the results in Table 8 show a different scenario. The best performing model in misogyny identification task, BERT, performs weaker than BOW and (Frenda et al., 2018) models. We speculate that this is due to the number of instances for each class. Recent studies (Edwards et al., 2020) showed that the performance of the pre-trained models (e.g. BERT) decreases marginally when the number of instances in the training data is less than ~5K, and this was evident for multi-class classification datasets. In this task, the total size of the training data is ~4K, and for most of the classes, the maximum number of instances is ~200.

Model	Acc.	Prec.	Rec.	F1
Majority class	0.52	0.06	0.12	0.09
BOW + TF-IDF	0.79	0.52	0.37	0.41
Frenda et al. (2018) model	0.81	0.62	0.38	**0.43**
LSTM	0.75	0.42	0.3	0.33
BERT	0.81	0.44	0.33	0.35

Table 8: Results of the categories classification task.

For the third task, the results in Table 9 show that all the models have a very competitive performance, with a small improvement for the (Frenda et al., 2018) model.

4.4 Multi-task Learning

In multi-task learning (MTL), a set of relevant tasks (two or more) are involved in the training process of a model to improve the performance on each of them (Caruana, 1997). MTL enables a model to use

Model	Acc.	Prec.	Rec.	F1
Majority class	0.52	0.17	0.33	0.23
BOW + TF-IDF	0.82	0.86	0.77	0.81
Frenda et al. (2018) model	0.85	0.88	0.8	**0.83**
LSTM	0.82	0.82	0.81	0.82
BERT	0.83	0.85	0.82	0.82

Table 9: Results of the target classification task.

cues from various tasks to improve each of them performance, or of a target task (Zhang and Abdul-Mageed, 2019). MTL has been employed in several NLP tasks (Kochkina et al., 2018; Majumder et al., 2019; Samghabadi et al., 2020). In this work, we use our three tasks in an MTL configuration to investigate whether the performance of the model on each of them will improve. Therefore, we use the BERT model in our experiment. In Figure 1 we illustrate the MTL configuration with an example.

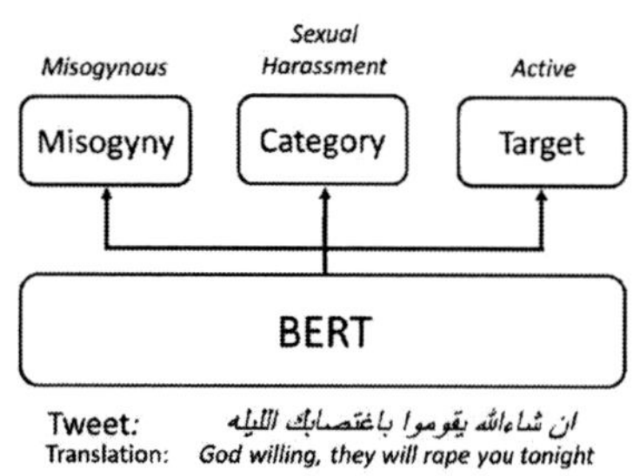

Figure 1: BERT model in an MTL configuration.

The MTL experiment results listed in Table 10 show that MTL improves the performance of both misogyny and target classification tasks clearly, with an average improvement of %4 on the F1 metric. However, the category classification task's performance does not improve and decreases slightly compared to the BERT performance without MTL (1% drop).

Task	Acc.	Prec.	Rec.	F1
Misogyny identification	0.9	0.9	0.9	0.9
Categories classification	0.82	0.42	0.32	0.34
Target classification	0.89	0.89	0.88	0.88

Table 10: Results of the MTL experiment using BERT model.

4.5 Error Analysis

Given the previous sections' results, we can notice that the models' performances in the second task are weak compared to the other two tasks. Thus, in this section, we investigate the causes of the miss-classified cases in the second task. A manual analysis allows us to see which category is the most difficult to be dealt with in the best performing system. Figure 2 reports the confusion matrix of gold labels (y-axis) vs. predicted labels (x-axis).

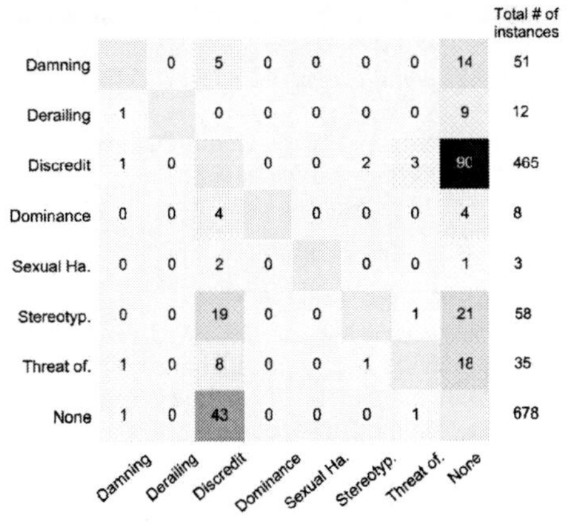

Figure 2: Confusion matrix of errors.

The manual analysis of the tweets shows that classification errors are due to five main factors:

1. **Weak predictions**: although the tweets have been annotated correctly, the model cannot always detect the misogyny category. The cause of this type of errors could be due to the model's generalizability; it could be noted that the model is not able to learn few training cases of some misogynous textual patterns; Besides, this type of errors is evident in the categories having the lowest number of instances in the training data such as *derailing*, *dominance*, and *sexual Harassment*.

2. **Mixed labels**: few tweets can belong to more than one misogyny category, but the annotators chose the most dominant one. In this type of errors, we find that the model sometimes predicts the other possible category. For instance, the tweet: "انتي مذيعه يا تقبريني خليكي بتلبي عزايم وولائم"[6] annotated as *Stereotyping & Objectification* because the author is offending the target women by asking her to stay at home to cook food. It can also be considered discredit since the tweet's beginning is discrediting the targeted woman for her performance as a journalist.

3. **Sarcasm**: many tweets annotated under one of the misogyny categories due to their sarcastic meaning. Unfortunately, the model is not able to detect the sarcastic sense. For instance, the tweet: "كيف صرتي مذيعة؟"[7] is sarcastically offending the target woman by meaning that she should not be a journalist.

4. **Unique damnation phrases**: some tweets use a unique way or a phrase to curse and attack women. Similar to other languages, the Arabic language contains many phrases for damnation. Apart from the well known phrases, some authors created their own phrases that need some cultural knowledge to be understood. An example on these cases is the tweet: "ان شاءالله بسقطو زلاعيمك على المسالك البولية"[8]. This tweet's indirect meaning is that the author prays to God that the journalist will be muted person.

5. **False misogyny cases**: as we are interested in detecting misogynistic tweets, Let-Mi also contains none-misogynistic tweets to classify both groups. Many of the none-misogynistic tweets are neutral tweets (e.g. opinions, questions, news, etc.), but there are also general offensive tweets; not against women. Some of these tweets are offences to the misogynist authors. The analysis shows that the model sometimes cannot discriminate between offensive tweets that target women and the universal ones. An example on this type is the following tweet: "J1 اشرف منكو ومن اللي خلفكو انتو اللي واطيين يا عبدت الفاسدين والحرامية"[9].

5 Conclusion and Future Work

This work proposes Let-Mi, the first misogyny detection dataset for the Levantine dialects of the Arabic language. The dataset is annotated manually by a set of Levantine native speakers. We present a detailed description of the whole annotation process. Additionally, we present an experimental evaluation of several machine learning systems, including SOTA systems. Also, we employ an MTL configuration to investigate its effect on the tasks. The

[6]Explanatory translation: are you a journalist! stay at home to cook food for others.

[7]Translation: How you became a journalist?

[8]Literal translation: God willing, your pharynx will fall on the urinary tract.

[9]Literal translation: J1 is more honest than you and your parents, you who are dirty, and slaves of the corrupt and thieves.

results show that the performances of the used systems are consistent with SOTA results on the other languages, and MTL improved the performance of the used model on two of the proposed tasks. In future work, we plan to create a multi-label version of our dataset for the categories classification task as we found that some tweets can be considered under two or more categories. Moreover, since we found many misogynistic tweets that are sarcastic in our analysis, we plan to study the correlation between sarcasm and misogyny tasks.

References

Monirah A. Al-Ajlan and Mourad Ykhlef. 2018. Optimized twitter cyberbullying detection based on deep learning. In *Proceedings of the 21st Saudi Computer Society National Computer Conference (NCC)*, pages 52–56.

Areej Al-Hassan and Hmood Al-Dossari. 2019. Detection of hate speech in social networks: A survey on multilingual corpus. *Computer Science & Information Technology (CS & IT)*, 9(2):83–100.

Azalden Alakrota, Liam Murray, and Nikola S.Nikolov. 2018. Dataset construction for the detection of antisocial behaviour in online communication in arabic. *Procedia Computer Science*, 142:174–181.

Nuha Albadi, Maram Kurdi, and Shivakant Mishra. 2018. Are they our brothers? analysis and detection of religious hate speech in the arabic twittersphere. In *Proceedings of IEEE/ACM International Conference on Advances in Social Networks Analysis and Mining (ASONAM)*, pages 69–76.

Wissam Antoun, Fady Baly, and Hazem Hajj. 2020. AraBERT: Transformer-based Model for Arabic Language Understanding. In *Proceedings of the 4th Workshop on Open-Source Arabic Corpora and Processing Tools, with a Shared Task on Offensive Language Detection*, pages 9–15.

Maria Anzovino, Elisabetta Fersini, and Paolo Rosso. 2018. Automatic identification and classification of misogynistic language on twitter. In *International Conference on Applications of Natural Language to Information Systems*, pages 57–64. Springer.

Data Aurora. 2019. Lebanon protest statistics. "https://lebanonprotests.com/report". Online; accessed 10-January-2021.

Rich Caruana. 1997. Multitask learning. *Machine learning*, 28(1):41–75.

Jacob Devlin, Ming-Wei Chang, Kenton Lee, and Kristina Toutanova. 2019. BERT: Pre-training of Deep Bidirectional Transformers for Language Understanding. In *Proceedings of the 2019 Conference of the North American Chapter of the Association for Computational Linguistics: Human Language Technologies, Volume 1 (Long and Short Papers)*, pages 4171–4186.

Aleksandra Edwards, Jose Camacho-Collados, Hélène De Ribaupierre, and Alun Preece. 2020. Go Simple and Pre-Train on Domain-Specific Corpora: On the Role of Training Data for Text Classification. In *Proceedings of the 28th International Conference on Computational Linguistics*, pages 5522–5529.

Michelle Ferrier and Nisha Garud-Patkar. 2018. Trollbusters: Fighting online harassment of women journalists. In *Mediating Misogyny*, pages 311–332. Springer.

Elisabetta Fersini, Debora Nozza, and Paolo Rosso. 2018a. Overview of the EVALITA 2018 Task on Automatic Misogyny Identification (AMI). In *EVALITA Evaluation of NLP and Speech Tools for Italian*, volume 12, page 59.

Elisabetta Fersini, Paolo Rosso, and Maria Anzovino. 2018b. Overview of the Task on Automatic Misogyny Identification at IberEval 2018. In *Third Workshop on Evaluation of Human Language Technologies for Iberian Languages (IberEval 2018)*, volume 2150, pages 214–228.

Simona Frenda, Bilal Ghanem, and Manuel Montes-y Gómez. 2018. Exploration of Misogyny in Spanish and English Tweets. In *3rd Workshop on Evaluation of Human Language Technologies for Iberian Languages (IberEval 2018)*, volume 2150, pages 260–267. CEUR-WS.

Elena Kochkina, Maria Liakata, and Arkaitz Zubiaga. 2018. All-in-one: Multi-task learning for rumour verification. In *Proceedings of the 27th International Conference on Computational Linguistics*, pages 3402–3413.

Klaus Krippendorff. 2011. Computing krippendorff's alpha-reliability.

Navonil Majumder, Soujanya Poria, Haiyun Peng, Niyati Chhaya, Erik Cambria, and Alexander Gelbukh. 2019. Sentiment and sarcasm classification with multitask learning. *IEEE Intelligent Systems*, 34(3):38–43.

Mary L McHugh. 2012. Interrater reliability: the kappa statistic. *Biochemia medica: Biochemia medica*, 22(3):276–282.

Mairead Eastin Moloney and Tony P Love. 2018. Assessing online misogyny: Perspectives from sociology and feminist media studies. *Sociology compass*, 12(5):e12577.

Hamdy Mubarak, Kareem Darwish, and Walid Magdy. 2017. Abusive language detection on arabic social media. In *Proceedings of the First Workshop on Abusive Language Online*, pages 52–56.

Hala Mulki, Hatem Haddad, Chedi Bechikh Ali, and Halima Alshabani. 2019. L-hsab: a levantine twitter dataset for hate speech and abusive language. In *Proceedings of the Third Workshop on Abusive Language Online*, pages 111–118.

John T. Nockleby. 2000. *Hate Speech*, volume 1. Encyclopedia of the American Constitution (2nd ed., edited by Leonard W. Levy, Kenneth L. Karst et al. New York: Macmillan, New York: Macmillan.

Bailey Poland. 2016. *Haters: Harassment, abuse, and violence online*. Lincoln: University of Nebraska Press.

Niloofar Safi Samghabadi, Parth Patwa, PYKL Srinivas, Prerana Mukherjee, Amitava Das, and Thamar Solorio. 2020. Aggression and misogyny detection using bert: A multi-task approach. In *Proceedings of the Second Workshop on Trolling, Aggression and Cyberbullying*, pages 126–131.

Anna Schmidt and Michael Wiegand. 2017. A survey on hate speech detection using natural language processing. In *Proceedings of the Fifth International Workshop on Natural Language Processing for Social Media*, pages 1–10.

Jamillah Sleiman and Mythili Menon. 2018. The changing of arabic terminology in times of war and displacement. *Proceedings of the Twenty-Ninth Western Conference on Linguistics*.

Abu Bakr Soliman, Kareem Eissa, and Samhaa R. El-Beltagy. 2017. Aravec: A Set of Arabic Word Embedding Models for Use in Arabic NLP. *Procedia Computer Science*, 117:256 – 265. Arabic Computational Linguistics.

Chiyu Zhang and Muhammad Abdul-Mageed. 2019. Multi-task Bidirectional Transformer Representations for Irony Detection. *arXiv preprint arXiv:1909.03526*.

Empathetic BERT2BERT Conversational Model: Learning Arabic Language Generation with Little Data

Tarek Naous, Wissam Antoun, Reem A. Mahmoud, and Hazem Hajj
Department of Electrical and Computer Engineering
American University of Beirut
Beirut, Lebanon
{tnn11,wfa07,ram79,hh63}@aub.edu.lb

Abstract

Enabling empathetic behavior in Arabic dialogue agents is an important aspect of building human-like conversational models. While Arabic Natural Language Processing has seen significant advances in Natural Language Understanding (NLU) with language models such as AraBERT, Natural Language Generation (NLG) remains a challenge. The shortcomings of NLG encoder-decoder models are primarily due to the lack of Arabic datasets suitable to train NLG models such as conversational agents. To overcome this issue, we propose a transformer-based encoder-decoder initialized with AraBERT parameters. By initializing the weights of the encoder and decoder with AraBERT pre-trained weights, our model was able to leverage knowledge transfer and boost performance in response generation. To enable empathy in our conversational model, we train it using the ArabicEmpatheticDialogues dataset and achieve high performance in empathetic response generation. Specifically, our model achieved a low perplexity value of 17.0 and an increase in 5 BLEU points compared to the previous state-of-the-art model. Also, our proposed model was rated highly by 85 human evaluators, validating its high capability in exhibiting empathy while generating relevant and fluent responses in open-domain settings.

1 Introduction

Conversational models with empathetic responding capabilities are crucial in making human-machine interactions closer to human-human interactions, as they can lead to increased engagement, more trust, and reduced frustration (Yalçın and DiPaola, 2018). These characteristics are highly desirable in open-domain conversational models as they can boost user satisfaction and make chatbots look less boorish. While empathy can be attributed to a range of behaviors, it can be generally described as the

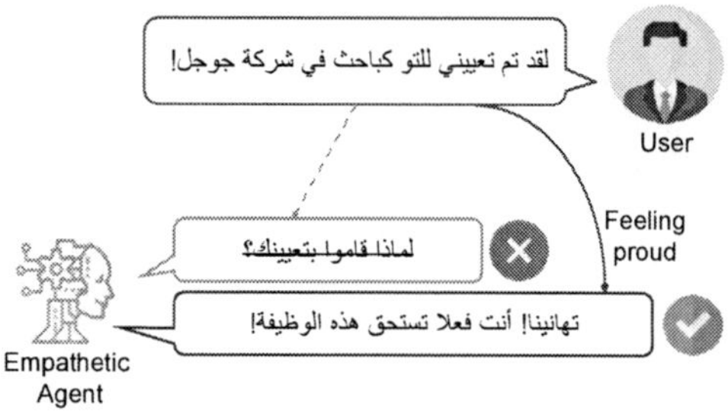

Figure 1: Example of empathetic behavior in a conversational agent.

innate human capacity of relating to another person's feelings and making sense of their emotional state (Yalçın, 2020). An important factor towards developing human-like dialogue agents is enabling their empathetic capability (Huang et al., 2020). To this end, there has been a significant interest in developing empathetic conversational models (Majumder et al., 2020; Sharma et al., 2020; Ma et al., 2020; Yalçın and DiPaola, 2019). These models infer the emotions of a human user and provide a suitable empathetic response. The desired behavior of an empathetic conversational agent is illustrated in Figure 1, where the empathetic agent recognizes that the user is feeling proud and, thus, generates an empathetic response that congratulates the user with enthusiasm.

Recent work in open-domain empathetic conversational models have adopted neural-based sequence generation approaches (Rashkin et al., 2019). These approaches are based on encoder-decoder neural network architectures such as Sequence-to-Sequence (Seq2Seq) recurrent neural network models (Shin et al., 2020) or transformers (Lin et al., 2020). Despite the significant work done in this direction, the focus so far has been mostly on the English language with fewer efforts being directed towards low-resource languages, such as

Proceedings of the Sixth Arabic Natural Language Processing Workshop, pages 164–172
Kyiv, Ukraine (Virtual), April 19, 2021.

Arabic. The first dataset for Arabic utterances and empathetic responses was recently introduced by Naous et al. (2020), where a Bidirectional Long Short-Term Memory (Bi-LSTM) Seq2Seq model was trained on the dataset. However, the model proposed by Naous et al. (2020) delivered sub-optimal performance due to the limited size of the dataset. The additional challenges in developing neural-based empathetic conversational models for Arabic is the lack of open-domain conversational data that can be used for pre-training (Li et al., 2017), and thus no availability of pre-trained conversational models that can be used directly for fine-tuning (Zhang et al., 2020b).

To address the challenges of small dataset size and lack of conversational resources, in terms of datasets and pre-trained models, we propose a transformer-based encoder-decoder model initialized with AraBERT (Antoun et al., 2020) pre-trained weights. Our work extends the English BERT2BERT architecture (Rothe et al., 2020) to Arabic response generation. We fine-tune our proposed model on the limited-sized dataset of empathetic responses in Arabic (Naous et al., 2020). By using the pre-trained weights of the AraBERT language model to initialize the encoder and decoder, our proposed BERT2BERT model is expected to leverage knowledge transfer and show enhanced performance in empathetic response generation compared to the baseline Bi-LSTM model proposed by Naous et al. (2020).

The rest of this paper is organized as follows: Section 2 reviews the recent literature on empathetic conversational models in both English and Arabic. Our proposed BERT2BERT approach for empathetic response generation is presented in Section 3, including the dataset and pre-processing steps. Section 4 analyzes the performance of our model and compares its results to several benchmark models. Concluding remarks and future directions are presented in Section 5.

2 Related Work

2.1 English Empathetic Conversational Models

The interest in enabling empathy in conversational agents has increased over the last few years with the introduction of the EmpatheticDialogues dataset by Rashkin et al. (2019). EmpatheticDialogues is a crowdsourced dataset of open-domain conversations where a group of workers was instructed to select an emotion, describe a situation where they have felt that way, and carry out a conversation related to the emotion. The authors used the conversations collected to train retrieval-based and generative-based models, which showed higher levels of empathy in their responses compared with models trained on spontaneous conversational data gathered from the Internet.

The release of EmpatheticDialogues (Rashkin et al., 2019) stimulated further research in this area with multiple attempts in the literature to improve the empathetic capability of conversational models. Shin et al. (2020) formulated the empathetic responding task as a reinforcement learning problem. The approach named "Sentiment look-ahead" employs a Seq2Seq policy model with Gated Recurrent Units to generate an empathetic response based on an input utterance and updates the policy using the REINFORCE method. Lin et al. (2020) fined-tuned a GPT model on the EmpatheticDialogues dataset. The GPT model was pre-trained on the BooksCorpus (Zhu et al., 2015) dataset, improving the NLU capability of the model, as well as on the PersonaChat (Zhang et al., 2018) dataset, allowing the model to have improved performance on response generation.

2.2 Arabic Empathetic Conversational Models

While many works have focused on enabling empathetic capabilities in conversational models for English, there are much fewer attempts to build similar models for Arabic. In general, research on Arabic conversational models is still in its infancy mainly due to the complexity of the language, and the lack of resources and pre-trained models that are available in abundance for English. Despite the availability of Arabic pre-trained language models such as hULMonA (ElJundi et al., 2019) and AraBERT (Antoun et al., 2020), which have proven useful for Arabic NLU tasks, the lack of pre-trained models for Arabic NLG makes the development of neural-based Arabic conversational models a challenging task. Hence, existing works on Arabic chatbots have mainly focused on retrieval-based methods (Ali and Habash, 2016) or rule-based approaches (Hijjawi et al., 2014; Fadhil and AbuRa'ed, 2019). While these approaches work well on task-oriented objectives, they are limited by the size of manually crafted rules they follow or the richness of the database they can retrieve responses from. This

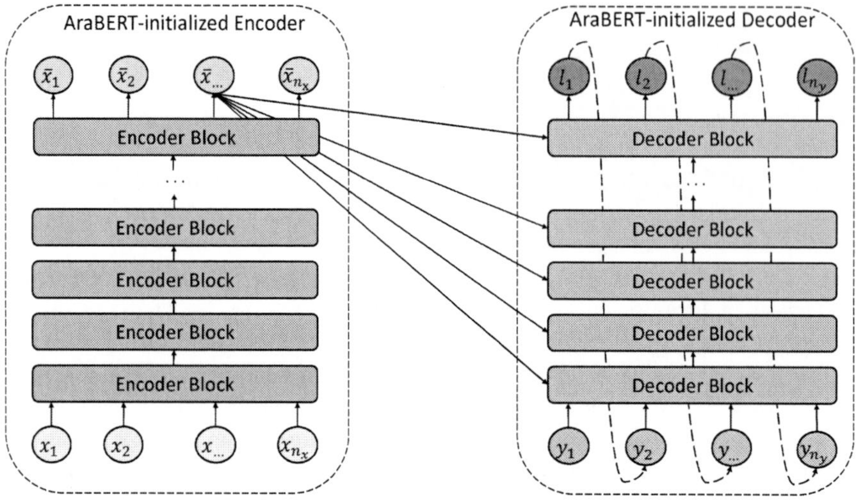

Figure 2: Architecture of the proposed BERT2BERT model initialized with AraBERT checkpoints for Arabic empathetic response generation.

makes it difficult for such types of models to operate well in open-domain conversational settings, where generative neural-based models would be more suitable.

Recently, the first empathy-driven Arabic conversational model was proposed by Naous et al. (2020) that released ArabicEmpatheticDialogues, a dataset of Arabic utterances and their corresponding empathetic responses. The authors trained a Seq2Seq model with bidirectional LSTM units on the dataset. While the model succeeded in generating empathetic responses, it showed an average Relevance score which indicates that the responses can sometimes go off-topic and may not be suitable responses for the emotional context of the input utterance. The limitations of this work were mainly due to the limited size of the dataset.

In this work, we adopt the BERT2BERT architecture (Rothe et al., 2020) and leverage the pre-trained AraBERT (Antoun et al., 2020) model to improve the performance of empathetic Arabic conversational models.

3 Proposed Method

3.1 Proposed BERT2BERT Model

Our proposed model for Arabic empathetic response generation is a transformer-based Seq2Seq model (Vaswani et al., 2017), which has been shown to boost performance on a several Seq2Seq tasks (Raffel et al., 2020; Lewis et al., 2019). However, such an architecture would require massive pre-training before being fine-tuned on the desired task (Zhang et al., 2020a). It was shown by Rothe et al. (2020) that warm-starting the transformer-based encoder-decoder model with the checkpoints of a pre-trained encoder (e.g. BERT) allows the model to deliver competitive results in sequence generation tasks while skipping the costly pre-training. Inspired by this idea, and due to the unavailability of Arabic conversational datasets that can be used for pre-training, we adopt the BERT2BERT architecture (Rothe et al., 2020), and warm-start the encoder and decoder with the AraBERT checkpoint (Antoun et al., 2020). The encoder-decoder attention is randomly initialized. The architecture of the proposed model is illustrated in Figure 2.

The input to the proposed model is a sequence $x = [x_1, x_2, \dots, x_{n_x}]$ of one-hot representations with a length of n_x tokens, chosen to be 150. This sequence is fed as input to an AraBERT initialized encoder. At the decoder side, the model generates an empathetic response represented by a sequence $y = [y_1, y_2, \dots, y_{n_y}]$, where the maximum output length n_y is also specified to be 150. We optimize the log-likelihood loss over the output tokens.

To generate empathetic responses from our model, we adopt the Top-K Sampling scheme (Fan et al., 2018) where, at each time step, the model randomly samples the K most likely candidates from the probability distribution of all words in the vocabulary. This decoding strategy has been

Emotion	Excited
Utterance	في الأسبوع الماضي كنا نشاهد كأس العالم ، وها هي كرواتيا تغلبت على البلد المضيف، روسيا
Response	رأيت تلك اللعبة. لقد فازوا بركلات الترجيح!
Emotion	**Furious**
Utterance	تخيل، لقد طلبت البطاطس المقلية و لكن تم تقديم البرغر بدلا من ذلك!
Response	إنها خدمة سيئة للغاية. ماذا فعلت؟ هل اشتكيت للمدير؟
Emotion	**Embarrassed**
Utterance	خرجت في نهاية الأسبوع الماضي و تعرضت لحادث كبير. خمن ماذا جرى
Response	هل أنت بخير؟ عليك أن تخبرني بما حدث

Table 1: Samples of utterances and empathetic responses from the ArabicEmpatheticDialogues dataset for three emotion labels: Excited, Furious, and Embarrassed

found more effective than conventional approaches such as beam search, which tends to yield common responses found repetitively in the training set or similar, slightly-varying versions of the same high-likelihood sequences (Ippolito et al., 2019).

3.2 Dataset

Grouped Emotion Labels	Complete Emotion Labels
Joy	Excited
	Proud
	Grateful
	Hopeful
	Confident
	Joyful
	Content
	Prepared
	Anticipating
Love	Caring
	Sentimental
	Trusting
	Faithful
	Nostalgic
Surprise	Surprised
	Impressed
Sadness	Sad
	Lonely
	Guilty
	Disappointed
	Devastated
	Embarrassed
	Ashamed
Anger	Angry
	Annoyed
	Furious
	Disgusted
	Jealous
Fear	Afraid
	Terrified
	Anxious
	Apprehensive

Table 2: Grouping of emotion labels in the ArabicEmpatheticDialogues dataset as per Parrott's characterization of tree-structured emotions (Parrott, 2001).

Pre-Segmentation
أنا فخور جدا بإبنتي لقد تخرجت للتو من كلية الهندسة
Post-Segmentation
أنا فخور جد+ا ب+ إبن +ت +ي لقد تخرج +ت ل+ ال+ تو من كلي +ة ال+ هندس +ة

Table 3: Example of an Arabic utterance segmentation using Farasa.

We use the ArabicEmpatheticDialogues dataset (Naous et al., 2020) which was translated from the English version introduced by Rashkin et al. (2019). ArabicEmpathicDialogues contains 36,628 samples of speaker utterances and their corresponding empathetic responses in Arabic. Each sample is also labeled with the emotion of the speaker's utterance. Three examples from the dataset for three different emotion labels are provided in Table 1. By training a sequence generation model on the samples of utterances and their corresponding responses from the dataset, the model will be able to infer the emotions in input utterances and provide suitable empathetic responses. Thus, the empathetic capability of the model would be enhanced.

The dataset is originally labeled with 32 emotion labels, many of which are very similar such as "joyful" and "content", or "angry" and "furious". To reduce the number of classes, we follow the tree-structured list of emotions defined by Parrott (2001) to map the 32 emotion labels to their 6 primary emotions which are "Joy", "Surprise", "Love", "Surprise", "Anger", and "Fear". This grouping is shown in Table 2.

To reduce lexical sparsity, the utterances and responses in the dataset are segmented using the Farasa segmenter (Abdelali et al., 2016). Given the morphological complexity of the Arabic language, segmentation is an important pre-processing step that can greatly enhance the performance of neural-based sequence generation models. An example of this process is shown in Table 3. By performing segmentation, the vocabulary size is drastically reduced from 47K tokens to around 13K tokens.

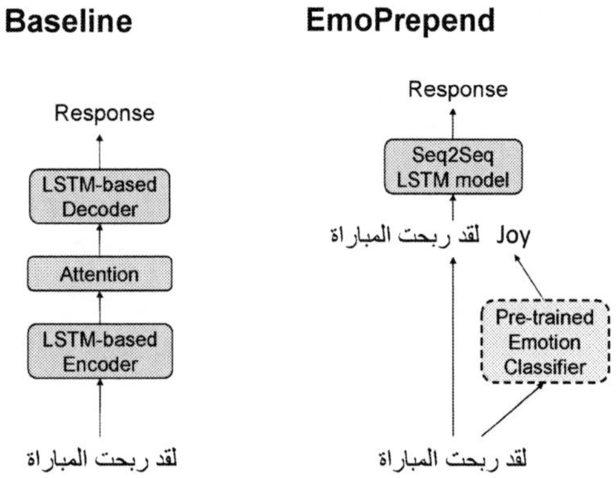

Figure 3: Architectures of the Baseline and EmoPrepend models used for comparative evaluation against the proposed BERT2BERT model.

4 Experiments & Results

We evaluate the proposed BERT2BERT model in comparison to three benchmark models. We conduct numerical as well as human evaluation of the different conversational models.

4.1 Benchmark Models

We train several neural-based sequence generation models on the ArabicEmpatheticDialogues dataset and consider them as benchmarks for performance comparison. The benchmark models are denoted as follows:

Baseline: The baseline model, illustrated in Figure 3, is a Seq2Seq Bi-LSTM model with Attention following the prior state-of-the-art model proposed by Naous et al. (2020).

EmoPrepend: In this setup, illustrated in Figure 3, we prepend the emotion label to each utterance before feeding it as input to the baseline model described above, and we denote this approach as EmoPrepend. This allows us to add supervised information to the data, without having to introduce any modifications to the architecture. The existing emotion labels have been prepended to the utterances in the train and validation sets. For the test set and at inference, we fine-tune AraBERT for emotion classification using the utterances and their labels in the dataset. The fine-tuned AraBERT model is then used as an external predictor to classify the emotion in the utterance and prepend it as a token before being used as an input to the EmoPrepend model. We note that the step of grouping emotion labels into 6 main labels, as discussed in Section 3, makes the emotion classification task easier.

Model	PPL	BLEU
Baseline (Naous et al., 2020)	38.6	0.5
EmoPrepend	24.1	3.16
BERT2BERT-UN	159.8	0.1
BERT2BERT	**17.0**	**5.58**

Table 4: Performance of the models on the test set in terms of PPL and BLEU score.

BERT2BERT-UN: which stands for BERT2BERT-Uninitialized. This model is a regular transformer-based encoder-decoder model that shares the same architecture of the BERT2BERT model shown in Figure 2, but **is not** initialized with AraBERT pre-trained weights.

4.2 Experimental Setup

The proposed BERT2BERT model was developed using the Huggingface transformers library[1]. We train the model for 5 epochs with a batch size of 32[2]. Model training was done on a 16GB V100 NVidia GPU. The Baseline Bi-LSTM Seq2Seq (Naous et al., 2020), EmoPrepend, and BERT2BERT-UN benchmark models were developed using the OpenNMT Library (Klein et al., 2017).

Dataset Partitioning: All models were trained and evaluated on common data splits of the ArabicEmpatheticDialogues. We randomly partitioned the dataset into 90% training, 5% validation, and 5% testing using a seed of 42.

4.3 Numerical Evaluation

Table 4 summarizes the perplexity (PPL) and Bilingual Evaluation Understudy (BLEU) scores for the proposed and benchmark models when evaluated on the test set. It is clear from the numerical evaluation results that the proposed BERT2BERT model consistently outperforms the benchmark models. This is reflected through both a lower PPL score and a higher BLEU score.

[1]https://github.com/huggingface/transformers

[2]https://github.com/aub-mind/Arabic-Empathetic-Chatbot

Model	Empathy	Relevance	Fluency
Baseline (Naous et al., 2020)	2.04	1.68	2.44
EmoPrepend	2.81	2.18	3.28
BERT2BERT	**4.0**	**3.59**	**4.30**

Table 5: Average evaluation of the collected human ratings.

Generated Response	Utterance	Emotion
أوه لا! ماذا حدث ؟	اليوم يوم سيئ جدا	Sadness
!من الرائع سماع ذلك ما الذي يجعلك سعيدا جدا حيال ذلك ؟	أنا سعيد جدا	Joy
أنا آسف جدا لسماع ذلك. هل أنت بخير ؟	لقد أصبت بفيروس كورونا	Fear
إنه لأمر رائع أنك فخور جدا بنفسك	أنا فخور جدا بكوني مهندس	Joy
تهانينا! ما هو العمل الشاق ؟	لقد تلقيت ترقية في عملي اليوم	Surprise
أنا اسف لسماع ذلك هل كان عيد ميلادك المفضل ؟	خلال عيد الميلاد قبل بضع سنوات، لم أحصل على أي هدايا	Sadness
أوه ، واو! يجب أن يكون ذلك مزعجا حقا	يستمر جاري في إحداث ضوضاء في الساعة الثانية صباحا	Anger
أوه ، واو ، أنا متأكد من أنك ستكون بخير	أختي ستتزوج الأسبوع القبل . أنا سعيد جدا لها ولكن في بعض الأحيان أشعر بشيء ثقيل في القلب	Sadness

Table 6: Examples of responses generated by the BERT2BERT model for multiple utterances with various emotional states and domain contexts.

With EmoPrepend, the addition of supervised information in the form of prepended emotion labels showed performance improvements in comparison to the Baseline model, reflected by an increase in 2.6 BLEU points and a reduction of 14.5 points in the PPL score. Nevertheless, the PPL score of EmoPrepend at 24.1 is still considered high and could potentially lead to sub-optimal performance. BERT2BERT showed significant performance improvements in comparison to the baseline Seq2Seq Bi-LSTM, highlighted by a much reduced PPL value of 17.0 and an increase in 5 BLEU points. BERT2BERT also achieved better scores than the EmoPrepend model.

The BERT2BERT-UN model resulted in a very high PPL score of 158.9 and very low BLEU score of 0.1. These poor results are due to the nature of transformer networks that require huge amounts of data samples to deliver good performance. The initialization of the BERT2BERT with pre-trained AraBERT weights showed very significant enhancements compared with the uninitialized BERT2BERT-UN model. This performance boost provided by the BERT2BERT model is expected given the fact that AraBERT's initialization parameters have been pre-trained on a massive 24 GB Arabic corpus.

The numerical results achieved by the BERT2BERT model are particularly impressive since, despite the limited size of the ArabicEmpatheticDialogues dataset, BERT2BERT was able to leverage knowledge transfer through fine-tuning to achieve state-of-art performance on the task of open-domain empathetic response generation in Arabic without requiring additional empathetic samples to train on, or pre-training conversational data.

4.4 Human Evaluation

Automated metrics such as PPL and BLEU scores are not sufficient alone to evaluate a model's ability to exhibit empathetic behavior. Given the unavailability of specific metrics to evaluate empathy in a conversational model, we resort to evaluation based on the judgment of human subjects. Through human evaluation, we can evaluate the emotional communication capability of the models, which is their ability to recognize emotion in the input utterance and generate a suitable expression of emotion in their corresponding response (Yalçın, 2019). To this end, we conducted a survey to collect ratings from 85 native Arabic speakers.

Generated Response	Utterance
أنا سعيد لسماع ذلك	مرحبا كيف حالك ؟
ماذا عنك ؟	ماذا تفعل ؟
أوه ، واو. أنا أحب الحيوانات الأليفة	ما اسمك ؟
لست متأكدا من أين ذهبت. هل ذهبت ؟	هل زرت لاس فيجاس من قبل ؟
هذا يبدو و كأنه عطلة نهاية أسبوع رائعة	سأذهب للتنزه قليلا و أعود بعد قليل

Table 7: Examples of responses generated by the BERT2BERT model for multiple utterances with neutral emotions.

The raters were shown various utterances and their corresponding responses generated by the Baseline, EmoPrepend, and BERT2BERT models. The BERT2BERT-UN model was excluded from the survey given its poor results in terms of numerical metrics. The raters were asked to evaluate each of the models' ability to show Empathy, Relevance, and Fluency in the generated response. The raters were asked to answer the following questions:

- Empathy: Does the generated response show an ability to infer the emotions in the given utterance?
- Relevance: How relevant is the generated response to the input utterance?
- Fluency: How understandable is the generated response? Is it linguistically correct?

For each question, the raters were asked to score the responses of the models on a scale of 0 to 5, where 0 reflects extremely poor performance and 5 reflects excellent performance.

The results of the survey are summarized in Table 5, where we report the average of the collected ratings. The EmoPrepend model showed a higher average score of Empathy and Relevance than the Baseline model. However, these scores are below 3, meaning the EmoPrepend model was seen to deliver below-average performance.

On the other hand, the average ratings of the BERT2BERT model can be considered high and are much superior to both the Baseline and the EmoPrepend models, which indicates BERT2BERT's ability to deliver highly empathetic responses while abiding by linguistic correctness. This is reflected in some examples of the generated responses by BERT2BERT that can be seen in Table 6. The responses demonstrate the model's ability to express empathetic, relevant, and fluent responses when prompted with input utterances with various emotional states and domain contexts, which also proves its ability to handle open-domain conversations.

4.5 Performance on Inputs with Neutral Emotional States

Despite the promising results achieved by the BERT2BERT model in generating relevant empathetic responses in open-domain settings, it was shown to poorly handle regular chit-chat utterances with neutral emotions, such as "Hey, how are you?" or "What are you doing?". Instead of providing a regular response, the BERT2BERT model will opt to generate an empathetic response as we show in Table 7. This issue can be explained by the fact that the model was fine-tuned on a dataset comprised of utterances with pure emotional context and corresponding empathetic responses. Moreso, the AraBERT-initialized parameters did not help mitigate this issue since AraBERT is pre-trained in a self-supervised fashion on news articles and later fine-tuned on a task-specific dataset that does not contain regular chit-chat samples. Thus, it is clear why the BERT2BERT model is not able to handle neutral chit-chat conversations, as it is outside the scope of the training data and the task at hand.

5 Conclusion

In this paper, we address the limitation in resources for Arabic conversational systems, in particular, empathetic conversations. Unlike the English language which has seen great advancements in language generation models due to large corpora and million parameter pre-trained models like GPT, Arabic is considered a low-resource language with limited availability of conversational datasets and pre-trained models for response generation.

We propose an empathetic BERT2BERT, a transformer-based model, of which the encoder and decoder are warm-started using AraBERT pre-trained parameters and fine-tuned for Arabic empathetic response generation using the ArabicEmpatheticDialogues dataset. By adopting this transfer learning strategy, the proposed BERT2BERT model was able to address the challenges of building an open-domain neural-based empathetic conversational model for a low resource language such as Arabic. BERT2BERT achieved significant performance improvements in comparison to three benchmark models, a baseline Seq2Seq Bi-LSTM model, a Seq2Seq Bi-LSTM model with prepended supervised information about the emotion label during the training process, and a transformer-based encoder-decoder that is not initialized with pre-trained weights.

The proposed BERT2BERT model achieved a low PPL value of 17.0, a BLEU score of 5.58, and was rated highly by human evaluators with a score of 4.3/5.0, reflecting its ability to generate empathetic, relevant, and fluent responses. Hence, our results show the ability to develop high-performing conversational models in low resource settings by adopting the BERT2BERT strategy.

Despite its high performance in empathetic response generation, BERT2BERT showed a limitation in its ability to handle regular chit-chat conversations with neutral emotional states. To this end, future directions include the development of a strategy that improves the model's ability to determine when an empathetic response is suitable and when it is not.

Acknowledgments

This work has been funded by the University Research Board (URB) at the American University of Beirut (AUB).

References

Ahmed Abdelali, Kareem Darwish, Nadir Durrani, and Hamdy Mubarak. 2016. Farasa: A fast and furious segmenter for arabic. In *Proceedings of the 2016 conference of the North American chapter of the association for computational linguistics: Demonstrations*, pages 11–16.

Dana Abu Ali and Nizar Habash. 2016. Botta: An arabic dialect chatbot. In *Proceedings of COLING 2016, the 26th International Conference on Computational Linguistics: System Demonstrations*, pages 208–212.

Wissam Antoun, Fady Baly, and Hazem Hajj. 2020. AraBERT: Transformer-based model for arabic language understanding. In *Proceedings of the 4th Workshop on Open-Source Arabic Corpora and Processing Tools, with a Shared Task on Offensive Language Detection*, pages 9–15.

Obeida ElJundi, Wissam Antoun, Nour El Droubi, Hazem Hajj, Wassim El-Hajj, and Khaled Shaban. 2019. hulmona: The universal language model in arabic. In *Proceedings of the Fourth Arabic Natural Language Processing Workshop*, pages 68–77.

Ahmed Fadhil and Ahmed AbuRa'ed. 2019. OlloBot - towards a text-based Arabic health conversational agent: Evaluation and results. In *Proceedings of the International Conference on Recent Advances in Natural Language Processing (RANLP 2019)*, pages 295–303.

Angela Fan, Mike Lewis, and Yann Dauphin. 2018. Hierarchical neural story generation. In *Proceedings of the 56th Annual Meeting of the Association for Computational Linguistics (Volume 1: Long Papers)*, pages 889–898.

Mohammad Hijjawi, Zuhair Bandar, Keeley Crockett, and David Mclean. 2014. ArabChat: an arabic conversational agent. In *2014 6th International Conference on Computer Science and Information Technology (CSIT)*, pages 227–237. IEEE.

Minlie Huang, Xiaoyan Zhu, and Jianfeng Gao. 2020. Challenges in building intelligent open-domain dialog systems. *ACM Transactions on Information Systems (TOIS)*, 38(3):1–32.

Daphne Ippolito, Reno Kriz, Joao Sedoc, Maria Kustikova, and Chris Callison-Burch. 2019. Comparison of diverse decoding methods from conditional language models. In *Proceedings of the 57th Annual Meeting of the Association for Computational Linguistics*, pages 3752–3762.

Guillaume Klein, Yoon Kim, Yuntian Deng, Jean Senellart, and Alexander M Rush. 2017. Opennmt: Open-source toolkit for neural machine translation. In *Proceedings of ACL 2017, System Demonstrations*, pages 67–72.

Mike Lewis, Yinhan Liu, Naman Goyal, Marjan Ghazvininejad, Abdelrahman Mohamed, Omer Levy, Ves Stoyanov, and Luke Zettlemoyer. 2019. Bart: Denoising sequence-to-sequence pre-training for natural language generation, translation, and comprehension. *arXiv preprint arXiv:1910.13461*.

Yanran Li, Hui Su, Xiaoyu Shen, Wenjie Li, Ziqiang Cao, and Shuzi Niu. 2017. Dailydialog: A manually labelled multi-turn dialogue dataset. In *Proceedings of the Eighth International Joint Conference on Natural Language Processing (Volume 1: Long Papers)*, pages 986–995.

Zhaojiang Lin, Peng Xu, Genta Indra Winata, Farhad Bin Siddique, Zihan Liu, Jamin Shin, and Pascale Fung. 2020. CAiRE: an end-to-end empathetic chatbot. In *AAAI*, pages 13622–13623.

Zhiqiang Ma, Rui Yang, Baoxiang Du, and Yan Chen. 2020. A control unit for emotional conversation generation. *IEEE Access*, 8:43168–43176.

Navonil Majumder, Pengfei Hong, Shanshan Peng, Jiankun Lu, Deepanway Ghosal, Alexander Gelbukh, Rada Mihalcea, and Soujanya Poria. 2020. Mime: Mimicking emotions for empathetic response generation. In *Proceedings of the 2020 Conference on Empirical Methods in Natural Language Processing (EMNLP)*, pages 8968–8979.

Tarek Naous, Christian Hokayem, and Hazem Hajj. 2020. Empathy-driven arabic conversational chatbot. In *Proceedings of the Fifth Arabic Natural Language Processing Workshop*, pages 58–68.

W Gerrod Parrott. 2001. *Emotions in social psychology: Essential readings*. Psychology Press.

Colin Raffel, Noam Shazeer, Adam Roberts, Katherine Lee, Sharan Narang, Michael Matena, Yanqi Zhou, Wei Li, and Peter J Liu. 2020. Exploring the limits of transfer learning with a unified text-to-text transformer. *Journal of Machine Learning Research*, 21(140):1–67.

Hannah Rashkin, Eric Michael Smith, Margaret Li, and Y-Lan Boureau. 2019. Towards empathetic open-domain conversation models: A new benchmark and dataset. In *Proceedings of the 57th Annual Meeting of the Association for Computational Linguistics*, pages 5370–5381.

Sascha Rothe, Shashi Narayan, and Aliaksei Severyn. 2020. Leveraging pre-trained checkpoints for sequence generation tasks. *Transactions of the Association for Computational Linguistics*, 8:264–280.

Ashish Sharma, Adam Miner, David Atkins, and Tim Althoff. 2020. A computational approach to understanding empathy expressed in text-based mental health support. In *Proceedings of the 2020 Conference on Empirical Methods in Natural Language Processing (EMNLP)*, pages 5263–5276.

Jamin Shin, Peng Xu, Andrea Madotto, and Pascale Fung. 2020. Generating empathetic responses by looking ahead the user's sentiment. In *ICASSP 2020-2020 IEEE International Conference on Acoustics, Speech and Signal Processing (ICASSP)*, pages 7989–7993. IEEE.

Ashish Vaswani, Noam Shazeer, Niki Parmar, Jakob Uszkoreit, Llion Jones, Aidan N Gomez, ukasz Kaiser, and Illia Polosukhin. 2017. Attention is all you need. In *Advances in neural information processing systems*, pages 5998–6008.

Özge Nilay Yalçın. 2019. Evaluating empathy in artificial agents. In *2019 8th International Conference on Affective Computing and Intelligent Interaction (ACII)*, pages 1–7. IEEE.

Özge Nilay Yalçın. 2020. Empathy framework for embodied conversational agents. *Cognitive Systems Research*, 59:123–132.

Özge Nilay Yalçın and Steve DiPaola. 2018. A computational model of empathy for interactive agents. *Biologically Inspired Cognitive Architectures*, 26:20–25.

Özge Nilay Yalçın and Steve DiPaola. 2019. M-path: a conversational system for the empathic virtual agent. In *Biologically Inspired Cognitive Architectures Meeting*, pages 597–607. Springer.

Jingqing Zhang, Yao Zhao, Mohammad Saleh, and Peter Liu. 2020a. Pegasus: Pre-training with extracted gap-sentences for abstractive summarization. In *International Conference on Machine Learning*, pages 11328–11339. PMLR.

Saizheng Zhang, Emily Dinan, Jack Urbanek, Arthur Szlam, Douwe Kiela, and Jason Weston. 2018. Personalizing dialogue agents: I have a dog, do you have pets too? In *Proceedings of the 56th Annual Meeting of the Association for Computational Linguistics (Volume 1: Long Papers)*, pages 2204–2213.

Yizhe Zhang, Siqi Sun, Michel Galley, Yen-Chun Chen, Chris Brockett, Xiang Gao, Jianfeng Gao, Jingjing Liu, and William B Dolan. 2020b. DIALOGPT: Large-scale generative pre-training for conversational response generation. In *Proceedings of the 58th Annual Meeting of the Association for Computational Linguistics: System Demonstrations*, pages 270–278.

Yukun Zhu, Ryan Kiros, Rich Zemel, Ruslan Salakhutdinov, Raquel Urtasun, Antonio Torralba, and Sanja Fidler. 2015. Aligning books and movies: Towards story-like visual explanations by watching movies and reading books. In *Proceedings of the IEEE International Conference on Computer Vision*, pages 19–27.

ALUE: Arabic Language Understanding Evaluation

Haitham Seelawi Ibraheem Tuffaha Mahmoud Gzawi Wael Farhan
Bashar Talafha Riham Badawi Zyad Sober Oday Al-Dweik
Abed Alhakim Freihat Hussein T. Al-Natsheh
Mawdoo3 Ltd, Amman, Jordan
{haitham.selawi,ibraheem.tuffaha,mahmoud.gzawi,wael.farhan,
bashar.talafha,riham.badawi,zyad.sober,oday.aldweik,
abedalhakim.freihat,h.natsheh}
@mawdoo3.com

Abstract

The emergence of Multi-task learning (MTL) models in recent years has helped push the state of the art in Natural Language Understanding (NLU). We strongly believe that many NLU problems in Arabic are especially poised to reap the benefits of such models. To this end, we propose the Arabic Language Understanding Evaluation Benchmark (ALUE), based on 8 carefully selected and previously published tasks. For five of these, we provide new privately held evaluation datasets to ensure the fairness and validity of our benchmark. We also provide a diagnostic dataset to help researchers probe the inner workings of their models. Our initial experiments show that MTL models outperform their singly trained counterparts on most tasks. But in order to entice participation from the wider community, we stick to publishing singly trained baselines only. Nonetheless, our analysis reveals that there is plenty of room for improvement in Arabic NLU. We hope that ALUE will play a part in helping our community realize some of these improvements. Interested researchers are invited to submit their results to our online, and publicly accessible leaderboard.

1 Introduction

Historically, research into the wide spectrum of problems in Natural Language Processing (NLP) and Understanding (NLU), has been highly compartmentalized, with each line of research attempting to tackle every single problem on its own, irrespective of the rest. However in recent years, the view has been shifting towards re-examining the whole field of NLP under a multitasking lens. This has manifested itself in the development of Multi-Task Learning (MTL) models, which are trained to optimize multiple losses, each for a different task, simultaneously.

This shift in paradigm was brought about by a confluence of various elements from the wide landscape of NLP research. For one, most core NLP tasks have been researched extensively with a significant slowdown in improvements under the banner of "singlism"! Another is the recent advances in contextual word embeddings, which was brought about in turn by the advent of a whole new class of neural network architectures, namely, the transformer, as described in the seminal paper of Vaswani et al. (2017).

We believe that the community of Arabic NLP is particularly poised to reap significant benefits from adopting this shift in paradigm. To this end, we seek to present a collection of 8 different Arabic-specific tasks, as part of a collective benchmark which we refer to as the Arabic Language Understanding Evaluation benchmark (ALUE). Similar to the General Language Understanding Evaluation (GLUE) benchmark (Wang et al., 2019b), the tasks we present in ALUE, are already available online and have featured in previous competitive workshops. To ensure fair use of the benchmark, we provide our privately held evaluation datasets for five of these tasks, in which we follow the respective original authors' annotation processes to a tee. In addition, we present an expert-constructed diagnostic dataset, to help researchers probe the inner workings of their models, and diagnose their shortcomings against a wide range of linguistic phenomena. We also present an automated and publicly published leaderboard on the internet[1], open to any researcher to directly submit the results of their models to. Last but not least, we include baseline results for several publicly available pre-trained Arabic models.

This paper aims to introduce our work to the Arabic NLP community. We hope it will provide an impetus that aids the research and development ef-

[1]www.alue.org

Proceedings of the Sixth Arabic Natural Language Processing Workshop, pages 173–184
Kyiv, Ukraine (Virtual), April 19, 2021.

forts related to Arabic MTL approaches, and leads to wider collaboration as well as healthy competition. In Section 2, we discuss related work, both from the point of view of MTL models and datasets. In Section 3, we discuss the tasks comprising the ALUE benchmark, and their respective datasets. Section 4 focuses on the diagnostic dataset, and the way it was constructed, and the rationale behind it. An overview of our selected baselines can be found in Section 5. Results and discussions of our work can be found under Section 6, followed by our conclusions in section 7.

2 Related Work

The idea of MTL is relatively new in NLP. One of the earliest oft-cited works in this regard was by Collobert et al. (2011), in which they trained a multi-layered neural model on different sentence tagging tasks, with a common sentence encoder shared between them all, achieving solid performance on all of the tasks in the process.

The shift in paradigm towards MTL, requires a shift in terms of benchmarking as well. The General Language Understanding Evaluation (Wang et al., 2019b) is one of the most widely used benchmarks for comparing MTL models in the English language. It consists of nine tasks that are based on previously published benchmarks/datasets, mainly focusing on NLU. A subsequent iteration of the benchmark, named SuperGlue (Wang et al., 2019a), extends the scope of focus of the original benchmark to more challenging tasks, including question answering and co-reference resolution, while including a human performance baseline. For both benchmarks, the organizers provide an automated leaderboard that serves to compare and showcase the latest advancements in the field.

One of the earliest successful employment of MTL in Arabic NLP was by (Zalmout and Habash, 2019). By using MTL in an Adversarial learning setting, they reported state of the art results in cross-dialectal morphological tagging. This was mainly achieved by learning dialect invariant features between MSA (high resource dialect), and Egyptian Arabic (low resource dialect). This, they argue, helps in knowledge-transfer from the former to the latter, thereby sidestepping the issue of resource scarcity that plagues many Arabic variants. They also note that the gain from such knowledge transfer approach is more significant the smaller the datasets are.

Another paper by Baniata et al. (2018) employs the idea of MTL in the context of Neural Machine Translation. For translation from dialectical Arabic to Modern Standard Arabic (MSA), the authors use a sequence-to-sequence architecture, where each source language has its own encoder. However, for the target language, only a single shared decoder is used. Using this setup they report better results. Using this setup, they report better results and are able to efficiently use smaller datasets.

Freihat et al. (2018) manually curated an Arabic corpus of 2 million words, that was simultaneously annotated for POS, NER, and segmentation. Using an MTL model trained to perform the three aforementioned tasks, the authors were able to achieve state of the art results on said tasks, and show that such a model can greatly simplify and enhance downstream tasks, such as lemmatization.

Using this setup, they report better results and are able to efficiently use smaller datasets.

3 Tasks and Datasets

ALUE incorporates a total of 8 tasks covering a wide spectrum of Arabic dialects and NLP/NLU problems. Below, we provide a brief description of each task; the nature of the problem, its original workshop, and the evaluation metrics used. If the task is one of the five we have provided our own private dataset for, then we will also discuss the annotation process we followed to generate said private dataset.

It is worth mentioning that some of these tasks were subtasks in their respective workshops, such as the **Emotion Classification** and **Sentiment Intensity Regression** subtasks from **SemEval-2018 Task 1**, and the **Offensive** and **Hate Speech** subtasks from **OSACT4 Shared Task on Offensive Language Detection**. However, for the purposes of ALUE, these will be treated as independent tasks rather than subtasks. Nevertheless, in the discussion below, we are going to list them under the name of the original workshop task they featured in first.

3.1 IDAT@FIRE2019 Irony Detection Task (FID)

The shared task of Irony Detection in Arabic Tweets (Ghanem et al., 2019) is based on a dataset of around 5,000 tweets. Each tweet is labeled with a "1" when it is ironic, holds satire, parody, sarcasm, or if the intended meaning is the contrary of the literal one. A label of "0" is given otherwise. This task will be evaluated using the F1 score.

3.2 MADAR Shared Task Subtask 1 (MDD)

This task is based on the MADAR Shared Task on Arabic Fine-Grained Dialect Identification (Bouamor et al., 2019). Each sentence is exclusively classified into one of 25 labels, corresponding to one city out of 25 predefined Arab cities. A 26th label is added for MSA. The data is sourced from the Basic Traveling Expression Corpus (Takezawa et al., 2007), with the same 2,000 sentences translated to the spoken dialect in each of the cities and MSA (Corpus-26). The metric of choice for this task is the F1-score.

3.3 NSURL-2019 Shared Task 8 (MQ2Q)

The Semantic Question Similarity in Arabic task (Seelawi et al., 2019) was presented in the First International Workshop on NLP Solutions for Under Resourced Languages (NSURL 2019). In this task, a pair of questions is assumed to be semantically similar if they have the same exact answer and meaning, which is denoted with a label of "1". A label of "0" is given otherwise. For this task, we develop a new evaluation dataset. We start by clustering a dataset of Arabic article titles into clusters of similar semantic meaning. From these, we select headlines that have a question format. Then by pairing questions from similar clusters, we obtain 29,254 similar question pairs. Non-similar question pairs were generated by pairing questions from clusters that are close but not similar in semantic meaning. This is done to ensure that the resultant dataset is challenging. We then select 4,000 of these pairs, with an equal representation of "0"s and "1"s. A final round of human validation on those question pairs is conducted to ensure the quality of the resulting dataset. The evaluation of this task is performed using an F1-score.

3.4 OSACT4 Shared Task on Offensive Language Detection (OOLD & OHSD)

The offensive Language Detection shared task (Mubarak et al., 2020) is based on a dataset that contains a total of 10,000 tweets, with 2 subtasks. The first is the Offensive Task **(OOLD)** where a tweet is labeled offensive if it consists of inappropriate language or imply insults or attacks against other people, and not offensive otherwise. The second is the HateSpeech Task **(OHSD)** in which offensive tweets from the subtask above are also considered hate speech if they are attacking a certain group based on nationality, ethnicity, gender, political or sports affiliation, religious belief, or other related characteristics. Otherwise, they are labeled as not hate speech.

For both of these tasks, we develop our own evaluation dataset, using the Abusive Language Detection on Arabic Social Media corpus (Al Jazeera) (Mubarak et al., 2017), which contains 32,000 comments. We refine this corpus with 8 multi-labeled fine-grained classes, namely: toxic, insult, threat, identity hate, sexual, racial, blasphemy, and politically incorrect. Each label of these is denoted with either "1" if the class applies, or "0" otherwise.

We then annotate these comments using the following guidelines: (i) offensive if 3 or more classes of insult, toxic, threat, identity hate, and/or sexual are present, (ii) hate speech if the same previous conditions were satisfied, but with the additional requirement of the racial class having a label of "1" too (iii) comments with 0 values across all the classes are labeled as not offensive nor hate speech (iv) anything else that fails to satisfy any of the previous conditions is discarded.

We select 1,000 sentences from the resultant dataset, with special care to achieve a similar distribution of the original one. Finally, a round of human validation is conducted to ensure the quality of the overall evaluation dataset. Both of these tasks are evaluated using the F1-score.

3.5 SemEval-2018 Task 1 - Affect in Tweets (SVREG & SEC)

The Affect in Tweets dataset (Mohammad et al., 2018) was introduced in the 2018 SemEval workshop. The task consists of five subtasks. For our purposes, we will only include two of these. The first is the Emotion Classification task **(SEC)** in which a tweet is classified using one or more of eleven possible labels that best capture the emotions expressed by it. These labels are anger, anticipation, disgust, fear, joy, love, optimism, pessimism, sadness, surprise, and trust. The second is the Sentiment Intensity Regression task **(SVREG)** in which participants are expected to predict the "valence" of a given tweet, using a real-valued score between "0" and "1", with "0" representing the most negative sentiment possible, while "1" being the most positive sentiment possible.

For both of these tasks, we develop privately held evaluation datasets. For SEC, our annotation process follows the convention described in SemEval-2018 (Mohammad et al., 2018). First, we select certain keywords, which collectively capture the 11 emotions. This is accomplished using various morphological forms and sub-phrases. A total of 18,000 tweets are then crawled using said keywords, each of which is subsequently labeled by four experienced annotators. A given emotion is then labeled as present with a "1", if two or more annotators agree. Otherwise, the emotion is labeled with a "0". 1,000 tweets are selected in a manner that resembles the distribution captured by the original dataset.

Our VREG evaluation dataset is based on the same 1,000 tweets selected for SEC. It is annotated using the Best-Worst Scaling (BWS) annotation methodology as described by Kiritchenko and Mohammad (2016). We combine these tweets and group them in tuples of four tweets each, according to the following set of rules: (i) No two 4-tuples should have the same four tweets. (ii) No duplicated tweets should exist within the same 4-tuple. (iii) All the tweets should have equal representation during the annotation process. As noted by the original authors, somewhere between 1,500 and 2,000 BWS questions should be sufficient to obtain reliable scores. Each of our tweets is present in 8 different 4-tuples, making a total of 2,000 BWS questions. Those tuples are then presented to the annotators who pick the tweet with the highest sentiment, as well as the lowest sentiment out of a given 4-tuple. Each 4-tuple is annotated by two different annotators.

Regression values are then obtained using the equation below:

$$V_i = 0.5 + 0.5((B_i - W_i)/T_i)$$

Where *Vi* is the regression value for the tweet *i*, *Bi* is the number of times that tweet *i* was voted as having the highest sentiment in a 4-tuple, and *Wi* representing the number of times it was voted as having the lowest sentiment. *Ti* is the number of times the tweet appears throughout all of the 4-tuples. It is worth noting that the *Vi* value obtained using the above equation will be between 0 and 1, inclusive.

For evaluation, we use the Jaccard similarity score and the Pearson correlation coefficient for SEC and VREG, respectively.

3.6 Cross-lingual Sentence Representations (XNLI)

This task is based on a dataset that was first presented by Conneau et al. (2018). It contains 7,500 textual entailment sentence pairs, each representing a hypothesis and a premise. These sentence pairs are labeled with either one of the following logical relationship labels: entailment, contradictory, or neutral. The data was originally labeled in the English language and then translated into 15 other languages including Arabic. It is split into 2,500 for development, and 5,000 for testing. The training data is meant to be the Multi-Genre Natural Language Inference (MultiNLI) corpus (Williams et al., 2018), which is available only in English. However, for the purposes of ALUE, we consider the 5,000 test dataset to be the training dataset, and the 2,500 development dataset to be the test dataset. The Evaluation metric for this task is accuracy.

3.7 How to Participate

Similar to GLUE, researchers interested in submitting their results to our leaderboard need to download and run their models, only using the training and, where available, the validation datasets, for each and every task. Once the results are obtained, and proper formatting and naming are adhered to, they can be submitted to our website[2]. The leaderboard shows each accepted team's submission performance per task. The final ranking is based on the unweighted average across all the tasks, not including the diagnostic dataset. Appendix B can be consulted for more details on the technology stack powering our leaderboard.

4 Diagnostics

Understanding a sentence depends on the capacity of the model to capture multiple underlying linguistic representations; changes in the logical, semantic, syntactic, and/or morphological features of a sentence can alter its meaning. These alterations can be described in terms of logical relationships (Bos and Markert, 2005). The Single-Task Training Benchmark by Wang et al. (2019b) shows varying weaknesses between different models when it comes to capturing the linguistic phenomena involved. For example, double negation is especially difficult for Contextualized Word Vectors such as Cove (McCann et al., 2017). Nonetheless, this seems to be somewhat ameliorated by

[2]www.alue.org

deep learning-based Contextualized Word representations such as ELMo (Peters et al., 2018). Yet, ELMo seems to struggle with Morphological Negation when compared to Cove.

The use of a manually annotated evaluation dataset that captures the diversity of such linguistic phenomena can help model designers better understand their models' generalization behavior, and work on improving them in the process. For this purpose, we create the ALUE diagnostic dataset; a high-quality, hand-labeled evaluation dataset, inspired by its GLUE counterpart (Wang et al., 2019b). It is composed of around 1,100 Arabic pairs of hypothesis and premise sentences. Each of these is labeled with their respective entailment relationship (entailment, contradiction, or neutral) and tagged with one or more category representing the host of linguistic phenomena they represent.

For the purposes of the evaluation of a given model's performance on the diagnostic dataset, we opted to follow GLUE's lead, and use the R3 metric (Gorodkin, 2004), for similar reasons (i.e. unbalanced class distribution in the diagnostic dataset labels). We also believe that the R3 readily helps with the investigation of systematic errors.

4.1 Annotation Process

We begin with the set of categories introduced in GLUE (Wang et al., 2019b)[3]. Each class describes a linguistic phenomenon that is important for NLU models to capture. Given that many of them are well described in the linguistics literature, they can be matched using syntactic/semantic patterns. Next, we look up for sentences expressing these patterns in a syntactically tagged Arabic corpus, with the help of WordNet relations. From these sentences, we construct sentence pairs, mostly by modifying the sub-phrases of a premise to produce a hypothesis reflecting the same linguistic phenomena in GLUE. For this purpose, we use three main sources, namely: Arabic Wikipedia, UN Multilingual Corpus V1.0 (Ziemski et al., 2016) and the corpus from the Arabic Linguistic Tool (ALP) (Freihat et al., 2018). This latter source is composed of syntactically annotated texts of various genres (e.g. news items, prose, literature, dialogues and TV podcasts) to ensure high coverage of spoken and written MSA. In addition, we manually translate the 330 artificially created examples from GLUE, which mostly express complex linguistic phenomena, and included them as part of our diagnostic dataset.

It must be noted that languages do not always describe similar linguistic phenomena in the same manner. This can lead to different entailments for equivalent translations. For instance, the agent of a verb in a passive construction is often mentioned in English, and when combined with Negation the entailment always yields a contradiction label: *John didn't break the vase* vs *The vase was broken by John*. The Arabic language tends to hide the agent of the verb in passive constructions which leads to a neutral label[4]: *John didn't break the vase* vs *The vase was broken*. With this in mind, during the annotation process, we took care of such peculiarities and, hence, ended up adding other categories. See appendix C.1 for more details.

5 Baselines

All of our baselines build on publicly released pre-trained word embeddings or models. These were carefully selected to represent a temporal cross-section of progress in Arabic NLP during the past few years; we start with fixed word-embeddings (i.e. AraVec, Soliman et al., 2017 and Fasttext, Joulin et al., 2017), and end with masked language models (i.e. Arabic-BERT, Safaya et al., 2020 and Multilingual-BERT, Turc et al., 2019), by way of sentence representations (i.e. Large Multilingual Universal Sentence Encoder, Yang et al., 2019) and the early starts of contextual embeddings (i.e. ELMoForManyLangs, Che et al., 2018; Fares et al., 2017).

For BERT based models, we use Huggingface (Wolf et al., 2019) for implementation, whereas for all other models, we use TensorFlow 2.0 (Abadi et al., 2015). However since the ELMoForManyLangs model is implemented in PyTorch, we decided to use its contextual embeddings without fine-tuning, as otherwise, we would have needed to implement it using PyTorch (Paszke et al., 2019). This would have effectively required from us to use three different deep-learning frameworks to implement all of our baselines. This, we reckon, would make the process of reproduction of our baselines much more complex for other researchers; as a matter of fact, as we trawled through the literature in search for Arabic pre-trained and publicly re-

[3]The full details of the annotation process for the diagnostics data are too long to be included here. Therefore we opted to provide them on our website.

[4]The logical inference is not centered on the agent of the verb, but the whole event.

leased models, we couldn't but notice the dearth of publicly released Arabic models especially those that capitalize on the latest advancements in NLP. We hope that our contributions through ALUE will help in this regard, by being a part of a conducive environment for the Arabic NLP community, to develop and publicly release state of the art MTL models.

We also note the lack of large corpora dedicated in full to Arabic and its varients. The majority of our selected baselines are pre-trained on dumps of Arabic Wikipedia and the Common Crawl (both of which are predominantly MSA in nature), while a few of them are trained on unreleased crawls with larger coverage of the various dialects of Arabic (i.e. ArabicBERT and AraVec). This makes our baselines a little harder to compare directly, but we hope that this highlights the peculiar challenges that Arabic NLP faces in this regard.

For all of our models, we embed our sentences into fixed-size vectors which in turn are fed into a feed-forward network that produces the final prediction. For the Universal Sentence Encoder (USE), this is readily achieved. However, for our AraVec, Fasttext and ELMO based models, in order to achieve the same step, we first consume the word embeddings using a BiLSTM. For the BERT based models, this is achieved somewhat indirectly, via the [CLS] token, which serves as a surrogate for sentence embeddings. More details on the exact architecture for each model per task, can be obtained via appendix A and the github repo where we release all our code[5]. The parameters used for each model might differ slightly, as we attempted to bring out the best performance possible from each to make our comparisons between them a little more fair.

6 Results and Discussion

Several key points in our work are worth analyzing, namely: (i) the baseline scores and the comparison of the different approaches, (ii) the analysis of the performance of our baseline models on the diagnostic dataset, and (iii) the comparative analysis between private and public evaluation datasets. This section goes through each of these key points in the same order as presented above.

6.1 Benchmark Results

Each one of our models was trained in a single-task fashion. To ensure reproducibility we used a random seed. While we strongly advocate for MTL models, we strategically eschewed training any such model for our baselines. This is mainly because our initial experiments show that it significantly boosts the performance on our benchmark, and as such, with the end goal of encouraging researchers to submit their results to ALUE, we decided to keep our baselines competitive enough to entice participation from the wide community, but simple enough to surpass. At the end of the day, we believe that baselines, as their name suggests, belong at the base of a leaderboard. The results obtained for each of our baselines are outlined in Table 1.

We note that, expectedly, BERT based models outperform all others by a large margin, with ArabicBERT's performance being the best across all tasks. This can be attributed in part, to the fact that it is trained on a large corpus composed of MSA as well as dialectical variants of Arabic. The importance of this factor is evident in tasks that are heavily skewed towards dialectical Arabic (i.e. OOLD and OHSD), where a simple model using twitter-based word representations such as AraVec (i.e. which has a heavy representation of dialectical words) outclassed Multi-lingual BERT, which was only trained on MSA. This strongly highlights the importance of pre-training data that covers the wide spectrum of Arabic variants in this time and age.

Interestingly, the difference in performance between Multi-BERT cased and uncased is somewhat negligible across all tasks except for those that require strong syntactical performance (i.e. MQ2Q and XNLI). This indicates that orthographic normalization in Arabic might impede a model's ability to achieve good syntactical modeling. We also suspect that the cased Multi-BERT model is indirectly benefiting from preserving the case for the other languages in the shared WordPiece vocabulary space it learns.

In a similar vein, the USE model performs very competitively on XNLI and MQ2Q. This is due to the fact the Natural Language Inference (NLI) is part of the pre-training method for said model.

[5]We release the code for our baselines publicly for reproducibility at the following GitHub repo: https://github.com/hseelawi/alue_baselines

Model	FID	MDD	MQ2Q	OOLD	OHSD	SVREG	SEC	XNLI	Avg	DIAG
ArabicBERT	**82.18**	59.66	**85.69**	**89.47**	**78.72**	**55.12**	**25.13**	60.96	**67.12**	**19.60**
ML-BERT Cased	81.61	**61.26**	83.24	80.33	70.54	33.85	14.02	**63.09**	60.99	19.00
ML-BERT Uncased	81.01	57.98	75.79	79.85	70.64	32.01	13.81	57.91	58.63	15.10
USE	76.90	23.40	76.50	76.30	68.20	36.50	14.80	57.10	53.71	13.90
ML-ELMo	77.00	52.10	70.50	71.60	62.88	24.90	14.40	50.00	52.92	09.60
AraVec	76.70	48.40	62.60	85.60	73.80	32.20	18.05	47.70	55.63	10.00
FastText	77.10	50.80	66.80	79.70	60.40	37.00	15.30	52.70	54.98	03.50

Table 1: Evaluation scores for our baseline models on the various ALUE tasks, with Pearson Correlation and Jaccard Index scores for SVREG and SEC tasks respectively, Matthews Correlation Coefficient for the Diagnostic dataset (DIAG), Accuracy for XNLI, and F1-score for the rest. Note that DIAG is not included in the average as it is not designed for direct model comparison.

Nonetheless, the model's very poor performance on dialect detection (i.e. MDD) reveals the inherent issues that sentence embedding models face in tasks where lexical information is important, as it tends to be discarded, in the process of embedding the full sentence into a single fixed-size vector. For such tasks, we can make the observation that models which use subword embeddings or some form of word morphological based tokenization tend to perform well, for the exact opposite reason, even for those that have been trained on MSA only (i.e. Multi-BERT).

The benefits of using subwords can be generalized to dialect-heavy tasks too, as can be seen in the case of the Multi-BERT and Fasttext models. This might be explained by the fact that subwords make better use of cognates across the different forms of Arabic. Additionally, there is no denying that the use of subwords mitigates the effects of non-standard orthography, amongst and across the various dialects. Nonetheless, their contributions might become less pronounced when dialectical Arabic is strongly present in the pre-training corpus. This is very evident in the case of the AraVec model, which, as alluded to above, outperforms all the models on three out of five of those tasks (i.e. SEC, OOLD, and OHSD), except for ArabicBERT, which even then, is heavily pre-trained on dialectical data.

6.2 Diagnostic Results Analysis

We report the performance of our models on the diagnostic dataset in Table 2.

For **coarse-grained** categories, ArabicBERT outperforms, on average, all other models with a considerable difference, although the overall performance across all models is low. The highest scores fall under the Predicate-Argument Structures category, with an average of 15, whereas the scores on Lexical Semantics seem to be the lowest with an 8.1 average. Interestingly, both versions of MultiBERT outperform ArabicBERT in world-knowledge, which depends on extra-linguistic information. This, perhaps, has something to do with the fact that they were trained on Wikipedia dumps of many languages. USE results seem to be high in World Knowledge compared to other coarse-grained categories as well.

For **fine-grained** categories, here again we can see the strong correlation between USE and Multi-BERT performance on Named Entities, which perhaps is underpinned by the same factors for their solid performance on World Knowledge. All of our models seem to exhibit very poor performance on Double Negation and Conditionals. This is probably due to the very rich diversity of tool-words used in Arabic to describe such phenomena, which makes it difficult for the models to make adequate generalizations. Of note is the fact that FastText seems to work especially well on Restrictivity, where all other models seem to struggle.

6.3 Private vs Public Set Analysis

Here we preform a comparative analysis between our private evaluation datasets and the original ones, to provide a better understanding of the involved baselines and datasets. First, we compute a correlation score between both, private and public results as displayed in Table 3. As expected, all of these scores are positively correlated but some datasets are more so than others. For instance, the strong correlation between the public and private evaluation datasets for MQ2Q can be explained by the fact that the only difference is in the diversity of the topics covered. On the other hand, while both the public and private evaluation datasets for SVREG and SEC are from the same source (i.e. tweets), they were collected at different points in

Model	All	LS	PAS	L	K	Quant	2N	Cond	Rest	Nom	NE
	Coarse-Grained					Fine-Grained					
ArabicBert	**19.6**	15	**28**	13.1	15	**48**	-17	-06	16	15	10
ML-BERT cased	19	**17**	20	12	**19**	45	-20	00	00	**34**	**23**
ML-BERT uncased	15.1	07	15	**13.5**	**19**	36	-12	-14	-10	10	06
USE	13.9	07	14	10	15	34	-30	-14	00	20	22
Elmo	9.6	14	10	09	10	08	-26	**10**	-12	14	00
AraVec	10	00	10	09	06	07	-37	-01	00	10	10
FastText	3.5	-02	08	02	-03	14	-37	-24	**30**	09	-06
AVG		8.1	**15**	9.8	11.6						

Table 2: The R3 results of our different baseline models on the diagnostic dataset. Scores are scaled by 100. The "All" score is the average of coarse-grained categories. Abbreviations are: Lexical Semantics (LS), Predicate-Argument Structure (PAS), Logic (L), World knowledge (k), Quantifiers (Quant), Double Negation (2N), Conditional (Cond), Restrictivity (Restr), Nominalization (Nom) and Named entities (NE). Here we only report results on the fine-grained classes that we find to be the most interesting.

Model	MQ2Q		SVREG		SEC		OOLD		OHSD	
	Private	Public	Private	Public	Private	Public	Private	Public	Private	Public
ArabicBERT	0.8569	0.9523	0.5512	0.8376	0.2513	0.5422	0.8947	0.9583	0.7872	0.9820
MultiBERT-cased	0.8324	0.9573	0.3385	0.7261	0.1402	0.4802	0.8033	0.9439	0.7054	0.9715
MultiBERT-uncased	0.7579	0.9389	0.3201	0.7274	0.1381	0.4739	0.7985	0.9453	0.7064	0.9772
USE	0.7650	0.8451	0.3650	0.7224	0.1480	0.2705	0.7630	0.7264	0.6820	0.5501
ELMo	0.7050	0.9018	0.2490	0.5550	0.1440	0.2850	0.7160	0.6119	0.6288	0.4930
FastText	0.6680	0.8869	0.3700	0.6480	0.1530	0.3221	0.7970	0.7059	0.6040	0.4770
AraVec	0.6260	0.8096	0.3220	0.6402	0.1805	0.3552	0.8560	0.7439	0.7380	0.6145
Correlation	**0.7757**		**0.8492**		**0.5012**		**0.6229**		**0.7151**	

Table 3: The evaluation scores for our baseline models on both, the private and public evaluation datasets. The last row shows the Pearson correlation coefficient for both sets across all the models for the corresponding task.

time. For SVREG, the scores on both evaluation datasets are highly correlated, yet there is a drastic gap between the results. This can be explained by the comparative nature of the BWS annotation process. Each tweet is labeled with a floating number that evaluates how its sentiment compares to the average or norm of the entire dataset. From the results, we can deduce that the overall sentiment of the public evaluation dataset is more positive than ours. The results on the SEC datasets seem to be the least correlated. This is because both versions of MultiBERT (cased and otherwise) achieve high scores on the original evaluation dataset, yet, curiously, they score the lowest on our evaluation dataset. Interestingly, in the case of OOLD and OHSD, the public and private evaluation datasets for both cases, have a strong positive correlation despite the fact that they were collected from two different sources; the original one is from Twitter while our dataset is from Aljazeera comments.

7 Conclusion

In this paper, we introduce the ALUE benchmark, with the purpose of providing a platform for researchers interested in pushing the state of the art in Arabic NLU. It consists of 8 previously published tasks, with 5 privately curated evaluation datasets to ensure the validity of the leaderboard. We evaluated the correctness of these 5 evaluation sets, finding a positive correlation between the ones we developed and the original ones. In addition, we built a novel diagnostic dataset that helps analyze the results of models against a comprehensive range of linguistic phenomena. Our initial experiments show that MTL approaches outperform their single-model-per-task counterparts, but to keep our leaderboard lucrative for participation, we decided to only use single-task models as our baselines. Our BERT baselines seem to outperform all other models, and especially so, when the pertraining data is not confined to MSA-dominant corpuses, but contain dialectical varieties of Arabic as well. For the diagnostic dataset, we found that our baselines struggle to capture many of the linguistic phenomena represented by the dataset itself, which suggests that there is plenty of room for improvement in the state of art for Arabic NLU. We hope that ALUE will be an integral part of the efforts to push said state of the art in the coming few years.

8 Acknowledgement

We would like to express our gratitude to our partners in this project, the MIND Lab at the American University of Beirut (AUB), and the CAMeL Lab at New York University Abu Dhabi. Their outstanding support and ongoing guidance was invaluable to the work presented in this paper. We would also like to thank the team members of Mawdoo3 AI data Annotation and Linguistics departments for their contributions in annotating the privately held evaluation datasets; namely: Manar Salous, Yasmin Al Momani, Othman Abu Saa', Mohammad Saleh and Mariam Arnaout. In addition, we thank Abdallah Abu Sham and Wael Gaith from Mawdoo3 for help in developing and deploying our leaderboard website. Finally, special thanks goes to Mawdoo3 Ltd. for supporting our research efforts and for making the evaluation datasets publicly available for further research on Arabic NLP/NLU.

References

Martín Abadi, Ashish Agarwal, Paul Barham, Eugene Brevdo, Zhifeng Chen, Craig Citro, Greg S. Corrado, Andy Davis, Jeffrey Dean, Matthieu Devin, Sanjay Ghemawat, Ian Goodfellow, Andrew Harp, Geoffrey Irving, Michael Isard, Yangqing Jia, Rafal Jozefowicz, Lukasz Kaiser, Manjunath Kudlur, Josh Levenberg, Dandelion Mané, Rajat Monga, Sherry Moore, Derek Murray, Chris Olah, Mike Schuster, Jonathon Shlens, Benoit Steiner, Ilya Sutskever, Kunal Talwar, Paul Tucker, Vincent Vanhoucke, Vijay Vasudevan, Fernanda Viégas, Oriol Vinyals, Pete Warden, Martin Wattenberg, Martin Wicke, Yuan Yu, and Xiaoqiang Zheng. 2015. TensorFlow: Large-scale machine learning on heterogeneous systems. Software available from tensorflow.org.

Laith H Baniata, Seyoung Park, and Seong-Bae Park. 2018. A neural machine translation model for arabic dialects that utilizes multitask learning (mtl). *Computational intelligence and neuroscience*, 2018.

Johan Bos and Katja Markert. 2005. Recognising textual entailment with logical inference. In *Proceedings of Human Language Technology Conference and Conference on Empirical Methods in Natural Language Processing*, pages 628–635, Vancouver, British Columbia, Canada. Association for Computational Linguistics.

Houda Bouamor, Sabit Hassan, and Nizar Habash. 2019. The madar shared task on arabic fine-grained dialect identification. In *Proceedings of the Fourth Arabic Natural Language Processing Workshop*, pages 199–207.

Wanxiang Che, Yijia Liu, Yuxuan Wang, Bo Zheng, and Ting Liu. 2018. Towards better UD parsing: Deep contextualized word embeddings, ensemble, and treebank concatenation. In *Proceedings of the CoNLL 2018 Shared Task: Multilingual Parsing from Raw Text to Universal Dependencies*, pages 55–64, Brussels, Belgium. Association for Computational Linguistics.

Ronan Collobert, Jason Weston, Léon Bottou, Michael Karlen, Koray Kavukcuoglu, and Pavel Kuksa. 2011. Natural language processing (almost) from scratch. *Journal of machine learning research*, 12(Aug):2493–2537.

Alexis Conneau, Ruty Rinott, Guillaume Lample, Adina Williams, Samuel R. Bowman, Holger Schwenk, and Veselin Stoyanov. 2018. Xnli: Evaluating cross-lingual sentence representations. In *Proceedings of the 2018 Conference on Empirical Methods in Natural Language Processing*. Association for Computational Linguistics.

Murhaf Fares, Andrey Kutuzov, Stephan Oepen, and Erik Velldal. 2017. Word vectors, reuse, and replicability: Towards a community repository of large-text resources. In *Proceedings of the 21st Nordic Conference on Computational Linguistics*, pages 271–276, Gothenburg, Sweden. Association for Computational Linguistics.

Abed Alhakim Freihat, Gabor Bella, Hamdy Mubarak, and Fausto Giunchiglia. 2018. A single-model approach for arabic segmentation, pos tagging, and named entity recognition. In *2018 2nd International Conference on Natural Language and Speech Processing (ICNLSP)*, pages 1–8. IEEE.

Bilal Ghanem, Jihen Karoui, Farah Benamara, Véronique Moriceau, and Paolo Rosso. 2019. Idat at fire2019: Overview of the track on irony detection in arabic tweets. In *Proceedings of the 11th Forum for Information Retrieval Evaluation*, pages 10–13.

Jan Gorodkin. 2004. Comparing two k-category assignments by a k-category correlation coefficient. *Computational biology and chemistry*, 28(5-6):367–374.

Armand Joulin, Édouard Grave, Piotr Bojanowski, and Tomáš Mikolov. 2017. Bag of tricks for efficient text classification. In *Proceedings of the 15th Conference of the European Chapter of the Association for Computational Linguistics: Volume 2, Short Papers*, pages 427–431.

Svetlana Kiritchenko and Saif M Mohammad. 2016. Capturing reliable fine-grained sentiment associations by crowdsourcing and best–worst scaling. In *Proceedings of NAACL-HLT*, pages 811–817.

Bryan McCann, James Bradbury, Caiming Xiong, and Richard Socher. 2017. Learned in translation: Contextualized word vectors. In *Advances in Neural Information Processing Systems*, pages 6294–6305.

Saif Mohammad, Felipe Bravo-Marquez, Mohammad Salameh, and Svetlana Kiritchenko. 2018. Semeval-2018 task 1: Affect in tweets. In *Proceedings of the 12th international workshop on semantic evaluation*, pages 1–17.

Hamdy Mubarak, Kareem Darwish, and Walid Magdy. 2017. Abusive language detection on arabic social media. In *Proceedings of the First Workshop on Abusive Language Online*, pages 52–56.

Hamdy Mubarak, Kareem Darwish, Walid Magdy, Tamer Elsayed, and Hend Al-Khalifa. 2020. Overview of osact4 arabic offensive language detection shared task. In *Proceedings of the 4th Workshop on Open-Source Arabic Corpora and Processing Tools, with a Shared Task on Offensive Language Detection*, pages 48–52.

Adam Paszke, Sam Gross, Francisco Massa, Adam Lerer, James Bradbury, Gregory Chanan, Trevor Killeen, Zeming Lin, Natalia Gimelshein, Luca Antiga, Alban Desmaison, Andreas Kopf, Edward Yang, Zachary DeVito, Martin Raison, Alykhan Tejani, Sasank Chilamkurthy, Benoit Steiner, Lu Fang, Junjie Bai, and Soumith Chintala. 2019. Pytorch: An imperative style, high-performance deep learning library. In H. Wallach, H. Larochelle, A. Beygelzimer, F. d'Alché-Buc, E. Fox, and R. Garnett, editors, *Advances in Neural Information Processing Systems 32*, pages 8024–8035. Curran Associates, Inc.

Matthew E Peters, Mark Neumann, Mohit Iyyer, Matt Gardner, Christopher Clark, Kenton Lee, and Luke Zettlemoyer. 2018. Deep contextualized word representations. In *Proceedings of NAACL-HLT*, pages 2227–2237.

Ali Safaya, Moutasem Abdullatif, and Deniz Yuret. 2020. Kuisail at semeval-2020 task 12: Bert-cnn for offensive speech identification in social media. In *Proceedings of the International Workshop on Semantic Evaluation (SemEval)*.

Haitham Seelawi, Ahmad Mustafa, Wael Farhan, and Hussein T. Al-Natsheh. 2019. NSURL-2019 task 8: Semantic question similarity in arabic. In *Proceedings of the First Workshop on NLP Solutions for Under Resourced Languages*, NSURL '19, Trento, Italy.

Abu Bakr Soliman, Kareem Eissa, and Samhaa R El-Beltagy. 2017. Aravec: A set of arabic word embedding models for use in arabic nlp. *Procedia Computer Science*, 117:256–265.

Toshiyuki Takezawa, Genichiro Kikui, Masahide Mizushima, and Eiichiro Sumita. 2007. Multilingual spoken language corpus development for communication research. In *International Journal of Computational Linguistics & Chinese Language Processing, Volume 12, Number 3, September 2007: Special Issue on Invited Papers from ISCSLP 2006*, pages 303–324.

Iulia Turc, Ming-Wei Chang, Kenton Lee, and Kristina Toutanova. 2019. Well-read students learn better: On the importance of pre-training compact models. *arXiv preprint arXiv:1908.08962v2*.

Ashish Vaswani, Noam Shazeer, Niki Parmar, Jakob Uszkoreit, Llion Jones, Aidan N Gomez, ukasz Kaiser, and Illia Polosukhin. 2017. Attention is all you need. In *Advances in neural information processing systems*, pages 5998–6008.

Alex Wang, Yada Pruksachatkun, Nikita Nangia, Amanpreet Singh, Julian Michael, Felix Hill, Omer Levy, and Samuel Bowman. 2019a. Superglue: A stickier benchmark for general-purpose language understanding systems. In *Advances in Neural Information Processing Systems*, pages 3261–3275.

Alex Wang, Amanpreet Singh, Julian Michael, Felix Hill, Omer Levy, and Samuel Bowman. 2019b. Glue: A multi-task benchmark and analysis platform for natural language understanding. In *7th International Conference on Learning Representations, ICLR 2019*.

Adina Williams, Nikita Nangia, and Samuel Bowman. 2018. A broad-coverage challenge corpus for sentence understanding through inference. In *Proceedings of the 2018 Conference of the North American Chapter of the Association for Computational Linguistics: Human Language Technologies, Volume 1 (Long Papers)*, pages 1112–1122. Association for Computational Linguistics.

Thomas Wolf, Lysandre Debut, Victor Sanh, Julien Chaumond, Clement Delangue, Anthony Moi, Pierric Cistac, Tim Rault, R'emi Louf, Morgan Funtowicz, and Jamie Brew. 2019. Huggingface's transformers: State-of-the-art natural language processing. *ArXiv*, abs/1910.03771.

Yinfei Yang, Daniel Cer, Amin Ahmad, Mandy Guo, Jax Law, Noah Constant, Gustavo Hernandez Abrego, Steve Yuan, Chris Tar, Yun-Hsuan Sung, et al. 2019. Multilingual universal sentence encoder for semantic retrieval. *arXiv*, pages arXiv–1907.

Nasser Zalmout and Nizar Habash. 2019. Adversarial multitask learning for joint multi-feature and multi-dialect morphological modeling. In *Proceedings of the 57th Annual Meeting of the Association for Computational Linguistics*, pages 1775–1786, Florence, Italy. Association for Computational Linguistics.

Michał Ziemski, Marcin Junczys-Dowmunt, and Bruno Pouliquen. 2016. The united nations parallel corpus v1. 0. In *Proceedings of the Tenth International Conference on Language Resources and Evaluation (LREC'16)*, pages 3530–3534.

A Additional Benchmark Details

Each of our baselines is adapted to each ALUE task as needed. As such, extra trainable layers are added to each model to consume its outputs, which in turn is trained to make task specific predictions.

Please consult the subsections below in addition to the publicly available github repo[6] for exact details on the fine-tuning process for each model.

A.1 BERT

All of our BERT models weights are fine-tuned per task, using the [CLS] token, along with a dropout layer followed by a linear output layer that is suitable for each task.

A.2 USE

The produced sentence representations are fed into a feed-forward network that is designed and trained independently for each task.

A.3 ELMo

Given that the size of embeddings produced by this model is 1024, we use a BiLSTM for each task with a hidden size of 1024 in both directions. The hidden states of the last token are then fed to the appropriate feed-forward network for a given task. No fine tuning of the ELMo model itself is done.

A.4 AraVec

We use the skip-gram model with 300 vector size of unigram type that is trained on 66.9M Arabic tweets. This is mainly because skip-gram embeddings provide better representations for less frequent words compared to continuous bag of words. The embedding of each token in a given sentence is fed into a BiLSTM and a feed-forward network, which are trained on each task separately, similar to ELMo.

A.5 FastText

These are pre-trained word embeddings that use subword information to avoid out-of-vocab issues. The Arabic model is mainly trained on Arabic Wikipedia dumps and Arabic content from the Common Crawl. They come in a fixed size of 300. We use these embeddings to train a BiLSTM and a feed-forward network for each task similar to ELMo and AraVec.

[6]https://github.com/hseelawi/alue_baselines

B Benchmark Website Details

Our online leaderboard is powered by CodaLab[7], but is self-hosted on our own servers. Many high caliber Arabic NLP/NLU workshops are typically hosted on Codalab, and as such many researchers in the field are already familiar with its interface. This was a deciding factor in selecting it to power our leaderboard.

C Additional Diagnostics Details

The Diagnostic dataset is composed of sentence pairs. Each, has a premise and hypothesis sentences, and tagged with an entailment label : entailment, neutral or contradiction, in addition to the linguistic phenomena involved in the relationship. Linguistic phenomena tags are divided into 4 coarse-grained categories: Lexical semantics (LS), predicate-argument structure (PAS), logic (L) and world-knowledge (K).

When applicable, coarse-grained categories are tagged with fine-grained categories. Each sentence-pair is followed by its inverse form to establish a confusion of the entailment.

C.1 Diagnostics Categories

The original GLUE diagnostic dataset uses 4 coarse-grained categories further divided into 33 fine-grained categories. For an explanation of these phenomena, please consult the related sections in the original GLUE paper by Wang et al. (2019b). In addition to these, we added the following fine-grained categories, some of which are specific to Arabic:

Lexical Implication: a verb Y is entailed by X if by doing X you must be doing Y:

- *Saeed is snoring* **entails but is not entailed by** *Saeed is a sleep.*

Topicalization: a syntactic movement where an argument is moved to the beginning of the sentence to put emphasis:

- *The city of Amman is located in Jordan* **entails and is entailed by** *The city of Amman, it is located in Jordan.*

Reciprocity: an alternation resulting in the realization of the object as a part of a conjoined subject.

[7]https://codalab.org/

- *Reptiles fight each other by biting and scratching* **entails and is entailed by** *Reptiles fight (each other) by biting and scratching.*

Causative/Inchoative: an alternation that expresses a change of state leading to the omission of the agent. This case is marked by the addition of an inchoative *n* morpheme in Arabic.

- *Saeed broke the vase* **entails but is not entailed by** *The vase broke.*

Adjectivation: use of relational adjectives instead of the entity they describe i.e. China/Chinese.

- *These technologies will help strengthen the Chinese social security system* **entails and is entailed by** *These technologies will help strengthen the social security system of China.*

Quranic Verses Semantic Relatedness Using AraBERT

Abdullah N. Alsaleh
University of Leeds
School of Computing
scanaa@leeds.ac.uk

Eric Atwell
University of Leeds
School of Computing
e.s.atwell@leeds.ac.uk

Abdulrahman Altahhan
University of Leeds
School of Computing
a.altahhan@leeds.ac.uk

Abstract

Bidirectional Encoder Representations from Transformers (BERT) has gained popularity in recent years producing state-of-the-art performances across Natural Language Processing tasks. In this paper, we used AraBERT language model to binary classify pairs of verses provided by the QurSim dataset to either be semantically related or not. We have pre-processed The QurSim dataset and formed three datasets for comparisons. Also, we have used both versions of AraBERT, which are AraBERTv0.2 and AraBERTv2, to recognise which version performs the best with the given datasets. The best results was AraBERTv0.2 with 92% accuracy score using a dataset comprised of label '2' and label '-1', the latter was generated outside of QurSim dataset.

1 Introduction

In recent years, Natural Language Processing (NLP) has been evolved with the introduction of Transformer architecture by Vaswani et al. (2017). BERT, built on the transformer layer, has showed and produced state-of-the-art accuracy in a number of NLP tasks such as machine translation and text classification (Devlin et al., 2019). There are two stages of BERT: pre-training and fine-tuning. Pre-training is used for masked language modeling and next sentence prediction. For fine-tuning, is to add one or more layers designed for specific task on top of the final encoder layer (Rogers et al., 2020). Google provides pre-trained models for English and other languages including Arabic. Several studies provide their own language model based on BERT to perform better on specific tasks. AraBERT is recently published that contributes to Arabic language model that is pre-trained to suit a wide range of Arabic NLP related tasks. In this paper, we have used AraBERT language model to classify QurSim dataset in semantic relatedness task. Section 2 will outline the related work in semantic similarity and relatedness while section 3 will discuss AraBERT. Section 4 will discuss QurSim dataset and filtration process. Finally, section 5 will showcase the results of using QurSim datasets using AraBERT.

2 Related Work

2.1 Semantic Similarity/Relatedness in Arabic and Quranic Text

Several studies that involved Arabic and Quranic text using different methods to extract semantic similarity or relatedness. Mohamed et al. (2015) built a system Al-Bayan for evaluating semantic interpreter between Arabic questions and answers. The system used Morphological Analysis and Disambiguation for Arabic (Habash et al., 2009) as preprocessing tool and Decision Tree Classifier to predict the label. The proposed system achieved 74.5% accuracy score. Another study by Al-Bataineh et al. (2019) presented a system to identify similar Arabic questions in Quora using ELMo (Peters et al., 2018), Word2vec (Mikolov et al., 2013a) (Mikolov et al., 2013b) and Sent2vec (Pagliardini et al., 2018). The dataset used for training word and sentence embeddings includes Mawdoo3 question-to-question (Q2Q) (Seelawi et al., 2019b) and Madar Dialect Q2Q (Bouamor et al., 2018) datasets. The study found that ELMo performed better with 93% in Modern Standard Arabic and 82% in Arabic Dialects compared to other models such as Sent2vec and Word2vec.

2.2 Semantic Similarity using BERT

There are studies that use BERT models for identifying semantic similarity between text. A team competing at NSURL-2019 used BERT model with pre-trained multilingual to detect similar Arabic questions (Al-Theiabat and Al-Sadi, 2019). The dataset used for this competition mostly from Madwoo3 (Seelawi et al., 2019a). The results showcased BERT model outperform other models with F1-Score of 95.92%. Another study by Peinelt et al.

Proceedings of the Sixth Arabic Natural Language Processing Workshop, pages 185–190
Kyiv, Ukraine (Virtual), April 19, 2021.

(2020) combines topic model and BERT (tBERT) to enhance semantic similarity detection and prediction between pairs of English sentences. Reimers and Gurevych (2019) presented Sentence-BERT (SBERT) that uses siamese and triplets network structure with modified pre-trained BERT to derive semantically meaningful text embeddings that can be compared using cosine-similarity. However, to the best of our knowledge there is no research on semantic similarity or relatedness using BERT or AraBERT on Holy Quran text.

3 AraBERT

AraBERT is an Arabic language model in which BERT was trained on a large Arabic corpus (Antoun et al., 2020). The dataset includes Arabic Wikipedia, 1.5 billion words from Arabic corpora (El-Khair, 2016) and the Open Source International Arabic News Corpus (Zeroual et al., 2019). The corpus covers news articles from several Arab news media with different topics and from different Arab countries. The size of the pre-training dataset is 70 million sentences that amounts to approximately 24GB of text (Antoun et al., 2020).

AraBERT has produced better results on various Arabic NLP tasks. In sentiment analysis, AraBERT performed better than mBERT, which is a multilingual BERT model developed by Google, on most tested datasets (Antoun et al., 2020). Also, AraBERT outperformed mBERT and TF-IDF on the new Twitter-based benchmark dataset for Arabic Sentiment Analysis (Alharbi et al., 2020). In Named Entity Recognition (NER), AraBERTv01 had better results over Bi-LSTM-CRF model with macro-F1 score of 84.2, in which AraBERT new state of the art for NER on ANERcorp (Antoun et al., 2020). AraBERT also outperformed other Arabic NER tools such MADAMIRA and FARASA in NER tasks using AQMAR and NEWS datasets (Helwe et al., 2020).

4 QurSim

QurSim is a work of Arabic text that pertains to the Holy Quran (Sharaf and Atwell, 2012). The dataset showcases 7679 pairs of verses that are similar or related verses according to comments of Ibn Kathir's Tafsir, which is highly respected for its interpretation of the Holy Quran. It also improves its dataset using lexical similarity approach such as Term Frequency-Inverse Document Frequency (TF-IDF). QurSim dataset classifies pairs of Quranic verses that are related into three classes.

Label '2' indicates that the two verses are strongly related and they share similar lexicon. Label '1' means that the two verses are related based on the main topics that were mentioned in these verses but they share less similar lexicon. Finally, label '0' is being classified as not obvious relation between verses as, for example, it draws analogies that are different from each other but they serve the same purpose. Label '2', '1' and '0' comprises 40.09%, 48.41% and 11.49% respectively of the total QurSim dataset.

4.1 Mapping QurSim dataset to Quranic Verses Text

The QurSim data contains numeric values that entail the location of chapters and verses. However, for this research, BERT needs text as inputs in order to perform its models including BERTforSequenceClassification. Therefore, We needed to map Quranic numeric verses to texts. A Quran dataset by Aloufi (2019) has been used to map the numeric verses to their texts. Then, the verses were manually checked to see if they are in correct order.

4.2 Dataset Filtration

4.2.1 Duplicated Pairs Elimination

We found there were duplicated pairs of verses in QurSim datasets with the total of 764 records of duplicated pairs of verses. When we examined the duplicates, there were 592 records of duplicated pairs were labelled the same but ordered differently. For example, chapter 2 verse 2 is paired with chapter 2 verse 3 and the pair is labelled '2' and vice versa, shown in Table 1. For this case, we opted to remove the duplicates since they were redundant considering that the relationship is naturally bidirectional.

ID	SS	SV	TS	TV	Label
91	2	2	2	3	1
98	2	3	2	2	1

Table 1: Duplicated pairs of verses with same label, where SS stands for source Soura (chapter) , SV is the source verse, TS is target Soura and TV is target verse

The other 172 records of duplicated pairs of verses were labelled differently. For example, chapter 1 verse 5 paired with chapter 73 verse 9 were labelled '2'; however, they were labelled '1' when ordered differently, shown in Table 2. Since the label assignments were mainly influenced by Ibn Kathir's Tafsir, it is difficult for the authors to interpret Ibn Kathirs's comments in order to assign which appropriate label to pair of verses. So, it was important for this research to remove all pairs of verses that were labelled differently to ensure the dataset.

ID	SS	SV	TS	TV	Label
66	1	5	73	9	2
7339	73	9	1	5	1

Table 2: Duplicated pairs of verses with different label, where SS stands for source Soura (chapter) , SV is the source verse, TS is target Soura and TV is target verse

4.2.2 Label '1' Pairs Removal

The purpose of the paper is to binary classify pairs of Quranic verses for semantic relatedness using AraBERT. Label '1' pairs are related, however, the degree of similarity/relatedness are weaker than label '2'. Pairs of verses that share the label '1' have fewer words and concepts in common, which could affect the results based on AraBERT limitation on classical Arabic.

> والوزن يومئذ الحق فمن ثقلت موازينه فأولئك هم المفلحون
>
> And the weighing [of deeds] that Day will be the truth. So those whose scales are heavy - it is they who will be successful. [7:8]
>
> فإذا نفخ في الصور فلا أنساب بينهم يومئذ ولا يتساءلون
>
> So when the Horn is blown, no relationship will there be among them that Day, nor will they ask about one another [23:101]

In this example, the two verses are labelled '1' and they are describing events that happen on the judgment day. Both verses are related in which they share the topic of judgement day; however, they are mentioning different events that happen on the judgement day. Both verses also do not share any Arabic lexical item except for يومئذ 'That Day' which references to the judgement day.

Also, this is a preliminary research to use the AraBERT model for semantic similarity and the authors chose the extreme similarity label, which is label '2', for training and testing. Therefore, pairs of verses that have been assigned label '1' were removed from the dataset. In future studies, the authors may expand to include and train label '1' for multi-classification research.

4.2.3 Dataset Balancing

After deducing duplicated pairs of verses and label '1', we found that the dataset was imbalanced between label '2' and '0'. Label '2' has 2548 records while label '0' has 857 records. This was an issue because the dataset is imbalanced and could produce poorly results as we will mention it in the results section. We also needed pairs of verses that are not related to train and test against label '2'. Therefore, we randomly generated 2548 pairs of verses from the Holy Quran that are not in the QurSim dataset and labelled them as '-1'. Since the QurSim dataset is according to Ibn Kathir's Tafsir, we assume that these randomly generated pairs of verses are not related according to Ibn Kathir. Therefore, it is fair to say that we are building a model to test the relatedness of pairs of verses that is only based on Ibn Kathir's opinions and interpretations.

5 Results and Discussions

5.1 Results

Dataset	Testing		Training	
	v02	v2	v02	v2
Label '2' Label '0'	90.2%	88.7%	88%	87%
Label '2' Label '-1'	**92.1%**	88.6%	88%	87%
Label '2' Label '0' & '-1'	87.9%	88.6%	87%	85%

Table 3: Results of both versions of AraBERT with three datasets.

We have experimented with the latest two different versions of AraBERT, which are AraBERTv0.2 and AraBERTv2 (Antoun et al., 2020). AraBERTv2 version uses Farasa to segment the words into stems, prefix and suffix. AraBERTv0.2 does not require any Farasa segmentation. We could not use the LARGE version of the models as we only used the BASE version due to hardware limitations. The BASE model of both AraBERT versions has 136M parameters and 200 million sentences with a size of 77G of text. Furthermore, there are three groups of experiments based on dataset parameters which we will entail in this section. Summary of the experiments are shown in Table 3.

The experiments were performed using Google Colab. AraBERT along with Transformers library were installed while performing the experiments. The model was fine tuned for semantic similarity task. All of the experiments have batch size of 32, learning rate is 2e-5 and 8 epochs.

The first dataset has label '2' and label '0' of QurSim dataset after the filtration process. Label '2' has 2548 records while label '0' has 857 records. The dataset was split into training set, validation set and testing set. The training set has 2052 records, the validation set has 229 records and the testing set has 1124 records. AraBERTv0.2 scored better accuracy score metric than AraBERTv2. Although the dataset is small and imbalanced, both AraBERT versions achieved good accuracy score, which is shown in Table 3.

The second dataset has label '2' from QurSim dataset and label '-1' for pairs that were generated randomly. Both labels have the same number of records, which are 2548 pairs of verses. The dataset was split into training set, validation set and testing set. The training set has 3072 records, the validation set has 342 records and the testing set has 1682 records. We found that AraBERTv0.2 performed better than AraBERTv2 with the accuracy score of 92%. AraBERTv0.2 scored the best accuracy score compared to the other datasets. This is due to generated pairs of verses labelled '-1' being not related.

The third and final dataset comprises of label '2' and label '0' augmented with '-1'. They also have the same number of records of 2548 pairs of verses. The reason to combine label '0' and label '-1' for the experiment is to test the BERT model if it would identify the label '0' and '-1' as one class. The dataset was again split into training set (3072 records), validation set (342 records) and testing set (1682 records). The results turned out to be worse than previous two for AraBERTv0.2 while AraBERTv2 maintaining consistency with its accuracy score, which similar to the previous two experiments.

ID	SS	SV	TS	TV	Label
5648	32	27	80	24	1
5649	32	27	80	25	1
5650	32	27	80	26	1
5651	32	27	80	27	1
5652	32	27	80	28	1
5653	32	27	80	29	1
5654	32	27	80	30	1
5655	32	27	80	31	1
5656	32	27	80	32	2

Table 4: Series of verses are related to a single verse

5.2 Discussion

Although the results were promising, we have looked at the output files of these experiments and we found common problems that we will examine in this section.

5.2.1 Dataset

In regards to the dataset, we found there are a series of verses that are discussing and describing a particular topic and are related to one verse. However, in the QurSim dataset, those series of verses are paired with a single verse, an example shown in Table 4.

> متاعا لكم ولأنعامكم
>
> [As] enjoyment [i.e., provision] for you, and for your livestock. [80:32]
>
> أولم يروا أنا نسوق الماء الى الأرض الجرز فنخرج به زرعا تأكل منه أنعامهم وأنفسهم أفلا يبصرون
>
> Do they not see how We conduct the water to a dry land, and with it We produce vegetation, from which their livestock eat, and themselves? Do they not see? [32:27]

In this example, both verses [80:32] and [32:27] are related as they are mentioning the livelihood for people and the cattle. In verse [32:27], Allah mentions His kindness by providing water to dry land, and herewith bring forth crops and vegetation for people and their cattle to eat. The verse [80:32] is the last verse of a series of verses describing the same meaning of verse [32:27]; however, they were broken into several small verses. Therefore, the model failed to predict that both verses are related.

5.2.2 Lexical Synonyms

We also found that in QurSim dataset, a very few pairs of verses that are strongly related have less similar words; however, they use different words to achieve the same meaning. Therefore, AraBERT did not predict a few of those verses to be related. Also, there are phrases in classical Arabic that are pertain to Islamic teachings that the model did not predict correctly between related verses.

> ثم جعلناه نطفة في قرار مكين
>
> Then We placed him as a sperm-drop [or "as a zygote"] in a firm lodging [i.e., the womb] [23:13]
>
> ألم نخلقكم من ماء مهين
>
> Did We not create you from a liquid disdained [or "insignificant fluid"]? [77:20]

For this example, both verses [23:13] and [77:20] are related as they mentioned sperm as part of human creation. In verse [23:13], Allah draws the analogy of the sperm or zygote as an insignificant fluid or a disdained liquid to serve the purpose of its weakness in comparison to the power of the Creator. The model did not understand the analogy and the context of these verses which is why the model failed to correctly predict to be related.

> قم اليل إلا قليلا
>
> Arise [to pray] the night, except for a little [73:2]
>
> تتجافى جنوبهم عن المضاجع يدعون
> ربهم خوفا وطمعا ومما رزقناهم ينفقون
>
> Their sides shun their beds, as they pray to their Lord, out of reverence and hope; and from Our provisions to them, they spend. [32:16]

As for this example, both verses [73:2] and [32:16] are related as they mention praying during the night; however, the model did not predict they were related. The verse [73:2] mentions "Arise the night" as staying up at night, which is correct literal translation; however, the phrase in the classical Arabic religious context entails that a person staying up the night to pray. Therefore, the model did not predict both verses to be related.

6 Conclusion

The paper presented experiments on the QurSim dataset using fine-tuned AraBERT model to classify pairs of verses either to be semantically related or not. The paper applied data filtration to the QurSim dataset to avoid redundancy and generate unrelated pairs of verses. Also, the paper used both versions of AraBERT and the experiments suggested that AraBERTv0.2 has better results than AraBERTv2 across all three datasets. The best performance was achieved by AraBERTv0.2 with 92% accuracy score. However, by examining the results, AraBERT could not identify some of the classical Arabic lexical synonyms and religious context which could be a result of classical Arabic limitation in the AraBERT corpus. Finally, this study has a lot of potential for improvement on both the datasets and fine-tuning the AraBERT model.

References

Hesham Al-Bataineh, Wael Farhan, Ahmad Mustafa, Haitham Seelawi, and Hussein T Al-Natsheh. 2019. Deep contextualized pairwise semantic similarity for arabic language questions. In *2019 IEEE 31st International Conference on Tools with Artificial Intelligence (ICTAI)*, pages 1586–1591. IEEE.

Hana Al-Theiabat and Aisha Al-Sadi. 2019. The inception team at NSURL-2019 task 8: Semantic question similarity in Arabic. In *Proceedings of The First International Workshop on NLP Solutions for Under Resourced Languages (NSURL 2019) co-located with ICNLSP 2019 - Short Papers*, pages 112–117, Trento, Italy. Association for Computational Linguistics.

Basma Alharbi, Hind Alamro, Manal Alshehri, Zuhair Khayyat, Manal Kalkatawi, Inji Ibrahim Jaber, and Xiangliang Zhang. 2020. Asad: A twitter-based benchmark arabic sentiment analysis dataset.

Khalid Aloufi. 2019. Quran dataset.

Wissam Antoun, Fady Baly, and Hazem Hajj. 2020. Arabert: Transformer-based model for arabic language understanding. In *LREC 2020 Workshop Language Resources and Evaluation Conference 11–16 May 2020*, page 9.

Houda Bouamor, Nizar Habash, Mohammad Salameh, Wajdi Zaghouani, Owen Rambow, Dana Abdulrahim, Ossama Obeid, Salam Khalifa, Fadhl Eryani, Alexander Erdmann, and Kemal Oflazer. 2018. The MADAR Arabic dialect corpus and lexicon. In *Proceedings of the Eleventh International Conference on Language Resources and Evaluation (LREC 2018)*, Miyazaki, Japan. European Language Resources Association (ELRA).

Jacob Devlin, Ming-Wei Chang, Kenton Lee, and Kristina Toutanova. 2019. Bert: Pre-training of deep bidirectional transformers for language understanding.

I. A. El-Khair. 2016. 1.5 billion words arabic corpus. *ArXiv*, abs/1611.04033.

Nizar Habash, Owen Rambow, and Ryan Roth. 2009. Mada+tokan: A toolkit for arabic tokenization, diacritization, morphological disambiguation, pos tagging, stemming and lemmatization. In *Proceedings of the Second International Conference on Arabic Language Resources and Tools*, Cairo, Egypt. The MEDAR Consortium.

Chadi Helwe, Ghassan Dib, Mohsen Shamas, and Shady Elbassuoni. 2020. A semi-supervised BERT approach for Arabic named entity recognition. In *Proceedings of the Fifth Arabic Natural Language Processing Workshop*, pages 49–57, Barcelona, Spain (Online). Association for Computational Linguistics.

Tomas Mikolov, Kai Chen, Greg Corrado, and Jeffrey Dean. 2013a. Efficient estimation of word representations in vector space.

Tomas Mikolov, Ilya Sutskever, Kai Chen, Greg Corrado, and Jeffrey Dean. 2013b. Distributed representations of words and phrases and their compositionality.

Reham Mohamed, Maha Ragab, Heba Abdelnasser, Nagwa M. El-Makky, and Marwan Torki. 2015. Albayan: A knowledge-based system for Arabic answer selection. In *Proceedings of the 9th International Workshop on Semantic Evaluation (SemEval 2015)*, pages 226–230, Denver, Colorado. Association for Computational Linguistics.

Matteo Pagliardini, Prakhar Gupta, and Martin Jaggi. 2018. Unsupervised learning of sentence embeddings using compositional n-gram features. *Proceedings of the 2018 Conference of the North American Chapter of the Association for Computational Linguistics: Human Language Technologies, Volume 1 (Long Papers)*.

Nicole Peinelt, Dong Nguyen, and Maria Liakata. 2020. tBERT: Topic models and BERT joining forces for semantic similarity detection. In *Proceedings of the 58th Annual Meeting of the Association for Computational Linguistics*, pages 7047–7055, Online. Association for Computational Linguistics.

Matthew E. Peters, Mark Neumann, Mohit Iyyer, Matt Gardner, Christopher Clark, Kenton Lee, and Luke Zettlemoyer. 2018. Deep contextualized word representations.

Nils Reimers and Iryna Gurevych. 2019. Sentence-bert: Sentence embeddings using siamese bert-networks.

Anna Rogers, Olga Kovaleva, and Anna Rumshisky. 2020. A primer in bertology: What we know about how bert works.

Haitham Seelawi, Ahmad Mustafa, Hesham Al-Bataineh, Wael Farhan, and Hussein T. Al-Natsheh. 2019a. Nsurl-2019 shared task 8: Semantic question similarity in arabic.

Haitham Seelawi, Ahmad Mustafa, Hesham Al-Bataineh, Wael Farhan, and Hussein T. Al-Natsheh. 2019b. NSURL-2019 task 8: Semantic question similarity in Arabic. In *Proceedings of The First International Workshop on NLP Solutions for Under Resourced Languages (NSURL 2019) co-located with ICNLSP 2019 - Short Papers*, pages 1–8, Trento, Italy. Association for Computational Linguistics.

Abdul-Baquee Sharaf and Eric Atwell. 2012. Qursim: A corpus for evaluation of relatedness in short texts.

Ashish Vaswani, Noam Shazeer, Niki Parmar, Jakob Uszkoreit, Llion Jones, Aidan N. Gomez, Lukasz Kaiser, and Illia Polosukhin. 2017. Attention is all you need.

I. Zeroual, Dirk Goldhahn, T. Eckart, and A. Lakhouaja. 2019. Osian: Open source international arabic news corpus - preparation and integration into the clarin-infrastructure. In *WANLP@ACL 2019*.

ARAELECTRA: Pre-Training Text Discriminators for Arabic Language Understanding

Wissam Antoun and **Fady Baly** and **Hazem Hajj**
American University of Beirut
{wfa07, fbg06, hh63}@aub.edu.lb

Abstract

Advances in English language representation enabled a more sample-efficient pre-training task by Efficiently Learning an Encoder that Classifies Token Replacements Accurately (ELECTRA). Which, instead of training a model to recover masked tokens, it trains a discriminator model to distinguish true input tokens from corrupted tokens that were replaced by a generator network. On the other hand, current Arabic language representation approaches rely only on pretraining via masked language modeling. In this paper, we develop an Arabic language representation model, which we name ARAELECTRA. Our model is pretrained using the replaced token detection objective on large Arabic text corpora. We evaluate our model on multiple Arabic NLP tasks, including reading comprehension, sentiment analysis, and named-entity recognition and we show that ARAELECTRA outperforms current state-of-the-art Arabic language representation models, given the same pretraining data and with even a smaller model size.

1 Introduction

Recently, pre-trained language representation models have demonstrated state-of-the-art performance on multiple NLP tasks and in different languages. Pre-training is commonly done via Masked Language Modeling (MLM) (Devlin et al., 2019; Liu et al., 2019; Conneau et al., 2019), where an input sequence has some of its tokens randomly hidden and the model is tasked to recover the original masked tokens. While this approach has proven successful, recent works have shown that MLM is not sample-efficient (Clark et al., 2020b), since the network only learns from the small subset of masked tokens per sequence (15% of the tokens in BERT). Clark et al. (2020b) proposed an approach called Efficiently Learning an Encoder that Classifies Token Replacements Accurately (ELECTRA). The method uses a pre-training technique based on replaced token detection (RTD) task is more efficient than MLM, and thus achieved state-of-the-art results on English benchmarks. RTD is a pre-training task where a model is tasked to distinguish true input tokens from synthetically generated ones. RTD solves the issue of the mismatch created in MLM, where the model only sees the `[MASK]` token during pre-training but not during fine-tuning. In ELECTRA, a small masked language generator network **G** is used to generate used to generate the corrupted tokens, and BERT-based discriminator model **D** predicts for whether a token is an original or a replacement.

Current state-of-the-art language representation models for Arabic employ MLM as a pre-training objective (Antoun et al., 2020; Safaya et al., 2020; Lan et al., 2020; Abdul-Mageed et al., 2020b; Chowdhury et al., 2020; Abdul-Mageed et al., 2020a). In this paper, we describe the process of pre-training a transformer encoder model for Arabic language understanding using the RTD objective, which we call ARAELECTRA. We also evaluate ARAELECTRA on multiple Arabic NLP tasks and show empirically that ARAELECTRA outperforms current state-of-the-art Arabic pre-trained models.

Our contributions can be summarized as follows:

- Pre-training the ELECTRA model on a large-scale Arabic corpus.
- Reaching a new state-of-the-art on multiple Arabic NLP tasks.
- Publicly releasing ARAELECTRA on popular NLP libraries.

The rest of the paper is organized as follows. Section 2 provides a review of previous Arabic language representation literature. Section 3 details

Proceedings of the Sixth Arabic Natural Language Processing Workshop, pages 191–195
Kyiv, Ukraine (Virtual), April 19, 2021.

the methodology used in developing ARAELECTRA. Section 4 describes the experimental setup, evaluation procedures, and experiment results. Finally, we conclude in Section 5.

2 Related Works

Recently, work on Arabic language representation have been on the rise due to the performance benefits that transfer learning approaches have brought. Early transfer learning approaches in Arabic relied on using pre-trained word embeddings i.e. AraVec (Soliman et al., 2017). Model-level transfer learning was shown to work on Arabic with hULMonA (ElJundi et al., 2019), a recurrent neural network-based language modeling approach. Antoun et al. (2020) and Safaya et al. (2020) improved on hULMonA, and pre-trained transformer-based models with MLM with large scale Arabic corpora. Other approaches addressed issues with the early BERT-based models such as training on code-switched English-Arabic corpora to improve performance on information retrieval tasks (Lan et al., 2020), and training on dialectal Arabic (DA) corpora to address the domain miss-match between MSA and DA during pre-training and fine-tuning (Abdul-Mageed et al., 2020b; Chowdhury et al., 2020).

We hence propose an Arabic ELECTRA-based language representation model pre-trained using the RTD objective on large MSA corpora.

3 ARAELECTRA: Methodology

In this paper, we develop an ELECTRA-based Arabic language representation model to improve the state-of-the-art in Arabic reading comprehension. We create ARAELECTRA a bidirectional transformer encoder model with 12 encoder layers, 12 attention heads, 768 hidden size, and 512 maximum input sequence length for a total of 136M parameters. The pre-training setup and dataset of ARAELECTRA are described in the following sections.

3.1 Pre-training Setup

While ARABERT was trained using the MLM objective, ARAELECTRA is pre-trained using the RTD objective. The RTD approach trains two neural network models, a generator **G** and a discriminator **D** or ARAELECTRA, as shown in Figure 1. **G** takes a corrupted input sequence, where random tokens are replaced with the `[MASK]` token, and learns to predict the original tokens that have been masked. The generator network **G** is in our case a small BERT model with 12 encoder layers, 4 attention heads, and 256 hidden size[1]. The discriminator network **D** then takes as input the recovered sequence from the output of **G** and tries to predict which tokens were replaced and which tokens are from the original text.

While this approach may look similar to a generative adversarial network (GAN) (Goodfellow et al., 2014), the generator network in ELECTRA is trained with maximum-likelihood instead of adversarial training to fool the discriminator and the input to the generator is not a random noise vector, but a corrupted sequence of tokens.

3.2 pre-training Dataset

We chose to pre-train on the same dataset as ARABERTv0.2 (Antoun et al., 2020), to make the comparison between models fair. The dataset is a collection of the Arabic corpora list below:

- The OSCAR corpus (Ortiz Suárez et al., 2020).
- The 1.5B words Arabic Corpus (El-Khair, 2016).
- The Arabic Wikipedia dump from September 2020.
- The OSIAN corpus (Zeroual et al., 2019).
- News articles provided by As-Safir newspaper.

The total size of the training dataset is 77GB or 8.8 billion words, and comprises mostly news articles. For validation, we use new Wikipedia articles that were published after the September 2020 dump.

The same wordpiece vocabulary from ARABERTv0.2 was used for tokenization.

3.3 Fine-tuning

Since the discriminator network has the same architecture and layers as a BERT model, we add a linear classification layer on top of ELECTRA's output, and fine-tune the whole model with the added layer on new tasks. ARAELECTRA's performance is validated on three Arabic NLP tasks i.e. question answering (QA), sentiment analysis (SA) and named-entity recognition (NER).

[1] In the generator, the input embeddings of size 768 are first projected into the generator hidden size with the addition of a linear layer.

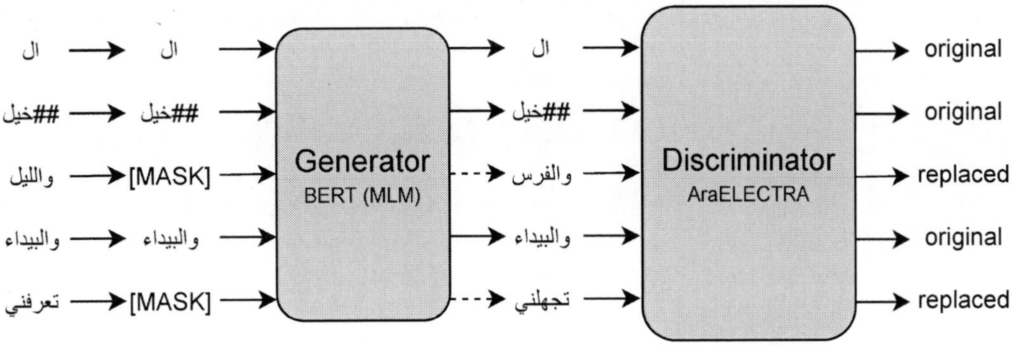

Figure 1: Replaced Token Detection pre-training task

4 Experiments and Evaluation

4.1 Experimental Setup

pre-training For pre-training, 15% of the 512 input tokens were masked. The model was pre-trained for 2 million steps with a batch size of 256. Pre-training took 24 days to finish on a TPUv3-8 slice. The learning rate was set to 2e-4, with 10000 warm-up steps.

Fine-tuning All the models were fine-tuned with batch size set to 32, maximum sequence length of 384, and a stride of 128 for QA, and a maximum sequence length of 256 for SA and NER. Experiments were only performed with the following learning rates [2e-5, 3e-5, 5e-5], since model specific hyper-parameter optimization is computationally expensive.

4.2 Datasets and other Models

4.2.1 Question Answering

The question answering task examines the model's reading comprehension and language understanding capabilities. The datasets of choice are the Arabic Reading Comprehension Dataset (ARCD) (Mozannar et al., 2019) and the Typologically Diverse Question Answering dataset (TyDiQA) (Clark et al., 2020a). Both datasets follow the SQuAD (Rajpurkar et al., 2016) format where the model is required to extract the span of the answer, given a question and a context.

The ARCD (Mozannar et al., 2019) training set consists of 48344 machine-translated questions and answers from English, with 693 questions and answers from the ARCD set. The test was performed on the remaining 702 questions from the ARCD set. From the TyDiQA (Clark et al., 2020a), we chose the Arabic examples from the training and development sets of subtask 2, for a total of 14508 pairs for training and 921 pairs for testing.

4.2.2 Sentiment Analysis

Arabic sentiment Analysis evaluation is done on the Arabic Sentiment Twitter Dataset for LEVantine (ArSenTD-Lev) (Baly et al., 2018). The dataset contains 4000 tweets written in the Levantine Arabic dialect and annotated for the sentiment (5 classes), topic, and sentiment target. The data was split 80-20 for training and testing.

4.2.3 Named-Entity Recognition

For Arabic NER recognition, the model is evaluated on the ANERcorp dataset (Benajiba et al., 2007), with the data split from CAMeL Lab (Obeid et al., 2020). The train split has 125,102 words and the test split has 25,008 words, labeled for organization (ORG), person (PER), location (LOC), and miscellaneous (MISC).

4.2.4 Reference Models

We evaluate our model against a collection of Arabic transformer models.

- ARABERTv0.1 (Antoun et al., 2020).
- ARABERTv0.2 base, large (Antoun et al., 2020).
- ARABIC-BERT base, medium, large (Safaya et al., 2020).
- ARABIC ALBERT base, large, xlarge[2].
- ARBERT (Abdul-Mageed et al., 2020a).

4.3 Results

Experimental results for the different datasets and models are shown in Table 1.

[2]https://github.com/KUIS-AI-Lab/Arabic-ALBERT/

Model	TyDiQA		ARCD		ArSenTD-LEV	ANERcorp
	EM	F1	EM	F1	F1	F1
AraBERTv0.1	68.51	82.86	31.62	67.45	53.56	83.14
AraBERTv0.2-base	73.07	85.41	32.76	66.53	55.71	83.70
AraBERTv0.2-large	73.72	86.03	36.89	**71.32**	56.94	83.08
Arabic-BERT-base	67.42	81.24	30.48	62.24	54.21	81.05
Arabic-BERT-large	70.03	84.12	33.33	67.28	55.32	82.15
Arabic-ALBERT-base	67.10	80.98	30.91	61.33	51.70	76.89
Arabic-ALBERT-large	68.07	81.59	34.19	65.41	54.62	79.61
Arabic-ALBERT-xlarge	71.12	84.59	**37.75**	68.03	54.15	81.13
ARBERT	71.55	83.69	31.62	65.93	53.52	83.33
AraELECTRA	<u>**74.91**</u>	<u>**86.68**</u>	<u>37.03</u>	<u>71.22</u>	<u>**57.20**</u>	<u>**83.95**</u>

Table 1: Performance of all tested model on the various Arabic downstream tasks. Overall best scores are highlighted in bold, while the best score within base-sized models is underlined.

The results show that ARAELECTRA achieved the highest performance on all tested datasets when compared to the other base models, and only fell short on ARCD to Arabic-ALBERT-xlarge, a model 4 times its size, in exact match scores, and to ARABERTv0.2-large in F1-score.

The performance difference between both QA datasets is due to the poor quality of the ARCD training examples, which are translated from English SQuAD. ARCD training examples also contained text in languages other than Arabic and English, which further reduced performance due to the occurrence of unknowns subwords and characters. It is also to be noted, that some training examples in Arabic TyDiQA contained HTML artifacts which appeared in the training context and answer.

As for the ArSenTD-LEV scores, all test Arabic models still struggle with fine-grained labelling of ArSenTD-Lev. Mainly because the dataset only contains 4K examples distributed between 5 sentiment classes and on 6 diverse topics, with high class-imbalance.

These results clearly demonstrate that ELECTRA's RTD objective achieves higher performance especially on QA tasks and improved semantic representation compared to MLM on Arabic text.

5 Conclusion

In this paper, we showed that pre-training using the RTD objective on Arabic text is more efficient and produces pre-trained language representation models better than the MLM objective. Our ARAELECTRA model improves the state-of-the-art for Arabic Question Answering, sentiment analysis and named-entity recognition, and achieves higher performance compared to other models pre-trained with the same dataset and with larger model sizes. Our model will be publicly available, along with our pre-training and fine-tuning code, in our repository github.com/aub-mind/arabert/tree/master/araelectra

Acknowledgments

The author would like to thank Tarek Naous for the constructive criticism of the manuscript. This research was supported by the University Research Board (URB) at the American University of Beirut (AUB), and by the TFRC program, which we thank for the free access to cloud TPUs. We also thank As-Safir newspaper for the data access.

References

Muhammad Abdul-Mageed, AbdelRahim Elmadany, and El Moatez Billah Nagoudi. 2020a. Arbert & marbert: Deep bidirectional transformers for arabic. *arXiv preprint arXiv:2101.01785*.

Muhammad Abdul-Mageed, Chiyu Zhang, AbdelRahim Elmadany, and Lyle Ungar. 2020b. Toward micro-dialect identification in diaglossic and code-switched environments. *arXiv preprint arXiv:2010.04900*.

Wissam Antoun, Fady Baly, and Hazem Hajj. 2020. Arabert: Transformer-based model for arabic language understanding. In *LREC 2020 Workshop Language Resources and Evaluation Conference 11–16 May 2020*, page 9.

Ramy Baly, Alaa Khaddaj, Hazem Hajj, Wassim El-Hajj, and Khaled Bashir Shaban. 2018. Arsentd-lev: A multi-topic corpus for target-based sentiment analysis in arabic levantine tweets. In *OSACT 3: The 3rd*

Workshop on Open-Source Arabic Corpora and Processing Tools, page 37.

Yassine Benajiba, Paolo Rosso, and José Miguel BenedíRuiz. 2007. Anersys: An arabic named entity recognition system based on maximum entropy. In *Computational Linguistics and Intelligent Text Processing*, pages 143–153, Berlin, Heidelberg. Springer Berlin Heidelberg.

Shammur Absar Chowdhury, Ahmed Abdelali, Kareem Darwish, Jung Soon-Gyo, Joni Salminen, and Bernard J. Jansen. 2020. Improving Arabic text categorization using transformer training diversification. In *Proceedings of the Fifth Arabic Natural Language Processing Workshop*, pages 226–236, Barcelona, Spain (Online). Association for Computational Linguistics.

Jonathan H. Clark, Eunsol Choi, Michael Collins, Dan Garrette, Tom Kwiatkowski, Vitaly Nikolaev, and Jennimaria Palomaki. 2020a. Tydi qa: A benchmark for information-seeking question answering in typologically diverse languages. *Transactions of the Association for Computational Linguistics*.

Kevin Clark, Minh-Thang Luong, Quoc V Le, and Christopher D Manning. 2020b. Electra: Pre-training text encoders as discriminators rather than generators. *arXiv preprint arXiv:2003.10555*.

Alexis Conneau, Kartikay Khandelwal, Naman Goyal, Vishrav Chaudhary, Guillaume Wenzek, Francisco Guzmán, Edouard Grave, Myle Ott, Luke Zettlemoyer, and Veselin Stoyanov. 2019. Unsupervised cross-lingual representation learning at scale. *arXiv preprint arXiv:1911.02116*.

Jacob Devlin, Ming-Wei Chang, Kenton Lee, and Kristina Toutanova. 2019. Bert: Pre-training of deep bidirectional transformers for language understanding. In *Proceedings of the 2019 Conference of the North American Chapter of the Association for Computational Linguistics: Human Language Technologies, Volume 1 (Long and Short Papers)*, pages 4171–4186.

Ibrahim Abu El-Khair. 2016. 1.5 billion words arabic corpus. *arXiv preprint arXiv:1611.04033*.

Obeida ElJundi, Wissam Antoun, Nour El Droubi, Hazem Hajj, Wassim El-Hajj, and Khaled Shaban. 2019. hulmona: The universal language model in arabic. In *Proceedings of the Fourth Arabic Natural Language Processing Workshop*, pages 68–77.

Ian Goodfellow, Jean Pouget-Abadie, Mehdi Mirza, Bing Xu, David Warde-Farley, Sherjil Ozair, Aaron Courville, and Yoshua Bengio. 2014. Generative adversarial nets. *Advances in neural information processing systems*, 27:2672–2680.

Wuwei Lan, Yang Chen, Wei Xu, and Alan Ritter. 2020. Gigabert: Zero-shot transfer learning from english to arabic. In *Proceedings of The 2020 Conference on Empirical Methods on Natural Language Processing (EMNLP)*.

Yinhan Liu, Myle Ott, Naman Goyal, Jingfei Du, Mandar Joshi, Danqi Chen, Omer Levy, Mike Lewis, Luke Zettlemoyer, and Veselin Stoyanov. 2019. Roberta: A robustly optimized bert pretraining approach. *arXiv preprint arXiv:1907.11692*.

Hussein Mozannar, Elie Maamary, Karl El Hajal, and Hazem Hajj. 2019. Neural Arabic question answering. In *Proceedings of the Fourth Arabic Natural Language Processing Workshop*, pages 108–118, Florence, Italy. Association for Computational Linguistics.

Ossama Obeid, Nasser Zalmout, Salam Khalifa, Dima Taji, Mai Oudah, Bashar Alhafni, Go Inoue, Fadhl Eryani, Alexander Erdmann, and Nizar Habash. 2020. CAMeL tools: An open source python toolkit for Arabic natural language processing. In *Proceedings of the 12th Language Resources and Evaluation Conference*, pages 7022–7032, Marseille, France. European Language Resources Association.

Pedro Javier Ortiz Suárez, Laurent Romary, and Benoît Sagot. 2020. A monolingual approach to contextualized word embeddings for mid-resource languages. In *Proceedings of the 58th Annual Meeting of the Association for Computational Linguistics*, pages 1703–1714, Online. Association for Computational Linguistics.

Pranav Rajpurkar, Jian Zhang, Konstantin Lopyrev, and Percy Liang. 2016. Squad: 100,000+ questions for machine comprehension of text. *arXiv preprint arXiv:1606.05250*.

Ali Safaya, Moutasem Abdullatif, and Deniz Yuret. 2020. KUISAIL at SemEval-2020 task 12: BERT-CNN for offensive speech identification in social media. In *Proceedings of the Fourteenth Workshop on Semantic Evaluation*, pages 2054–2059, Barcelona (online). International Committee for Computational Linguistics.

Abu Bakr Soliman, Kareem Eissa, and Samhaa R El-Beltagy. 2017. Aravec: A set of arabic word embedding models for use in arabic nlp. *Procedia Computer Science*, 117:256–265.

Imad Zeroual, Dirk Goldhahn, Thomas Eckart, and Abdelhak Lakhouaja. 2019. Osian: Open source international arabic news corpus-preparation and integration into the clarin-infrastructure. In *Proceedings of the Fourth Arabic Natural Language Processing Workshop*, pages 175–182.

ARAGPT2: Pre-Trained Transformer for Arabic Language Generation

Wissam Antoun and **Fady Baly** and **Hazem Hajj**
American University of Beirut
{wfa07, fbg06, hh63}@aub.edu.lb

Abstract

Recently, pre-trained transformer-based architectures have proven to be very efficient at language modeling and understanding, given that they are trained on a large enough corpus. Applications in language generation for Arabic are still lagging in comparison to other NLP advances primarily due to the lack of advanced Arabic language generation models. In this paper, we develop the first advanced Arabic language generation model, AraGPT2, trained from scratch on a large Arabic corpus of internet text and news articles. Our largest model, ARAGPT2-MEGA, has 1.46 billion parameters, which makes it the largest Arabic language model available. The MEGA model was evaluated and showed success on different tasks including synthetic news generation, and zero-shot question answering. For text generation, our best model achieves a perplexity of 29.8 on held-out Wikipedia articles. A study conducted with human evaluators showed the significant success of AraGPT2-mega in generating news articles that are difficult to distinguish from articles written by humans. We thus develop and release an automatic discriminator model with a 98% percent accuracy in detecting model-generated text. The models are also publicly available[1], hoping to encourage new research directions and applications for Arabic NLP.

1 Introduction

Few years ago, Natural language processing (NLP) was revolutionized with the introduction of multi-head self-attention transformer architecture (Vaswani et al., 2017). The transformer achieved superior performance compared to recurrent neural networks several NLP tasks including machine translation, sentence classification with BERT (Devlin et al., 2019), and ELECTRA (Clark et al., 2020b), and sentence completion with GPT-2 (Radford et al., 2019), GROVER (Zellers et al., 2019), and CTRL (Keskar et al., 2019). Recent works have shown that larger models pre-trained on larger datasets can further improve performance i.e. RoBERTa (Liu et al., 2019), and XLM-R (Conneau et al., 2019).

On the other hand, work on Arabic language modeling has mostly targeted natural language understanding (NLU) by pre-training transformer-based models using the Masked Language Modeling (MLM) task i.e. ARABERT (Antoun et al., 2020a). In contrast, Arabic text generation or causal language modeling hasn't received much attention. Few works such as hULMonA (ElJundi et al., 2019) used next word prediction as a pre-training task in for transfer learning in Arabic text classification. (Khooli, 2020) and (Doiron, 2020) leveraged the existing GPT2 English model and adapted it for Arabic using text from the Arabic Wikipedia dumps, which is sub-optimal for Arabic.

In this paper, the first advanced language generation models built from the grounds up on Arabic language have been developed. The process of pre-training ARAGPT2, a GPT-2 transformer model for the Arabic language is described. The model comes in 4 size variants: **base** (135M[2]), **medium** (370M), **large** (792M) and **mega** (1.46B[3]), which allows the exploration of ARAGPT2 in multiple applications with different data availability and computational constraints. The perplexity measure is used to automatically evaluate ARAGPT2. Furthermore, a human-based evaluation is provided, which highlights the ability of ARAGPT2 to deceive human evaluators. Finally, an ARAELECTRA (Antoun et al., 2020b) based detector is devel-

[1] Pretrained variants of ARAGPT2 (base, medium, large, mega) and discriminator are publicly available on github.com/aub-mind/arabert/tree/master/aragpt2

[2] Million Parameters

[3] Billion Parameters

Proceedings of the Sixth Arabic Natural Language Processing Workshop, pages 196–207
Kyiv, Ukraine (Virtual), April 19, 2021.

oped and released. It is able to consistently identify news articles written by ARAGPT2. Making such powerful models publicly available to the Arabic research community enables research in rising Arabic NLP fields i.e Conversational Agents (Naous et al., 2020), Detection of Automatic News Generation Detection (Harrag et al., 2020)...

Our contributions can be summarized as follows:

- A methodology to pre-train a billion-size GPT2 model on a large-scale Arabic corpus.
- An automatic discriminator that achieves a 98% accuracy in detecting model-generated synthetic text.
- The four variants of ARAGPT2 are released on popular NLP libraries, along with the automatic ARAGPT2 discriminator.

The rest of the paper is structured as follows. Section 2 provides a concise review of previous literature on Arabic language modeling. Section 3 details the methodology used in developing ARAGPT2. Section 4 describes the experimental setup, evaluation procedures and results. In addition, the approach to build a machine-generated text discriminator is presented in Section 5. Finally, a conclusion of the work and implications are mentioned in Section 6.

2 Related Works

2.1 English and Non-Arabic Language modeling

GPT-1 (Radford et al., 2018) showed that Causal Language Modeling[4] is an effective pre-training technique that improves a model's generalization capabilities. GPT-2 then showed that using a larger model trained on a larger dataset surpasses the state-of-the-art of many tasks in a zero-shot setting, where a model solves a task without receiving any training on that task. Taking the scaling approach to the extreme led to the creation of GPT-3 (Brown et al., 2020), with 175 billion parameter model, also trained with CLM using terabytes of internet text. GPT-3 explored the idea of few-shot learning, where a model is given examples from a new task as a text prompt, which unlocks new capabilities at test time. It was later shown that a carefully designed GPT-3 prompt allows the model to generate website designs, scramble/unscramble words... The advantage of scaling model sizes and training datasets comes with drawbacks, particularly the high computational cost, in addition to the huge corpora required for pre-training. It was estimated that training GPT-2 and GPT-3 costs $43K and $4.6M respectively, without any hyper-parameter tuning. These drawbacks restricted the availability of large pre-trained models to English mainly and a handful of other languages i.e. ruGPT3[5] for Russian, and Chinese 1.5B GPT2 (Zhang, 2019).

2.2 Arabic Language modeling

Work on Arabic causal language modeling has been mostly limited to automatic speech recognition (ASR) systems. Since the language modeling component in ASR systems is a key module that ensures that the output text adheres with the statistical structure of language. Work on Arabic language models in ASR systems has mostly relied on N-grams language models. (Ali et al., 2014) built an N-grams language model (LM) using GALE training data transcripts of 1.4M words. More recent work in Arabic ASR implemented a recurrent neural network as an LM, using 130M tokens, and achieved a perplexity of 481 compared to 436 for a 4-gram LM (Khurana et al., 2019). Hamed et al. (2017) developed a code-switched Arabic-English language model using tri-gram LM and provided performance superior compared to two separate monolingual LMs. The code-switched LM was trained on 2.3M sentences or 13M words and achieved a perplexity of 275.

With the rising popularity of transfer learning in NLP, Arabic CLM was used as a pre-training task for an Arabic universal LM, hULMonA (ElJundi et al., 2019). The model was then fine-tuned on different downstream text classification tasks. hULMonA is a 3 stack of AWD-LSTM[6] layers (Howard and Ruder, 2018), trained on 600K Wikipedia article pre-segmented using the MADAMIRA Arabic morphological analyzer and disambiguator (Pasha et al., 2014).

Masked Language Modeling (MLM) has been useful as a pre-training task for several Arabic NLU models. Masked Language Modeling (MLM) is a slightly different objective than CLM that requires a system to predict a masked word within a sequence compared to CLM which predicts the missing word at the end of a sequence. MLM

[4]This is the regular Language Modeling objective where the model learns the probability of a word given the previous context. The CLM acronym is used to distinguish from masked language modeling (MLM).

[5]https://github.com/sberbank-ai/ru-gpts/

[6]ASGD Weight-Dropped LSTM

was used in models such as ARABERT (Antoun et al., 2020a), Arabic-BERT (Safaya et al., 2020), Arabic-ALBERT[7], GigaBERT (Lan et al., 2020), MarBERT (Abdul-Mageed et al., 2020), and QARiB (Chowdhury et al., 2020). Only two works have attempted to create an Arabic transformer causal language model. Khooli (2020) and Doiron (2020) finetuned the OpenAI GPT2-base model on Arabic Wikipedia, which was mainly trained on English text. Doiron (2020) also continued training on a collection of dialectal Arabic datasets, in order to create a dialectal Arabic GPT2. While this approach has shown the capability to generate Arabic text, it is sub-optimal for Arabic and is useful in cases where the training data is scarce.

Our proposed model is hence, the first Arabic transformer-based causal language model trained from scratch on the largest Arabic corpora available at the time of writing.

3 ARAGPT2: Methodology

ARAGPT2 is a stacked transformer-decoder model trained using the causal language modeling objective. The model is trained on 77GB of Arabic text. ARAGPT2 comes in four variants as detailed in Table 1, with the smallest model, **base**, having the same size as ARABERT-base which makes it accessible for the larger part of researchers. Larger model variants (**medium**, **large**, **xlarge**) offer improved performance but are harder to fine-tune and computationally more expensive. The ARAGPT2-detector is based on the pre-trained ARAELECTRA model fine-tuned on the synthetically generated dataset. More details on the training procedure and dataset are provided in the following sections.

3.1 Model

ARAGPT2 closely follows GPT2's variant architectures and training procedure. Table 1 shows the different model sizes, number of heads, number of layers, parameter count, and optimizer used for each model variant. All models are trained with context sizes of 1024 tokens. The LAMB (You et al., 2019) optimizer is used in the **base** and **medium** models only, since it allows using large batch sizes without worrying about training divergence. Using LAMB and Adam (Kingma and Ba, 2014) to train the **large** and **mega** variants isn't possible on TPUv3 due to the optimizer's high memory requirements, since memory cost scales linearly with the number of parameters. The limitations were overcome by following the training procedure of the GROVER model (Zellers et al., 2019) by using the Adafactor optimizer (Shazeer and Stern, 2018), which reduces memory requirements by factoring the second-order momentum parameters into a tensor product of two vectors. The GROVER architecture was also used instead of GPT2's, in which the layer normalization order in the transformer block is changed.

3.2 Dataset

The training dataset is a collection of the publicly available Arabic corpora listed below:

- The unshuffled OSCAR corpus (Ortiz Suárez et al., 2020).
- The Arabic Wikipedia dump from September 2020.
- The 1.5B words Arabic Corpus (El-Khair, 2016).
- The OSIAN corpus (Zeroual et al., 2019).
- News articles provided by As-safir newspaper.

Preprocessing First, the corpus was filtered by removing short documents with less than 3 sentences, and documents with more than 20% repeated sentences. URLs, emails, and user mentions were also replaced with special tokens. All diacritics, and elongations were removed as well, while punctuation and non-alphabetic characters were padded with white-spaces. Moreover, the '<|endoftext|>' token is appended at the end of each document. The total dataset size is 77GB with 8.8B words[8]. The majority of the training data is comprised of Arabic news article, which is mostly written in MSA. The corpus also contains a small set of English words i.e. named entities, which are kept without lower-casing. Subsequently, a Byte-level byte-pair-encoding (BPE) tokenizer is trained with 64000 vocabulary size on all of our preprocessed dataset, using the optimized BPE implementation from the HuggingFace library (Wolf et al., 2020). Finally, the BPE encoding is applied on the preprocessed dataset, which results in a total of 9.7M training examples with 1024 sub-word tokens each.

[7]https://github.com/KUIS-AI-Lab/Arabic-ALBERT/

[8]Word count was done after preprocessing, where white space is inserted before and after punctuations, brackets, numbers... which increased the total word count

Model	Size	Architecture	Context Size	Emb. Size	Heads	Layers	Optimizer
Base	135M	GPT2	1024	768	12	12	LAMB
Medium	370M	GPT2	1024	1024	16	24	LAMB
Large	792M	GROVER	1024	1280	20	36	Adafactor
Mega	1.46B	GROVER	1024	1536	24	48	Adafactor

Table 1: ARAGPT2 model variants with sizes, architecture and optimizer

Model	Batch Size	Learning Rate	Steps	Time (days)	PPL
Base	1792	1.27e-3	120K	1.5	55.8
Medium*	80	3e-4	1M	23	45.7
Large	256	1e-4	220K	3	36.6
Mega	256	1e-4	780K	9	**29.8**

Table 2: ARAGPT2 training details and validation perplexity. ***Medium** was trained on a TPUv3-8 with a small batch size, since the model was not converging with a large batch size

4 Experiments and Evaluation

4.1 Pre-training Setup

All models were trained on a TPUv3-128 slice[9] with different batch sizes and the total number of steps as shown in Table 2. **Base** and **mega** were trained for approximately 20 epochs, while **medium** and **large** were trained for 10 and 6 epochs respectively, due to TPU access limitations.

4.2 Numerical Evaluation

For the validation dataset, the Arabic Wikipedia articles that were published after August 2020 were used, since older articles were included in the September Wikipedia dump. The perplexity score was selected as a numerical evaluation metric since it measures the degree of 'uncertainty' a model has assigning probabilities to the test text. Table 2 shows that, unsurprisingly, validation perplexity keeps improving with larger model sizes. In fact, the model is still under-fitting the validation set from Wikipedia. The generation capabilities of the different variants of ARAGPT2 is illustrated through the selected examples in Appendix A.

4.3 Zero-Shot Evaluation

During zero-shot task evaluation, the model is only given a natural language instruction to motivate and ground the task, without any back-propagation happening. The task of searching and finding the best input prompt, also known as "prompt engineering", is hard. Since the search space is practically infinite, and the performance is highly sensitive to changes in the prompt. The zero-shot performance of ARAGPT2-Mega is evaluated on two tasks, question answering, and translation. ARAGPT2-MEGA correctly answers 25% of the trivia questions but fails in English-to-Arabic translation. Details on the datasets, prompts, and evaluation are presented in Appendix B.

[9]TPUv3-128 has a total of 2TB of HBM memory with 16GB per core. TPUs were freely provided by the TFRC program.

4.4 Evaluating the Human Ability to Detect Machine-Generated Text

The gold standard for evaluating a model's language generation capability is human evaluation. We presented 74 Arabic-speaking subjects from various social media with a survey designed to test the average-human ability to distinguish between machine-generated and human-written text and thus testing the model's ability to deceive a human subject. The survey had a total of 8 news articles, 4 machine-generated using ARAGPT2-Mega and 4 written by humans. Each category was split into long and short text, which allows us to test the long-term generation coherency. In addition, the human evaluators are allowed to add justification for each answer.

The survey results, Figure 1, show that ARAGPT2-Mega successfully fooled approx. 60% of the respondents, with longer passages having a higher error rate than short passages. In the provided explanations, some subjects relied on punctuation mistakes, coherence, and repetition issues, while others spotted factual inaccuracies. However, the results also show that humans were misclassifying human-written 50% the time (chance level performance), while also citing factual inconsistencies, grammatical errors, and unusual writing styles[10].

These surprising results show that ARAGPT2 can accurately generate human-like text while

[10]Survey results are available on our GitHub repository.

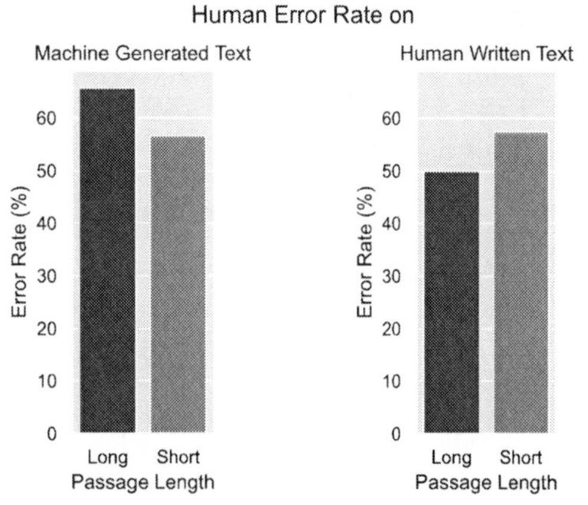

Figure 1: Survey results showing human error rates on machine generated *(left)* and human written text *(right)*

maintaining grammatical correctness that can fool the average reader. It should be noted that there exist some tools, i.e. the Giant Language model Test Room (GLTR) (Gehrmann et al., 2019), that allows humans to study the statistical distributional differences in text generated by GPT2-based models and human-written text. Figure 5 in Appendix C displays a visualization of token-level information created by GLTR with text generated by AraGPT2 and on human-written articles.

5 Automatic Detection of Machine Generated Text

Large language models could have a significant societal impact if used for malicious purposes, such as automating the generation of misleading news articles, fake reviews, or high-quality phishing messages. The survey in Section 4.4, showcases the failure of the average-human to consistently detect machine-generated text, which motivates the problem of automatic detection of AraGPT2-generated text. Related work on the detection of machine-generated text by Jawahar et al. (2020) indicates that automatic detectors like the GROVER-detector (Zellers et al., 2019) and the RoBERTA-detector (Solaiman et al., 2019) have better success than human evaluators. In addition, previous work on detecting Arabic GPT2 (Khooli, 2020) auto-generated tweets, achieved 98.7% accuracy, by fine-tuning an AraBERTv0.1 (Antoun et al., 2020a) based classifier (Harrag et al., 2020).

Our detector is based on the pre-trained AraELECTRA (Antoun et al., 2020b) model, which we fine-tuned on a dataset created by combining 1500 human-written news articles, with 1500 articles generated by AraGPT2-Mega. For article generation, we only provided the model with a short prompt of 25 words. We created two versions of the dataset, one with short texts (150 tokens) and one with long texts (500 tokens), in order to evaluate the impact of the text's length.

Fine-tuned AraELECTRA achieves 98.7% and 94.9% F1-score on long and short text respectively[11], which indicates that longer text is easier to detect than short text. The high scores achieved by AraELECTRA can be explained by the fact that machine-generated text tends to be more predictable compared to human-written text (see Appendix C, Fig. 5). The difference in text predictability can be easily exploited by a language model to detect machine-generated text. Another contributing factor is that AraELECTRA was pre-trained on the exact same dataset as AraGPT2.

6 Conclusion

AraGPT2 is the first advanced Arabic language generation model based on the transformer architecture. The model was trained on the largest publicly available collection of filtered Arabic corpora. The model was evaluated using the perplexity measure which measures how well a probability model predicts a sample. Results show that AraGPT2 is able to produce high quality Arabic text that is coherent, grammatically correct and syntactically sound.

It is important to note that AraGPT2, like many ML models, has ethical implications and can be used maliciously i.e. automatic fake news generation, modeling the dataset inherent biases... To help detect misuse of the model, a detector model that is tasked to detect output generated by AraGPT2 is also released. More importantly, our hopes that publicly releasing AraGPT2 will open up doors for new research possibilities for the Arabic NLP community.

Acknowledgments

This research was supported by the University Research Board (URB) at the American University of Beirut (AUB), and by the TFRC program for providing free access to cloud TPUs. Many thanks to As-Safir newspaper for the data access, and also thanks to Nick Doiron for the insightful discussions.

[11]The trained model will be publicly available in our repository

References

Muhammad Abdul-Mageed, Chiyu Zhang, AbdelRahim Elmadany, and Lyle Ungar. 2020. Toward micro-dialect identification in diaglossic and code-switched environments. *arXiv preprint arXiv:2010.04900*.

Ahmed Ali, Yifan Zhang, Patrick Cardinal, Najim Dahak, Stephan Vogel, and James Glass. 2014. A complete kaldi recipe for building arabic speech recognition systems. In *2014 IEEE spoken language technology workshop (SLT)*, pages 525–529. IEEE.

Wissam Antoun, Fady Baly, and Hazem Hajj. 2020a. Arabert: Transformer-based model for arabic language understanding. In *LREC 2020 Workshop Language Resources and Evaluation Conference 11–16 May 2020*, page 9.

Wissam Antoun, Fady Baly, and Hazem Hajj. 2020b. Araelectra: Pre-training text discriminators for arabic language understanding.

Tom B Brown, Benjamin Mann, Nick Ryder, Melanie Subbiah, Jared Kaplan, Prafulla Dhariwal, Arvind Neelakantan, Pranav Shyam, Girish Sastry, Amanda Askell, et al. 2020. Language models are few-shot learners. *arXiv preprint arXiv:2005.14165*.

Shammur Absar Chowdhury, Ahmed Abdelali, Kareem Darwish, Jung Soon-Gyo, Joni Salminen, and Bernard J. Jansen. 2020. Improving Arabic text categorization using transformer training diversification. In *Proceedings of the Fifth Arabic Natural Language Processing Workshop*, pages 226–236, Barcelona, Spain (Online). Association for Computational Linguistics.

Jonathan H. Clark, Eunsol Choi, Michael Collins, Dan Garrette, Tom Kwiatkowski, Vitaly Nikolaev, and Jennimaria Palomaki. 2020a. Tydi qa: A benchmark for information-seeking question answering in typologically diverse languages. *Transactions of the Association for Computational Linguistics*.

Kevin Clark, Minh-Thang Luong, Quoc V Le, and Christopher D Manning. 2020b. Electra: Pre-training text encoders as discriminators rather than generators. *arXiv preprint arXiv:2003.10555*.

Alexis Conneau, Kartikay Khandelwal, Naman Goyal, Vishrav Chaudhary, Guillaume Wenzek, Francisco Guzmán, Edouard Grave, Myle Ott, Luke Zettlemoyer, and Veselin Stoyanov. 2019. Unsupervised cross-lingual representation learning at scale. *arXiv preprint arXiv:1911.02116*.

Jacob Devlin, Ming-Wei Chang, Kenton Lee, and Kristina Toutanova. 2019. Bert: Pre-training of deep bidirectional transformers for language understanding. In *Proceedings of the 2019 Conference of the North American Chapter of the Association for Computational Linguistics: Human Language Technologies, Volume 1 (Long and Short Papers)*, pages 4171–4186.

Nick Doiron. 2020. Making a mini gpt-2 with dialect prompts.

Ibrahim Abu El-Khair. 2016. 1.5 billion words arabic corpus. *arXiv preprint arXiv:1611.04033*.

Obeida ElJundi, Wissam Antoun, Nour El Droubi, Hazem Hajj, Wassim El-Hajj, and Khaled Shaban. 2019. hulmona: The universal language model in arabic. In *Proceedings of the Fourth Arabic Natural Language Processing Workshop*, pages 68–77.

Sebastian Gehrmann, Hendrik Strobelt, and Alexander M Rush. 2019. Gltr: Statistical detection and visualization of generated text. *arXiv preprint arXiv:1906.04043*.

Injy Hamed, Mohamed Elmahdy, and Slim Abdennadher. 2017. Building a first language model for code-switch arabic-english. *Procedia Computer Science*, 117:208–216.

Fouzi Harrag, Maria Dabbah, Kareem Darwish, and Ahmed Abdelali. 2020. Bert transformer model for detecting Arabic GPT2 auto-generated tweets. In *Proceedings of the Fifth Arabic Natural Language Processing Workshop*, pages 207–214, Barcelona, Spain (Online). Association for Computational Linguistics.

Jeremy Howard and Sebastian Ruder. 2018. Universal language model fine-tuning for text classification. *arXiv preprint arXiv:1801.06146*.

Ganesh Jawahar, Muhammad Abdul-Mageed, and Laks Lakshmanan, V.S. 2020. Automatic detection of machine generated text: A critical survey. In *Proceedings of the 28th International Conference on Computational Linguistics*, pages 2296–2309, Barcelona, Spain (Online). International Committee on Computational Linguistics.

Nitish Shirish Keskar, Bryan McCann, Lav R Varshney, Caiming Xiong, and Richard Socher. 2019. Ctrl: A conditional transformer language model for controllable generation. *arXiv preprint arXiv:1909.05858*.

Abed Khooli. 2020. gpt2-small-arabic.

Sameer Khurana, Ahmed Ali, and James Glass. 2019. Darts: Dialectal arabic transcription system. *arXiv preprint arXiv:1909.12163*.

Diederik P Kingma and Jimmy Ba. 2014. Adam: A method for stochastic optimization. *arXiv preprint arXiv:1412.6980*.

Wuwei Lan, Yang Chen, Wei Xu, and Alan Ritter. 2020. Gigabert: Zero-shot transfer learning from english to arabic. In *Proceedings of The 2020 Conference on Empirical Methods on Natural Language Processing (EMNLP)*.

Yinhan Liu, Myle Ott, Naman Goyal, Jingfei Du, Mandar Joshi, Danqi Chen, Omer Levy, Mike Lewis, Luke Zettlemoyer, and Veselin Stoyanov. 2019. Roberta: A robustly optimized bert pretraining approach. *arXiv preprint arXiv:1907.11692*.

Hussein Mozannar, Elie Maamary, Karl El Hajal, and Hazem Hajj. 2019. Neural Arabic question answering. In *Proceedings of the Fourth Arabic Natural Language Processing Workshop*, pages 108–118, Florence, Italy. Association for Computational Linguistics.

Tarek Naous, Christian Hokayem, and Hazem Hajj. 2020. Empathy-driven Arabic conversational chatbot. In *Proceedings of the Fifth Arabic Natural Language Processing Workshop*, pages 58–68, Barcelona, Spain (Online). Association for Computational Linguistics.

Pedro Javier Ortiz Suárez, Laurent Romary, and Benoît Sagot. 2020. A monolingual approach to contextualized word embeddings for mid-resource languages. In *Proceedings of the 58th Annual Meeting of the Association for Computational Linguistics*, pages 1703–1714, Online. Association for Computational Linguistics.

Arfath Pasha, Mohamed Al-Badrashiny, Mona Diab, Ahmed El Kholy, Ramy Eskander, Nizar Habash, Manoj Pooleery, Owen Rambow, and Ryan Roth. 2014. MADAMIRA: A fast, comprehensive tool for morphological analysis and disambiguation of Arabic. In *Proceedings of the Ninth International Conference on Language Resources and Evaluation (LREC'14)*, pages 1094–1101, Reykjavik, Iceland. European Language Resources Association (ELRA).

Matt Post. 2018. A call for clarity in reporting BLEU scores. In *Proceedings of the Third Conference on Machine Translation: Research Papers*, pages 186–191, Belgium, Brussels. Association for Computational Linguistics.

Alec Radford, Karthik Narasimhan, Tim Salimans, and Ilya Sutskever. 2018. Improving language understanding by generative pre-training.

Alec Radford, Jeffrey Wu, Rewon Child, David Luan, Dario Amodei, and Ilya Sutskever. 2019. Language models are unsupervised multitask learners. *OpenAI*.

Ali Safaya, Moutasem Abdullatif, and Deniz Yuret. 2020. KUISAIL at SemEval-2020 task 12: BERT-CNN for offensive speech identification in social media. In *Proceedings of the Fourteenth Workshop on Semantic Evaluation*, pages 2054–2059, Barcelona (online). International Committee for Computational Linguistics.

Noam Shazeer and Mitchell Stern. 2018. Adafactor: Adaptive learning rates with sublinear memory cost. *arXiv preprint arXiv:1804.04235*.

Irene Solaiman, Miles Brundage, Jack Clark, Amanda Askell, Ariel Herbert-Voss, Jeff Wu, Alec Radford, Gretchen Krueger, Jong Wook Kim, Sarah Kreps, et al. 2019. Release strategies and the social impacts of language models. *arXiv preprint arXiv:1908.09203*.

Jörgrg Tiedemann. 2012. Parallel data, tools and interfaces in opus. In *Proceedings of the Eight International Conference on Language Resources and Evaluation (LREC'12)*, Istanbul, Turkey. European Language Resources Association (ELRA).

Ashish Vaswani, Noam Shazeer, Niki Parmar, Jakob Uszkoreit, Llion Jones, Aidan N Gomez, ukasz Kaiser, and Illia Polosukhin. 2017. Attention is all you need. *Advances in neural information processing systems*, 30:5998–6008.

Thomas Wolf, Lysandre Debut, Victor Sanh, Julien Chaumond, Clement Delangue, Anthony Moi, Pierric Cistac, Tim Rault, Rémi Louf, Morgan Funtowicz, Joe Davison, Sam Shleifer, Patrick von Platen, Clara Ma, Yacine Jernite, Julien Plu, Canwen Xu, Teven Le Scao, Sylvain Gugger, Mariama Drame, Quentin Lhoest, and Alexander M. Rush. 2020. Transformers: State-of-the-art natural language processing. In *Proceedings of the 2020 Conference on Empirical Methods in Natural Language Processing: System Demonstrations*, pages 38–45, Online. Association for Computational Linguistics.

Yang You, Jing Li, Sashank Reddi, Jonathan Hseu, Sanjiv Kumar, Srinadh Bhojanapalli, Xiaodan Song, James Demmel, Kurt Keutzer, and Cho-Jui Hsieh. 2019. Large batch optimization for deep learning: Training bert in 76 minutes. *arXiv preprint arXiv:1904.00962*.

Rowan Zellers, Ari Holtzman, Hannah Rashkin, Yonatan Bisk, Ali Farhadi, Franziska Roesner, and Yejin Choi. 2019. Defending against neural fake news. In *Advances in neural information processing systems*, pages 9054–9065.

Imad Zeroual, Dirk Goldhahn, Thomas Eckart, and Abdelhak Lakhouaja. 2019. Osian: Open source international arabic news corpus-preparation and integration into the clarin-infrastructure. In *Proceedings of the Fourth Arabic Natural Language Processing Workshop*, pages 175–182.

Zhibo Zhang. 2019. Gpt2-ml: Gpt-2 for multiple languages. `https://github.com/imcaspar/gpt2-ml`.

A Generated Samples from ARAGPT2

Prompt

أحدث حصول لقاح شركة " أوكسفورد " البريطانية على الموافقة في موطنه ، حالة من الارتياح في العالم ، نظرا إلى فعاليته في وقاية الجسم من وباء كورونا ، فضلا عن سعره المناسب وسهولة تخزينه اللافتة مقارنة بالتطعيمات الأخرى المتاحة في السوق الدولية . وبحسب شبكة " سكاي نيوز " البريطانية فإن هذا الموافقة على هذا اللقاح تعني الشيء الكثير للعالم وليست مجرد خبر عادي .

Generated Text 1

وقالت الشبكة إن هذه هي المرة الأولى التي يحصل فيها لقاح مضاد لكورونا على موافقة منظمة الصحة العالمية ، كما أنها المرة الأولى التي تحصل فيها شركة بريطانية على مثل هذه الموافقة منذ أكثر من 20 عاما . وأضافت أن الشركة حصلت أيضا على موافقة إدارة الغذاء والدواء الأميركية (FDA) لقاحها المضاد لفيروس زيكا الذي تم تطويره بالتعاون مع شركة " غلاكسو سميثكلاين " للأدوية وشركة " سانوفي أفنتيس " الفرنسية للصناعات الدوائية . وأشارت إلى أنه لم يتم حتى الآن الإعلان عن أي حالات إصابة بكورونا بين البشر في الولايات المتحدة أو غيرها من دول العالم . ونقلت الشبكة عن المدير التنفيذي لشركة " جلاكسو سميث كلاين " قوله : " نحن سعداء للغاية بحصولنا على هذه الموافقة لأن ذلك يعني أننا تمكنا من تحقيق هدفنا المتمثل في حماية أكبر عدد ممكن من الناس من الإصابة بفيروس كورونا " . وأضاف : " نأمل أن نتمكن من إنتاج المزيد من اللقاحات المضادة لهذا الفيروس وغيره من الأمراض المعدية المنتشرة في جميع أنحاء العالم خلال السنوات القليلة المقبلة "

يذكر أن فيروس كورونا المسبب لمتلازمة الشرق الأوسط التنفسية هو أحد الفيروسات التي تصيب الجهاز التنفسي ، ولا توجد حتى الآن على مستوى العالم معلومات دقيقة عن مصدر هذا الفيروس ولا طرق انتقاله ، كما لا يوجد تطعيم وقائي أو مضاد حيوي لعلاجه . لكن مراكز السيطرة على الأمراض والوقاية منها بالولايات المتحدة الأميركية كانت قد أعلنت في وقت سابق من الشهر الجاري أن لقاحا تجريبيا أنتجته شركة " نوفارتس " السويسرية أثبت فاعليته في الوقاية من مرض متلازمة الشرق الأوسط التنفسية (MERS - CoV) لدى الأطفال والبالغين الذين يعانون من أعراض شبيهة بأعراض الانفلونزا . وكانت منظمة الصحة العالمية قد أعلنت في شهر سبتمبر أيلول الماضي تسجيل أول حالة وفاة ناجمة عن الإصابة بفيروس كورونا في المملكة العربية السعودية ، حيث توفي رجل يبلغ من العمر 69 عاما كان يعاني من عدة أمراض مزمنة جراء إصابته بهذا الفيروس . وكان الرجل قد نقل إلى مستشفى الملك فيصل التخصصي ومركز الأبحاث في مدينة الرياض بعد شعوره بأعراض تنفسية حادة أدت إلى دخوله في غيبوبة وتوفي بعد يومين من إدخاله المستشفى . وقال الدكتور علاء العلوان المدير العام للمكتب التنفيذي لمجلس وزراء الصحة لدول مجلس التعاون ورئيس اللجنة الخليجية لمكافحة الأمراض المعدية إنه بناء على ما أعلنته منظمة الصحة العالمية فقد تمت الموافقة على طلب وزارة الصحة بالمملكة العربية السعودية لتزويدها باللقاح الواقي

Generated Text 2

وقالت الشبكة إن هذه هي المرة الأولى التي يحصل فيها لقاح مضاد لفيروس كوفيد - 19 على موافقة منظمة الصحة العالمية ، ما يعني أنه سيكون متاحا للجميع خلال الأسابيع القليلة المقبلة .وأضافت أن هذا اللقاح الذي يحمل اسم " تاميفلو " (Tamiflu) تم تطويره بالتعاون مع شركة " غلاكسو سميث كلاين " (GlaxoSmithKline) وشركة " سانوفي باستور " (Sanofi Pasteur) الفرنسية ، وهما شركتان تابعتان لمجموعة " أسترا زينيكا " (AstraZeneca) الدوائية .وقال رئيس قسم الأمراض المعدية في منظمة الصحة العالمية ديفيد نابارو : " نحن مسرورون للغاية بحصول هذا اللقاح على الموافقة النهائية من قبل إدارة الأغذية والعقاقير الأمريكية (FDA) ومنظمة الصحة العالمية (WHO) " . وأضاف : " إنه نبأ سار لجميع العاملين في مجال الرعاية الصحية والمرضى الذين سيستفيدون من هذا اللقاح " .من جهته ، قال الرئيس التنفيذي لشركة " غلاكسوسميث كلاين " ، بروس أرمسترونغ : " إننا سعداء جدا بهذا الخبر السار ، ونحن واثقون من أننا سنتمكن من إنتاج كميات كبيرة من هذا اللقاح لتلبية الطلب العالمي المتزايد عليه " .وتابع قائلا : " لقد عملنا بشكل وثيق مع وزارة الصحة العامة في المملكة المتحدة لضمان الحصول على الموافقات التنظيمية اللازمة لهذا اللقاح ، ونأمل أن نتمكن من إنتاجه بكميات كافية لتلبية احتياجات المرضى في جميع أنحاء العالم " .يشار إلى أن فيروس كورونا المسبب لمتلازمة الشرق الأوسط التنفسية (MERS - CoV) هو أحد الفيروسات التي تصيب الجهاز التنفسي ، ولا توجد حتى الآن على مستوى العالم معلومات دقيقة عن مصدر هذا الفيروس ولا طرق انتقاله ، كما لا يوجد تطعيم وقائي أو مضاد حيوي لعلاجه . لكن هناك العديد من الإجراءات والاحتياطات التي يمكن اتخاذها للحد من خطر الإصابة به ، مثل الإقلال من مخالطة المرضى وغسل اليدين بانتظام وتجنب لمس العين والأنف والفم واستخدام المناديل عند السعال أو العطس وتغطية الفم والأنف أثناء السعال أو العطاس وتغطية الأنف والفم عند العطس أو السعال باستخدام منديل والتخلص منه مباشرة في سلة النفايات وعدم مشاركة الآخرين في أدوات الطعام والشراب غير المستخدمة بعد غسلها جيدا والحرص على غسل اليدين بالصابون والماء الدافئ لمدة 20 ثانية على الأقل ثم شطفها بالماء البارد وتجفيف اليدين بمنشفة نظيفة والابتعاد عن أماكن الازدحام والتجمعات البشرية قدر الإمكان .يذكر أن منظمة الصحة العالمية كانت قد أعلنت الأسبوع الماضي أن عدد حالات الإصابة المؤكدة بفيروس كورونا الجديد ارتفع إلى 991 حالة ، توفي منها 563 شخصا منذ اكتشاف المرض في شهر سبتمبر أيلول 2012 .

Figure 2: Random unseen context about coronavirus vaccine(top). Followed by two generated samples bu ARAGPT2-mega. Generated text 1 ($top_p = 0.95$), Generated text 2 ($top_p = 1$)

Prompt

يحكى أن مزارعا مخادعا قام ببيع بئر الماء الموجود في أرضه لجاره مقابل مبلغ كبير من المال ، وعندما جاء المزارع الذي اشترى البئر ليستخدم الماء الموجود فيه في اليوم التالي قال له الرجل المخادع : اذهب من هنا أيها الرجل فأنا قد بعتك البئر لكنني لم أبعك الماء الموجود فيه ، دهش الرجل مما سمع وتوجه إلى القاضي ليشتكي المزارع المخادع له بعد محاولات عديدة لإقناعه بأن البئر والماء الذي فيه من حقه

Generated Text 1

وأن عليه أن يدفع المبلغ الذي اشتراه به ثمنا للبئر ، لكن القاضي رفض الشكوى وقال للرجل المخادع : لقد اشتريت منك البئر لكنك لم تشتر مني الماء .وفي يوم من الأيام وبينما كان أحد المزارعين يجلس على إحدى شرفات منزله المطلة على حديقة مليئة بالأشجار رأى رجلا قادما نحوه وبيده كيس مليء بالحلوى فسلم عليه وسأله عن سبب مجيئه إليه فأخبره الرجل بأنه يريد أن يعطيه بعض الحلوى التي يحبها ، فقال له المزارع : حسنا سأعطيك ما تريد بشرط واحد وهو أن لا تخبر أحدا بهذا الأمر أبدا ، وافق الرجل على شرط المزارع وأعطاه الكيس المملوء بالحلوى ، وقبل أن يغادر المزرعة سأله المزارع قائلا : هل تعلم يا سيدي بأنني رجل فقير ولا أملك مالا لأحصل على الحلوى ؟ فأجابه الرجل : نعم أعلم ذلك ولكن المشكلة هي أنني لا أستطيع أن أعطيك الحلوى دون أن تخبرني بذلك ، ضحك المزارع قليلا ثم قال للرجل : إذا أخبرتني قبل أن تعطيني الحلوى فلن أسمح لك بأخذ أي شيء منها حتى لو كان هذا الشيء هو ثمن الحلوى التي أعطيتك إياها .أخبر المزارع جاره بما حدث معه وطلب منه أن يوصله إلى القاضي لعله يجد حلا لمشكلته ، ذهب جار المزارع إلى القاضي وأخبره بما حدث مع جاره ، فسأله القاضي مستغربا : لماذا فعلت ذلك ؟ أجابه الجار : لأنني أريد أن أعرف كيف حصلت على الحلوى دون أن تأخذها مني ودون أن تعطيها لأحد غيرك !وبالفعل عندما وصل الجار إلى القاضي طلب منه القاضي أن يريه الصندوق الذي يحتوي على الحلوى ، نظر القاضي إلى الصندوق فوجد بداخله صندوقا آخر كبيرا مليئا بالحلوى ، تعجب القاضي من محتويات الصندوق لكنه سرعان ما قرر أن يفتح الصندوق ليرى ماذا يوجد بداخله ، فتح القاضي الصندوق فوجده مملوءا بالحلوى وقد كتب عليه عبارة تقول : " هذه الحلوى لمن يستطيع الحصول عليها فقط " ، استغرب القاضي من محتوى الصندوق وقرر أن يعيد فتحه مرة أخرى ليجد بداخله صندوقا ثالثا مليئا بالحلوى أيضا ، سأل القاضي صاحب الصندوقين عما يحتويه كل صندوق فأجاب صاحب الصندوق الثالث قائلا : إن هذين الصندوقين مخصصان للفقراء الذين لا يستطيعون الحصول على الحلوى ، أما الصندوقين الآخرين فهما مخصصان للأغنياء الذين يستطيعون الحصول على تلك الحلوى .

Prompt

يحكى أن الأسد ملك الغابة وأقوى سكانها كان ذات يوم نائما ، عندما بدأ فأر صغير يعيش في الغابة نفسها بالركض حوله والقفز فوقه وإصدار أصوات مزعجة ، مما أقلق نوم الأسد ودفعه للاستيقاظ ، وعندما قام الأسد من نومه كان غاضبا ، فوضع قبضته الضخمة فوق الفأر ، وزمجر وفتح فمه ينوي ابتلاع الفأر الصغير بلقمة واحدة ، صاح الفأر عندها بصوت يرتجف من الخوف راجيا أن يعفو الأسد عنه ، وقال :

Generated Text 1

" سامحني يا ملك الغابة ، أرجوك سامحني ، فأنا لا أستطيع العيش بدونك " .أجاب الأسد قائلا : " أنا ملك الغابة ، وأنت أيها الفأر الصغير مجرد تابع لي ، ولا تستطيع عمل أي شيء دون إذني ، أما أنا فأستطيع أن أعمل ما أشاء وأعيش كما أشاء ، ولكن بشرط واحد وهو أن تساعدني على القضاء على جميع الفئران التي تعيش في الغابة " .فقال الفأر : " نعم سيدي ، سأفعل كل ما تأمرني به ، وسأقضي على جميع الفئران الموجودة في الغابة ، وسآتي بك إلى هنا لتعيش معي وتاكل من طعامي وتشرب من مائى وتنام في فراشي " .ضحك الأسد ضحكة عالية ثم قال للفأر : " هل أنت موافق ؟ " ، فقال الفأر : " لقد سمعت هذا الكلام منذ قليل فقط ، ولكني لم أكن أعرف أنك ملك الغابة وسيدها ، وأن لك سلطانا علي الحيوانات كلها ، لذلك أرجو منك أن تسمح لي بأن أعيش معك تحت سقف واحد وتحت حماية سلطانك وملكك " .فرح الأسد كثيرا بالفكرة ، وطلب من الفأر أن يذهب معه إلى بيته ليعيشا معا حياة سعيدة هانئة ، وبالفعل ذهب الفأر مع الأسد إلى بيت الأسد الذي رحب به أجمل ترحيب ، وأعطاه قطعة كبيرة من الخشب ليصنع منها سريرا كبيرا له ولزوجته وأولاده ، وهكذا عاش الفأر مع الأسد في سعادة وهناء .وبعد فترة قصيرة من الزمن ، مرض الأسد مرضا شديدا ، ولم يعد قادرا على تحمل المزيد من الأعباء الملقاة على عاتقه ، فطلب من الفأر أن يساعده في حمل سريره الثقيل والذهاب به إلى الطبيب ، فوافق الفأر على الفور ، وذهب مسرعا إلى الطبيب ليخبره بأنه مصاب بمرض خطير يحتاج إلى جراحة عاجلة ، لكنه رفض إجراء الجراحة خوفا من غضب الأسد عليه وانتقامه منه ، لكن الفأر أصر على الذهاب إلى الطبيب لإجراء الجراحة ، وفي أثناء ذلك سمع صوت الأسد يناديه ويقول له : " ماذا تريد مني يا ملك الغابة ؟ " ، فأجابه الفأر : " أريد أن أحملك على ظهري لأذهب بك إلى الطبيب حتى يشخص حالتك ويصف لك العلاج المناسب لحالتك " .نظر الأسد إلى الفأر مبتسما وقال له : " هيا بنا يا صديقي العزيز لنذهب

Figure 3: Random unseen contexts about children stories. Followed by a generated sample by ARAGPT2-mega with $top_p = 0.95$

Prompt 1 (Cooking Recipes)

فتة الدجاج اللبنانية طريقة التحضير نضع الدجاج في قدر من الماء مع البصل والهيل وورق الغار والملح والفلفل الأسود ونسلقه على نار متوسطة حتى ينضج تماما . صفي الدجاج من المرق ونفتته ونضعه جانبا ثم نصفي المرق ونضعه في وعاء . نحمي الزيت ونقلي فيه الخبز حتى يصبح ذهبيا ومقرمشا .

Generated Text

نوزع شرائح الفليفلة الخضراء والحمراء والخضراء والبندورة المقشرة والمفرومة فوق الخبز ، ثم نرش فوقها القليل من البقدونس المفروم والصنوبر المحمص . ندهن صينية فرن بالقليل من الزيت ونرشها بالقليل من الطحين ثم ندخل الصينية إلى فرن محمى مسبقا على حرارة 180 درجة مئوية لمدة تتراوح بين 15 و 20 دقيقة أو حتى يحمر وجه الصـينية . نخرج الصـينية من الفرن ونتركها لتبرد قليلا ثم نقطعها ونقدمها ساخنة .

Prompt 2 (Short Conversation - Greeting)

مرحبا كيف حالك ؟

Generated Text

ان شاء الله بخير . اليوم جبتلكم لعبة حلوة كتير و هي عبارة عن مجموعة من الكرات الملونة بألوان مختلفة , كل ما عليك فعله هو الضغط على الكرة التي تريد أن ترميها في المكان المخصص لها ثم اضغط عليها مرة أخرى

Prompt 3 (Wikipedia-style)

لبنان تعد الجمهورية اللبنانية دولة عربية عاصمتها بيروت ، وتقع على الشاطئ المطل على الجزء الشرقي للبحر الأبيض المتوسط ، وتعد واحدة من أكثر البلدان المكتظة بالسكان ، وبالعودة إلى تاريخها فهي تعتبر موطنا لأقدم الحضـارات البشـرية في الألفية الثالثة قبل الميلاد خاصـة المنطقة السـاحلية منها ، فكانت من أهم المراكز الثقافية والتجارية في ذلك الوقت ، وكان لتضـاريسـها الوعرة دورا مهما على مر التاريخ في لجوء عدة جماعات إليها ، وأعلنت كدولة جمهورية عام 1926 م ، وفي عام 1946 م حصلت لبنان على استقلالها بعد الانتداب الفرنسي .

Generated Text

[١][٢]تعد اللغة العربية هي اللغة الرسـمية للبلاد ، بالإضـافة إلى وجود لغتين رسـميتين أخريين هما الإنجليزية والفرنسـية ، أما الديانة السـائدة في البلاد فهي الإسلام ، حيث يشكل المسلمون حوالي 96 % من إجمالي عدد السكان ، ويتوزع الباقون على الطوائف المسيحية والديانات الأخرى ، ومن أبرز المعالم السياحية في لبنان مدينة بيروت التي تعد عاصـمة البلاد ومركزها الثقافي والاقتصـادي ، كما يوجد بها العديد من المواقع الأثرية الهامة مثل مغارة جعيتا ، وقلعة بعلبك ، وبرج إيفل ، ومتحف سرسق ، وقصر بيت الدين الذي يعد واحدا من أقدم القصـور التاريخية في العالم ، وغيرها الكثير من المعالم المميزة . [٣]تعتمد السـياحة في لبنان بشـكل أسـاسـي على الطبيعة الخلابة والمناخ المعتدل صيفا وشتاء ، لذلك فإن أغلب السياح يفضلون قضـاء عطلتهم الصيفية في المناطق الجبلية والسـاحلية للاستمتاع بالمناظر الطبيعية الخلابة والمناظر المائية الرائعة ، بينما يفضـــل البعض الآخر التوجه إلى المدن والمناطق الداخلية للتمتع بمناخها المعتدل والاستجمام في أحضان الطبيعة الساحرة

Figure 4: Random unseen contexts on miscellaneous topics. Followed by a generated sample by ARAGPT2-mega with $top_p = 0.95$

B Zero-Shot Learning

B.1 Question Answering

In zero-shot factoid question answering, the information contained within the language model can be queried. The model is tested on the Arabic examples from the TyDiQA (Clark et al., 2020a) validation dataset (921 examples), and on the test set of ARCD (Mozannar et al., 2019) (702 examples). Hence, the model os provided with the following prompt: *"Answer the following question:"* - "أجب عن السؤال التالي:" , followed by the question, then the phrase *"The answer is"* - "الجواب هو:". It is also possible to append the phrase *"in the year"* - "في عام", if the expected answer is a year, as shown in Table 3.

Table 3: The input prompt for question answering

أجب عن السؤال التالي : متى عرضت أول حلقة من مسلسل بافي قاتلة مصاصي الدماء ؟ الجواب هو في عام *Answer the following question: When was the first episode of the series Buffy the Vampire Slayer shown? The answer is in the year*

The answer length is set to be the same as the gold answer length, and a repetition penalty is applied as in CTRL (Keskar et al., 2019), which penalizes the probability scores of previously generated tokens. A 'no repeat tri-gram' strategy that inhibits the model from generating the same tri-gram more than once has also been employed. Note that the context passage is not provided, which forces the model to rely only on the information gained during pretraining.

The model achieves a 3.93% exact-match score and an F1-score of 14.51% on TyDiQA, and 4.07% exact-match score and 13.88% F1-score on ARCD. Since exact-match and F1-score misses answers that are correct but are worded differently (as shown in Table 4). A subset of 500 answers from the best TyDiQA run is selected, and scored manually. Manual scoring shows that AraGPT2 correctly answered 24.6% of the questions. The model was particularly good in countries and capitals question, year of birth and death, and some geography. Yet it was failing mostly on questions about quantities i.e. population counts, area, age... The predefined answer length negatively affected the generated answers in some cases, which is a limitation of the current approach.

Table 4: Examples of correct answers that have zero exact match score.

Question	من هو ألفرد نوبل ؟ *Who is Alfred Nobel?*
Predicted Answer	مخترع الديناميت ، ومخترع *Inventor of the dynamite, and the inventor of*
Ground Truth	مهندس ومخترع وكيميائي سويدي *An engineer and an inventor and a Swedish chemist*
Question	متى تاسس الاتحاد الدولي لكرة القدم ؟ *When was the FIFA founded?*
Predicted Answer	١٩٠٤ م . *1904 AD*
Ground Truth	٢١ مايو من العام ١٩٠٤ *21 May of the year 1904*
Question	من هو إدغار ديغا ؟ *Who is Edgar Degas?*
Predicted Answer	أنه فنان تشكيلي فرنسي ، ولد في باريس عام *He is a French visual artist, born in*
Ground Truth	فنان تشكيلي و رسام و نحات فرنسي *Visual artist and painter and sculptor*

B.2 Translation

A experiments has also been conducted to test the translation capability of AraGPT2 by appending the prompt *"What is the translation of this sentence ?:"* - "ما هي ترجمة هذه الجملة ؟:" to the sentence from the source language, in order to induce the translation behavior of the model. We then apply greedy decoding to get the generated target sentence. Evaluation is performed on 5000 randomly selected pairs from the English-Arabic Tatoeba (Tiedemann, 2012) dataset. The model achieved only 1.32 BLEU score[12]. The low score is due to the scarce representation of English words in the vocabulary, since most words were split into single characters. Additionally, given that the prompt design greatly affects the model's zero-shot performance, our prompt design might have been suboptimal. Nevertheless, this negative result encourages research into prompt engineering for Arabic language models, which we leave as future work.

[12]Using the sacrebleu scorer (Post, 2018)

C GLTR Analysis and Visualizations

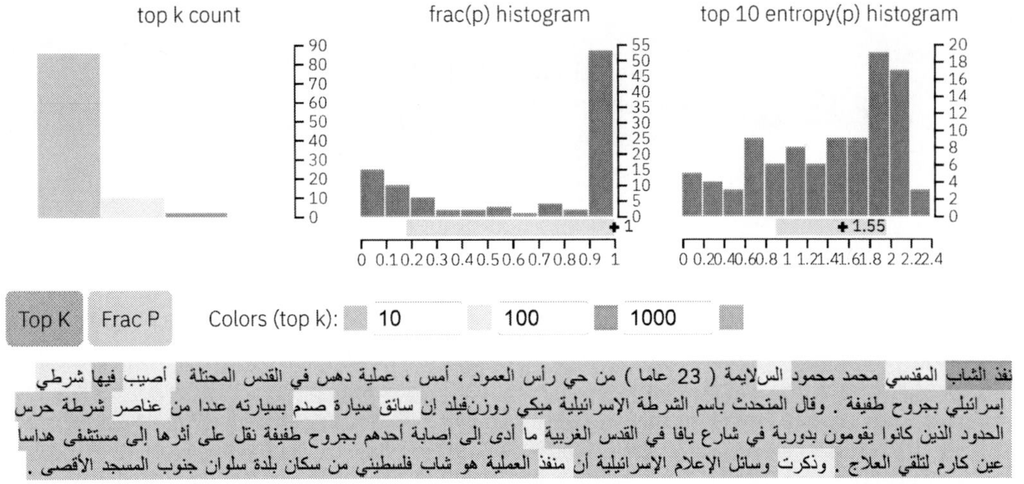

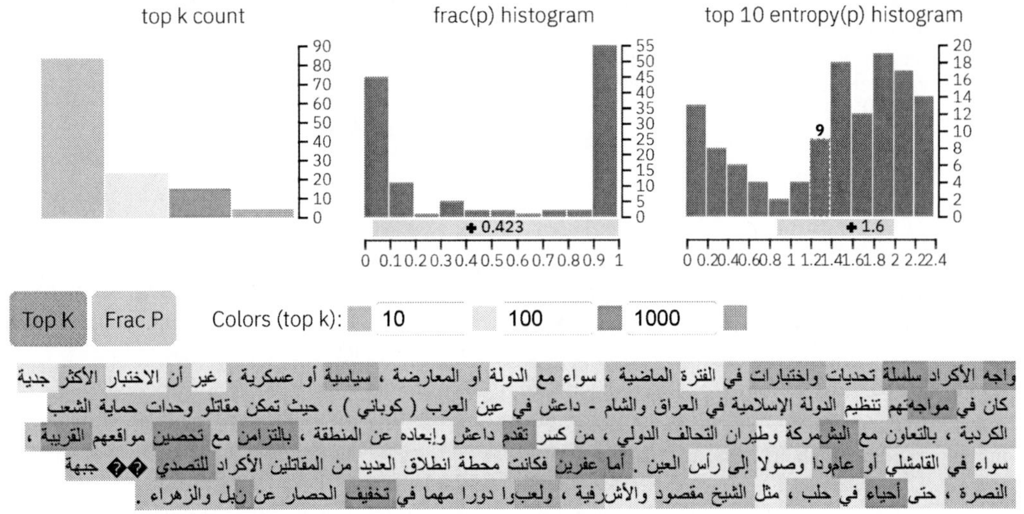

(b) Human-Written Text

Figure 5: It is clear that the machine generated text in (a) is mostly green and yellow highlighted, while in the human-written text, (b), an increase in red and purple highlighted words can be noticed. P.S.: We use ARAGPT2-base as the backend model in GLTR

QuranTree.jl: A Julia package for Quranic Arabic Corpus

Al-Ahmadgaid B. Asaad
UnionBank of the Philippines, Inc.
alahmadgaid@gmail.com

Abstract

QuranTree.jl is an open-source package for working with the Quranic Arabic Corpus (Dukes and Habash, 2010). It aims to provide Julia APIs as an alternative to the Java APIs of JQuranTree. QuranTree.jl currently offers functionalities for intuitive indexing of chapters, verses, words and parts of words of the Qur'an; for creating custom transliteration; for character dediacritization and normalization; and, for handling the Morphological Features. Lastly, it can work well with Julia's TextAnalysis.jl[1] and Python's CAMeL Tools (Obeid et al., 2020).

1 Introduction

The Quranic Arabic Corpus (Dukes and Habash, 2010) provides a complete annotation of the Morphological Features of the Qur'an. These features include part-of-speech tags, morphological segments, semantic ontology, and syntactic analysis using dependency graph. The corpus can be accessed through either the Java package, JQuranTree, or by downloading it as a Text (.txt) file from:

https://corpus.quran.com/

The corpus was made to produce a resource that enables further analysis of the Qur'an, the 1,400 year old central religious text of Islam. The 77,430 words of the Qur'an form a distinct genre difficult to compare to other texts of Arabic; and processing Quranic Arabic is a unique challenge from a computational point of view, since it differs significantly from Modern Standard Arabic (MSA) (Dukes and Habash, 2010).

In an effort to make the corpus accessible computationally, Dukes and Habash (2010) developed the Java package, JQuranTree. It includes APIs for accessing and analyzing the said corpus in its Arabic form, through the Uthmani distribution of the Tanzil[2] project. This distribution is encoded as a Orthographic Object Model, that is *immutable* and follows the following hierarchy: Document → Chapter → Verse → Token → Character → Diacritic. The package uses extended[3] Buckwalter (Buckwalter, 2002) encoding as transliteration for the Qur'an's Arabic texts, whilst also offering Simple Encoding[4] as another type of Arabic to Roman mapping. Lastly, JQuranTree supports APIs for Search and Analysis table for analyzing the corpus.

While JQuranTree provides all the fundamental functionalities for working with the corpus, it is, however, not easily accessible to researchers with little to no experience in programming. This is mainly due to the programming language used for the APIs, which is Java. Indeed, it is a powerful language but is only taught to *engineering* and *computer science* students, and rarely used in other non-engineering or non-IT courses. As such, it is therefore safe to assume, that most non-engineering or non-IT researchers who started coding for their research papers, are likely to be users of a high-level programming languages (relative to Java), like R, Python or Julia.

High-level languages are, by design, easier to learn compared to low-level languages. This is because high-level languages are often, if not always, aimed at abstracting some complexities of a low-level languages. On top of that, algorithms and models for scientific computing are often implemented in high-level programming languages. This is the motivation of QuranTree.jl, by providing APIs on a high-level language as an alternative module to JQuranTree's Java APIs, without com-

[1] https://github.com/JuliaText/TextAnalysis.jl

[2] http://tanzil.net/docs/tanzil_project

[3] https://corpus.quran.com/java/buckwalter.jsp

[4] https://corpus.quran.com/java/simpleencoding.jsp

Proceedings of the Sixth Arabic Natural Language Processing Workshop, pages 208–212
Kyiv, Ukraine (Virtual), April 19, 2021.

promising on the speed and robustness of the latter library.

While the availability of the Text file for the Quranic Arabic Corpus meant that anyone can load it into their favorite programming languages for analysis, it requires, however, heavy text processing on the Morphological Features, an advanced task for non-engineering researchers. It is, therefore, part of this project to abstract these complexities by providing intuitive high-level APIs.

Lastly, the fact that there are other libraries (*see* discussions in Section 2) dedicated for handling the Quranic datasets, simply suggests that there are growing interest for such tool, especially with the proliferation of computational approaches to *learning from the data.*

2 Related Work

There have been efforts on bringing the Qur'an into packages of a high-level languages for accessible analyses. For R language, for example, Heiss (2019) came up with the *quRan* library. The said library provides four types of datasets encoded as R data frames for the Qur'an: two in Arabic texts (with and without diacritics), and two as English translations (Saheeh International and Yusuf Ali). Each data frame contains columns describing the *descriptive* feature of the Surah or Chapter; for example, features like Surah ID, Ayah ID, Surah Title, etc.; and other indicator features like if a Sajdah is obligatory for the verse, or if it is recommended. As such, *quRan* lacks columns for Morphological Features of the Qur'an, which is useful for further analysis of the linguistic style of the said scripture.

For Python, on the other hand, Yousef et al. (2018) came up with *PyQuran*, which unlike *quRan*, this package provides extra utilities for analyses. For example, APIs for character dediacritization; Buckwalter transliteration; other functionalities like grouping letters based on its diacritics; and, search functionalities. However, like the *quRan*, *PyQuran* is not using the Quranic Arabic Corpus (Dukes and Habash, 2010), and thus lacking Morphological Features as well, which again are useful for the analysis of the linguistic style of the Qur'an, a step further than just the descriptive part.

3 Design and Implementation

QuranTree.jl is an open-souce library consisting of a set of Julia APIs for working with the Quranic Arabic Corpus (Dukes and Habash, 2010), and in this section, we are going to discuss the design and implementation of the package.

3.1 Design Philosophy

The main philosophy on the design of the QuranTree.jl, is to make it *Julia with little-else*. That is, as much as possible the package should only provide the nuts and bolts, so users won't have difficulty in learning the package and give them the opportunity to create their own wrappers for specific functionalities. Further, this philosophy should also revolve around the three main design features: *speed*, *robustness* and *modularity*.

3.2 Implementation

QuranTree.jl was implemented on top of Julia, a new general-purpose programming language with heavy emphasis on numerical and high-performance computing (Bezanson et al., 2017). There are several reasons as to why Julia was a good choice for the project, all of which are geared towards the three design features mentioned. In its core, Julia aims to solve the *two-language problem*, which describes the process where high-level languages like R and Python are often used for prototyping, and then are rewritten to low-level languages like Java and C at the operationalization stage, for optimal performance. In short, Julia aims to be as fast as C but with the friendly syntax like that of Python (or other high-level programming languages). The choice of Julia therefore addresses the first design principle, which is *speed*. Moving on, the expressive type trait of Julia makes it a good choice for creating a *robust* and *scalable* package. Note that, the type trait of Julia is optional, so Python and R users can easily skip it. Another trait of Julia is *Multiple-Dispatch*, a feature that enables users to create interface to other Julia libraries with minimal effort. This built-in feature plus the extensive Julia's interoperability packages like PyCall.jl and RCall.jl, enables QuranTree.jl to connect to other languages as well, making the package *modular*.

4 Installation

QuranTree.jl is a registered Julia package with source code available on Github[5], and can be installed in the Julia REPL as follows:

[5]`https://github.com/alstat/QuranTree.jl`

```
using Pkg
Pkg.add("QuranTree")
```

Or by pressing `]` in the said REPL and then enter `add QuranTree` to run the installation.

5 Package Features

At the time of writing, QuranTree.jl has the following features:

1. Indexing - Intuitive indexing for Chapters, Verses, Words and Parts of Words.
2. Transliteration - Buckwalter (Buckwalter, 2002) as default; has function for creating custom transliterator; and, can update transliteration in 1 line of code.
3. Morphological features - Complete type for all Morphological Features and Parts of Speech.
4. Seamless transition between Arabic and Buckwalter (or custom transliteration).
5. Simple Encoding[6]
6. Character Normalization - For both Arabic and Buckwalter (or custom transliteration).
7. Character Dediacritization - For both Arabic and Buckwalter (or custom transliteration).
8. Utilities - Function for displaying detailed description of the Morphological Features.
9. Modularity and Type-Safe - Can easily interoperate with Python (using PyCall.jl) and R (using RCall.jl) for packages that are not yet in Julia; Type-safe like JQuranTree.
10. Others - Read-only array for raw datasets (Quranic Arabic Corpus and Tanzil[7] Data).

In the following subsections, we will discuss how the design principles (*robustness*, *modularity*, and *speed*) are implemented in the package.

[6]https://corpus.quran.com/java/simpleencoding.jsp

[7]http://tanzil.net/docs/tanzil_project

5.1 *Robustness*: Morphological Features

Among the main efforts in the Quranic Arabic Corpus project, is the morphological annotation of the Qur'an down to the level of every part of every word. The definition for the tags of the Morphological Features are detailed in Dukes and Habash (2010), including the tags for Parts of Speech. In QuranTree.jl, all tags from the said article are defined as Julia's immutable `struct`s. For example, the type for Indicative and Subjunctive Verb features are express as part of a hierarchy of types shown in Figure 1. This hierarchy of types allows users to create methods for particular type or group of types. For example, methods for the parent type `AbstractVerb` are shared across all Verb types under it.

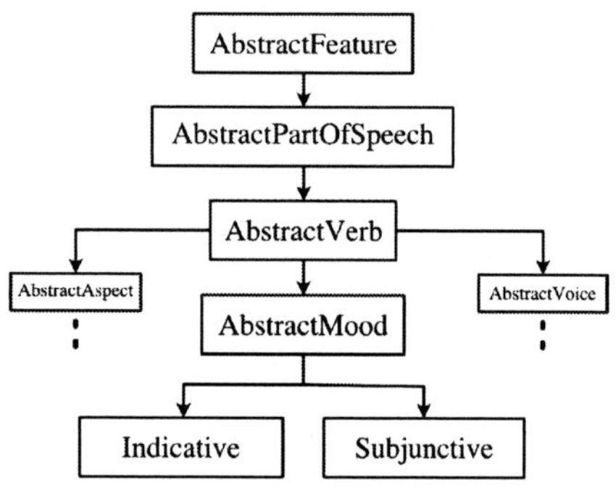

Figure 1: QuranTree.jl's Verb Mood Type Hierarchy.

These type hierarchy are useful for searching or filtering the corpus based on the Morphological Features as will be shown later. The Morphological Features in its raw form is a `String` that looks like this:

```
"STEM|POS:N|LEM:{som|ROOT:smw|M|GEN"
```

QuranTree.jl's `parse(Features, x)` parses String `x` into a Morphological Features object with `Features` as its type. This parsed input will have methods for processing the morphological annotations. For example, to check whether the parsed features is a particular Part of Speech, is done through the method `isfeature(parsed_x, Masculine)`, which checks whether the parsed features contains Masculine as part of the description of the token.

The expressive type system for the Morphological Features of the QuranTree.jl, allows users to create *robust* wrappers based on these types – something that is lacking in other high-level languages like R and Python, where both have the risks of accepting any input to any defined wrappers or functions due to lack of type capabilities, out-of-the-box.

5.2 *Modularity*: Working with NLP packages

In studying the linguistic style of the Qur'an, computationally, researchers are expected to use some Natural Language Processing algorithms. QuranTree.jl was designed to be as modular as possible to existing NLP toolkits both in Julia and other programming languages. Succeeding subsections will illustrate how to use QuranTree.jl with Julia's leading NLP toolkit (TextAnalysis.jl[8]), and how it interoperate with recently released Python's leading (in terms of features) Universal Arabic NLP toolkit, the CAMeL Tools (Obeid et al., 2020).

5.2.1 TextAnalysis.jl

TextAnalysis.jl is the leading (in terms of features) library for analyzing texts in Julia. It offers utilities for basic NLP modeling but with close integration to Flux.jl (Innes, 2018) — Julia's leading (in terms of popularity) Deep Learning library. TextAnalysis.jl is specifically useful for creating feature matrix that can later be used as input to any Machine Learning models. An example of this, is on applying TextRank on summarizing Qur'an's Chapter 18 (The Cave) detailed in QuranTree.jl's documentation[9]. TextAnalysis.jl, however, was built for general text analyses, and working with specific feature of a language is obviously a limitation. For example in Arabic, disambiguation of *all-consonants* token is a problem in itself, which does not occur in English (default language assumed in TextAnalysis.jl) or other non-Semitic languages.

5.2.2 CAMeL Tools

At the time of writing, by far, the first package to offer toolkit for Universal Arabic NLP in terms of features, is the project from New York University Abu Dhabi, known as the CAMeL Tools (Obeid et al., 2020). The said library is written in Python, and offers a suite of tools for handling and modeling Arabic texts. For example, it has methods for analyzing, generating and reinflecting a given Morphological Features of a token. The said package has functions for the following: Disambiguator, Tagger, Tokenizers, Dialectic Identification, Sentiment Analysis and Named Entity Recognization. All tailored specifically for Arabic language.

QuranTree.jl can take advantage of the Python APIs available in CAMeL Tools. This is possible with the extensive list of Julia's interoperation libraries to other languages, including Python via the package PyCall.jl. As an example, Figure 2 illustrates the disambiguation of a dediacritized *basmala*. In this figure, CAMeL APIs work seamlessly in Julia, specifically with QuranTree.jl's APIs like: `dediac`, `encode` and `normalize`.

```
[42]: using PyCall
      @pyimport camel_tools.disambig.mle as camel

[43]: mled = camel.MLEDisambiguator.pretrained()

[43]: PyObject <camel_tools.disambig.mle.MLEDisamb
      iguator object at 0x7fbc48912820>

[44]: dvrs = dediac(vrs)

[44]: "بسم ٱلله ٱلرحمن ٱلرحيم"

[45]: dis = mled.disambiguate(split(dvrs));
      out = [d[2][1][2]["diac"] for d in dis]
      out = join(out, " ")

[45]: "بِسَمّ لله الرَّحْمٰن الرَّحِيم"

[46]: encode(out)

[46]: "bisam~ All~`h AlraHom`n AlraHiym"

[47]: encode(vrs)

[47]: "bisomi {ll~ahi {lr~aHoma`ni {lr~aHiymi"

[48]: normalize(encode(vrs))

[48]: "bisomi All~ahi Alr~aHomaAni Alr~aHiymi"
```

Figure 2: CAMeL Tools' disambiguation on dediacritized *basmala*.

As shown in the figure, the simplicity of the `@pyimport` macro enables users to use Python APIs with little boilerplate. Further, this seamless interoperability allows QuranTree.jl to be modular since Julia APIs can now work well with Python APIs from the CAMeL Tools.

Needless to say, all other functionalities in CAMeL Tools not illustrated here are also accessible to QuranTree.jl.

5.3 *Speed*: Experiment

Finally, for the third design feature, we attempt to compare CAMeL Tools' APIs on transliteration and dediacritization against the QuranTree.jl's APIs. The task is to transliterate the Uthmani Corpus to Buckwalter, then dediacritized, then encode again to its Arabic form. The task was replicated

[8]https://github.com/JuliaText/TextAnalysis.jl

[9]https://alstat.github.io/QuranTree.jl/dev/man/nlp/text_summarization/

for 16 times and summarized into the following table:

Metric	CAMeL Tools	QuranTree.jl
Min	342.3ms	418.3ms
Mean	352.4ms	434.9ms
Median	350.6ms	436.2ms
Max	375.6ms	452.7ms

Table 1: Speed of CAMeL Tools vs QuranTree.jl in milliseconds (ms).

While QuranTree.jl is aimed at *speed*, at the time of writing, the transliteration and dediacritization APIs are not well optimized compared to that of CAMeL Tools, as evident in the table. Indeed, this optimization is still a work-in-progress.

6 Conclusion and Future Work

In conclusion, QuranTree.jl provides the nuts and bolts for doing Arabic text analysis for the Quranic Arabic Corpus in Julia, with the main advantage of being able to work seamlessly with existing Julia's general NLP toolkit, TextAnalysis.jl; and seamlessly interoperate with other packages outside Julia, like CAMeL Tools. This *modularity* has indeed been part of the main design principles of the package, along with the *robustness* provided by the expressive type system of Julia, and of course the inherited *speed* – still a work-in-progress for the package.

There are still room for improvements, however, given the fact that QuranTree.jl was just recently added to Julia's package registry, at the time of writing. Among the future works, the first one is the standardization of the mappings for dediacritization and normalization functionalities. Specifically, to align QuranTree.jl to JQuranTree and CAMeL Tools to avoid confusion and unnecessary adjustments; second, the binary encoding of the Text (.txt) files of the raw data in the backend; third, the development of a pure Julia library for Universal Arabic NLP, with close integration to QuranTree.jl. This is a huge effort but will indeed complete the Arabic NLP toolkit for Julia; and lastly, any suggestions to further improve the package are welcome, simply open an issue in the Github repository[10].

[10] `https://github.com/alstat/QuranTree.jl`

References

Jeff Bezanson, Alan Edelman, Stefan Karpinski, and Viral B Shah. 2017. Julia: A fresh approach to numerical computing. *SIAM review*, 59(1):65–98.

Tim Buckwalter. 2002. Buckwalter arabic morphological analyzer version 1.0. Linguistic Data Consortium, University of Pennsylvania.

Kais Dukes and Nizar Habash. 2010. Morphological annotation of quranic arabic. In *Proceedings of the International Conference on Language Resources and Evaluation, LREC 2010, 17-23 May 2010, Valletta, Malta*. European Language Resources Association.

Andrew Heiss. 2019. andrewheiss/quran: Initial cran release.

Mike Innes. 2018. Flux: Elegant machine learning with julia. *Journal of Open Source Software*, 3(25):602.

Ossama Obeid, Nasser Zalmout, Salam Khalifa, Dima Taji, Mai Oudah, Bashar Alhafni, Go Inoue, Fadhl Eryani, Alexander Erdmann, and Nizar Habash. 2020. CAMeL tools: An open source python toolkit for Arabic natural language processing. In *Proceedings of the 12th Language Resources and Evaluation Conference*, pages 7022–7032, Marseille, France. European Language Resources Association.

Waleed A. Yousef, Taha M. Madbouly, Omar M. Ibrahime, Ali H. El-Kassas, Ali O. Hassan, and Abdallah R. Albohy. 2018. Pyquran: The python package for quranic analysis. https://hci-lab.github.io/PyQuran-Private.

Automatic Romanization of Arabic Bibliographic Records

Fadhl Eryani and **Nizar Habash**
Computational Approaches to Modelling Language (CAMeL) Lab
New York University Abu Dhabi, UAE
{fadhl.eryani,nizar.habash}@nyu.edu

Abstract

International library standards require cataloguers to tediously input Romanization of their catalogue records for the benefit of library users without specific language expertise. In this paper, we present the first reported results on the task of automatic Romanization of *undiacritized* Arabic bibliographic entries. This complex task requires the modeling of Arabic phonology, morphology, and even semantics. We collected a 2.5M word corpus of parallel Arabic and Romanized bibliographic entries, and benchmarked a number of models that vary in terms of complexity and resource dependence. Our best system reaches 89.3% exact word Romanization on a blind test set. We make our data and code publicly available.

Description	Tag	Romanized Entry	Arabic Entry
Author details	100a*	Taymūr, Aḥmad,	تيمور، احمد،
	100d	1871-1930,	1871-1930،
	100e	author.	مؤلف.
Title details	245a*	Qabr al-imām al-Suyūṭī wa-taḥqīq mawḍiʻihi /	قبر الإمام السيوطي وتحقيق موضعه /
	245c*	bi-qalam al-faqīr ilayhi taʻālá Aḥmad Taymūr.	بقلم الفقير إليه تعالى أحمد تيمور.
Place of production	264a*	al-Qāhirah :	القاهرة :
	264b*	al-Maṭbaʻah al-Salafīyah wa-Maktabatuhā,	المطبعة السلفية ومكتبتها،
	264c	1346 [H.], [1927? M.]	1346 [هـ]، [1927؟ م.]
Physical description	300a	24 pages, 1 unnumbered leaf of plates :	24 صفحة، 1 ورقة لوحات غير مرقمة :
	300b	illustrations, maps	مصورات، خرائط ؛
	300c		24 سم
Subject - name	600a*	Suyūṭī,	السيوطي،
	600d	1445-1505.	1445-1505.
Subject - topic	650a	Tombs	القبور
	650z	Egypt	مصر
	650z	Cairo.	القاهرة.

Figure 1: A bibliographic record for Taymūr (1927?) in Romanized and original Arabic forms.

1 Introduction

Library catalogues comprise a large number of bibliographic records consisting of entries that provide specific descriptions of library holdings. Records for Arabic and other non-Roman-script language materials ideally include Romanized entries to help researchers without language expertise, e.g., Figure 1. There are many Romanization standards such as the ISO standards used by French and other European libraries, and the ALA-LC (American Library Association and Library of Congress) system (Library of Congress, 2017) widely adopted by North American and UK affiliated libraries. These Romanizations are applied manually by librarians across the world – a tedious error-prone task.

In this paper, we present, to our knowledge, the first reported results on automatic Romanization of *undiacritized* Arabic bibliographic entries. This is a non-trivial task as it requires modeling of Arabic phonology, morphology and even semantics. We collect and clean a 2.5M word corpus of parallel Arabic and Romanized bibliographic entries, and evaluate a number of models that vary in terms of complexity and resource dependence. Our best system reaches 89.3% exact word Romanization on a blind test set. We make our data and code publicly available for researchers in Arabic NLP.[1]

2 Related Work

Arabic Language Challenges Arabic poses a number of challenges for NLP in general, and the task of Romanization in particular. Arabic is morphologically rich, uses a number of clitics, and is written using an Abjad script with optional diacritics, all leading to a high degree of ambiguity. The Arabic script does not include features such as capitalization which is helpful for NLP in a range of Roman script languages. There are a number of enabling technologies for Arabic that can help, e.g., MADAMIRA (Pasha et al., 2014), Farasa (Abde-

[1] https://www.github.com/CAMeL-Lab/Arabic_ALA-LC_Romanization

Proceedings of the Sixth Arabic Natural Language Processing Workshop, pages 213–218
Kyiv, Ukraine (Virtual), April 19, 2021.

Split	Bib Records	Entries	Words
Train	85,952 (80%)	479,726	~2M
Dev	10,744 (10%)	59,964	~250K
Test	10,743 (10%)	59,752	~250K
Total	107,439	599,442	~2.5M

Table 1: Corpus statistics and data splits.

lali et al., 2016), and CAMeL Tools (Obeid et al., 2020). In this paper we use MADAMIRA to provide diacritics, morpheme boundaries and English gloss capitalization information as part of a rule-based Romanization technique.

Machine Transliteration *Transliteration* refers to the mapping of text from one script to another. Romanization is specifically transliteration into the Roman script (Beesley, 1997). There are many ways to transliterate and Romanize, varying in terms of detail, consistency, and usefulness. Commonly used name transliterations (Al-Onaizan and Knight, 2002) and so-called Arabizi transliteration (Darwish, 2014) tend to be lossy and inconsistent while strict orthographic transliterations such as Buckwalter's (Buckwalter, 2004) tend to be exact but not easily readable. The ALA-LC transliteration is a relatively easy to read standard that requires a lot of details on phonology, morphology and semantics. There has been a sizable amount of work on mapping Arabizi to Arabic script using a range of techniques from rules to neural models Chalabi and Gerges (2012); Darwish (2014); Al-Badrashiny et al. (2014); Guellil et al. (2017); Younes et al. (2018); Shazal et al. (2020). In this paper we make use of a number of insights and techniques from work on Arabizi-to-Arabic script transliteration, but apply them in the opposite direction to map from Arabic script to a complex, detailed and strict Romanization. We compare rule-based and corpus-based techniques including a Seq2Seq model based on the publicly available code base of Shazal et al. (2020).

3 Data Collection

Sources We collected bibliographic records from three publicly available xml dumps stored in the machine-readable cataloguing (MARC) standard, an international standard for storing and describing bibliographic information. The three data sources are the Library of Congress (LC) (10.5M), the University of Michigan (UMICH) (680K), and New York University Abu Dhabi's Arabic Collections Online (ACO) (12K), amounting to 11.2 million records in total.

Extraction From these collections, we extracted 107,493 records that are specifically tagged with the Arabic language code (MARC 008 "ara").

Filtering Within the extracted records we filter out some of the entries using two strategies. First, we used a list of 33 safe tags (determined using their definitions and with empirical sampling check) to eliminate all entries that include a mix of translations, control information, and dates. The star-marked tags in Figure 1 are all included, while the rest are filtered out. Second, we eliminated all entries with mismatched numbers of tokens. This check was done after a cleaning step that corrected for common errors and inconsistencies in many entries such as punctuation misalignment and incorrect separation of the conjunction +و *wa+*[2] 'and' clitic. As a result of this filtering, a small number of additional records are eliminated since all their entries were eliminated. The total number of retained records is 107,439. The full details on extraction and filtering are provided as part of the project's public github repo (see footnote 1).

Data Splits Finally, we split the remaining collection of records into Train, Dev, and Test sets. Details on the number of records, entries, and words they contain is presented in Table 1. We make our data and data splits available (see footnote 1).

4 Task Definition and Challenges

As discussed above, there are numerous ways to "transliterate" from one script to another. In this section we focus on the Romanization of undiacritized Arabic bibliographic entries into the ALA-LC standard. Our intention is to highlight the important challenges of this task in order to justify the design choices we make in our approaches. For a detailed reference of the ALA-LC Arabic Romanization standard, see (Library of Congress, 2012).

Phonological Challenges While Romanizing Arabic consonants is simple, the main challenge is in identifying unwritten phonological phenomena, e.g., short vowels, under-specified long vowels, consonantal gemination, and nunnation, all of which require modeling Arabic diacritization.

[2]Strict orthographic transliteration using the HSB scheme (Habash et al., 2007).

Morphosyntactic Challenges Beyond basic diacritization modeling, the task requires some morphosyntactic modeling: examples include (a) proclitics such as the definite article, prepositions and conjunctions are marked with a hyphen, (b) case endings are dropped, except before pronominal enclitics, (c) the silent Alif, appearing in some masculine plural verbal endings, is ignored, and (d) the Ta-Marbuta ending can be written as *h* or *t* depending on the morphosyntactic state of the noun. For more information on Arabic morphology, see (Habash, 2010).

Semantic Challenges Proper nouns need to be marked with capitalization on their first non-clitic alphabetic letter. Since Arabic script does not have "capitalizations", this effectively requires named-entity recognition. The Romanization of the word القاهرة *AlqAhrħ* 'Cairo' as *al-Qāhirah* in Figure 1 illustrates elements from all challenge types.

Special Cases The Arabic ALA-LC guidelines include a number of special cases, e.g., the word بن *bn* 'son of' is Romanized as *ibn*, and proper noun عمرو *ςmrw* is Romanized as *'Amr*.

5 Romanization Models

We compare multiple Romanization models built using four basic techniques with different expectation about training data availability, contextual modeling, and system complexity. The models are listed in Table 2.

CharTrans Technique Our baseline technique is an extremely simple character transliteration approach utilizing regular expressions and exception lists. This technique is built based on the ALA-LC guidelines, and is inspired by the work of Biadsy et al. (2009); it comprises 104 regex, 13 exceptions, and one capitalization rule (for entry-initial words). This technique accepts diacritized, undiacritized or partially diacritized input. Model **Rules Simple** uses CharTrans only.

MorphTrans Technique This technique relies on the morphological disambiguation system MADAMIRA (Pasha et al., 2014) to provide diacritization, morpheme boundaries, POS tags and English glosses for the Arabic input. Morpheme boundaries are used to identify clitic hyphenation points. POS tags and capitalization in English glosses are used to decide on what to capitalize in the transliteration. We strip diacritical morphological case endings, but keep other diacritics. We utilize the CharTrans technique to finalize the Romanization starting with the diacritized, hyphenated and capitalization marked words. For words unknown to the morphological analyzer, we simply back off to the CharTrans technique. Model **Rules Morph** uses MorphTrans with CharTrans backoff.

MLE Technique Unlike the previous two techniques, MLE (maximum likelihood estimate) relies on the parallel training data we presented in Section 3. This simple technique works on white-space and punctuation tokenized entries and learns simple one-to-one mapping from Arabic script to Romanization. The most common Romanization for a particular Arabic script input in the training data is used. The outputs are detokenized to allow strict matching alignment with the input. Faced with OOV (out of vocabulary), we back off to the MorphTrans technique (Model **MLE Morph**) or CharTrans Technique (Model **MLE Simple**). In Table 2, we also study the performance of **MLE Simple** with different corpus sizes.

Seq2Seq Technique Our last technique also relies on existing training data. We use an encoder-decoder character-level sequence-to-sequence architecture closely following Shazal et al. (2020) (although in reverse direction).

The encoder consists of two gated recurrent unit (GRU) layers (Cho et al., 2014) with only the first layer being bidirectional, and the decoder has two GRUs with attention (Luong et al., 2015). For the input, we used character embeddings concatenated with embeddings of the words in which the characters appear. For all other setting details, see Shazal et al. (2020)'s Line2Line model. We also show how **Seq2Seq** performs with different corpus sizes in Table 2.

The Seq2Seq technique is known for occasionally dropping tokens, which in our case leads to misalignment with the Arabic input. To handle this issue in model **Seq2Seq**, we align its output and fill such gaps using the outputs produced by three other techniques, thus creating models **Seq2Seq+Rules Morph**, **Seq2Seq+MLE Simple**, and **Seq2Seq+MLE Morph**. The alignment technique we use relies on minimizing character-edit distance between present words to identify missing ones.

Model	Corpus Size	Morph Trans	Char Trans	Dev Exact	Dev CI	Dev CPI	Test Exact	Test CI	Test CPI
Rules Simple	0		✓	16.2	17.4	17.8	16.1	17.3	17.7
Rules Morph	0	✓	✓	67.4	83.5	84.8	67.4	83.6	84.9
MLE Simple 1/64	31K		✓	63.6	69.8	71.1			
MLE Simple 1/32	63K		✓	68.5	75.1	76.4			
MLE Simple 1/16	125K		✓	73.0	79.9	81.3			
MLE Simple 1/8	250K		✓	75.6	82.8	84.2			
MLE Simple 1/4	500K		✓	80.3	87.2	88.6			
MLE Simple 1/2	1M		✓	82.7	89.5	90.9			
MLE Simple	2M		✓	84.0	90.7	92.1	84.1	90.8	92.2
MLE Morph	2M	✓	✓	84.7	91.6	93.0	84.8	91.7	**93.2**
Seq2Seq 1/64	31K			6.3	7.5	10.2			
Seq2Seq 1/32	63K			28.3	31.0	38.1			
Seq2Seq 1/16	125K			64.9	69.1	70.5			
Seq2Seq 1/8	250K			75.5	79.6	80.9			
Seq2Seq 1/4	500K			82.5	85.8	87.1			
Seq2Seq 1/2	1M			85.9	88.6	90.1			
Seq2Seq	2M			87.2	89.7	90.9	87.3	89.8	91.0
Seq2Seq + Rules Morph	2M	✓	✓	88.8	91.6	92.9	88.9	91.7	93.0
Seq2Seq + MLE Simple	2M		✓	**89.2**	**91.8**	**93.1**	**89.3**	**91.9**	**93.2**
Seq2Seq + MLE Morph	2M	✓	✓	**89.2**	**91.8**	**93.1**	**89.3**	**91.9**	**93.2**

Table 2: Dev and Test Romanization word accuracy (%). (CI = case-insensitive, and CPI = case and punctuation-insensitive)

Comparing the Techniques The CharTrans and MorphTrans techniques do not need parallel data, while the MLE and Seq2Seq techniques do. Furthermore, the MorphTrans and Seq2Seq techniques make use of available context: in MorphTrans, we use context-aware monolingual morphological disambiguation; and in Seq2Seq we model parallel examples in context. In contrast, neither the MLE technique nor the CharTrans technique use the context of the words being mapped.

6 Experimental Results

Table 2 presents the Dev and Test results for the models discussed in the previous section. All results are in terms of three word accuracy metrics: exact match (Exact), case-insensitive match (CI), and case and punctuation-insensitive match (CPI).

The **Rules Simple** baseline manages to correctly produce an exact answer in close to 1/6th of all the cases. **Rules Morph**, which uses no training data, misses about 1/3rd of all exact transliteration matches; however, about half of the errors are from capitalization issues.

The **MLE Simple** with 2M words cuts the error from Rules Morph by 51% (Exact) and 44% (CI). Notably **Rules Morph** outperforms **MLE Simple** with 31K words in Exact match, and **MLE Simple** with 250K words in CI match.

The **MLE Morph** model improves over **MLE Simple** by ~1% absolute in all metrics (5% and 10% error reduction in Exact and CI, respectively).

The **Seq2Seq** model outperforms the **MLE Morph** model by 2.5% absolute (16% error reduction) in Exact match, but under-performs in CI match. The **Seq2Seq** performance is comparatively much poorer with less data. With 31K words, **MLE Simple**'s performance is 10 times better than **Seq2Seq**; and their performance only becomes comparable with 250K words.

We observe that ~2% of the **Seq2Seq** output words are missing, contributing negatively to the system's results. Of the three models that address this issue through alignment and combination, **Seq2Seq+Rules Morph**, **Seq2Seq+MLE Simple**, and **Seq2Seq+MLE Morph**, the last two using the MLE technique are the best performers overall in Exact match. It's noteworthy that in CPI match, **MLE Morph**'s performance is almost equivalent to the best systems' performance.

Error Type		Counts	Source	Prediction	Target
Gold 52	**Romanization**	34	إبراهيم	Ibrāhīm	Ibrāhim
			الأشقر	al-Ashqar	Ashqar
			ندوات	Nadawāt	Nadwāt
	Alignment	8	أحمد بو حسن.	Aḥmad Bū Ḥasan.	Bū Ḥasan, Aḥmad.
	Source	5	الطبع	al-Ṭab‘	al-Ṭab‘ah
	Translation	5	شعر.	shi‘r.	Poems.
System 48	**Romanization**	36	الريف	al-Rayf	al-rīf
			حدث	ḥadath	Ḥaddatha
			خسارة،	Khassārah,	Khasārah.
	Hallucination	10	الادارية.	Taṣal-Idārīyah.	al-Idārīyah.
	Valid variant	2	السوفياتي	al-Sūfyātī	al-Sūfiyātī

Table 3: Error types, counts, and examples on a sample of 100 **Seq2Seq+MLE Morph** predictions.

The CPI metric values are consistently higher than CI by ∼1.3% absolute for all models.

Blind test results presented in the right hand side of Table 2 are consistent with Dev results.

7 Error Analysis

We classified a sample of 100 word errors (ignoring capitalization and punctuation) from the Dev set of our best performing model (**Seq2Seq+MLE Morph**). Our classification results are presented in Table 3 along with representative examples.

Gold Errors We found 52 gold errors, where the human-provided target reference is incorrect. Romanization errors such as typos, incorrect vowelization, and dropped definite articles, constitute roughly 65% of gold errors. The rest of the errors include issues such as first and last name flipping which we classify as an alignment issue, Arabic input source typos, and errors in which the target is a translation instead of a Romanization. Notably, we observe that our **Seq2Seq+MLE Morph** model generates correct predictions for 85% of all gold error cases.

System Errors Romanization errors make up 75% of system errors. The vast majority of these mistakes are due to wrong prediction of vowels or gemination. An additional 21% of the errors is due to Seq2Seq model hallucinations of characters unsupported by the source input. We also encountered 2 predictions that did not match the target reference but are correct variants. In ∼44% of system error cases, outputs generated by the **MLE Morph** or **Rules Morph** models are in fact correct, but were not chosen during alignment and combination because of existing Seq2Seq answers.

8 Conclusions and Future Work

We presented a new task for Arabic NLP, namely the Romanization of Arabic bibliographic records. Our extracted corpus and benchmark data splits, as well as our code base will be publicly available.

In the future, we plan to create an online Romanization interface to assist librarians. As more data is created efficiently, better models can be created.

We also plan to exploit the latent annotations in bibliographic records for improving Arabic NLP tools, e.g. using vowelization for automatic diacritization and possible morphological disambiguation (Habash et al., 2016), marked clitics for tokenization, and Roman-script capitalization for Arabic named entity recognition.

Acknowledgments

This work was carried out on the High Performance Computing resources at New York University Abu Dhabi (NYUAD). We thank Salam Khalifa, Ossama Obeid, Justin Parrott, and Alexandra Provo for helpful conversations. And we especially thank Elie Kahale for introducing us to this interesting challenge during the Winter Institute in Digital Humanities at NYUAD.

References

Ahmed Abdelali, Kareem Darwish, Nadir Durrani, and Hamdy Mubarak. 2016. Farasa: A fast and furious segmenter for Arabic. In *Proceedings of the Conference of the North American Chapter of the Association for Computational Linguistics (NAACL)*, pages 11–16, San Diego, California.

Mohamed Al-Badrashiny, Ramy Eskander, Nizar Habash, and Owen Rambow. 2014. Automatic transliteration of romanized Dialectal Arabic. In *Proceedings of the Conference on Computational Natural Language Learning (CoNLL)*, pages 30–38, Ann Arbor, Michigan.

Yaser Al-Onaizan and Kevin Knight. 2002. Machine Transliteration of Names in Arabic Text. In *Proceedings of the Workshop on Computational Approaches to Semitic Languages (CASL)*.

Kenneth R. Beesley. 1997. Romanization, Transcription and Transliteration. Http://www.xrce.xerox.com/Research-Development/Historical-projects/Linguistic-Demos/Arabic-Morphological-Analysis-and-Generation/Romanization-Transcription-and-Transliteration.

Fadi Biadsy, Nizar Habash, and Julia Hirschberg. 2009. Improving the Arabic Pronunciation Dictionary for Phone and Word Recognition with Linguistically-Based Pronunciation Rules. In *Proceedings of the Conference of the North American Chapter of the Association for Computational Linguistics (NAACL)*, pages 397–405, Boulder, Colorado.

Tim Buckwalter. 2004. Buckwalter Arabic Morphological Analyzer Version 2.0. LDC catalog number LDC2004L02, ISBN 1-58563-324-0.

Achraf Chalabi and Hany Gerges. 2012. Romanized Arabic transliteration. In *Proceedings of the Second Workshop on Advances in Text Input Methods*, pages 89–96, Mumbai, India. The COLING 2012 Organizing Committee.

Kyunghyun Cho, Bart van Merriënboer, Çağlar Gülçehre, Dzmitry Bahdanau, Fethi Bougares, Holger Schwenk, and Yoshua Bengio. 2014. Learning phrase representations using rnn encoder–decoder for statistical machine translation. In *Proceedings of the Conference on Empirical Methods in Natural Language Processing (EMNLP)*, pages 1724–1734, Doha, Qatar.

Kareem Darwish. 2014. Arabizi Detection and Conversion to Arabic. In *Proceedings of the Workshop for Arabic Natural Language Processing (WANLP)*, pages 217–224, Doha, Qatar.

Imane Guellil, cal Azouaou Fai Mourad Abbas, and Fatiha Sadat. 2017. Arabizi transliteration of Algerian Arabic dialect into Modern Standard Arabic. In *Social MT 2017/First workshop on social media and user generated content machine translation*.

Nizar Habash, Anas Shahrour, and Muhamed Al-Khalil. 2016. Exploiting Arabic diacritization for high quality automatic annotation. In *Proceedings of the Tenth International Conference on Language Resources and Evaluation (LREC'16)*, pages 4298–4304, Portorož, Slovenia. European Language Resources Association (ELRA).

Nizar Habash, Abdelhadi Soudi, and Tim Buckwalter. 2007. On Arabic Transliteration. In A. van den Bosch and A. Soudi, editors, *Arabic Computational Morphology: Knowledge-based and Empirical Methods*, pages 15–22. Springer, Netherlands.

Nizar Y Habash. 2010. *Introduction to Arabic natural language processing*. Morgan & Claypool Publishers.

Library of Congress. 2012. Arabic Romanization Table. `https://www.loc.gov/catdir/cpso/romanization/arabic.pdf`.

Library of Congress. 2017. ALA-LC Romanization Tables. `https://www.loc.gov/catdir/cpso/roman.html`.

Thang Luong, Hieu Pham, and Christopher Manning. 2015. Effective approaches to attention-based neural machine translation. In *Proceedings of the Conference on Empirical Methods in Natural Language Processing (EMNLP)*, pages 1412–1421, Lisbon, Portugal.

Ossama Obeid, Nasser Zalmout, Salam Khalifa, Dima Taji, Mai Oudah, Bashar Alhafni, Go Inoue, Fadhl Eryani, Alexander Erdmann, and Nizar Habash. 2020. CAMeL tools: An open source python toolkit for Arabic natural language processing. In *Proceedings of the 12th Language Resources and Evaluation Conference*, pages 7022–7032, Marseille, France. European Language Resources Association.

Arfath Pasha, Mohamed Al-Badrashiny, Mona Diab, Ahmed El Kholy, Ramy Eskander, Nizar Habash, Manoj Pooleery, Owen Rambow, and Ryan Roth. 2014. MADAMIRA: A fast, comprehensive tool for morphological analysis and disambiguation of Arabic. In *Proceedings of the Language Resources and Evaluation Conference (LREC)*, pages 1094–1101, Reykjavik, Iceland.

Ali Shazal, Aiza Usman, and Nizar Habash. 2020. A unified model for Arabizi detection and transliteration using sequence-to-sequence models. In *Proceedings of the Fifth Arabic Natural Language Processing Workshop*, pages 167–177, Barcelona, Spain (Online). Association for Computational Linguistics.

Ahmad Taymūr. 1927? Qabr al-imām al-Suyūṭī wa-taḥqīq mawḍiʿihi. Arabic Collections Online: `http://hdl.handle.net/2333.1/m37pvs4b`.

Jihene Younes, Emna Souissi, Hadhemi Achour, and Ahmed Ferchichi. 2018. A sequence-to-sequence based approach for the double transliteration of Tunisian dialect. *Procedia Computer Science*, 142:238 – 245. Arabic Computational Linguistics.

SERAG: Semantic Entity Retrieval from Arabic knowledge Graphs

Saher Esmeir
Bloomberg L.P.
London, United Kingdom
sesmeir2@bloomberg.net

Abstract

Knowledge graphs (KGs) are widely used to store and access information about entities and their relationships. Given a query, the task of entity retrieval from a KG aims at presenting a ranked list of entities relevant to the query. Lately, an increasing number of models for entity retrieval have shown a significant improvement over traditional methods. These models, however, were developed for English KGs. In this work, we build on one such system, named KEWER, to propose SERAG (Semantic Entity Retrieval from Arabic knowledge Graphs). Like KEWER, SERAG uses random walks to generate entity embeddings. DBpedia-Entity v2 is considered the standard test collection for entity retrieval. We discuss the challenges of using it for non-English languages in general and Arabic in particular. We provide an Arabic version of this standard collection, and use it to evaluate SERAG. SERAG is shown to significantly outperform the popular BM25 model thanks to its multi-hop reasoning.

1 Introduction

Recent years have witnessed a rapid growth in the use of KGs. Both large-scale graphs that connect millions of entities through billions of relationships and smaller domain-specific KGs have become widely available. One way to access the information stored in KGs is through a dedicated query language, such as SPARQL. This, however, requires proficiency with the syntax of the language and knowledge of the exact schema of the database. Given a query in natural language, the task of entity retrieval aims at presenting a ranked list of entities relevant to the query. Consider, for example, the query "museums in Arab capitals". Figure 1 shows how the subgraph around the entity *E3*, labelled "Egyptian Museum", supports its relevance to the query. This complex, indirect relationship is not represented textually in any single document.

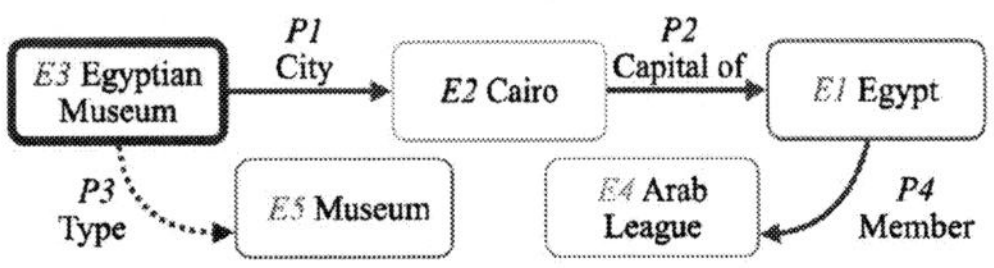

Figure 1: Given the query "museums in Arab capitals", the relevance of the entity *E3* (Egyptian Museum) is supported by the information along two paths.

The current standard test collection for entity search is DBpedia-Entity v2 (DEv2). It is provided with the performance results of a dozen baseline methods (Hasibi et al., 2017). Lately, Nikolaev and Kotov (2020) presented KEWER, a system that significantly outperformed previous methods on DEv2. KEWER, nevertheless, was developed for and tested on English KGs. In this work, we build on it and propose SERAG,[1] a method for **S**emantic **E**ntity **R**etreival from **A**rabic knowledge **G**raphs. To evaluate SERAG, we create and share a Modern Standard Arabic (MSA) version of DEv2. To our knowledge, this is the first attempt to offer DEv2 in a non-English language. SERAG is shown to perform well on Arabic DEv2 and to significantly improve on the classic BM25 retriever.

Contributions The notable contributions of this work are: (1) introducing a new Arabic test collection for entity retrieval by translating queries from DEv2 and leveraging DBpedia's inter-language links,[2] and (2) proposing a method for entity retrieval from Arabic KGs and evaluating it on the new test collection.

2 Background and Related Work

There are several attempts in literature to define KGs (Ehrlinger and Wöß, 2016; Fensel et al., 2020).

[1] سراج (sirāj) is Arabic for a lantern.

[2] The translated queries and usage directions can be found at https://doi.org/10.5281/zenodo.4560653.

Proceedings of the Sixth Arabic Natural Language Processing Workshop, pages 219–225
Kyiv, Ukraine (Virtual), April 19, 2021.

In this work, we follow Färber et al. (2018) and view a KG as a finite set of RDF triples in the form of subject-predicate-object (s, p, o).

Graph Embedding Graph embeddings transform nodes and edges into a low dimension vector space while preserving structural information, an idea that was adopted from language modeling. Cai et al. (2018) survey various graph embedding methods. These methods, however, focus on the relational structure of the graph and do not leverage the information present in the surface forms of entities and predicates. Consider again the graph in Figure 1. *P1* links *E3* and *E2*, but there is additional information in the labels attached to those.

Entity Retrieval Since the introduction of DEv2, several works have reported significant progress on entity retrieval. Naseri et al. (2018) explored enriching entity representations using information from related entities. Kadilierakis et al. (2020) adapted Elasticsearch[3] for supporting keyword search over RDF datasets. Gerritse et al. (2020) studied utilizing Wikipedia2Vec (Yamada et al., 2020) for entity reranking. Nikolaev and Kotov (2020) proposed KEWER, a system that employs joint word and entity embeddings to rank entities. KEWER was evaluated on DEv2 but can be applied to any KG and does not require a large textual corpus.

Question Answering (QA) QA systems are concerned with automatically providing answers to natural language questions. Such systems have been integrated in search engines and virtual assistants. Answers may be constructed by querying a structured database or pulled from an unstructured collection of documents. Inspired by DrQa (Chen et al., 2017), Mozannar et al. (2019) presented SOQAL, a system for open domain factual Arabic QA using Wikipedia. SOQAL was evaluated on two novel datasets: Arabic Reading Comprehension Dataset and a machine translated version of Stanford QA Dataset. Samy et al. (2019) overview the work done in Arabic QA and recommend tools and linguistic resources for future systems.

Question Answering over Knowledge Graphs A special case of QA is KGQA, where the information source is a KG. Unlike entity retrieval, the input for a KGQA system must be structured as a question, and the output is typically one or more answers formed as text. Chakraborty et al. (2019) provides a recent survey on neural methods for KGQA. Abu Taha (2015) and Albarghothi et al. (2017) designed systems for domain specific Arabic KGQA. The tasks of entity retrieval and KGQA may overlap when the query is a question, and the relevant answers are named entities from a KG. DEv2, our chosen test collection, has a category focusing on this special case.

3 Dataset

Queries DEv2 consists of 467 natural language queries, each with a list of DBpedia entities, scored based on relevance (0: irrelevant, 1: relevant, and 2: highly relevant). The scores are collected using crowdsourcing. In total, there are 49280 query-entity pairs. Table 1 details the four different groups the queries are categorized into. The set creators also offer a "stopped" version[4] which includes the same queries, with stop patterns and punctuation marks removed. Similarly to previous works, we use the stopped version.

DBpedia DBpedia provides structured content from the information available on Wikipedia. The test collection is based on DBpedia version 2015-10, released in 2016.[5] The English edition describes 6.2M entities, of which 4.6M have abstracts (required by DEv2), and has 1.1B RDF triples.

DBpedia Arabic An Arabic chapter was added to DBpedia in 2015.[6] Ismail et al. (2016) introduced an Arabic endpoint for the chapter and provided a comparison between the Arabic and English editions. While there are later releases, we restrict ourselves to the same release as DEv2 due to the time sensitivity of some queries. The number of entities with abstracts in the Arabic chapter of 2015-10 is 368K (8% of the English chapter). This reflects the gap in coverage between the English and corresponding Arabic editions of Wikipedia. The gap has narrowed since and is expected to narrow further thanks to the increasing popularity of Wikipedia Arabic and to the efforts by the Wikimedia Foundation (Redi et al., 2021).

DBPedia Arabic Challenges Prior to its release, several works identified challenges in the path towards an Arabic DBpedia (Al-Feel, 2013; Bahanshal and Al-Khalifa, 2013). Lakshen et al. (2018)

[3] https://www.elastic.co

[4] https://github.com/iai-group/DBpedia-Entity

[5] http://wiki.dbpedia.org/datasets

[6] http://wiki.dbpedia.org/join/chapters

Category	Description	Example	#queries	#Arabic
SemSearch-ES	Named entity queries	brooklyn bridge	113	7
INEX-LD	IR-style keyword queries	electronic music genres	99	23
QALD2	Natural language questions	Who is the mayor of Berlin?	140	56
ListSearch	Seek a particular list of entities	Campuses of Indiana University	115	53

Table 1: Query categories in DEv2 and in Arabic DEv2.

discuss challenges in quality assessment of DBpedia Arabic and list issues regarding accuracy, consistency, and relevancy. When working with the DBpedia files, we apply standard text preprocessing, similar to Obeid et al. (2020) and Mohammad et al. (2017). We also replace all instances of Farsi Ye with Arabic Yā'.[7] Finally, and due to the inconsistent use of the definite article "al", we remove it from the beginning of words. Prior to retrieval, we apply the same preprocessing to the queries.

Searching DBpedia Arabic vs. English Given the challenges and smaller coverage of Arabic DBpedia, an alternative would be to translate queries from Arabic into English, search the English KG and map the retrieved entities to Arabic ones using DBpedia's inter-language links. While this approach may work for some tasks, we view it as limited. At least 30% of DBpedia Arabic entities do not have a counterpart in English and capture unique information of high interest to Arabic users. Furthermore, while Wikipedia English allows only one article per entry, content across chapters varies. The availability of other sources and the different points of view mean that Arabic articles are not necessarily a direct translation of English ones. They may include additional or conflicting information.[8] Forcing a search through English content prevents utilization of this diversity and richness. Finally, our aim in this work is to provide a solution for entity retrieval from any Arabic KG, not only the ones that have an English edition.

Entity Coverage For each query, DEv2 provides a list of relevant and irrelevant entities, obtained through pooling and crowdsourcing. It does not, therefore, guarantee coverage of all relevant entities, and no system will be rewarded for ranking high a relevant but unjudged entity. This problem is

```
<http://ar.dbpedia.org/resource/ابن_خلدون>
<http://www.w3.org/2002/07/owl#sameAs>
<http://dbpedia.org/resource/Ibn_Khaldun>
```

Figure 2: Entity mapping in DBpedia.

exacerbated when mapping entities across chapters.

Arabic DEv2 Entities Because we wanted to keep the relevance scores provided in DEv2, we used DBpedia's inter-language files to programmatically map English entity IDs to their Arabic counterparts. Figure 2 demonstrates how the mapping between the English and Arabic entities of Ibn Khaldun is defined. Once mapped, English entities were not used for retrieval or ranking, and SERAG only relied on the Arabic graph. Due to lower coverage, however, many entities were not mapped. Out of the 16700 relevant entities, only 3025 were successfully mapped to Arabic and a large number of queries did not have a single mapped relevant entity. A query is included in Arabic DEv2 if the number of Arabic relevant entities is at least 10, or if at least half of the relevant entities were mapped. Consequentially, Arabic DEv2 consists of 139 queries. Table 1 shows the number of queries in each category of the Arabic set.

Query Translation Considerations Having chosen the queries, the next step is translation to Arabic. We opted for human translation by native Arabic speakers in our organization, rather than machine translation (MT). Many of the queries are not necessarily structured as valid sentences and present a challenge to MT.[9] We wanted the queries in Arabic to be as close as possible to English, including (mis)structure. Furthermore, MT would have presented a significant gender bias. Arabic uses gender-specific terms, while MT is designed to generate a single output text. Even if a translation model is debiased, a query with a single gender term will result in biased

[7]The two look identical when connected ـيـ, but have different Unicode values.

[8]Consider, for example, the popular dish "Mujaddara". As of Jan 2021, its place of origin according to the the Arabic article is "Mashriq" but "Persia or India" in the English one.

[9]For example, query INEX_LD-2012327: "Beloved author African-American Nobel Prize Literature".

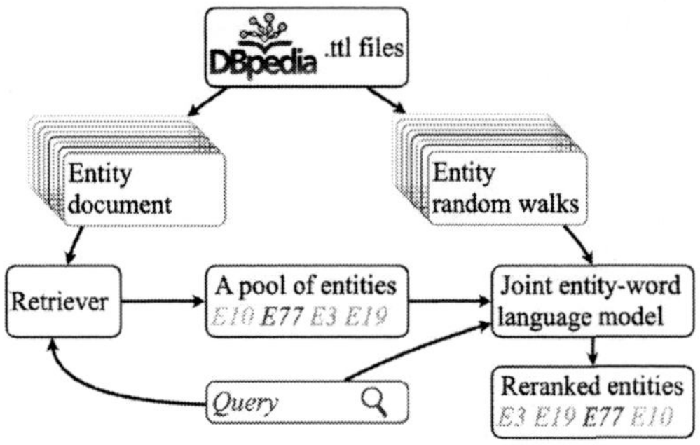

Figure 3: Entity retrieval and re-ranking framework

```
<http://ar.dbpedia.org/resource/المتحف_المصري>
<http://ar.dbpedia.org/property/مدينة>
<http://ar.dbpedia.org/resource/القاهرة>
<http://ar.dbpedia.org/property/العاصمة>
<http://ar.dbpedia.org/resource/مصر>
--------------------------------------------
المتحف المصري مدينة
<http://ar.dbpedia.org/property/القاهرة>
العاصمة مصر
```

Figure 4: A sample random walk (top) and its corresponding generated sentence (bottom). Some, but not all, of the IDs are replaced with their surface form.

retrieval. Habash et al. (2019) proposed to extend MT's output with gender-specific re-inflections. We believe their work is very promising, but it is currently limited to first-person sentences. To avoid such bias, our translators were asked to concatenate both forms where relevant. This, however, comes at a price: the queries are less natural and the duplication may introduce a new bias. An alternative approach, which we plan to explore in future work, is to choose one form at random and rely on the retriever to escape gender bias by leveraging morphological analyzers and language models.

4 Method

SERAG, our proposed framework for Arabic entity retrieval, is inspired by KEWER. As illustrated in Figure 3, for each entity, DBpedia is used to generate (1) a document formed of directly linked textual information (recipe provided with DEv2), and (2) a set of random walks starting at that entity. Given a query, BM25 scores entities based on the relevance of their documents to the query. It does not, however, utilize information about the graph structure or entities indirectly connected.

To enhance the ranking, a word2vec (Mikolov et al., 2013) model is built using the random walks. Each walk consists of entities and predicates along a path in the Arabic DBpedia graph. Entities appear in their entity ID form (e.g., E3) with a probability p and replaced with their surface form (e.g., Egyptian Museum[10]) otherwise. Each walk is considered a sentence and all sentences are concatenated into one corpus, used to train the word2vec model. Hence, the vocabulary of the model includes both words and entity IDs. Figure 4 illustrates how random walks and sentences are formed.

We use a standard, two-stage ranking approach: given a query q, we first select 1000 entities using BM25, then we rerank them using embeddings. Let e be an entity retrieved by BM25, v_e its embedding, and v_q the embedding of q. The final score of e with respect to q is based on a mix of its BM25 score and the embeddings' cosine similarity:

$$MM(q,e) = \beta \cdot \cos(v_q, v_e) + (1-\beta) \cdot BM25(e)$$

In our implementation, we modified KEWER's code to allow for Arabic KGs. To keep everything in Python, we reimplemented the document generator and used gensim (Řehůřek and Sojka, 2010) for BM25. While KEWER also uses BM25F (Zhiltsov et al., 2015), a fielded version of BM25, in this work we only consider BM25. KEWER tunes the parameters of BM25 and β, the mixture weight, using a 5-fold split. Our data, however, is prohibitively small. Therefore, SERAG is tested in an unsupervised setup using the default values of gensim, a fixed $\beta = 0.9$, chosen to give random walks a higher impact, and the default values KEWER uses for the number of walks (100), their length (10), and p (0.1). We are confident that SERAG will benefit from parameter tuning and hope to include it when a larger dataset becomes available.

5 Experiments and Discussion

The evaluation metric of DEv2 is Normalized Discounted Cumulative Gain (nDCG) at ranks 10 and 100. Table 2 compares the performance of BM25 and SERAG. SERAG yields better results across all categories. In total, its advantage is found to be statistically significant (paired t-test with $\alpha = 0.05$).

In Section 3 we noted that DEv2 in general, and Arabic DEv2 in particular, do not offer judgements for all relevant entities. Buckley and Voorhees (2004) introduced bpref, a retrieval measure designed specifically for incomplete judgment sets.

[10]SERAG uses the Arabic surface form: المتحف المصري

	nDCG@10		nDCG@100	
Cat	**BM25**	**SERAG**	**BM25**	**SERAG**
Sem	0.186	**0.324**	0.321	**0.463**⋆
INEX	0.215	**0.284**⋆	0.293	**0.365**⋆
QALD	0.149	**0.198**⋆	0.213	**0.267**⋆
List	0.174	**0.216**⋆	0.256	**0.293**⋆
Total	0.172	**0.226**⋆	0.248	**0.303**⋆

Table 2: Normalized Discounted Cumulative Gain. Best results are in **bold**. ⋆ indicates a statistically significant improvements (paired t-test with $\alpha = 0.05$).

It only considers the relative ranks of relevant and nonrelevant judged entities. We applied bpref to the first 10 and 100 retrieved entities. In both cases, SERAG outperformed BM25 (0.17 vs. 0.142 for top 10 and 0.336 vs. 0.314 for top 100). To the best of our knowledge, bpref has not been used to evaluate English DEv2 systems.

Query Analysis To demonstrate the effectiveness of SERAG, we analyze several sample queries. Consider query `SemSearch_LS-50` "wonders of the ancient world". Of the highly relevant entities (score 2), BM25 ranks only one in the top 10, namely "Hanging Gardens of Babylon" (ranked 8th). SEARG ranks this entity higher (3rd) and also lists "Temple of Artemis" as 10th. Other highly relevant entities outside the top 10 were also ranked higher by SERAG. "Great Pyramid of Giza", for instance, was ranked 30th by SERAG and 59th by BM25. As another example, consider query `INEX_LD-2012383` "famous computer scientists disappeared at sea". In this case there is only one relevant entity, namely "Jim Gray (computer scientist)". SERAG ranks it first, while BM25 ranks it 5th.

Arabic DEv2 Challenges Compared to the results reported in literature for English DEv2, Arabic DEv2 proved to be more challenging, and the retrieval effectiveness, as measured by nDCG, was generally lower. Recall the query "wonders of the ancient world". While SERAG listed only two highly relevant entities in the top 10, KEWER listed five, including, for example, "Great Pyramid of Giza". Overall, for about a third of the queries, both BM25 and SERAG failed to rank a relevant entity in the top 10. We believe this is because:

- As discussed in Section 3, Arabic DBpedia is much smaller. Some relevant information is missing or mismapped.
- Arabic's morphological richness presents a challenge to NLP in general and IR in particular (Habash, 2010; Shaalan et al., 2018). This richness leads to MSA verbs with upwards of 5,400 forms, making the task of word-level representation extremely difficult.
- Diacritics are typically omitted in Wikipedia, resulting in morphological ambiguity.[11] Fadel et al. (2019) proposed Translation over Diacritization to assist NLP tasks in such cases.
- Inconsistent choices of synonyms make retrieval much harder. For example, Nobel prize winners are referred to in three ways.[12]
- Spelling of named entities vary. For instance, Google is transcribed in three forms.[13]
- DEv2 was created for English DBpedia. In the pooling stage, entities were obtained using runs of previous methods, optimized for English documents. In the crowdsourcing stage, annotators only considered English content.

6 Conclusions

There has been significant progress in offering tools and resources for Arabic NLP applications. In this work, we addressed the task of entity retrieval from an Arabic KG. Our contribution is twofold. We introduced an Arabic version of DEv2, the standard test collection for entity retrieval and then proposed SERAG, a system for end-to-end entity retrieval from Arabic KGs.

We believe Arabic DEv2 can already be used as a benchmark for KG entity retrieval. It is, however, only the first step. We hope to collaborate with the community to expand both the queries and relevant entities. A fresher dump of Wikipedia Arabic should be considered in order to increase coverage. We also plan to translate the collection to other languages and create a multi-lingual set.

While SERAG was shown to improve over BM25, we observed that Arabic entity retrieval faced unique challenges. To address those, we plan to employ the recently introduced Arabic NLP toolkit (Obeid et al., 2020) and utilize pretrained language models such as ArabicBert (Safaya et al., 2020) and AraBert (Antoun et al., 2020).

[11] The word عقد, for instance, can take over a dozen combinations of diacritics, each with multiple meanings.

[12] حاصلون، حائزون، فائزون

[13] جوجل، غوغل، قوقل

References

Alaa W. Abu Taha. 2015. An ontology-based arabic question answering system submitted. Master's thesis, Faculty of Information Technology, Islamic University of Gaza.

Haytham Al-Feel. 2013. A step towards the arabic dbpedia. *International Journal of Computer Applications*, 80:27–33.

Ali Albarghothi, Feras Khater, and Khaled Shaalan. 2017. Arabic question answering using ontology. *Procedia Computer Science*, 117:183–191.

Wissam Antoun, Fady Baly, and Hazem Hajj. 2020. AraBERT: Transformer-based model for Arabic language understanding. In *Proceedings of the 4th Workshop on Open-Source Arabic Corpora and Processing Tools, with a Shared Task on Offensive Language Detection*, pages 9–15, Marseille, France. European Language Resource Association.

Alia O. Bahanshal and Hend S. Al-Khalifa. 2013. Toward recipes for arabic dbpedia. In *Proceedings of International Conference on Information Integration and Web-Based Applications & Services*, IIWAS '13, pages 331–335, New York, NY, USA. Association for Computing Machinery.

Chris Buckley and Ellen M. Voorhees. 2004. Retrieval evaluation with incomplete information. In *Proceedings of the 27th Annual International ACM SIGIR Conference on Research and Development in Information Retrieval*, SIGIR '04, pages 25–32, New York, NY, USA. Association for Computing Machinery.

H. Cai, V. W. Zheng, and K. Chang. 2018. A comprehensive survey of graph embedding: Problems, techniques, and applications. *IEEE Transactions on Knowledge & Data Engineering*, 30(09):1616–1637.

Nilesh Chakraborty, D. Lukovnikov, Gaurav Maheshwari, Priyansh Trivedi, Jens Lehmann, and Asja Fischer. 2019. Introduction to neural network based approaches for question answering over knowledge graphs. *ArXiv*, abs/1907.09361.

Danqi Chen, Adam Fisch, Jason Weston, and Antoine Bordes. 2017. Reading Wikipedia to answer open-domain questions. In *Proceedings of the 55th Annual Meeting of the Association for Computational Linguistics (Volume 1: Long Papers)*, pages 1870–1879, Vancouver, Canada. Association for Computational Linguistics.

Lisa Ehrlinger and Wolfram Wöß. 2016. Towards a definition of knowledge graphs. In *Joint Proceedings of the Posters and Demos Track of the 12th International Conference on Semantic Systems - SEMANTiCS2016 and the 1st International Workshop on Semantic Change & Evolving Semantics (SuCCESS'16) co-located with the 12th International Conference on Semantic Systems (SEMANTiCS 2016), Leipzig, Germany, September 12-15, 2016*, volume 1695 of *CEUR Workshop Proceedings*. CEUR-WS.org.

Ali Fadel, Ibraheem Tuffaha, Bara' Al-Jawarneh, and Mahmoud Al-Ayyoub. 2019. Arabic text diacritization using deep neural networks. *CoRR*, abs/1905.01965.

Michael Färber, Frederic Bartscherer, Carsten Menne, and Achim Rettinger. 2018. Linked data quality of dbpedia, freebase, opencyc, wikidata, and yago. *Semantic Web*, 9:77–129.

Dieter Fensel, Umutcan Şimşek, Kevin Angele, Elwin Huaman, Elias Kärle, Oleksandra Panasiuk, Ioan Toma, Jürgen Umbrich, and Alexander Wahler. 2020. *Introduction: What Is a Knowledge Graph?*, pages 1–10. Springer International Publishing, Cham.

Emma J. Gerritse, Faegheh Hasibi, and Arjen P. de Vries. 2020. Graph-embedding empowered entity retrieval. *Advances in Information Retrieval*, pages 97–110.

Nizar Habash, Houda Bouamor, and Christine Chung. 2019. Automatic gender identification and reinflection in Arabic. In *Proceedings of the First Workshop on Gender Bias in Natural Language Processing*, pages 155–165, Florence, Italy. Association for Computational Linguistics.

Nizar Y. Habash. 2010. Introduction to arabic natural language processing. *Synthesis Lectures on Human Language Technologies*, 3(1):1–187.

Faegheh Hasibi, Fedor Nikolaev, Chenyan Xiong, Krisztian Balog, Svein Erik Bratsberg, Alexander Kotov, and Jamie Callan. 2017. Dbpedia-entity v2: A test collection for entity search. In *Proceedings of the 40th International ACM SIGIR Conference on Research and Development in Information Retrieval*, SIGIR '17, pages 1265–1268. ACM.

Ahmed Salama Ismail, Haytham Al-Feel, and Hoda M. O. Mokhtar. 2016. Introducing a new arabic endpoint for dbpedia internationalization project. In *Proceedings of the 20th International Database Engineering & Applications Symposium*, IDEAS '16, pages 284–289, New York, NY, USA. Association for Computing Machinery.

Giorgos Kadilierakis, Pavlos Fafalios, Panagiotis Papadakos, and Yannis Tzitzikas. 2020. Keyword search over rdf using document-centric information retrieval systems. In *The Semantic Web*, pages 121–137, Cham. Springer International Publishing.

Guma Abdulkhader Lakshen, Valentina Janev, and Sanja Vraneš. 2018. Challenges in quality assessment of arabic dbpedia. In *Proceedings of the 8th International Conference on Web Intelligence, Mining and Semantics*, WIMS '18, New York, NY, USA. Association for Computing Machinery.

Tomas Mikolov, Ilya Sutskever, Kai Chen, Greg Corrado, and Jeffrey Dean. 2013. Distributed representations of words and phrases and their compositionality. In *Proceedings of the 26th International Conference on Neural Information Processing Systems - Volume 2*, NIPS'13, pages 3111–3119, Red Hook, NY, USA. Curran Associates Inc.

Abu Bakr Mohammad, Kareem Eissa, and Samhaa El-Beltagy. 2017. Aravec: A set of arabic word embedding models for use in arabic nlp. *Procedia Computer Science*, 117:256–265.

Hussein Mozannar, Elie Maamary, Karl El Hajal, and Hazem Hajj. 2019. Neural Arabic question answering. In *Proceedings of the Fourth Arabic Natural Language Processing Workshop*, pages 108–118, Florence, Italy. Association for Computational Linguistics.

Shahrzad Naseri, John Foley, J. Allan, and Brendan T. O'Connor. 2018. Exploring summary-expanded entity embeddings for entity retrieval. In *CIKM Workshops*.

Fedor Nikolaev and Alexander Kotov. 2020. Joint word and entity embeddings for entity retrieval from a knowledge graph. In *Advances in Information Retrieval*, pages 141–155, Cham. Springer International Publishing.

Ossama Obeid, Nasser Zalmout, Salam Khalifa, Dima Taji, Mai Oudah, Bashar Alhafni, Go Inoue, Fadhl Eryani, Alexander Erdmann, and Nizar Habash. 2020. CAMeL tools: An open source python toolkit for Arabic natural language processing. In *Proceedings of the 12th Language Resources and Evaluation Conference*, pages 7022–7032, Marseille, France. European Language Resources Association.

Miriam Redi, Martin Gerlach, Isaac Johnson, Jonathan Morgan, and Leila Zia. 2021. A taxonomy of knowledge gaps for wikimedia projects (second draft). *ArXiv*.

Radim Řehůřek and Petr Sojka. 2010. Software Framework for Topic Modelling with Large Corpora. In *Proceedings of the LREC 2010 Workshop on New Challenges for NLP Frameworks*, pages 45–50, Valletta, Malta. ELRA.

Ali Safaya, Moutasem Abdullatif, and Deniz Yuret. 2020. Kuisail at semeval-2020 task 12: Bert-cnn for offensive speech identification in social media. *ArXiv*, abs/2007.13184.

Heba Samy, Ehab E. Hassanein, and Khaled Shaalan. 2019. Arabic question answering: A study on challenges, systems, and techniques. *International Journal of Computer Applications*, 181(44):6–14.

Khaled Shaalan, Sanjeera Siddiqui, Manar Alkhatib, and Azza Monem. 2018. *Challenges in Arabic Natural Language Processing*, chapter Chapter 3. World Scientific Publishing Company.

Ikuya Yamada, Akari Asai, Jin Sakuma, Hiroyuki Shindo, Hideaki Takeda, Yoshiyasu Takefuji, and Yuji Matsumoto. 2020. Wikipedia2Vec: An efficient toolkit for learning and visualizing the embeddings of words and entities from Wikipedia. In *Proceedings of the 2020 Conference on Empirical Methods in Natural Language Processing: System Demonstrations*, pages 23–30, Online. Association for Computational Linguistics.

Nikita Zhiltsov, Alexander Kotov, and Fedor Nikolaev. 2015. Fielded sequential dependence model for ad-hoc entity retrieval in the web of data. In *Proceedings of the 38th International ACM SIGIR Conference on Research and Development in Information Retrieval*, SIGIR '15, pages 253–262, New York, NY, USA. Association for Computing Machinery.

Introducing A large Tunisian Arabizi Dialectal Dataset for Sentiment Analysis

Chayma Fourati **Hatem Haddad** **Abir Messaoudi**

Moez Ben Haj Hmida **Aymen Ben Elhaj Mabrouk** **Malek Naski**
iCompass, Tunisia
{chayma,hatem,abir,moez,aymen,malek}@icompass.digital

Abstract

On various Social Media platforms, people tend to use the informal way to communicate, or write posts and comments: their local dialects. In Africa, more than 1500 dialects and languages exist. Particularly, Tunisians talk and write informally using Latin letters and numbers rather than Arabic ones. In this paper, we introduce a large common-crawl-based Tunisian Arabizi dialectal dataset dedicated for Sentiment Analysis. The dataset consists of a total of 100k comments (about movies, politic, sport, etc.) annotated manually by Tunisian native speakers as Positive, Negative, and Neutral. We evaluate our dataset on sentiment analysis task using the Bidirectional Encoder Representations from Transformers (BERT) as a contextual language model in its mul-tilingual version (mBERT) as an embedding technique then combining mBERT with Convolutional Neural Network (CNN) as classifier. The dataset is publicly available[1].

1 Introduction

While being so diverse and rich, Arabic language and particularly Arabic dialects, are still under represented and not yet fully exploited. Arabizi is a term describing a system of writing Arabic using English characters. This term comes from two words "arabi" (Arabic) and "Engliszi" (English). Arabizi is the representation of Arabic sounds using Latin letters and numbers to replace the non existing equivalent ones (Mulki et al., 2017). Particularly in Tunisia, this way of writing was introduced in (Fourati et al., 2020) as "Tunizi".

In this paper, we introduce a large Tunizi dataset available freely in order to help Tunisian and other researchers interested in the Natural Language Processing (NLP) field. This dataset contains 100k Tunizi comments collected from crowd-sourcing and built for the sentiment analysis task. Indeed, the dataset's comments are manually annotated by Tunisian native speakers as positive, negative, or neutral. This dataset can be also used for other NLP subtasks such as dialect identification, named entities recognition, etc.

In this paper, we present the motivation of our work, the Tunizi way of writing, previous related work, data composition including the data collection, preprocessing, annotation, and the data statistics. Then, we present experiments performed using our dataset for the Sentiment Analysis (SA) task. Finally, we present the conclusion and future work.

2 Tunizi

Tunizi was referred in (Fourati et al., 2020) as "the Tunisian Arabic text written using Latin characters and numerals rather than Arabic letter". This type of writing is most used on social media platforms since it presents an easier way to communicate. Also, since the Tunisian dialect already contains French and English words, people tend to use Tunizi for easier typing of non formal texts. However, not all Arabic letters have a Latin equivalent representation such as the character "ق" or "ح". These characters are expressed using numbers instead in the Tunizi representation. Tunisians have high contact culture where online social networks play a key role in facilitating social communication (Skandrani et al., 2011). For instance, due to the linguistic situation specific to each country, Tunisians generally use the french background when writing in Tunizi, whereas, other Arabic countries like Egypt would use English. For example the word اشتريت would be written in Tunizi as "chrit" whereas as "ishtareet" in Arabizi.

In Table 1, some examples of Arabic letters and their Tunizi equivalent are presented.

[1]https://zenodo.org/record/4275240.YDew1-oo9H4

Proceedings of the Sixth Arabic Natural Language Processing Workshop, pages 226–230
Kyiv, Ukraine (Virtual), April 19, 2021.

Arabic	Arabizi	Tunizi
ح	7	7
خ	5 or 7'	5 or kh
ذ	d' or dh	dh
ش	$ or sh	ch
ث	t' or th or 4	th
غ	4'	gh or 8
ع	3	3
ق	8	9

Table 1: Arabic letters and equivalent Arabizi and Tunizi representation

In (Abidi, 2019), a study was conducted on 1,2M social media Tunisian comments including 16M words and 1M unique words states the following: 53% of the comments used Romanized alphabet, 34% used Arabic alphabet, and 13% used script-switching. The study states, also, that 87% of the comments based on Romanized alphabet are Tunizi, while the rest are French and English. Some examples of Tunizi sentences with different polarities (positive, negative, and neutral) are presented in Table 2.

3 Related Work

In (Mdhaffar et al., 2017), a Tunisian dataset entitled TSAC (Tunisian Sentiment Analysis Corpus) was presented. This dataset combines 17366 positive/negative Tunisian Facebook comments written in Arabic and Tunizi. TSAC includes only 9196 comments written in Tunizi. However, Tunizi comments are not balanced with 3856 negative comments (41%) and 5340 positive comments (59%). The doc2vec algorithm was used to produce document embeddings of Tunisian Arabic and Tunizi comments. The generated embeddings were fed to train a Multi-Layer Perceptron (MLP) classifier performing a F-measure values of 78%.

In (Chader et al., 2019), authors proposed a transliteration method from Arabizi to MSA in order to evaluate sentiment analysis of Arabizi Algerian dialect. The best achieved performances was 87% of F-score using the Support Vector Machine.

In (Taha, 2020), a work on Lebanese Arabizi was performed. In order to create Sentiment Analysis experiments, a dataset was collected from Twitter and manually labelled as positive and negative. The dataset resulted in 2.9K Tweets: 801 positive, 881 negative, and 1.2K neutral Arabizi tweets. Comments used for Sentiment analysis experiments are of size 1.6K balanced as 800 positive, and 800 negative tweets. A Sentiment Analysis task is, then, performed using a lexicon-based approach. The lexicon created was first of size 1.6K words and was expanded until achieved 80K words. The lexicon-based approach using the original lexicon classified only 23% of the tweets. Unclassified tweets are classified as positive or negative randomly. The classification using the original lexicon achieved 60% F1-score. Classification achieved a coverage of 63% of the tweets with an F1-score of 78% in one of the expanded versions of the lexicon.

In (Fourati et al., 2020), a Tunisian Arabizi Sentiment Analysis dataset called "Tunizi" was introduced. This work provided 9k sentences annotated as positive and negative. TUNIZI is a balanced and representative dataset that covers different topics collected from Youtube social network. However, the dataset is not enough large to be used for deep learning approaches.

In (Baert et al., 2020), a work focuses on the Arabizi form of writing. The work creates a large dataset (LAD) of size 7.7M written in Arabizi collected from Arabizi tweets using Egyptian keywords as seeds. LAD was used for pretraining a BERT language model called "BAERT". A subset of LAD entitled SALAD of size 1700 was annotated for sentiment analysis. The subset was used for fine-tuning BAERT. SALAD contains tweets annotated as Positive, Negative, Neutral, Conflict and ConflictTxtvsEm (tweets where the comments have a conflict in the text and the emoji symbol) . However, the dataset is not balanced and very limited to be used for deep learning approaches. Tunizi dataset (Fourati et al., 2020) was also used for fine-tuning BAERT model. Fine-tuning on Tunizi and SALAD (3 classes) performed 83.8% and 74.4% of F1-score respectively. In order to perform better performances, such experiments would require larger annotated datasets.

In (Gugliotta et al., 2021), the authors present a multi-task sequence prediction system for Tunisian Arabizi. A dataset was annotated for several subtasks: text classification, tokenization, PoS tagging and encoding of Tunisian Arabizi into CODA* Arabic orthography. Nevertheless, the dataset was not annotated for sentiment analysis task.

Previous work proposed relatively small datasets to be used for deep learning approaches. Hence, our contributions can be summarized as: the first release of a Tunizi large-scale Common-Crawl-based

Tunizi Comment	MSA Translation	English Translation	Polarity
ma7leha lbo93a	ما احلى هذا المكان	This place is nice	Positive
5ayeb el loun	اللون بشع	The color is bad	Negative
bech nemchi nenta5eb	سوف انتخب	I will go vote	Neutral
5edma 3alamiya 5ouya	عمل رائع يا أخي	Great job bro	Positive

Table 2: Tunizi example comments and their Modern Standard Arabic (MSA) and English translations.

dataset[2], annotated manually for sentiment analysis task and training the dataset using neural networks and attention mechanisms for the Sentiment Analysis.

4 Tunisian Arabizi dataset

This dataset is composed of one instance presented as text comments, and labeled as positive, negative, or neutral. In this work, we use crowd-sourcing from social media until we reached 100k comments.

4.1 Data Collection

Because of the lack of available Tunisian dialect data (books, wikipedia, etc.), we use a Common-Crawl-based dataset extracted from social media. It is collected from comments on various social networks. The chosen posts included sports, politics, comedy, TV shows, TV series, arts and Tunisian music videos such that the dataset is representative and contains different types of ages, background, writing, etc. This data does not include any confidential information since it is collected from comments on public Social Media posts. However, negative comments may include offensive or insulting content. This dataset relates directly to people from different regions, different ages and different genders.

A filter was applied to ensure that only Latin-based comments are included. The extracted data was preprocessed by removing links, emoji symbols, and punctuations. Examples of comments before and after preprocessing are in Table 3.

4.2 Annotation Policy

The collected comments were manually annotated using an overall polarity: positive, negative and neutral. The annotation task was divided equally on ten Tunisian native speakers: two males PhD holders, aged 43 and 42; two females and one male, one aged 24 and two aged 26 working as research and development Artificial Intelligence engineers and five engineering students: four females, and one male aged 23.

Sentiment is an extremely multi-faceted phenomenon. For this reason, "light" comprehensive guidelines covering the most frequent potentially ambiguous cases were presented to the annotators with the aim of ensuring high enough agreement.

4.3 Dataset Statistics

We divided the dataset into separate training, validation and test datasets, with a ratio of 7:1:2 with a balanced split where the number of comments from positive class and negative class are almost the same. Table 4 presents statistics of the dataset including number of positive, number of negative, and number of neutral comments. Statistics of the train, validation, and test datasets for each label are presented in Table 5.

5 Experiments

To evaluate the dataset, two experiments were conducted:

- MBERT (Devlin et al., 2018) as language model and a classifier:

  We decided to use the Bidirectional Encoder Representations from Transformers (BERT) as a contextual language model in its multilingual version (MBERT) as an embedding technique. MBERT contains more than 10 languages including English, French and Arabic. Using the BERT tokenizer, we map words to their indexes and representations in the BERT embedding matrix. These representations are used to feed the MBERT classifier. Filter sizes used for all experiments are 2,3,4,5,6.

- MBERT as language model and Convolutional Neural Network (CNN) as classifier: Using the BERT tokenizer, we map words to their indexes and representations in the BERT embedding matrix. These representations are used to feed a CNN classifier.

[2]https://zenodo.org/record/4275240.YDew1-oo9H4

Before preprocessing	After preprocessing
3saall to9telll nmout 3liha!!!	3saall to9telll nmout 3liha
odkhlou lel google www.google.com	odkhlou lel google
ma3ejbetnich el 7al9a lyoum ☺	ma3ejbetnich el 7al9a lyoum

Table 3: Examples before and after preprocessing

Charactertistic	Statistic
#positive	52 711
#negative	43 767
#neutral	3 522
Total Comments	**100K**
#words	996 782
#unique words	189 257

Table 4: Dataset Statistics

Charactertistic	Train	Validation	Test
#positive	38 239	4 824	9 648
#negative	29 295	4 824	9 648
#neutral	2 466	352	704
Total Comments	**70K**	**10K**	**20K**

Table 5: Train, Validation and Test Datasets Statistics

Since the neutral class have less comments than the positive and negative ones, the same experiments were conducted on only two classes of the dataset: positive and negative. Hence statistics of the new sub-dataset are presented in table 6. The sub dataset was also divided for train, dev, and test as 7:1:2 where the train, dev, and test dataset are balanced.

Charactertistic	Statistic
Total Comments	**96 478**
#words	971 932
#unique words	208 464

Table 6: Binary labeled dataset

Experiments results on the binary and multi-label classification, are presented in table 7 and 8 respectively. Each table presents results of two experiments where MBERT is used as an embedding and a classifier and MBERT as an embedding and CNN as a classifier.

Our dataset showed that the Bidirectional encoder representations from transformers (BERT) as a contextual language model in its multilingual version (Devlin et al., 2018) as an embedding technique followed by CNN for classification outperforms the BERT as an embedding and a classifier when tested on the whole dataset for multi-label classification. The best result for Sentiment Analysis performed 80.3% accuracy and F1 micro score. However, F1 macro score achieved 58.0% because the neutral class contains less comments than the positive and negative ones. However, MBERT as an embedding and a classifier outperforms MBERT as an embedding and CNN as a classifier for binary classification when omitting the neutral class. Results achieved better performances and have led to an increase in all performance measures. Since this sub-dataset is balanced. Hence, accuracy, F1-Macro, and, F1-Micro metrics achieved 82.9%.

Model	Acc.	F1-Mic.	F1-Mac.
MBERT	**0.829**	**0.829**	**0.829**
MBERT & CNN	0.822	0.822	0.821

Table 7: SA results on binary classification

Model	Acc.	F1-Mic.	F1-Mac.
MBERT	0.79	0.79	0.558
MBERT & CNN	**0.803**	**0.803**	**0.580**

Table 8: SA results on multi-label classification

6 Conclusion

In this work, we present the largest dataset dedicated for the Tunisian Arabizi, annotated as positive, negative, and neutral and preprocessed for Sentiment Analysis subtask. Such datasets can be used for further NLP activities. We also experiment deep learning models using our dataset. This dataset could improve performances of several works dedicated for the Tunisian dialect in the NLP field. As a future work, we plan to build and release other large underrepresented African and Arabic datasets in order to help the NLP community further build machine learning and deep learning models.

References

Karima Abidi. 2019. *Automatic building of multilingual resources from social networks : application to Maghrebi dialects (Doctoral dissertation).* Ph.D. thesis, University of Lorraine, Nancy, France.

Gaétan Baert, Souhir Gahbiche, Guillaume Gadek, and Alexandre Pauchet. 2020. Arabizi language models for sentiment analysis. In *Proceedings of the 28th International Conference on Computational Linguistics*, pages 592–603, Barcelona, Spain (Online). International Committee on Computational Linguistics.

Asma Chader, Lanasri Dihia, Leila Hamdad, Mohamed Belkheir, and Wassim Hennoune. 2019. Sentiment analysis for arabizi: Application to algerian dialect. pages 475–482.

Jacob Devlin, Ming-Wei Chang, Kenton Lee, and Kristina Toutanova. 2018. BERT: pre-training of deep bidirectional transformers for language understanding. *CoRR*, abs/1810.04805.

Chayma Fourati, Abir Messaoudi, and Hatem Haddad. 2020. Tunizi: a tunisian arabizi sentiment analysis dataset. In *AfricaNLP Workshop, Putting Africa on the NLP Map. ICLR 2020, Virtual Event*, page arXiv:3091079.

Elisa Gugliotta, Marco Dinarelli, and Olivier Kraif. 2021. Multi-task sequence prediction for tunisian arabizi multi-level annotation.

Salima Mdhaffar, Fethi Bougares, Yannick Estève, and Lamia Hadrich-Belguith. 2017. Sentiment Analysis of Tunisian Dialects: Linguistic Ressources and Experiments. In *Third Arabic Natural Language Processing Workshop (WANLP)*, pages 55–61, Valence, Spain.

Hala Mulki, Hatem Haddad, and Ismail Babaoglu. 2017. Modern trends in arabic sentiment analysis: A survey. *Traitement Automatique des Langues*, 58(3):15–39.

Hamida Skandrani, Abdelfattah Triki, and Boudour Baratli. 2011. Trust in supply chains, meanings, determinants and demonstrations: A qualitative study in an emerging market context. *Qualitative Market Research: An International Journal*, 14:391–409.

Tobaili Taha. 2020. *Sentiment Analysis for the Low-Resourced Latinised Arabic "Arabizi"*. Ph.D. thesis, TheOpen University.

AraFacts: The First Large Arabic Dataset of Naturally-Occurring Professionally-Verified Claims

Zien Sheikh Ali, Watheq Mansour, Tamer Elsayed, and Abdulaziz Al-Ali
Computer Science and Engineering Department, Qatar University
{zs1407404, wm1900793, telsayed, a.alali}@qu.edu.qa

Abstract

We introduce **AraFacts**, the first large Arabic dataset of naturally-occurring claims collected from 5 Arabic fact-checking websites, e.g., Fatabyyano and Misbar, covering claims since 2016. Our dataset consists of 6,222 claims along with their factual labels and additional metadata, such as fact-checking article content, topical category, and links to posts or Web pages spreading the claim. Since the data is obtained from various fact-checking websites, we standardize the original claim labels to provide a unified label rating for all claims. Moreover, we provide revealing dataset statistics and motivate its use by suggesting possible research applications. The dataset is made publicly available for the research community.

1 Introduction

Fake news and misinformation are considered among the greatest threats to nations. The spread of fake news can cause manipulation in public opinion, which has adverse consequences to politics and journalism. Moreover, the recent COVID-19 pandemic revealed how medical misinformation could easily harm the health of people (Islam et al., 2020). Notable development has been made in automated fact-checking systems over the past years. However, one of the main limitations of Arabic automated fact-checking systems is the lack of Arabic datasets. Recently several Arabic fact-checking websites (e.g., Fatabyyano and Misbar) have emerged to help combat the spread of rumors and fake news, especially over social media. They constitute a valuable resource of naturally-occurring fact-checked claims in the Arab world. The claims are annotated and verified by professional fact-checkers and journalists, making them a reliable source of information. While the verified information about those rumors is posted on those websites and their corresponding social media accounts, they are not gathered and unified as a dataset that can be used to develop automated systems. In this paper, we introduce **AraFacts**, the first large Arabic Fact-checking dataset of naturally-occurring and professionally-verified claims. We crawl 6,222 claims along with their factual labels, description, and additional metadata, from 5 different fact-checking websites, and make them available to the research community in a normalized form. The contributions of our work are two-fold:

- We extract and publicly share[1] about 6k claims with their original and normalized factual labels along with their metadata.
- We propose several research applications for which our dataset can be utilized.

The rest of the paper is organized as follows. Section 2 summarizes related work. Section 3 describes the data collection process. Section 4 provides data analysis. Section 5 outlines some research applications, and Section 6 concludes.

2 Related Work

Several datasets of naturally occurring claims have been previously proposed, but mostly in English. For example, MultiFC dataset (Augenstein et al., 2019) includes 38,918 claims and their metadata from 26 different fact-checking websites. Similarly, Liar dataset (Wang, 2017) consists of 12,836 claims collected from PolitiFact.[2] FakeNewsNet (Shu et al., 2017a,b) is a mutli-dimensional data repository that contains 23,196 fact-checked articles from PolitiFact and GossipCop.[3] It also includes additional social context related to the checked claims.

Other datasets that focus on topic-specific claims were published recently. FakeCovid (Shahi and Nandini, 2020) dataset covers 5,182 multilingual fact-checked claims from 92 different fact-

[1] https://gitlab.com/bigirqu/AraFacts/
[2] https://www.politifact.com/
[3] https://www.gossipcop.com/

Proceedings of the Sixth Arabic Natural Language Processing Workshop, pages 231–236
Kyiv, Ukraine (Virtual), April 19, 2021.

checking websites, all related to COVID-19. Moreover, PUBHEALTH dataset Kotonya and Toni (2020) consists of 11,832 claims public health-related claims attained from 8 different websites.

Over the past few years, there has been an increased interest in task-specific Arabic applications leading to the release of several Arabic datasets. Most of these are built for tasks such as check-worthiness of tweets, evidence retrieval, and claim verification (Barrón-Cedeno et al., 2020; **?**).

Additionally, the Arabic News Stance dataset (ANS) (Khouja, 2020) supports claim verification and stance prediction. The dataset is generated using existing Arabic news titles from ANT corpus (Chouigui et al., 2017). The limitation with ANS is that it requires manual annotation to generate claims from news titles. Elmadany et al. (2020) address this limitation with the AraNews dataset. AraNews uses Arabic articles from online news data to automatically generate Arabic manipulated text.

Baly et al. (2018) proposed a corpus consisting of 422 fact-checked Arabic claims and documents associated with the claims. The corpus supports multiple tasks such as stance detection and fact-checking. **AraFacts** differs from their work in two ways; it covers a larger number of claims and all claims are professionally fact-checked.

While several datasets were constructed for different tasks that are related to fact-checking, to the best of our knowledge, **AraFacts** is the largest Arabic dataset that leverages emerging Arabic fact-checking websites as a source of annotated professionally-verified information.

3 Data Collection

In this section, we describe the process of selecting fact-checking websites, crawling the verification articles, and constructing the **AraFacts** dataset.

3.1 Fact-checking websites

We chose fact-checking websites that are either verified by the International Fact-Checking Network (IFCN) or popular in the Arab region. IFCN certification indicates that the website complies with IFCN's code of ethics. The following websites were selected as data sources: **1) Fatabyyano**[4] is an IFCN-certified fact-checking organization that launched in 2016. Fatabyyano collaborates with Facebook as a third-party fact-checker to debunk fake-news, rumors, and conspiracy theories using Facebook's claim rating system.[5] **2) FactuelAFP Arabic**[6] is the Arabic bureau of the French press news service. Their team consists of journalists and fact-checkers. It aims to debunk false statements, videos, or images that appear online. It is certified by IFCN and collaborates with Facebook. **3) Misbar**[7] is a popular independent Arabic fact-checking platform. It uses an 8-point claim rating system to label claims online. **4) Maharat-news fact-o-meter**[8] is an IFCN-certified fact-checking website that focuses on investigating rumors online and in real-life using a 3-point claim rating system. **5) Verify-Sy**[9] is a media platform that specializes in detecting and debunking false news and media by experienced journalists.

3.2 Data Extraction

From every fact-checking website, we crawled all fact-checking articles and extracted their claims, labels, and metadata. We also extracted the claim type using some indicative search keywords. The claim type identifies if the claim refers to textual information or if the claim is paired with visual information (such as a video or an image). For example; The claim *MISB_2941* is referring to a fake image shown in Figure 2.

While parsing the content of the HTML pages, some challenges were faced. One challenge was that websites like Verify-Sy do not explicitly label the veracity of the claim. To address this challenge, we reviewed the website's editorial policy and inspected a subset of the claims manually. We concluded that all claims are, in fact, false. Moreover, not all metadata fields were available on all websites. Table 1 shows the number of crawled claims per website and a summary of available metadata.

3.3 Veracity and Category Normalization

Another faced challenge was the varying claim rating system adopted by the different websites. We proposed a normalized claim rating to achieve a standard rating for all claims in **AraFacts**. We also used a normalized rating for the categories of the claims.

To normalize the veracity label of the claim, we used the label normalization method presented by

[4]https://Fatabyyano.net/

[5]http://bit.ly/2LnD1Rk

[6]https://factcheck.afp.com/ar/list

[7]https://misbar.com/

[8]https://maharat-news.com/fact-o-meter

[9]https://www.verify-sy.com/

Table 1: Summary of the amount of claims extracted from each website and some of their metadata

Website	Number of Claims	Image or Video Claims	Extracted Metadata			
			Pages with Claim URLs	Avg. no. of claim URLs	Pages with Evidence URLs	Avg. no. of Evidence URLs
Misbar	2,952	1,974	2,946	6.4	2,945	2.6
Fatabyyano	1,503	930	905	2.2	1,449	4.7
FactuelAFP	973	824	514	2.4	461	3.8
Verify-sy	707	403	179	1.1	86	0.3
Maharat-news	87	10	62	1.1	0	0.0

Khouja (2020) with some variation. We set our own claim rating scheme consisting of four labels *(False, Partly-False, Sarcasm, True)* and mapped original labels to them. To do so, we referred to the source websites' methodology, manually inspected a subset of the claims, then finally did the mapping of 27 distinct original labels to four normalized labels. We adopted a similar mapping technique to map 35 distinct topical categories to 8 normalized categories: *(Politics, News, Health, Social, Religion, General Sciences, Arts & Culture, and Other)*. More details on our claim and category normalization can be found in **AraFacts** repository.

The normalization process was performed by two authors of this work independently; then, disagreements were discussed and resolved.

3.4 Dataset Construction

After extracting claim information and normalizing the veracity labels and categories, we assigned a unique ID to each claim. We finally merged the crawled information for each website into one database with the following schema: 1) **Claim-ID:** ID of the claim. 2) **Claim:** Text of the claim. 3) **Source:** Name of the fact-checking website from which the claim was crawled. 4) **Description:** Detailed description of the claim. 5) **Source-label:** The veracity label of the claim as it appears in the fact-checking website. 6) **Normalized-label:** Normalized claim label. 7) **Source-category:** Topical category of the claim as it appears in the fact-checking website. 8) **Normalized-category:** Normalized topical category of the claim. 9) **Date:** Article publication date. 10) **Source URL:** URL of the article. 11) **Claim URLs:** URLs to web pages spreading the claim. 12) **Evidence URLs:** URLs referenced by the fact-checker to justify their annotation. 13) **Claim type:** Indicates whether the claim refers to text, an image or a video.

Additionally, we extracted the content of the fact-checking article and included it in **AraFacts**. Figure 1 shows an example claim with some attributes.

ClaimID: MIS_2550
Claim:
ترامب خلال مقطع فيديو يدعو إلى ترقب مفاجأة بداية يناير/كانون الأول الجاري، والاستمتاع بالعرض
Description:
تداولت حسابات وصفحات على موقع التواصل الاجتماعي تويتر، منذ تاريخ 29 ديسمبر/كانون الأول المنصرم، مقطع فيديو للرئيس الأميركي دونالد ترامب، ادعت فيه بأنّه قال هناك مفاجأة ستحدث بداية يناير/كانون الثاني عام 2021 تم التوقيع عليها، وعلى الجميع انتظارها والاستمتاع بالعرض، وأوضحت المنشورات أن هناك قنبلة سيفجرها ترامب مع بداية شهر يناير الجاري
Source: Misbar
Date: 2021-01-02
Source_label: مضلل
Normalized_label: Partly-false
Source_category: سياسة
Normalized_category: Politics
Source_url: https://misbar.com/factcheck/2021/01/02/فاجأةيناير-التي-أعلن-عنها-ترامب-كذبت-من-وعود-حملته-الانتخابية

Figure 1: An example claim from **AraFacts**.

قرار الامم المتحدة
بخصوص اللاجئين في اليونان وبعد اجتماع اميركا
وبريطانيا واستراليا وكندة لمناقشة وضع اللاجئين في
اليونان قرر في تاريخ2021/3/5 بفتح جميع طلبات
اعادة توطين ابتدائن بتاريخ2021/2/24 ولحتى نهاية
2021/3/4

Το ψήφισμα των Ηνωμένων Εθνών σχετικά με τους πρόσφυγες στην Ελλάδα και μετά τη συνάντηση της Αμερικής, της Βρετανίας, της Αυστραλίας και του Καναδά για να συζητήσουν το καθεστώς των προσφύγων στην Ελλάδα, αποφάσισαν στις 3/3/2021 να ανοίξουν όλες τις αιτήσεις επανεγκατάστασης από τις 24/2/2021 και για το τέλος της συνεδρίασης της 3/4/2021.

Figure 2: An example claim from **AraFacts** that has a fake image. Claim MISB_2941 refers to this image claiming that UN decided to open applications for refugee resettlement in Greece.

4 Data Analysis

In this section, we perform further analysis on the collected claims. Table 1 gives an overall summary of the collected claims and some of the ex-

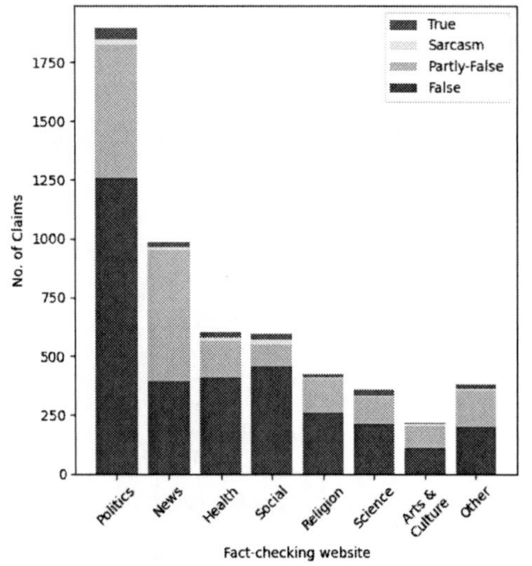

Figure 3: Distribution of normalized labels and categories.

Table 2: Top 5 source domains of claims.

Domain	% of URLs
facebook.com	54.5%
twitter.com	25.0%
perma.cc	4.1%
archive.vn	3.1%
youtube.com	3.1%

tracted metadata. In addition to the number of claims, for each website, we report the number of claims that have a refer to visual information (image or video), number of claims that have embedded claim URLs, average number of embedded URLs per claim, number of claims that have embedded evidence URLs, and average number of evidence URLs per claim.

Figure 3 illustrates the distribution of the normalized labels over the normalized categories. Most claims are political or news, and false claims are expectedly dominating in all categories.

We also examined the original source domains of the claims from the embedded claim URLs. Table 2 lists the most frequent 5 claim URLs. It is worthwhile noting that social media platforms constitute the main source of claims and rumors in the dataset.

Figure 4 shows the distribution of the claims over publication time. We notice that the majority of the claims were published in 2020; this is due to the

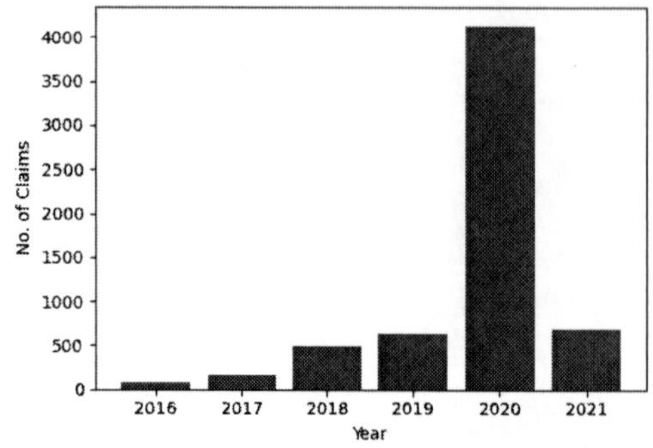

Figure 4: Claims distribution over time.

Figure 5: Most frequent 100 words in claims.

fact the most fact-checking websites in our dataset were launched in the past two years. Figure 5 shows the most frequent 100 words in the claim text. We notice a mix of political figures, religious entities, and country names among others.

Finally, we analyze the types of extracted claims. Figure 6 shows the frequency of the different types of claims (Text claims, Image claims, and Video claims) for each fact-checking website. Interestingly, the two most contributing fact-checking websites (Misbar and Fatabyyano) contain more visual claims than textual.

5 Example Use Cases

This section provides example use cases and research problems that can be supported by **AraFacts**.

5.1 Claim Verification

One of the main automated fake news detection tasks is claim verification. The task is defined as follows: given a claim, predict its veracity. The metadata can be used as features to classify the claim, such as claim source URLs. While we provide four normalized veracity labels of the claim, the original veracity labels can still be utilized following

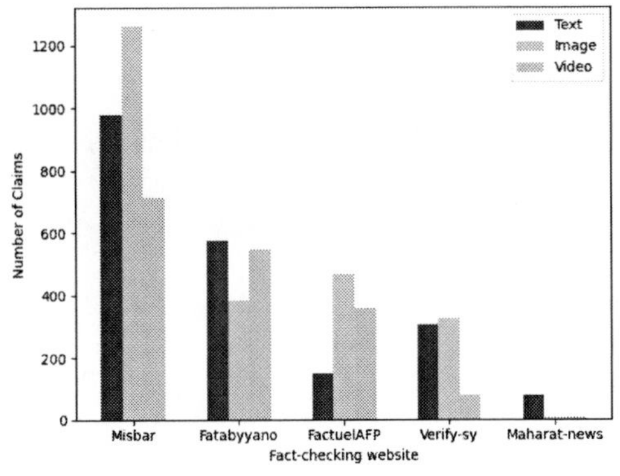

Figure 6: Type of claims published by each fact-checking website

a Multi-Task Learning (MLT) approach similar to Augenstein et al. (2019) MLT claim verification approach.

5.2 Claim Retrieval

The claim retrieval task is defined as follows: given a claim, check whether this claim has already been checked. The importance of this problem stems from the fact that many posted claims over social media platforms are just repetitions of previously fact-checked old claims. Having a system that addresses this problem can help combat the spread of those circulating claims over social media.

5.3 Evidence Retrieval

The task is defined as follows: given a claim, retrieve evidential sentences that help in verifying or debunking the claim. As we provide the content of the fact-checking articles and the URLs of evidence pages of claims, **AraFacts** can be extended by further annotating evidence sentences from the evidence pages to support such task.

5.4 Image-based Fact-checking

The task is defined as follows; given a claim that is mainly about an image, predict the factuality of the claim using the image and claim. This task has been explored for English claims (Zlatkova et al., 2019), but it has not been studied in Arabic yet. While **AraFacts** does not include the images related to the claims, we indicate the claim type and provide the URL to the fact-checking articles where the images can be extracted and paired with the claims.

6 Conclusion

In this paper, we introduce **AraFacts**, the first large Arabic dataset of naturally-occurring claims covering about 6k claims published since 2016 and already annotated by professional fact-checkers from 5 different Arabic fact-checking websites over several topical categories. The dataset supports many research tasks such as claim verification, claim retrieval, also evidence retrieval. We made our dataset publicly available to the research community, and we plan for periodic crawling to augment the newly verified claims from existing and new fact-checking websites. We believe that **AraFacts** will serve as a valuable resource for future studies on fact-checking, such as fake image detection. Our future work will focus on evaluating and utilizing **AraFacts** for several fact-checking tasks to contribute the Arabic-based work in that domain.

Acknowledgments

This work was made possible by NPRP grant No.: NPRP11S-1204-170060 from the Qatar National Research Fund (a member of Qatar Foundation). The statements made herein are solely the responsibility of the authors.

References

Isabelle Augenstein, Christina Lioma, Dongsheng Wang, Lucas Chaves Lima, Casper Hansen, Christian Hansen, and Jakob Grue Simonsen. 2019. Multifc: A real-world multi-domain dataset for evidence-based fact checking of claims. In *Proceedings of the 2019 Conference on Empirical Methods in Natural Language Processing and the 9th International Joint Conference on Natural Language Processing (EMNLP-IJCNLP)*, pages 4677–4691.

Ramy Baly, Mitra Mohtarami, and James Glass. 2018. Integrating stance detection and fact checking in a unified corpus. In *Proceedings of NAACL-HLT*, pages 21–27.

Alberto Barrón-Cedeno, Tamer Elsayed, Preslav Nakov, Giovanni Da San Martino, Maram Hasanain, Reem Suwaileh, Fatima Haouari, Nikolay Babulkov, Bayan Hamdan, Alex Nikolov, et al. 2020. Overview of checkthat! 2020: Automatic identification and verification of claims in social media. In *International Conference of the Cross-Language Evaluation Forum for European Languages*, pages 215–236. Springer.

Amina Chouigui, Oussama Ben Khiroun, and Bilel Elayeb. 2017. Ant corpus: an arabic news text collection for textual classification. In *2017 IEEE/ACS*

14th International Conference on Computer Systems and Applications (AICCSA), pages 135–142. IEEE.

AbdelRahim Elmadany, Muhammad Abdul-Mageed, Tariq Alhindi, et al. 2020. Machine generation and detection of arabic manipulated and fake news. In *Proceedings of the Fifth Arabic Natural Language Processing Workshop*, pages 69–84.

Md Saiful Islam, Tonmoy Sarkar, Sazzad Hossain Khan, Abu-Hena Mostofa Kamal, SM Murshid Hasan, Alamgir Kabir, Dalia Yeasmin, Mohammad Ariful Islam, Kamal Ibne Amin Chowdhury, Kazi Selim Anwar, et al. 2020. Covid-19–related infodemic and its impact on public health: A global social media analysis. *The American Journal of Tropical Medicine and Hygiene*, 103(4):1621.

Jude Khouja. 2020. Stance prediction and claim verification: An arabic perspective. In *Proceedings of the Third Workshop on Fact Extraction and VERification (FEVER)*, pages 8–17.

Neema Kotonya and Francesca Toni. 2020. Explainable automated fact-checking for public health claims. In *Proceedings of the 2020 Conference on Empirical Methods in Natural Language Processing (EMNLP)*, pages 7740–7754, Online. Association for Computational Linguistics.

Gautam Kishore Shahi and Durgesh Nandini. 2020. FakeCovid – a multilingual cross-domain fact check news dataset for covid-19. In *Workshop Proceedings of the 14th International AAAI Conference on Web and Social Media*.

Kai Shu, Amy Sliva, Suhang Wang, Jiliang Tang, and Huan Liu. 2017a. Fake news detection on social media: A data mining perspective. *ACM SIGKDD Explorations Newsletter*, 19(1):22–36.

Kai Shu, Suhang Wang, and Huan Liu. 2017b. Exploiting tri-relationship for fake news detection. *arXiv preprint arXiv:1712.07709*.

William Yang Wang. 2017. "liar, liar pants on fire": A new benchmark dataset for fake news detection. In *Proceedings of the 55th Annual Meeting of the Association for Computational Linguistics (Volume 2: Short Papers)*, pages 422–426.

Dimitrina Zlatkova, Preslav Nakov, and Ivan Koychev. 2019. Fact-checking meets fauxtography: Verifying claims about images. In *Proceedings of the 2019 Conference on Empirical Methods in Natural Language Processing and the 9th International Joint Conference on Natural Language Processing (EMNLP-IJCNLP)*, pages 2099–2108, Hong Kong, China. Association for Computational Linguistics.

Improving Cross-Lingual Transfer for Event Argument Extraction with Language-Universal Sentence Structures

Minh Van Nguyen and Thien Huu Nguyen
Department of Computer and Information Science
University of Oregon, Eugene, Oregon, USA
{minhnv,thien}@cs.uoregon.edu

Abstract

We study the problem of Cross-lingual Event Argument Extraction (CEAE). The task aims to predict argument roles of entity mentions for events in text, whose language is different from the language that a predictive model has been trained on. Previous work on CEAE has shown the cross-lingual benefits of universal dependency trees in capturing shared syntactic structures of sentences across languages. In particular, this work exploits the existence of the syntactic connections between the words in the dependency trees as the anchor knowledge to transfer the representation learning across languages for CEAE models (i.e., via graph convolutional neural networks – GCNs). In this paper, we introduce two novel sources of language-independent information for CEAE models based on the semantic similarity and the universal dependency relations of the word pairs in different languages. We propose to use the two sources of information to produce shared sentence structures to bridge the gap between languages and improve the cross-lingual performance of the CEAE models. Extensive experiments are conducted with Arabic, Chinese, and English to demonstrate the effectiveness of the proposed method for CEAE.

1 Introduction

Event Argument Extraction (EAE) aims to classify argument roles of entity mentions for events in text. For example, given the sentence *"He **died** of injuries from a grenade attack by a fellow soldier"*, the task requires systems to identify the entity mention *"a fellow soldier"* as the *Agent* of the event *Die*, which is triggered by the verb *"died"*. EAE is an important component of event extraction (EE) that has been extensively studied with different approaches (Ji and Grishman, 2008; Liao and Grishman, 2011a; Li et al., 2014; Nguyen and Grishman, 2015b; Nguyen et al., 2016; Nguyen and Grishman, 2018; Liu et al., 2018; Zhang et al., 2019b; Wang et al., 2019). Cross-lingual Event Argument Extraction (CEAE) is an instance of EAE that considers the setting where test languages (i.e., target languages) are different from training languages (i.e., source languages). The goal is to transfer knowledge in source languages, where data is abundant, to low-resource target languages. The previous work on CEAE (Subburathinam et al., 2019) has shown the existence of shared syntactic structures of sentences across languages, which are useful for cross-lingual transfer. In particular, with the multilingual word embeddings, Subburathinam et al. (2019) develop a model based on Graph Convolutional Networks (GCNs) (Kipf and Welling, 2017; Zhang et al., 2018), which operates on universal dependency trees to capture the shared structures.

Notably, the use of the dependency trees of the sentences for GCNs in (Subburathinam et al., 2019) essentially treats the existence of the syntactic connections between the words in the universal dependency trees as the language-universal knowledge that can be exploited to bridge the gap between languages for EAE. In (Subburathinam et al., 2019), such syntactic connection existences are formalized via the adjacency matrices $A^{dep} = \{a^{dep}_{ij}\}_{i,j=1..N}$ of the dependency trees (i.e., N is the number of words in the input sentence and $a^{dep}_{ij} = 1$ if the i-th and j-th words are connected in the dependency tree) that would be consumed by GCNs for representation learning. We call A^{dep} the *syntax-based structures* of the sentences for convenience (as a^{dep}_{ij} is based on the syntactic connection of the words).

As such, in this work, we introduce two novel sources of information as the language anchors, which are complementary to the syntactic connections A^{dep}, to enable GCNs to learn better language-general representations for EAE. The first source of information relies on the semantic similarities of the pairs of words in the input

Proceedings of the Sixth Arabic Natural Language Processing Workshop, pages 237–243
Kyiv, Ukraine (Virtual), April 19, 2021.

sentence to induce the *semantic-based structures* $A^{sem} = \{a_{ij}^{sem}\}_{i,j=1..N}$ for GCNs. The rationale for such semantic-based structures is that despite the vocabulary differences between languages, the semantic similarity of the words is a language-invariant concept and can be leveraged to enhance the cross-lingual knowledge transfer for EAE. In this work, we rely on the multilingual representation vectors of the words to facilitate such semantic similarity computation for a_{ij}^{sem} in different languages. For the second source of information, we propose to employ the syntactic dependency relations between the words (e.g., *nsubj*, *conj*) in the dependency trees to obtain the *relation-based structures* $A^{rel} = \{a_{ij}^{rel}\}_{i,j=1..N}$ for EAE with GCNs. Specifically, $A^{rel} = \{a_{ij}^{rel}\}_{i,j=1..N}$ is an extension of A^{dep} that further considers the natures (i.e., the relations) of the syntactic connections between the words (i.e., instead of using only the existence of the connections as in A^{dep}). Similar to the semantic-based structures, we argue that the syntactic dependency relations from the universal dependency trees are also language-independent and can be helpful for our CEAE problem. To this end, we employ the embeddings of the dependency relations to compute the relation-based structure scores a_{ij}^{rel}. Note that all the structures A^{dep}, A^{sem}, and A^{rel} are fed into GCN models for representation learning in this work. Finally, we conduct extensive experiments to demonstrate the benefits of the proposed sentence structures, leading to the state-of-the-art performance for CEAE with Arabic, Chinese, and English as the experiment languages. To our knowledge, this is the first work to examine semantic-based and relation-based structures for EAE.

2 Related Work

EAE and EE have been extensively studied for English in the monolingual context of Event Extraction, featuring both the traditional machine learning models (Patwardhan and Riloff, 2009; Liao and Grishman, 2011b; Li et al., 2013; Yang and Mitchell, 2016) and the recent advanced deep learning models (Chen et al., 2015; Sha et al., 2018; Wang et al., 2019; Zhang et al., 2019a; Nguyen and Nguyen, 2019; Lai and Nguyen, 2019; Lai et al., 2020; Pouran Ben Veyseh et al., 2020). Only a few works have considered cross-lingual learning for EAE (Chen and Ji, 2009; Hsi et al., 2016; Subburathinam et al., 2019).

Cross-lingual transfer learning has also been examined for the other related tasks of EAE, including multilingual relation extraction (Kim et al., 2010; Qian et al., 2014; Faruqui and Kumar, 2015; Lin et al., 2017; Zou et al., 2018; Wang et al., 2018) and semantic role labeling (Mulcaire et al., 2018, 2019; Liu et al., 2019). However, none of these works explores edge-based attention GCN as we do.

Finally, our work is also related to the recent text structure models for other NLP tasks, including relation extraction (Sahu et al., 2019; Tran et al., 2020), event factuality prediction (Veyseh et al., 2019), and text summarization (Balachandran et al., 2020).

3 Model

We formalize EAE as a multi-class classification problem. Let $W = w_1, w_2, ..., w_N$ be a sentence (of N words) with w_t as the trigger word and w_a as the argument candidate (i.e., an entity mention) ($1 \leq t, a \leq N$). The goal of EAE is to predict the role y^* of w_a for the event triggered by w_t.

Following (Subburathinam et al., 2019), we use the UDPipe toolkit (Straka and Straková, 2017) to obtain the universal dependency tree for W, the part of speech (POS) tags and BIO entity type tags for the words in W. For convenience, let R be the set of universal dependency relations and E be the matrix for the embedding vectors of such dependency relations where E_r indicates the embedding vector for $r \in R$.

In the first step for cross-lingual EAE, each word w_i in W is represented by the concatenation vector x_i of three language-universal embedding vectors: $x_i = [x_i^w, x_i^p, x_i^e, x_i^d]$ where x_i^w is the multilingual word embedding for w_i from MUSE (Joulin et al., 2018), x_i^p is the embedding vector for the POS tag of $w_i \in W$, x_i^e is the embedding vector for the entity type tag of w_i, and x_i^d is the embedding vector E_{r_i} for the dependency relation r_i between w_i and its governor. The POS tag and entity type tag embeddings are initialized randomly and learned via training. After this step, the input sentence W would be transformed into a sequence of representation vectors $X = x_1, x_2, \ldots, x_N$. As presented in the introduction, our CEAE model involves three major sentence structures (i.e., A^{dep}, A^{sem}, and A^{rel}) that would be consumed by the GCN models to perform CEAE. We describe these components in detail below.

Models	Cross-lingual (training/test languages)									Monolingual		
	en/ch	en/ar	ch/en	ch/ar	ar/en	ar/ch	en+ch/ar	en+ar/ch	ch+ar/en	en	ch	ar
GCN	**59.0**	61.8	51.6	60.6	43.1	50.1	63.1	**60.1**	51.9	63.9	59.3	64.0
RSGCN	58.4	**62.9**	**53.9**	**63.3**	**48.0**	**52.6**	**64.0**	59.1	**55.5**	**64.9**	**63.7**	**66.9**

Table 1: F1 scores of the models on the test data.

Models	en/ch	en/ar	ch/en	ch/ar	ar/en	ar/ch
RSGCN	**55.3**	**63.3**	**56.0**	**63.8**	**50.5**	**53.8**
-A^{rel}	53.1	60.0	52.6	61.8	49.6	52.0
-A^{sem}	53.5	61.5	54.0	62.6	48.7	53.1
-A^{sem}-A^{rel}	53.8	61.4	52.3	59.4	47.6	51.9

Table 2: F1 scores of the models on the development data.

3.1 Language-Universal Sentence Structures

A sentence structure in this work refers to a real-valued matrix $A = \{a_{ij}\}_{i,j=1..N}$ capturing the levels of interactions/dependencies between the pairs of words in W. In particular, the score $a_{ij} \in A$ represents the contribution that the representation vector of w_j would provide for the representation vector computation of w_i in W according to some information source/perspective (e.g., syntax or semantic). Our goal in this work is to obtain the sentence structures for W based on the language-independent knowledge (thus called language-universal sentence structures) to enable cross-lingual representation learning for EAE. As such, three types of sentence structures are utilized in this work:

(i) Syntax-based Sentence Structures (denoted by $A^{dep} = \{a_{ij}^{dep}\}_{i,j=1..N}$): This structure is inherited from (Subburathinam et al., 2019) to capture the syntactic connections of the words in the dependency tree T of W. In particular, $a_{ij}^{dep} = 1$ only if w_i and w_j are connected in T.

(ii) Semantic-based Sentence Structures (denoted by $A^{sem} = \{a_{ij}^{sem}\}_{i,j=1..N}$): As mentioned in the introduction, this type of structures aims to leverage the semantic similarities between pairs of words as the universal knowledge across languages for CEAE. In this work, we use the multilingual word embedding vectors x_i^w to capture the semantic representations of the words w_i. The semantic-based structure score a_{ij}^{sem} is then computed by: $a_{ij}^{sem} = \tanh\left(u^\top(x_i^w \odot x_j^w)\right)$ where $\odot$ is the element-wise product and u is a learnable vector.

(iii) Relation-based Sentence Structures (denoted by $A^{rel} = \{a_{ij}^{rel}\}_{i,j=1..N}$): The syntax-based structures A^{dep} only consider the syntactic connections of the words to generate the structure scores. In this work, we note that the dependency relations (e.g., *nsubj*, *conj*) between the words in the universal dependency trees are also the language-independent concepts. To this end, we propose to further exploit such dependency relations to obtain the relation-based structure scores a_{ij}^{rel} for CEAE: $a_{ij}^{rel} = \tanh(v^\top E_{r_{ij}})$ if w_i and w_j are connected in T and 0 otherwise (here r_{ij} is the dependency relation between w_i and w_j in T). Here, v is a learnable vector.

Note that we normalize A_{dep} via the neighbor sizes of the words, and A_{sem}, A_{rel} via the softmax function to ensure that the weights corresponding to a word w_i (i.e., a_{ij}^* for $j = 1..N$) sum to 1.

3.2 Graph Convolutional Neural Networks

In order to exploit the aforementioned sentence structures for representation learning for CEAE, we propose to first combine the structures via a linear combination, leading to a richer structure $A = \{a_{ij}\}_{i,j=1..N}$:

$$A = \gamma_1 A^{dep} + \gamma_2 A^{sem} + (1 - \gamma_1 - \gamma_2)A^{rel} \quad (1)$$

Afterward, we follow (Subburathinam et al., 2019) to feed A into a GCN model for representation learning. In particular, the GCN model in this work involves L layers. The representation vector h_i^l for the word $w_i \in W$ at the l-th layer ($1 \leq l \leq L$) is computed via: $h_i^l = \text{ReLU}(\sum_{j=1}^{N} a_{ij}(W^l h_j^{l-1} + b^l))$ where h_i^0 is set to x_i for all $1 \leq i \leq N$, and W^l and b^l are the learnable weight matrices and bias vectors at the l-th layer.

In the next step, an overall representation vector V is computed based on hidden vectors in the last layer of the GCN model via: $V = [h_a^L, h_t^L, \text{max\_pooling}(h_1^L, \ldots, h_N^L)]$. This vector is sent into an one-layer feed-forward network to

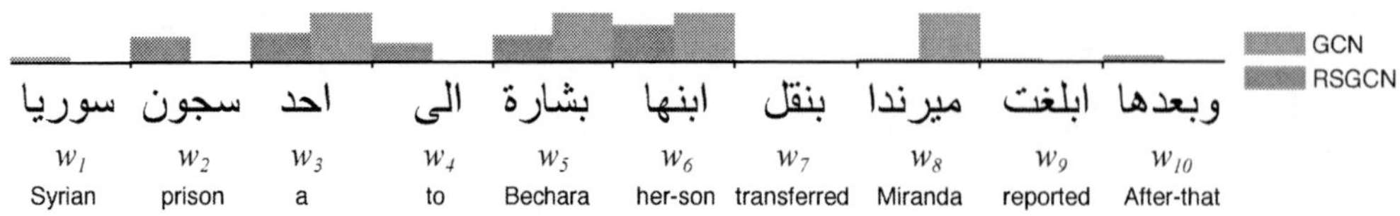

Figure 1: Visualization of the weights of the words with respect to the trigger word w_7 (i.e., a_{7j} and a_{7j}^{dep}).

estimate the distribution $P(.|W, w_a, w_t)$ over all the possible argument roles for our CEAE problem. Finally, the negative log-likelihood $L = -\log P(y^*|W, w_a, w_t)$ is used as the loss function to train the models in this work.

4 Experiments

4.1 Dataset and Hyper-parameters

Following (Subburathinam et al., 2019), we evaluate the models in this work using the multilingual ACE 2005 dataset where the EAE data is provided for three languages, i.e., Arabic (*ar*), Chinese (*ch*), and English (*en*). We use the preprocessed data and the train/dev/test split provided by (Subburathinam et al., 2019) to ensure a fair comparison. The development data is used to finetune hyper-parameters. In particular, we use 30 dimensions for the POS and entity type embeddings, 30 dimensions for the dependency relation embeddings (that are initialized randomly and updated during training), 200 dimensions for the hidden vector of GCN, 2 layers for the GCN model, the bath size of 50 for mini-batching, 0.5 for the learning rate for the SGD optimizer, and 0.9 for the learning rate decay. For the novel sentence structures, we observe that $\gamma_1 = 0.6$ and $\gamma_2 = 0.1$ leads to the best performance of the proposed model on the development data.

4.2 Comparison with the State of the Art

This section compares the proposed model (called **RSGCN** – Rich Sentence Structure-based GCN) with the GCN-based model in (Subburathinam et al., 2019) (called **GCN**). In particular, the models are trained on the training datasets for one or two of the three language (i.e., *en*, *ch* and *ar*) that are then evaluated on the test datasets for the other languages. Table 1 reports the performance of the models. As we can see, the proposed model RSGCN significantly outperforms GCN on seven over nine cross-lingual settings, and interestingly also on all the monolingual settings with substantial performance gaps ($p < 0.01$). This clearly demonstrates the advantages of the proposed semantic-based and relation-based structures for CEAE.

4.3 Ablation Study

To assess the contributions of the novel semantic-based (A^{sem}) and relation-based (A^{rel}) structures in this work, we exclude each of them from RSGCN and evaluate the performance of the remaining model on development data. This ablation study is conducted over six different cross-lingual settings, i.e., six choices for different source and target language.

Table 2 shows that both structures A^{sem} and A^{rel} are necessary for the proposed model as removing any of them would hurt the performance across different language pairs. We also observe that for most language pairs (e.g., *en/ar*, *ch/en*), excluding A^{rel} would lead to a deeper performance drop than those for removing A^{sem}, thus demonstrating the more importance of A^{rel} over A^{sem}. We attribute this to the fact that the A^{rel} structure is based on explicit structural information (i.e., dependency relations) which could be more valuable for the structure transfer.

4.4 Analysis

To understand the effect of the proposed structures, we analyze the examples from the development data of the setting *en/ar* that RSGCN makes correct predictions but GCN does not. Among others, we find that the proposed sentence structures help RSGCN assign more appropriate structure scores for the words for better representation learning. Consider Figure 1 as an example where a rough translation for the sentence is *"After that, Miranda was informed that her son Bechara had been transferred to a Syrian prison"*. In this example, the word w_7 (i.e., *"transferred"*) is the trigger of the event *"Movement-Transport"*, and the word w_6 (i.e., *"her son"*) is the argument with the role *"Artifact"*.

As shown in the figure, both RSGCN and GCN assign the highest score for the most important word w_6 (i.e., *"her son"*). However, in addition to that, GCN also considers the words w_5 (i.e.,

"Bechara"), w_3 (i.e., *"a"*), and w_8 (i.e., *"Miranda"*) as equally important as w_6. This is problematic as the irrelevant words w_3 and w_5 for argument role identification might introduce noise into the representation vectors. Even worse, the high score for w_8 might cause the model to incorrectly predict *"Miranda"* as the argument in this case. To this end, the proposed sentence structures help RSGCN to mitigate such issues by re-distributing the scores so *"her son"* can have the highest score and the confusing word *"Miranda"* is almost canceled (with the nearly zero score), eventually leading to the success of RSGCN on this example.

5 Conclusion and Future Work

We introduce two novel sentence structures for cross-lingual EAE with GCNs based on the semantic similarity and the universal dependency relations of the words in the input sentences. The experiments demonstrate the benefits of the proposed sentence structures that lead to the state-of-the-art performance for different experiments scenarios for CEAE. In the future, we plan to apply the proposed model to other related tasks, e.g., cross-lingual relation extraction (Veyseh et al., 2020). In addition, motivated by the recent introduction of high-performance multilingual NLP toolkits, e.g., Trankit (Nguyen et al., 2021), we expect to extend our work to other languages to better demonstrate the benefits of the proposed models. Finally, we will also explore the performance of our models when recent pre-trained multilingual language models, e.g., multilingual BERT (Devlin et al., 2019), are employed to encode input texts for different languages.

Acknowledgments

This research has been supported by the Army Research Office (ARO) grant W911NF-17-S-0002. This research is also based upon work supported by the Office of the Director of National Intelligence (ODNI), Intelligence Advanced Research Projects Activity (IARPA), via IARPA Contract No. 2019-19051600006 under the Better Extraction from Text Towards Enhanced Retrieval (BETTER) Program. The views and conclusions contained herein are those of the authors and should not be interpreted as necessarily representing the official policies, either expressed or implied, of ARO, ODNI, IARPA, the Department of Defense, or the U.S. Government. The U.S. Government is authorized to reproduce and distribute reprints for governmental purposes notwithstanding any copyright annotation therein. This document does not contain technology or technical data controlled under either the U.S. International Traffic in Arms Regulations or the U.S. Export Administration Regulations.

References

Vidhisha Balachandran, Artidoro Pagnoni, Jay Yoon Lee, Dheeraj Rajagopal, Jaime Carbonell, and Yulia Tsvetkov. 2020. Structsum: Incorporating latent and explicit sentence dependencies for single document summarization. In *arXiv preprint arXiv:2003.00576*.

Yubo Chen, Liheng Xu, Kang Liu, Daojian Zeng, and Jun Zhao. 2015. Event extraction via dynamic multi-pooling convolutional neural networks. In *ACL*.

Zheng Chen and Heng Ji. 2009. Can one language bootstrap the other: a case study on event extraction. In *Workshop on Semi-Supervised Learning for Natural Language Processing*.

Jacob Devlin, Ming-Wei Chang, Kenton Lee, and Kristina Toutanova. 2019. Bert: Pre-training of deep bidirectional transformers for language understanding. In *ACL*.

Manaal Faruqui and Shankar Kumar. 2015. Multilingual open relation extraction using cross-lingual projection. In *NAACL-HLT*.

Andrew Hsi, Yiming Yang, Jaime Carbonell, and Ruochen Xu. 2016. Leveraging multilingual training for limited resource event extraction. In *COLING*.

Heng Ji and Ralph Grishman. 2008. Refining event extraction through cross-document inference. In *ACL*.

Armand Joulin, Piotr Bojanowski, Tomas Mikolov, Hervé Jégou, and Edouard Grave. 2018. Loss in translation: Learning bilingual word mapping with a retrieval criterion. In *EMNLP*.

Seokhwan Kim, Minwoo Jeong, Jonghoon Lee, and Gary Geunbae Lee. 2010. A cross-lingual annotation projection approach for relation detection. In *COLING*.

Thomas N. Kipf and Max Welling. 2017. Semi-supervised classification with graph convolutional networks. In *ICLR*.

Viet Dac Lai and Thien Huu Nguyen. 2019. Extending event detection to new types with learning from keywords. In *Proceedings of the 5th Workshop on Noisy User-generated Text (W-NUT) at EMNLP 2019*.

Viet Dac Lai, Tuan Ngo Nguyen, and Thien Huu Nguyen. 2020. Event detection: Gate diversity and syntactic importance scores for graph convolution neural networks. In *EMNLP*.

Qi Li, Heng Ji, Yu Hong, and Sujian Li. 2014. Constructing information networks using one single model. In *EMNLP*.

Qi Li, Heng Ji, and Liang Huang. 2013. Joint event extraction via structured prediction with global features. In *ACL*.

Shasha Liao and Ralph Grishman. 2011a. Acquiring topic features to improve event extraction: in preselected and balanced collections. In *RANLP*.

Shasha Liao and Ralph Grishman. 2011b. Acquiring topic features to improve event extraction: in preselected and balanced collections. In *RANLP*.

Yankai Lin, Zhiyuan Liu, and Maosong Sun. 2017. Neural relation extraction with multi-lingual attention. In *ACL*.

Nelson F. Liu, Matt Gardner, Yonatan Belinkov, Matthew E. Peters, and Noah A. Smith. 2019. Linguistic knowledge and transferability of contextual representations. In *NAACL-HLT*.

Xiao Liu, Zhunchen Luo, and Heyan Huang. 2018. Jointly multiple events extraction via attention-based graph information aggregation. In *EMNLP*.

Phoebe Mulcaire, Jungo Kasai, and Noah A. Smith. 2019. Polyglot contextual representations improve crosslingual transfer. In *NAACL-HLT*.

Phoebe Mulcaire, Swabha Swayamdipta, and Noah A. Smith. 2018. Polyglot semantic role labeling. In *ACL*.

Minh Nguyen, Viet Lai, Amir Pouran Ben Veyseh, and Thien Huu Nguyen. 2021. Trankit: A light-weight transformer-based toolkit for multilingual natural language processing. In *EACL (System Demonstrations)*.

Thien Huu Nguyen, Kyunghyun Cho, and Ralph Grishman. 2016. Joint event extraction via recurrent neural networks. In *NAACL-HLT*.

Thien Huu Nguyen and Ralph Grishman. 2015b. Event detection and domain adaptation with convolutional neural networks. In *ACL-IJCNLP*.

Thien Huu Nguyen and Ralph Grishman. 2018. Graph convolutional networks with argument-aware pooling for event detection. In *AAAI*.

Trung Minh Nguyen and Thien Huu Nguyen. 2019. One for all: Neural joint modeling of entities and events. In *AAAI*.

Siddharth Patwardhan and Ellen Riloff. 2009. A unified model of phrasal and sentential evidence for information extraction. In *ACL*.

Amir Pouran Ben Veyseh, Tuan Ngo Nguyen, and Thien Huu Nguyen. 2020. Graph transformer networks with syntactic and semantic structures for event argument extraction. In *EMNLP Findings*.

Longhua Qian, Haotian Hui, Yanan Hu, Guodong Zhou, and Qiaoming Zhu. 2014. Bilingual active learning for relation classification via pseudo parallel corpora. In *ACL*.

Sunil Kumar Sahu, Fenia Christopoulou, Makoto Miwa, and Sophia Ananiadou. 2019. Inter-sentence relation extraction with document-level graph convolutional neural network. In *ACL*.

Lei Sha, Feng Qian, Baobao Chang, and Zhifang Sui. 2018. Jointly extracting event triggers and arguments by dependency-bridge rnn and tensor-based argument interaction. In *AAAI*.

Milan Straka and Jana Straková. 2017. Tokenizing, pos tagging, lemmatizing and parsing ud 2.0 with udpipe. In *CoNLL*.

Ananya Subburathinam, Di Lu, Heng Ji, Jonathan May, Shih-Fu Chang, Avirup Sil, and Clare Voss. 2019. Cross-lingual structure transfer for relation and event extraction. In *EMNLP-IJCNLP*.

Hieu Minh Tran, Minh Trung Nguyen, and Thien Huu Nguyen. 2020. The dots have their values: Exploiting the node-edge connections in graph-based neural models for document-level relation extraction. In *EMNLP Findings*.

Amir Pouran Ben Veyseh, Franck Dernoncourt, Dejing Dou, and Thien Huu Nguyen. 2020. Exploiting the syntax-model consistency for neural relation extraction. In *ACL*.

Amir Pouran Ben Veyseh, Thien Huu Nguyen, and Dejing Dou. 2019. Graph based neural networks for event factuality prediction using syntactic and semantic structures. In *ACL*.

Xiaozhi Wang, Xu Han, Yankai Lin, Zhiyuan Liu, and Maosong Sun. 2018. Adversarial multi-lingual neural relation extraction. In *COLING*.

Xiaozhi Wang, Ziqi Wang, Xu Han, Zhiyuan Liu, Juanzi Li, Peng Li, Maosong Sun, Jie Zhou, and Xiang Ren. 2019. Hmeae: Hierarchical modular event argument extraction. In *EMNLP-IJCNLP*.

Bishan Yang and Tom M. Mitchell. 2016. Joint extraction of events and entities within a document context. In *NAACL-HLT*.

Junchi Zhang, Yanxia Qin, Yue Zhang, Mengchi Liu, and Donghong Ji. 2019a. Extracting entities and events as a single task using a transition-based neural model. In *IJCAI*.

Tongtao Zhang, Heng Ji, and Avirup Sil. 2019b. Joint entity and event extraction with generative adversarial imitation learning. In *Data Intelligence*.

Yuhao Zhang, Peng Qi, and Christopher Manning. 2018. Graph convolution over pruned dependency trees improves relation extraction. In *EMNLP*.

Bowei Zou, Zengzhuang Xu, Yu Hong, and Guodong Zhou. 2018. Adversarial feature adaptation for cross-lingual relation classification. In *COLING*.

NADI 2021:
The Second Nuanced Arabic Dialect Identification Shared Task

Muhammad Abdul-Mageed, Chiyu Zhang, AbdelRahim Elmadany, Houda Bouamor,[†] Nizar Habash[‡]
The University of British Columbia, Vancouver, Canada
[†]Carnegie Mellon University in Qatar, Qatar
[‡]New York University Abu Dhabi, UAE
{muhammad.mageed, a.elmadany}@ubc.ca chiyuzh@mail.ubc.ca
hbouamor@cmu.edu nizar.habash@nyu.edu

Abstract

We present the findings and results of the Second Nuanced Arabic Dialect Identification Shared Task (NADI 2021). This Shared Task includes four subtasks: country-level Modern Standard Arabic (MSA) identification (Subtask 1.1), country-level dialect identification (Subtask 1.2), province-level MSA identification (Subtask 2.1), and province-level sub-dialect identification (Subtask 2.2). The shared task dataset covers a total of 100 provinces from 21 Arab countries, collected from the Twitter domain. A total of 53 teams from 23 countries registered to participate in the tasks, thus reflecting the interest of the community in this area. We received 16 submissions for Subtask 1.1 from five teams, 27 submissions for Subtask 1.2 from eight teams, 12 submissions for Subtask 2.1 from four teams, and 13 Submissions for subtask 2.2 from four teams.

1 Introduction

Arabic is the native tongue of $\sim$ 400 million people living the Arab world, a vast geographical region across Africa and Asia. Far from a single monolithic language, Arabic has a wide number of varieties. In general, Arabic could be classified into three main categories: (1) Classical Arabic, the language of the Qur'an and early literature; (2) Modern Standard Arabic (MSA), which is usually used in education and formal and pan-Arab media; and (3) dialectal Arabic (DA), a collection of geopolitically defined variants. Modern day Arabic is usually referred to as *diglossic* with a so-called 'High' variety used in formal settings (MSA), and a 'Low' variety used in everyday communication (DA). DA, the presumably 'Low' variety, is itself a host of variants. For the current work, we focus on geography as an axis of variation where people from various sub-regions, countries, or even provinces within the same country, may be using Arabic differently.

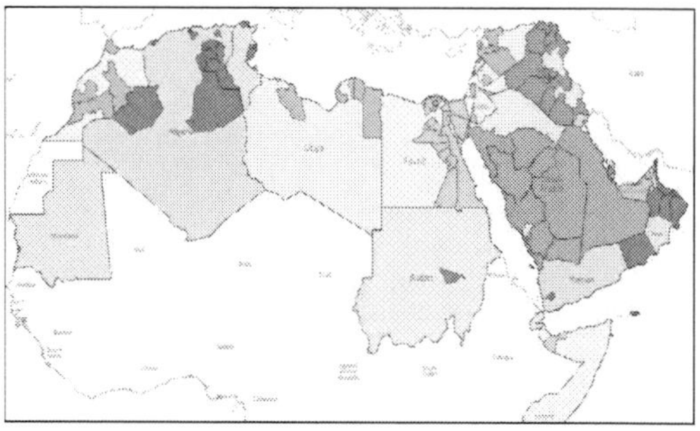

Figure 1: A map of the Arab World showing thr 21 countries and 100 provinces in the NADI 2021 datasets. Each country is coded in color different from neighboring countries. Provinces within each country are coded in a more intense version of the same color as the country.

The Nuanced Arabic Dialect Identification (NADI) series of shared tasks aim at furthering the study and analysis of Arabic variants by providing resources and organizing classification competitions under standardized settings. The First Nuanced Arabic Dialect Identification (NADI 2020) Shared Task targeted 21 Arab countries and a total of 100 provinces across these countries. NADI 2020 consisted of two subtasks: *country-level* dialect identification (Subtask 1) and *province-level* detection (Subtask 2). The two subtasks depended on Twitter data, making it the first shared task to target naturally-occurring fine-grained dialectal text at the sub-country level. The Second Nuanced Arabic Dialect Identification (NADI 2021) is similar to NADI 2020 in that it also targets the same 21 Arab countries and 100 corresponding provinces and is based on Twitter data. However, NADI 2021 has four subtasks, organized into country level and

Proceedings of the Sixth Arabic Natural Language Processing Workshop, pages 244–259
Kyiv, Ukraine (Virtual), April 19, 2021.

province level. For each classification level, we afford both MSA and DA datasets as Table 1 shows.

Variety	Country	Province
MSA	Subtask 1.1	Subtask 2.1
DA	Subtask 1.2	Subtask 2.2

Table 1: NADI 2021 subtasks.

We provided participants with a new Twitter labeled dataset that we collected exclusively for the purpose of the shared task. The dataset is publicly available for research.[1] A total of 53 teams registered for the shard task, of whom 8 unique teams ended up submitting their systems for scoring. We allowed a maximum of five submissions per team. We received 16 submissions for Subtask 1.1 from five teams, 27 submissions for Subtask 1.2 from eight teams, 12 submissions for Subtask 2.1 from four teams, and 13 Submissions for subtask 2.2 from four teams. We then received seven papers, all of which we accepted for publication.

This paper is organized as follows. We provide a brief overview of the computational linguistic literature on Arabic dialects in Section 2. We describe the two subtasks and dataset in Sections 3 and Section 4, respectively. And finally, we introduce participating teams, shared task results, and a high-level description of submitted systems in Section 5.

2 Related Work

As we explained in Section 1, Arabic has three main categories: CA, MSA, and DA. While CA and MSA have been studied extensively (Harrell, 1962; Cowell, 1964; Badawi, 1973; Brustad, 2000; Holes, 2004), DA has received more attention only in recent years.

One major challenge with studying DA has been rarity of resources. For this reason, most pioneering DA works focused on creating resources, usually for only a small number of regions or countries (Gadalla et al., 1997; Diab et al., 2010; Al-Sabbagh and Girju, 2012; Sadat et al., 2014; Smaïli et al., 2014; Jarrar et al., 2016; Khalifa et al., 2016; Al-Twairesh et al., 2018; El-Haj, 2020). A number of works introducing multi-dialectal data sets and regional level detection models followed (Zaidan and Callison-Burch, 2011; Elfardy et al., 2014; Bouamor et al., 2014; Meftouh et al., 2015).

[1]The dataset is accessible via our GitHub at: https://github.com/UBC-NLP/nadi.

Arabic dialect identification work as further sparked by a series of shared tasks offered as part of the VarDial workshop. These shared tasks used speech broadcast transcriptions (Malmasi et al., 2016), and integrated acoustic features (Zampieri et al., 2017) and phonetic features (Zampieri et al., 2018) extracted from raw audio. Althobaiti (2020) is a recent survey of computational work on Arabic dialects.

The Multi Arabic Dialects Application and Resources (MADAR) project (Bouamor et al., 2018) introduced finer-grained dialectal data and a lexicon. The MADAR data were used for dialect identification at the city level (Salameh et al., 2018; Obeid et al., 2019) of 25 Arab cities. An issue with the MADAR data, in the context of DA identification, is that it was commissioned and not naturally occurring. Several larger datasets covering 10-21 countries were also introduced (Mubarak and Darwish, 2014; Abdul-Mageed et al., 2018; Zaghouani and Charfi, 2018). These datasets come from the Twitter domain, and hence are naturally-occurring.

Several works have also focused on socio-pragmatics meaning exploiting dialectal data. These include sentiment analysis (Abdul-Mageed et al., 2014), emotion (Alhuzali et al., 2018), age and gender (Abbes et al., 2020), offensive language (Mubarak et al., 2020), and sarcasm (Abu Farha and Magdy, 2020). Concurrent with our work, (Abdul-Mageed et al., 2020c) also describe data and models at country, province, and city levels.

The first NADI shared task, NADI 2020 (Abdul-Mageed et al., 2020b), comprised two subtasks, one focusing on 21 Arab countries exploiting Twitter data, and another on 100 Arab provinces from the same 21 countries. As is explained in (Abdul-Mageed et al., 2020b), the NADI 2020 datasets included a small amount of non-Arabic and also a mixture of MSA and DA. For NADI 2021, we continue to focus on 21 countries and 100 provinces. However, we breakdown the data into MSA and DA for a stronger signal. This also gives us the opportunity to study each of these two main categories independently. In other words, in addition to dialect and sub-dialect identification, it allows us to investigate the extent to which MSA itself can be teased apart at the country and province levels. Our hope is that NADI 2021 will support exploring variation in geographical regions that have not been studied before.

3 Task Description

The NADI shared task consists of four subtasks, comprising two levels of classification–country and province. Each level of classification is carried out for both MSA and DA. We explain the different subtasks across each classification level next.

3.1 Country-level Classification

- **Subtask 1.1: Country-level MSA.** The goal of Subtask 1.1 is to identify country level MSA from short written sentences (tweets). NADI 2021 Subtask 1.1 is novel since no previous works focused on teasing apart MSA by country of origin.

- **Subtask 1.2: Country-level DA.** Subtask 1.2 is similar to Subtask 1.1, but focuses on identifying country level *dialect* from tweets. Subtask 1.2 is similar to previous works that have also taken country as their target (Mubarak and Darwish, 2014; Abdul-Mageed et al., 2018; Zaghouani and Charfi, 2018; Bouamor et al., 2019; Abdul-Mageed et al., 2020b).

We provided labeled data to NADI 2021 participants with specific training (TRAIN) and development (DEV) splits. Each of the 21 labels corresponding to the 21 countries is represented in both TRAIN and DEV. Teams could score their models through an online system (codalab) on the DEV set before the deadline. We released our TEST set of unlabeled tweets shortly before the system submission deadline. We then invited participants to submit their predictions to the online scoring system housing the gold TEST set labels. Table 2 shows the distribution of the TRAIN, DEV, and TEST splits across the 21 countries.

3.2 Province-level Classification

- **Subtask 2.1: Province-level MSA.** The goal of Subtask 2.1 is to identify the specific state or province (henceforth, *province*) from which an MSA tweet was posted. There are 100 province labels in the data, and provinces are unequally distributed among the list of 21 countries.

- **Subtask 2.2: Province-level DA.** Again, Subtask 2.2 is similar to Subtask 2.1, but the goal is identifying the province from which a *dialectal* tweet was posted.

While the MADAR shared task (Bouamor et al., 2019) involved prediction of a small set of cities, NADI 2020 was the first to propose automatic dialect identification at geographical regions as small as provinces. Concurrent with NADI 2020, (Abdul-Mageed et al., 2020c) introduced the concept of *microdialects*, and proposed models for identifying language varieties defined at both province and city levels. NADI 2021 follows these works, but has one novel aspect: We introduce province-level identification for MSA and DA independently (i.e., each variety is handled in a separate subtask). While province-level sub-dialect identification may be challenging, we hypothesize province-level MSA might be even more difficult. However, we were curious to what extent, if possible at all, a machine would be successful in teasing apart MSA data at the province-level.

In addition, similar to NADI 2020, we acknowledge that province-level classification is somewhat related to geolocation prediction exploiting Twitter data. However, we emphasize that geolocation prediction is performed at the level of *users*, rather than tweets. This makes our subtasks different from geolocation work. Another difference lies in the way we collect our data as we will explain in Section 4. Tables 11 and 12 (Appendix A) show the distribution of the 100 province classes in our MSA and DA data splits, respectively. ***Importantly, for all 4 subtasks, tweets in the TRAIN, DEV and TEST splits come from disjoint sets.***

3.3 Restrictions and Evaluation Metrics

We follow the same general approach to managing the shared task as our first NADI in 2020. This includes providing participating teams with a set of restrictions that apply to all subtasks, and clear evaluation metrics. The purpose of our restrictions is to ensure fair comparisons and common experimental conditions. In addition, similar to NADI 2020, our data release strategy and our evaluation setup through the CodaLab online platform facilitated the competition management, enhanced timeliness of acquiring results upon system submission, and guaranteed ultimate transparency.[2]

Once a team registered in the shared task, we directly provided the registering member with the data via a private download link. We provided the data in the form of the actual tweets posted to the Twitter platform, rather than tweet IDs. This

[2]`https://codalab.org/`

Country	Provinces	MSA (Subtasks 1.1 & 2.1)					DA (Subtasks 1.2 & 2.2)				
		Train	DEV	TEST	Total	%	Train	DEV	TEST	Total	%
Algeria	9	1,899	427	439	2,765	8.92	1,809	430	391	2,630	8.48
Bahrain	1	211	51	51	313	1.01	215	52	52	319	1.03
Djibouti	1	211	52	51	314	1.01	215	27	7	249	0.80
Egypt	20	4,220	1,032	989	6,241	20.13	4,283	1,041	1,051	6,375	20.56
Iraq	13	2,719	671	652	4,042	13.04	2,729	664	664	4,057	13.09
Jordan	2	422	103	102	627	2.02	429	104	105	638	2.06
Kuwait	2	422	103	102	627	2.02	429	105	106	640	2.06
Lebanon	3	633	155	141	929	3.00	644	157	120	921	2.97
Libya	6	1,266	310	307	1,883	6.07	1,286	314	316	1,916	6.18
Mauritania	1	211	52	51	314	1.01	215	53	53	321	1.04
Morocco	4	844	207	205	1,256	4.05	858	207	212	1,277	4.12
Oman	7	1,477	341	357	2,175	7.02	1,501	355	371	2,227	7.18
Palestine	2	422	102	102	626	2.02	428	104	105	637	2.05
Qatar	1	211	52	51	314	1.01	215	52	53	320	1.03
KSA	10	2,110	510	510	3,130	10.10	2,140	520	522	3,182	10.26
Somalia	2	346	63	102	511	1.65	172	49	55	276	0.89
Sudan	1	211	48	51	310	1.00	215	53	53	321	1.04
Syria	6	1,266	309	306	1,881	6.07	1,287	278	288	1,853	5.98
Tunisia	4	844	170	176	1,190	3.84	859	173	212	1,244	4.01
UAE	3	633	154	153	940	3.03	642	157	158	957	3.09
Yemen	2	422	88	102	612	1.97	429	105	106	640	2.06
Total	**100**	**21,000**	**5,000**	**5,000**	**31,000**	**100**	**21,000**	**5,000**	**5,000**	**31,000**	**100**

Table 2: Distribution of classes and data splits over our MSA and DA datasets for the four subtasks.

guaranteed comparison between systems exploiting identical data. For all four subtasks, we provided clear instructions requiring participants not to use any external data. That is, teams were required to only use the data we provided to develop their systems and no other datasets regardless how these are acquired. For example, we requested that teams do not search nor depend on any additional user-level information such as geolocation. To alleviate these strict constraints and encourage creative use of diverse (machine learning) methods in system development, we provided an unlabeled dataset of 10M tweets in the form of tweet IDs. This dataset is in addition to our labeled TRAIN and DEV splits for the four subtasks. To facilitate acquisition of this unlabeled dataset, we also provided a simple script that can be used to collect the tweets. We encouraged participants to use these 10M unlabeled tweets in any way they wished.

For all four subtasks, the official metric is macro-averaged F_1 score obtained on blind test sets. We also report performance in terms of macro-averaged precision, macro-averaged recall and accuracy for systems submitted to each of the four subtasks. Each participating team was allowed to submit up to five runs for each subtask, and only the highest scoring run was kept as representing the team. Although official results are based only on a blind TEST set, we also asked participants to report their results on the DEV set in their papers. We setup four CodaLab competitions for scoring participant systems.[3] We will keep the Codalab competition for each subtask live post competition, for researchers who would be interested in training models and evaluating their systems using the shared task TEST set. For this reason, we will not release labels for the TEST set of any of the subtasks.

4 Shared Task Datasets

We distributed two Twitter datasets, one in MSA and another in DA. Each tweet in each of these two datasets has two labels, one label for country level and another label for province level. For example, for the MSA dataset, the same tweet is assigned one out of 21 country labels (Subtask 1.1) and one out of 100 province labels (Subtask 2.1). The same applies to DA data, where each tweet is assigned a country label (Subtask 1.2) and a province label (Subtask 2.2). Similar to MSA, the tagset for DA data has 21 country labels and 100 province labels.

[3] Links to the CodaLab competitions are as follows: Subtask 1.1: https://competitions.codalab.org/competitions/27768, Subtask 1.2: https://competitions.codalab.org/competitions/27769, Subtask 2.1: https://competitions.codalab.org/competitions/27770, Subtask 2.2: https://competitions.codalab.org/competitions/27771.

In addition, as mentioned before, we made available an unlabeled dataset for optional use in any of the four subtasks. We now provide more details about both the labeled and unlabeled data.

4.1 Data Collection

Similar to NADI 2020, we used the Twitter API to crawl data from 100 provinces belonging to 21 Arab countries for 10 months (Jan. to Oct., 2019).[4] Next, we identified users who consistently and *exclusively* tweeted from a single province during the whole 10 month period. We crawled up to 3,200 tweets from each of these users. We select only tweets assigned the Arabic language tag (`ar`) by Twitter. We lightly normalize tweets by removing usernames and hyperlinks, and add white space between emojis. Next, we remove retweets (i.e., we keep only tweets and replies). Then, we use character-level string matching to remove sequences that have < 3 Arabic tokens.

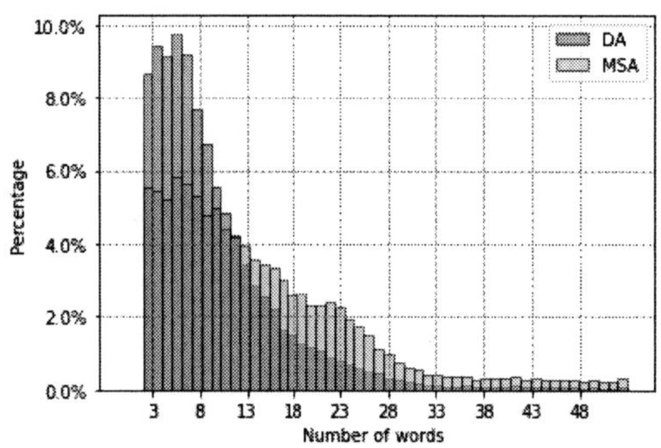

Figure 2: Distribution of tweet length (trimmed at 50) in words in NADI-2021 labeled data.

Since the Twitter language tag can be wrong sometimes, we apply an effective in-house language identification tool on the tweets and replies to exclude any non-Arabic. This helps us remove posts in Farsi (`fa`) and Persian (`ps`) which Twitter wrongly assigned an Arabic language tag. Finally, to tease apart MSA from DA, we use the dialect-MSA model introduced in Abdul-Mageed et al. (2020a) (acc= 89.1%, F1= 88.6%).

4.2 Data Sets

To assign labels for the different subtasks, we use user *location* as a proxy for *language variety labels* at both country and province levels. This applies to both our MSA and DA data. That is, we label tweets from each user with the country and province from which the user consistently posted for the *whole* of the 10 months period. Although this method of label assignment is not ideal, it is still a reasonable approach for easing the bottleneck of data annotation. For both the MSA and DA data, across the two levels of classification (i.e., country and province), we randomly sample 21K tweets for training (TRAIN), 5K tweets for development (DEV), and 5K tweets for testing (TEST). These three splits come from three disjoint sets of users. We distribute data for the four subtasks directly to participants in the form of actual tweet text. Table 2 shows the distribution of tweets across the data splits over the 21 countries, for all subtasks. We provide the data distribution over the 100 provinces in Appendix A. More specifically, Table 11 shows the province-level distribution of tweets for MSA (Subtask 2.1) and Table 12 shows the same for DA (Subtask 2.2). We provide examples DA tweets from a number of countries representing different regions in Table 3. For each example in Table 3, we list the province it comes from. Similarly, we provide example MSA data in Table 4.

Unlabeled 10M. We shared 10M Arabic tweets with participants in the form of tweet IDs. We crawled these tweets in 2019. Arabic was identified using Twitter language tag (`ar`). This dataset does not have any labels and we call it UNLABELED 10M. We also included in our data package released to participants a simple script to crawl these tweets. Participants were free to use UNLABELED 10M for any of the four subtasks in any way they they see fits.[5] We now present shared task teams and results.

5 Shared Task Teams & Results

5.1 Our Baseline Systems

We provide two simple baselines, Baseline I and Baseline II, for each of the four subtasks. **Baseline I** is based on the majority class in the TRAIN data for each subtask. It performs at $F_1 = 1.57\%$ and $accuracy = 19.78\%$ for Subtask 1.1, $F_1 = 1.65\%$ and $accuracy = 21.02\%$ for Subtask 1.2, $F_1 = 0.02\%$ and $accuracy = 1.02\%$ for Subtask

[4]Although we tried, we could not collect data from Comoros to cover all 22 Arab countries.

[5]Datasets for all the subtasks and UNLABELED 10M are available at `https://github.com/UBC-NLP/nadi`. More information about the data format can be found in the accompanying README file.

Country	Province	Tweet
Algeria	Bouira	شحال راكي تبيعي فيه... نحي ندي كونتيتي
	Khenchela	شحال يقلبو النم هاذوك لي يقدسو الراپرز ،!
	Oran	راك زعفان مزية ربحتوا
Egypt	Alexandria	بس مش زي ما هنقدر نعدي حياتنا
	Minya	بص انا كل مضميري هيبقي صاحي هجيلك تقتلهولي
	Sohag	انا معنديش حد يفسحنى زي الوليه
KSA	Ar-Riyad	و يعدين تجلسون تلعبون سماش !!
	Ash-Sharqiyah	يابن الحلال اسمهم رجال فقراويه مايفهمون تبي حريمهم تفهم
	Tabuk	طيب ايش دخل الوزارة هذي وفاه طبيعيه
Morocco	Marrakech-Tensift-Al-Haouz	مافي ربح ولا كرش العصبية اشرب بنادول عشان ارتاح
	Meknes-Tafilalet	مراداون إنيخ أداخ إعفو ربي خ إمداكلن لحاجت !!!!
	Souss-Massa-Draa	أبيه نسيتهم ڭاع حتى هما متشيعيين بزاف
Oman	Ash-Sharqiyah	يحصلج انتي اصلاً حد يعلق لج.
	Dhofar	اسمعي قران ، ميبي تغفين عليه
	Musandam	ماني بقايل غلاتك هقوه وخابت بقول عين الحسود الله يجازيها
Palestine	Gaza-Strip	احنا اليوم عاملين مفتول وانتو ؟؟
	West-Bank	اتفقنا ع هيك
	West-Bank	اليوم كنت فيهم بجننو
Sudan	Khartoum	صرت عادي اشوف أشياء تقهرني واسكت. لأني ادري لو تكلمت م راح القي شي برضيني صرت انهي كلامي...
	Khartoum	من وين جبتي كلامك دا..... إستندتي علي شنو إنه لو قتلنا ح نكون قتلة...
	Khartoum	انا شكلي حأتبع سياسة قصي وابلك من طرف.
UAE	Abu-Dhabi	يحسبني لاهِي عنه و أنا ملتهي به
	Dubai	يلي يبا خوتي بالطيب خاويته
	Ras-Al-Khaymah	ل موسم نخربها بالاخر وما تدري شو المشكلة الأساسية احسك مني مليت

Table 3: Randomly picked DA tweets from select provinces and corresponding countries.

2.1, and F_1 = 0.02% and $accuracy$ = 1.06% for Subtask 2.2.

Baseline II is a fine-tuned multi-lingual BERT-Base model (mBERT)[6]. More specifically, we fine-tune mBERT for 20 epochs with a learning rate of $2e-5$, and batch size of 32. The maximum length of input sequence is set as 64 tokens. We evaluate the model at the end of each epoch and choose the best model on our DEV set. We then report the best model on the TEST set. Our best mBERT model obtains F_1 = 14.15% and $accuracy$ = 24.76% on Subtask 1.1, F_1 = 18.02% and $accuracy$ = 33.04% on Subtask 1.2, F_1 = 3.39% and $accuracy$ = 3.48% on Subtask 2.1, and F_1 = 4.08% and $accuracy$ = 4.18% on Subtask 2.2 as Tables 6, 7, 8, and 9, respectively.

5.2 Participating Teams

We received a total of 53 unique team registrations. After evaluation phase, we received a total of 68 submissions. The breakdown across the subtasks is as follows: 16 submissions for Subtask 1.1 from five teams, 27 submissions for Subtask 1.2 from eight teams, 12 submissions for Subtask 2.1 from four teams, and 13 submissions for Subtask 2.2 from four teams. Of participating teams, seven teams submitted description papers, all of which we accepted for publication. Table 5 lists the seven teams.

[6]https://github.com/google-research/bert

Country	Province	Tweet
Algeria	Biskra	عندك حق جلال .اصبح مستحيل
	Oran	انتظرتك طويلا على عتبة اللقاء جهزت خطابا ... و عتابا .. و ما اردت غير عناقا .. اخبرتك كثيرا ... انني اريد ان ابكي... اوغى
	Ouargla	أجمل شيئ هو البساطة فألف تحية لعائلة أبو تريك
Egypt	Faiyum	الان يرحل عن ربوعك فارس مهزوم
	Minya	من الأذكار، أعوذ بكلمات الله التامة من كل شيطان وهامة ومن كل عين لامة
	Red-Sea	اللهم بشرني بالجنه ، اللهم ارزقني الفردوس الاعلى من غير حساب ولا سابقة عذاب
KSA	Al-Madinah	ومن جميل ما قيل في السّلام : سلاماً على من مَرَ على مُرِنَا مُحَلَاه .
	Ar-Riyad	اللهُم إجعلني من الذين إذا أحسنوا إستبشروا وإذا أساءوا أستغفًا.
	Jizan	لا إله إلا أنت سُبحانك إنك على كل شئ وكيل
Morocco	Marrakech-Tensift-Al-Haouz	اصلا متى مر يوم بدون لا اتضايق ؟
	Meknes-Tafilalet	اللهم اجعل أيامنا كلها أعيادًا بطاعتك .. وامطر على قلوبنا فرحًا لا ينتهي
Oman	Ad-Dhahirah	النور نورك اخي
	Muscat	يحفظه ويطول لنا بعمره..اشتقنا لطلته الغالية عسى ربي يلبسه ثوب الصحة والعافية
Palestine	Gaza-Strip	معبرة جدا ..لا فض فوك
	West-Bank	بارك الله فيك ابو جود
	West-Bank	الصراحه هذا واقعنا العربي
Sudan	Khartoum	لا يا عزيزي الحرب بدأها الترابي .. وقبل وصول الترابي لرئاسة الوزراء كانت الحركة الاسلامية تطبخ الصراع و تخلق الصراع تجهيزا للحرب بقيادة الترابي
	Khartoum	اللهم إني استودعتك مستقبلي فأجعله أجمل مما تمنيت
UAE	Dubai	بعض مما عندكم يا فندم
	Ras-Al-Khaymah	لاجديد ميسي يجلد مدريد
	Ras-Al-Khaymah	نشاطنا وأفكارنا بالإيجاب أو بالسلب تشبه المغناطيس ، و نحن نحاول أن نتجنب المشاكل تستمر المشاكل في الحدوث وقد تزداد سوءاً

Table 4: Randomly picked MSA tweets from select provinces and corresponding countries.

Team	Affiliation	Tasks
AraDial_MJ (Althobaiti, 2021)	Taif Uni, KSA	1.2
Arizona (Issa, 2021)	Uni of Arizona, USA	1.2
CairoSquad (AlKhamiss et al., 2021)	Microsoft, Egypt	all
CS-UM6P (El Mekki et al., 2021)	Mohammed VI Polytech, Morocco	all
NAYEL (Nayel et al., 2021)	Benha Uni, Egypt	all
Phonemer (Wadhawan, 2021)	Flipkart Private Limited, India	all
Speech Trans (Lichouri et al., 2021)	CRSTDLA, Algeria	1.1, 1.2

Table 5: List of teams that participated in one or more of the four subtasks *and* submitted a system description paper.

5.3 Shared Task Results

Table 6 presents the best TEST results for all 5 teams who submitted systems for Subtask 1.1. Based on the official metric, $macro - F_1$, CairoSquad obtained the best performance with 22.38% F_1 score. Table 7 presents the best TEST results of each of the eight teams who submitted systems to Subtask 1.2. Team CairoSquad achieved the best F_1 score that is 32.26%. Table 8 shows the best TEST results for all four teams who submitted systems for Subtask 2.1. CairoSquad achieved the best performance with 6.43% F_1 score.

Table 9 provides the best TEST results of each of the four teams who submitted systems to Subtask 2.2. CairoSquad also achieved the best perfor-

Team	F_1	Acc	Precision	Recall
CairoSquad	22.38(1)	35.72(1)	31.56(1)	20.66(1)
Phonemer	21.79(2)	32.46(3)	30.03(3)	19.95(2)
CS-UM6P	21.48(3)	33.74(2)	30.72(2)	19.70(3)
Speech Translation	14.87(4)	24.32(4)	18.95(4)	13.85(4)
Our Baseline II	14.15	24.76	20.01	13.21
NAYEL	12.99(5)	23.24(5)	15.09(5)	12.46(5)
Our Baseline I	1.57	19.78	0.94	4.76

Table 6: Results for Subtask 1.1 (country-level MSA). The numbers in parentheses are the ranks. The table is sorted on the $macro - F1$ score, the official metric.

Team	F_1	Acc	Precision	Recall
CairoSquad	32.26(1)	51.66(1)	36.03(1)	31.09(1)
CS-UM6P	30.64(2)	49.50(2)	32.91(2)	30.34(2)
Phonemer	24.29(4)	44.14(3)	30.24(3)	23.70(4)
Speech Translation	21.49(5)	40.54(5)	26.75(5)	20.36(6)
Arizona	21.37(6)	40.46(6)	26.32(6)	20.78(5)
AraDial_MJ	18.94(7)	35.94(8)	21.58(8)	18.28(7)
NAYEL	18.72(8)	37.16(7)	21.61(7)	18.12(8)
Our Baseline II	18.02	33.04	18.69	17.88
Our Baseline I	1.65	21.02	1.00	4.76

Table 7: Results for Subtask 1.2 (province-level MSA)

Team	F_1	Acc	Precision	Recall
CairoSquad	6.43(1)	6.66(1)	7.11(1)	6.71(1)
Phonemer	5.49(2)	6.00(2)	6.17(2)	6.07(2)
CS-UM6P	5.35(3)	5.72(3)	5.71(3)	5.75(3)
NAYEL	3.51(4)	3.38(4)	4.09(4)	3.45(4)
Our Baseline II	3.39	3.48	3.68	3.49
Our Baseline I	0.02	1.02	0.01	1.00

Table 8: Results for Subtask 2.1 (country-level DA).

Team	F_1	Acc	Precision	Recall
CairoSquad	8.60(1)	9.46(1)	9.07(1)	9.33(1)
CS-UM6P	7.32(2)	7.92(2)	7.73(2)	7.95(2)
NAYEL	4.55(3)	4.80(3)	4.71(3)	4.55(4)
Phonemer	4.37(4)	5.32(4)	4.49(4)	5.19(3)
Our Baseline II	4.08	4.18	4.54	4.22
Our Baseline I	0.02	1.06	0.01	1.00

Table 9: Results for Subtask 2.2 (province-level DA).

mance with 8.60%.[7]

5.4 General Description of Submitted Systems

In Table 10, we provide a high-level description of the systems submitted to each subtask. For each team, we list their best score of each subtask, the features employed, and the methods adopted/developed. As can be seen from the table, the majority of the top teams have used Transformers. Specifically, team CairoSquad and CS-UM6P developed their system utilizing MARBERT (Abdul-Mageed et al., 2020a), a pre-trained Transformer language model tailored to Arabic dialects and the domain of social media. Team Phonemer utilized AraBERT (Antoun et al., 2020a) and AraELECTRA (Antoun et al., 2020b). Team CairSquad apply adapter modules (Houlsby et al., 2019) and vertical attention to MARBERT fine-tuning. CS-UM6P fine-tuned MARBERT on country-level and province-level jointly by multi-task learning. The rest of participating teams have either used a type of neural networks other than Transformers or resorted to linear machine learning

[7]The full sets of results for Subtask 1.1, 1.2, 2.1, and 2.2 are in Tables 13, 14, 15 and 15, respectively, in Appendix A.

Team	F_1	Features						Techniques					
		N-gram	TF-IDF	Linguistics	Word embeds	PMI	Sampling	Classical ML	Neural nets	Transformer	Ensemble	Multitask	Semi-super
SUBTASK 1.1													
CairoSquad	22.38									✓	✓		
Phonemer	21.79									✓			
CS-UM6P	21.48									✓		✓	
Speech Trans	14.87	✓	✓				✓	✓	✓		✓		
NAYEL	12.99		✓					✓	✓				
SUBTASK 1.2													
CairoSquad	32.26									✓	✓		
CS-UM6P	30.64									✓		✓	
Phonemer	24.29									✓			
Speech Trans	21.49	✓	✓				✓	✓	✓		✓		
Arizona	21.37			✓	✓				✓				
AraDial_MJ	18.94	✓	✓		✓	✓		✓	✓		✓		✓
NAYEL	18.72		✓					✓	✓				
SUBTASK 2.1													
CairoSquad	6.43									✓	✓		
Phonemer	5.49									✓			
CS-UM6P	5.35									✓		✓	
NAYEL	3.51		✓					✓	✓				
SUBTASK 2.2													
CairoSquad	8.60									✓	✓		
CS-UM6P	7.32									✓		✓	
NAYEL	4.55		✓					✓	✓				
Phonemer	4.37									✓			

Table 10: Summary of approaches used by participating teams. PMI: poinwise mutual information. Classical ML refers to any non-neural machine learning methods such as naive Bayes and support vector machines. The term "neural nets" refers to any model based on neural networks (e.g., FFNN, RNN, and CNN) except Transformer models. Transformer refers to neural networks based on a Transformer architecture such as BERT. The table is sorted by official metric , $macro - F_1$. We only list teams that submitted a description paper. "Semi-super" indicates that the model is trained with semi-supervised learning.

models, usually with some form of ensembling.

6 Conclusion and Future Work

We presented the findings and results of the NADI 2021 shared task. We described our datasets across the four subtasks and the logistics of running the shared task. We also provided a panoramic description of the methods used by all participating teams. The results show that distinguishing the language variety of short texts based on small geographical regions of origin is possible, yet challenging. The total number of submissions during official evaluation (n=68 submissions from 8 unique teams), as well as the number of teams who registered and acquired our datasets (n=53 unique teams) reflects a continued interest in the community and calls for further work in this area.

In the future, we plan to host a third iteration of the NADI shared task that will use new datasets and encourage novel solutions to the set of problems introduced in NADI 2021. As results show all the fours subtasks remain very challenging, and we hope that encouraging further solutions will help advance work in this area.

Acknowledgments

We gratefully acknowledge the support of the Natural Sciences and Engineering Research Council of Canada, the Social Sciences Research Council of Canada, Compute Canada, and UBC Sockeye.

References

Ines Abbes, Wajdi Zaghouani, Omaima El-Hardlo, and Faten Ashour. 2020. Daict: A dialectal Arabic irony corpus extracted from twitter. In *Proceedings of The 12th Language Resources and Evaluation Conference*, pages 6265–6271.

Muhammad Abdul-Mageed, Hassan Alhuzali, and Mohamed Elaraby. 2018. You tweet what you speak: A city-level dataset of Arabic dialects. In *Proceedings of the Language Resources and Evaluation Conference (LREC)*, Miyazaki, Japan.

Muhammad Abdul-Mageed, Mona Diab, and Sandra Kübler. 2014. Samar: Subjectivity and sentiment analysis for Arabic social media. *Computer Speech and Language*, 28(1):20–37.

Muhammad Abdul-Mageed, AbdelRahim Elmadany, and El Moatez Billah Nagoudi. 2020a. ARBERT & MARBERT: Deep Bidirectional Transformers for Arabic. *arXiv preprint arXiv:2010.04900.*

Muhammad Abdul-Mageed, Chiyu Zhang, Houda Bouamor, and Nizar Habash. 2020b. NADI 2020: The First Nuanced Arabic Dialect Identification Shared Task. In *Proceedings of the Fifth Arabic Natural Language Processing Workshop (WANLP 2020)*, pages 97–110, Barcelona, Spain.

Muhammad Abdul-Mageed, Chiyu Zhang, AbdelRahim Elmadany, and Lyle Ungar. 2020c. Micro-dialect identification in diaglossic and code-switched environments. In *Proceedings of the 2020 Conference on Empirical Methods in Natural Language Processing (EMNLP)*, pages 5855–5876.

Ibrahim Abu Farha and Walid Magdy. 2020. From Arabic Sentiment Analysis to Sarcasm Detection: The ArSarcasm Dataset. In *Proceedings of the 4th Workshop on Open-Source Arabic Corpora and Processing Tools, with a Shared Task on Offensive Language Detection*, pages 32–39.

Rania Al-Sabbagh and Roxana Girju. 2012. YADAC: Yet another Dialectal Arabic Corpus. In *Proceedings of the Eighth International Conference on Language Resources and Evaluation (LREC-2012)*, pages 2882–2889.

Nora Al-Twairesh, Rawan Al-Matham, Nora Madi, Nada Almugren, Al-Hanouf Al-Aljmi, Shahad Alshalan, Raghad Alshalan, Nafla Alrumayyan, Shams Al-Manea, Sumayah Bawazeer, Nourah Al-Mutlaq, Nada Almanea, Waad Bin Huwaymil, Dalal Alqusair, Reem Alotaibi, Suha Al-Senaydi, and Abeer Alfutamani. 2018. SUAR: Towards building a corpus for the Saudi dialect. In *Proceedings of the International Conference on Arabic Computational Linguistics (ACLing).*

Hassan Alhuzali, Muhammad Abdul-Mageed, and Lyle Ungar. 2018. Enabling deep learning of emotion with first-person seed expressions. In *Proceedings of the Second Workshop on Computational Modeling of People's Opinions, Personality, and Emotions in Social Media*, pages 25–35.

Badr AlKhamiss, Mohamed Gabr, Muhammed El-Nokrashy, and Khaled Essam. 2021. Adapting MARBERT for Improved Arabic Dialect Identification: Submission to the NADI 2021 Shared Task. In *Proceedings of the Sixth Arabic Natural Language Processing Workshop (WANLP 2021).*

Maha J Althobaiti. 2020. Automatic Arabic dialect identification systems for written texts: A survey. *arXiv preprint arXiv:2009.12622.*

Maha J. Althobaiti. 2021. Country-level Arabic Dialect Identification Using Small Datasets with Integrated Machine Learning Techniques and Deep Learning Models. In *Proceedings of the Sixth Arabic Natural Language Processing Workshop (WANLP 2021).*

Wissam Antoun, Fady Baly, and Hazem Hajj. 2020a. Arabert: Transformer-based model for arabic language understanding. In *Proceedings of the 4th Workshop on Open-Source Arabic Corpora and Processing Tools, with a Shared Task on Offensive Language Detection*, pages 9–15.

Wissam Antoun, Fady Baly, and Hazem Hajj. 2020b. AraELECTRA: pre-training text discriminators for arabic language understanding. *arXiv preprint arXiv:2012.15516.*

MS Badawi. 1973. Levels of contemporary Arabic in Egypt. *Cairo: Dâr al Ma'ârif.*

Houda Bouamor, Nizar Habash, and Kemal Oflazer. 2014. A multidialectal parallel corpus of Arabic. In *Proceedings of the Language Resources and Evaluation Conference (LREC)*, Reykjavik, Iceland.

Houda Bouamor, Nizar Habash, Mohammad Salameh, Wajdi Zaghouani, Owen Rambow, Dana Abdulrahim, Ossama Obeid, Salam Khalifa, Fadhl Eryani, Alexander Erdmann, and Kemal Oflazer. 2018. The MADAR Arabic Dialect Corpus and Lexicon. In *Proceedings of the Language Resources and Evaluation Conference (LREC)*, Miyazaki, Japan.

Houda Bouamor, Sabit Hassan, and Nizar Habash. 2019. The MADAR shared task on Arabic fine-grained dialect identification. In *Proceedings of the Fourth Arabic Natural Language Processing Workshop*, pages 199–207.

Kristen Brustad. 2000. *The Syntax of Spoken Arabic: A Comparative Study of Moroccan, Egyptian, Syrian, and Kuwaiti Dialects.* Georgetown University Press.

Mark W. Cowell. 1964. *A Reference Grammar of Syrian Arabic.* Georgetown University Press, Washington, D.C.

Mona Diab, Nizar Habash, Owen Rambow, Mohamed Altantawy, and Yassine Benajiba. 2010. COLABA: Arabic dialect annotation and processing. In *LREC workshop on Semitic language processing*, pages 66–74.

Mahmoud El-Haj. 2020. Habibi - a multi dialect multi national Arabic song lyrics corpus. In *Proceedings of the 12th Language Resources and Evaluation Conference*, pages 1318–1326, Marseille, France.

Abdellah El Mekki, Abdelkader El Mahdaouy, Kabil Essefar, Nabil El Mamoun, Ismail Berrada, and Ahmed Khoumsi. 2021. CS-UM6P @ NADI'2021: BERT-based Multi-Task Model for Country and Province Level MSA and Dialectal Arabic Identification. In *Proceedings of the Sixth Arabic Natural Language Processing Workshop (WANLP 2021)*.

Heba Elfardy, Mohamed Al-Badrashiny, and Mona Diab. 2014. Aida: Identifying code switching in informal Arabic text. In *Proceedings of the Conference on Empirical Methods in Natural Language Processing (EMNLP)*, pages 94–101, Doha, Qatar.

Hassan Gadalla, Hanaa Kilany, Howaida Arram, Ashraf Yacoub, Alaa El-Habashi, Amr Shalaby, Krisjanis Karins, Everett Rowson, Robert MacIntyre, Paul Kingsbury, David Graff, and Cynthia McLemore. 1997. CALLHOME Egyptian Arabic transcripts LDC97T19. Web Download. Philadelphia: Linguistic Data Consortium.

R.S. Harrell. 1962. *A Short Reference Grammar of Moroccan Arabic: With Audio CD*. Georgetown classics in Arabic language and linguistics. Georgetown University Press.

Clive Holes. 2004. *Modern Arabic: Structures, Functions, and Varieties*. Georgetown Classics in Arabic Language and Linguistics. Georgetown University Press.

Neil Houlsby, Andrei Giurgiu, Stanislaw Jastrzebski, Bruna Morrone, Quentin De Laroussilhe, Andrea Gesmundo, Mona Attariyan, and Sylvain Gelly. 2019. Parameter-efficient transfer learning for nlp. In *International Conference on Machine Learning*, pages 2790–2799. PMLR.

Elsayed Issa. 2021. Country-level Arabic dialect identification using RNNs with and without linguistic features. In *Proceedings of the Sixth Arabic Natural Language Processing Workshop (WANLP 2021)*.

Mustafa Jarrar, Nizar Habash, Faeq Alrimawi, Diyam Akra, and Nasser Zalmout. 2016. Curras: an annotated corpus for the Palestinian Arabic dialect. *Language Resources and Evaluation*, pages 1–31.

Salam Khalifa, Nizar Habash, Dana Abdulrahim, and Sara Hassan. 2016. A Large Scale Corpus of Gulf Arabic. In *Proceedings of the Language Resources and Evaluation Conference (LREC)*, Portorož, Slovenia.

Mohamed Lichouri, Mourad Abbas, Khaled Lounnas, Besma Benaziz, and Aicha Zitouni. 2021. Arabic Dialect Identification based on Weighted Concatenation of TF-IDF Transformers. In *Proceedings of the Sixth Arabic Natural Language Processing Workshop (WANLP 2021)*.

Shervin Malmasi, Marcos Zampieri, Nikola Ljubešić, Preslav Nakov, Ahmed Ali, and Jörg Tiedemann. 2016. Discriminating between similar languages and arabic dialect identification: A report on the third dsl shared task. In *Proceedings of the third workshop on NLP for similar languages, varieties and dialects (VarDial3)*, pages 1–14.

Karima Meftouh, Salima Harrat, Salma Jamoussi, Mourad Abbas, and Kamel Smaili. 2015. Machine translation experiments on padic: A parallel Arabic dialect corpus. In *Proceedings of the Pacific Asia Conference on Language, Information and Computation*.

Hamdy Mubarak and Kareem Darwish. 2014. Using Twitter to collect a multi-dialectal corpus of Arabic. In *Proceedings of the Workshop for Arabic Natural Language Processing (WANLP)*, Doha, Qatar.

Hamdy Mubarak, Kareem Darwish, Walid Magdy, Tamer Elsayed, and Hend Al-Khalifa. 2020. Overview of osact4 Arabic offensive language detection shared task. In *Proceedings of the 4th Workshop on Open-Source Arabic Corpora and Processing Tools, with a Shared Task on Offensive Language Detection*, pages 48–52.

Hamada Nayel, Ahmed Hassan, Mahmoud Sobhi, and Ahmed El-Sawy. 2021. Data-Driven Approach for Arabic Dialect Identification. In *Proceedings of the Sixth Arabic Natural Language Processing Workshop (WANLP 2021)*.

Ossama Obeid, Mohammad Salameh, Houda Bouamor, and Nizar Habash. 2019. ADIDA: Automatic dialect identification for Arabic. In *Proceedings of the 2019 Conference of the North American Chapter of the Association for Computational Linguistics (Demonstrations)*, pages 6–11, Minneapolis, Minnesota. Association for Computational Linguistics.

Fatiha Sadat, Farnazeh Kazemi, and Atefeh Farzindar. 2014. Automatic identification of Arabic language varieties and dialects in social media. *Proceedings of SocialNLP*, page 22.

Mohammad Salameh, Houda Bouamor, and Nizar Habash. 2018. Fine-grained Arabic dialect identification. In *Proceedings of the International Conference on Computational Linguistics (COLING)*, pages 1332–1344, Santa Fe, New Mexico, USA.

Kamel Smaïli, Mourad Abbas, Karima Meftouh, and Salima Harrat. 2014. Building resources for Algerian Arabic dialects. In *Proceedings of the Conference of the International Speech Communication Association (Interspeech)*.

Anshul Wadhawan. 2021. Dialect Identification in Nuanced Arabic Tweets Using Farasa Segmentation and AraBERT. In *Proceedings of the Sixth Arabic Natural Language Processing Workshop (WANLP 2021)*.

Wajdi Zaghouani and Anis Charfi. 2018. ArapTweet: A Large Multi-Dialect Twitter Corpus for Gender, Age and Language Variety Identification. In *Proceedings of the Language Resources and Evaluation Conference (LREC)*, Miyazaki, Japan.

Omar F Zaidan and Chris Callison-Burch. 2011. The Arabic online commentary dataset: an annotated dataset of informal Arabic with high dialectal content. In *Proceedings of the 49th Annual Meeting of the Association for Computational Linguistics: Human Language Technologies: short papers-Volume 2*, pages 37–41. Association for Computational Linguistics.

Marcos Zampieri, Shervin Malmasi, Nikola Ljubešić, Preslav Nakov, Ahmed Ali, Jörg Tiedemann, Yves Scherrer, and Noëmi Aepli. 2017. Findings of the vardial evaluation campaign 2017.

Marcos Zampieri, Shervin Malmasi, Preslav Nakov, Ahmed Ali, Suwon Shon, James Glass, Yves Scherrer, Tanja Samardzic, Nikola Ljubešić, Jörg Tiedemann, et al. 2018. Language identification and morphosyntactic tagging: The second vardial evaluation campaign. In *Proceedings of the Fifth Workshop on NLP for Similar Languages, Varieties and Dialects (VarDial 2018)*, pages 1–17.

Appendices

A Data

We provide the distribution Distribution of the NADI 2021 MSA data over provinces, by country (Subtask 2.1), across our our data splits in Table 11. Similarly, Table 12 shows the distribution of the DA data over provinces for all countries (Subtask 2.2) in our data splits.

B Shared Task Teams & Results

We provide full results for all four subtasks. Table 13 shows full results for Subtask 1.1, Table 14 for Subtask 1.2, Table 15 for Subtask 2.1, and Table 16 for Subtask 2.2.

Province Name	TRAIN	DEV	TEST	Province Name	TRAIN	DEV	TEST
ae_Abu-Dhabi	211	51	51	kw_Jahra	211	52	51
ae_Dubai	211	52	51	lb_Akkar	211	52	39
ae_Ras-Al-Khaymah	211	51	51	lb_North-Lebanon	211	51	51
bh_Capital	211	51	51	lb_South-Lebanon	211	52	51
dj_Djibouti	211	52	51	ly_Al-Butnan	211	52	51
dz_Batna	211	52	51	ly_Al-Jabal-al-Akhdar	211	52	52
dz_Biskra	211	52	51	ly_Benghazi	211	51	51
dz_Bouira	211	12	51	ly_Darnah	211	52	51
dz_Béchar	211	52	31	ly_Misrata	211	52	51
dz_Constantine	211	51	51	ly_Tripoli	211	51	51
dz_El-Oued	211	52	51	ma_Marrakech-Tensift-Al-Haouz	211	51	51
dz_Khenchela	211	52	51	ma_Meknes-Tafilalet	211	52	52
dz_Oran	211	52	51	ma_Souss-Massa-Draa	211	52	51
dz_Ouargla	211	52	51	ma_Tanger-Tetouan	211	52	51
eg_Alexandria	211	51	51	mr_Nouakchott	211	52	51
eg_Aswan	211	52	51	om_Ad-Dakhiliyah	211	51	51
eg_Asyut	211	52	51	om_Ad-Dhahirah	211	32	51
eg_Beheira	211	52	51	om_Al-Batnah	211	51	51
eg_Beni-Suef	211	52	51	om_Ash-Sharqiyah	211	51	51
eg_Dakahlia	211	51	51	om_Dhofar	211	52	51
eg_Faiyum	211	52	51	om_Musandam	211	52	51
eg_Gharbia	211	52	51	om_Muscat	211	52	51
eg_Ismailia	211	52	51	ps_Gaza-Strip	211	51	51
eg_Kafr-el-Sheikh	211	52	20	ps_West-Bank	211	51	51
eg_Luxor	211	52	51	qa_Ar-Rayyan	211	52	51
eg_Minya	211	51	51	sa_Al-Madinah	211	51	51
eg_Monufia	211	52	51	sa_Al-Quassim	211	51	51
eg_North-Sinai	211	52	51	sa_Ar-Riyad	211	51	51
eg_Port-Said	211	51	51	sa_Ash-Sharqiyah	211	51	51
eg_Qena	211	51	51	sa_Asir	211	51	51
eg_Red-Sea	211	52	51	sa_Ha'il	211	51	51
eg_Sohag	211	51	51	sa_Jizan	211	51	51
eg_South-Sinai	211	51	51	sa_Makkah	211	51	51
eg_Suez	211	51	51	sa_Najran	211	51	51
iq_Al-Anbar	211	51	51	sa_Tabuk	211	51	51
iq_Al-Muthannia	211	52	51	sd_Khartoum	211	48	51
iq_An-Najaf	211	51	51	so_Banaadir	211	52	51
iq_Arbil	211	52	51	so_Woqooyi-Galbeed	135	11	51
iq_As-Sulaymaniyah	187	52	51	sy_Aleppo	211	51	51
iq_Babil	211	52	51	sy_As-Suwayda	211	51	51
iq_Baghdad	211	51	51	sy_Damascus-City	211	51	51
iq_Basra	211	51	51	sy_Hama	211	52	51
iq_Dihok	211	52	51	sy_Hims	211	52	51
iq_Karbala	211	52	40	sy_Lattakia	211	52	51
iq_Kirkuk	211	52	51	tn_Ariana	211	51	51
iq_Ninawa	211	52	51	tn_Bizerte	211	15	51
iq_Wasit	211	51	51	tn_Mahdia	211	52	23
jo_Aqaba	211	52	51	tn_Sfax	211	52	51
jo_Zarqa	211	51	51	ye_Aden	211	51	51
kw_Hawalli	211	51	51	ye_Ibb	211	37	51

Table 11: Distribution of the NADI 2021 MSA data over provinces, by country, across our TRAIN, DEV, and TEST splits (Subtask 2.1).

Province Name	TRAIN	DEV	TEST	Province Name	TRAIN	DEV	TEST
ae_Abu-Dhabi	214	52	52	kw_Jahra	215	53	53
ae_Dubai	214	53	53	lb_Akkar	215	53	14
ae_Ras-Al-Khaymah	214	52	53	lb_North-Lebanon	215	52	53
bh_Capital	215	52	52	lb_South-Lebanon	214	52	53
dj_Djibouti	215	27	7	ly_Al-Butnan	214	52	53
dz_Batna	215	34	10	ly_Al-Jabal-al-Akhdar	215	53	53
dz_Biskra	215	53	53	ly_Benghazi	214	52	52
dz_Bouira	215	26	53	ly_Darnah	215	53	53
dz_Béchar	215	53	11	ly_Misrata	214	52	53
dz_Constantine	215	52	53	ly_Tripoli	214	52	52
dz_El-Oued	215	53	52	ma_Marrakech-Tensift-Al-Haouz	214	52	53
dz_Khenchela	89	53	53	ma_Meknes-Tafilalet	215	50	53
dz_Oran	215	53	53	ma_Souss-Massa-Draa	215	53	53
dz_Ouargla	215	53	53	ma_Tanger-Tetouan	214	52	53
eg_Alexandria	214	52	52	mr_Nouakchott	215	53	53
eg_Aswan	214	52	52	om_Ad-Dakhiliyah	214	52	53
eg_Asyut	214	53	53	om_Ad-Dhahirah	215	40	53
eg_Beheira	214	52	52	om_Al-Batnah	214	52	53
eg_Beni-Suef	214	52	52	om_Ash-Sharqiyah	214	52	53
eg_Dakahlia	214	52	52	om_Dhofar	214	53	53
eg_Faiyum	214	52	53	om_Musandam	215	53	53
eg_Gharbia	214	52	53	om_Muscat	215	53	53
eg_Ismailia	214	52	53	ps_Gaza-Strip	214	52	52
eg_Kafr-el-Sheikh	215	52	53	ps_West-Bank	214	52	53
eg_Luxor	214	52	52	qa_Ar-Rayyan	215	52	53
eg_Minya	214	52	53	sa_Al-Madinah	214	52	52
eg_Monufia	215	52	53	sa_Al-Quassim	214	52	52
eg_North-Sinai	215	52	53	sa_Ar-Riyad	214	52	52
eg_Port-Said	214	52	52	sa_Ash-Sharqiyah	214	52	52
eg_Qena	214	52	53	sa_Asir	214	52	52
eg_Red-Sea	214	52	53	sa_Ha'il	214	52	52
eg_Sohag	214	52	52	sa_Jizan	214	52	53
eg_South-Sinai	214	52	53	sa_Makkah	214	52	52
eg_Suez	214	52	52	sa_Najran	214	52	53
iq_Al-Anbar	214	52	52	sa_Tabuk	214	52	52
iq_Al-Muthannia	215	53	53	sd_Khartoum	215	53	53
iq_An-Najaf	215	53	53	so_Banaadir	136	40	2
iq_Arbil	215	53	53	so_Woqooyi-Galbeed	36	9	53
iq_As-Sulaymaniyah	153	32	53	sy_Aleppo	215	52	23
iq_Babil	215	53	53	sy_As-Suwayda	214	53	53
iq_Baghdad	214	52	52	sy_Damascus-City	214	52	53
iq_Basra	214	52	53	sy_Hama	215	53	53
iq_Dihok	215	53	30	sy_Hims	214	53	53
iq_Karbala	215	53	53	sy_Lattakia	215	15	53
iq_Kirkuk	215	53	53	tn_Ariana	214	52	53
iq_Ninawa	215	53	53	tn_Bizerte	215	16	53
iq_Wasit	214	52	53	tn_Mahdia	215	52	53
jo_Aqaba	215	52	53	tn_Sfax	215	53	53
jo_Zarqa	214	52	52	ye_Aden	214	52	53
kw_Hawalli	214	52	53	ye_Ibb	215	53	53

Table 12: Distribution of the NADI 2021 DA data over provinces, by country, across our TRAIN, DEV, and TEST splits (Subtask 2.2).

Team	F_1	Acc	Precision	Recall
CairoSquad	22.38(1)	35.72(1)	31.56(3)	20.66(1)
CairoSquad	21.97(2)	34.90(2)	30.01(7)	20.15(2)
Phonemer	21.79(3)	32.46(6)	30.03(6)	19.95(4)
Phonemer	21.66(4)	31.70(7)	28.46(8)	20.01(3)
CS-UM6P	21.48(5)	33.74(4)	30.72(5)	19.70(5)
CS-UM6P	20.91(6)	33.84(3)	31.16(4)	19.09(6)
Phonemer	20.78(7)	32.96(5)	37.69(1)	18.42(8)
CS-UM6P	19.80(8)	31.68(8)	26.69(9)	19.04(7)
Speech Translation	14.87(9)	24.32(11)	18.95(14)	13.85(9)
Speech Translation	14.50(10)	24.06(12)	20.24(12)	13.24(10)
Speech Translation	14.48(11)	24.88(9)	22.88(10)	13.17(11)
NAYEL	12.99(12)	23.24(14)	15.09(15)	12.46(12)
NAYEL	11.84(13)	23.74(13)	19.42(13)	10.92(13)
NAYEL	10.29(14)	24.60(10)	33.11(2)	9.83(14)
NAYEL	10.13(15)	18.32(15)	11.31(16)	9.76(15)
NAYEL	7.73(16)	24.06(12)	21.07(11)	8.37(16)

Table 13: Full results for Subtask 1.1 (country-level MSA). The numbers in parentheses are the ranks. The table is sorted on the *macro* F_1 score, the official metric.

Team	F_1	Acc	Precision	Recall
CairoSquad	32.26(1)	51.66(1)	36.03(1)	31.09(1)
CairoSquad	31.04(2)	51.02(2)	35.01(2)	30.62(2)
CS-UM6P	30.64(3)	49.50(4)	32.91(6)	30.34(3)
CS-UM6P	30.14(4)	48.94(5)	33.20(4)	30.21(4)
CS-UM6P	29.08(5)	50.30(3)	34.99(3)	29.04(5)
IDC team	26.10(6)	42.70(9)	27.04(11)	25.88(6)
Phonemer	24.29(7)	44.14(6)	30.24(7)	23.70(7)
IDC team	24.00(8)	40.08(14)	25.57(15)	23.29(9)
Phonemer	23.56(9)	43.32(8)	28.05(10)	23.34(8)
Phonemer	22.72(10)	43.46(7)	28.13(9)	22.55(10)
Speech Translation	21.49(11)	40.54(10)	26.75(12)	20.36(12)
Arizona	21.37(12)	40.46(12)	26.32(13)	20.78(11)
Speech Translation	21.14(13)	40.32(13)	25.43(16)	20.16(14)
Speech Translation	21.09(14)	40.50(11)	26.29(14)	20.02(15)
Arizona	20.48(15)	40.04(15)	24.09(17)	20.22(13)
Arizona	19.85(16)	39.90(16)	22.89(18)	19.66(16)
AraDial_MJ	18.94(17)	35.94(22)	21.58(22)	18.28(17)
NAYEL	18.72(18)	37.16(20)	21.61(21)	18.12(18)
AraDial_MJ	18.66(19)	35.54(23)	21.45(23)	18.03(19)
AraDial_MJ	18.09(20)	37.22(19)	21.84(20)	17.55(20)
AraDial_MJ	18.06(21)	38.48(17)	22.70(19)	17.39(21)
IDC team	16.33(22)	29.82(25)	18.04(25)	16.10(22)
NAYEL	16.31(23)	38.08(18)	32.94(5)	15.91(23)
NAYEL	14.41(24)	32.78(24)	20.16(24)	14.11(24)
NAYEL	13.16(25)	36.96(21)	30.00(8)	13.83(25)
NAYEL	12.81(26)	26.48(26)	14.32(26)	12.66(26)
AraDial_MJ	4.34(27)	12.64(27)	4.33(27)	4.70(27)

Table 14: Full results for Subtask 1.2 (province-level MSA).

Team	F_1	Acc	Precision	Recall
CairoSquad	6.43(1)	6.66(1)	7.11(1)	6.71(1)
CairoSquad	5.81(2)	6.24(2)	6.26(2)	6.33(2)
Phonemer	5.49(3)	6.00(3)	6.17(3)	6.07(3)
Phonemer	5.43(4)	5.96(4)	6.12(4)	6.02(4)
CS-UM6P	5.35(5)	5.72(6)	5.71(7)	5.75(6)
Phonemer	5.30(6)	5.84(5)	5.97(6)	5.90(5)
CS-UM6P	5.12(7)	5.50(7)	5.24(8)	5.53(7)
CS-UM6P	4.72(8)	5.00(8)	5.97(5)	5.02(8)
NAYEL	3.51(9)	3.38(10)	4.09(9)	3.45(10)
NAYEL	3.47(10)	3.56(9)	3.53(10)	3.60(9)
NAYEL	3.16(11)	3.28(11)	3.38(12)	3.40(11)
NAYEL	3.15(12)	3.06(12)	3.43(11)	3.07(12)

Table 15: Full results for Subtask 2.1 (country-level DA).

Team	F_1	Acc	Precision	Recall
CairoSquad	8.60(1)	9.46(1)	9.07(1)	9.33(1)
CairoSquad	7.88(2)	8.78(2)	8.27(2)	8.66(2)
CS-UM6P	7.32(3)	7.92(4)	7.73(4)	7.95(3)
CS-UM6P	7.29(4)	8.04(3)	8.17(3)	7.90(4)
CS-UM6P	5.30(5)	6.90(5)	7.00(5)	6.82(5)
NAYEL	4.55(6)	4.80(10)	4.71(6)	4.55(10)
NAYEL	4.43(7)	4.88(9)	4.59(8)	4.62(9)
Phonemer	4.37(8)	5.32(6)	4.49(9)	5.19(6)
Phonemer	4.33(9)	5.26(7)	4.44(10)	5.14(7)
Phonemer	4.23(10)	5.20(8)	4.21(11)	5.08(8)
NAYEL	3.92(11)	4.12(12)	4.05(12)	4.00(12)
NAYEL	3.02(12)	3.10(13)	3.19(13)	3.19(13)
CS-UM6P	2.90(13)	4.20(11)	4.68(7)	4.13(11)

Table 16: Full results for Subtask 2.2 (province-level DA).

Adapting MARBERT for Improved Arabic Dialect Identification: Submission to the NADI 2021 Shared Task

Badr AlKhamissi*
Independent
badr [at] khamissi.com

Mohamed Gabr*
Microsoft EGDC
mohamed.gabr [at] microsoft.com

Muhammed ElNokrashy
Microsoft EGDC
muelnokr [at] microsoft.com

Khaled Essam
Mendel.ai
khaled.essam [at] mendel.ai

Abstract

In this paper, we tackle the Nuanced Arabic Dialect Identification (NADI) shared task (Abdul-Mageed et al., 2021) and demonstrate state-of-the-art results on all of its four subtasks. Tasks are to identify the geographic origin of short Dialectal (DA) and Modern Standard Arabic (MSA) utterances at the levels of both country and province. Our final model is an ensemble of variants built on top of MARBERT that achieves an F1-score of 34.03% for DA at the country-level development set—an improvement of 7.63% from previous work.

1 Introduction

The Arab World is a vast geographical region that covers North Africa and Southwest Asia, boasting a population of around 400M that speak different derivatives of a common language. However, by virtue of its size and cultural variety, there exists a dialect continuum across the region wherein the language varieties of neighboring peoples may differ slightly, but distant regions can become mutually unintelligible. This continuum is referred to as Dialectal Arabic (DA) and is the "Low" variety of modern Arabic *diglossia*. On the other hand, the "High" variety is referred to as Modern Standard Arabic (MSA) and is used in formal settings such as academia, mass media, and legislation—and is taught through the formal education system in most Arab countries. This standard variant emerged gradually, but most notably with the advent of the printing press in the 19th century. It diverged from Classical Arabic (CA) into a more simple version that is now used across the Arab World.

The modern vernacular dialects (DA) differ along several dimensions, including pronunciation, syntax, morphology, vocabulary, and even orthography. Dialects may be heavily influenced by previously dominant local languages. For example, Egyptian variants are influenced by the Coptic language, while Sudanese variants are influenced by the Nubian language.

In this paper, we study the classification of such variants and describe our model that achieves state-of-the-art results on all of the four Nuanced Arabic Dialect Identification (NADI) subtasks (Abdul-Mageed et al., 2021). The task focuses on distinguishing both MSA and DA by their geographical origin at both the country and province levels. The data is a collection of tweets covering 100 provinces from 21 Arab countries. The code has been made open-source and available on GitHub[1].

2 Related Work

The first efforts to collect and label dialectal Arabic data goes back to 1997 (Gadalla, 1997). However, studying DA in NLP started to gain traction in recent years as more digital Arabic data became available, especially with the rise of online chatting platforms that place no restrictions on the syntax, style, or formality of the writing. Zaidan and Callison-Burch (2014) labelled the Arabic Online Commentary Dataset (AOC) through crowd-sourcing, then built a model to classify even more crawled data. Abdelali et al. (2020) provided the QADI dataset by automatically collecting dialectal Arabic tweets and labelling them based on descriptions of the author accounts, while trying to reduce the recall of written MSA and inappropriate tweets. Abu Farha and Magdy (2020) provided ArSarcasm: a dataset of labelled tweets. Originally for sarcasm detection, it also contains labels for sentiment and dialect detection. Labelled dialectal Arabic challenges

* Equal contribution.

[1] https://github.com/mohamedgabr96/NeuralDialectDetector

Proceedings of the Sixth Arabic Natural Language Processing Workshop, pages 260–264
Kyiv, Ukraine (Virtual), April 19, 2021.

such as MADAR (Bouamor et al., 2019) and NADI (Abdul-Mageed et al., 2020b, 2021) (which started in 2020) shed light on the underlying challenges of the task. Both comprise labelled Arabic tweets but with class sets of different granularities.

Talafha et al. (2020) presents a solution that won the 2020 NADI shared task (Subtask 1.2) by continuing training AraBERT (Antoun et al., 2020) using Masked Language Modelling (MLM) on 10M unlabelled tweets, then fine-tuning on the dialect identification task. On the other hand, the solution that won Subtask 2.2 uses a hierarchical classifier that takes as input a weighted combination of TF-IDF and AraBERT features to first classify the country, then invokes an ArabBERT-based, country-specific, province-level classifier to detect the province (El Mekki et al., 2020).

The large size of pretrained Transformer models hinders their applicability in many use cases. The usual number of parameters in such a model lies between 150M and 300M and needs between 500MB and 1GB of space to be stored. A novel technique to address these issues is proposed by Houlsby et al. (2019)—bottleneck layers ("adapters") are added to each transformer layer as an alternative to fine-tuning the entire pre-trained model when optimizing for downstream tasks (Houlsby et al., 2019; Bapna and Firat, 2019; Pfeiffer et al., 2021). Only these additional parameters (which can be 1% or less of the size of the main model) need to be stored per downstream task, given that they are the only layers changing. Besides being light-weight and scalable, adapters offer several advantages over traditional approaches of transfer-learning: (1) They learn modular representations that are compatible with other layers of the transformer, (2) They avoid interfering with pre-trained knowledge, mitigating catastrophic forgetting and catastrophic inference—two common downsides of multi-task learning (Pfeiffer et al., 2020).

3 Datasets & Subtasks

Dataset	Country	Province
MSA	Subtask 1.1	Subtask 2.1
DA	Subtask 1.2	Subtask 2.2

Table 1: Subtask ID per Dataset and Granularity Level

The second NADI shared task consists of four subtasks on two datasets (see Table 1). Each consists of 21k tweets for training, 5k for development

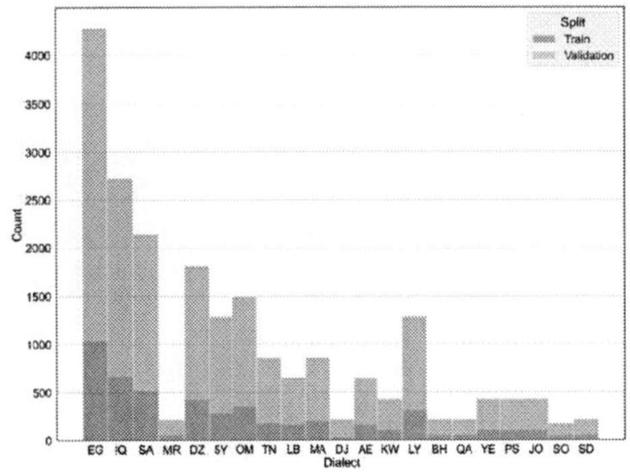

Figure 1: Train/Dev Corpora Sizes per Country (DA)

and 5k for testing collected from a disjoint set of users (Abdul-Mageed et al., 2021). Both datasets are labelled at two levels of granularity: country, and province. The NADI task is the first to focus on sub-country level dialects. However, the data is extremely unbalanced, even at the country-level (see Figure 1), with the most frequent class being Egypt (4283 instances), and the least common class being Somalia (172 instances). The data comes preprocessed with URLs replaced with the token 'URL' and Twitter mentions replaced with the token 'USER'. One of the main challenges of Arabic Dialect Identification is the high similarity of dialects in short utterances; many short phrases are commonly used in all dialects. Since the tweets are collected "in the wild" and DA is not formally defined (the same word can be written in a variety of ways), this makes it even more challenging to capture the meaning of a logical word unit across its different forms.

4 System Description

Our model builds on MARBERT—a publicly available transformer model trained on 1B multi-dialectal Arabic tweets (Abdul-Mageed et al., 2020a). It follows the $\text{BERT}_{\text{BASE}}$ architecture (Devlin et al., 2019) with 163M parameters and similarly uses WordPiece tokenization (Wu et al., 2016). To optimize it for the task at hand, we introduce changes to the architecture and training regimen as described below. Note that, due to time and compute constraints, all hyperparameters were optimized on the development set of Subtask 1.2 then applied as-is to the other three subtasks. We report the result of the best ensemble for each subtask.

General The experiments described below all use the following configuration: The classification head is a softmax layer over the CLS vector of the last layer $\mathbf{z}_L$ (with a dropout rate of 30% during training). The base learning rate of the classification head is set higher ($1e{-}2$) than the rest of the trainable parameters ($5e{-}6$). The LR schedule is warmed up linearly over 250 steps, then decayed once every 10 gradient updates following an inverse-square-root scheme to the minimum $0.01 \cdot LR_{\text{base}}$. We use the Adam optimizer with decoupled weight regularization (Loshchilov and Hutter, 2019). During training, we evaluate the model every 100 mini-batches of size 32, and halt if the dev macro-F1 score does not improve for 10 consecutive evaluations. The maximum sequence length is 90 for the DA dataset and 110 for the MSA dataset.

Fine-tuning We fine-tune the full MARBERT transformer using the base configuration.

Adapters Here we embed two additional layers at each transformer block (one after the Multi-Head Attention module and one after the FFN module) following the Houlsby et al. (2019) architecture. This allows us to preserve the pre-trained embedded knowledge in the MARBERT layers, which are trained on a rich corpus with less bias towards specific dialects. The final architecture of a transformer block is illustrated in Figure 5.

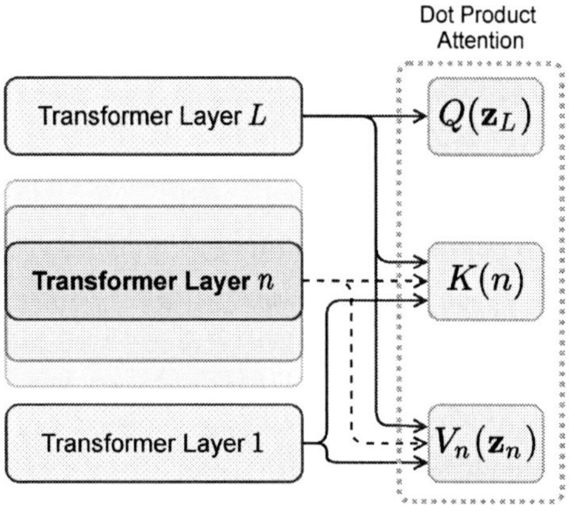

Figure 2: Vertical Attention

Vertical Attention (VAtt) The MARBERT model has $L = 12$ transformer layers. For each $n \in L$, let $\mathbf{z}_n$ be the CLS token at level n (after the adapter). Let k_n be a static learned positional embedding for level n. Apply a scaled dot-product based attention module where: query is $Q(\mathbf{z}_L)$, keys are $\{K(k_n)\}_n^L$, and values are $\{V_n(\mathbf{z}_n)\}_n^L$. This attends over the layers' sentence representations by content-to-level (depth) addressing. We introduce this to allow choice of the abstraction level. See Figure 2.

Ensembling We create an ensemble of multiple models on combinations of the following architectural variables:

- Whether Vertical Attention is used.
- Training adapters or fine-tuning full model.

The soft-max outputs of the models are aggregated together by doing an element-wise multiplication. The best ensemble provide 1.13% F1 boost over the best solo model (see Table 2).

5 Results

Models	DEV		TEST	
	Acc.	F1	Acc.	F1
Adapters	***52.48***	32.10	50.62	30.78
+VAtt	52.28	31.73	***51.08***	30.09
Fine-tuning	51.02	32.23	50.28	30.41
+VAtt	50.07	***32.90***	49.42	***31.30***
Ensemble	**53.42**	**34.03**	**51.66**	**32.26**

Table 2: Ablation study (Subtask 1.2)

The results table shows that the best F1 score is obtained by ensembling the following list of model configurations (all of which use a maximum sequence length of 90): (1) Fine-tuning, (2) Adapters + VAtt, (3) Fine-tuning + VAtt, and (4) Fine-tuning using a linear learning rate schedule instead of the inverse-square-root scheme. Among solo models, the best performer is the fully fine-tuned variant with Vertical Attention, with an F1 score of 32.90 on the development set.

6 Discussion

The confusion matrix of the Ensemble in Subtask 1.2 (Table 2) shows over-prediction of Egyptian and Saudi Arabian, reflecting their over-representation in training (Figure 1). The matrix suggests that the dialects most confused together are often from geographically close countries. For example: Tunisia and Libya, and Qatar and Bahrain. Gulf countries also show high confusion.

Considering the sequence length in words for correct and wrong predictions, we find that correctly predicted sentences tend to be longer than

Subtask	Models	DEV		TEST	
		Acc.	F1	Acc.	F1
1.1	**Ours**	**39.06**	**23.52**	**35.72**	**22.38**
1.2	MARBERT	48.86	26.40	48.40	29.14
	Ours	**53.42**	**34.03**	**51.66**	**32.26**
2.1	**Ours**	**7.04**	**6.73**	**6.66**	**6.43**
2.2	MARBERT	7.91	5.23	8.48	6.28
	Ours	**10.74**	**10.02**	**9.46**	**8.60**

Table 3: Results compared to previous SOTA. MARBERT taken from Abdul-Mageed et al. (2020a).

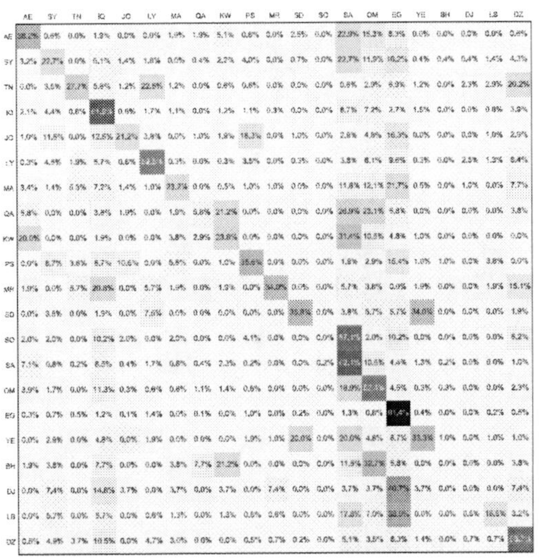

Figure 3: Confusion matrix of the predictions of the best performing model in subtask 1.2.

	Mean/Variance (λ)	Median
Correct	7.16	5.45
Wrong	4.22	3.40
All	4.10	3.26

Table 4: Sequence length (fitted to an Erlang distribution)

the means of all and of wrongly predicted sentences (fit as an Erlang distribution). The numbers were computed after removing the special USER and URL tokens.

7 Conclusion

In this paper, we present a solution that provides a new state-of-the-art on all of the NADI subtasks. Inserting adapters at each of the MARBERT transformer layers preserved the original pre-trained knowledge, stemming from a rich corpus of tweets, while still embedding task knowledge. To further improve the model's performance, we vertically at-

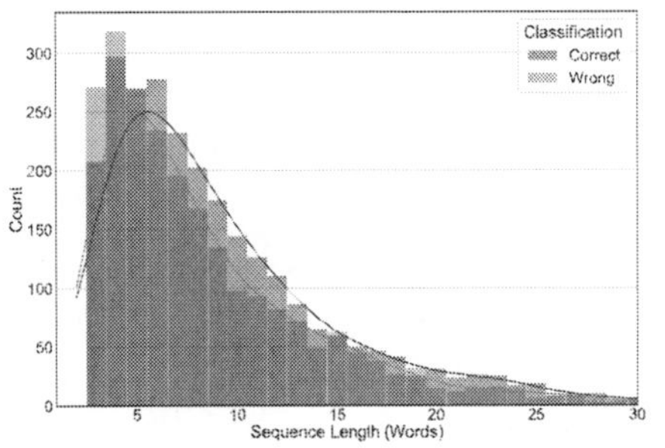

Figure 4: Distribution of length for correct and wrong classifications in subtask 1.2 trimmed at the tail after length > 30.

tend on all of the CLS token hidden-states coming out of each of the transformer layers instead of just using the top layer's output. We ensemble models on two design variables: Whether fine-tuning is full or through adapters, and whether Vertical Attention is used. The bias towards dominating classes in the task dataset remains a significant issue that is still not mitigated. As a future work, we would like to employ adapter fusion (Pfeiffer et al., 2021) to attenuate this bias.

References

Ahmed Abdelali, Hamdy Mubarak, Younes Samih, Sabit Hassan, and Kareem Darwish. 2020. Arabic dialect identification in the wild.

Muhammad Abdul-Mageed, AbdelRahim Elmadany, and El Moatez Billah Nagoudi. 2020a. Arbert & marbert: Deep bidirectional transformers for arabic. *arXiv preprint arXiv:2101.01785*.

Muhammad Abdul-Mageed, Chiyu Zhang, Houda Bouamor, and Nizar Habash. 2020b. NADI 2020: The First Nuanced Arabic Dialect Identification Shared Task. In *Proceedings of the Fifth Arabic Natural Language Processing Workshop (WANLP 2020)*, Barcelona, Spain.

Muhammad Abdul-Mageed, Chiyu Zhang, Abdel-Rahim Elmadany, Houda Bouamor, and Nizar Habash. 2021. NADI 2021: The Second Nuanced Arabic Dialect Identification Shared Task. In *Proceedings of the Sixth Arabic Natural Language Processing Workshop (WANLP 2021)*.

Ibrahim Abu Farha and Walid Magdy. 2020. From Arabic sentiment analysis to sarcasm detection: The ArSarcasm dataset. In *Proceedings of the 4th Workshop on Open-Source Arabic Corpora and Processing Tools, with a Shared Task on Offensive Language Detection*, pages 32–39, Marseille, France. European Language Resource Association.

Wissam Antoun, Fady Baly, and Hazem Hajj. 2020. Arabert: Transformer-based model for arabic language understanding.

Ankur Bapna and Orhan Firat. 2019. Simple, scalable adaptation for neural machine translation. In *Proceedings of the 2019 Conference on Empirical Methods in Natural Language Processing and the 9th International Joint Conference on Natural Language Processing (EMNLP-IJCNLP)*, pages 1538–1548, Hong Kong, China. Association for Computational Linguistics.

Houda Bouamor, Sabit Hassan, and Nizar Habash. 2019. The MADAR shared task on Arabic fine-grained dialect identification. In *Proceedings of the Fourth Arabic Natural Language Processing Workshop*, pages 199–207, Florence, Italy. Association for Computational Linguistics.

Jacob Devlin, Ming-Wei Chang, Kenton Lee, and Kristina Toutanova. 2019. BERT: Pre-training of deep bidirectional transformers for language understanding. In *Proceedings of the 2019 Conference of the North American Chapter of the Association for Computational Linguistics: Human Language Technologies, Volume 1 (Long and Short Papers)*, pages 4171–4186, Minneapolis, Minnesota. Association for Computational Linguistics.

Abdellah El Mekki, Ahmed Alami, Hamza Alami, Ahmed Khoumsi, and Ismail Berrada. 2020. Weighted combination of BERT and n-GRAM features for nuanced Arabic dialect identification. In *Proceedings of the Fifth Arabic Natural Language Processing Workshop*, pages 268–274, Barcelona, Spain (Online). Association for Computational Linguistics.

Hassan and Gadalla. 1997. Callhome egyptian arabic transcripts ldc97t19.

Neil Houlsby, Andrei Giurgiu, Stanislaw Jastrzebski, Bruna Morrone, Quentin de Laroussilhe, Andrea Gesmundo, Mona Attariyan, and Sylvain Gelly. 2019. Parameter-efficient transfer learning for nlp.

Ilya Loshchilov and Frank Hutter. 2019. Decoupled weight decay regularization. In *International Conference on Learning Representations*.

Jonas Pfeiffer, Aishwarya Kamath, Andreas Rücklé, Kyunghyun Cho, and Iryna Gurevych. 2021. Adapterfusion: Non-destructive task composition for transfer learning.

Jonas Pfeiffer, Andreas Rücklé, Clifton Poth, Aishwarya Kamath, Ivan Vulić, Sebastian Ruder, Kyunghyun Cho, and Iryna Gurevych. 2020. AdapterHub: A Framework for Adapting Transformers. In *Proceedings of the 2020 Conference on Empirical Methods in Natural Language Processing (EMNLP 2020): Systems Demonstrations*, pages 46–54, Online. Association for Computational Linguistics.

Bashar Talafha, Mohammad Ali, Muhy Eddin Za'ter, Haitham Seelawi, Ibraheem Tuffaha, Mostafa Samir, Wael Farhan, and Hussein T. Al-Natsheh. 2020. Multi-dialect arabic bert for country-level dialect identification.

Yonghui Wu, Mike Schuster, Zhifeng Chen, Quoc Le, Mohammad Norouzi, Wolfgang Macherey, Maxim Krikun, Yuan Cao, Qin Gao, Klaus Macherey, Jeff Klingner, Apurva Shah, Melvin Johnson, Xiaobing Liu, ukasz Kaiser, Stephan Gouws, Yoshikiyo Kato, Taku Kudo, Hideto Kazawa, and Jeffrey Dean. 2016. Google's neural machine translation system: Bridging the gap between human and machine translation.

Omar F. Zaidan and Chris Callison-Burch. 2014. Arabic dialect identification. *Computational Linguistics*, 40(1):171–202.

A Appendices

A.1 System Architecture

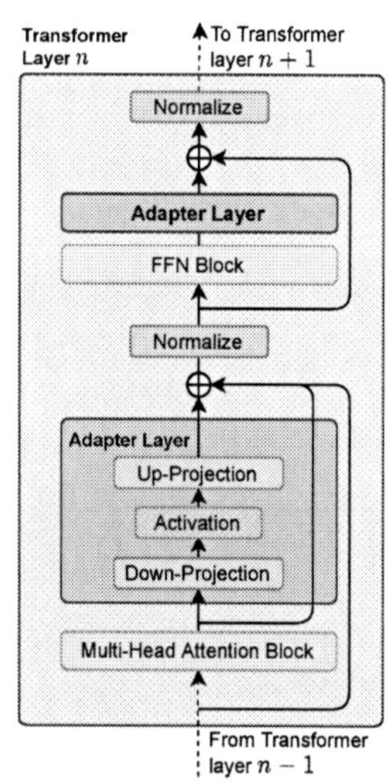

Figure 5: Details of the used model's architecture, specifically looking at one transformer layer. All layers are of the same architecture.[2]

[2]Diagrams generated using `diagrams.net` (draw.io).

Country-level Arabic Dialect Identification Using Small Datasets with Integrated Machine Learning Techniques and Deep Learning Models

Maha J. Althobaiti
Department of Computer Science, Taif University, KSA
maha.j@tu.edu.sa

Abstract

Arabic is characterised by a considerable number of varieties including spoken dialects. In this paper, we presented our models developed to participate in the NADI subtask 1.2 that requires building a system to distinguish between 21 country-level dialects. We investigated several classical machine learning approaches and deep learning models using small datasets. We examined an integration technique between two machine learning approaches. Additionally, we created dictionaries automatically based on Pointwise Mutual Information and labelled datasets, which enriched the feature space when training models. A semi-supervised learning approach was also examined and compared to other methods that exploit large unlabelled datasets, such as building pre-trained word embeddings. Our winning model was the Support Vector Machine with dictionary-based features and Pointwise Mutual Information values, achieving an 18.94% macros-average F1-score.

1 Introduction

Arabic Dialect Identification (ADI) no doubt caught the attention of researchers (Althobaiti, 2020a,b). Recently, many events and campaigns have been organised to handle ADI and all associated challenges (Molina et al., 2016; Malmasi et al., 2016; Zampieri et al., 2017; Bouamor et al., 2019; Abdul-Mageed et al., 2020, 2021). Dialectal Arabic (DA) started to appear online in text form with the rise of Web 2.0, which has allowed users to generate online content, such as social media posts, blogs, discussion forums, and emails. However, the ADI problem has become challenging due to a lack of data to represent a wide spectrum of Arabic dialects and their complex taxonomy. In this paper, we examined the possibility of exploiting small datasets in order to build an ADI system with solid performance. We experimented with an integration technique between two classical Machine Learning (ML) approaches. We also automatically created dictionaries based on Pointwise Mutual Information (PMI) and labelled datasets. We exploited the automatically created dictionaries to enrich the feature space when training the models. A semi-supervised learning paradigm, namely, co-training was also designated to exploit the noisy and unlabelled data available hugely online. We also investigated another approach to leverage large unlabelled data, such as building pre-trained word embeddings to be used later in the training process. Two Deep Learning (DL) models, the Gated Recurrent Unit (GRU) and the Bidirectional Long-Short Term Memory (BiLSTM), were investigated along with a co-training method and word embeddings (either pre-trained, or learned during training).

2 Datasets

The dataset used in this paper is the NADI corpus, consisting of 31,000 labelled tweets and encompassing 21 country-level Arabic dialects. The dataset is divided into three parts: 68% for training (21,000 tweets), 16% for the development set (5,000 tweets), and 16% for the test set (5,000 tweets). The NADI shared task organisers also shared with participating teams around 10M unlabelled tweets.

The text pre-processing steps are essential in any Natural Language Processing (NLP) application and may affect positively or negatively the final outputs. The pre-processing pipeline we followed in our study before training our proposed models includes tokenising, the removal of stop words and one-character words, and cleaning the texts. The cleaning step involves the removal of diacritical marks, non-alphanumeric characters including emojis and excessive white spaces.

Proceedings of the Sixth Arabic Natural Language Processing Workshop, pages 265–270
Kyiv, Ukraine (Virtual), April 19, 2021.

3 Feature Extraction

In this section, we illustrate the extracted features and the text representation of the input data before feeding them to the proposed models.

3.1 Pointwise Mutual Information (PMI)

The PMI represents a statistical measure of association strength between two events x and y, given their individual and joint distributions (Manning et al., 1999). In our study, the PMI was utilised to assess the significance of specific words to their corresponding Arabic dialects by measuring the correlation between the word and that Arabic dialect. Mathematically, it is the log of the probability of the word being utilised in a certain Arabic dialect divided by the product of the probability of the word and the probability of that Arabic dialect independently.

$$pmi(w, T_{dialect}) = \log \frac{p(w, T_{dialect})}{p(w) * p(T_{dialect})}$$

Where w is a word in the corpus and $T_{dialect}$ represents the tweets from Arabic dialects in the corpus. To compute the required probabilities for the words and Arabic dialects, we relied on the training corpus of the NADI shared task for the country-level DA identification as illustrated in Section 2. The words with the highest PMI scores for a particular dialect have a high probability to appear in tweets of that specific Arabic dialect. On the other hand, the negative PMI score between a word and a certain Arabic dialect indicates the lack of relatedness between this word and that dialect. Clearly, the use of PMI helps to rank the words in the dataset according to their degree of association to each Arabic dialect. We used PMI scores to train some of our proposed models, as follows:

1. Dictionary-based features: We automatically created a dictionary for each Arabic dialect by exploiting the labelled training data and the PMI scores of the dataset's vocabulary in relation to relevant Arabic dialects. That is, only words with positive PMI scores higher than 1.5 were automatically added to the dictionary of each dialect. Consequently, the dictionary of each Arabic dialect includes only dialectal words that correlate most to that dialect. The distribution of the subtask 1.2 dataset, however, is not balanced. In addition, the tweets of each country may be biased to the topics mentioned in this dataset's tweets. Thus, the unbalanced data and limited topics may result in some MSA words with positive PMI values higher than 1.5. To this end, we utilised the MSA corpus provided by the NADI organisers for the subtask 1.1 in order to prevent MSA words from being included in the dictionary of each dialect. The dictionary-based features are used as binary features to indicate whether the word in a tweet exists in the dictionary of an Arabic dialect or not.

2. Tweet's PMI value: Each example in the dataset (i.e., each tweet) has been given a total PMI value, calculated by summing the PMI score of each word in the tweet with each Arabic dialect. That is, for each tweet, 21 PMI values have been computed, which represent the strength of the whole tweet's association with each of the 21 Arabic dialects.

3.2 Word Embeddings

Distributed representations of text at various levels of granularity, including words and sentences, have become the dominant method for vectorising textual data for various NLP tasks (Mikolov et al., 2013b,a, 2018; Pennington et al., 2014; Zahran et al., 2015; Abdul-Mageed et al., 2018). Word embedding representation captures a considerable number of semantic and syntactic word relationships where the words are vectorised by training a neural network on a large corpus. In our study, we vectorised the words of the corpus using two methods of embeddings :

(1) Pre-trained embeddings on 300K Twitter data: We built a word vectors model using 300K tweets from the 10M unlabelled tweets provided by the NADI shared task organisers. The Continuous Bag of Words (CBOW) algorithm was adopted for training the model with the number of dimensions of the embeddings set to 100 (i.e., default value). Other hyper-parameters were set as follows: the window size = 5 and the minimum count of words to consider = 5. We built the word2vec model using the Gensim toolkit in Python (Rehurek and Sojka, 2010). We adopted the same pre-processing steps illustrated in Section 2.

(2) Learned embeddings during the training of the ADI system: The word embeddings layer is learned jointly with a neural network model during training the model on the NADI shared task corpus of country-level dialectal identification.

3.3 Other Features

We used the Term Frequency-Inverse Document Frequency (TFIDF) to represent text when we modelled our ADI systems using classical machine learning approaches. The TFIDF is another numerical measure that represents how important a word is to a specific Arabic dialect. The importance increases proportionally to the number of times the word appears in an Arabic dialect, but is offset by the number of times a word appears in other Arabic dialects (Jones, 1972; Yun-tao et al., 2005; Schütze et al., 2008).

We also utilised word unigram, bigrams, and trigrams as features, as well as the character n-grams where n ranges from 2 to 5.

4 System Description

This section presents the approaches we employed in our experiments to examine various traditional ML and DL models when working on country-level ADI problem, covering 21 countries, with small datasets and various features.

4.1 Classical Machine Learning

Support Vector Machine: We utilised the Support Vector Machine (SVM) to perform the country-level ADI task. The 21 dictionaries built automatically, as explained in Section 3, are used as binary features fed to the SVM in conjunction with other features like Tweet's PMI values and TFIDF vectors, as well as character (2-5)-grams and word (1-3)-grams.

Integrated Machine Learning Technique: It involves integrating two classical ML approaches, where the predictions of one are exploited as additional features to train the second machine learning method. We utilised the Logistic Regression (LR) model as a first classifier whereby its predictions were fed, in conjunction with other features, to the SVM model.

Ensemble Classifier: The final decision of the ensemble classifier employed for country-level ADI relies on hard voting of three individual classifiers: SVM, LR, and a Random Forest (RF).

The features utilised to train each individual classifier in the integrated ML Method and ensemble classifier are: dictionary-based features, Tweet's PMI values, character (2-5)-grams, word (1-3)-grams, as well as TFIDF as a way to represent texts.

Co-Training: We attempted to add additional training data to the limited amount of NADI labelled data (a total of 21,000 training tweets) for country-level DA identification (Blum and Mitchell, 1998). To this end, we utilised an automatic labelling approach, namely co-training to annotate additional data without human intervention. Although the NADI organisers shared 10M unlabelled tweets with the participating teams, we decided to label only 300K tweets.

In our study, the co-training involves the use of three classifiers: LR, SVM, and RF in order to label the same tweet with labels l_1, l_2, and l_3. The tweet is finally labelled l if $l = l_1 = l_2 = l_3$. That is, the tweet will be labelled and included in the final corpus only when the three classifiers agree. We called the 300 annotated tweets that resulted from the co-training technique the $CoTraining_{labelled}$ corpus.

4.2 Deep Learning

GRU: The Gated Recurrent Unit (GRU) was also examined in our study for the country-level DA identification. Our GRU-based model consists of a GRU layer with 50 units. A softmax layer is applied on top for classification (No. of epochs = 30). For word vectors, an embedding layer was added to the beginning of the network with dimensions equal to 100. In addition, we carried out another experiment in which we initialised the words with pre-trained word embeddings on the $CoTraining_{labelled}$ corpus.

BiLSTM: We developed a Bidirectional Long-Short Term Memory (BiLSTM) network, consisting of 50 hidden units, followed by a fully connected layer with 50 hidden units. Lastly, a dense layer with 21 hidden units and softmax activation function was utilised to predict the country of the dialect. We used 300 as input sequence length, 0.1 for dropout rate, and 30 for epochs. We specified *Adam* as the optimisation algorithm and *categorical_crossentropy* as the loss function. Two experiments were conducted: one using the word embeddings learned during the training, and the other using initialised values of words with pre-trained embeddings on the $CoTraining_{labelled}$ corpus. In both cases of word embeddings the dimension was equal to 100.

In order to examine the co-training method and to make experimental evaluations of various methods, the $CoTraining_{labelled}$ corpus was utilised to implement multiple classical ML and DL models, as well as integrated ML techniques with the same settings as explained in previous subsections.

5 Results

We conducted several experiments in which we examined various classical ML and DL models to perform multi-way ADI using small datasets. We also examined various features, as explained in Section 3 and Section 4. We started with character (2-5)-grams and word (1-3)-grams as features to develop an SVM model. We created dictionaries automatically based on Pointwise Mutual Information and labelled datasets. Including the automatically generated dictionaries in the feature space to train the SVM model boosted the model's performance especially in terms of *recall* measure. The use of dictionaries alone as binary features increased the performance of the SVM model, but adding the Tweet's PMI values to the features set yielded the better SVM performance. Furthermore, we experimented with an integration approach between SVM and LR, as well as set of features including dictionary-based features and PMI values. This approach outperformed the SVM model in terms of precision, as expected, but fell behind slightly in terms of *recall* and *F1-score*. We also experimented with the ensemble method by combining the decisions of three individual classifiers: LR, SVM, and RF. The ensemble classifier with dictionary-based features and Tweet's PMI values surpassed the performance of all models in terms of *precision*, a predictable outcome as the ensemble classifier relied on hard voting. Moreover, the BiLSTM and GRU-based models fell short in comparison to classical ML techniques. The small dataset of 21,000 tweets may significantly affect the overall performance of the DL models.

Table 1 shows the performance of various classical ML and DL models evaluated on development and test sets. Table 2 shows the performance of the models when training on the $CoTraining_{labelled}$ corpus that consists of 300K annotated tweets. The increase in training data size by implementing the co-training labelling method resulted in a drop in the overall performance of all models. The classical ML techniques with PMI values and dictionary-based features still outperformed DL models, even on the 300K annotated tweets. This can be attributed to the fact that labelling new tweets was conducted automatically based on other models trained on a small dataset (i.e., NADI training data). We also considered the available unlabelled tweets as resources to build a pre-trained word embeddings model to initialise the word values in DL models, as explained in Section 3. In order to build the pre-trained word embeddings we used $CoTraining_{labelled}$ corpus, the same data employed to train the models to compare both the co-training automatic labelling approach and the use of pre-trained word embeddings model. The results clearly showed that the two techniques performed on par. For example, the BiLSTM-based model achieved *macro-average F1-score* equal to 12.85 when using NADI training data and word embeddings vectors, which are pre-trained on the $CoTraining_{labelled}$ corpus. On the other hand, using $CoTraining_{labelled}$ corpus as the training data of the BiLSATM model resulted in 12.63 *macro-average F1-score*.

Method	Dev Set		Test Set	
	F1	**ACC**	**F1**	**ACC**
SVM,c2-5,w1-3,dict,PMI	18.71	35.68	18.94	35.94
SVM,c2-5,w1-3,dict	18.52	35.54	18.66	35.53
SVM,c2-5,w1-3	17	35.22	-	-
Integrated ML,c2-5,w1-3,dict,PMI	17.87	36.74	18.06	38.47
Integrated ML,c2-5,w1-3,dict	17.57	36.86	18.08	37.21
Ensemble,c2-5,w1-3,dict	17.45	37.26	-	-
Ensemble,c2-5,w1-3,dict,PMI	17.23	37.48	-	-
BiLSTM, WE_{layer}	13.2	26.16	-	-
GRU, WE_{layer}	12.85	29.14	-	-

Table 1: The performance of classical ML and DL models trained on NADI subtask 1.2 corpus and evaluated on development and test sets. "c2-5" indicates character n-grams where n=2-5, "w1-3" indicates word n-grams where n=1-3, "dict" indicates dictionary-based features, "PMI" is Tweet's PMI value, and "WE_{layer}" indicates word embeddings learned during the training.

6 Discussion and Analysis

We analysed the outputs of various models on the development dataset. We noticed that many mislabelled tweets are short in length and do not contain

Method	F1	P	R	ACC
Integrated ML,c2-5,w1-3,dict	14.45	17.12	15.88	24.6
SVM,c2-5,w1-3,dict,PMI	14.2	17.09	15.4	24.14
SVM,c2-5,w1-3	14.04	16.45	15.63	23.76
BiLSTM, $WE_{pretrained}$	12.85	13.89	14.17	35.8
BiLSTM, WE_{layer}	12.63	14.24	13.13	22.96
GRU, WE_{layer}	11.51	12.3	13.71	26.68
GRU, $WE_{pretrained}$	11.5	12.73	13.35	36.3

Table 2: The performance of classical ML and DL models trained on $CoTraining_{labelled}$ corpus and evaluated on the development set. "c2-5" indicates character n-grams where n=2-5, "w1-3" indicates word n-grams where n=1-3, "dict" indicates dictionary-based features, "PMI" is Tweet's PMI value, "WE_{layer}" indicates word embeddings learned during the training, and "$WE_{pretrained}$" indicates the use of pre-trained word embeddings.

any distinctive dialectal Arabic words (i.e, words primarily used in one Arabic dialect and can be used to distinguish that dialect from others). For example, the tweet (حتى تكمل اكيد) is labelled as "Iraq" in the corpus but predicted as "Saudi Arabic" by our system of integrated ML technique. In addition, we noticed that a number of tweets contain obvious distinctive dialectal words, however, the model failed to identify the correct dialect. This can be partially attributed to the fact that the training data for NADI subtask 1.2 is small and for 6 out of 21 dialects, the number of training samples is less than 250. On the other hand, although the automatically created dictionaries led to better performance for the classical ML techniques, these dictionaries were collected based on a small dataset (labelled data of NADI subtask 1.2 training corpus). The unbalanced distribution of samples per country in the corpus led to obtaining words with high PMI values for some Arabic dialects and with low PMI values for others, although the words are shared between these dialects. For example, the word (مافيش) is used in Egypt and Yemen, so the PMI values between the word and the two Arabic dialects should not be high , since it is shared between the two dialects. However, the word's PMI value was high with the Yemeni dialect (1.167) and relatively low with Egyptian (0.322), because the number of Egypt samples in the corpus is 4283 while Yemen has only 429 samples. We expect that a large corpus with relatively even numbers of Arabic dialect samples will result in dictionaries with a considerable number of entries and better PMI values.

Normalisation is one of the preprocessing steps when building NLP applications. For dialectal Arabic normalisation is a vital step that should be taken into consideration according to the Arabic NLP application's needs. In order to reduce the data sparsity and increase its accuracy, one should take normalisation of some Arabic letters into account, especially when building pre-trained word embeddings or learning them during the training process.

7 Conclusion

In this paper, we investigated the possibility of exploiting small datasets in order to build a strongly performing ADI system, by integrating various machine learning approaches. We also created dictionaries automatically based on Pointwise Mutual Information and labelled datasets, which enriched the feature space when training models. A semi-supervised learning paradigm, namely co-training was also examined as a way to leverage the large and noisy unlabelled dialectal Arabic datasets. Another approach examined in this study to exploit large unlabelled datasets was building pre-trained word embeddings model to be used later in the training process. Both approaches to leverage large and noisy unlabelled data showed similar results and performed on par. Our winning model was the Support Vector Machine with dictionary-based features and PMI values, achieving 18.94% macros-average F1-score on the NADI subtask 1.2 test set. In terms of precision, the integration method that merged two classical machine learning algorithms surpassed all models with precision equal to 22.70%. We also concluded that pre-processing text is a vital step before building any dialectal Arabic models and needs to be further investigated to understand its side effects and benefits.

References

Muhammad Abdul-Mageed, Hassan Alhuzali, and Mohamed Elaraby. 2018. You tweet what you speak: A city-level dataset of arabic dialects. In *Proceedings of the Eleventh International Conference on Language Resources and Evaluation (LREC 2018)*, pages 3653–3659.

Muhammad Abdul-Mageed, Chiyu Zhang, Houda Bouamor, and Nizar Habash. 2020. NADI 2020: The First Nuanced Arabic Dialect Identification Shared Task. In *Proceedings of the Fifth Arabic Natural Language Processing Workshop*, pages 97–110.

Muhammad Abdul-Mageed, Chiyu Zhang, Abdel-Rahim Elmadany, Houda Bouamor, and Nizar Habash. 2021. NADI 2021: The Second Nuanced Arabic Dialect Identification Shared Task. In *Proceedings of the Sixth Arabic Natural Language Processing Workshop (WANLP 2021)*.

Maha J Althobaiti. 2020a. Automatic Arabic Dialect Identification Systems for Written Texts: A Survey. *International Journal of Computational Linguistics (IJCL)*, 11(3):61–89.

Maha J Althobaiti. 2020b. Automatic Arabic Dialect Identification Systems for Written Texts: A Survey. *arXiv preprint arXiv:2009.12622*.

Avrim Blum and Tom Mitchell. 1998. Combining labeled and unlabeled data with co-training. In *Proceedings of the eleventh annual conference on Computational learning theory*, pages 92–100.

Houda Bouamor, Sabit Hassan, and Nizar Habash. 2019. The MADAR shared task on Arabic fine-grained dialect identification. In *Proceedings of the Fourth Arabic Natural Language Processing Workshop*, pages 199–207.

Karen Sparck Jones. 1972. A statistical interpretation of term specificity and its application in retrieval. *Journal of documentation*.

Shervin Malmasi, Marcos Zampieri, Nikola Ljubešić, Preslav Nakov, Ahmed Ali, and Jörg Tiedemann. 2016. Discriminating between similar languages and arabic dialect identification: A report on the third dsl shared task. In *Proceedings of the Third Workshop on NLP for Similar Languages, Varieties and Dialects (VarDial3)*, pages 1–14.

Christopher D Manning, Christopher D Manning, and Hinrich Schütze. 1999. *Foundations of statistical natural language processing*. MIT press.

Tomas Mikolov, Kai Chen, Greg Corrado, and Jeffrey Dean. 2013a. Efficient estimation of word representations in vector space. In *Proceedings of the International Conference on Learning Representations (ICLR 2013)*, pages 1–12.

Tomáš Mikolov, Édouard Grave, Piotr Bojanowski, Christian Puhrsch, and Armand Joulin. 2018. Advances in Pre-Training Distributed Word Representations. In *Proceedings of the Eleventh International Conference on Language Resources and Evaluation (LREC 2018)*, pages 52–55.

Tomas Mikolov, Ilya Sutskever, Kai Chen, Greg S Corrado, and Jeff Dean. 2013b. Distributed Representations of Words and Phrases and their Compositionality. *Advances in Neural Information Processing Systems*, 26:3111–3119.

Giovanni Molina, Fahad AlGhamdi, Mahmoud Ghoneim, Abdelati Hawwari, Nicolas Rey-Villamizar, Mona Diab, and Thamar Solorio. 2016. Overview for the Second Shared Task on Language Identification in Code-Switched Data. In *Proceedings of the Second Workshop on Computational Approaches to Code Switching*, pages 40–49.

Jeffrey Pennington, Richard Socher, and Christopher D Manning. 2014. Glove: Global vectors for word representation. In *Proceedings of the 2014 conference on empirical methods in natural language processing (EMNLP)*, pages 1532–1543.

Radim Rehurek and Petr Sojka. 2010. Software framework for topic modelling with large corpora. In *In Proceedings of the LREC 2010 workshop on new challenges for NLP frameworks*, pages 46–50.

Hinrich Schütze, Christopher D Manning, and Prabhakar Raghavan. 2008. *Introduction to information retrieval*, volume 39. Cambridge University Press Cambridge.

Zhang Yun-tao, Gong Ling, and Wang Yong-cheng. 2005. An improved TF-IDF approach for text classification. *Journal of Zhejiang University-Science A*, 6(1):49–55.

Mohamed A Zahran, Ahmed Magooda, Ashraf Y Mahgoub, Hazem Raafat, Mohsen Rashwan, and Amir Atyia. 2015. Word representations in vector space and their applications for arabic. In *International Conference on Intelligent Text Processing and Computational Linguistics*, pages 430–443. Springer.

Marcos Zampieri, Shervin Malmasi, Nikola Ljubešić, Preslav Nakov, Ahmed Ali, Jörg Tiedemann, Yves Scherrer, and Noëmi Aepli. 2017. Findings of the VarDial evaluation campaign 2017. In *Proceedings of the fourth workshop on NLP for similar languages, varieties and dialects*.

BERT-based Multi-Task Model for Country and Province Level Modern Standard Arabic and Dialectal Arabic Identification

Abdellah El Mekki[1] **Abdelkader El Mahdaouy**[1] **Kabil Essefar**[1]
Nabil El Mamoun[2] **Ismail Berrada**[1] **Ahmed Khoumsi**[3]
[1]School of Computer Sciences, Mohammed VI Polytechnic University, Morocco
[2]Faculty of Sciences Dhar EL Mahraz, Sidi Mohamed Ben Abdellah University, Morocco
[3]Dept. Electrical & Computer Engineering, University of Sherbrooke, Canada
{firstname.lastname}@um6p.ma
ahmed.khoumsi@usherbrooke.ca

Abstract

Dialect and standard language identification are crucial tasks for many Arabic natural language processing applications. In this paper, we present our deep learning-based system, submitted to the second NADI shared task for country-level and province-level identification of Modern Standard Arabic (MSA) and Dialectal Arabic (DA). The system is based on an end-to-end deep Multi-Task Learning (MTL) model to tackle both country-level and province-level MSA/DA identification. The latter MTL model consists of a shared Bidirectional Encoder Representation Transformers (BERT) encoder, two task-specific attention layers, and two classifiers. Our key idea is to leverage both the task-discriminative and the inter-task shared features for country and province MSA/DA identification. The obtained results show that our MTL model outperforms single-task models on most subtasks.

1 Introduction

The Arabic language is spoken by approximately 400 million people and characterized by different varieties. On the one hand, people of the Arab world tend to use Modern Standard Arabic (MSA) as a communication channel in formal situations (e.g. media, religion, education). On the other hand, Arabic dialects are usually used for informal communication in daily life. These dialects differ, to varying degrees, from one region to another.

Generally, existing research works categorized DA into four regions (Maghreb, Egypt, Gulf, and Levant) based on the coarse-grained taxonomy (Zaidan and Callison-Burch, 2014). Recently, several research studies classified DA into more fine-grained varieties such as country-level dialects (Salameh et al., 2018; Bouamor et al., 2019; Abdul-Mageed et al., 2020b).

In the last few years, Arabic dialect identification has gained much attention (Bouamor et al., 2019; El Mekki et al., 2020; Abdul-Mageed et al., 2020b,c). Identifying the dialect of an end-user is a very important task in many applications such as user profiling, personalized customer support, etc. Nevertheless, due to the nature and the structure of DA as well as MSA (Al-Sughaiyer and Al-Kharashi, 2004; Habash, 2010; Habash et al., 2012), this task faces several challenges.

Previous works on DA identification mainly focused on the use of traditional machine learning models (Abu Kwaik and Saad, 2019; Meftouh et al., 2019) and single-task deep learning models (Talafha et al., 2020). (El Mekki et al., 2020) introduced hierarchical models that perform the training and prediction of the country-level and province-level classification based on a sequential process. Recently, (Abdul-Mageed et al., 2020c) shown the effectiveness of MTL using MARBERT, a transformer-based language model pre-trained on a massive dataset of 128GB Arabic tweets, for both country-level and province-level DA identification.

In this paper, we tackle both the DA and MSA identification of the second NADI (Nuanced Arabic Dialect Identification) shared tasks: Country-level MSA identification, country-level DA identification, province-level MSA identification, and province-level DA identification (Abdul-Mageed et al., 2021). Our submitted system consists of an end-to-end deep MLT model that predicts both the province and the country of a given Arabic tweet. Our model leverages MARBERT's contextualized word embedding (Abdul-Mageed et al., 2020a) with two task-specific attention layers that extract the task-discriminative features. The latter features are then concatenated with the encoder's pooled embedding ([CLS] embedding) and are fed to the task classifiers. Thus, the core idea of our approach is to combine both task-discriminative and

Proceedings of the Sixth Arabic Natural Language Processing Workshop, pages 271–275
Kyiv, Ukraine (Virtual), April 19, 2021.

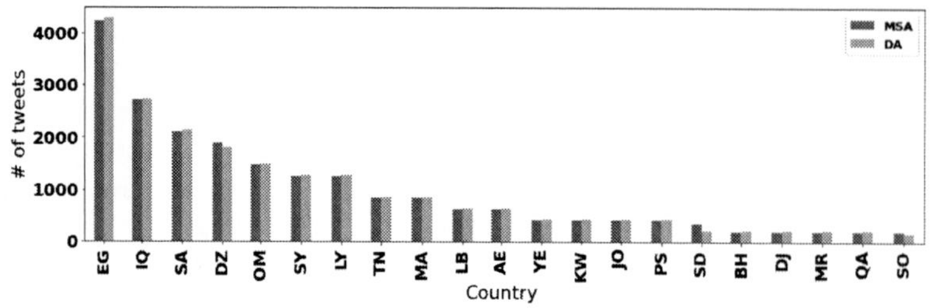

Figure 1: Label distribution of the training set for the country-level classification subtasks. Country code following the ISO 3166-1 alpha-2 (Wikipedia, 2020)

inter-task shared features for country and province MSA/DA identification. The obtained results show that our MTL model outperforms its single-task counterpart on all evaluated subtasks. These results prove the effectiveness of combining task-specific features and inter-task shared features for country-level and province-level MSA and DA identification.

The rest of this paper is organized as follows. Section 2 describes the NADI shared task's datasets. Section 3 presents our proposed method. Section 4 summarizes the obtained results for both subtask 1 and subtask 2. In Section 5, we discuss these results. Finally, the conclusion is given in section 6.

2 Data

The second NADI shared task consists of four subtasks on MSA and DA country-level as well as province-level identification. Table 1 presents the four subtasks of NADI'2020.

Table 1: NADI'2021 DA and MSA identification subtasks

Data	Country-level	Province-level
MSA	Subtask 1.1	Subtask 2.1
DA	Subtask 1.2	Subtask 2.2

For both MSA and DA subtasks, the organizers of NADI'2021 provided a dataset of 31,000 labeled tweets covering 21 Arab countries and 100 Arab provinces. The training set consists of 21,000 tweets, while the rest 10,000 are equally distributed between the development and test sets. Finally, each tweet is assigned a single country label and a single province label. Figure 1 shows that the distribution of tweets for the country-level classification subtasks is unbalanced. Furthermore, Egypt, Iraq and Saudi Arabia countries have the highest number of tweets, while Mauritania, Qatar and Somalia have the lowest one.

3 Method

Our multi-task model, for both tasks, consists of three main components: BERT encoder (MARBERT pre-trained language model), two task-specific attention layers, and two task classifiers.

3.1 BERT Encoder

The input tweets are encoded using a Bidirectional Encoder Representation from Transformers (BERT) model (Devlin et al., 2019). BERT employs multiple transformer blocks to encode the input text. This model is trained on large textual corpora by jointly optimizing the Masked Language Model (MLM) and the Next Sentence Prediction (NSP) objectives. Fine-tuning BERT model on the downstream tasks has shown state-of-the-art performances in many NLP applications.

In order to avoid domain shift, our end-to-end model for NADI'2021 uses MARBERT. In fact, MARBERT (Abdul-Mageed et al., 2020a) is a variation of BERT pre-trained on a large Arabic Twitter dataset (1 billion tweets) using only MLM objective (tweets are short).

3.2 Task-specific attention layer

Two task-specific attention layers are used to reward tokens' hidden representation (contextual embedding) that contributes to the correct classification of tweets for the country-level and province-level tasks. These layers operate on top of the contextualized word embedding of the BERT encoder $H = [h_1, h_2, ..., h_n] \in \mathbb{R}^{n \times d}$, where n is the sequence length and d is the embedding dimension. Hence, each task-specific attention layer (Bahdanau et al., 2015; Yang et al., 2016) can attend to some parts of the tweet to extract the task-discriminative features. The attention mechanism is given by:

$$C = tanh(HW_a)$$
$$\alpha = softmax(C^T W_\alpha)$$
$$v = \alpha \cdot H^T$$

where $W_a \in \mathbb{R}^{d \times 1}$, $W_\alpha \in \mathbb{R}^{n \times n}$ are the attention mechanism's learnable parameters, $C \in \mathbb{R}^{n \times 1}$ and $\alpha \in [0, 1]^n$ weights the word hidden representations according to their relevance to the task, v represents the task-relevant information contained in a tweet.

3.3 Task classifier

The task classifier consists of one hidden layer and one output layer. The pooled output ($h_{[CLS]}$ embedding) and the vector v, obtained using the task-specific attention layer, are concatenated and passed to the task classifier. The latter outputs the predicted task label.

3.4 Multi-task learning objective

Our MTL model is trained to jointly optimize both tasks' cross-entropy losses. For the country-level MSA/DA identification, our model minimizes:

$$L_{Country}(\hat{y}^c, y^c) = -\sum_{i=1}^{N}\sum_{j=1}^{l} y_{ij}^c log(\hat{y}_{ij}^c)$$

where y_{ij}^c is the ground-truth label, $\hat{y}_{ij}^c$ is the predicted label, N is the number of training samples, and l is the number of countries ($l = 21$).
For the province-level MSA/DA identification, our model is trained to minimize:

$$L_{Province}(\hat{y}^p, y^p) = -\sum_{i=1}^{N}\sum_{j=1}^{k} y_{ij}^p log(\hat{y}_{ij}^p)$$

where y_{ij}^p is the ground-truth label, $\hat{y}_{ij}^p$ is the predicted label, and k is the number of provinces ($k = 100$).
Thus, the final loss of our model is:

$$L = L_{Country} + L_{Province}$$

Finally, our model is trained using Adam optimizer (Kingma and Ba, 2014), with a learning rate of 1×10^{-5}. Based on several experiments, the batch size and the number of epochs are set to 16 and 5, respectively. For tweets cleaning, we have implemented the same preprocessing pipeline that is used by MARBERT which consists of diacritics removal and mention substitution by USER token.

4 Results

In our experiments, we have investigated multiple models, starting from traditional machine learning techniques to transformer-based approaches. The obtained results show that MARBERT significantly outperforms the other approaches. For a fair comparison, our single-task model employs an attention layer over the contextualized word embedding of MARBERT and concatenates its outputs with the [CLS] token embedding for MSA and DA identification subtasks. It is worth mentioning that incorporating an attention layer into single-task and MTL models improves the results compared to performing the classification using only the [CLS] token embedding representation.

Table 2 presents the Macro-averaged F1-scores and the accuracies achieved using our evaluated single-task and MTL models on the four subtasks. The obtained results show that our attention-based multi-task model largely outperforms the single-task model on all subtasks' Dev set and Test set. For MSA identification, at the country-level and province-level, our MTL model achieves F1-score performance increments of 1.49% and 0.35% respectively over the single-task model on the Dev set, while it achieves F1-score performance increments of 0.47% and 0.63% respectively over the single-task model for the Test set. For DA identification, at the country-level and province-level, the MTL model leads to F1-score performance increments of 0.42% and 0.42% over the single-task model, respectively on the Dev set, while it achieves increments of 1.57% and 2.02%, respectively on the Test set. This can be explained by the fact that our MTL model leverages signals from related tasks and boosts the performance of both. Moreover, through the task-specific attention layers, the MTL model extracts the task-discriminative features. Furthermore, employing task-specific features and global-shared features ([CLS] embedding) improves the performance of our MTL model.

5 Discussion

In order to analyze the results and explain the lower performance of our MTL model on some subtasks, Figure 2 draws the confusion matrices for DA and MSA identification at the country-level on the Dev set. The matrices highlight a number of strengths and weaknesses of our final model. On the one hand, the model performs well for countries with

	Dev/Test	Single-task model F1	Single-task model Accuracy	Multi-task model F1	Multi-task model Accuracy
Subtask 1.1	Dev	21.56	34.35	**23.05**	**37.80**
	Test	20.90	33.73	**21.47**	**33.84**
Subtask 1.2	Dev	31.62	48.48	**32.04**	**51.28**
	Test	29.07	49.50	**30.64**	**50.30**
Subtask 2.1	Dev	6.05	6.63	**6.40**	**6.85**
	Test	4.72	5.00	**5.35**	**5.72**
Subtask 2.2	Dev	8.88	9.60	**9.40**	**9.84**
	Test	5.30	6.90	**7.32**	**7.92**

Table 2: Scores of our models (%) for the 4 subtasks (dev-sets and test-sets).

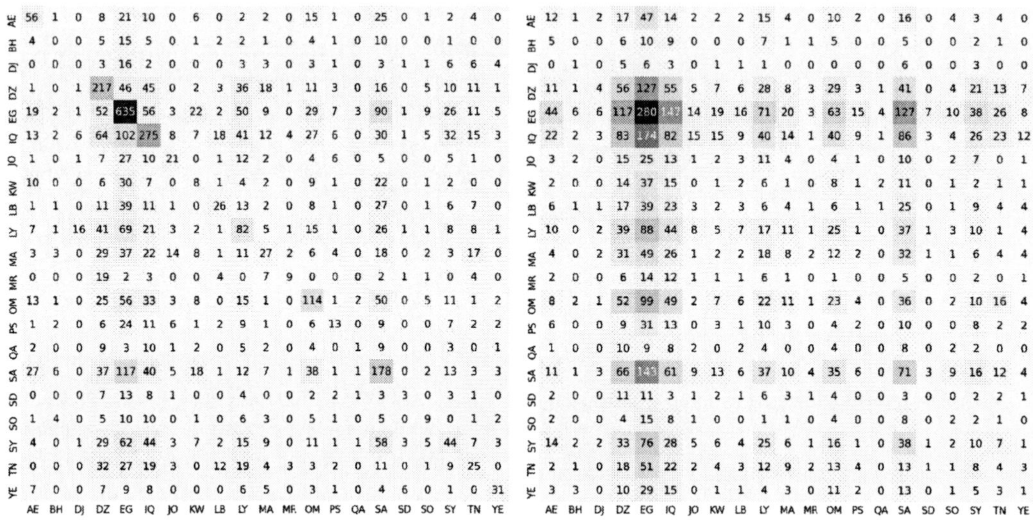

(a) MSA identification

(b) DA identification

Figure 2: The confusion matrices of our MTL model on the Dev set for country-level DA and MSA identification.

a high number of training examples such as Egypt, Algeria, and Iraq. On the other hand, the model shows poor performance in predicting true positives for countries with a low number of training examples, as it is the case of Djibouti and Bahrain. Moreover, the MSA country-level identification is a very challenging subtask since it is hard to find patterns to discriminate between countries and provinces based on standard language. Also, the model tends to make incorrect predictions for countries that are geographically close since their dialects have some minor differences (e.g. the Gulf countries) compared to other Arab countries.

6 Conclusion

In this paper, we introduced our submitted system to the second NADI shared task. We proposed an MTL model for joint country-level and province-level identification of MSA and DA tweets. The model is based on the state-of-the-art MARBERT encoder and uses two task-specific attention layers to extract the task-discriminative features. The obtained results have shown that our MTL model outperforms the single-task model on all subtasks for both evaluation measures (Macro-F1 and accuracy).

Future research work will focus on developing task-interaction and class-interaction modules and mechanisms for coarse-grained and fine-grained DA and MSA identification.

References

Muhammad Abdul-Mageed, AbdelRahim Elmadany, and El Moatez Billah Nagoudi. 2020a. ARBERT & MARBERT: Deep bidirectional transformers for arabic. *arXiv preprint arXiv:2101.01785*.

Muhammad Abdul-Mageed, Chiyu Zhang, Houda Bouamor, and Nizar Habash. 2020b. NADI 2020: The First Nuanced Arabic Dialect Identification Shared Task. In *Proceedings of the Fifth Arabic Natural Language Processing Workshop (WANLP 2020)*, Barcelona, Spain.

Muhammad Abdul-Mageed, Chiyu Zhang, Abdel-Rahim Elmadany, Houda Bouamor, and Nizar Habash. 2021. NADI 2021: The Second Nuanced Arabic Dialect Identification Shared Task. In *Proceedings of the Sixth Arabic Natural Language Processing Workshop (WANLP 2021)*.

Muhammad Abdul-Mageed, Chiyu Zhang, Abdel-Rahim Elmadany, and Lyle Ungar. 2020c. Toward micro-dialect identification in diaglossic and code-switched environments. In *Proceedings of the 2020 Conference on Empirical Methods in Natural Language Processing (EMNLP)*, pages 5855–5876, Online. Association for Computational Linguistics.

Kathrein Abu Kwaik and Motaz Saad. 2019. ArbDialectID at MADAR shared task 1: Language modelling and ensemble learning for fine grained Arabic dialect identification. In *Proceedings of the Fourth Arabic Natural Language Processing Workshop*, pages 254–258, Florence, Italy. Association for Computational Linguistics.

Imad A. Al-Sughaiyer and Ibrahim A. Al-Kharashi. 2004. Arabic morphological analysis techniques: A comprehensive survey. *Journal of the American Society for Information Science and Technology*, 55(3):189–213.

Dzmitry Bahdanau, Kyunghyun Cho, and Yoshua Bengio. 2015. Neural machine translation by jointly learning to align and translate. *CoRR*, abs/1409.0473.

Houda Bouamor, Sabit Hassan, and Nizar Habash. 2019. The MADAR shared task on Arabic fine-grained dialect identification. In *Proceedings of the Fourth Arabic Natural Language Processing Workshop*, pages 199–207.

Jacob Devlin, Ming-Wei Chang, Kenton Lee, and Kristina Toutanova. 2019. BERT: Pre-training of deep bidirectional transformers for language understanding. In *Proceedings of the 2019 Conference of the North American Chapter of the Association for Computational Linguistics: Human Language Technologies, Volume 1 (Long and Short Papers)*, pages 4171–4186, Minneapolis, Minnesota. Association for Computational Linguistics.

Abdellah El Mekki, Ahmed Alami, Hamza Alami, Ahmed Khoumsi, and Ismail Berrada. 2020. Weighted combination of BERT and n-GRAM features for nuanced Arabic dialect identification. In *Proceedings of the Fifth Arabic Natural Language Processing Workshop*, pages 268–274, Barcelona, Spain (Online). Association for Computational Linguistics.

Nizar Habash, Mona Diab, and Owen Rambow. 2012. Conventional orthography for dialectal Arabic. In *Proceedings of the Eighth International Conference on Language Resources and Evaluation (LREC-2012)*, pages 711–718, Istanbul, Turkey. European Languages Resources Association (ELRA).

Nizar Y Habash. 2010. *Introduction to Arabic natural language processing*, volume 3. Morgan & Claypool Publishers.

Diederik P. Kingma and Jimmy Ba. 2014. Adam: A method for stochastic optimization. Cite arxiv:1412.6980Comment: Published as a conference paper at the 3rd International Conference for Learning Representations, San Diego, 2015.

Karima Meftouh, Karima Abidi, Salima Harrat, and Kamel Smaili. 2019. The SMarT classifier for Arabic fine-grained dialect identification. In *Proceedings of the Fourth Arabic Natural Language Processing Workshop*, pages 259–263, Florence, Italy. Association for Computational Linguistics.

Mohammad Salameh, Houda Bouamor, and Nizar Habash. 2018. Fine-grained Arabic dialect identification. In *Proceedings of the 27th International Conference on Computational Linguistics*, pages 1332–1344, Santa Fe, New Mexico, USA. Association for Computational Linguistics.

Bashar Talafha, Mohammad Ali, Muhy Eddin Za'ter, Haitham Seelawi, Ibraheem Tuffaha, Mostafa Samir, Wael Farhan, and Hussein Al-Natsheh. 2020. Multi-dialect Arabic BERT for country-level dialect identification. In *Proceedings of the Fifth Arabic Natural Language Processing Workshop*, pages 111–118, Barcelona, Spain (Online). Association for Computational Linguistics.

Zichao Yang, Diyi Yang, Chris Dyer, Xiaodong He, Alex Smola, and Eduard Hovy. 2016. Hierarchical attention networks for document classification. In *Proceedings of the 2016 Conference of the North American Chapter of the Association for Computational Linguistics: Human Language Technologies*, pages 1480–1489, San Diego, California. Association for Computational Linguistics.

Omar F. Zaidan and Chris Callison-Burch. 2014. Arabic dialect identification. *Computational Linguistics*, 40(1):171–202.

Country-level Arabic dialect identification using RNNs with and without linguistic features

Elsayed Issa[1*] **Mohammed AlShakhori**[1†] **Reda Al-Bahrani**[2**] **Gus Hahn-Powell**[1§]

[1]University of Arizona

[2]Independent Researcher

{*elsayedissa,†mkalshakhori,§hahnpowell}@email.arizona.edu
**reda.bahrani@gmail.com

Abstract

This work investigates the value of augmenting recurrent neural networks with feature engineering for the Second Nuanced Arabic Dialect Identification (NADI) Subtask 1.2: Country-level DA identification. We compare the performance of a simple word-level LSTM using pretrained embeddings with one enhanced using feature embeddings for engineered linguistic features. Our results show that the addition of explicit features to the LSTM is detrimental to performance. We attribute this performance loss to the bivalency of some linguistic items in some text, ubiquity of topics, and participant mobility.

1 Introduction

Arabic exhibits *diglossia*—the existence of two spoken varieties of a language side by side in a community (Ferguson, 1959); while there are a multitude of informal regional varieties, Modern Standard Arabic (MSA) serves as the chief formal variety. Not only the existence of the two spoken varieties is a complex situation for linguists to investigate (Bassiouney, 2009), but it is more complex for data scientists to classify text data of such a language. While phonological differences are apparent in speech, the distinction is lost in writing, as all varieties use the same orthographic system.

Additionally, short vowels in the orthographic system are represented by a diacritic above each phoneme as "أَحَبَّ" meaning "he loved"; recently, however, these vocalic diacritics are dropped from any word as in "احب." The omission is common in news articles, institutional texts, and most obviously on social media platforms. This issue causes what we term *bivalent linguistic unit*, which means that a written text without any vocalic diacritic can belong to any dialect depending on its readers' dialects even if it is written in a local context, a concept that we adopt from (Woolard, 1998). With so few orthographic contrasts, classifying written varieties (MSA, Arabic regional dialects) poses a challenge.

Over the years, there have been several attempts at classifying Arabic dialects, starting from classical natural language processing methods to deep learning whether throughout individual work or shared tasks such as MADAR series (Bouamor et al., 2019), which continued to enhance Arabic dialect identification followed by the NADI series starting in 2019 (Abdul-Mageed et al., 2020). In 2013, Elfardy and Diab (2013) implemented a supervised system for identifying MSA and Egyptian Arabic at the sentence level, by predicting the level of formality of a sentence harvested from the web. Observing the lack of the other Arabic dialects' representation in previous work, Zaidan and Callison-Burch (2014) constructed a corpus focused on including other Arabic varieties. Using n-gram and word character models, they were able to evaluate annotators' biases towards labeling text written in their own dialects.

Deep Learning (DL) methods have revolutionized tasks such as large-scale language modeling (Bengio et al., 2003; Dauphin et al., 2017; Jozefowicz et al., 2016), language identification (Joulin et al., 2017), and sentiment analysis (Dong et al., 2014; Severyn and Moschitti, 2015; Araque et al., 2017). The orthographic overlap between MSA and regional dialects has posed a serious challenge to past work on fine-grained dialect identification. Elaraby and Abdul-Mageed (2018) demonstrated that both recurrent and convolutional neural networks can surpass linear models such as logistic regression, multinomial Naive Bayes, and linear kernel support vector machines (SVM) classifiers. Other methods such as word vector modeling are able to identify some linguistic features of Arabic

Proceedings of the Sixth Arabic Natural Language Processing Workshop, pages 276–281
Kyiv, Ukraine (Virtual), April 19, 2021.

tweet corpus (Abdul-Mageed et al., 2018).

2 Data

In our experiments, we restricted ourselves to using only the official Twitter corpus provided by the Second NADI Shared Task (Abdul-Mageed et al., 2021). As a preprocessing step, we normalized all partitions of the data by removing non-Arabic words, emojis, links, and excess white space. After normalization, we tokenized the tweets using Keras (Chollet et al., 2015). 10% of the training partition was set aside for monitoring validation loss in an effort to avoid overfitting through early stopping.[1]

3 Experiments

In this work, we explored two approaches[2] to fine-grained dialect classification. The first one involved using pretrained word embeddings as the input to an LSTM (Hochreiter and Schmidhuber, 1997) used to encode each tweet. In Experiment 2, we combined the LSTM from Experiment 1 with a feed-forward neural network that encodes a concatenation of low-dimensional dense embeddings representing explicit linguistic features. These linguistic features were used side-by-side with the word-level RNN from Experiment 1 with the aim of supplementing our input with features deemed salient to dialect classification.

3.1 Experiment 1: CBOW and LSTM

The neural architecture used for Experiment 1, shown in Figure 1, consists of pretrained word embeddings and an LSTM to model sequential information. We compared two different sets of available word embeddings: Aravec (Soliman et al., 2017) and Mazajak (Abu Farha and Magdy, 2019). Both sets of pretrained word embeddings were developed using Twitter data with different vocabulary, vector, and corpus sizes. Although both Aravec and Mazajak achieved similar results, the Mazajak word embeddings trained using Continuous Bag of Words (CBOW) (n = 100M tweets) achieved the optimal results in these experiments. As a result, an embedding matrix of the shape [maximum features, embedding size] was created to serve as the weights in the embedding layer in our neural network model.

[1]The early stopping patience was set to 2.

[2]Code: `github.com/clu-ling/wanlp-2021`

Our neural architecture for Experiment 1 consists of three layers.[3] Input to the first layer is restricted to a maximum 80 tokens. The second layer is an embedding layer initialized using the pretrained Mazajak word embeddings. The third layer is an LSTM layer with 300 units, a dropout rate of 0.3, and a recurrent dropout rate of 0.2.

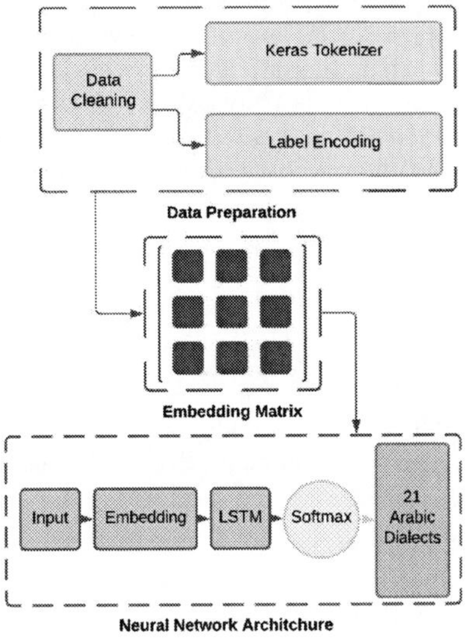

Figure 1: Experiment 1 - The Pipeline for the Arabic Identification System involves 1) data preparation, 2) the extraction of embedding matrix from the CBOW, and 3) a neural network with three layers.

3.2 Experiment 2: Engineered features

Experiment 2 extends the architecture of Experiment 1 by injecting linguistic information using engineered features to learn low-dimensional dense embeddings. These linguistic units are unique distinctive features that signify each dialect from each other. These features vary in terms of their linguistic types starting from demonstrative markers to degree markers. Figure 2 shows the architecture of this two-component network.

The first component works the same way as the model in the Experiment 1 in which the embedding layer receives its weights from the embedding matrix of the pretrained word embeddings. The second component takes a binary vector representing features present in a document (tweet). We use 56 linguistic to represent all 21 Arabic dialects. The input vector of the 56 binary values is

[3]The hyperparameters used are as follows: embedding size of 300, vocabulary size of 50000, batch size of 64, and maximum sequence length of 80.

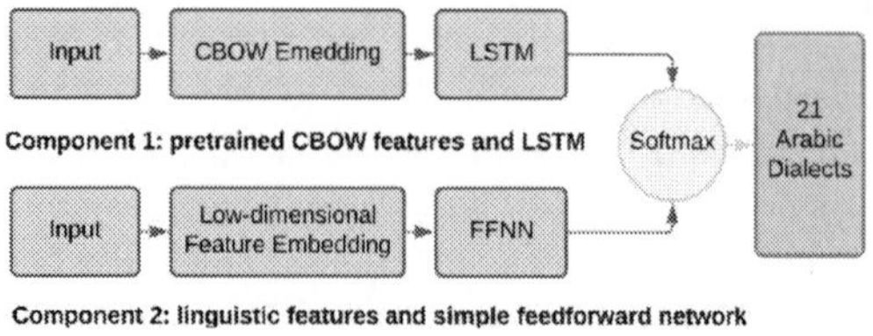

Figure 2: Experiment 2 - the two-component architecture combining word embeddings with embeddings learned for explicit linguistic features. One input consists of pretrained word embeddings fed into an LSTM. The second input is a concatenation of learned embeddings for linguistic features. Finally, the two inputs are combined through concatenation prior to classification.

used to select low-dimensional feature embeddings which are concatenated and fed through a simple feed-forward network consisting of two 100-unit hidden layers with ReLU activation followed by an element-wise multiplication before being concatenated to the output of the LSTM described in Experiment 1.

Table 1 shows a sample of engineered linguistic features. These simple features represent expressions and terms commonly used in each dialect. If one of these features is present, it is assigned 1 otherwise 0. Though here we only report results for the model using positive features, we also explored learning representations for the absence of features (NOT_X).

Dialect	Sample features	Gloss
Iraqi	خوش	ok / good
Saudi	كذا	like this
Moroccan	ديال / ديالي	of-genitive

Table 1: A small sample of the engineered linguistic features for Egyptian, Iraqi, Saudi, Moroccan dialects from DA_Subtask 1.2.Each binary feature was used to learn a dense low-dimensional embedding.

4 Results & Discussion

We evaluated the architectures from both experiments on development data provided for the task. Based on the performance of the two systems, our submission for the shared task uses the architecture from Experiment 1 which does not incorporate any engineered linguistic features.

Our results, shown in Table 2, emphasize the main findings of this article: linguistic features (at least of the forms explored) do not provide sufficient information for fine-grained Arabic dialect identification. Rather, we believe that pretrained word embeddings and models such as BERT are amongst the optimal solutions for feature extraction for Arabic dialectal classification.

Metric (macro)	Model 1	Model 2
Accuracy	41.36	37.82
Precision	30.12	21.65
Recall	21.56	18.72
F1	22.10	18.60

Table 2: Results of the development data for Experiment 1 & 2. The F1 score for Experiment 1 (our simpler model consisting of pretrained word embeddings and an LSTM) outperforms the Experiment 2 architecture which incorporated engineered linguistic features.

There are several observations that underscore the decline in the performance of our model in Experiment 2. Though we treated Experiment 1 as a baseline system to dialect/language identification, it achieved a better macro F1 score than our proposed hybrid method in Experiment 2 which incorporates simple engineered features. This suggests that pretrained word embeddings already provide richer information than what was encoded in our engineered features.

From a linguistic perspective, we believe that explicitly modeling salient features is a promising direction for improving our model; however, there are are a number of reasons this approach was unsuccessful here.

Sparse features Our system has few features relative to the number of classes, and the frequency feature in the corpus (and thus their coverage) is low. That is, these features are insufficient to cover the set of documents available for each dialect.

Genre Much of the data is characterized by what we call *global genre*—meaning that the content of the text contains global shared topics such as sports and popular culture. For instance, examples 3, 4, and 5 in Table 3 indicate that the content of the tweets is governed by a global genre topic which imposes less presence of the local linguistic features of the participants' dialects. In order to improve performance through feature engineering, the content of the data has to be characterized by more *local genre*. Sociologists have shown that participants of different linguistic communities in

No	Label	Tweet	Gloss	Type
1.	Oman	هههههه بايخه هههههه	hahaha stale joke hahaha	bivalent linguistic units
2.	Syria	هههه لاتصدق بس تستاهل	haha don't believe but you deserve	bivalent linguistic units
3.	Syria	ميسي وضعية الميت	Messi ... the state of being dead	global genre
4.	Iraq	اعطي المزيد من الوقت لميسي ونيمار راح يكون البرسا ديناميت	more time to Messi & Nymear, Barca will be dynamite	global genre
5.	Algeria	ميسي ونيمار طلب يا حبيبي	oh my dear, Messi & Nymar are demands	global genre
6.	Algeria	شلون تفوز بالابطال و انت مدربك فالفيردي	How will you win the Europe Champion while the coach is Valverde?	participant mobility
7.	Djibouti	بدنا ترند في كل مكان اليسا في أعياد بيروت	We want a trend everywhere Alissa_in_Beriut_festival	participant mobility
8.	Iraq	لا عاد الحساويين دبغين	Oh the Hassawi people are not likable	shared Gulf lexical items
9.	Oman	عيل اجمل وجه راح اتامله	a guy with good-looking face that I like to stare at	cross-dialect linguistic units

Table 3: A sample of the tweets from the labeled data subtask 1.2. The above tweets are either linguistically constrained or governed by participant mobility. Tweets that are linguistically *bivalent* as 1 & 2 can be classified in any dialect. *Globally genre tweets* as in 3-5 are governed by a global topic rather a local one in the region of the dialect. The *shared Gulf lexical item* indicates that some linguistic segments are shared by other dialects in the same region. No. 9 presents a sample of how one lexical item can be semantically different from another language.

social events exhibit global identities by projecting shared linguistic features; however, the local identities of the same participants emerge by projecting more local linguistic features as long as the topic touches their personality or their communities (De Fina, 2000; Schilling-Estes, 2004; Bucholtz and Hall, 2005; Bucholtz, 2010; Benor, 2010; Becker, 2009, *inter alia*). Modeling these kinds of linguistic features seems a promising direction for future research.

Location granularity A number of the features included in this work are regional, rather than unique to a single dialect. An example of such a situation is example 8 in Table 3 in which an Iraqi participant shares the same linguistic features "عاد" that are found in the Saudi dialect. Similarly, some word-level features exhibit different behavior across dialects. For instance, Gulf states use heavily the word "عيل" as "then," shown in Table 3 example 9, but this word semantically means "child" in the Egyptian dialect data. Such *cross-dialect linguistic units* require more sophisticated feature engineering to adequately model.

Dataset design This is a challenging dataset. Consider, for instance, the topic of *participant mobility*. Examples 6 and 7 show some linguistic items that belong to different dialects compared to the location of the tweets. In this sense, the word "بدنا" in example 7 is a Levantine lexicon, rather than a Djibouti one. While examining the training data, we came across tweets that, to a native speaker, could just as easily be classified into *any* dialect (see examples 1 & 2). Sociolinguists characterize these samples as *bivalent linguistic units* (Woolard, 1998). Such datapoints may provide very little signal for their assigned class.

Impoverished features Rather than incorporating general linguistic features, our approach focused on devising distinctive word-level features that signify each dialect. Considering the complexity of the task, our preliminary features are inadequate both in terms of their number (56) and distribution across linguistic levels (morphology, syntax, etc.). There are several Arabic morphological analysis tools that could be used to greatly enrich and expand our set of features (Habash et al., 2012; Obeid et al., 2020). In the same respect, Bouamor et al. (2019) presented a large parallel corpus of 25 Arabic city dialects in the travel domain and a lexicon of 1,045 concepts with an average of 45 words from 25 cities per concept. While the approach presented here does not make use of these resources, our architecture was designed with extensibility in mind. We hope to explore this avenue in future work.

5 Conclusion

In this work, we report results for two experiments: one that uses pretrained CBOW word embeddings with an LSTM, and another that integrates linguistic features as low-dimensional feature embeddings fed through a simple feed-forward network. The two experiments are used to classify Arabic tweets for the Second Nuanced Arabic Dialect Identification (NADI) Subtask 1.2.: Country-level DA identification. The results show that rare linguistic features do not enhance the performance of an LSTM with pretrained CBOW word embeddings. These results emphasize the importance of pretrained models in NLP tasks related to Arabic dialects.

References

Muhammad Abdul-Mageed, Hassan Alhuzali, and Mohamed Elaraby. 2018. You tweet what you speak: A city-level dataset of arabic dialects. In *Proceedings of the Eleventh International Conference on Language Resources and Evaluation (LREC 2018).*

Muhammad Abdul-Mageed, Chiyu Zhang, Houda Bouamor, and Nizar Habash. 2020. NADI 2020: The First Nuanced Arabic Dialect Identification Shared Task. In *Proceedings of the Fifth Arabic Natural Language Processing Workshop (WANLP 2020)*, Barcelona, Spain.

Muhammad Abdul-Mageed, Chiyu Zhang, Abdel-Rahim Elmadany, Houda Bouamor, and Nizar Habash. 2021. NADI 2021: The Second Nuanced Arabic Dialect Identification Shared Task. In *Proceedings of the Sixth Arabic Natural Language Processing Workshop (WANLP 2021).*

Ibrahim Abu Farha and Walid Magdy. 2019. Mazajak: An online Arabic sentiment analyser. In *Proceedings of the Fourth Arabic Natural Language Processing Workshop*, pages 192–198, Florence, Italy. Association for Computational Linguistics.

Oscar Araque, Ignacio Corcuera-Platas, J Fernando Sánchez-Rada, and Carlos A Iglesias. 2017. Enhancing deep learning sentiment analysis with ensemble techniques in social applications. *Expert Systems with Applications*, 77:236–246.

Reem Bassiouney. 2009. Arabic sociolinguistics: Topics in diglossia, gender. *Identity, and Politics. Georgetown University Press.*

Kara Becker. 2009. /r/and the construction of place identity on new york city's lower east side 1. *Journal of Sociolinguistics*, 13(5):634–658.

Yoshua Bengio, Réjean Ducharme, Pascal Vincent, and Christian Janvin. 2003. A neural probabilistic language model. *The journal of machine learning research*, 3:1137–1155.

Sarah Bunin Benor. 2010. Ethnolinguistic repertoire: Shifting the analytic focus in language and ethnicity 1. *Journal of Sociolinguistics*, 14(2):159–183.

Houda Bouamor, Sabit Hassan, and Nizar Habash. 2019. The MADAR shared task on Arabic fine-grained dialect identification. In *Proceedings of the Fourth Arabic Natural Language Processing Workshop*, pages 199–207.

Mary Bucholtz. 2010. *White kids: Language, race, and styles of youth identity.* Cambridge University Press.

Mary Bucholtz and Kira Hall. 2005. Identity and interaction: A sociocultural linguistic approach. *Discourse studies*, 7(4-5):585–614.

François Chollet et al. 2015. Keras. `https://keras.io`.

Yann N Dauphin, Angela Fan, Michael Auli, and David Grangier. 2017. Language modeling with gated convolutional networks. In *International conference on machine learning*, pages 933–941. PMLR.

Anna De Fina. 2000. Orientation in immigrant narratives: The role of ethnicity in the identification of characters. *Discourse Studies*, 2(2):131–157.

Li Dong, Furu Wei, Chuanqi Tan, Duyu Tang, Ming Zhou, and Ke Xu. 2014. Adaptive recursive neural network for target-dependent twitter sentiment classification. In *Proceedings of the 52nd annual meeting of the association for computational linguistics (volume 2: Short papers)*, pages 49–54.

Mohamed Elaraby and Muhammad Abdul-Mageed. 2018. Deep models for arabic dialect identification on benchmarked data. In *Proceedings of the Fifth Workshop on NLP for Similar Languages, Varieties and Dialects (VarDial 2018)*, pages 263–274.

Heba Elfardy and Mona Diab. 2013. Sentence level dialect identification in arabic. In *Proceedings of the 51st Annual Meeting of the Association for Computational Linguistics (Volume 2: Short Papers)*, pages 456–461.

Charles A Ferguson. 1959. Diglossia. *WORD*, 15(2):325–340.

Nizar Habash, Ramy Eskander, and Abdelati Hawwari. 2012. A morphological analyzer for egyptian arabic. In *Proceedings of the twelfth meeting of the special interest group on computational morphology and phonology*, pages 1–9.

Sepp Hochreiter and Jürgen Schmidhuber. 1997. Long short-term memory. *Neural Computation*, 9(8):1735–1780.

Armand Joulin, Edouard Grave, Piotr Bojanowski, and Tomas Mikolov. 2017. Bag of tricks for efficient text classification. In *Proceedings of the 15th Conference of the European Chapter of the Association for Computational Linguistics: Volume 2, Short Papers*, pages 427–431, Valencia, Spain. Association for Computational Linguistics.

Rafal Jozefowicz, Oriol Vinyals, Mike Schuster, Noam Shazeer, and Yonghui Wu. 2016. Exploring the limits of language modeling. *arXiv preprint arXiv:1602.02410.*

Ossama Obeid, Nasser Zalmout, Salam Khalifa, Dima Taji, Mai Oudah, Bashar Alhafni, Go Inoue, Fadhl Eryani, Alexander Erdmann, and Nizar Habash. 2020. Camel tools: An open source python toolkit for arabic natural language processing. In *Proceedings of the 12th language resources and evaluation conference*, pages 7022–7032.

Natalie Schilling-Estes. 2004. Constructing ethnicity in interaction. *Journal of Sociolinguistics*, 8(2):163–195.

Aliaksei Severyn and Alessandro Moschitti. 2015. Twitter sentiment analysis with deep convolutional neural networks. In *Proceedings of the 38th international ACM SIGIR conference on research and development in information retrieval*, pages 959–962.

Abu Bakr Soliman, Kareem Eissa, and Samhaa R El-Beltagy. 2017. Aravec: A set of arabic word embedding models for use in arabic nlp. *Procedia Computer Science*, 117:256–265.

Kathryn A Woolard. 1998. Simultaneity and bivalency as strategies in bilingualism. *Journal of linguistic anthropology*, 8(1):3–29.

Omar F Zaidan and Chris Callison-Burch. 2014. Arabic dialect identification. *Computational Linguistics*, 40(1):171–202.

Arabic Dialect Identification based on Weighted Concatenation of TF-IDF Features

Mohamed Lichouri, Mourad Abbas, Khaled Lounnas, Besma Benaziz, Aicha Zitouni
Computational Linguistics Department / CRSTDLA, Algiers, Algeria
{m.lichouri,m.abbas,k.lounnas,b.benaziz,a.zitouni}@crstdla.dz

Abstract

In this paper, we analyze the impact of weighted concatenation of TF-IDF features for the Arabic Dialect Identification task. This study is performed for two subtasks: subtask 1.1 (country-level MSA) and subtask 1.2 (country-level DA) identification. The classifiers supporting our comparative study are Linear Support Vector Classification (LSVC), Linear Regression (LR), Perceptron, Stochastic Gradient Descent (SGD), Passive Aggressive (PA), Complement Naive Bayes (CNB), MutliLayer Perceptron (MLP), and RidgeClassifier. In the evaluation phase, our system gives F_1 scores of 14.87% and 21.49%, for country-level MSA and DA identification respectively, which is very close to the average F_1 scores achieved by the submitted systems and recorded for both subtasks (18.70% and 24.23%).

1 Introduction

Nowadays, the study of Arabic dialects has become the focus of many researches, and many workshops have been dedicated for this interesting topic. One of the noteworthy works are those featured in MADAR 2019 (Bouamor et al., 2019), we can mention (Ragab et al., 2019; Abbas et al., 2019; Přibáň and Taylor, 2019) where authors used machine learning techniques combined with resemble classifier or major voting rules to enhance the performance of the used models. The MADAR 2019 has been followed by NADI 2020 in which more dialects from 100 Arab provinces have been covered (Abdul-Mageed et al., 2020). In Talafha et al. (2020); El Mekki et al. (2020); Gaanoun and Benelallam (2020), authors adopted the combination of ngrams and TF-IDF features. An analysis of the impact of preprocessing and n-grams on automatic classification of Tweets that mention medications has been presented in Lichouri and Abbas (2020b). In (Lichouri et al., 2020), the authors studied the effect of TF-IDF features and morphological process on profiling fake news spreaders on Twitter. In some works, because of the imbalanced nature of the used dataset, there is a need to apply sampling techniques: upsampling the minority class as presented in Beltagy et al. (2020) using the Scikit-Learn library (Pedregosa et al., 2011), or the use of oversampling techniques from imblearn toolbox (Lemaître et al., 2017) like: Random Over-Sampler (ROS), Synthetic Minority Oversampling Technique (SMOTE) and Adaptive Synthetic (ADASYN) as described in Lichouri and Abbas (2020a). In this work, we combined multiple classifiers, using a combination of ngrams and TF-IDF as features (Lichouri et al., 2018) with the same concept as suggested in Abu Kwaik and Saad (2019); Touileb (2020) by using a weighted concatenation of these features. We also readapted the oversampling approach proposed in Lichouri and Abbas (2020a), in addition to the morphological preprocessing steps that we applied like stemming, lemmatization and pos tagging. This paper is structured as follows: In section 2, a description of the used dataset is presented. The applied cleaning steps and preprocessing are explained in section 3. In section 4, we present the proposed approach and discuss the findings. Finally, we conclude in section 5.

2 Description of the Dataset

The used dataset in this shared task of NADI 2021 (Abdul-Mageed et al., 2021) is an extension of the previous shared task (Abdul-Mageed et al., 2020). It is composed of two parts, the first one includes tweets written in Modern Standard Arabic (MSA), and the second one in the local Arabic Dialects (DA). These two subsets (MSA and DA) include tweets from 21 Arab countries and 100 provinces.

Proceedings of the Sixth Arabic Natural Language Processing Workshop, pages 282–286
Kyiv, Ukraine (Virtual), April 19, 2021.

	MSA subset				DA subset			
	Train	**Dev**	**Test**	**Total**	**Train**	**Dev**	**Test**	**Total**
# sentences	21,000	5,000	5,000	31,000	21,000	5,000	5,000	31,000
# words	233.4k	65.4k	63.1k	408.2k	168.3k	45.7k	44.7k	258.7k
Max # word per sentence	49	58	57	-	51	58	59	-
Min # word per sentence	1	1	1	-	1	1	1	-
Max # char per sentence	592	382	285	-	268	279	283	-
Min # char per sentence	1	2	1	-	1	2	2	-

Table 1: Dataset statistics after applying some pre-processing steps

We divided these subsets into three parts: train, dev and test, for which we addressed some statistics in Table 1, after applying a number of pre-processing steps. As can be noticed from Table 1, the minimum number of words and characters per sentence in the training and development sets is 1. This information is useful to determine the number "n" of grams to be selected in the features extraction phase.

3 Data Cleaning and Preprocessing

In most NLP tasks, dealing with tweets necessitates cleaning before analysis and processing. Hence we applied some simple surface cleaning steps including Arabic Letter Normalizer (ALN) and the removal of: punctuation (RP), emojis (i.e., emoticons, symbols & pictographs, transport & map symbols and flags (iOS)) (RE), stop words (RSW), Arabic diacritics (RAD), Latin letter (RLL) and words (RLW), repeated words (RRW) and chars (RRC). We used also three morphological preprocessing steps: WordNetLemmatizer (Lem), ISRI Arabic Stemmer (Stem) and PosTagger (PosTag) of NLTK[1].

After a series of experiments in order to investigate the impact of all the possible combinations of the different aforementioned cleaning processes, we kept the best configuration which is composed of emojis removal, diacritics removal, repeated words removal, in addition to the stemming process. Furthermore, we selected the features which yielded the best performance after testing a huge number of n-grams combinations (200 experiments). These features have been transformed using the TF-IDF vectorizer and concatenated with (see Table 2) and without (see Table 3) a weighted union function.

4 Proposed system

It should be noted from Figure 1, that we first combined all the aforementioned preprocessing steps to generate all the possible textual presentations, after that we applied a second combination between n-grams (n=1 to 10) and tokenizer (word, char, char with boundary, union of the three) to generate all the possible vector features. Then we fed these features to the best oversampling procedures (i.e., ADASYN) which were applied before training our three best classifiers (LSVC, RDG, SGD). Finally we used an resemble classifier (i.e., majority voting rule) which takes as input the three predictions and applies a majority voting rule to predict the dialect. We divided our work into three setups. In the first setup, we conducted an empirical comparison of some classifiers (Pedregosa et al., 2011), namely: Linear Support Vector Classification (LSVC), Linear Regression (LR), Perceptron, Stochastic Gradient Descent (SGD), Passive Aggressive (PA), Complement Naive Bayes (CNB), MutliLayer Perceptron (MLP), and RidgeClassifier. We used these classifiers in their default setup except for the SGD classifier for which we examined the performance in function of runs number. In the first setup, we used three types of features independently, it is about the TF-IDF features of ngrams for words, chars and char_wb. Using different values of n (ngrams) resulted in diverse feature vectors using the eight aforementioned classifiers. We then ranked the best "features+classifiers" combinations according to the obtained F_1 scores, in order to use them in the following setups.

The second setup is based on the first one, since we concatenate the best "features+classifiers", mentioned above, without weighting. The best performance is obtained by three classifiers, as shown in Table 2.

[1]https://www.nltk.org/index.html

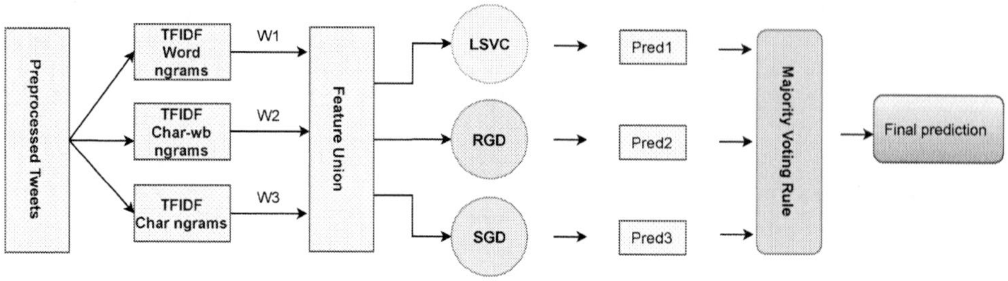

Figure 1: Proposed system based on weighted concatenation approach

	MSA		DA	
Model	Configuration	F_1	Configuration	F_1
SVC	unionVect(1, 5, 2, 10, 2, 8)	14.70	unionVect(1, 3, 1, 4, 2, 4)	21.81
SGD	unionVect(1, 2, 1, 4, 1, 9)	15.28	unionVect(1, 3, 1, 4, 2, 4)	21.85
RDG	unionVect(1, 2, 1, 5, 1, 9)	14.73	unionVect(1, 2, 1, 4, 2, 4)	20.68

Table 2: Obtained results in the dev phase while applying a concatenation without weighting. unionVect takes as inputs different values of n (ngrams)

	MSA		DA	
Model	weights	F_1	weights	F_1
SVC	0.8 0.6 0.5	14.89	0.8 0.4 0.8	21.25
SGD	0.8 0.8 0.8	14.84	0.8 0.5 0.8	18.98
RDG	0.8 0.7 0.8	14.85	0.8 0.5 0.8	19.76
Comb.	0.8 0.7 0.8	14.90	0.8 0.5 0.8	20.09

Table 3: Obtained results in the dev phase while applying a concatenation by weighting the three analyzers (char, char_wb, word). The selected values of n are (1, 5, 1, 7, 1, 9).

According to the results shown in Table 3, the three best classifiers are SVC, SGD and RDG, run with their default parameters. The best results for both MSA and DA are obtained by SGD classifer with an F_1-score of 15.28% and 21.85%, respectively. For the first subtask, the concatenation of: word bigrams (1, 2), char 4-grams (1, 4) and char_wb 9-grams (1, 9) gave the best results. Whereas, in the second subtask, the best performance was achieved using a concatenation of: word 3-grams (1, 3), char 4-grams (1, 4) and char_wb "bigrams, 3-grams and 4-grams" (2, 4).

In the third setup, we applied weighted concatenation of the features used in the second setup. We used multiple values of the weights: w1, w2 and w3 for word, char, and char_wb analyzers, respectively. The best performance is recorded for both MSA and DA subtasks using a majority voting rule on the three classifiers SVC, SGD, and RDG with an F_1-score of 14.90% and 20.09%, respectively. The best performance for the second subtask is achieved using the SVC classifier with an F_1-score of 21.25%. We summarize the results in Table 3.

As a final step, and in order to improve the results achieved in the third setup, we investigated the impact of oversampling approaches (i.e., ROS, SMOTE, ADASYN) to tackle the issue of imbalanced data (see Figure 1). It should be noted that the configurations reported in Table 5 are defined in Table 4.

For the first subtask (MSA), we obtained these performances by applying a set of surface and morphological preprocessing followed by a union of (word 5-grams, char (2,8) grams and char_wb (2,10)) multiplied by a vector weights (1.3, 1.3, 1), in addition to the intern parameters of SGD classifier(l1_ratio=0.25, loss='modified_huber',penalty='elasticnet'). We obtained F_1=16.30% (dev) F_1=14.50% (test).

For the second subtask (DA), we included the ADASYN oversampling technique to the configuration used in the first subtask while changing the preprocessing, ngrams range used by unionVect, vector weight as well as the parameters of

<table>
<tr><th>Configs</th><th>Preprocess</th><th>Union</th><th>Weights</th><th>Oversampling</th><th>SGD</th></tr>
<tr><td>Conf1</td><td rowspan="3">RSW, RAD, ALN, RRW, RLL, Stem, Lem</td><td rowspan="3">1, 5, 2, 8, 2, 10</td><td>1.3, 1.3, 0.9</td><td rowspan="3">N/A</td><td rowspan="3">l1_ratio=0.25, loss='modified_huber', penalty='elasticnet'</td></tr>
<tr><td>Conf2</td><td>1.3, 1.3, 1.0</td></tr>
<tr><td>Conf3</td><td>1.3, 1.3, 1.9</td></tr>
<tr><td>Conf4</td><td rowspan="3">RE, RAD, RRW, Stem</td><td rowspan="3">1, 3, 1, 4, 2, 4</td><td rowspan="3">1.8, 0.7, 1.8</td><td>ratio='minority'</td><td rowspan="3">max_iter=2000, shuffle=False</td></tr>
<tr><td>Conf5</td><td>ratio='minority', random_state=222</td></tr>
<tr><td>Conf6</td><td>ratio='minority', random_state=333}</td></tr>
</table>

Table 4: Configurations used in the 4th setup

<table>
<tr><th>Subtasks</th><th>Configuration</th><th>Conf1</th><th>Conf2</th><th>Conf3</th><th>Conf4</th><th>Conf5</th><th>Conf6</th></tr>
<tr><td rowspan="2">Subtask 1.1</td><td>Dev</td><td>15.86</td><td>16.28</td><td>16.30</td><td rowspan="2" colspan="3">N/A</td></tr>
<tr><td>Test</td><td>14.47</td><td>14.87</td><td>14.50</td></tr>
<tr><td rowspan="2">Subtask 1.2</td><td>Dev</td><td rowspan="2" colspan="3">N/A</td><td>22.81</td><td>22.94</td><td>23.01</td></tr>
<tr><td>Test</td><td>21.08</td><td>21.49</td><td>21.13</td></tr>
</table>

Table 5: Performance (F1) achieved using weighted concatenation and oversampling techniques for both subtasks.

the SGD classifier. We obtained performance equal to 23.01% and 21.13% for development and test phases, respectively.

5 Conclusion

In this paper, we described our two submitted systems for identifying Arabic dialects, using twitter texts collected from 21 Arabic countries. We carried out an empirical comparison study by conducting 200 experiments in which we used several combinations of features, and preprocessing steps as stemming, lemmatization and part of speech tagging. We used a simple classification technique comprising three classifiers: LSVC, RDG and SGD. We addressed the issue of imbalanced data using a set of oversampling methods. Furthermore, We tried to investigate the impact of concatenating TF-IDF features with and without weight vector.

References

Mourad Abbas, Mohamed Lichouri, and Abed Alhakim Freihat. 2019. St madar 2019 shared task: Arabic fine-grained dialect identification. In *Proceedings of the Fourth Arabic Natural Language Processing Workshop*, pages 269–273.

Muhammad Abdul-Mageed, Chiyu Zhang, Houda Bouamor, and Nizar Habash. 2020. Nadi 2020: The first nuanced arabic dialect identification shared task. *arXiv preprint arXiv:2010.11334*.

Muhammad Abdul-Mageed, Chiyu Zhang, Abdel-Rahim Elmadany, Houda Bouamor, and Nizar Habash. 2021. NADI 2021: The Second Nuanced Arabic Dialect Identification Shared Task. In *Proceedings of the Sixth Arabic Natural Language Processing Workshop (WANLP 2021)*.

Kathrein Abu Kwaik and Motaz K Saad. 2019. Arbdialectid at madar shared task 1: Language modelling and ensemble learning for fine grained arabic dialect identification. In *Proceedings of the Fourth Arabic Natural Language Processing Workshop*, Proceedings of the Fourth Arabic Natural Language Processing Workshop. Association for Computational Linguistics.

Ahmad Beltagy, Abdelrahman Wael, and Omar ElSherief. 2020. Arabic dialect identification using bert-based domain adaptation. *arXiv preprint arXiv:2011.06977*.

Houda Bouamor, Sabit Hassan, and Nizar Habash. 2019. The madar shared task on arabic fine-grained dialect identification. In *Proceedings of the Fourth Arabic Natural Language Processing Workshop*, pages 199–207.

Abdellah El Mekki, Ahmed Alami, Hamza Alami, Ahmed Khoumsi, and Ismail Berrada. 2020. Weighted combination of bert and n-gram features for nuanced arabic dialect identification. In *Proceedings of the Fifth Arabic Natural Language Processing Workshop*, pages 268–274.

Kamel Gaanoun and Imade Benelallam. 2020. Arabic dialect identification: An arabic-bert model with data augmentation and ensembling strategy. In *Proceedings of the Fifth Arabic Natural Language Processing Workshop*, pages 275–281.

Guillaume Lemaître, Fernando Nogueira, and Christos K. Aridas. 2017. Imbalanced-learn: A python toolbox to tackle the curse of imbalanced datasets in machine learning. *Journal of Machine Learning Research*, 18(17):1–5.

Mohamed Lichouri and Mourad Abbas. 2020a. Simple vs oversampling-based classification methods for fine grained arabic dialect identification in twitter. In *Proceedings of the Fifth Arabic Natural Language Processing Workshop*, pages 250–256.

Mohamed Lichouri and Mourad Abbas. 2020b. Speechtrans@ smm4h'20: Impact of preprocessing and n-grams on automatic classification of tweets that mention medications. In *Proceedings of the Fifth Social Media Mining for Health Applications Workshop & Shared Task*, pages 118–120.

Mohamed Lichouri, Mourad Abbas, and Besma Benaziz. 2020. Profiling fake news spreaders on twitter based on tfidf features and morphological process.

Mohamed Lichouri, Mourad Abbas, Abed Alhakim Freihat, and Dhiya El Hak Megtouf. 2018. Word-level vs sentence-level language identification: Application to algerian and arabic dialects. *Procedia Computer Science*, 142:246–253.

F. Pedregosa, G. Varoquaux, A. Gramfort, V. Michel, B. Thirion, O. Grisel, M. Blondel, P. Prettenhofer, R. Weiss, V. Dubourg, J. Vanderplas, A. Passos, D. Cournapeau, M. Brucher, M. Perrot, and E. Duchesnay. 2011. Scikit-learn: Machine learning in Python. *Journal of Machine Learning Research*, 12:2825–2830.

Pavel Přibáň and Stephen Taylor. 2019. Zcu-nlp at madar 2019: Recognizing arabic dialects. In *Proceedings of the Fourth Arabic Natural Language Processing Workshop*, pages 208–213.

Ahmad Ragab, Haitham Seelawi, Mostafa Samir, Abdelrahman Mattar, Hesham Al-Bataineh, Mohammad Zaghloul, Ahmad Mustafa, Bashar Talafha, Abed Alhakim Freihat, and Hussein Al-Natsheh. 2019. Mawdoo3 ai at madar shared task: Arabic fine-grained dialect identification with ensemble learning. In *Proceedings of the Fourth Arabic Natural Language Processing Workshop*, pages 244–248.

Bashar Talafha, Mohammad Ali, Muhy Eddin Za'ter, Haitham Seelawi, Ibraheem Tuffaha, Mostafa Samir, Wael Farhan, and Hussein T Al-Natsheh. 2020. Multi-dialect arabic bert for country-level dialect identification. *arXiv preprint arXiv:2007.05612*.

Samia Touileb. 2020. Ltg-st at nadi shared task 1: Arabic dialect identification using a stacking classifier. In *Proceedings of the Fifth Arabic Natural Language Processing Workshop*, pages 313–319.

Machine Learning-Based Approach for Arabic Dialect Identification

Mahmoud S. Ali, Ahmed H. Ali, Ahmed A. El-Sawy, Hamada A. Nayel
Department of Computer Science
Faculty of Computers and Artificial Intelligence
Benha University
{mahmoud.hassan,ahmed.ali,ahmed.el_sawy,hamada.ali}@fci.bu.edu.eg

Abstract

This paper describes our systems submitted to the Second Nuanced Arabic Dialect Identification Shared Task (NADI 2021). Dialect identification is the task of automatically detecting the source variety of a given text or speech segment. There are four subtasks, two subtasks for country-level identification and the other two subtasks for province-level identification. The data in this task covers a total of 100 provinces from all 21 Arab countries and come from the Twitter domain. The proposed systems depend on five machine-learning approaches namely Complement Naïve Bayes, Support Vector Machine, Decision Tree, Logistic Regression and Random Forest Classifiers. F_1 macro-averaged score of Naïve Bayes classifier outperformed all other classifiers for development and test data.

1 Introduction

Today, huge amounts of data in text, picture, and video format are posted to social network sites, the general web, and mobile devices. Social networks like Twitter are based on interactions with fast temporal dynamics which generate a large variety of contents with their own characteristics which are difficult to compute with classical tools used on traditional texts like essays and articles (Sun et al., 2019).

This article focuses on dialect identification, which is a technology critical in tasks such as author profiling and other NLP downstream tasks such as sentiment analysis, POS tagging, text summarization, among others. In dialect identification, we face some questions: how to find differences in writing style on social networks between men and women, age groups, or location. The answers to these questions are important for the new problem we face in the era of social networks such as fake news, plagiarism, and identity theft (Mansour et al., 2020).

Recently, research community concerning Arabic natural language processing focussed on dialect identification for Arabic(Bouamor et al., 2019; Salameh et al., 2018; Abdul-Mageed et al., 2021, 2020). A shared task for Nuanced Arabic Dialect Identification (NADI 2020) has been organized to identify the dialect in Arabic Tweets.

We propose five models to perform Dialect Identification for Arabic tweets. The Term Frequency Inverse Document Frequency (TF/IDF) algorithm is implemented for feature extraction after preprocessing process. Complement Naïve Bayes (CNB), Decision Tree (DT), Logistic Regression (LR), Random Forest (RF), and Support Vector Machine (SVM) classifiers are used in the classification step. The results of development set showing that CNB classifier outperforms all other classifiers.

2 Data

The NADI 2021 datasets were the main corpus used for training and testing the system (Abdul-Mageed et al., 2021). The NADI 2021 datasets are in both Modern Standard Arabic (MSA) and dialectal Arabic (DA). For each of these varieties, the dataset is partitioned into three parts, the training part of 21,000 tweets, development of 5,000 tweets, and test set of 5,000 tweets The data sets are labeled in two levels: the first level (country level) of 21 countries and the second level (provinces level) of 100 provinces. The test set was published unlabelled, and the system output was evaluated by the NADI shared task team. The training set was used to train our models while the development set was used to optimize models' parameters. The distribution of data over the country and province classes is unbalanced.

Proceedings of the Sixth Arabic Natural Language Processing Workshop, pages 287–290
Kyiv, Ukraine (Virtual), April 19, 2021.

3 System Architecture

As shown in Figure 1, our system composed of four main stages. These are: Text Preprocessing, Feature Extraction, Classification, Evaluation and Testing. Text preprocessing, where we make some cleaning and corrections on input as we will explain next. In the second stage important features from all documents have been selected. The third stage is classification, in which we classify each vector in the feature vectors to its correct class (correct Arabic dialect). The model has been tested in evaluation stage. At last, a blind test set has been used to predict the correct class (Arabic dialect).

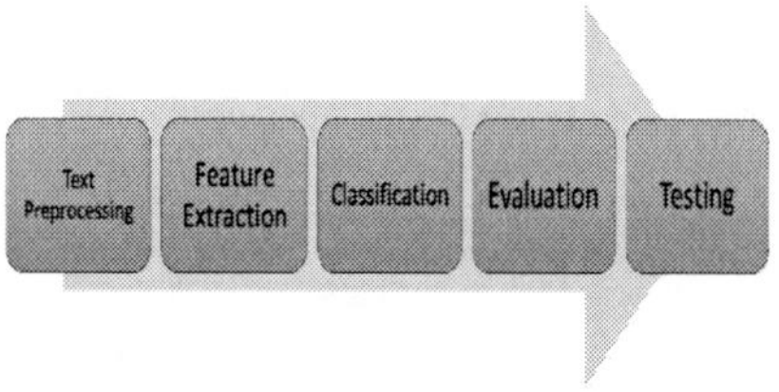

Figure 1: Stages of our system

3.1 Text Preprocessing

Arabic tweets are very noisy, so we removed URLs, emojis, Latin-characters, numbers, mentions, and any non-Arabic characters. Arabic hashtags were kept as they are, because they might contain important information (Touileb, 2020; Nayel, 2019). Preprocessing is a step used in almost all NLP applications (Ananthakrishnan et al., 2019; Nayel et al., 2019). In the proposed models, this stage consists of some steps as the following:

- Non-Arabic letter removal, which is achieved by deleting English letters, special symbols, numbers, Twitter markup, Emoticons, repetition letters etc.
- Text refinement, which is carried out to normalize different forms of some Arabic characters to unique form like," ي " (an Arabic letter pronounced Yaa) and " ى " to be " ي", removing redundant Arabic forms like, " ال " (pronounced al and it is used as determiner), and excessive character repetitions, Kashida "tatweel" and diacritics.
- Removing Punctuation, in which we removed punctuation marks such as $\{'+','\#','-','\$',...\}$ which are increasing the dimension of feature space with redundant features.
- Reduction of letter repetition, because all tweets in Twitter do not follow the standard rules of the language especially Arabic language. A common manner of users is to repeat a specific letter in a word. Cleaning the tokens from these redundant letters helps in feature space reduction. In our experiments, the letter is assumed to be redundant if it is repeated more than two times. For example the words " ههههههه " ("hahahah" i.e. giggles) and " عاللللللم " (i.e. "global") containing redundant letter and will be reduced to " هه " and " عالم " respectively.

The class distribution is highly imbalanced, which could make a model biased towards certain classes. Therefore, random up-sampling for each data class was applied to match the size of the majority class, the Egyptian class (Aliwy et al., 2020).

3.2 Feature Extraction

In this study, we use TF/IDF with unigram features (words) to represent each tweet as a feature vector, and the value of each cell in the vector is the weight of each feature within each tweet vector and is determined by the following formula:

$$w_{ij} = tf_{ij} * \log\left(\frac{N+1}{df_i+1}\right)$$

where, w_{ij} is the weight of word i in vector j, tf_{ij} is the count of word i in document j, N is the total number of tweets, and df_i is the count of word i in all tweets.

In TF/IDF, we used unigram model, which deal with a single word as a token. For example, the sentence "ريال مدريد كان الأفضل", which means Real Madrid was the best, has the following set of features { الأفضل ، كان، مدريد ، ريال }.

3.3 Classification

The classification step was achieved by voting among five well-known and very different five classifiers (CNB, DT, LR, RF, and SVM). The dataset has two levels of classification, country-level with 21 class and province-level with 100 province. Each province related to one of 21 countries. The

Complement Naive Bayes (CNB) classifier was designed to correct the "severe assumptions" made by the standard Multinomial Naive Bayes classifier. It is particularly suited for imbalanced data sets and this is actually proved in the results.

Decision Tree (DT) classifier uses a decision tree as a predictive model to go from observations about an item represented in the branches to conclusions about the item's target value that is represented in the leaves. Logistic regression (LR) is a statistical model that in its basic form uses a logistic function to model a binary dependent variable. Random Forest (RF) is a meta estimator that fits a number of decision tree classifiers on various sub-samples of the dataset and uses averaging to improve the predictive accuracy and control over-fitting.

Support Vector Machine (SVM) is a linear classifier which uses training samples or vectors close to the boundaries of classes as support vectors. SVM implemented for different NLP tasks effectively. SVM can be used for classifying non-linear data using kernel functions such as, Gaussian, RBF, or Linear (Nayel, 2020).

Algorithm	Country Level		Province Level	
	MSA	**DA**	**MSA**	**DA**
CNB	14.06	21.34	4.16	4.39
DT	11.23	12.19	3.33	3.23
LR	9.15	12.49	3.56	4.51
RF	13.17	14.30	4.09	3.88
SVM	11.37	15.97	3.82	4.73

Table 1: F_1-score of our models on DEV data.

Subtask	**1.1**	**1.2**	**2.1**	**2.2**
Rank	5	8	4	3
Precision	15.09	21.61	4.09	4.71
Recall	12.46	18.12	3.46	4.55
F_1-score	12.99	18.72	3.51	4.55
Accuracy	23.24	37.16	3.38	4.80

Table 2: Performance of our models on TEST data.

4 Results

We propose five machine learning algorithms for the task: CNB, DT, LR, RF and SVM classifiers. All algorithms were implemented on NADI shared task data set. There are four subtask: 1.1 for MSA-country-level, 1.2 for DA-country-level, 2.1 for MSA-province-level, and 2.2 for DA-province-level. The F_1score is the evaluation metric for all subtasks. The Complement Naïve Bayes (CNB) classifier outperformed all other classifiers in all subtasks and achieved the highest F_1-score ratio for the development set data. Table 1 shows the results for all runs of the development set classification.

The results of test set is given in Table 2. Concerning the evaluation of our submissions for test data, our model achieved 5th rank for subtask 1.1, 8th rank for subtask 1.2, 4th rank for subtask 2.1, and 3rd rank for subtask 2.2 among all submissions as shown in Table 2.

5 Discussion

We provided a description of our different models we developed for NADI 2021. The dataset of 21 country-level classes and 100 province-level classes were used to evaluate the systems. There were four subtasks, two subtasks for identifying MSA and two subtasks for identifying DA. The F_1-score results of classification were relatively low because:

1. The MSA data used in different Arabic countries may have a significant degree of similarity,

2. Some dialects are very close to some other dialects,

3. Tweet ambiguity, resulting from use of MSA or dialect sequences where the same sentence can be spoken in different countries but is written the same way,

4. The dialects of some provinces may be closer to those of a different neighbouring country than it is to the country to which the province belongs,

5. Use of location as a proxy for dialect may not be straightforward as organizers indicate in NADI 2020.

6 Conclusion

We can conclude that Arabic dialect identification is one of the most challenging tasks for many reasons mentioned. This paper proposed five classifier models for identifying Arabic dialect in Twitter. The results of training using Complement Naïve Bayes classifier achieved the best F_1 macro-averaged score as it is very good to deal with NLP depending on Naïve Bayes rule. In future work, different weighting scores can be used to improve the performance of classification, such as word embeddings.

References

Muhammad Abdul-Mageed, Chiyu Zhang, Houda Bouamor, and Nizar Habash. 2020. NADI 2020: The first nuanced Arabic dialect identification shared task. In *Proceedings of the Fifth Arabic Natural Language Processing Workshop (WANLP 2020)*, pages 97–110, Barcelona, Spain (Online). Association for Computational Linguistics.

Muhammad Abdul-Mageed, Chiyu Zhang, Abdel-Rahim Elmadany, Houda Bouamor, and Nizar Habash. 2021. NADI 2021: The Second Nuanced Arabic Dialect Identification Shared Task. In *Proceedings of the Sixth Arabic Natural Language Processing Workshop (WANLP 2021)*.

Ahmed Aliwy, Hawraa Taher, and Zena AboAltaheen. 2020. Arabic dialects identification for all Arabic countries. In *Proceedings of the Fifth Arabic Natural Language Processing Workshop*, pages 302–307, Barcelona, Spain (Online). Association for Computational Linguistics.

Haritha Ananthakrishnan, Akshaya Ranganathan, D. Thenmozhi, and Chandrabose Aravindan. 2019. Arabic author profiling and deception detection using traditional learning methodologies with word embedding. In *Working Notes of FIRE 2019 - Forum for Information Retrieval Evaluation, Kolkata, India, December 12-15, 2019*, volume 2517 of *CEUR Workshop Proceedings*, pages 100–104. CEUR-WS.org.

Houda Bouamor, Sabit Hassan, and Nizar Habash. 2019. The madar shared task on arabic fine-grained dialect identification. In *Proceedings of the Fourth Arabic Natural Language Processing Workshop*, pages 199–207.

Moataz Mansour, Moustafa Tohamy, Zeyad Ezzat, and Marwan Torki. 2020. Arabic dialect identification using BERT fine-tuning. In *Proceedings of the Fifth Arabic Natural Language Processing Workshop*, pages 308–312, Barcelona, Spain (Online). Association for Computational Linguistics.

Hamada Nayel. 2020. NAYEL at SemEval-2020 task 12: TF/IDF-based approach for automatic offensive language detection in Arabic tweets. In *Proceedings of the Fourteenth Workshop on Semantic Evaluation*, pages 2086–2089, Barcelona (online). International Committee for Computational Linguistics.

Hamada A. Nayel. 2019. NAYEL@APDA: Machine Learning Approach for Author Profiling and Deception Detection in Arabic Texts. In *Working Notes of FIRE 2019 - Forum for Information Retrieval Evaluation, Kolkata, India, December 12-15, 2019*, volume 2517 of *CEUR Workshop Proceedings*, pages 92–99. CEUR-WS.org.

Hamada A. Nayel, Walaa Medhat, and Metwally Rashad. 2019. BENHA@IDAT: Improving Irony Detection in Arabic Tweets using Ensemble Approach. In *Working Notes of FIRE 2019 - Forum for Information Retrieval Evaluation, Kolkata, India, December 12-15, 2019*, volume 2517 of *CEUR Workshop Proceedings*, pages 401–408. CEUR-WS.org.

Mohammad Salameh, Houda Bouamor, and Nizar Habash. 2018. Fine-grained arabic dialect identification. In *Proceedings of the 27th International Conference on Computational Linguistics*, pages 1332–1344.

Yutong Sun, Hui Ning, Kaisheng Chen, Leilei Kong, Yunpeng Yang, Jiexi Wang, and Haoliang Qi. 2019. Author profiling in arabic tweets: An approach based on multi-classification with word and character features. In *Working Notes of FIRE 2019 - Forum for Information Retrieval Evaluation, Kolkata, India, December 12-15, 2019*, volume 2517 of *CEUR Workshop Proceedings*, pages 105–109. CEUR-WS.org.

Samia Touileb. 2020. LTG-ST at NADI shared task 1: Arabic dialect identification using a stacking classifier. In *Proceedings of the Fifth Arabic Natural Language Processing Workshop*, pages 313–319, Barcelona, Spain (Online). Association for Computational Linguistics.

Dialect Identification in Nuanced Arabic Tweets Using Farasa Segmentation and AraBERT

Anshul Wadhawan
Flipkart Private Limited
anshul.wadhwan@flipkart.com

Abstract

This paper presents our approach to address the EACL WANLP-2021 Shared Task 1: Nuanced Arabic Dialect Identification (NADI). The task is aimed at developing a system that identifies the geographical location(country/province) from where an Arabic tweet in the form of modern standard Arabic or dialect comes from. We solve the task in two parts. The first part involves pre-processing the provided dataset by cleaning, adding and segmenting various parts of the text. This is followed by carrying out experiments with different versions of two Transformer based models, AraBERT and AraELECTRA. Our final approach achieved macro F1-scores of 0.216, 0.235, 0.054, and 0.043 in the four subtasks, and we were ranked second in MSA identification subtasks and fourth in DA identification subtasks.

1 Introduction

Spoken by about 500 million people around the world, Arabic is the biggest part of the Semitic language family. Being the official language of almost 22 countries belonging to the Middle-East North Africa (MENA) region, it is not only an integral member of the six official UN languages, but also fourth most used language on the Internet (Guellil et al., 2019). Middle East contributes to 164 million internet users and North Africa contributes to 121 million internet users. Comparing with other languages, Arabic language has received little attention in modern computational linguistics, despite its religious, political and cultural significance. However, with rapid development of tools and techniques delivering state-of-the-art performance in many language processing tasks, this negligence is being taken care of.

The presence of various dialects and complex morphology are some of the distinguishing factors prominent in the Arabic language. Also, the informal nature of conversations on social media and the differences in Modern Standard Arabic (MSA) and Dialectical Arabic (DA), both significantly increase this complexity. While DA is used for informal daily communication, MSA is used for formal writing. Social media is the home for both of these forms, with the former being the most common form. Lack of data is the primary reason why many of the Arabic dialects remain understudied. With the availability of diverse data belonging to 21 Arab countries, this bottleneck can be diminished. The Nuanced Arabic Dialect Identification (NADI), with this goal, is the task of automatic detection of the source variety of a given text or speech segment.

Previously, on the lines of Arabic dialect identification, there have been approaches focusing on coarse-grained regional varieties such as Levantine or Gulf (Elaraby and Abdul-Mageed, 2018; Zaidan and Callison-Burch, 2014; Elfardy and Diab, 2013) or country level varieties (Bouamor et al., 2019; Zhang and Abdul-Mageed, 2019). There have been tasks that involved city level classification on human translated data (Salameh et al., 2018). Some tasks have focused on country and province level classification simultaneously (Abdul-Mageed et al., 2020).

In this paper, we present our process to tackle the WANLP-2021 Shared Task 1. The paper is organised in the following way: Section 2 presents the problem statement and details of the provided dataset. Section 3 describes a modularised process that we inculcate as part of methodology. Section 4 describes the experiments that were conducted, with detailed statistics about the dataset, system settings and results of these experiments. A brief conclusion of the paper with the potential prospects of our study are presented in Section 5.

Proceedings of the Sixth Arabic Natural Language Processing Workshop, pages 291–295
Kyiv, Ukraine (Virtual), April 19, 2021.

2 Task Definition

The WANLP-2021 Shared Task 1 (Abdul-Mageed et al., 2021) is based on a multi-class classification problem where the aim is to recognize which country or province an Arabic tweet in the form of modern standard Arabic or dialect belongs to. The task targets dialects at the province-level, and also focuses on naturally-occurring fine-grained dialects at the sub-country level. The NADI 2021 task promotes efforts made towards distinguishing both modern standard Arabic (MSA) and dialects (DA) according to their geographical origin, focusing on fine-grained dialects with new datasets. The provided data comes from the domain of Twitter and covers 100 provinces from 21 Arab countries. The task is divided into 4 subtasks as described below:

Subtask 1.1: Country-level MSA identification
Subtask 1.2: Country-level DA identification
Subtask 2.1: Province-level MSA identification
Subtask 2.2: Province-level DA identification

The training dataset has a total of 21,000 tweet, validation and test datasets have 5,000 tweets each. Every example belongs to one of 100 provinces of 21 Arab countries. Additional 10M unlabeled tweets are provided that can be used in developing the systems for either or both of the tasks. F-score, Accuracy, Precision and Recall are the evaluation metrics. However, the official metric of evaluation is the Macro Averaged F-score.

3 Methodology

We present our methodology in two parts. The first part in the methodology is data preprocessing. This is followed by experimenting with different transformer based models for the task at hand. Both these parts have been described in detail in the following sub sections.

3.1 Data Pre-Processing

Transformer based models, that we plan to fine tune on our dataset, are pre-trained on processed rather than raw data. Owing to the variations in expression of opinions among users belonging to different parts of the world, the tweets fetched from the website are a clear representation of these variations. We find these variations on randomly checking the given examples in different forms. It is common for users to use slang words on the Twitter platform, and post non-ascii characters like emojis. Also, spelling errors, user mentions and URLs are prominent in tweets of most users. These parts within the tweets do not contribute to being informative towards deciding the geographical location of the tweet as they correspond to noise. Thus, the given dataset is cleaned in the following ways, so that the data used for fine tuning has a similar distribution to that used for the pre-training process:

1. Perform Farasa segmentation (for select models only) (Abdelali et al., 2016).
2. Replace all URLs with [رابط], emails with [بريد], mentions with [مستخدم].
3. Remove HTML line breaks and markup, unwanted characters like emoticons, repeated characters (> 2) and extra spaces.
4. Insert whitespace before and after all non Arabic digits or English Digits and Alphabet and the 2 brackets, and between words and numbers or numbers and words.

3.2 Transformer Based Models

The domains of speech recognition (Graves et al., 2013) and computer vision (Krizhevsky et al., 2012) have largely utilised different deep learning techniques and produced significant improvements over the traditional machine learning techniques. In the domain of natural language processing, most deep learning based techniques until now utilised word vector representations (Bengio et al., 2003; Yih et al., 2011; Mikolov et al., 2013) for different classification tasks. Lately, transformer based approaches have shown significant progress towards many NLP benchmarks (Vaswani et al., 2017), including text classification (Chang et al., 2020), owing to their ability to build proficient language models. As an output of the pre-training process, embeddings are produced which are utilised for finer tasks.

3.2.1 AraBERT

AraBERT is an Arabic pretrained language model based on Google's BERT architecture (Antoun et al.). There are six versions of the model: AraBERTv0.1-base, AraBERTv0.2-base, AraBERTv0.2-large, AraBERTv1-base, AraBERTv2-base and AraBERTv2-large. For these variations, the model parameters with respect to the pre-training process have been depicted in Table 1.

Model	Size		Pre-Segmentation	Dataset		
	MB	Params		#Sentences	Size	#Words
AraBERTv0.2-base	543MB	136M	No	200M	77GB	8.6B
AraBERTv0.2-large	1.38G	371M	No	200M	77GB	8.6B
AraBERTv2-base	543MB	136M	Yes	200M	77GB	8.6B
AraBERTv2-large	1.38G	371M	Yes	200M	77GB	8.6B
AraBERTv0.1-base	543MB	136M	No	77M	23GB	2.7B
AraBERTv1-base	543MB	136M	Yes	77M	23GB	2.7B

Table 1: Model Pre-training Parameters

3.2.2 AraELECTRA

Being a method for self-supervised language representation learning, ELECTRA has the ability of making use of lesser computations for the task of pre-training transformers (Antoun et al., 2020). Similar to the objective of discriminator of a Generative Adversarial Network, ELECTRA models are trained with the goal of distinguishing fake input tokens from the real ones. On the Arabic QA dataset, AraELECTRA achieves state-of-the-art results.

For all new AraBERT and AraELECTRA models, the same pretraining data is used. The dataset that is used for pre-training, before the application of Farasa Segmentation, has a total of 82,232,988,358 characters or 8,655,948,860 words or 200,095,961 lines, and has a size of 77GB. Initially, several websites like OSCAR unshuffled and filtered, Assafir news articles, Arabic Wikipedia dump from 2020/09/01, The OSIAN Corpus and The 1.5B words Arabic Corpus, were crawled to create the pre-training dataset. Later, unshuffled OSCAR corpus, after thorough filtering, was added to the previous dataset used in AraBERTv1 without including the data from the above mentioned crawled websites to create the new dataset.

Country	DA		MSA	
	Train	Dev	Train	Dev
Algeria	1809	430	1899	427
Bahrain	215	52	211	51
Djibouti	215	27	211	52
Egypt	4283	1041	4220	1032
Iraq	2729	664	2719	671
Jordan	429	104	422	103
Kuwait	429	105	422	103
Lebanon	644	157	633	155
Libya	1286	314	1266	310
Mauritania	215	53	211	52
Morocco	858	207	844	207
Oman	1501	355	1477	341
Palestine	428	104	422	102
Qatar	215	52	211	52
Saudi_Arabia	2140	520	2110	510
Somalia	172	49	346	63
Sudan	215	53	211	48
Syria	1287	278	1266	309
Tunisia	859	173	844	170
UAE	642	157	633	154
Yemen	429	105	422	88

Table 2: Country Level Data Distribution

4 Experiments

We experiment with eight transformer based models using the given training and validation sets. We calculate the final test predictions by fine tuning the most efficient model, which is decided by the scores produced above, with the concatenated labeled training and validation splits. This is followed by evaluating the test set on this fine tuned model. This section presents the Country-level dataset distribution, system settings, results of our research followed by a descriptive analysis of our system.

Parameter	Value
Learning Rate	1e-5
Epsilon (Adam optimizer)	1e-8
Maximum Sequence Length	256
Batch Size (for base models)	40
Batch Size (for large models)	4
#Epochs	5

Table 3: Parameter Values

Model	Subtask 1.1		Subtask 1.2		Subtask 2.1		Subtask 2.2	
	F1	A	F1	A	F1	A	F1	A
AraBERTv0.1-base	0.283	0.324	0.338	0.390	0.024	0.028	0.025	0.037
AraBERTv0.2-base	0.300	0.344	0.382	0.427	0.038	0.042	0.035	0.051
AraBERTv0.2-large	0.304	0.343	0.362	0.413	0.022	0.030	0.029	0.041
AraBERTv1-base	0.281	0.318	0.306	0.377	0.032	0.040	0.019	0.033
AraBERTv2-base	0.309	0.347	0.389	0.432	0.029	0.038	0.034	0.048
AraBERTv2-large	0.315	0.346	0.416	0.450	0.001	0.010	0.001	0.010
AraELECTRA-base-generator	0.106	0.231	0.165	0.285	0.005	0.018	0.006	0.022
AraELECTRA-base-discriminator	0.192	0.281	0.280	0.375	0.007	0.020	0.006	0.026

Table 4: Validation Set Results

	M-F1	A	P	R
Subtask 1.1	0.216	0.317	0.321	0.189
Subtask 1.2	0.235	0.433	0.280	0.233
Subtask 2.1	0.054	0.060	0.061	0.060
Subtask 2.2	0.043	0.053	0.044	0.051

Table 5: Test Set Results

4.1 Dataset

The country-wise distribution of the provided training and validation splits, for both the tasks of MSA and DA, are shown in Table 2.

4.2 System Settings

We make use of pre-trained AraBERT and AraELECTRA models, with the names of bert-base-arabert, bert-base-arabertv01, bert-large-arabertv2, bert-base-arabertv2, bert-large-arabertv02, bert-base-arabertv02, araelectra-base-generator and araelectra-base-discriminator for fine-tuning the transformer based models. We use hugging-face[1] API to fetch the pre-trained transformer based models, and then fine tuned the same on our dataset. The hyper parameters used for fine tuning these models have been specified in Table 3.

4.3 Results and Analysis

For all subtasks, the performance results of proposed models on the provided validation set with reference to accuracy(A) and weighted F1 scores(F1) are shown in Table 4.

From Table 4, we conclude that:

1. For most of the subtasks, one of the base models performs almost as good as the best performing large model.
2. AraELECTRA models seem to perform worse than all AraBERT models, possibly due to their specialization in handling GAN related tasks, which are different from classification based tasks.
3. AraBERTv2-large out performs all other models for subtasks 1.1 and 1.2. For subtasks 2.1 and 2.2, AraBERTv0.2-base produces the best results on the validation set.

From the above results, we choose AraBERTv2-large for subtasks 1.1, 1.2 and AraBERTv0.2-base for subtasks 2.1, 2.2 to be the primary models to fine tune on the concatenated training and validation set as well as carry out inferences on the unseen dataset. The final test set results in terms of Macro F1 Score(M-F1), Recall(R), Accuracy(A) and Precision(P) are specified in Table 5.

5 Conclusion and Future Work

In this paper, we present a comprehensive overview of the approach that we employed to solve the EACL WANLP-2021 Shared Task 1. We tackle the given problem in two parts. The first part involves pre processing the given data by modifying various parts of the text. The second part involves experimenting with different versions of two Transformer based networks, AraBERT and AraELECTRA, all pre-trained on Arabic text. Our final submissions for the four subtasks are based on the best performing version of AraBERT model. With Macro Averaged F1-Score as the final evaluation criteria, our approach fetches a private leaderboard rank of 2 for MSA identification and 4 for DA identification. In the future, we aim to utilise other features relevant for classification tasks like URLs, emoticons, and experiment with ensembles of transformer based and word vector based input representations.

[1] `https://huggingface.co/transformers/`

References

Ahmed Abdelali, Kareem Darwish, Nadir Durrani, and Hamdy Mubarak. 2016. Farasa: A fast and furious segmenter for Arabic. In *Proceedings of the 2016 Conference of the North American Chapter of the Association for Computational Linguistics: Demonstrations*, pages 11–16, San Diego, California. Association for Computational Linguistics.

Muhammad Abdul-Mageed, Chiyu Zhang, Houda Bouamor, and Nizar Habash. 2020. NADI 2020: The First Nuanced Arabic Dialect Identification Shared Task. In *Proceedings of the Fifth Arabic Natural Language Processing Workshop (WANLP 2020)*, Barcelona, Spain.

Muhammad Abdul-Mageed, Chiyu Zhang, Abdel-Rahim Elmadany, Houda Bouamor, and Nizar Habash. 2021. NADI 2021: The Second Nuanced Arabic Dialect Identification Shared Task. In *Proceedings of the Sixth Arabic Natural Language Processing Workshop (WANLP 2021)*.

Wissam Antoun, Fady Baly, and Hazem Hajj. Arabert: Transformer-based model for arabic language understanding. In *LREC 2020 Workshop Language Resources and Evaluation Conference 11–16 May 2020*, page 9.

Wissam Antoun, Fady Baly, and Hazem Hajj. 2020. Araelectra: Pre-training text discriminators for arabic language understanding.

Yoshua Bengio, Réjean Ducharme, Pascal Vincent, and Christian Janvin. 2003. A neural probabilistic language model. *J. Mach. Learn. Res.*, 3(null):1137–1155.

Houda Bouamor, Sabit Hassan, and Nizar Habash. 2019. The madar shared task on arabic fine-grained dialect identification. In *Proceedings of the Fourth Arabic Natural Language Processing Workshop*, pages 199–207.

Wei-Cheng Chang, Hsiang-Fu Yu, Kai Zhong, Yiming Yang, and Inderjit Dhillon. 2020. Taming pretrained transformers for extreme multi-label text classification.

Mohamed Elaraby and Muhammad Abdul-Mageed. 2018. Deep models for Arabic dialect identification on benchmarked data. In *Proceedings of the Fifth Workshop on NLP for Similar Languages, Varieties and Dialects (VarDial 2018)*, pages 263–274, Santa Fe, New Mexico, USA. Association for Computational Linguistics.

Heba Elfardy and Mona Diab. 2013. Sentence level dialect identification in Arabic. In *Proceedings of the 51st Annual Meeting of the Association for Computational Linguistics (Volume 2: Short Papers)*, pages 456–461, Sofia, Bulgaria. Association for Computational Linguistics.

Alex Graves, Abdel rahman Mohamed, and Geoffrey Hinton. 2013. Speech recognition with deep recurrent neural networks.

Imane Guellil, Houda Saâdane, Faical Azouaou, Billel Gueni, and Damien Nouvel. 2019. Arabic natural language processing: An overview. *Journal of King Saud University - Computer and Information Sciences*.

Alex Krizhevsky, Ilya Sutskever, and Geoffrey E. Hinton. 2012. Imagenet classification with deep convolutional neural networks. In *Proceedings of the 25th International Conference on Neural Information Processing Systems - Volume 1*, NIPS'12, page 1097–1105, Red Hook, NY, USA. Curran Associates Inc.

Tomas Mikolov, Ilya Sutskever, Kai Chen, Greg Corrado, and Jeffrey Dean. 2013. Distributed representations of words and phrases and their compositionality. In *Proceedings of the 26th International Conference on Neural Information Processing Systems - Volume 2*, NIPS'13, page 3111–3119, Red Hook, NY, USA. Curran Associates Inc.

Mohammad Salameh, Houda Bouamor, and Nizar Habash. 2018. Fine-grained arabic dialect identification. In *Proceedings of the 27th International Conference on Computational Linguistics*, pages 1332–1344.

Ashish Vaswani, Noam Shazeer, Niki Parmar, Jakob Uszkoreit, Llion Jones, Aidan N. Gomez, Lukasz Kaiser, and Illia Polosukhin. 2017. Attention is all you need.

Wen-tau Yih, Kristina Toutanova, John C. Platt, and Christopher Meek. 2011. Learning discriminative projections for text similarity measures. In *Proceedings of the Fifteenth Conference on Computational Natural Language Learning*, pages 247–256, Portland, Oregon, USA. Association for Computational Linguistics.

Omar F. Zaidan and Chris Callison-Burch. 2014. Arabic dialect identification. *Computational Linguistics*, 40(1):171–202.

Chiyu Zhang and Muhammad Abdul-Mageed. 2019. No army, no navy: BERT semi-supervised learning of Arabic dialects. In *Proceedings of the Fourth Arabic Natural Language Processing Workshop*, pages 279–284, Florence, Italy. Association for Computational Linguistics.

Overview of the WANLP 2021 Shared Task on Sarcasm and Sentiment Detection in Arabic

Ibrahim Abu Farha[1], Wajdi Zaghouani[2] and Walid Magdy[1,3]
[1]School of Informatics, The University of Edinburgh, Edinburgh, United Kingdom
[2]College of Humanities and Social Sciences, Hamad Bin Khalifa University, Doha, Qatar
[3]The Alan Turing Institute, London, United Kingdom
i.abufarha@ed.ac.uk
wzaghouani@hbku.edu.qa
wmagdy@inf.ed.ac.uk

Abstract

This paper provides an overview of the WANLP 2021 shared task on sarcasm and sentiment detection in Arabic. The shared task has two subtasks: sarcasm detection (subtask 1) and sentiment analysis (subtask 2). This shared task aims to promote and bring attention to Arabic sarcasm detection, which is crucial to improve the performance in other tasks such as sentiment analysis. The dataset used in this shared task, namely ArSarcasm-v2, consists of 15,548 tweets labelled for sarcasm, sentiment and dialect. We received 27 and 22 submissions for subtasks 1 and 2 respectively. Most of the approaches relied on using and fine-tuning pre-trained language models such as AraBERT and MARBERT. The top achieved results for the sarcasm detection and sentiment analysis tasks were 0.6225 F1-score and 0.748 F_1^{PN} respectively.

1 Introduction

Work on opinion mining and subjective language analysis has been prominent in the natural language processing (NLP) field during the last two decades. One of the main tasks in this area is sentiment analysis (SA). One of the early works on SA is (Pang et al., 2002), where the authors analysed the sentiment in movie reviews. Following that, and embarked with the popularity of social media, SA became one of the popular topics in NLP. Most of the work on SA targeted English, while other languages, including Arabic, lagged behind. In the last decade, researchers on Arabic NLP started targeting SA such as the work of Abdul-Mageed et al. (2011). Since then, there have been numerous works on Arabic SA such as the works of (Abdulla et al., 2013; Alayba et al., 2018; Abdul-Mageed, 2019; Al-Smadi et al., 2019; Abu Farha and Magdy, 2021). Work on Arabic SA has been hindered by many challenges such as the large variation in dialects (Habash, 2010; Darwish et al., 2014) and the complex morphology of the language (Abdul-Mageed et al., 2011). With the advancement of work on SA, researchers started tackling the challenges affecting this task such as sarcasm (Hussein, 2018). Sarcasm can be defined as a form of verbal irony that is intended to express contempt or ridicule (Joshi et al., 2017). Sarcasm is considered one of the main challenges for SA systems since it implies expressing the opinion in an indirect way, where the intended meaning is different from the literal one (Wilson, 2006).

There have been several related works on English sarcasm detection including datasets such as the works reported in (Abercrombie and Hovy, 2016; Barbieri et al., 2014a,b; Filatova, 2012; Ghosh et al., 2015; Joshi et al., 2016; Oprea and Magdy, 2020) and detection systems such as (Rajadesingan et al., 2015; Joshi et al., 2015; Amir et al., 2016). Currently, there are few attempts to work on Arabic sarcasm. Those include the work by soukhria2017, a shared task on irony detection Ghanem et al. (2019) along with the participants' submissions and dialectal sarcasm datasets by Abbes et al. (2020); Abu Farha and Magdy (2020).

In this shared task, we offer our sarcasm and sentiment detection in Arabic task that is co-organised with the WANLP 2021 workshop on Arabic NLP. The goal of the shared task is to provide resources and encourage researchers to work on Arabic sarcasm detection. The shared task has two subtasks, sarcasm detection (subtask 1) and sentiment analysis (subtask 2). We provided the participant with a new dataset (ArSarcasm-v2), which is publicly available[1]. The dataset is annotated for sarcasm, sentiment and dialect. We received 27 submissions for subtask 1 and 22 submissions for subtask 2. This paper provides an overview of the shared task

[1]ArSarcasm-v2 is available at: http://github.com/iabufarha/ArSarcasm-v2

Proceedings of the Sixth Arabic Natural Language Processing Workshop, pages 296–305
Kyiv, Ukraine (Virtual), April 19, 2021.

and the achieved results by the participants along with their approaches.

Most of the approaches used by participants were based on fine-tuning pre-trained language models. A small number of participants utilised other deep learning and conventional machine learning algorithms. The top team in the sarcasm detection task was BhamNLP (Alharbi and Lee, 2021), who achieved an F1-score of 0.6225 over the sarcastic class. While the top team in the sentiment analysis task was CS-UM6P (El Mahdaouy et al., 2021), who achieved F_1^{PN} of 0.748.

2 Related Work

Our shared task offers two subtasks on Arabic Sarcasm and sentiment detection. In the following, we discuss the literature in both tasks within the Arabic NLP community.

2.1 Arabic Sarcasm Classification

Arabic sarcasm did not receive the same degree of attention as English. The work on Arabic sarcasm detection is limited to a few works. soukhria2017 were the first to work on Arabic sarcasm/irony detection. In their work, they created a corpus of sarcastic Arabic tweets, which they collected using a set of political keywords. They filtered the sarcastic tweets using distant supervision, where they relied on some markers such as the Arabic equivalent of #sarcasm such as #سخرية, #مسخرة, #تهكم and #استهزاء. The final dataset consists of 5,479, 1,733 of which are sarcastic/ironic. They experimented with various classifiers such as SVM, Naive Bayes, Logistic Regression, Linear Regression. Random Forest was the best model, where it achieved an F1-score of 0.73. ghanem2019idat organised a shared task on Arabic sarcasm/irony detection. They prepared their dataset through collecting tweets related to different topics such as the US elections. Then they filtered out tweets that contain sarcastic hashtags, where they used the same hashtags used by soukhria2017. To prepare the final dataset, the authors sampled tweets from both the sarcastic and non-sarcastic portions, then they manually annotated them. The final dataset consists of 5,030 tweets, 2,614 of which are sarcastic. The shared task saw the participation of 18 teams. The first place was obtained by Khalifa and Hussein (2019), where they achieved an F1-score of 0.85. In their work, they relied on a set of features that include word n-grams, topic modelling features, sentiment features, statistical features and word embeddings. They experimented with multiple classifiers such as BiLSTM, Random Forest, XGBoost. Their best model was an ensemble of XGBoost, neural network and Random Forest. In a recent work by Abu Farha and Magdy (2020), the authors proposed ArSarcasm dataset for sarcasm detection, which contains around 10K tweets out of which around 1,600 are sarcastic. They presented a basic baseline that uses BiLSTM and achieved a F-score of 0.46 over the sarcastic class. Another recent study, Abbes et al. (2020) created a corpus of ironic tweets, namely DAICT. To prepare the corpus, the authors followed the same approach used by Ghanem et al. (2019) the corpus consists of 5,358 tweets distributed as follows: 4,809 sarcastic, 435 non-sarcastic and 114 labelled as ambiguous.

2.2 Arabic Sentiment Analysis

Unlike Arabic sarcasm detection, Arabic sentiment analysis (SA) has been under the researchers' radar for a while. Early work on Arabic SA such as in Abdul-Mageed et al. (2011); Abbasi et al. (2008), focused on modern standard Arabic (MSA). Since then, researchers started targeting dialectal Arabic (DA) such as the work of Mourad and Darwish (2013), where the authors introduced an expandable Arabic sentiment lexicon along with a corpus of tweets. Other datasets include the works of Kiritchenko et al. (2016); Rosenthal et al. (2017); Elmadany et al. (2018). Other works focused on proposing and comparing various approaches for Arabic SA (El-Beltagy et al., 2017; Al-Smadi et al., 2019; Abdulla et al., 2013; Alayba et al., 2018; Abu Farha and Magdy, 2019).

A recent comprehensive study by Abu Farha and Magdy (2021) provides a thorough comparative analysis of the available approaches on SA. In their work, they compared a large variety of models on three benchmark datasets. Their analysis shows that deep learning models combined with word embeddings achieve much better performance compared to classical machine learning models, such as SVMs. However, their experiments show that the utilisation of transformer-based language model achieves better results the best deep learning model architecture that uses word-embeddings. They show that using a fine-tuned AraBERT(Antoun et al., 2020) outperforms all existing classical and deep learning models on all the three benchmark datasets they examined.

Set	Sarcasm		Sentiment			Total
	Sarcastic	Non-sarcastic	Positive	Negative	Neutral	
Training	2,168	10,380	2,180	4,621	5,747	12,548
Testing	821	2,179	575	1,677	748	3,000
Total	2,989	12,559	2,577	6,298	6,495	15,548

Table 1: Statistics of training and testing sets, showing the number of examples for both sarcasm detection and sentiment analysis tasks.

Dialect	Sarcastic	Non-Sarcastic	Negative	Positive	Neutral	Total
MSA	1,523	9,362	3,986	1,890	5,009	10,885
Egypt	1,085	1,896	1,564	524	893	2,981
Gulf	214	752	411	192	363	966
Levant	152	519	312	143	216	671
Maghreb	15	30	25	6	14	45
Total	2,989	12,559	6,298	2,755	6,495	15,548

Table 2: Statistics of ArSarcasm-v2 dataset showing the distribution of sarcasm and sentiment over the dialects.

3 Dataset

The shared task provides the ArSarcasm-v2, which is a new dataset for Arabic sarcasm detection. The dataset is an extension of the original ArSarcasm dataset (Abu Farha and Magdy, 2020).

3.1 Resources

ArSarcasm-v2 uses the whole original ArSarcasm dataset (Abu Farha and Magdy, 2020) as part of its training data. The original ArSarcasm consists of 10,547 tweets, 1,682 of which are sarcastic. Additional sarcastic tweets are added to the ArSarcasm-v2 dataset from the DAICT dataset (Abbes et al., 2020), which represents a corpus of ironic/sarcastic tweets. DAICT contains 5,358 tweets, 4,809 of which are ironic/sarcastic.

Since the goal is to extend the larger ArSarcasm, and because DAICT is mostly sarcastic, a new set of random tweets were collected over the period November-December 2020. The tweets where collected using the Twitter streaming API with the language filter set to Arabic ("lang:ar"). Since sarcasm is usually present in percentage, the new tweets were used to balance out DAICT.

3.2 Annotation

For the annotation process, we used appen[2] crowdsourcing platform. ArSarcasm represents the majority portion of ArSarcasm-v2. Thus, the goal was to annotate the new portions to have similar labels to ArSarcasm. Additionally, DAICT was only annotated for sarcasm/irony, thus a new annotation was needed. To ensure consistency with ArSarcasm, we followed the same procedure and used the same guidelines to annotated the new portions. The original ArSarcasm paper defined sarcasm as *an utterance that is used to express ridicule, where the intended meaning is different from the apparent one*. Appendix A shows the guidelines (in Arabic) that have been shown to annotators.

Since DAICT is only annotated for sarcasm/irony, it was used as a pool of sarcastic examples which were balanced with the set of random Arabic tweets. A new set of 5,000 tweets, 2,500 of which are from DAICT, were annotated. The annotators were asked to provide three labels for each tweet as the following:

- **Sarcasm:** sarcastic or non-sarcastic.
- **Sentiment:** positive, negative or neutral.
- **Dialect:** Egyptian, Gulf, Levantine, Maghrebi or Modern Standard Arabic (MSA).

Only annotators with an Arab origin were allowed to participate. This was verified through their profile (usage of the Arabic language). Each tweet was annotated by at least three different annotators. The quality of annotation was monitored using a set of 100 hidden test questions that appear randomly during the task, each of those questions has the correct label for sentiment, sarcasm and

[2]https://www.appen.com/

dialect. If the performance of an annotator in these test questions dropped below 80%, this annotator is eliminated and all the labels he/she provided are also ignored. Agreement among annotators was 78.9% for sentiment, 87.3% for sarcasm and 77.0% for dialects.

3.3 Dataset Statistics

The new ArSarcasm-v2 dataset consists of 15,548 tweets, 10,547 of them were taken from the original ArSarcasm dataset while the rest (5,001 tweets) from DAICT and the new collection of tweets. These additional 5,001 tweets were split into two parts: 2,001 tweets added to the original ArSarcasm to form the set of training data of 12,548 tweets, and the remaining 3000 were used as the test set, as shown in Table 1. Each of the tweets has three labels for sarcasm, sentiment and dialect. Tables 1 and 2 show the statistics of the new dataset, where we can see that 19.2% of the data is sarcastic (2,989 tweets). Also, the annotation shows that most of the data is either in MSA or Egyptian dialect while the Maghrebi dialect is under-represented with only 45 tweets.

4 Shared Task

This section provides an overview of the shared task, the description of the subtasks and the evaluation metrics.

4.1 Tasks Description

The shared task on sarcasm detection and sentiment analysis in Arabic contains two subtasks as follows:

- **Sarcasm Detection (subtask 1)**: the goal is to identify whether a tweet is sarcastic or not.
- **Sentiment Analysis (subtask 2)**: the goal is to classify the tweet to one of the sentiment classes: positive, negative or neutral.

The data for both subtasks was provided as train/test split without a specific development set. Table 1 shows the statistics of the two sets. The training set consists of 12,548 tweets, while the testing set consists of 3,000 tweets. The participants had access to the tweets' text and the dialect label during the testing phase.

4.2 Evaluation Metrics

The main evaluation metric for subtask 1 (sarcasm detection) is the F1-score of the sarcastic class only (F1-sarcastic), since it is the main class to be detected. Sarcasm is usually present in small percentages in the data, thus the task is an imbalanced classification task. F1-sarcastic is calculated using the following equation:

$$F_1^{sarcastic} = 2 \cdot \frac{P^{sarcastic} \cdot R^{sarcastic}}{P^{sarcastic} + R^{sarcastic}}, \quad (1)$$

Where $P^{sarcastic}$, $R^{sarcastic}$ are the precision and recall with respect to the sarcastic class.

For the sentiment analysis, the macro F1-score over the positive and negative classes was used (F_1^{PN}). It is worth noting that the neutral class is excluded from the metric calculation and not the whole task. Thus miss-classified neutral tweets will lead to the increase of false positives for the positive or negative class, and thus should lead to the reduction of the F_1^{PN} value. This metric is the main adapted measure in multiple sentiment analysis shared tasks in different languages (Kiritchenko et al., 2016; Rosenthal et al., 2017).

F_1^{PN} is calculated using the following equation:

$$F^{PN} = \frac{1}{2}(F_1^P + F_1^N), \quad (2)$$

Where F_1^P, F_1^N are the F_1 with respect to the positive and negative classes respectively, while the neutral class is ignored.

4.3 Participating Teams

The shared task saw the participation of 30 unique teams. The sarcasm detection task (subtask 1) received 27 submissions, while the sentiment analysis task (subtask 2) received 22 submissions. Table 3 shows the list of the participating teams whose papers were accepted[3].

4.4 Shared Task Results

Tables 4 and 5 show the results of both subtask 1 and subtask 2 respectively. The results are sorted in descending order based on the official metric of the corresponding subtask, where F1-sarcastic and F_1^{PN} are the official metrics for subtask 1 and subtask 2 respectively. For each team, only the last submission was considered for the leaderboard. For subtask 1 (sarcasm detection), BhamNLP Alharbi and Lee (2021) achieved first place with an F1-sarcastic of 0.6225. For subtask 2 (sentiment analysis), CS-UM6P El Mahdaouy et al. (2021) team achieved first place with an F_1^{PN} of 0.748.

[3]We received system description papers from only 17 of the participating teams.

Team	Affiliation of the first author	Subtask(s)
AIMTechnologies	A.I.M Technologies	1, 2
ALI-B2B-AI	Alibaba Group, China	1, 2
ArabicProcessors (Gaanoun and Benelallam, 2021)	INSEA, Morocco	1, 2
BhamNLP (Alharbi and Lee, 2021)	University of Birmingham, King Abdulaziz University	1, 2
CS-UM6P (El Mahdaouy et al., 2021)	Mohammed VI Polytechnic University, Morocco	1, 2
DeepBlueAI (Song et al., 2021)	DeepBlue Technology (Shanghai) Co., Ltd, China	1, 2
DM-JUST(dalya) (Faraj and Abdullah, 2021)	Jordan University of Science and Technology, Jordan	1
Fatemah (Husain and Uzuner, 2021)	Kuwait University, Kuwait	1, 2
iCompass (Naski et al., 2021)	iCompass, Tunisia	1, 2
IDC (Israeli et al., 2021)	The Data Science Institute, Interdisciplinary Center, Israel	1, 2
ITAM	University Mohamed First, Oujda, Morocco	1, 2
Juha (Abuzayed and Al-Khalifa, 2021)	iWAN research group, Saudi Arabia	1, 2
Laila & Daliyah (Laila) (Bashmal and Alzeer, 2021)	King Saud University, Saudi Arabia	1
Naglaa Abdelhade (Naglaa)	Assiut university, Egypt	2
NAYEL (Nayel et al., 2021)	Benha University, Egypt	1, 2
Phonemer (Wadhawan, 2021)	Flipkart Private Limited	1, 2
rematchka (Abdel-Salam, 2021)	Computer Engineering, Cairo University, Egypt	1, 2
SalamBERT (Husain and Uzuner, 2021)	Kuwait University, Kuwait	1, 2
Serpente (Ghoul and Lejeune, 2021)	Sorbonne University, France	1, 2
SpeechTrans (Lichouri et al., 2021)	CRSTDLA Research Center, Algeria	1, 2
SPPU_AASM (Hengle et al., 2021)	Pune University, India	1, 2
ZTeam (Elagbry et al., 2021)	Helwan University, Egypt	1, 2

Table 3: The list of participating teams who provided their affiliation details along with the citation for those who submitted a system description paper. Runs that did not provide any details on their affiliation are not listed, but their results are listed in Tables 4 and 5.

4.5 Approaches by Top Submissions

The participating teams used a variety of approaches for both subtasks. Most of the teams used pre-trained language models such as AraBERT (Antoun et al., 2020) and MARBERT (Abdul-Mageed et al., 2020). Abu Farha and Magdy (2021), provide an extensive comparison of pre-trained language models on ArSarcasm-v2 dataset. A few of the participants used deep learning and conventional machine learning approaches. All the teams, that are participating in the two subtasks, used the same architecture for both tasks.

For the sarcasm detection task, BhamNLP (Alharbi and Lee, 2021) team was ranked first with an F1-sarcastic of 0.6225. In their approach, they used a multi-task learning architecture that is trained for sarcasm and sentiment classification. The model is based on both MARBERT and a CNN-LSTM model, where the output of each of these models is concatenated and fed to the final output layer. The CNN-LSTM used both word and character embeddings. The second place (SPPU-AASM) (Hengle et al., 2021) used an ensemble of AraBERT and CNN-BiLSTM model, which achieved an F1-sarcastic of 0.614. The third place (DeepBlueAI) (Song et al., 2021) used an ensemble of AraBERT and XLM-R, which achieved an F1-sarcastic of 0.6127.

For the sentiment analysis task, CS-UM6P team El Mahdaouy et al. (2021) achieved first place with an F_1^{PN} of 0.748. Their model is based on MARBERT-based Multi-Task Learning with task attention interaction layer for sarcasm and sentiment detection. The model used MARBERT as an encoder to produce sentence embeddings. Those embeddings are fed into separate attention and output layers specific to each task. The second place was obtained by DeepBlueAI (Song et al., 2021) with an F_1^{PN} of 0.7392. They used a similar architecture to the ones used for sarcasm detection. The third place was obtained by (rematchka) Abdel-Salam (2021) fine-tuned MARBERT for sentiment classification and achieved an F_1^{PN} of 0.7321.

4.6 Other Interesting Approaches

salambert-arsarcasm built their on the hypothesis that tweets with negative sentiment and tweets with sarcasm content are more likely to have offensive content. Thus, they pre-trained AraBERT (Antoun et al., 2020) on offensive language data then fine-tuned it for the target task. In (Israeli et al., 2021), the authors filtered the data through down sampling the non-sarcastic class. Their hypothesis is that the test set would be similar to the extra portions added to the original ArSarcasm. Thus, for both ArSarcasm and the added tweets, they built a

Rank	Team	F1-sarcastic	Accuracy	Macro-F1	Precision	Recall
1	BhamNLP	0.6225	0.7700	0.7286	0.7193	0.7460
2	SPPU-AASM	0.6140	0.7410	0.7096	0.7031	0.7447
3	DeepBlueAI	0.6127	0.7830	0.7310	0.7279	0.7345
4	CS-UM6P	0.6000	0.7680	0.7183	0.7122	0.7268
5	dalya	0.5989	0.7830	0.7251	0.7268	0.7235
6	Laila	0.5968	0.7063	0.6829	0.6874	0.7337
7	Phonemer	0.5872	0.7830	0.7200	0.7264	0.7147
8	AIMTechnolgies	0.5852	0.7467	0.7014	0.6934	0.7174
9	IDC	0.5677	0.7670	0.7041	0.7062	0.7022
10	rematchka	0.5662	0.7803	0.7095	0.7231	0.7004
11	UBC	0.5468	0.7723	0.6974	0.7119	0.6880
12	SalamBERT	0.5348	0.7727	0.6922	0.7128	0.6807
13	Juha	0.5191	0.6980	0.6495	0.6443	0.6661
14	ZTeam	0.5189	0.7533	0.6765	0.6858	0.6700
15	ALI-B2B-AI	0.5139	0.7617	0.6780	0.6965	0.6678
16	ArabicProcessors	0.5086	0.7797	0.6833	0.7296	0.6665
17	MMFOUAD	0.5056	0.6917	0.6408	0.6360	0.6557
18	Fatemah	0.5041	0.7607	0.6732	0.6950	0.6622
19	Kalawy	0.4870	0.7247	0.6494	0.6514	0.6476
20	rehab88	0.4870	0.7247	0.6494	0.6514	0.6476
21	iCompass	0.4860	0.7730	0.6702	0.7195	0.6543
22	Serpente	0.4109	0.7630	0.6313	0.7116	0.6194
23	SpeechTrans	0.3371	0.7287	0.5833	0.6359	0.5802
24	AhmedAbdou	0.2542	0.7340	0.5462	0.6486	0.5569
25	ITAM	0.2509	0.7253	0.5414	0.6218	0.5517
26	NAYEL	0.2440	0.7460	0.5457	0.7048	0.5602
27	rematchka	0.1657	0.7047	0.4932	0.5497	0.5185

Table 4: Results achieved by participants in subtask 1 (sarcasm detection). The main metric is the F1-score of the sarcastic class (F1-sarcastic).

topic model for each dialect and removed irrelevant topics from ArSarcasm. Additionally, they utilised a language model to augment the data with new sarcastic examples. The augmentation was done through replacing and adding new words. Finally, they fine-tuned MARBERT model (Abdul-Mageed et al., 2020) for each dialect. Other participants used BERT models in different ways. The majority of the participants used ensemble methods, where the combined BERT-based models with other models. While most participants used the same architecture for both tasks, some participants relied on multi-task learning to train the model on both tasks simultaneously such as in Alharbi and Lee (2021); El Mahdaouy et al. (2021).

5 Conclusion and Future Directions

This paper provides an overview of the shared task on sarcasm detection and sentiment analysis in Arabic. We provide an overview of the current state of research on Arabic sarcasm. The paper provides an overview of the new ArSarcasm-v2 dataset which was used for the shared task. We also provide a high-level description of the top participating teams in the shared task. The aim of this shared task is to encourage researchers to work on Arabic sarcasm, which was reflected by the popularity of the task and having 27 run submissions and 17 system description papers discussing different approaches applied on this task.

We hope that this task would not be the last on Arabic Sarcasm detection. More datasets on Arabic Sarcasm would further help the development of better detection models. In addition, much work is still required for this challenging task, since as it is noticed, the state-of-the-art performance is 0.62 F-score, which shows that there is large room of improvement to be achieved.

Rank	Team	F_1^{PN}	Accuracy	Macro-F1	Precision	Recall
1	CS-UM6P	0.7480	0.7107	0.6625	0.6660	0.6713
2	DeepBlueAI	0.7392	0.7037	0.6570	0.6591	0.6714
3	rematchka	0.7321	0.6957	0.6587	0.6498	0.6748
4	Phonemer	0.7255	0.6983	0.6531	0.6515	0.6623
5	IDC	0.7190	0.6923	0.6446	0.6429	0.6582
6	ArabicProcessors	0.7145	0.6817	0.6439	0.6362	0.6693
7	Juha	0.7139	0.6853	0.6297	0.6362	0.6513
8	iCompass	0.7085	0.6743	0.6423	0.6393	0.6488
9	UBC	0.7081	0.6760	0.6346	0.6274	0.6452
10	SPPU-AASM	0.7073	0.6840	0.6232	0.6421	0.6388
11	BhamNLP	0.7014	0.6753	0.6296	0.6287	0.6570
12	Fatemah	0.6877	0.6630	0.6210	0.6136	0.6318
13	AIMTechnolgies	0.6850	0.6677	0.6236	0.6213	0.6263
14	ALI-B2B-AI	0.6556	0.6333	0.5955	0.5873	0.6159
15	Serpente	0.6506	0.6473	0.5784	0.5899	0.5710
16	SalamBERT	0.6259	0.6073	0.5635	0.5580	0.5813
17	ZTeam	0.6241	0.6053	0.5545	0.5578	0.5786
18	NAYEL	0.5936	0.5980	0.5291	0.5434	0.5207
19	SpeechTrans	0.5787	0.5923	0.5222	0.5321	0.5161
20	Naglaa	0.5638	0.5793	0.5158	0.5646	0.5068
21	GOF	0.4288	0.5147	0.4275	0.5764	0.4546
22	ITAM	0.3845	0.5293	0.3768	0.4054	0.3983

Table 5: Results achieved by participants in subtask 2 (sentiment analysis). The main metric is the macro average of the F1-scores of the positive and negative classes (F_1^{PN}).

References

Ahmed Abbasi, Hsinchun Chen, and Arab Salem. 2008. Sentiment analysis in multiple languages: Feature selection for opinion classification in web forums. *ACM Transactions on Information Systems (TOIS)*, 26(3):1–34.

Ines Abbes, Wajdi Zaghouani, Omaima El-Hardlo, and Faten Ashour. 2020. DAICT: A dialectal Arabic irony corpus extracted from Twitter. In *Proceedings of the 12th Language Resources and Evaluation Conference*, pages 6265–6271, Marseille, France. European Language Resources Association.

Reem Abdel-Salam. 2021. Wanlp 2021 shared-task: Towards irony and sentiment detection in arabic tweets using multi-headed-lstm-cnn-gru and marbert. In *Proceedings of the Sixth Arabic Natural Language Processing Workshop*.

Muhammad Abdul-Mageed. 2019. Modeling arabic subjectivity and sentiment in lexical space. *Information Processing & Management*, 56(2):291–307.

Muhammad Abdul-Mageed, Mona T. Diab, and Mohammed Korayem. 2011. Subjectivity and sentiment analysis of modern standard arabic. In *Proceedings of the 49th Annual Meeting of the Association for Computational Linguistics: Human Language Technologies: Short Papers - Volume 2*, HLT '11, pages 587–591, Stroudsburg, PA, USA. Association for Computational Linguistics.

Muhammad Abdul-Mageed, AbdelRahim Elmadany, and El Moatez Billah Nagoudi. 2020. Arbert & marbert: Deep bidirectional transformers for arabic. *arXiv preprint arXiv:2101.01785.*

N. A. Abdulla, N. A. Ahmed, M. A. Shehab, and M. Al-Ayyoub. 2013. Arabic sentiment analysis: Lexicon-based and corpus-based. In *2013 IEEE Jordan Conference on Applied Electrical Engineering and Computing Technologies (AEECT)*, pages 1–6.

Gavin Abercrombie and Dirk Hovy. 2016. Putting sarcasm detection into context: The effects of class imbalance and manual labelling on supervised machine classification of twitter conversations. In *Proceedings of the ACL 2016 Student Research Workshop*, pages 107–113.

Ibrahim Abu Farha and Walid Magdy. 2019. Mazajak: An online Arabic sentiment analyser. In *Proceedings of the Fourth Arabic Natural Language Processing Workshop*, pages 192–198, Florence, Italy. Association for Computational Linguistics.

Ibrahim Abu Farha and Walid Magdy. 2020. From Arabic sentiment analysis to sarcasm detection: The ArSarcasm dataset. In *Proceedings of the 4th Workshop on Open-Source Arabic Corpora and Processing Tools, with a Shared Task on Offensive Language*

Detection, pages 32–39, Marseille, France. European Language Resource Association.

Ibrahim Abu Farha and Walid Magdy. 2021. Benchmarking transformer-based language models for arabicsentiment and sarcasm detection. In *Proceedings of the Sixth Arabic Natural Language Processing Workshop*.

Ibrahim Abu Farha and Walid Magdy. 2021. A comparative study of effective approaches for arabic sentiment analysis. *Information Processing Management*, 58(2):102438.

Abeer Abuzayed and Hend Al-Khalifa. 2021. Sarcasm and sentiment detection in arabic tweets using bert-based models and data augmentation. In *Proceedings of the Sixth Arabic Natural Language Processing Workshop*.

Mohammad Al-Smadi, Bashar Talafha, Mahmoud Al-Ayyoub, and Yaser Jararweh. 2019. Using long short-term memory deep neural networks for aspect-based sentiment analysis of Arabic reviews. *International Journal of Machine Learning and Cybernetics*, 10(8):2163–2175.

Abdulaziz M. Alayba, Vasile Palade, Matthew England, and Rahat Iqbal. 2018. A combined cnn and lstm model for arabic sentiment analysis. In *Machine Learning and Knowledge Extraction*, pages 179–191, Cham. Springer International Publishing.

Abdullah I. Alharbi and Mark Lee. 2021. Multi-task learning using a combination of contextualised and static word embeddings for arabic sarcasm detection and sentiment analysis. In *Proceedings of the Sixth Arabic Natural Language Processing Workshop*.

Silvio Amir, Byron C. Wallace, Hao Lyu, Paula Carvalho, and Mário J. Silva. 2016. Modelling context with user embeddings for sarcasm detection in social media. In *Proceedings of The 20th SIGNLL Conference on Computational Natural Language Learning*, pages 167–177, Berlin, Germany. Association for Computational Linguistics.

Wissam Antoun, Fady Baly, and Hazem Hajj. 2020. AraBERT: Transformer-based model for Arabic language understanding. In *Proceedings of the 4th Workshop on Open-Source Arabic Corpora and Processing Tools, with a Shared Task on Offensive Language Detection*, pages 9–15, Marseille, France. European Language Resource Association.

Francesco Barbieri, Francesco Ronzano, and Horacio Saggion. 2014a. Italian irony detection in twitter: a first approach. In *The First Italian Conference on Computational Linguistics CLiC-it*, page 28.

Francesco Barbieri, Horacio Saggion, and Francesco Ronzano. 2014b. Modelling sarcasm in twitter, a novel approach. In *Proceedings of the 5th Workshop on Computational Approaches to Subjectivity, Sentiment and Social Media Analysis*, pages 50–58.

Laila Bashmal and Daliyah H. Alzeer. 2021. Arsarcasm shared task: An ensemble bert model for sarcasm detection in arabic tweets. In *Proceedings of the Sixth Arabic Natural Language Processing Workshop*.

Kareem Darwish, Walid Magdy, et al. 2014. Arabic information retrieval. *Foundations and Trends® in Information Retrieval*, 7(4):239–342.

Samhaa R. El-Beltagy, Mona El Kalamawy, and Abu Bakr Soliman. 2017. NileTMRG at SemEval-2017 task 4: Arabic sentiment analysis. In *Proceedings of the 11th International Workshop on Semantic Evaluation (SemEval-2017)*, pages 790–795, Vancouver, Canada. Association for Computational Linguistics.

Abdelkader El Mahdaouy, Abdellah El Mekki, Nabil El Mamoun, Kabil Essefar, Ismail Berrada, and Ahmed Khoumsi. 2021. Deep multi-task model for sarcasm detection and sentiment analysis in arabic language. In *Proceedings of the Sixth Arabic Natural Language Processing Workshop*.

Hazem E. Elagbry, Shimaa Attia, Ahmed Abdel-Rahman, Ahmed Abdel-Ate, and Sandra Girgis. 2021. A contextual word embedding for arabic sarcasm detection with random forests. In *Proceedings of the Sixth Arabic Natural Language Processing Workshop*.

AbdelRahim A Elmadany, Hamdy Mubarak, and Walid Magdy. 2018. Arsas: An arabic speech-act and sentiment corpus of tweets. In *OSACT 3: The 3rd Workshop on Open-Source Arabic Corpora and Processing Tools*, page 20.

Dalya Faraj and Malak Abdullah. 2021. Sarcasmdet at sarcasm detection task 2021 in arabic using arabert pretrained model. In *Proceedings of the Sixth Arabic Natural Language Processing Workshop*.

Elena Filatova. 2012. Irony and sarcasm: Corpus generation and analysis using crowdsourcing. In *Lrec*, pages 392–398. Citeseer.

Kamel Gaanoun and Imade Benelallam. 2021. Sarcasm and sentiment detection in arabic language: A hybrid approach combining embeddings and rule-based features. In *Proceedings of the Sixth Arabic Natural Language Processing Workshop*.

Bilal Ghanem, Jihen Karoui, Farah Benamara, Véronique Moriceau, and Paolo Rosso. 2019. Idat at fire2019: Overview of the track on irony detection in arabic tweets. In *Proceedings of the 11th Forum for Information Retrieval Evaluation*, pages 10–13.

Debanjan Ghosh, Weiwei Guo, and Smaranda Muresan. 2015. Sarcastic or not: Word embeddings to predict the literal or sarcastic meaning of words. In *proceedings of the 2015 conference on empirical methods in natural language processing*, pages 1003–1012.

Dhaou Ghoul and Gaël Lejeune. 2021. Sarcasm and sentiment detection in arabic: investigating the interest of character-level features. In *Proceedings of the Sixth Arabic Natural Language Processing Workshop*.

Nizar Y. Habash. 2010. Introduction to arabic natural language processing. *Synthesis Lectures on Human Language Technologies*, 3(1):1–187.

Amey Hengle, Atharva Kshirsagar, Shaily Desai, and Manisha Marathe. 2021. Combining context-free and contextualized word representations for arabic sarcasm detection and sentiment identification. In *Proceedings of the Sixth Arabic Natural Language Processing Workshop*.

Fatmeh Husain and Ozlem Uzuner. 2021. Leveraging offensive language for sarcasm and sentiment detection in arabic. In *Proceedings of the Sixth Arabic Natural Language Processing Workshop*.

Doaa Mohey El-Din Mohamed Hussein. 2018. A survey on sentiment analysis challenges. *Journal of King Saud University - Engineering Sciences*, 30(4):330 – 338.

Abraham Israeli, Yotam Nahum, Shai Fine, and Kfir Bar. 2021. The idc system for the sentiment classification and sarcasm detection in arabic. In *Proceedings of the Sixth Arabic Natural Language Processing Workshop*.

Aditya Joshi, Pushpak Bhattacharyya, and Mark J Carman. 2017. Automatic sarcasm detection: A survey. *ACM Computing Surveys (CSUR)*, 50(5):73.

Aditya Joshi, Vinita Sharma, and Pushpak Bhattacharyya. 2015. Harnessing context incongruity for sarcasm detection. In *Proceedings of the 53rd Annual Meeting of the Association for Computational Linguistics and the 7th International Joint Conference on Natural Language Processing (Volume 2: Short Papers)*, pages 757–762.

Aditya Joshi, Vaibhav Tripathi, Pushpak Bhattacharyya, and Mark Carman. 2016. Harnessing sequence labeling for sarcasm detection in dialogue from tv series 'friends'. In *Proceedings of The 20th SIGNLL Conference on Computational Natural Language Learning*, pages 146–155.

M. Khalifa and Noura Hussein. 2019. Ensemble learning for irony detection in arabic tweets. In *FIRE*.

Svetlana Kiritchenko, Saif Mohammad, and Mohammad Salameh. 2016. Semeval-2016 task 7: Determining sentiment intensity of english and arabic phrases. In *Proceedings of the 10th international workshop on semantic evaluation (SEMEVAL-2016)*, pages 42–51.

Mohamed Lichouri, Mourad Abbas, Besma Benaziz, Aicha Zitouni, and Khaled Lounnas. 2021. Preprocessing solutions for detection of sarcasm and sentiment for arabic. In *Proceedings of the Sixth Arabic Natural Language Processing Workshop*.

Ahmed Mourad and Kareem Darwish. 2013. Subjectivity and sentiment analysis of modern standard arabic and arabic microblogs. In *Proceedings of the 4th workshop on computational approaches to subjectivity, sentiment and social media analysis*, pages 55–64.

Malek Naski, Abir Messaoudi, Hatem Haddad, Moez Ben Haj Hmida, Chayma Fourati, and Aymen Ben Elhaj Mabrouk. 2021. icompass at shared task on sarcasm and sentiment detection in arabic. In *Proceedings of the Sixth Arabic Natural Language Processing Workshop*.

Hamada Nayel, Eslam Amer, Aya Allam, and Hanya Abdallah. 2021. Machine learning-based model for sentiment and sarcasm detection. In *Proceedings of the Sixth Arabic Natural Language Processing Workshop*.

Silviu Oprea and Walid Magdy. 2020. isarcasm: A dataset of intended sarcasm. In *Proceedings of the 58th Annual Meeting of the Association for Computational Linguistics*, pages 1279–1289.

Bo Pang, Lillian Lee, and Shivakumar Vaithyanathan. 2002. Thumbs up?: sentiment classification using machine learning techniques. In *Proceedings of the ACL-02 conference on Empirical methods in natural language processing-Volume 10*, pages 79–86. Association for Computational Linguistics.

Ashwin Rajadesingan, Reza Zafarani, and Huan Liu. 2015. Sarcasm detection on twitter: A behavioral modeling approach. In *Proceedings of the Eighth ACM International Conference on Web Search and Data Mining*, pages 97–106. ACM.

Sara Rosenthal, Noura Farra, and Preslav Nakov. 2017. SemEval-2017 task 4: Sentiment analysis in Twitter. In *Proceedings of the 11th International Workshop on Semantic Evaluation*, SemEval '17, Vancouver, Canada. Association for Computational Linguistics.

Bingyan Song, Chunguang Pan, Wang Shengguang, and Luo Zhipeng. 2021. Deepblueai at wanlp-eacl2021 task 2: A deep ensemble-based method for sarcasm and sentiment detection in arabic. In *Proceedings of the Sixth Arabic Natural Language Processing Workshop*.

Anshul Wadhawan. 2021. Arabert and farasa segmentation based approach for sarcasm and sentiment detection in arabic tweets. In *Proceedings of the Sixth Arabic Natural Language Processing Workshop*.

Deirdre Wilson. 2006. The pragmatics of verbal irony: Echo or pretence? *Lingua*, 116(10):1722.

A Annotation Guidelines

هدف البحث :تجميع المعلومات لتطوير التحليل الاوتوماتيكي للعواطف و الآراء.

الفوائد :هذا البحث لن يفيدك بشكل مباشر لكن سوف يفيد المجتمع بشكل عام من حيث تطوير كيفية تحليل الكمبيوتر للغات البشرية. قد يؤدي ذلك الى تطوير برامج تحليل اراء وأحاسيس متطورة، بالإضافة الى تطوير بحث الانترنت.

هذه المهمة تهدف إلى تصنيف التغريدات (تويت) بناء على ما تحتويه من عواطف (مشاعر) إلى تغريدات ذات محتوى إيجابي أو سلبي أو محايد، بالإضافة إلى تصنيفها في حال احتوت على سخرية أو تهكم.

بالإضافة إلى ذلك سوف يقوم المشارك باختيار الى اي لهجة تنتمي هذه التغريدة.

الخطوات:

1. قم بقراءة التغريدة
2. قم باختيار نوع الشعور في التغريدة (ايجابي ، سلبي ، محايد) حيث نص السؤال (sentiment)
3. قم باختيار فيما إذا كانت التغريدة تحتوي على تهكم أو سخرية حيث نص السؤال (sarcasm)
4. اختيار لهجة التغريدة حيث نص السؤال (dialect)

أمثلة:

النصوص الإيجابية هي التي تحتوي بطابعها شعورا إيجابيا تهنئة أو مناسبة أو ربح او أي حدث يبعث أو يبشر بالخير و التفاؤل.

1. تصفيات كاس العالم سويسرا و مدري مين المهم مباريات حلوووه
2. محمد صلاح يستحق افضل لاعب

النص السلبي هو الذي يعبر عن شيء سلبي أو محزن أو أي خبر سيء أو سلبي بالاضافة الى التعبير عن الغضب او الانفعال. فيما يلي بعض الأمثلة:

1. مفيش حماس خالص في تصفيات كاس العالم مش حاسس باي حاجة خالص
2. انا مع مقاطعة الانتخابات ما لم يكن هناك مسار ثوري حقيقي يحقق اهداف ثورة يناير

النص الحيادي (المحايد) هو الذي لا يحتوي على تعبيرات إيجابية أو سلبية. فيما يلي بعض الأمثلة:

1. هو لعب كام ماتش في تصفيات كاس العالم؟
2. الرئيس السيسي: الغرب يعتقد اننا ضد حقوق الانسان . و اقول لهم : لا.. نحن امة تريد العيش بسلام

فيما يتعلق السخرية أو التهكم فتكون عندما يكون المقصود بالنص عكس المكتوب ويكون الغرض هو السخرية من شيء بطريقة غير مباشر. فيما يلي بعض الأمثلة:

1. التصفيات اللي قعد اسويها بحياتي اقوي من تصفيات كاس العالم
2. ابني شايل 3 مواد في الجامعة. حاجة تشرف

Figure 1: A sample of the guidelines provided to the annotators.

WANLP 2021 Shared Task: Towards Irony and Sentiment detection in Arabic tweets using Multi-headed-LSTM-CNN-GRU and MaRBERT

Reem Abdel-Salam
Computer Engineering, Cairo University
reem.abdelsalam13@gmail.com

Abstract

Irony and Sentiment detection is important to understand people's behavior and thoughts. Thus it has become a popular task in natural language processing (NLP). This paper presents results and main findings in WANLP 2021 shared tasks one and two. The task was based on the ArSarcasm-v2 dataset (Abu Farha et al., 2021). In this paper, we describe our system Multi-headed-LSTM-CNN-GRU and also MARBERT (Abdul-Mageed et al., 2021) submitted for the shared task, ranked 10 out of 27 in shared task one achieving 0.5662 F1-Sarcasm and ranked 3 out of 22 in shared task two achieving 0.7321 F1-PN under CodaLab username "rematchka". We experimented with various models and the two best performing models are a Multi-headed CNN-LSTM-GRU in which we used prepossessed text and emoji presented from tweets and MARBERT.

1 Introduction

Text on social media as Twitter and Facebook involves the usage of expressive and figurative languages like irony and sarcasm. A text is considered ironic if it is intended to mean the opposite of what it literally expresses. While sentiment is the interpretation and classification of emotions (positive, negative, and neutral) within text. Irony detection has recently become more relevant due to its importance in extracting information from texts. For example, In order to move beyond the literal match of user queries, irony detection will enhance information retrieval with new operators to allow non-literal retrieval of creative expressions. Sentiment analysis has been an important topic in the literature for a while. The interest in Sentiment analysis arises due to the wide and increase in usage of social media platforms, and online shopping. Companies can benefit from understanding the feedback and thoughts of their customers. The sixth workshop for Arabic Natural Language Processing co-located with EACL 2021, had two shared tasks: Sarcasm and Sentiment Detection in Arabic tweets. The shared task on sarcasm detection is a binary classification where it is required to identify whether a piece of text is sarcastic or not. While shared task in sentiment detection is multi-class classification, where it is required to identify sentiment of a piece of text as positive or negative or neutral. In this paper, we describe the work we performed on both shared tasks. MARBERT, and Multi-headed-LSTM-CNN-GRU models [1] were used in this study. The rest of this paper is structured as follows: section 2 discusses the related work that has been performed on automatic sarcasm and Irony detection, section 3 describes the dataset used in this shared task, section 4 discusses the approach we used in our study, and section 6 discusses the results we obtained.

2 Related Work

There have been large attempts in the literature to tackle irony and sentiment detection. Most of the work is biased towards machine learning approaches, with few attempts to use deep learning approaches. A Recent work (Abdul-Mageed et al., 2021) proposed two powerful bidirectional based transformers models ARBERT and MARBERT. The models were trained and evaluated based on Arbenchmark which consists of 41 datasets targeting 5 different tasks/task clusters including irony and sarcasm tasks. In (Karoui et al., 2017), the authors used a random forest classifier based on some set of features, in which they believe are powerful, for irony detection. The set of features are surface features, Sentiment features, Shifter fea-

[1]The source code for the developed models can be found through: https://github.com/rematchka/Irony-and-Sarcasm-detection-in-Arabic-tweets

Proceedings of the Sixth Arabic Natural Language Processing Workshop, pages 306–311
Kyiv, Ukraine (Virtual), April 19, 2021.

tures, and Contextual features. In another work (Khalifa and Hussein, 2019), the authors used ensemble learning in irony detection in Arabic tweets. The ensemble learning consists of three ensemble models. The first ensemble model uses different machine learning classifiers which uses TF-IDF word n-gram features, topic modeling features, bag-of-words, and sentiment features. The second ensemble model uses 8 different Word-level Bi-LSTM while the third ensemble model is a combination of both the first and second ensemble models. Moreover Alayba et al. (2018) proposed CNN-LSTM model for Arabic semantic analysis. The authors tested their model on two datasets, ArTwitter (Abdulla et al., 2013) and Arabic Health Services (Alayba et al., 2017) datasets, where they achieved accuracies of 88.1% and 94.3% respectively. Elshakankery and Ahmed (2019) proposed HILATSA for Arabic semantic analysis. HILATSA combines lexicon-based and machine learning approaches. The authors experimented with several datasets in their work as ASTD (Nabil et al., 2015) and ArTwitter. The authors made use of Different classifiers, which varied from using classical machine learning to deep learning models. In another study (Al-Smadi et al., 2019), the authors proposed two models: a character-level bidirectional LSTM along with a conditional random field classifier (Bi-LSTM-CRF) for aspect opinion target expressions extraction, and an aspect-based LSTM for aspect sentiment polarity classification. They tested their model on Arabic hotels' reviews (Elnagar et al., 2018) dataset, they achieved an F-score of 70%.

3 Data

This Section shows the used dataset in the shared task. We used ArSarcasm-v2 dataset (Abu Farha et al., 2021), which was provided in the training phase by ArSarcasm Shared Task. The dataset is a Twitter text with labels "FALSE" and "TRUE" for the first shared task and "POS", "NEG", and "NEU" for the second shared task. The dataset provided in the training phase contains 12548 training examples, while the test set provided in the test phase consists of 3000 examples.

Table 1 shows the statistics of ArSarcasm-v2 dataset. Most of the dialect examples presented in the dataset are either MSA or Egyptian, while there are few examples of the Maghrebi dialect. Based on labels distribution, the dataset provided is imbalanced, since it has 2168 examples for True around 17.3% and 10380 examples for False around 82.7%, in irony detection task, and 4621, 5747, 2180 around 36.8%, 45.8% and 17.4% for Negative, Neutral, Positive examples, in sentiment detection task, respectively. Emoji distribution in the provided training data was analyzed, it was found that there are 1524 examples that contain emojis, where the maximum length was 219 emojis. Therefore it could be concluded that there are examples of pure emoji or do not contain a large amount of text.

4 Methodology

This section discusses the details required for reproducing the results. It mentions the preprocessing steps, the architecture of the classifiers used, and hyperparameter values.

4.1 Preprocessing

Processing data is essential in order to extract useful information and improve data quality, which directly affects model performance. Especially when dealing with text messages from various dialects and non-standard language. Our processing pipeline goes as follows:

1. Removal of URLs, mentions, emails, dates, numbers, punctuation, English letters, stop words found in NLTK (Bird, 2006), and the emojis.
2. Diacritic removal, letter normalization
3. Conversion of emojis presented into text.
4. Unifying similar Arabic characters such as Hamza and Yaa

4.2 Proposed Models

In this section, we show the key models used in the two shared tasks. We used the Multi-headed-LSTM-CNN-GRU model and MARBET (Abdul-Mageed et al., 2021) as our baseline models. In addition to other experimental models that were not effective based on train-validation-test split used.

4.2.1 Multi-headed-LSTM-CNN-GRU Model

In this model, Arabic news embedding (Altowayan and Tao, 2016) was used as text representation in addition to emoji2vec (Eisner et al., 2016) for emoji information presented in the examples. These embeddings were then fed to a deep learning model which comprises the Bidirectional LSTM-CNN model, Bidirectional GRU-CNN model, and CNN-LSTM model. Processed clean text and emojis

Dialect	Non-Sarcastic	Sarcastic	Negative	Neutral	Positive	Total
msa	7634	928	2671	4486	1405	8562
egypt	1745	930	1376	793	506	2675
gulf	487	157	264	259	121	644
levant	486	138	285	197	142	624
magreb	28	15	25	12	6	43
Total	10380	2168	4621	5747	2180	12548

Table 1: Dataset statistics for sarcasm and sentiment over the dialects and labels

Model	Accuracy	F1-Score	Precision	Recall	Shared Task
MARBERT	0.944	0.899	0.892	0.908	1
MARBERT	0.8730	0.858	0.856	0.861	2
Multi-headed-LSTM-CNN-GRU	0.955	0.9259	0.928	0.924	1
Multi-headed-LSTM-CNN-GRU	0.873	0.795	0.699	0.923	2
Multi-headed-LSTM-CNN-GRU with TF-IDF 2-grams	0.822	0.762	0.776	0.752	1
CNN-LSTM with dialect information	0.836	0.834	0.834	0.834	1

Table 2: Results on our initial development set in shared task one and two, based on our splitting criteria when evaluating models

Model	F1-PN	Accuracy	Macro-F1	Precision	Recall
MARBERT	0.7321	0.6957	0.6587	0.6498	0.6748

Table 3: Leaderboard results on Provided test set for shared task two

Model	F1-Sarcastic	Accuracy	Macro-F1	Precision	Recall
MARBERT	0.5662	0.7803	0.7095	0.7231	0.7004
Multi-headed-LSTM-CNN-GRU model	0.1657	0.7047	0.4932	0.5497	0.5185

Table 4: Leaderboard results on provided test set for shared task one

were inputted to the network. Clean text is processed in two branches Bidirectional LSTM-CNN model and the Bidirectional GRU-CNN model. The output of both branches are concatenated and passed through the batch norm layer, then dense layer. emoji is processed using the CNN-LSTM model. The output of the processed emoji layer is concatenated with a dense layer. At this step, the output is passed to two fully connected layers as shown in figure1.

4.2.2 MARBERT Model

MARBERT model (Abdul-Mageed et al., 2021) was fine-tuned on the provided dataset. MARBERT model is a bidirectional transformer-based model.

4.2.3 Various Deep learning models

For shared task one and two, experiments were conducted on other models as CNN-LSTM model with Arabic news embedding, CNN-LSTM model with emoji embeddings, another version of Multi-headed CNN-LSTM-GRU where one input was processed text and the other input was dialect or TF-IDF of 2-grams.

4.2.4 Machine learning models

Experiments were conducted on SVM model and logistic regression model. The pipeline goes as follows: examples were processed as discussed in the previous subsection. For each example and its extracted emoji (if exists) we get their vector rep-

Model	F1-Sarcastic	Accuracy	Macro-F1	Precision	Recall
Multi-headed-LSTM-CNN-GRU model	0.42	0.69	0.60	0.43	0.41
Multi-headed-LSTM-CNN-GRU with TF-IDF 2-grams	0.30	0.72	0.56	0.47	0.23
Multi-headed-LSTM-CNN-GRU with Dialect information	0.18	0.73	0.51	0.54	0.11
SVM with concatenated features	0.47	0.52	0.51	0.34	0.79
Linear regression with add features	0.46	0.49	0.49	0.32	0.78

Table 5: Non official results on provided test set for shared task one, after competitions has ended

Model	F1-PN	Accuracy	Macro-F1	Precision	Recall
Multi-headed-LSTM-CNN-GRU model	0.55	0.527	0.48	0.48	0.49
SVM with concatenated features	0.54	0.55	0.47	0.47	0.46
Linear regression with concatenated features	0.5	0.53	0.45	0.45	0.46

Table 6: Non official results on provided test set for shared task two, after competitions has ended

resentation based on Arabic news embeddings and emoji2vec embeddings. We then obtain features either by concatenating examples vector representation with emoji vector representation or by adding them together.

5 Experimental Setup

Experiments were conducted via Python and Tensorflow framework, running on Google Colab resources, which are Nvidia Tesla P100-PCIE-16GB GPU, Intel ® Xeon ® CPU @ 2.20 GHz, and 12GB RAM. We used 70%-10%-20% strategy for train-validation-test splits respectively for the training phase. Eventually, we had 8783 examples for the training set, 753 examples for the validation set, and 3012 examples for the test set. All of the presented models were trained on the same dataset and splitting criteria. In the Multi-headed CNN-LSTM-GRU model, weights were initialized with He Initialization. Adam optimizer with a 0.0001 learning rate was used, with cross-entropy as a loss function. The model was trained for 150 epochs which took around 2-3 hours of training, with 32 batch sizes. For the MARBERT model, it was fine-tuned for 5 epochs using the initial learning rate 2e-06, with a batch size of 32 with Adam weight decay optimizer and cross-entropy loss function. Precision, recall, f-score (f1-sarcastic for shared task one, and macro average f1-score for shared task two), and accuracy were used as evaluation metrics.

6 Results and Discussion

6.1 Development phase results

Table 2 shows that Multi-headed-LSTM-CNN-GRU outperforms MARBERT based on our splitting criteria in shared task one, while MARBERT outperforms in shared task two. We believe that if ensemble learning were to be used, it will perform better as it will incorporate all information needed in both shared tasks from dialect, processed text, and emojis. We didn't include SVM and linear regression model scores as their F1-Sarcastic were below 0.2.

6.2 Official leaderboard results

The leaderboard results for shared task one official metric was based on F-score of the sarcastic class, while for shared task two, it was based on F-PN (Macro average of the F-score of the positive and negative classes). precision, recall, f-score, accuracy were also used for evaluation. As shown in table 4, based on the leaderboard in shared task one MARBERT model achieved 0.5662 F1-Sarcastic,

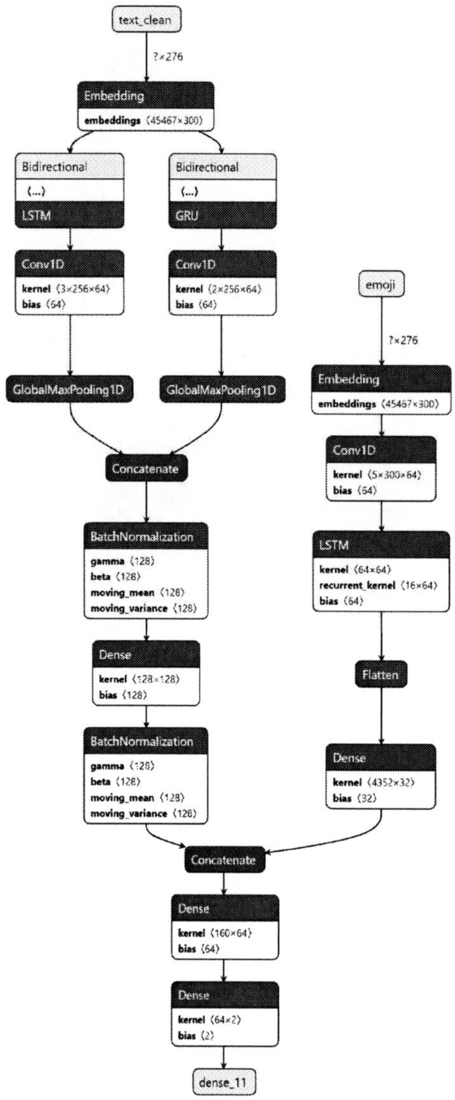

Figure 1: Model architecture

0.7803 Accuracy, 0.7095 Macro-F1, 0.7231 Precision, and 0.7004 recall, placing in 10th place among the submitted models, while Multi-headed-LSTM-CNN-GRU model achieved 0.1657, 0.7047, 0.4932, 0.5497, and 0.5185 for F1-Sarcastic, Accuracy, Macro-F1, Precision, Recall respectively, being placed in 27th place in the leaderboard.

The MARBERT model outperforms the Multi-headed-LSTM-CNN-GRU in F1-Sarcastic metric and has 8% accuracy loss on the test set. We believe that this shake in the leaderboard happened as MARBERT trained on multiple datasets and uses dialect information in addition to text, while Multi-headed-LSTM-CNN-GRU uses emoji and text. It was found that the distribution of emoji in the test set examples is not high as in train set examples, around 487 examples, with a maximum length of 71 emoji. In shared task two as shown in table 3 based on the leaderboard, MARBERT model achieved 0.732 F1-PN, 0.6957 accuracy, 0.6587 Macro-F1, 0.6498 precision, and 0.6748 recall on the leaderboard.

6.3 Non-official results

After the submission, we evaluated our models, on the provided test set and their annotations. As shown in table 5, for shared task one, a slightly modified version from the Multi-headed-LSTM-CNN-GRU model could achieve a higher F1-Sarcastic score. We believe that by fine-tuning the model by incorporating class imbalance, emoji distribution, and architecture tuning could achieve a competitive accuracy, F1-score as MARBERT model. Surprisingly, SVM model outperformed the Multi-headed-LSTM-CNN-GRU model on shared task one. For shared task two, table 6 shows Multi-headed-LSTM-CNN-GRU model, SVM, and logistic regression performance on test set. It could be concluded that most of models in shared task two have similar F1-PN, and accuracy score. Multi-headed-LSTM-CNN-GRU model performed well on shared task two than on shared task one.

7 Conclusion

In this paper, the results and the main findings of ArSarcasm shared task one and two, on identifying irony and sentiment in Arabic tweets were presented, in which different experiments were carried out with MARBERT and Multi-headed-LSTM-CNN-GRU model. Information presented in text as emojis were used to improve model performance. However, hyperparameter optimization and the usage of pre-trained word embeddings for the Multi-headed-LSTM-CNN-GRU network showed its effectiveness and impressive results for a small model compared to the pre-trained MARBERT model based on Bert and transformers. Future work will include investigating text representations, improving the deep learning model, and exploring different architectures.

References

Muhammad Abdul-Mageed, AbdelRahim Elmadany, and El Moatez Billah Nagoudi. 2021. Arbert & marbert: Deep bidirectional transformers for arabic. *ArXiv*, abs/2101.01785.

Nawaf A. Abdulla, N. A. Ahmed, Mohammed A. Shehab, and Mahmoud Al-Ayyoub. 2013. Arabic sentiment analysis: Lexicon-based and corpus-based. *2013 IEEE Jordan Conference on Applied Electrical Engineering and Computing Technologies (AEECT)*, pages 1–6.

Ibrahim Abu Farha, Wajdi Zaghouani, and Walid Magdy. 2021. Overview of the wanlp 2021 shared task on sarcasm and sentiment detection in arabic. In *Proceedings of the Sixth Arabic Natural Language Processing Workshop*.

Mohammad Al-Smadi, Bashar Talafha, Mahmoud Al-Ayyoub, and Y. Jararweh. 2019. Using long short-term memory deep neural networks for aspect-based sentiment analysis of arabic reviews. *International Journal of Machine Learning and Cybernetics*, pages 1–13.

Abdulaziz M. Alayba, V. Palade, Matthew England, and R. Iqbal. 2018. A combined cnn and lstm model for arabic sentiment analysis. *ArXiv*, abs/1807.02911.

Abdulaziz M. Alayba, Vasile Palade, Matthew England, and Rahat Iqbal. 2017. Arabic language sentiment analysis on health services. *CoRR*, abs/1702.03197.

A. Aziz Altowayan and L. Tao. 2016. Word embeddings for arabic sentiment analysis. *2016 IEEE International Conference on Big Data (Big Data)*, pages 3820–3825.

Steven Bird. 2006. Nltk: The natural language toolkit. *ArXiv*, cs.CL/0205028.

Ben Eisner, Tim Rocktäschel, Isabelle Augenstein, Matko Bosnjak, and S. Riedel. 2016. emoji2vec: Learning emoji representations from their description. *ArXiv*, abs/1609.08359.

Ashraf Elnagar, Yasmin S. Khalifa, and Anas Einea. 2018. Hotel arabic-reviews dataset construction for sentiment analysis applications.

Kariman Elshakankery and M. Ahmed. 2019. Hilatsa: A hybrid incremental learning approach for arabic tweets sentiment analysis. *Egyptian Informatics Journal*, 20:163–171.

Jihen Karoui, F. Benamara, and Véronique Moriceau. 2017. Soukhria: Towards an irony detection system for arabic in social media. In *ACLING*.

M. Khalifa and Noura Hussein. 2019. Ensemble learning for irony detection in arabic tweets. In *FIRE*.

Mahmoud Nabil, Mohamed A. Aly, and A. F. Atiya. 2015. Astd: Arabic sentiment tweets dataset. In *EMNLP*.

Sarcasm and Sentiment Detection In Arabic Tweets Using BERT-based Models and Data Augmentation

Abeer Abuzayed and Hend Al-Khalifa
iWAN Research Group
College of Computer and Information Sciences
King Saud University
aabuzayed1@students.iugaza.edu.ps, hendk@ksu.edu.da

Abstract

In this paper, we describe our efforts on the shared task of sarcasm and sentiment detection in Arabic (Abu Farha et al., 2021). The shared task consists of two subtasks: Sarcasm Detection (Subtask 1) and Sentiment Analysis (Subtask 2). Our experiments were based on fine-tuning seven BERT-based models with data augmentation to solve the imbalanced data problem. For both tasks, the MARBERT BERT-based model with data augmentation outperformed other models with an increase of the F-score by 15% for both tasks which shows the effectiveness of our approach.

1 Introduction

Sarcasm is a form of figurative language, where the speaker expresses his/her thoughts in a sarcastic way. The process of sarcasm detection relies on understanding people's true sentiments and opinions. Application of sarcasm detection can be beneficial in several NLP applications, such as marketing research, opinion mining and information categorization.

In recent years, sarcasm detection has received considerable attention in the NLP community (Joshi, 2016). Different approaches were used for sarcasm detection; Early approaches for sarcasm detection used feature-based machine learning models (Ghosh et al., 2018). Recently, deep learning methods have been applied for this task (Ghosh et al., 2020). For a comprehensive survey on sarcasm and irony detection see (Joshi et al., 2017). However, work on Arabic sarcasm detection is still in its early stages with very few works. There are few efforts on Arabic sarcasm detection such as the works of (Karoui et al., 2017); (Ghanem et al., 2020) and the recent efforts to build standard datasets for sarcasm detection such as (Abbes et al., 2020) and (Abu Farha and Magdy, 2020).

The current small size of the shared task labeled data-set and its imbalance nature makes it extremely difficult to build effective detection systems. Also, the context of the current sarcasm tweets does not have enough information to decide on its state which indeed makes the tasks more challenging.

In this paper, we describe the system submitted for the shared task on sarcasm detection and sentiment analysis in Arabic. We approached this challenge first by experimenting with different classical machine learning classifiers such as Support Vector Machines (SVMs), XGBoost, Random Forest that are trained on tf-idf features. Then, we experimented with different Deep Neural Networks (DNNs) along with character and word-level features. Finally, we conducted experiments on several BERT-based models such as MARBERT and QARiB. We took the most promising BERT-based models results for subtask 1 and subtask 2 on the training set, which was MARBERT for both of them and tested it with a new augmented dataset.

The rest of the paper is organized as follows: Section 2, describes the dataset. In section 3, we describe our approach in tackling the problem. Section 4 provides and discusses the results of subtask 1 and subtask 2. And in section 5, we provide a conclusion of our work.

Proceedings of the Sixth Arabic Natural Language Processing Workshop, pages 312–317
Kyiv, Ukraine (Virtual), April 19, 2021.

2 Dataset

The ArSarcasm-v2 dataset (Abu Farha et al., 2021) released for both shared tasks by the competition organizers is the same containing 12,548 training tweets. In addition to 3000 tweets for testing. The dataset was annotated for sarcasm detection task (Subtask 1) with the label "TRUE" for sarcastic tweets and "FALSE" for not sarcastic tweets. For the second shared task (Subtask 2) on sentiment analysis the labels are (NEU, NEG or POS) for neutral, negative or positive, respectively. Table 1 illustrates the label distributions for both tasks. It can be seen that the training dataset is quite imbalanced having only about 17% of the tweets labeled as sarcastic (TRUE) and 17% of them labeled as positive (POS).

Task	Class	Training set
Sarcasm Detection	TRUE FALSE	**2168** 10380
Sentiment Analysis	NEU NEG POS	5747 4621 **2180**

Table 1: Label distributions for both tasks.

3 System

This section provides a description of the different data preprocessing steps, models we used in the experiments, and our data augmentation approach.

3.1 Preprocessing:

For the preprocessing we have done 4 major steps to prepare the dataset as follows:

1. **Cleaning:** we removed all of the diacritics such as (tashdid, fatha, damma, kasra, etc.), English and Arabic punctuations, English words and numbers, URLS and USER mention tokens.
2. **Elongation removal:** any repeated character for more than twice was removed. For example, the word "أموووووت" becomes "أموت" after the preprocessing.
3. **Letter normalisation:** letters which appeared in different forms were transformed into a single form. For example, {آأإ} was replaced with {ا}, {ى} with {ي} ,{ة} with {ه} and {گ} with {ك}.
4. **Extract #hashtag keywords:** we removed the hash sign"#" and replace the underscore "_" within a hashtag with a white space to extract understandable key words, For instance, "#باسم_طلع_حرامي" turns into " باسم طلع حرامي".

3.2 Models

The past few years have witnessed a huge revolution in building various bidirectional transformer-based models, particularly for Arabic. Where they perform as powerful transfer learning tools that help in improving a wide range of natural language processing (NLP) tasks such as text classification, question answering, named entity recognition (NER), etc. While fine-tuning BERT-based models achieved state-of-the-art results on various downstream NLP tasks we will experiment the following BERT- based models:

- **MARBERT and ArBERT**: released by (Abdul-Mageed at el., 2020). Both are built based on the BERT-based model except for MARBERT which does not use the next sentence prediction (NSP) objective as it is trained on tweets which are basically short. ArBERT was trained on a collection of Arabic datasets which are mostly books and articles written in Modern Standard Arabic (MSA) with 6.5B tokens. While MARBERT trained on both Dialectal (DA) and MSA tweets and has 15.6B tokens. Additionally, MARBERT and ArBERT were experimented on ArSarcasm dataset (Abu Farha and Magdy, 2020).
- **QARiB** (QCRI Arabic and Dialectal BERT): was trained on a collection of Arabic tweets and sentences of text written on MSA with a total token number of 14B (Abdelali et al., 2020)[1].
- **AraBERTv02:** It was trained on Arabic corpora consisting of internet text and news articles of (8.6B tokens) (Antoun et al., 2020).
- **GigaBERTv3:** is a bilingual BERT for English and Arabic. It was pre-trained in a corpus (Gigaword, Oscar and Wikipedia) with ~10B tokens (Lan et al., 2020).
- **Arabic BERT:** was trained on about 8.2B words of MSA and dialectical Arabic too. (Safaya et al., 2020).

[1] https://github.com/qcri/QARiB

- **mBERT** (BERT multilingual base model (cased)): pretrained model supports 104 languages including Arabic was pre-trained on the entire Wikipedia for each language. (Devlin et al., 2018).

Our architecture as shown in Figure 1 is mainly based on fine-tuning the BERT- based models mentioned above. In our initial experiment MARBERT outperforms the other BERT-based models followed by QARiB. Thus, we decided to improve the performance of these two best models by adopting data augmentation techniques (described below) to solve the imbalanced data issue. In our experiments, all of the BERT- based models were fine-tuned with the same settings. The training set was splitted into 80% for training our models and 20% for validation. Where each model was trained for 5 epochs with a learning rate of 2e-06, maximum sequence length equals the maximum length seen in the training set and a batch size of 32. Google Colab free GPU and Huggingface pytorch versions of the previous mentioned models were used.

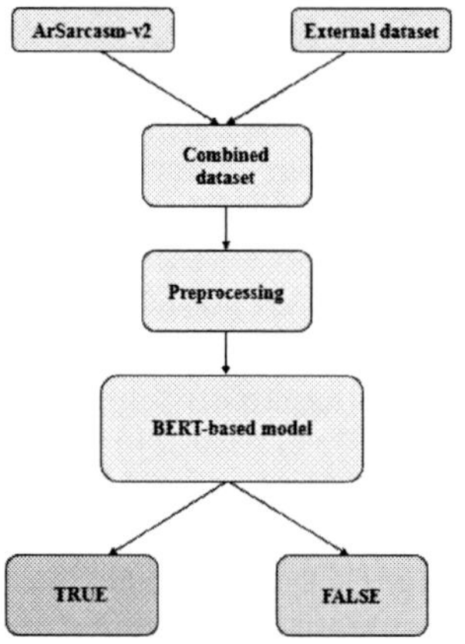

Figure 1: BERT- based model with data augmentation for sarcasm detection.

3.3 Data Augmentation

It is indicated that the sarcastic utterance usually has a negative implicit sentiment (Abu Farha at el., 2020). Moreover, from the provided dataset we found that 1939 (about 89%) of the tweets labeled as sarcastic and negative at the same time. Consequently, we hypothesis that every negative tweet can be sarcastic too. To investigate our hypothesis we used ASAD sentiment dataset (Alharbi at el., 2020) annotated with three sentiment labels (positive, negative and neutral). We could successfully retrieve 29924 tweets using the public tweet ids shared by the authors.

For sarcasm detection shared task, we replaced the labels annotated as “negative” with the label “TRUE” and replaced “positive” labels with “FALSE”. This produced an extra 4930 "FALSE" tweets and 4739 "TRUE" added to the original dataset which made the total number of the training set 22,217 tweets.

For the sentiment analysis task, we used the same dataset (which is basically annotated for sentiment) to provide the original training dataset with more positive and negative examples. A dataset of 4930 positive and 4739 negative examples were combined with the original training dataset and then tested on the best performing BERT-based model achieved by training them on the original training set.

4 Results and Discussion

In this section, we present and analyse the results of our experiments for subtask 1 and 2.

4.1 Results

The evaluation metrics used to test our system are F-score of the sarcastic class for subtask1 and macro-average F-score of the positive and negative classes (F-PN) for subtask 2. Both metrics were specified by the competition organizers.

4.1.1 Subtask 1:

Table 2 shows the results on the validation set in addition to the time the models took to train. MARBERT outperforms the other models with 0.647 F1-score on sarcastic class followed by QARIB with 0.597 F1-score. While mBERT gives the lowest F1- score of 0.411. The results of using MARBERT and QARiB with data augmentation are shown in Table 3. Data augmentation improves results by about 15% for both MARBERT and QARiB. This shows the effectiveness of our hypothesis to augment the dataset.

Model	F1-sarcastic	Training time (min: sec)
MARBERT	**0.65**	06:01
ArBERT	0.57	10:48
QARIB	0.60	10:25
AraBERTv02	0.56	10:07
GigaBERT	0.51	11:18
Arabic BERT	0.53	10:40
mBERT	0.41	06:30

Table 2: Results on original dataset for subtask 1.

Model	F1- sarcastic (valid set)	Training time (min: sec)
MARBERT	**0.80**	18:27
QARIB	0.75	18:00

Table 3: Results with data augmentation on subtask 1.

4.1.2 Subtask 2:

Similarly, the results of subtask 2 are shown in Table 4, QARiB achieved slightly higher F-PN score than MARBERT however, it has higher overfitting than MARBERT. Thus, we decided to try MARBERT with data augmentation. Expanding dataset size improves the performance of MARBERT by 15% as shown in Table 5 which also shows the effectiveness of our data augmentation approach.

Model	F-PN	Training time (min: sec)
MARBERT	0.71	05:59
QARIB	0.73	09:58

Table 4: Results on original dataset for subtask 2.

Model	F-PN (valid set)	Training time (min: sec)
MARBERT	**0.86**	19:28

Table 5: Results with data augmentation on subtask 2.

4.2 Official Results:

Based on the results above for both tasks we submitted the results of MARBERT on the test set. Table 6 presents the results of the MARBERT on the test set as reported by the competition organizers, compared to the results on the validation set. Obviously, there is a significant decrease in the model performance on the test set for both tasks, this is likely because of the overfitting issue.

Subtask 1		Subtask 2	
F1-sarcastic (valid set)	F1-sarcastic (test set)	F-PN (valid set)	F-PN (test set)
0.80	0.52	0.86	0.71

Table 6: Results of submitted model (MARBERT) for both tasks.

4.3 Error Analysis:

For further analysis for our proposed model results, extra error analysis is conducted to check where the model failed to correctly classify the tweets and try to find the reasons behind this mis-classifitcion. We randomly check a sample of 50 mis-classified examples. Table 7 lists some mis-classified tweets by our best performing model on sarcasm detection task. We found that there are several reasons for classifying sarcastic tweets as not sarcastic and vice versa. We summarise these reasons as follows:

- **Human annotation** is not 100% correct because annotators' cultures and backgrounds diversity might not be considered in the annotation process. For example, we believe that tweets 2 and 5 should be annotated as FALSE/ not sarcastic and TRUE respectively.
- **The absence of context:** in some tweets the context is missed and it was not possible for our model to understand the context and predict the label correctly. In examples 4 and 6 "Justin Bieber" is mentioned and it is expected that there is some special event happened, however, it is not clear using only one tweet. Thus, our model failed to classify both examples correctly. In addition, some tweets have media content and URLs which definitely clarify the context more which is not considered in this dataset.

	Tweet	True label	Predicted label
1	" بريطانيا السعودية واخد بالك 😁😁😁أنت"	TRUE	FALSE
2	"#شبكة_أخبار_المعارك أطفال اصيبوا نتيجة الغارات الروسية على مدينة #حلب صباح اليوم حسبنا الله ونعم والوكيل https://t.co/JHhjktp7qu"	TRUE	FALSE
3	" اجتماع لوزراء الخارجيه ف الجامعة العربيه اللي مقرها القاهرة. كل دول مش جايين لمصر دول جايين لجامعة الدول العربية. بسيطة☺"	TRUE	FALSE
4	" الصوره متلاعبين فيها دامجين ملامح زين مالك و جستن بيبر"	TRUE	FALSE
5	" يعني على اساس لو ما حلف الناتو والسعودية وتركيا وقطر كنتوا اساسن حسنتوا تسيطروا على مخفر"	FALSE	TRUE
6	" جستن بيبر فرع اليمن"	FALSE	TRUE
7	"حلقة فيها لفتة للشهيد "جبران تويني" ليك مين بين ضيوفها !! مسخرة !"	FALSE	TRUE
8	"االقسم بالله قمة المسخره ماهم عرفين يخترعو عذر لكن الرجال حيردو عليهم في الملعب"	FALSE	TRUE

Table 7: Examples of mis-clasffied tweets for sarcasm class.

- **Usage of sarcastic keywords:** tweets 7 and 8 use the keywords "مسخرة" which means "sarcasm", but the tweet itself is not sarcastic. It is likely our system picked up the sarcastic word but failed to take into account the context in which the word was used.
- **Emojis are not processed**: as we left the emojis in tweets without any kind of preprocessing, we noticed that some emojis impact the classification process. For instance, in examples 1 and 3 it is probably that the emojis (😁 and 🙂) give positive indication for our model that the tweets are not sarcastic, thus our model failed to classify them as sarcastic.

	Tweet	True label	Predicted label
1	"بيونسيه في أناقة مكياجها العيون – مجلة رنود https://t.co/UbnwcotH5v"	POS	NEU
2	"غوتشي 💞 https://t.co/vR5sY36zdA"	POS	NEU
3	"تهنئة لكل طالب وطالبة قضوا ما يزيد عن 150 يوماً معتصمين وواجهوا كل انواع التنكيل #جامعة_النيل"	POS	NEG
4	"وغاب عني وفراقه حبيبي شيء تآني ..عذاب مش بآلكلام احكيه 💔#اليسا https://t.co/LNjehLMxsQ "	POS	NEG
5	"# قروس يقولكم هاتوا ميسي وسواريز ونيمار 😎بيجلدهم مثل ماجلد الهلال في ثلاث ايام رايح جاي 😎 #الاهلي_برشلونه https://t.co…"	NEG	POS
6	" انشالله ما الاقي نفسي بتيك 😂😂 توك بعد جم يوم"	NEG	POS

Table 8: Examples of mis-clasffied tweets for sentiment class.

Similarly, we examined a random sample of mis-classified tweets for subtask 2 and investigated them as shown in Table 8. We found some reasons similar to the previous findings for sarcasm detection task. We argue that there are some errors in the annotations process such as examples number 1 and 2 should be NEU (neutral) instead of positive. Also, the usage of negative terms in positive context impacts the model performance. Negative terms such as "تنكيل" in example 3 and "عذاب" in example 4 were recognized by our system but without any further understanding of the context where they were mentioned. Finally, positive emojis such as (😎 and 😂) in examples 5 and 6 respectively are likely to skew the polarity of the sentence and reverse its detected sentiment.

5 Conclusion

In this paper we experimented with seven BERT-Based models and we augmented the shared task data set to identify the sentiment of a tweet or detect if a tweet is sarcasm. We achieved promising results for sarcasm detection and sentiment identification by MARBERT model with data augmentation. Our error analysis indicates certain types of errors in the dataset and in the annotation that can be addressed in the future.

Last but not least, if we had more time to work on this shared task, we will build a lexicon for sarcasm, try other approaches for data augmentation and also revise the annotation in the dataset, since we found several tweets were mis-annotated.

References

Abbes, I., Zaghouani, W., El-Hardlo, O. & Ashour, 2020. DAICT: A Dialectal Arabic Irony Corpus Extracted from Twitter. LREC 2020.

Abdul-Mageed, M., Elmadany, A. and Nagoudi, E.M.B., 2020. ARBERT & MARBERT: Deep Bidirectional Transformers for Arabic. arXiv preprint arXiv:2101.01785.

Abu Farha, I. and Magdy, W., 2020. From Arabic Sentiment Analysis to Sarcasm Detection: The ArSarcasm Dataset. OSACT4 - LREC 2020.

Abu Farha, I., Zaghouani, W. and Magdy, W., 2021. Overview of the WANLP 2021 Shared Task on Sarcasm and Sentiment Detection in Arabic. *Proceedings of the Sixth Arabic Natural Language Processing Workshop.*

Alharbi, B., Alamro, H., Alshehri, M., Khayyat, Z., Kalkatawi, M., Jaber, I.I. and Zhang, X., 2020. ASAD: A Twitter-based Benchmark Arabic Sentiment Analysis Dataset. arXiv preprint arXiv:2011.00578.

Antoun, W., Baly, F., and Hajj, H., 2020. AraBERT: Transformer-based Model for Arabic Language Understanding. *LREC 2020 Workshop Language Resources and Evaluation Conference.*

Devlin, J., Chang, M.W., Lee, K. and Toutanova, K., 2018. Bert: Pre-training of deep bidirectional transformers for language understanding. arXiv preprint arXiv:1810.04805.

Ghanem, B., Karoui, J., Benamara, F., Rosso, P. and Moriceau, V., 2020, April. Irony detection in a multilingual context. In *European Conference on Information Retrieval* (pp. 141-149). Springer, Cham.

Ghosh, D., Fabbri, A.R. and Muresan, S., 2018. Sarcasm analysis using conversation context. *Computational Linguistics*, *44*(4), pp.755-792.

Ghosh, D., Vajpayee, A. and Muresan, S., 2020. A report on the 2020 sarcasm detection shared task. *arXiv preprint arXiv:2005.05814*.

Joshi, A., Bhattacharyya, P., & Carman, M. J. (2017). Automatic sarcasm detection: A survey. ACM Computing Surveys (CSUR), 50(5), 73. American Psychological Association. 1983. *Publications Manual.* American Psychological Association, Washington, DC.

Karoui, J., Zitoune, F.B. and Moriceau, V., 2017. Soukhria: Towards an irony detection system for arabic in social media. *Procedia Computer Science*, *117*, pp.161-168.

Lan, W., Chen, Y., Xu, W. and Ritter, A., 2020, November. An Empirical Study of Pre-trained Transformers for Arabic Information Extraction. In *Proceedings of the 2020 Conference on Empirical Methods in Natural Language Processing (EMNLP)* (pp. 4727-4734).

Safaya, A., Abdullatif, M. and Yuret, D., 2020, December. Kuisail at semeval-2020 task 12: Bert-cnn for offensive speech identification in social media. *In Proceedings of the Fourteenth Workshop on Semantic Evaluation (pp. 2054-2059).*

Multi-task Learning Using a Combination of Contextualised and Static Word Embeddings for Arabic Sarcasm Detection and Sentiment Analysis

Abdullah I. Alharbi
School of Computer Science
University of Birmingham, UK
King Abdulaziz University, KSA
aia784@cs.bham.ac.uk

Mark Lee
School of Computer Science
University of Birmingham, UK
m.g.lee@cs.bham.ac.uk

Abstract

Sarcasm detection and sentiment analysis are important tasks in Natural Language Understanding. Sarcasm is a type of expression where the sentiment polarity is flipped by an interfering factor. In this study, we exploited this relationship to enhance both tasks by proposing a multi-task learning approach using a combination of static and contextualised embeddings. Our proposed system achieved the best result in the sarcasm detection subtask (Abu Farha et al., 2021).

1 Introduction

Social media platforms, such as Twitter, provide the public with an opportunity to share their thoughts and feelings with others through short posts of text. This has created a rich area of research to examine for linguistic expressions used on social media and explore expressions of emotion (sarcasm, humour, offense, etc.). 'Sarcasm' is defined as a figurative type of language where the expression is meant to communicate the opposite of its literal meaning. Within SA, detecting sarcasm is vital as sarcasm typically implies a negative feeling although the positive language is used. This conflict between what is said and what is meant creates a complicated challenge for SA tasks (Bouazizi and Otsuki Ohtsuki, 2016).

Compared to English, only a few studies have been made on Arabic sarcasm detection. Among the studies completed in this area are research by Karoui et al. (2017) and a shared task study by Ghanem et al. (2019). Recently, efforts have been made by Abu Farha and Magdy (2020) and Abbes et al. (2020) to create standard datasets to support sarcasm detection. In the WANLP-2021 Workshop, a shared task ('Sarcasm and Sentiment Detection in Arabic') (Abu Farha et al., 2021) was organised to contribute to the development of this area. Two sub-tasks are included in the shared task. The first will be to identify whether a tweet is sarcastic or not, and the second will be to determine if the tweet is expressing a neutral, positive or negative feeling.

Some substantial difficulties are presented by the shared task. Specifically, the targeted classes are distributed in an unbalanced way and the tweets used are in various dialects and even sub-dialects. Arabic dialects can be significantly different and they lack the established language rules found in Modern Standard Arabic (MSA). To deal with these difficulties, we propose a combined approach that uses three models. By using this combination, we believe we will be able to benefit from the strengths of each model and overcome their weaknesses.

The remainder of this paper is organised as follows. Section 2 comprises an overview of the methodology for our proposed system. Section 3 describes the dataset for the shared task. Section 4 provides experimental results, including the experimental set-up though which the proposed system was tested and a discussion of the outcomes. Finally, Section 5 concludes the paper with suggestions for future research.

2 Method

As described above, our proposed methodology consists of three models. These are the Static Word Embeddings (SWE) , Contextualized Embeddings (MARBERT) and Multi-Task Learning (MTL) models. The following three subsections explain each of these and how our proposed system incorporates them.

2.1 Pre-processing

We adopted the pre-processing techniques that have been undertaken and described by several researchers (Abu Farha and Magdy, 2019; Duwairi and El-Orfali, 2014). First, any unknown symbols

Proceedings of the Sixth Arabic Natural Language Processing Workshop, pages 318–322
Kyiv, Ukraine (Virtual), April 19, 2021.

or non-Arabic characters were removed (e.g. punctuation marks, diacritics, etc.). However, emojis were kept as we believe that they are important for sarcasm and sentiment classification tasks. Several letters that appeared in different forms in the original tweets were normalised. Thereafter, they were rendered into a single form. For instance, the 'hamza' on characters {أ,إ} was replaced with the {ا}, and the 't marbouta' {ة} was replaced with {ه}.

2.2 Static Word Embeddings (SWE)

One primary approach recently applied to the tasks of NLP is word embedding (Zhang et al., 2014; Devlin et al., 2014; Bordes et al., 2014; Lin et al., 2015). Word embedding involves the representation of text as dense vectors and captures semantic similarities between words by positioning them closely together within vectors. Each word is encoded in a real-valued vector, which features hundreds of dimensions. In our work, we used two different level of word embeddings, word-level and character-level embeddings.

Word-level Embeddings: We used a pre-trained word embedding model for Arabic: Ara2Vec (Soliman et al., 2017). The Ara2Vec word embeddings is a well-known open-source tool made up of six Arabic models. Data was obtained from Wikipedia, Twitter and Common Crawl (webpage crawl data) to train Ara2Vec. Although it a significant number of words were used to train Ara2Vec, it is not possible for such a word-level model to recognise every word used in real life. This results in the out-of-vocabulary (OOV) problem, where such resources cannot identify rare words. This is a major shortcoming of word-level embedding models.

Character-level Embeddings: The large number of Arabic dialects spoken in the Arab world can produce worse OOV problems compared to other languages. As a result, resources need to have a better understanding of Arabic dialects to be useful for sarcasm detection and SA tasks. We have found that word-level embeddings offer more value when it comes to semantic similarities, but character-level embeddings are better able to encode word morphology variants and position them more closely in the vector spaces. Thus, we used a pre-trained three-gram character representation model (CE) proposed by Alharbi and Lee (2020), which obtained competitive results in Arabic affect tasks. CE has been generated by training FastText (Bojanowski et al., 2017) on a large dataset of 10 million tweets. This corpus includes various affect words (sentiments and emotions, with different level of intensity) in different Arabic dialects. Table 1 shows a summary of important information about each of these models.

As a baseline, we employed the Convolutional Neural Network (CNN) proposed by Kim (2014). This deep learning architecture separately used one of the aforementioned static word embeddings (AraVec or CE) for initialising the embedding layer weights. These weights were then updated during the training process so they would be more appropriate for the task. This was followed by the application of different filters and kernels in order to generate a collection of features that were max pooled. Finally, these features were passed to the fully connected softmax layer for the classification task. In addition to the CNN network, we also used two different deep learning architectures: Long Short Term Memory (LSTM) network and combining CNN with LSTM network, following the proposed method by Wang et al. (2016). These algorithms were integrated with other models, which are detailed in the following subsections.

Model	level	Domain	Size
Ara2Vec	word	General	77M tweets
CE	character	Emotion	10M tweets

Table 1: The static word embeddings utilised for our systems.

2.3 Contextualized Embeddings Model (MARBERT):

Given the importance of context to determining whether an expression is intended to be sarcastic or not, we decided to use contextualised language models to help us with the shared task. One of these models is the Bidirectional Encoder Representation from Transformer (BERT) model, created by the Google research team, which has had great success with a range of NLP tasks (Devlin et al., 2019). As the dataset of this shared task contains different Arabic dialects, we use a model designed especially for tasks in Arabic dialects, the MARBERT model (Abdul-Mageed et al., 2020). MARBERT has been pre-trained on a significant dataset that includes 6B tweets, which achieves state-of-the-art results in

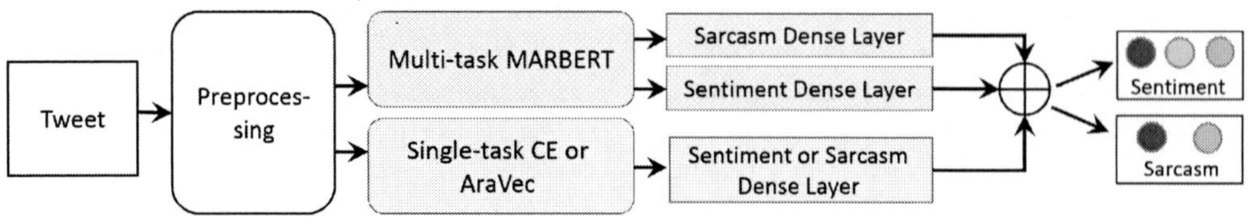

Figure 1: The proposed system architecture.

different Arabic-language NLP tasks. This model uses 12 attention headers, 12 encoder blocks and 768 hidden dimensions. It can handle sequences up to a maximum of 512 tokens, which, when entered into the model, generate a representation of the sequence. The first sequence token is the [CLS] , which contains targeted classification embedding.

We used MARBERT for the single task as a whole following the same implementation as that provided by the authors to target each subtask alone. In addition, we use the sentence embeddings of MARBERT in multi-task learning, as explained below.

2.4 Multi-task Learning (MTL) Model:

Multitask learning is an approach to inductive transfer that enhances generalisation by using the domain knowledge found in the training signals of similar tasks as an inductive bias. The intuition behind MTL is that a useful feature for one task will be useful and thus predictive for other, similar tasks (Caruana, 1997). At present, most research focuses on either detecting sarcasm or classifying sentiments. There has been little research into the idea that these two elements influence each other (Majumder et al., 2019; Zhang and Abdul-Mageed, 2019). We exploit this relationship to enhance both tasks (sarcasm detection and sentiment classification).

We propose a system that integrates an MTL approach with a combination of the aforementioned models (SWE and MARBERT). Figure 1 illustrates the architecture of the proposed method. To combine static and contextualised word embeddings, we followed Alghanmi et al. (2020) by simply concatenating representations obtained from MARBERT and SWE. However, our system enhances this combination of representations by additionally exploiting MTL in both tasks. Furthermore, in order to overcome issues with OOV, we use n-gram character word embeddings instead of just word-level embeddings.

To this end, we extracted the contextualised vectors (average of 12 hidden layers) after fine-tuning the model on the train dataset for each task. The dimension of these vectors after concatenation was 1536 (768 dimensions for each task). For SWE, we obtained the tweet vectors by averaging the real-value word vectors derived from the pre-trained models as a single task. our assumption in only using a single task for SWE instead of MTL is that to provide the target task with more weight. These static vectors were then used as input features into a deep learning architecture, as explained above. At this step, these two types of tweet representations (multi-task MARBERT and single-task SWE) were concatenated. To avoid overfitting, a dropout layer with a 0.5 drop rate was applied. Finally, a dense layer of number-of-classes output was set in place through the exploitation of softmax as an activation function to produce the final output.

3 Data Description

The shared task's organisers released the train and test datasets (ArSarcasm-v2) for both tasks, namely, subtask 1 - sarcasm detection and subtask 2 - sentiment analysis (Abu Farha et al., 2021). The train dataset contained 12,548 tweets while the test dataset consisted of 3,000 tweets. For subtask 1, the tweets were manually annotated using the term 'True' for sarcastic tweets and 'False' for tweets that were not sarcastic. For subtask 2, the tweets were designated as 'NEG' for negative class, 'NEU' for Neutral and 'POS' for positive. An overview of the dataset is provided in Tables 2 and 3.

Dataset	True	False	Total
Training	2168	10380	12,548
Test	821	2179	3000

Table 2: Distribution of classes in Subtask 1.

Dataset	NEG	NEU	POS	Total
Training	4621	5747	2180	12,548
Test	1677	748	575	3000

Table 3: Distribution of classes in Subtask 2.

4 Experiment Results

4.1 Results and Evaluation

Since no labelled development or test dataset was available, we decided to use five-fold cross-validation on the training dataset for evaluation purposes. However, our best model was trained on all training datasets for the final submission for both tasks. The official evaluation metric for subtask 1 was the F-score of the sarcastic class (F1-sarcastic) and the macro average of the F-score of the positive and negative classes (F-PN) for subtask 2.

Table 4 presents the models' performance using the average of cross-validation for both subtasks. For the sarcasm detection task, the best result (0.632) was obtained by the proposed system, which integrates MTL with MARBERT and then combines with SWE in the CNN-LSTM network architecture. From this result, it is evident that the MTL model is important for the sarcasm detection task. In addition, the character-level embeddings (CE) achieve better results compared with the word-level embeddings (AraVec) for the baseline model (CNN). Therefore, we decided to use CE as the static word embeddings for the MTL model. We submitted the predication classes based on the MTL-CNN-LSTM system, which achieved state-of-the-art compared with the other systems proposed by other participants.

For the SA subtask, Table 4 shows the results for all models, where the proposed system obtained the best result on the cross-validation metric. However, using MARBERT as a single-task obtained a very close result based on the five-fold cross-validation evaluation. The MTL-CNN-LSTM system has also been submitted for the SA subtask, which ranked 11th out of 27 participants. We believe this result should be studied as a future work by investigating different setup settings and, more importantly, to analyse errors on the test dataset.

4.2 Submission Results

For both aforementioned subtasks, we (BhamNLP team) submitted the predication classes based on the MTL-CNN-LSTM model. For the sarcasm detection subtask (1), the proposed model achieved state-of-the-art compared with the other systems proposed by other participants. For the SA subtask (2), the model achieved a macro F1-PN of 0.701 on the test set. Table 5 presents the official results achieved by our proposed model (MTL-CNN-LSTM) on the test set for Subtasks 1 and 2.

Model	Sarcasm (F1-sarcastic)	Sentiment (F-PN)
CNN-AraVec	0.486	0.534
CNN-CE	0.498	0.604
MARBERT	0.609	0.702
MTL-CNN	0.603	0.666
MTL-LSTM	0.619	0.698
MTL-CNN-LSTM	**0.632**	**0.713**

Table 4: Performance of the different models using the mean of five-fold Cross-Validation for Subtasks 1 and 2.

Task	Main Metric	Result	Rank
Sarcasm	F1-sarcastic	0.623	1st
Sentiment	F-PN	0.701	11th

Table 5: Main metric results obtained by the proposed model on the test set for both subtasks 1 and 2.

5 Conclusions

In this work, we described an MTL approach using a combination of static and contextualised word embeddings. The proposed system achieved the best result in sarcasm detection subtask and ranked 11th in SA task. In future studies, we will investigate the impact of sarcasm on SA task to enhance the performance of our proposed system for SA task. Additionally, advanced pre-possessing techniques should be applied as we observed some multi-words need to be segmented and treated. Also, instead of removing all punctuation symbols, some of these marks (e.g. question marks and exclamation marks) may be useful especially for the sarcasm detection task.

References

Ines Abbes, Wajdi Zaghouani, Omaima El-Hardlo, and Faten Ashour. 2020. DAICT: A dialectal Arabic irony corpus extracted from Twitter. In *Proceedings of the 12th Language Resources and Evaluation Conference*, pages 6265–6271, Marseille, France. European Language Resources Association.

Muhammad Abdul-Mageed, AbdelRahim Elmadany, and El Moatez Billah Nagoudi. 2020. ARBERT & MARBERT: Deep bidirectional transformers for Arabic.

Ibrahim Abu Farha and Walid Magdy. 2019. Mazajak: An online Arabic sentiment analyser. In *Proceedings of the Fourth Arabic Natural Language Processing Workshop*, pages 192–198, Florence, Italy. Association for Computational Linguistics.

Ibrahim Abu Farha and Walid Magdy. 2020. From Arabic sentiment analysis to sarcasm detection: The ArSarcasm dataset. In *Proceedings of the 4th Workshop on Open-Source Arabic Corpora and Processing Tools, with a Shared Task on Offensive Language Detection*, pages 32–39, Marseille, France. European Language Resource Association.

Ibrahim Abu Farha, Wajdi Zaghouani, and Walid Magdy. 2021. Overview of the WANLP 2021 shared task on sarcasm and sentiment detection in Arabic. In *Proceedings of the Sixth Arabic Natural Language Processing Workshop*.

Israa Alghanmi, Luis Espinosa Anke, and Steven Schockaert. 2020. Combining BERT with static word embeddings for categorizing social media. In *Proceedings of the Sixth Workshop on Noisy User-generated Text (W-NUT 2020)*, pages 28–33, Online. Association for Computational Linguistics.

Abdullah I. Alharbi and Mark Lee. 2020. Combining character and word embeddings for affect in Arabic informal social media microblogs. In *Natural Language Processing and Information Systems*, pages 213–224, Cham. Springer International Publishing.

Piotr Bojanowski, Edouard Grave, Armand Joulin, and Tomas Mikolov. 2017. Enriching word vectors with subword information. *Transactions of the Association for Computational Linguistics*, 5:135–146.

Antoine Bordes, Sumit Chopra, and Jason Weston. 2014. Question Answering with Subgraph Embeddings. In *Proceedings of the 2014 Conference on Empirical Methods in Natural Language Processing (EMNLP)*, pages 615–620.

M. Bouazizi and T. Otsuki Ohtsuki. 2016. A pattern-based approach for sarcasm detection on twitter. *IEEE Access*, 4:5477–5488.

Rich Caruana. 1997. Multitask Learning. *Machine Learning*.

Jacob Devlin, Ming-Wei Chang, Kenton Lee, and Kristina Toutanova. 2019. BERT: pre-training of deep bidirectional transformers for language understanding. In *Proceedings of the 2019 Conference of the North American Chapter of the Association for Computational Linguistics: Human Language Technologies, Volume 1 (Long and Short Papers)*, pages 4171–4186, Minneapolis. Association for Computational Linguistics.

Jacob Devlin, Rabih Zbib, Zhongqiang Huang, Thomas Lamar, Richard Schwartz, and John Makhoul. 2014. Fast and robust neural network joint models for statistical machine translation. In *Proceedings of the 52nd Annual Meeting of the Association for Computational Linguistics (Volume 1: Long Papers)*, volume 1, pages 1370–1380.

Rehab Duwairi and Mahmoud El-Orfali. 2014. A study of the effects of preprocessing strategies on sentiment analysis for Arabic text. *Journal of Information Science*, 40(4):501–513.

Bilal Ghanem, Jihen Karoui, F. Benamara, Véronique Moriceau, and P. Rosso. 2019. Idat at fire2019: Overview of the track on irony detection in Arabic tweets. *Proceedings of the 11th Forum for Information Retrieval Evaluation*.

Jihen Karoui, Farah Banamara Zitoune, and Véronique Moriceau. 2017. SOUKHRIA: Towards an irony detection system for Arabic in social media. *Procedia Computer Science*, 117:161–168. Arabic Computational Linguistics.

Yoon Kim. 2014. Convolutional neural networks for sentence classification. In *Proceedings of the 2014 Conference on Empirical Methods in Natural Language Processing (EMNLP)*, pages 1746–1751, Doha, Qatar. Association for Computational Linguistics.

Chu-Cheng Lin, Waleed Ammar, Chris Dyer, and Lori Levin. 2015. Unsupervised POS Induction with Word Embeddings. In *Proceedings of the 2015 Conference of the North American Chapter of the Association for Computational Linguistics: Human Language Technologies*, pages 1311–1316.

N. Majumder, S. Poria, H. Peng, N. Chhaya, E. Cambria, and A. Gelbukh. 2019. Sentiment and sarcasm classification with multitask learning. *IEEE Intelligent Systems*, 34(3):38–43.

Abu Bakr Soliman, Kareem Eissa, and Samhaa R El-Beltagy. 2017. AraVec: A set of Arabic word embedding models for use in Arabic NLP. *Procedia Computer Science*, 117:256–265.

Xingyou Wang, Weijie Jiang, and Zhiyong Luo. 2016. Combination of convolutional and recurrent neural network for sentiment analysis of short texts. In *Proceedings of COLING 2016, the 26th International Conference on Computational Linguistics: Technical Papers*, pages 2428–2437, Osaka, Japan. The COLING 2016 Organizing Committee.

Chiyu Zhang and Muhammad Abdul-Mageed. 2019. Multi-task bidirectional transformer representations for irony detection.

Jiajun Zhang, Shujie Liu, Mu Li, Ming Zhou, and Chengqing Zong. 2014. Bilingually-constrained phrase embeddings for machine translation. In *Proceedings of the 52nd Annual Meeting of the Association for Computational Linguistics (Volume 1: Long Papers)*, volume 1, pages 111–121.

ArSarcasm Shared Task: An Ensemble BERT Model for Sarcasm Detection in Arabic Tweets

Laila Bashmal
King Saud University
Riyadh, Saudi Arabia
lailabashmal@outlook.com

Daliyah H. Alzeer
Taif University
Taif, Saudi Arabia
dr.dalya.h@gmail.com

Abstract

Detecting Sarcasm has never been easy for machines to process. In this work, we present our submission of the sub-task1 of the shared task on the sarcasm and sentiment detection in Arabic organized by the 6th Workshop for Arabic Natural Language Processing (Abu Farha et al., 2021). In this work, we explored different approaches based on BERT models. First, we fine-tuned the AraBERTv02 model for the sarcasm detection task. Then, we used the Sentence-BERT model trained with contrastive learning to extract representative tweet embeddings. Finally, inspired by how the human brain comprehends the surface and the implicit meanings of sarcastic tweets, we combined the sentence embedding with the fine-tuned AraBERTv02 to further boost the performance of the model. Through the ensemble of the two models, our team ranked 5th out of 27 teams on the shared task of sarcasm detection in Arabic, with an F1-score of %59.89 on the official test data. The obtained result is %2.36 lower than the 1st place which confirms the capabilities of the employed combined model in detecting sarcasm.

1 Introduction

What is sarcasm? According to Cambridge Dictionary, it is "the use of remarks that clearly mean the opposite of what they say, made in order to hurt someone's feelings or to criticize something in a humorous way" (Cambridge, 2021). Former research in psychology and neurology reports that the mind requires the use of two distinct regions to process sarcasm as it implies a contradicting meaning to the literal one (Shamay-Tsoory, 2005). According to Capelli and her colleagues, the ability to analyze sarcasm develops from childhood. In their early stages, children are not able to perceive sarcasm by the text alone and it has to be accompanied by intonation for clearer understanding. Unlike adults who identify sarcasm effortlessly with intonation or from the text alone (Capelli et al., 1990). Megan Dress and her colleagues noticed that there are regional differences in the use of sarcasm when other demographic factors were controlled (Dress et al., 2008). Moreover, Yoritaka Akimoto and his colleague concluded in their paper that there are individual differences in the intended use of sarcasm that affects the processing and interpretation of verbal irony (Ivanko et al., 2004). From this perspective, we can understand the challenging aspect of processing the different meanings of sarcasm with machines.

Automatic sarcasm detection is the process of identifying if the text has a sarcastic meaning or not. This process is an essential step in the sentiment analysis task which requires a clear understanding of the intended meaning of the text. Over the years, researchers have proposed several methods to detect sarcastic features in texts. Applying several algorithms like gradient boosting (Ahuja et al., 2018), using linguistic features (González-Ibáñez et al., 2011), using incongruity phenomenon for creating a sarcasm detection system (Joshi et al., 2015), A2Text-Net deep learning model (Liu et al., 2019), and using a model based on embeddings from a language model (Ilić et al., 2018).

In Gonzalez's paper and Joshi's paper, they both utilized linguistic features to assess sarcasm detection in written texts. Furthermore, Liyuan Liu and Suzana Ili separately investigated two different deep learning methods for the sake of better sarcastic detection. Liu's and his colleagues' model used a hypothesis layer and a feature processing layer to test the hypothesis and to select the supported features before training a neural network for detection. Moving to Suzana Ili ́s paper, she and her colleagues found that the word-level representations model lacks the richness that embeddings from language models or ELMo have.

Proceedings of the Sixth Arabic Natural Language Processing Workshop, pages 323–328
Kyiv, Ukraine (Virtual), April 19, 2021.

Dialect	Non-Sarcastic	Sarcastic	Negative	Neutral	Positive	Total
Egyptian	1,745	930	1,376	793	506	2,675
Gulf	487	157	264	259	121	644
Levantine	486	138	285	197	142	624
Maghrebi	28	15	25	12	6	43
MSA	7,634	928	2,671	4,486	1405	8,562
Total	10,380	2,168	4,621	5,747	2,180	12,548

Table 1: ArSarcasm-v2 Training Dataset Statistics for Sarcasm and Sentiment over the Dialects (Abu Farha et al., 2021).

Accordingly, they used the ELMo model to investigate the sarcastic features in textual data.

Even more, Arabic sarcasm detection is lagging behind in the field of sarcastic detection in NLP. Some efforts have been done such as Jihen Karoui and her colleagues who worked to detect irony in Arabic tweets (Karoui et al., 2017).

Our goal in this task is to classify Arabic tweets into sarcastic or not sarcastic by taking into account the direct and the overall meaning of the tweet. To this end, we explored the use of the BERT model in three different ways. First, we performed a knowledge-transfer from AraBERTv02 to a sarcasm detection task. Secondly, we employed Sentence-BERT trained model with the contrastive loss for extracting representative sentence-level embedding for sarcasm. Finally, mimicking the way the human brain processes the surface and intended meaning of a sentence in two different regions, we processed the data into two different models and the outputs of the two models were then concatenated into a one-tuned ensemble model by stacking a classifier on top of them.

2 Dataset and Methodology

2.1 Dataset Description

The shared task of sarcasm and sentiment detection in Arabic is based on the ArSarcasm-v2 dataset (Abu Farha et al., 2021). Table 1 shows some statistics of the released training set. The dataset is provided with dialects and sentiment labels. In total, it consists of 12,548 tweets with 2168 sarcastic tweets and 10380 non-sarcastic ones. The test set, which contains 3000 tweets, was released without labels for evaluation purposes.

2.2 Preprocessing

2.2.1 Cleaning

Hashtags and mentions: For the hashtags and mentions, we tried to extract hand-crafted features and tested if they would have any relation between the number of hashtags and mentions and the sarcasm in the tweet text. However, we did not notice any significant relation. Accordingly, we removed them from tweets for smoother analysis.

English letters, digits, punctuations, and Arabic diacritics: Similarly, we tried to extract handcrafted features from the links, digits, and punctuations. Again, we did not notice any relevant connections between these features and the sarcasm in the tweet. Therefore, we removed the English letters and some punctuation. We also performed Arabic-letters normalization. This includes removing diacritics and normalizing different forms of Alef, Ya, and Ha each to a canonical form.

2.2.2 Emoji decoding

Unlike verbal sarcasm, written words do not have any intonations to help in detecting sarcasm (Kreuz and Caucci, 2007). Therefore, in textual contexts, emojis can help to provide us with emotional signals if these tweets have sarcastic features or not (Subramanian et al., 2019). Consequently, we decoded the emojis and their emotions by using the emojis' descriptions data (Emo). Since the emoji descriptions are in English, they were translated into Arabic using google translate API. We manually recheck the translated meaning to Arabic for more accuracy. For decoding, the emoji in each tweet is replaced with its equivalent textual description in Arabic.

2.3 Methodology

In this section, we provide details about the different BERT models we used in the experiments. These models are AraBERTv02, Sentence-BERT, and the Full-model that combines the two models.

2.3.1 AraBERTv02

Pre-trained bidirectional transformer-based models, known as BERT, represent the state-of-the-art

أنا راجع من الساحل وسأسعى للحضور بإذن الله ألف مبروك (not sarcasm)	بكم البرنامج السياحي من والى في فرنسا (not sarcasm)	similar
ويندوز 10 بيعمل تقريبا كل حاجه بمزاجه والموضوع مخيف (sarcasm)	أليس من المُضحك عندما يُحاضرك أحدهم عن الأخلاق والذوقيات وهو أكثر من يفتقر إليهما (sarcasm)	similar
ويندوز 10 بيعمل تقريبا كل حاجه بمزاجه والموضوع مخيف (sarcasm)	بكم البرنامج السياحي من والى في فرنسا (not sarcasm)	dissimilar

Figure 1: Dataset for Sentence-BERT Model

model in Natural Language Processing (NLP) and have proven to be successful on several NLP related tasks (Devlin et al., 2019).Unlike previous text representation models, BERT employs a self-attention mechanism method to capture long-range interactions among words in a text and enables the model to derive its contextual meanings. In order to employ this model in our task which has a relatively small dataset, we performed a transfer learning and fine-tuned a BERT model pre-trained on a very large corpus. We specifically used the AraBERTv02 base model (Antoun et al.). It is the second version of AraBERT that was pre-trained on 200 million Arabic sentences. The AraBERTv02 base model consists of 12 encoder layers with a hidden dimension of 768 and 12 attention heads. After performing a hyper-parameters search, we trained AraBERTv02 on a sarcasm detection task with the following hyper-parameters: the learning rate was set to 2e-05, the batch size is 16, the accumulation steps is 2, and fine-tuned the model with 2 iterations.

2.3.2 Sentence-BERT

Sentence-BERT is a siamese/triplet architecture that is based on BERT. It was mainly developed for information retrieval and paraphrasing tasks (Reimers and Gurevych, 2019). It accepts two (or more) sentences as inputs and projects each sentence to a vector space so that the semantically similar sentences are as close as possible to each other. One of the issues with word embeddings models is that they represent the semantic meaning of each word and lack the richness to represent the overall meaning of the piece of text. To overcome this obstacle, the sentence embeddings models solve the issue by showing the representation of the semantic meaning of an entire sentence. This representation is useful for applications where the implicit meaning of a sentence is different from the literal meaning of the sentence, especially in understanding the intended meaning of sarcastic sentences.

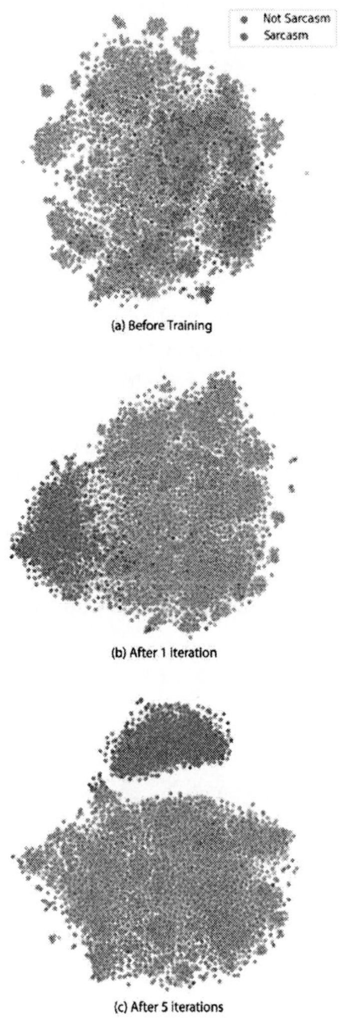

Figure 2: Sentence Embeddings Visualization via t-SNE: (a) Before Training the Sentence-Bert model;(b) After Training with 1 Iteration; (c) After Training with 5 Iterations.

Method	F1-score	Precision	Recall	Accuracy
BOW + LR classifier	45.88±2.07	39.78±1.68	55.28±3.10	78.02±1.50
TF-IDF + LR classifier	49.66±2.04	42.22±3.16	61.50±5.90	78.52±2.22
Sentence embedding + LR classifier	57.88±0.66	62.00±0.25	54.64±1.02	86.30±0.12
Fine-tuning BERT	61.06±0.99	64.40±1.14	58.20±2.49	86.78±0.23
Fine-tuning BERT and Sentence embedding	62.27±0.52	70.05±3.68	56.28±1.82	85.36±0.54

Table 2: Results on Validiation Set According to Different Methods.

For the implementation, we used the AraBERTv02 base model to adapt Sentence-BERT for sarcasm detection in the Arabic language (Antoun et al.). We fine-tuned the model to generate embeddings for the sarcasm detection task. For the sake of preparing the dataset for the siamese architecture, we rearranged the sentences in the dataset as pairs where similar sentences are given the label 1 and dissimilar sentences are given the label 0 as shown in the table (Figure 1).

We used a contrastive loss. Thus, if two tweets are expressing similar meanings, their embedding vectors are mapped to be closed to each other while maximizing the distance between the embedding of tweets with different meanings. Figure 2 shows how the sentence embeddings are mapped during the training phase. Finally, each tweet is represented by a fixed-size vector of its learned embedding.

2.3.3 Full-Model:

The architecture of the full model is shown in figure 3. The output of the fine-tuned BERT model is concatenated with the sentence embeddings obtained from the Sentence-BERT. This combined representation is then fed to an external classifier. The classifier consists of two linear layers: one with GELU activation and the second with a sigmoid activation to predict the sarcasm label. We fine-tuned the model using an SGD optimizer with a learning rate of 1e-04 for five iterations.

3 Experimental Results

The results of the five experiments of the method are shown in table 2 in the validation set. We split the dataset into two where %80 of the dataset is used for training and %20 is used for validation. In all experiments, we reported the results in terms of F1-score, recall, precision, and accuracy. F1-score is the official metric in this task, which combines the recall (TP/TP+FN) and the precision (TP/TP+FP) metrics. TP, FN, and FP refer respectively to the true positives, false negatives, and false positives. F1-score is given as 2 × (Precision × Recall)/(Precision + Recall) and it is more suitable than the accuracy for the binary classification task when the dataset is highly imbalanced.

3.1 Results of Baseline Methods

As a first attempt, we implemented a few baseline models, specifically the logistic regression(LR) classifier with TF-IDF and BOW word encodings. As shown in Table 2, BOW yields an F1-score of %45.88 compared to %49.66 to TF-IDF. These results indicate that the traditional word encodings methods are insufficient to model the complex meanings in sarcastic tweets.

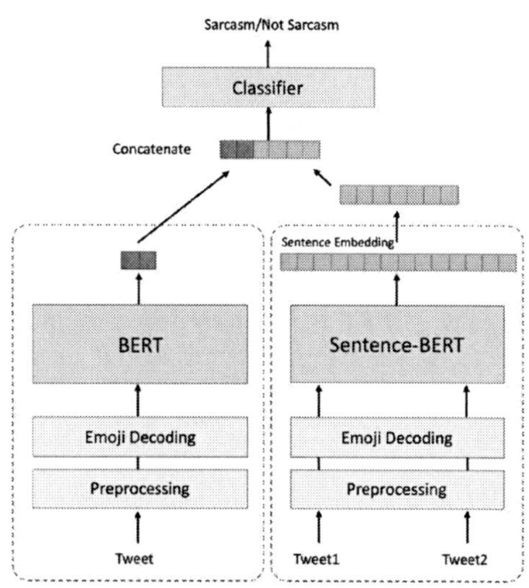

Figure 3: The Chart of the Full-Model that Combines the BERT Model and the Sentence-BERT Model. The Outputs of the Two Models are Concatenated and Fed into an External Classifier.

3.2 Results on the validation set

Next, we compared the results of the different BERT-based models on the validation set. As shown in Table 2, the results indicate that using BERT-based models can remarkably increase the

	F1-sarcastic	Accuracy	Macro-F1	Precision	Recall
Full-model	59.89	78.30	72.51	72.68	72.35

Table 3: Official Results Achieved by the Full-Model on the Test Set for the Sarcasm Detection task.

F1 score and the accuracy compared to traditional word encodings methods. Specifically, using sentence embeddings extracted from Sentence-BERT has improved the F1-score from %49.66 with TF-IDF to %57.88 using the same classifier. Moreover, fine-tuning AraBERTv02 with few iterations shows also a significant improvement with %61.06 F1-score. Finally, by simply combining the outputs of the fine-tuned AraBERTv02 and Sentence-BERT embeddings, the F1 score has increased to %62.27 and with a %1.42 decrease in the accuracy. This indicates that concatenating learned Sentence-BERT embeddings with BERT models has promising capabilities in detecting sarcasm.

3.3 Official Results on the Test set

Finally, we reported our submission results of the shared task on sarcasm detection in Arabic subtask-1 (Abu Farha et al., 2021). We submitted the full-model outputs as our primary submission, which achieved a %59.89 F1-sarcastic score (ranked 5th out of 27). The detailed results on the test set are shown in Table 3.

4 Conclusion

We presented our submission on the shared task on sarcasm detection and sentiment analysis in Arabic to tackle the problem of detecting sarcasm in Arabic. We explored different models based on BERT. We utilized a fine-tuning BERT and a Sentence-BERT to generate sentence embeddings that can be effective in detecting sarcasm. The final submission model combined the AraBERTv02 model and a representation obtained from a Sentence-BERT model to determine the sarcastic meaning of tweets. In the future, we will work on improving the performance of the model by exploring more sentence representation techniques.

References

Full Emoji List, v13.1, `https://unicode.org/emoji/charts/full-emoji-list.html`, note = Accessed: 2021-02-01.

Ibrahim Abu Farha, Wajdi Zaghouani, and Walid Magdy. 2021. Overview of the wanlp 2021 shared task on sarcasm and sentiment detection in arabic. In *Proceedings of the Sixth Arabic Natural Language Processing Workshop*.

Ravinder Ahuja, Shantanu Bansal, Shuvam Prakash, Karthik Venkataraman, and Alisha Banga. 2018. Comparative study of different sarcasm detection algorithms based on behavioral approach. *Procedia Computer Science*, 143:411–418. 8th International Conference on Advances in Computing Communications (ICACC-2018).

Wissam Antoun, Fady Baly, and Hazem Hajj. Arabert: Transformer-based model for arabic language understanding. In *LREC 2020 Workshop Language Resources and Evaluation Conference 11–16 May 2020*, page 9.

University Press Cambridge. 2021. *Cambridge Dictionary*. Cambridge University Press.

Carol A. Capelli, Noreen Nakagawa, and Cary M. Madden. 1990. How children understand sarcasm: The role of context and intonation. *Child Development*, 61(6):1824–1841.

Jacob Devlin, Ming-Wei Chang, Kenton Lee, and Kristina Toutanova. 2019. BERT: Pre-training of deep bidirectional transformers for language understanding. In *Proceedings of the 2019 Conference of the North American Chapter of the Association for Computational Linguistics: Human Language Technologies, Volume 1 (Long and Short Papers)*, pages 4171–4186, Minneapolis, Minnesota. Association for Computational Linguistics.

Megan L. Dress, Roger J. Kreuz, Kristen E. Link, and Gina M. Caucci. 2008. Regional variation in the use of sarcasm. *Journal of Language and Social Psychology*, 27(1):71–85.

Roberto González-Ibáñez, Smaranda Muresan, and Nina Wacholder. 2011. Identifying sarcasm in twitter: A closer look. In *Proceedings of the 49th Annual Meeting of the Association for Computational Linguistics: Human Language Technologies*, pages 581–586, Portland, Oregon, USA. Association for Computational Linguistics.

Suzana Ilić, Edison Marrese-Taylor, Jorge Balazs, and Yutaka Matsuo. 2018. Deep contextualized word representations for detecting sarcasm and irony. In *Proceedings of the 9th Workshop on Computational Approaches to Subjectivity, Sentiment and Social Media Analysis*, pages 2–7, Brussels, Belgium. Association for Computational Linguistics.

Stacey L. Ivanko, Penny M. Pexman, and Kara M. Olineck. 2004. How sarcastic are you?: Individual differences and verbal irony. *Journal of Language and Social Psychology*, 23(3):244–271.

Aditya Joshi, Vinita Sharma, and Pushpak Bhattacharyya. 2015. Harnessing context incongruity for sarcasm detection. In *Proceedings of the 53rd Annual Meeting of the Association for Computational Linguistics and the 7th International Joint Conference on Natural Language Processing (Volume 2: Short Papers)*, pages 757–762, Beijing, China. Association for Computational Linguistics.

Jihen Karoui, Farah Banamara Zitoune, and Véronique Moriceau. 2017. Soukhria: Towards an irony detection system for arabic in social media. *Procedia Computer Science*, 117:161–168. Arabic Computational Linguistics.

Roger J. Kreuz and Gina M. Caucci. 2007. Lexical influences on the perception of sarcasm. FigLanguages '07, page 1–4, USA. Association for Computational Linguistics.

L. Liu, J. L. Priestley, Y. Zhou, H. E. Ray, and M. Han. 2019. A2text-net: A novel deep neural network for sarcasm detection. In *2019 IEEE First International Conference on Cognitive Machine Intelligence (CogMI)*, pages 118–126.

Nils Reimers and Iryna Gurevych. 2019. Sentence-bert: Sentence embeddings using siamese bert-networks. In *Proceedings of the 2019 Conference on Empirical Methods in Natural Language Processing*. Association for Computational Linguistics.

Tomer R. Aharon-Peretz J. Shamay-Tsoory, S G. 2005. The neuroanatomical basis of understanding sarcasm and its relationship to social cognition. *Neuropsychology*, 19(3):288–300.

Jayashree Subramanian, Varun Sridharan, Kai Shu, and Huan Liu. 2019. Exploiting emojis for sarcasm detection. In *Social, Cultural, and Behavioral Modeling - 12th International Conference, SBP-BRiMS 2019, Proceedings*, pages 70–80. Springer Verlag.

Sarcasm and Sentiment Detection in Arabic: Investigating the Interest of Character-level Features

Dhaou Ghoul
STIH Lab, Sorbonne University, Paris
dhaou.ghoul@gmail.com

Gaël Lejeune
STIH Lab, Sorbonne University, Paris
gael.lejeune@paris-sorbonne.fr

Abstract

We present three methods developed for the Shared Task on Sarcasm and Sentiment Detection in Arabic. We present a baseline that uses character n-gram features. We also propose two more sophisticated methods: a recurrent neural network with a word level representation and an ensemble classifier relying on word and character-level features. We chose to present results from an ensemble classifier but it was not very successful as compared to the best systems : 22th/37 on sarcasm detection and 15th/22 on sentiment detection. It finally appeared that our baseline could have easily been tuned and achieve much better results.

1 Introduction

Arabic language is one of the most widely spoken language in the world, currently considered as the fifth language (Chung, 2008) with more than 330 million speakers. It is the official language in more than 22 countries and is therefore an important language to handle for NLP systems. Its written form is commonly referred as Literary Arabic and divided into two categories: Classical Arabic and Modern Standard Arabic (MSA). But Arabic has in fact many variants and research effort have been made on tasks like Arabic Dialects Identification(Abdul-Mageed et al., 2020). More fine-grained tasks have been tackled by the NLP community and this paper describes our participation to such a task : the Shared Task on Sarcasm and Sentiment Detection in Arabic(Abu Farha et al., 2021). This shared task focuses on analysing tweets and identifying the sentiment (negative, positive or neutral) and whether a tweet is sarcastic or not. More precisely, the task are defined as follows:

- **Subtask 1:** (Sarcasm Detection): Identifying whether a tweet is sarcastic or not, this is a binary classification task.
- **Subtask 2:** (Sentiment Analysis): Identifying the sentiment of a tweet and assigning one of three labels (Positive, Negative, Neutral), multiclass classification task.

The paper is organized as follows: Section 2, describes the dataset and Section 3 is devoted to the methods we developed. Section 4 details our results, future directions are given in Section 5.

2 Data

The dataset for both tasks is a combination of the ArSarcasm (Abu Farha and Magdy, 2020) and DAICT (Abbes et al., 2020), we used a 30% subset of the training data to get a dev set. Statistics on the resulting data are shown in Table 1.

Datasets	Train	Dev	Test
# lines	9,549	3,000	3,000
# words	144,158	45,047	51,478
# characters	1,822,547	570,592	552,871

Table 1: Size of the Train, Dev and Test sets

The distribution of labels (sarcasm and sentiment label) is rather imbalanced. In subtask-1, sarcastic tweets represent only 17% of the data (1666 sarcastic VS 7883 non-sarcastic). In subtask-2, positive tweets only represent 18% of the data and negative tweets represent no more than 37%. Hereafter we present some examples of labelled tweets.

Sarcastic : بيقولك أخر مره فاز فيها الزمالك علي الأهلي كانت أيام ما كان الحكم بيصفر بصباعه (They say that Zamalak's last victory against Al-Ahly happened when the referees had to use their fingers to whistle).

Positive : طلعنا من حلب الشرقية بسلام و الحمدلله (We came out of East Aleppo in peace, thank God)

Proceedings of the Sixth Arabic Natural Language Processing Workshop, pages 329–333
Kyiv, Ukraine (Virtual), April 19, 2021.

Negative: لبنان: ''سخرية'' من تعيين رجل وزيرا لشؤون المرأة. (Lebanon: "mocking" a male nominated as women's affairs minister)

Neutral: في حدا نازل على حلب في ورق ضروري لازم ابعته و شكرا. (Is there anyone going to Aleppo, I have important papers to send there. Thank you)

3 Methods developed for both tasks

We did not developed a specific method for each task, we rather tried to find features that could be useful for both tasks. We first present a simple baseline (Section 3.1) that shows the interest of character-level features. Afterwards we develop more sophisticated methods: a simple Deep Learning approach (Section 3.2) and an ensemble classifier taking advantage of both character-level and word-level features (Section 3.3).

3.1 Word-based or character-based models ?

The purpose of this method is to see how much simple baselines can be competitive for such tasks. In particular, it seemed important to see how much important is tokenization in NLP pipelines. We compared word-level representations and character-level representations with various classifiers (Multinomial Naive Bayes, Decision trees, Random Forest, Logistic regressions and SVM). It appeared that, except for the MNB classifier, word-based models only outperforms character-based models when the n-gram size is too small (using only 1-grams for instance) or way too big (using only N-grams with $N > 8$ for instance). It is not surprising since, without lemmatization, words are just a subset of all the character n-grams of a text. This observation is coherent with previous work showing the interest of character-level models for various NLP tasks (Nakov and Tiedemann, 2012; Kuru et al., 2016; Buscaldi et al., 2018).

Due to the restricted space we will just exhibit the results for the best classifier which was Logistic Regression. Figure 1 exhibits the influence of N-gram size on the results for both tasks. We can make two comments out of this figure : (i) unigrams are useful for classification even if they are not the best features by themselves and (ii) there is a plateau when the maximal size is set to 5, afterwards the results do not improve much (and even drop for the sarcasm detection task). This result leaded us to choose n-grams from 1 to 5 for our ensemble method (Section 3.3). This method was

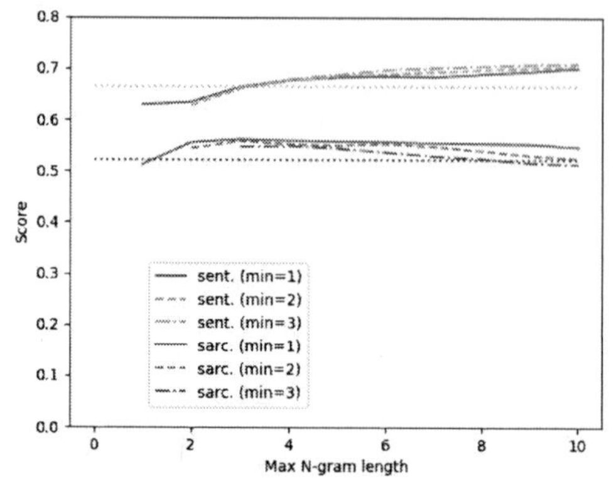

Figure 1: Results on subtask 1 (sarc., lower curves) and subtask2 (sent., upper curves) wrt. minimal size (min) and maximal size (abscissa) of character n-grams, the horizontal lines represent the best baseline with word uni-grams

supposed to act as a baseline but finally, using tf-idf and weighting the classes made this baseline even better that our two other methods.

3.2 A deep Learning approach

To build this system we used the ARAVEC pre-trained embeddings proposed by *Soliman et al.* ARAVEC is composed of three models trained trained with Word2Vec skip-gram and CBOW (Mikolov et al., 2013) on three different types of textual data in Arabic: tweets, web pages and Wikipedia articles (Soliman et al., 2017). We used the 100-dimensional Twitter N-Grams model since it seemed to better fit to this task.

The network is composed as follows: the input layer, an embedding layer, two LSTM layers and two Dense layers. To prevent over-fitting we add a dropout layer after each LSTM layer and the first dense layer. We use the pre-mentioned ARAVEC embeddings to enrich the representation. The final output is passed into one hidden layer and followed by a softmax output layer. There have been 10 epochs for the training.

3.3 Voting Ensemble Classifier with word and character-level features

We use the method developed for the 2020 NADI challenge (Ghoul and Lejeune, 2020). To build and train the model, we used the FEATUREUNION in SCIKIT-LEARN (Pedregosa et al., 2011) which allows to combine easily different n-gram representations at the word level and the character level as shown in Figure 2. To train this model,we concatenate three vectors with the following features (weigthed with TF-IDF): word n-grams (1 to 5-grams), character n-grams (1 to 4-grams) and character n-grams inside words (1 to 5-grams).

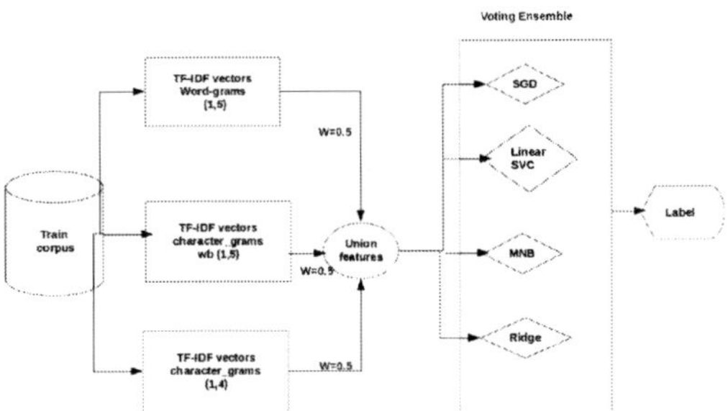

Figure 2: Model of the Ensemble Classifier

In this method, we use a set of simple classifiers to build an ensemble voting classifier that uses predicted class labels for majority rule voting. This ensemble is a combination of the following classifiers (`pen` stands for `penalty`):

- SGDClassifier ($\alpha = 10^{-5}$, `pen`='l2')
- LinearSVC (`pen`='l2', Tolerance $=10^{-3}$
- Multinomial Naive Bayes ($\alpha = 10^{-2}$)
- Ridge Classifier ($\alpha = 1$)

4 Results and Discussion

4.1 Subtask1: Sarcasm Detection

The results obtained by our models on the dev and test set are presented in Table 2. We chose to focus on the ensemble classifier since it showed a better accuracy on both subtask-1 and subtask-2. Figure 3 shows the result of this ensemble classifier on the dev set as a confusion matrix. We can see that this system has not been able to handle the imbalance in the dataset and had a strong tendency to yield False negatives (363). The number of False Positives (96) is much lower, that can lead to the conclusion that this system has been unable to find appropriate features for lowering silence. Combining multiple classifiers is promising but it seems that weighting the classes, as we finally did for the character-level method would have been more efficient.

It seems interesting to check for discrepancies in annotations. An important number of tweets contains words that belong to the sarcastic lexicon, for instance : ههههههههههه (laughing). The train/dev data contains 135 tweets with this word. Among these tweets, there are 32 tweets were not annotated as sarcastic. Some of them seem to have a wrong annotation, see for example:

- ههههههههههههههههههههههههههههههلا بس اضحك ع الي يقول ديبالا خليفة ميسي (hahaha. Non, I'm laughing on the guy who said Dybala will be the next Messi).
- سامي عنان والا كوفي عنان ؟؟ أعتقد إن مرتضي لـه يـد في الموضوع ده هههههههههههههههه. (Sami Anan or Kofi Annan ?? I think Morteza is involved in this matter, Hahahaha)

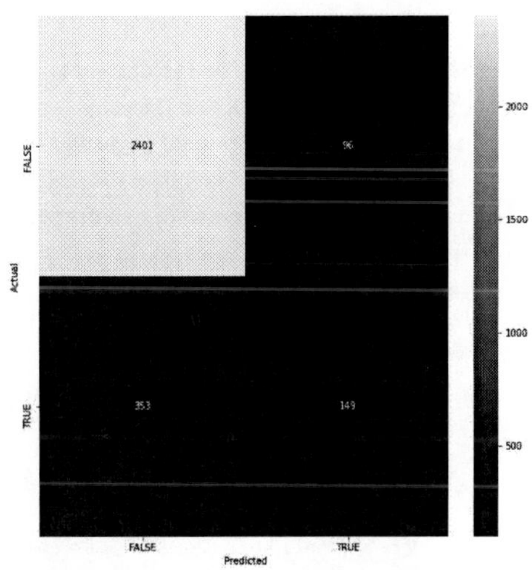

Figure 3: Confusion Matrix on the sarcasm dev set for the ensemble method

4.2 Subtask2: Sentiment Analysis

For this subtask, we use the exact same three methods. Table 3 shows that according to macro-F the best model is the voting Ensemble Classifier with an F-score (POS and NEG) of 65.06%. Surprisingly, the character-level method performed much better on the test than on the dev set and achieved better resultts than the ensemble method on the test set.

Method	**Trained on**	**Tested on**	**Macro P.**	**Macro R.**	**Macro F.**	**Acc.**	**F1 Sarc.**
Voting Ensemble	Train Set	Dev Set	**73.65**	62.78	65.48	**84.93**	39.60
	Train+Dev	Test Set	**71.16**	**61.94**	**63.13**	**76.30**	41.09
Deep Learning	Train Set	Dev Set	68.50	62.93	64.76	83.19	27.49
	Train+Dev	Test Set	72.41	58.80	58.87	75.77	32.50
Character Level	Train Set	Dev Set	66.39	**72.93**	**68.19**	78.80	49.81
	Train+Dev	Test Set	66.39	69.76	66.73	70.30	**55.83**

Table 2: Results of our three methods for Subtask1 (Sarcasm) in different training configurations (in blue the best scores, in bold the results of the submitted system, the main metric is in red)

Method	**Trained on**	**Tested on**	**Macro P.**	**Macro R.**	**Macro F.**	**Acc.**	**F. PN**
Voting Ensemble	Train Set	Dev Set	**71.27**	**65.79**	**67.26**	**71.19**	63.37
	Train+Dev	Test Set	**58.99**	**57.10**	**57.84**	**64.73**	65.06
Deep Learning	Train Set	Dev Set	68.40	60.54	62.23	67.06	58.15
	Train+Dev	Test Set	55.72	54.09	54.45	59.77	59.27
Character Level	Train Set	Dev Set	64.39	64.91	64.63	67.65	63.78
	Train+Dev	Test Set	59.40	55.60	56.85	62.80	**71.47**

Table 3: Results of our three methods for Subtask2 (Sentiment) in different training configurations (in blue the best scores, in bold the results of the submitted system, the main metric is in red)

The confusion matrix on the dev set is presented in Figure 4 shows that positive tweets were harder to predict with only 230 True Positives, 90 False Positives and 306 False Negatives. Recall has been issue in all the experiments we performed.

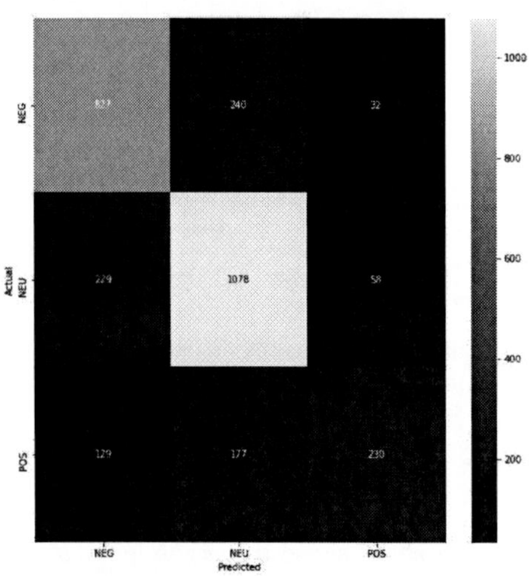

Figure 4: Confusion Matrix on the Sentiment dev set for the ensemble method

	Precision	Recall	F1-score
NEG	69.95	74.98	72.38
NEU	72.03	79.11	75.40
POS	71.83	43.28	54.02
Macro	71.27	65.79	67.26
Micro	71.23	71.19	70.47

Table 4: Classification report for the Voting Classifier on the Dev set for Subtask2 (acc. : 71.19%)

5 Conclusion

In this paper, we described three systems developed for the Shared Task on Sarcasm and Sentiment Detection in Arabic. We tried to show the interest of combining word-level and character-level features. In order to ease the choice of the type of character n-grams used as features we developed a baseline with a Logistic Regression classifier using character n-grams. It helped us to find an appropriate combination of features to produce the ensemble method whose results were submitted to this shared task. It appeared that adding tf-idf and class weighting made this baseline better than the ensemble method, showing maybe the interest of digging into character-level features.

References

Ines Abbes, Wajdi Zaghouani, Omaima El-Hardlo, and Faten Ashour. 2020. DAICT: A dialectal Arabic irony corpus extracted from Twitter. In *Proceedings of the 12th Language Resources and Evaluation Conference*, pages 6265–6271, Marseille, France. European Language Resources Association.

Muhammad Abdul-Mageed, Chiyu Zhang, Houda Bouamor, and Nizar Habash. 2020. NADI 2020: The first nuanced Arabic dialect identification shared task. In *Proceedings of the Fifth Arabic Natural Language Processing Workshop*, pages 97–110, Barcelona, Spain (Online). Association for Computational Linguistics.

Ibrahim Abu Farha and Walid Magdy. 2020. From Arabic sentiment analysis to sarcasm detection: The ArSarcasm dataset. In *Proceedings of the 4th Workshop on Open-Source Arabic Corpora and Processing Tools, with a Shared Task on Offensive Language Detection*, pages 32–39, Marseille, France. European Language Resource Association.

Ibrahim Abu Farha, Wajdi Zaghouani, and Walid Magdy. 2021. Overview of the wanlp 2021 shared task on sarcasm and sentiment detection in arabic. In *Proceedings of the Sixth Arabic Natural Language Processing Workshop*.

Davide Buscaldi, Joseph Le Roux, and Gaël Lejeune. 2018. Modèles en Caractères pour la Détection de Polarité dans les Tweets. In *Atelier DEFT 2018*, Rennes, France.

Wingyan Chung. 2008. Web searching in a multilingual world. *Commun. ACM*, 51(5):32–40.

Dhaou Ghoul and Gaël Lejeune. 2020. Voting Classifier vs Deep learning method in Arabic Dialect Identification. In *: Proceedings of the Fifth Arabic Natural Language Processing Workshop, COLING 2020*, Barcelone, Spain.

Onur Kuru, Ozan Arkan Can, and Deniz Yuret. 2016. CharNER: Character-level named entity recognition. In *Proceedings of COLING 2016, the 26th International Conference on Computational Linguistics: Technical Papers*, pages 911–921, Osaka, Japan. The COLING 2016 Organizing Committee.

Tomas Mikolov, Kai Chen, Greg Corrado, and Jeffrey Dean. 2013. Efficient estimation of word representations in vector space.

Preslav Nakov and Jörg Tiedemann. 2012. Combining word-level and character-level models for machine translation between closely-related languages. In *Proceedings of the 50th Annual Meeting of the Association for Computational Linguistics (Volume 2: Short Papers)*, pages 301–305, Jeju Island, Korea. Association for Computational Linguistics.

F. Pedregosa, G. Varoquaux, A. Gramfort, V. Michel, B. Thirion, O. Grisel, M. Blondel, P. Prettenhofer, R. Weiss, V. Dubourg, J. Vanderplas, A. Passos, D. Cournapeau, M. Brucher, M. Perrot, and E. Duchesnay. 2011. Scikit-learn: Machine learning in Python. *Journal of Machine Learning Research*, 12:2825–2830.

Abu Bakr Soliman, Kareem Eissa, and Samhaa R. El-Beltagy. 2017. Aravec: A set of arabic word embedding models for use in arabic nlp. *Procedia Computer Science*, 117:256 – 265. Arabic Computational Linguistics.

Deep Multi-Task Model for Sarcasm Detection and Sentiment Analysis in Arabic Language

Abdelkader El Mahdaouy[1] **Abdellah El Mekki**[1] **Nabil El Mamoun**[2]
Kabil Essefar[1] **Ismail Berrada**[1] **Ahmed Khoumsi**[3]
[1]School of Computer Sciences, Mohammed VI Polytechnic University, Morocco
[2]Faculty of Sciences Dhar EL Mahraz, Sidi Mohamed Ben Abdellah University, Morocco
[3]Dept. Electrical & Computer Engineering, University of Sherbrooke, Canada
{firstname.lastname}@um6p.ma
ahmed.khoumsi@usherbrooke.ca

Abstract

The prominence of figurative language devices, such as sarcasm and irony, poses serious challenges for Arabic Sentiment Analysis (SA). While previous research works tackle SA and sarcasm detection separately, this paper introduces an end-to-end deep Multi-Task Learning (MTL) model, allowing knowledge interaction between the two tasks. Our MTL model's architecture consists of a Bidirectional Encoder Representation from Transformers (BERT) model, a multi-task attention interaction module, and two task classifiers. The overall obtained results show that our proposed model outperforms its single-task counterparts on both SA and sarcasm detection subtasks.

1 Introduction

The popularity of the Internet and the unprecedented reach of social media platforms allow users to express their opinions on a wide range of topics. Thereby, Sentiment Analysis (SA) has become a cornerstone for many applications such as digital marketing, product review analysis, customer feedback, social media monitoring, etc. SA consists of determining the expressed sentiment (positive, negative, or neutral) conveyed by a text or a piece of text.

Over the past decade, significant research advances have been achieved for Arabic SA (Badaro et al., 2019; Al-Ayyoub et al., 2019; Oueslati et al., 2020; Abu Farha and Magdy, 2021). However, the mutual interaction and impact of figurative language devices, like sarcasm and irony, and Arabic SA remain under-explored (Abu Farha and Magdy, 2020, 2021; Abbes et al., 2020). These latter devices allow us to express ourselves intelligently beyond the literal meaning of words. Although the literature uses the terms irony and sarcasm interchangeably, they have different meanings and there is no consensus on their definition (Farías et al., 2016; Hernández Farías and Rosso, 2017; Zhang et al., 2019). Both sarcasm and irony devices pose a real challenge for SA as they can reverse the expressed sentiment polarity from positive to negative (Hernández Farías and Rosso, 2017; Abu Farha and Magdy, 2020, 2021). Therefore, there is an urgent need to develop sarcasm-aware SA tools.

Previous research works on Arabic SA and sarcasm detection have dealt with both tasks separately (Ghanem et al., 2019, 2020; Abbes et al., 2020; Abu Farha and Magdy, 2020). Abbes et al. (2020) have built a corpus for irony and sarcasm detection in Arabic language from twitter using a set of ironic hashtags. Unlike the previous work of Karoui et al. (2017) that have relied on ironic hashtags to label the tweets, the annotation is performed manually by two Arabic language specialists. Abu Farha and Magdy (2021) have presented an overview of existing Arabic SA methods and approaches, and a benchmarking using three existing datasets. Their results have shown that most of the evaluated models perform poorly on the SemEval and ASTD datasets. Due to the label inconsistencies discovered, they have re-annotated the previously mentioned datasets for SA and sarcasm detection. In addition to the highly subjective nature of SA task, they have reported a large performance drop in the case of sarcastic tweets (Abu Farha and Magdy, 2020, 2021).

Following the recent breakthroughs in Arabic Natural Language Processing (NLP), achieved using AraBERT model (Antoun et al., 2020), Abdul-Mageed et al. (2020) have introduced two Arabic transformer-based language models, namely ARBERT and MARBERT. ARBERT is trained on large textual corpora of Modern Standar Arabic (MSA), while MARBERT is trained on 1 billion DA and MSA tweets corpus. They have shown new cutting edge performances on wide range of DA

Proceedings of the Sixth Arabic Natural Language Processing Workshop, pages 334–339
Kyiv, Ukraine (Virtual), April 19, 2021.

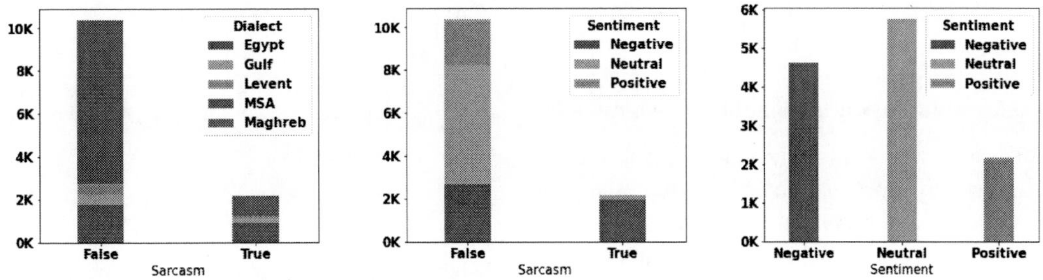

(a) Distribution of sarcastic tweets per region

(b) Distribution of sarcastic tweets per sentiment polarity

(c) Distribution of sentiment polarities

Figure 1: ArSarcasm-v2 dataset: distribution of sarcastic tweets and their sentiment polarities. True and False denote sarcastic and non-sarcastic tweets, respectively.

and MSA NLP tasks (AraBench datasets), including, among others, SA and sarcasm detection.

In this paper, we present our end-to-end deep MTL model, submitted to SA and sarcasm detection in Arabic language shared task (Abu Farha et al., 2021). Our approach is based on MARBERT (Abdul-Mageed et al., 2020), and a multi-task attention interaction module. The latter consists of two task-specific attention layers for extracting task-discriminative features, and of a Sigmoid interaction layer (Lan et al., 2017) for allowing interaction and knowledge sharing between sarcasm detection and SA. The task-interaction is performed using the task-specific attention outputs, a learnable shared matrix, and the Sigmoid activation. The obtained results show that our MTL model surpasses the other evaluated single-task and MTL models. Besides, the incorporation of an attention mechanism and the task-interaction boosts the performance of both sarcasm detection and SA.

The rest of the paper is organized as follows. Section 2 presents the shared task's dataset. Section 3 introduces the proposed method. In Section 4, we present the obtained results for both sarcasm detection and SA subtasks. Section 5 discusses the obtained results. Finally, Section 6 concludes the paper.

2 Data

The ArSarcasm Shared Task consists of two subtasks for sarcasm detection and SA in Arabic language (Abu Farha et al., 2021). The shared task's dataset, ArSarcasm-v2, is built from the previously introduced datasets for sarcasm and irony detection (Abbes et al., 2020; Abu Farha and Magdy, 2020). The provided dataset consists of 12,548 and 3,000 tweets for the training set and test set, respectively. The task's dataset is annotated for SA and sarcasm detection as well as the regional dialect of the tweets.

Figure 1 presents the distribution of sarcastic tweets and their sentiment polarities (Figures 1a and 1c). The distribution of all sentiment polarities in the dataset is illustrated in 1c. The dataset is unbalanced for both subtasks. Most sarcastic tweets are written in MSA and Egyptian dialect (Figure 1a), and are labeled with a negative sentiment (Figure 1b). Furthermore, approximately half of the tweets convey a neutral sentiment (Figure 1c).

3 Method

Our multi-task model consists of three main components: BERT encoder, a multi-task attention interaction module, and two task classifiers.

3.1 BERT Encoder

Fine-tuning Bidirectional Encoder Representation from Transformers (BERT) model on downstream tasks has shown a new wave of state-of-the-art performances in many NLP applications (Devlin et al., 2019). BERT model's architecture consists of multiple transformer encoders for learning contextualized word embedding of a given input text. It is trained on large textual corpora using two self-supervised objectives, namely the Masked Language Model (MLM) and the Next Sentence Prediction (NSP).

The encoder of our MTL model is the pre-trained MARBERT (Abdul-Mageed et al., 2020). MARBERT is fed with a sequence of wordpeices $[t_1, t_2, ..., t_n]$ of the input tweet, where n is the sequence length. It outputs the tweet embedding $h_{[CLS]}$ ([CLS] token embedding) and the contextualized word embedding of the input tokens

$H = [h_1, h_2, ..., h_n] \in \mathbb{R}^{nxd}$. Both $h_{[CLS]}$ and h_i have the same hidden dimension d.

3.2 Multi-task attention interaction module

This module consists of two task-specific attention layers (task-specific context-rich representation) and a Sigmoid task-interaction layer.

The task-specific sentence representation $v_* \in \mathbb{R}^{1xd}$ (e.g. v_{sarc} and v_{sent}) is obtained using the attention mechanism over the contextualized word embedding matrix H :

$$C = tanh(HW^a)$$

$$\alpha = softmax(C^T W^\alpha)$$

$$v_* = \alpha \cdot H^T$$

where $W^a \in \mathbb{R}^{dx1}$ and $W^\alpha \in \mathbb{R}^{nxn}$ are the learnable parameters of the attention mechanism. $C \in \mathbb{R}^{nx1}$ and $\alpha \in [0,1]^n$ weights words hidden representations according to their relevance to the task.

The task interaction mechanism (Lan et al., 2017) is performed using a learnable shared matrix $W^i \in \mathbb{R}^{dxd}$ and a bias vector $b^i \in \mathbb{R}^d$. The interaction of both task are given by:

$$v'_{sarc} = v_{sarc} \odot \sigma(W^i v_{sent} + b^i) \quad (1)$$

$$v'_{sent} = v_{sent} \odot \sigma(W^i v_{sarc} + b^i) \quad (2)$$

where v_{sarc} and v_{sent} are the output of the sarcasm task-specific attention layer and the sentiment task-specific attention layer, respectively. $\odot$ is the element-wise product.

3.3 Task classifier

We employ two task classifiers F_{sarc} and F_{sent} for sarcasm detection and SA, respectively. Each classifier consists of one hidden layer and one output layer. They are fed with the concatenation of the pooled output embedding and the task output of the multi-task attention interaction module v'_* (e.g. v'_{sarc} and v'_{sent}). The outputs of the task classifiers are given by:

$$\hat{y}_{sarc} = F_{sarc}([h_{[CLS]}, v'_{sarc}]) \quad (3)$$

$$\hat{y}_{sent} = F_{sarc}([h_{[CLS]}, v'_{sent}]) \quad (4)$$

3.4 Multi-task learning objective

We train our MTL model to jointly minimize the binary cross-entropy loss $\mathcal{L}_{BCE}$, for sarcasm detection, and the cross-entropy loss $\mathcal{L}_{CE}$, for SA. The total loss is given by:

$$\mathcal{L} = \mathcal{L}_{BCE}(y_{sarc}, \hat{y}_{sarc}) + \mathcal{L}_{CE}(y_{sent}, \hat{y}_{sent}) \quad (5)$$

where $\hat{y}_*$ is the predicted output and y_* is the ground truth label.

4 Results

In this section, we present the experiment settings and the obtained results.

4.1 Experiment settings

We have compared our model (MTL_ATTINTER) with two single-task models (ST and ST_ATT) and two MTL models (MTL and MTL_ATT).

- **ST** consists of MARBERT with one classification layer.
- **ST_ATT** employs the attention mechanism on top of the contextualized word embedding of MARBERT. The classification is performed using the attention layer output and the [CLS] token embedding.
- **MTL** is similar to **ST** model and uses classification layer for each task.
- **MTL_ATT** is the MTL counterpart of **ST_ATT** model.

We have implemented the MARBERT' tweets preprocessing pipeline (Abdul-Mageed et al., 2020). The evaluated models have been trained using Adam optimizer with a learning rate of 5×10^{-6}. Based on several experiments, the batch size and the number of epochs have been fixed to 64 and 5, respectively. Besides, we have used 80% and 20% of the provided training data for training set and development set, respectively. For comparison purposes, we have used the macro-average Precision, Recall, F1, and F1 score of positive and negative ($F1^{PN}$) evaluation measures. We have also employed the Accuracy and the F1 score of the sarcastic tweets ($F1^{Sarc}$).

4.2 Experiment results

Table 1 shows the obtained models' performances for both SA and sarcasm detection. The best results, for each evaluation measure, are highlighted with

		Sarcasm					Sentiment				
		Precision	**Recall**	**Accuracy**	**F1**	**F1^{Sarc}**	**Precision**	**Recall**	**Accuracy**	**F1**	**F1^{PN}**
ST	**Dev**	0.7649	*0.7683*	0.8673	0.7666	0.6132	0.7422	0.7519	0.7641	0.7465	0.7284
	Test	0.706	0.708	0.768	0.707	0.573	0.672	0.667	0.713	**0.665**	0.749
ST_ATT	**Dev**	0.7736	0.7588	0.8622	0.7658	0.6156	*0.7541*	0.7429	0.7629	*0.7479*	0.7253
	Test	0.724	**0.722**	**0.778**	0.723	0.598	0.664	0.665	0.709	0.661	0.742
MTL	**Dev**	0.7935	0.7611	0.8633	0.7753	0.6347	0.7424	0.748	*0.7649*	0.7448	0.7288
	Test	0.725	0.714	0.771	0.719	0.599	**0.676**	0.656	0.703	0.662	0.736
MTL_ATT	**Dev**	0.8064	0.7581	0.8606	0.7778	0.6421	0.7478	*0.7524*	*0.7649*	0.7465	0.7326
	Test	**0.741**	0.72	0.773	**0.728**	**0.617**	0.663	0.676	**0.717**	0.66	**0.752**
MTL_ATTINTER	**Dev**	*0.8106*	0.766	*0.8661*	*0.7846*	*0.6522*	0.7511	0.7414	0.7582	0.7436	*0.7358*
	Test	0.7268	0.7122	0.7680	0.7183	0.6000	0.6713	**0.7183**	0.7107	0.6625	0.7480

Table 1: Models evaluation on both SA and sarcasm detection subtasks

	Sarcasm					Sentiment				
	Precision	**Recall**	**Accuracy**	**F1**	**F1^{Sarc}**	**Precision**	**Recall**	**Accuracy**	**F1**	**F1^{PN}**
MTL_ATTINTER	0.7268	0.7122	0.7680	0.7183	0.6000	0.6713	**0.7183**	0.7107	0.6625	0.7480

Table 2: The obtained results of our **Official** submission

italic font and bold fond for the dev set and the test set, respectively. The overall obtained results show that MTL models outperform their single-task counterparts for most evaluation measures. In fact, incorporating attention mechanism into both ST_ATT and MTL_ATT improves the F1, F1^{Sarc} and F1^{PN}. The former compute the F1 score for sarcastic tweets only, while the latter consider only positive and negative sentiment.

MTL_ATTINTER and MTL_ATT achieve the best performances for most evaluation measures on both the dev and the test sets of sarcasm detection sub-task. Specifically, they show far better F1 performance for the sarcastic class prediction. For SA, the other evaluated models achieve slightly better performance. However, MTL_ATTINETER and MTL_ATT yield the best F1^{PN} performances on the dev set and the test set. Therefore, our proposed model excels in detecting sarcastic tweets as well as predicting positive and negative sentiments.

Official results

Since one submission was allowed, we have submitted the results of our MTL_ATTINETER model. Table 2 shows the official submission results. Our system is top ranked on SA Sub-task and has secured the fourth position among submitted systems for sarcasm detection.

5 Discussion

To investigate the strengths and weaknesses of our model, we have analyzed the confusion matrix of each subtask (Figures 2a and 2b) as well as the confusion matrices of sentiment analysis among sarcastic and non-sarcastic tweets respectively (Figures 2d and 2c). The analysis of these matrices shows that our MTL model leverages signals from both tasks and boosts the performances. This can be explained by the fact that most sarcastic tweets convey a negative sentiment. Besides, negative tweets tend to have a large probability of being sarcastic than the positive ones. This could be also deduced from Table 1, where MTL models achieve the best F1^{Sarc} and F1^{PN} scores compared to single-task models.

6 Conclusion

In this paper, we have proposed an end-to-end deep Multi-Task Learning model for SA and sarcasm detection. Our model leverages the MARBERT's contextualized word embedding with a multi-task attention interaction module. The aim is to allow task-interaction and knowledge sharing for both SA and sarcasm detection. Our model shows very promising results on both subtasks. Therefore, it proves the effectiveness of using task-specific attention layers as well as the task-interaction mechanism in multi-task learning.

Future research work will focus on developing

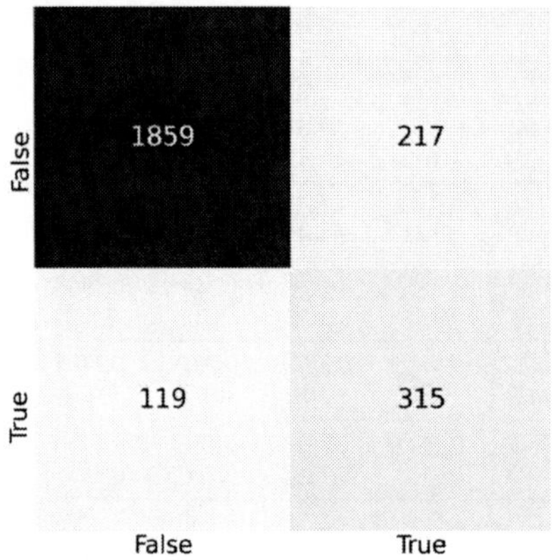

(a) Confusion matrix of the sarcasm detection task

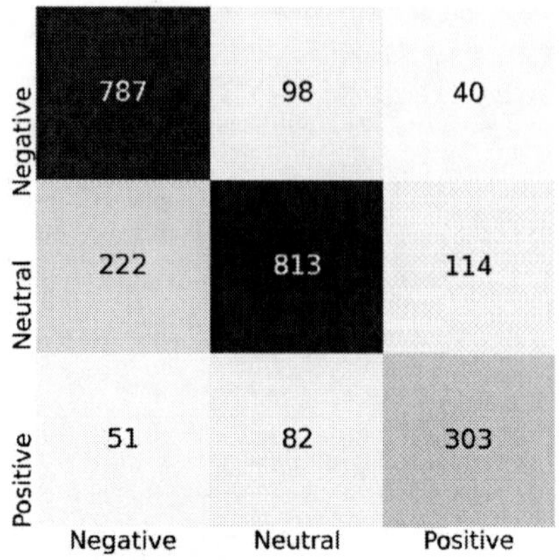

(b) Confusion matrix of SA task

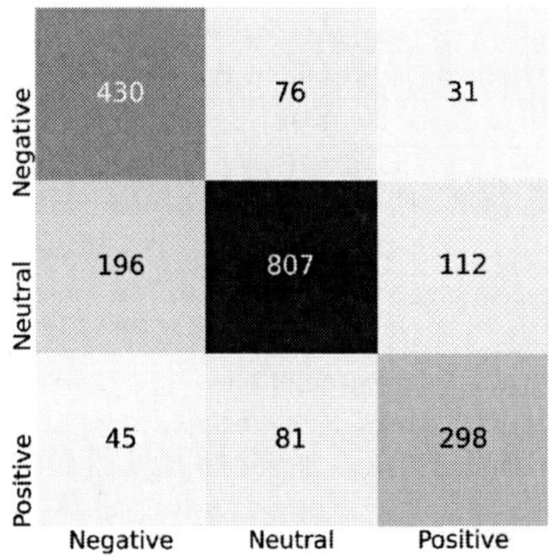

(c) Confusion matrix of SA among non-sarcastic tweets

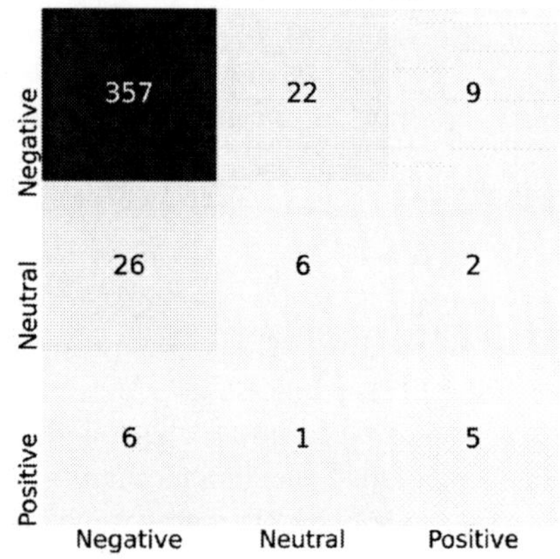

(d) Confusion matrix of SA among sarcastic tweets

Figure 2: The confusion matrices of our MTL model's prediction on both SA and sarcasm detection tasks

task-interaction and class-interaction modules and mechanisms for SA and sarcasm detection.

References

Ines Abbes, Wajdi Zaghouani, Omaima El-Hardlo, and Faten Ashour. 2020. DAICT: A dialectal arabic irony corpus extracted from twitter. In *Proceedings of The 12th Language Resources and Evaluation Conference, LREC 2020, Marseille, France, May 11-16, 2020*, pages 6265–6271. European Language Resources Association.

Muhammad Abdul-Mageed, AbdelRahim Elmadany, and El Moatez Billah Nagoudi. 2020. Arbert & marbert: Deep bidirectional transformers for arabic. *arXiv preprint arXiv:2101.01785*.

Ibrahim Abu Farha and Walid Magdy. 2020. From arabic sentiment analysis to sarcasm detection: The arsarcasm dataset. In *Proceedings of the 4th Workshop on Open-Source Arabic Corpora and Processing Tools, with a Shared Task on Offensive Language Detection*, pages 32–39.

Ibrahim Abu Farha and Walid Magdy. 2021. A comparative study of effective approaches for arabic sentiment analysis. *Information Processing Management*, 58(2):102438.

Ibrahim Abu Farha, Wajdi Zaghouani, and Walid Magdy. 2021. Overview of the wanlp 2021 shared task on sarcasm and sentiment detection in arabic. In *Proceedings of the Sixth Arabic Natural Language Processing Workshop*.

Mahmoud Al-Ayyoub, Abed Allah Khamaiseh, Yaser Jararweh, and Mohammed N. Al-Kabi. 2019. A comprehensive survey of arabic sentiment analysis. *Information Processing & Management*, 56(2):320 – 342. Advance Arabic Natural Language Processing (ANLP) and its Applications.

Wissam Antoun, Fady Baly, and Hazem Hajj. 2020. Arabert: Transformer-based model for arabic language understanding. In *LREC 2020 Workshop Language Resources and Evaluation Conference 11–16 May 2020*, page 9.

Gilbert Badaro, Ramy Baly, Hazem Hajj, Wassim El-Hajj, Khaled Bashir Shaban, Nizar Habash, Ahmad

Al-Sallab, and Ali Hamdi. 2019. A survey of opinion mining in arabic: A comprehensive system perspective covering challenges and advances in tools, resources, models, applications, and visualizations. *ACM Trans. Asian Low-Resour. Lang. Inf. Process.*, 18(3).

Jacob Devlin, Ming-Wei Chang, Kenton Lee, and Kristina Toutanova. 2019. BERT: Pre-training of deep bidirectional transformers for language understanding. In *Proceedings of the 2019 Conference of the North American Chapter of the Association for Computational Linguistics: Human Language Technologies, Volume 1 (Long and Short Papers)*, pages 4171–4186, Minneapolis, Minnesota. Association for Computational Linguistics.

Delia Irazú Hernańdez Farías, Viviana Patti, and Paolo Rosso. 2016. Irony detection in twitter: The role of affective content. *ACM Trans. Internet Technol.*, 16(3).

Bilal Ghanem, Jihen Karoui, Farah Benamara, Véronique Moriceau, and Paolo Rosso. 2019. Idat at fire2019: Overview of the track on irony detection in arabic tweets. In *Proceedings of the 11th Forum for Information Retrieval Evaluation*, FIRE '19, page 10–13, New York, NY, USA. Association for Computing Machinery.

Bilal Ghanem, Jihen Karoui, Farah Benamara, Paolo Rosso, and Véronique Moriceau. 2020. Irony detection in a multilingual context. In *Advances in Information Retrieval - 42nd European Conference on IR Research, ECIR 2020, Lisbon, Portugal, April 14-17, 2020, Proceedings, Part II*, volume 12036 of *Lecture Notes in Computer Science*, pages 141–149. Springer.

Delia Irazú Farias Hernández Farías and Paolo Rosso. 2017. Chapter 7 - irony, sarcasm, and sentiment analysis. In Federico Alberto Pozzi, Elisabetta Fersini, Enza Messina, and Bing Liu, editors, *Sentiment Analysis in Social Networks*, pages 113–128. Morgan Kaufmann, Boston.

Jihen Karoui, Farah Banamara Zitoune, and Véronique Moriceau. 2017. Soukhria: Towards an irony detection system for arabic in social media. *Procedia Computer Science*, 117:161–168. Arabic Computational Linguistics.

Man Lan, Jianxiang Wang, Yuanbin Wu, Zheng-Yu Niu, and Haifeng Wang. 2017. Multi-task attention-based neural networks for implicit discourse relationship representation and identification. In *Proceedings of the 2017 Conference on Empirical Methods in Natural Language Processing, EMNLP 2017, Copenhagen, Denmark, September 9-11, 2017*, pages 1299–1308. Association for Computational Linguistics.

Oumaima Oueslati, Erik Cambria, Moez Ben HajHmida, and Habib Ounelli. 2020. A review of sentiment analysis research in arabic language. *Future Generation Computer Systems*, 112:408 – 430.

Shiwei Zhang, Xiuzhen Zhang, Jeffrey Chan, and Paolo Rosso. 2019. Irony detection via sentiment-based transfer learning. *Information Processing Management*, 56(5):1633–1644.

A contextual word embedding for Arabic sarcasm detection with random forests

Hazem E. Elagbry, Shimaa Attia, Ahmed Abdel-Rahman, Ahmed Abdel-Ate, Sandra Girgis
Faculty of Computer Science and Artificial Intelligence
Helwan University, Egypt
{hazememad, Shimaa_20170268, Ahmed_20170044, Ahmed_20170056, totajo1999}@fci.helwan.edu.eg

Abstract

Sarcasm detection is of great importance in understanding people's true sentiments and opinions. Many online feedbacks, reviews, social media comments, etc. are sarcastic. Several researches have already been done in this field, but most researchers studied the English sarcasm analysis compared to the researches are done in Arabic sarcasm analysis because of the Arabic language challenges. In this paper, we propose a new approach for improving Arabic sarcasm detection. Our approach is using data augmentation, contextual word embedding and random forests model to get the best results. Our accuracy in the shared task on sarcasm and sentiment detection in Arabic was 0.5189 for F1-sarcastic as the official metric using the shared dataset ArSarcasm-V2 (Abu Farha, et al., 2021).

1 Introduction

Sarcasm detection is the process of classifying whether the text (i.e., a full document, a single sentence, a word, etc.) is sarcastic or not. Sarcastic writing is a common way for people to share their sentiment in many online texts (i.e., social media, reviews, posts, comments, etc.). This linguistic phenomenon has much significance for tasks such as sentiment analysis and opinion mining. Sarcasm detection has received much research attention in other languages especially in the English language, but the Arabic language still lags behind. A few efforts have done in Arabic sarcasm detection such as the works of (Al-Ghadhban, et al., 2017, May) and the shared task held by (Ghanem, et al., 2019). There have been some recent efforts to build standard datasets for this task such as (Farha & Magdy, 2020) but still not enough to get good results. A lot of challenges we face when dealing with Arabic sarcasm analysis such as 1) lack of datasets, 2) Imbalanced classes, 3) lack of pre-preprocessing tools (i.e., autocorrect, stemmer, etc.) for Arabic language, 4) diversity of dialects which affects the results. Most recent methods and approaches (i.e., machine-learning or deep learning) use one of the following two intermediate representations[1] for language modeling.

Firstly, and the very common intermediate representation which proved its efficiency in many experiments is TF-IDF (term frequency-inverse document frequency). TF-IDF is a very good way to start your initial representation because it has a lot of advantages such as 1) Ease of computing, 2) extracting the most descriptive terms in a document and 3) you can easily compute the similarity using it. But with all of this, there is a very big disadvantage such as it cannot capture semantic in the given text which affects the algorithms effectiveness.

Secondly, is another very good intermediate representation that proved its effectiveness called word embedding. Fixed word embeddings solve the problem of capturing the semantic of a word that we faced in TF-IDF intermediate representation by providing a fixed embedding to every word which was too useful (examples: word2vec, fastText). The limitations of the fixed word embeddings are that they cannot provide us with the information about words meaning in different

[1] Note that there are more than these ways in the literature but we have mentioned the commonly used techniques.

Proceedings of the Sixth Arabic Natural Language Processing Workshop, pages 340–344
Kyiv, Ukraine (Virtual), April 19, 2021.

contexts when setting a fixed embedding to every word.

Finally, to solve this problem there is a very good language modeling technique which is called contextual word embedding. Contextual word embeddings set a different embedding to the same word according to its meaning in the context which handles the problem of diversity of a single word meaning. In literature, several researches focus on enhancing the Arabic natural language understanding such as (Antoun, et al., 2020; Abdul-Mageed, et al., 2020).

In this paper, we attempt to extract contextual word embedding using Ara-Bert (Antoun, et al., 2020) then feed it to an ensemble learning method called random forests classifier. We provide the git hub link of the code used to extract the contextual embeddings[2].

2 Data

The data we have used to get our results in this shared task are: Ar-Sarcasm-V2 (Abu Farha, et al., 2021), emojis dataset, stop words dataset, and unseen dataset from the shared task on sarcasm and sentiment detection in Arabic as a test set to test our results.

2.1 Data Description

The training dataset was 12548 tweets that is given from the shared task on sarcasm and sentiment detection in Arabic (Abu Farha, et al., 2021) which has the following columns: 1) Sarcasm: this column value is binary (i.e., for every single tweet True if the tweet is sarcastic and False if it isn't sarcastic), 2) Sentiment: this column contains 3 classes POS, NEG, NEU for positive, negative, neutral respectively, 3) Dialect: this column contains 5 different dialects one of these 5 values was assigned to every tweet the values are: MSA, Gulf, Egypt, Levant, Magreb.

Emojis dataset is publicly available from Kaggle[3]. It contains 4159 different emoji with the following columns: 1) Emoji, 2) Name of the emoji in English, 3) Group of the emoji, 4) Sup-group of the emoji, 5) Code-point that represents the emoji. We have used the emoji dataset because they are expressive and all of us use them every day in our tweets, Facebook posts, and here in our dataset.

Stop words is a publicly available dataset which is consisting of two lists of Arabic stop words developed while working on this paper: (El-Khir, 2017). Finally, the Unseen dataset contains 3000 tweets with a column that contains the dialect of each tweet.

We have used an 80/20 split to prepare the training and validation sets in addition to using augmentation techniques which we are going to talk about in section 2.2.

2.2 Data Augmentation

In our dataset, there was a big class imbalance, because the dataset contains 10380 non-sarcastic tweets against 2168 sarcastic tweets with a total number of 12548 tweets. According to this situation we performed different data augmentation techniques inspired by (Liu, et al., 2014, June) to solve this issue such as:

1- Oversampling: we have done this by duplicating a random number of tweets to reach 6018 sarcastic tweets.

2- Undersampling: after this, we removed part of the non-sarcastic class samples to change number of samples from 10380 non-sarcastic to 6018 non-sarcastic tweets.

This made the two classes have the same number of samples with a total number of 12036 tweets.

2.3 Data Preprocessing

We have built a function to detect patterns and clean our text using regular expression package in python. We have removed the following patterns: Users (any name after @ symbol), English letters, Numbers (English or Arabic), Special characters / Punctuations, replace each emoji with its Arabic name without duplicating, Leading spaces (before and after the tweet), dropping empty tweets.

Because our emoji dataset was in English language not in Arabic and our shared task focus in the Arabic language, we have translated the dataset to the Arabic language.

[2] arabert/AraBert_output_Embeddings_PyTorch.ipynb at master · aub-mind/arabert · GitHub

[3] Link of the dataset: Full Emoji Database | Kaggle

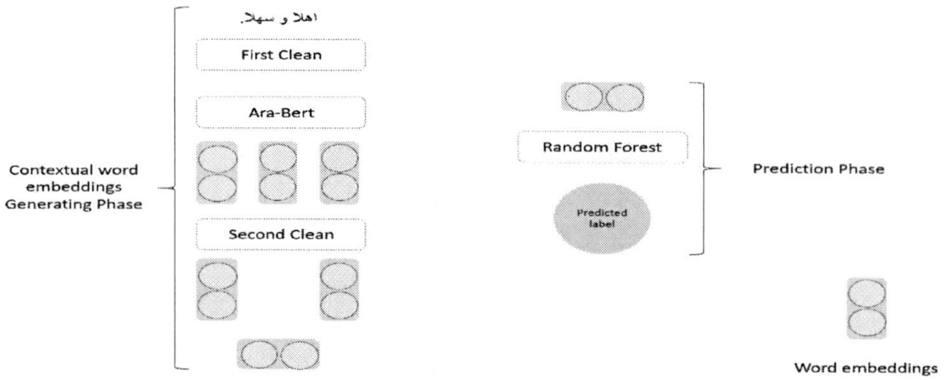

Figure 1: Illustration of our random forest model with the generation of contextual embeddings.

3 System

In our approach, we have used the pre-trained algorithm Ara-Bert for extracting the contextual word embeddings that we have talked about in section 1. BERT is designed to pre-train deep bidirectional representations from unlabeled text by jointly conditioning on both left and right context in all layers (Devlin, et al., 2018). According to BERT's state-of-the-art results, it is a big deal to include it in our classification task, but there is a problem which is BERT alone is not enough and there are limits to it for getting state-of-the-art results. So, and because of Ara-Bert powerful in natural language understanding and its huge corpus which is trained with. We have used Ara-Bert for language modeling (i.e., extracting contextual embeddings) with its base-configuration. $BERT_{BASE}$ consists of (L=12, H=768, A=12, Total Parameters=110M). In this notation, we denote the number of layers (i.e., Transformer blocks) as L, the hidden size as H, and the number of self-attention heads as A.

Till now we did not remove stop words or performing any stemming for our data. We did this removes and stemming after extracting the word embeddings because contextual word embeddings rely on extracting different embeddings for the same word in different contexts, and even ال in Arabic language can affect our understanding of the context. According to this assumption, we have implemented a second text cleaning/preprocessing after extracting our contextual word embeddings.

We have made another interesting mechanism for doing something very close to the stemming which we are going to discuss here. Ara-BERT's input is not a feature but is a sequence of words that is tokenized with a pre-trained Ara-BERT tokenizer. The Ara-BERT tokenizer is created with a word piece model. In this tokenization every word has one of the following forms: 1) the word still the same which means that this word is in BERT's vocabulary, 2) the word will come with a # sign which means that this word is part of a bigger word (i.e., the original word is not in its vocabulary so, BERT split the word into a group of subwords with #), 3) the word with a + sign means that this word is a prefix or suffix to another word (i.e., الكتاب the ال here is a prefix so it will appear like كتاب + ال). According to this form, we have used it to perform stemming especially with dialects which are very hard to stem by removing every word that has the + sign. After this second cleaning, we get the average of word embeddings to get our sentence embeddings with vector size of 768 feature.

After second cleaning and to avoid empty tweets in train or test set, we have removed every empty tweet after saving its index and assign to this tweet a False label which means it is not sarcastic by default.

Finally, we feed this sentence embedding to random forests (which is an ensemble learning method for classification, regression, and other

Hyperparameter	Value
Number of estimators	100
Max depth	None
criterion	Gini

Table 1: This table shows us part of random forest hyperparameters

tasks) with its default hyperparameters configuration using scikit-learn package in python see Table [1].

We provide the code[4] of our approach for publicly use to push the Arabic classification tasks to another state-of-the-art accuracy.

4 Results

In this section, we are going to discuss the key results of our approach by sharing with you our evaluation metrics with its key results in section 4.1, then the official metrics of the shared task on sarcasm and sentiment detection in Arabic with its key results in section 4.2.

4.1 Training Results

This section contains our evaluation before submitting the answers and see the final results (i.e., it is not the official metrics). Tables [2] shows our results using contextual word embeddings as our intermediate representation. We have split the Ar-SarcasmV2 (Abu Farha, et al., 2021) data after data augmentation into 80% as a training set and 20% as a test set. This shows us that the random forests using contextual word embeddings scored the with 93% F1-score for each class (i.e., True or False).

	Precision	Recall	F1-Score
False	0.96	0.90	0.93
True	0.90	0.96	0.93

Accuracy			0.93
Macro AVG	0.93	0.93	0.93
Weighted AVG	0.93	0.93	0.93

Table 2: This table shows us the results of using random forests with contextual word embeddings

As we see here the accuracy of 0.93 is a very high accuracy which will affect our judgment of the real performance of our model, and the main reason for this kind of error (i.e., fake high accuracy) is that we have augmented our dataset before splitting it. Like we have said in section 2.2 the oversampling technique that we have used was by duplicating the minor class (i.e., sarcastic class). Thus, the test set was containing data which is most of it duplicated tweets from the training set and this is why these fake results are here (i.e., our model does not perform this well). So, be aware and don't augment the data before splitting it.

4.2 Official Results

This section shares the shared task evaluation metrics using our submitted model which is random forests ensemble learning with contextual word embeddings. Table [3] shows our results for F1-Sarcastic (the official metric), Accuracy, Macro F1, precision, and recall in the unseen test dataset and we have got the following results:

F1-Sarcastic	Accuracy	Macro-F1
0.5189	0.7533	0.6765

Precision	Recall
0.6858	0.6700

Table 3: this table shares our submitted model official metrics in the shared task

For clarification purposes (i.e., showing the big difference between TF-IDF and contextual word embeddings). Table [4] shows the results of using TF-IDF in test data which are very bad in comparison with word embeddings in Table [3].

F1-Sarcastic	Accuracy	Macro-F1
0.41	0.73	0.62

Precision	Recall
0.51	0.34

Table 4: this table shares the results when using the TF-IDF as an intermediate representation

5 Discussion

Our observations and experiments show that in Arabic sarcasm detection 2 main challenges affect the accuracy, validation, and our improvement such as 1) the dataset was too small, 2) dealing with dialects was making this harder (EX. stemming was a very challenging problem when dealing with dialects)

To our knowledge, a very small number of researches are studying the effectiveness of

[4] Link of our colab: https://colab.research.google.com/drive/1GgVpke8wY9aOiiVeYni6VGAcxqFxPEeQ?usp=sharing

Contextual word embeddings in Arabic which are very helpful in dealing with different dialects and unseen data, and the most interesting example for such effectiveness is Ara-Bert which reaches a very good accuracy in dialects while he was trained in MSA corpus.

Dealing with incorrectly entered data especially in social media was incredible and very challenging (i.e., if a user wrote ' لامن حقك ' the tokenization phase will treat this 3 words as a 2 words ' لامن ' and ' حقك ' but if he wrote ' لا من حقك ' with a space between every word the tokenization phase will treat this as 3 words not two 'لا', 'من' and 'حقك') there always a problem when dealing with every step in pre-processing with dialects.

For the above reasons, our next steps are like the following: 1) Focusing more on preprocessing problems (i.e., produce an algorithm for stemming dialects, autocorrect Arabic words), 2) Looking for more data to get better accuracy and validation, 3) we have tried a machine learning approach which is not very good in capturing the amount of information that the contextual word embeddings transfer (i.e., it is like a bottleneck). So, one of our important next steps is dealing with the problem using deep learning models.

6 Conclusion

Our task allowed us to explore a lot of challenges with natural language processing in Arabic. We believe that Arabic natural language processing applications such as sarcasm detection, sentiment analysis, POS, etc. has a lot of areas to be investigated and developed. In our paper, we tried to overcome the problem of dialects and semantic diversity for every word in different contexts by generating a contextual word embedding using Ara-Bert which achieved very good results just using random forests ensemble learning with its initial scikit-learn configuration.

We hope that problems such as POS, Autocorrect, and such important problems take a more interest to solve it because we believe that such problems are a big deal when we talk about enhancing the accuracy of other tasks like: sentiment or sarcasm analysis.

7 References

Liu, P., Chen, W., Ou, G., Wang, T., Yang, D. and Lei, K., 2014, June. Sarcasm detection in social media based on imbalanced classification. In *International Conference on Web-Age Information Management* (pp. 459-471). Springer, Cham.

Elrazzaz, M., Elbassuoni, S., Shaban, K. and Helwe, C., 2017, July. Methodical evaluation of arabic word embeddings. In *Proceedings of the 55th Annual Meeting of the Association for Computational Linguistics (Volume 2: Short Papers)* (pp. 454-458).

Farha, I.A. and Magdy, W., 2020, May. From Arabic Sentiment Analysis to Sarcasm Detection: The ArSarcasm Dataset. In *Proceedings of the 4th Workshop on Open-Source Arabic Corpora and Processing Tools, with a Shared Task on Offensive Language Detection* (pp. 32-39).

Joshi, A., Tripathi, V., Patel, K., Bhattacharyya, P. and Carman, M., 2016. Are word embedding-based features useful for sarcasm detection?. *arXiv preprint arXiv:1610.00883.*

Antoun, W., Baly, F. and Hajj, H., 2020. Arabert: Transformer-based model for arabic language understanding. *arXiv preprint arXiv:2003.00104.*

Devlin, J., Chang, M.W., Lee, K. and Toutanova, K., 2018. Bert: Pre-training of deep bidirectional transformers for language understanding. *arXiv preprint arXiv:1810.04805.*

Al-Ghadhban, D., Alnkhilan, E., Tatwany, L. and Alrazgan, M., 2017, May. Arabic sarcasm detection in Twitter. In *2017 International Conference on Engineering & MIS (ICEMIS)* (pp. 1-7). IEEE.

Ghanem, B., Karoui, J., Benamara, F., Moriceau, V. and Rosso, P., 2019, December. Idat at fire2019: Overview of the track on irony detection in arabic tweets. In *Proceedings of the 11th Forum for Information Retrieval Evaluation* (pp. 10-13).

El-Khair, I.A., 2017. Effects of stop words elimination for Arabic information retrieval: a comparative study. *arXiv preprint arXiv:1702.01925.*

Abu Farha, I., Zaghouani, W., and Magdy, W. 2021. Overview of the WANLP 2021 Shared Task on Sarcasm and Sentiment Detection in Arabic. In Proceedings of the Sixth Arabic Natural Language Processing Workshop.

Abdul-Mageed, M., Elmadany, A. and Nagoudi, E.M.B., 2020. ARBERT & MARBERT: Deep Bidirectional Transformers for Arabic. arXiv preprint arXiv:2101.01785.

SarcasmDet at Sarcasm Detection Task 2021 in Arabic using AraBERT Pretrained Model

Dalya Faraj
Department of Computer Science
Jordan University of Science
and Technology
Irbid, Jordan
dfalnore18@cit.just.edu.jo

Malak Abdullah
Department of Computer Science
Jordan University of Science
and Technology
Irbid, Jordan
mabdullah@just.edu.jo

Abstract

This paper presents one of the top five winning solutions for the Shared Task on Sarcasm and Sentiment Detection in Arabic (sub-task1 Sarcasm Detection). The goal of the sub-task is to identify whether a tweet is sarcastic or not. Our solution has been developed using ensemble technique with AraBERT pre-trained model. This paper describes the architecture of the submitted solution in the shared task. It also provides in detail the experiments and the hyperparameters tuning that lead to this outperforming result. Besides, the paper discusses and analyzes the results by comparing all the models that we have trained or tested to build a robust model in a table design. Our model is ranked fifth out of 27 teams with an F1-score of 0.5989 of the sarcastic class. It is worth mentioning that our model achieved the highest accuracy score of 0.7830 in this competition.

Keywords: Arabic, Sentiment Analysis, Sarcasem, NLP, AraBERT.

1 Introduction

Sarcasm, bullying, and offense are critical topics that dramatically increase in social media, leading to countless problems, whether on the personal or community level. Irony and sarcasm use positive words commonly applied in public life to make fun, ridicule, or annoy someone, either directly or indirectly (González-Ibánez et al., 2011). Detecting sarcasm depends on the sentence context and understanding the current situation, which can be challenging to be discovered using traditional techniques. With the development of artificial intelligence (AI) methods, specifically natural language processing (NLP), predicting and reducing such words that denote sarcasm are investigated thoroughly using sentiment and emotion analysis methodologies (Abdullah et al., 2018; Ogudo and Nestor, 2019; Cheng and Tsai, 2019).

Sentiment analysis (SA) refers to the use of natural language processing, text analysis, and linguistics to identify, extract, quantify, and systematically determine whether a sentence or a document is positive or negative (Duwairi and El-Orfali, 2014; Al-Ayyoub et al., 2019). SA techniques have been applied to utilize the process of predicting whether the text contains sarcasm and offensive words within it (Feldman, 2013).

The lack of resources and annotated datasets for the Arabic language is considered one of the challenges in this field (Abdullah and Hadzikadic, 2017; Abdulla et al., 2013). For detecting sarcasm, a group of researchers (Abu Farha et al., 2021) provided new datasets for the shared task on Sarcasm and Sentiment Detection in Arabic (WANLP 2021). The shared task includes two subtasks: the Sarcasm Detection sub-task for detecting if the tweet is sarcastic or not. The Sentiment Analysis sub-task, which is focused on analyzing tweets then identifying their sentiment.

This paper presents the SarcasemDet team model at the WANLP 2021 Shared Task for subtask 1 (Sarcasm Detection). Our solution system (SarcasmDet) is one of the top five teams among 27 participated teams. The proposed approach uses the pre-trained language model AraBERT (Antoun et al.). We also have experimented with several pre-trained language models using the simple transformers library. It is worth mentioning that using the hard-voting ensemble technique has increased the performance of the model, remarkably.

The rest of the paper goes as follows. Section 2 overviews and discusses the existed work

Proceedings of the Sixth Arabic Natural Language Processing Workshop, pages 345–350
Kyiv, Ukraine (Virtual), April 19, 2021.

related to this research. Section 3 illustrates the shared task and describes the dataset. Section 4 displays our solution architecture and preprocessing method to achieve the best accuracy score in this task. Section 5 presents the experiments with hyperparameters tuning analysis. Section 6 presents the results. Finally, in section 7, the Conclusion.

2 Related Work

There are numerous resources on sarcasm detection in English and European languages, but there is a lack of resources and datasets in the Arabic language. The focus on detecting sarcasm in the Arabic language emerged in recent years. In (Karoui et al., 2017), the researchers were among the first people to provide a dataset to detect sarcasm in Arabic. They collected Arabic tweets of different Arabic dialects, such as Egyptian, Syrian and Saudi dialects. They cleaned the dataset, 5,479 tweets, including 1733 irony, and added four features for each tweet: surface, sentiment, shifter, and internal context features. The experiments showed that the Random Forest classifier achieved high accuracy with 72.76% to detect sarcasm in the Arabic language tweets.

Another sarcasm dataset in the Arabic language is provided by (Farha and Magdy, 2020). This dataset contains sarcasm, sentiment, and dialect labels incorporating 10,547 rows of tweets where 16% are sarcastic tweets. The researchers applied the Bidirectional LSTM (biLSTM) deep learning approach to achieve an F1-score of 0.46, which indicates the hardness of detecting sarcasm in Arabic.

Various machine learning mechanisms have been used to detect sarcasm and offensive in Arabic tweets. In (Al-Ghadhban et al., 2017), the authors used the supervised Naïve Bayes Multinomial Text algorithm to detect the sarcasm in Arabic tweets. They collected 344 rows of tweets data manually, where 238 out of them are sarcastic tweets, and 106 are nonsarcastic tweets. To evaluate the NB model, they used recall, precision, f1-score metrics, and the resultant outputs are 0.659, 0.710, and 0.676, respectively.

In (Hassan et al., 2020), the researchers participated in the SemEval 2020 Task 12 Arabic offensive language dataset for two subtasks: offensive language detection and hate speech detection. They were the winning solution system for discovering offensive language in the Arabic language. The dataset they used contains 10,000 rows of tweets data manually labeled for offensiveness (OFF or NOT OFF). They applied several deep and machine learning algorithms, such as DNN, CNN, RNN, and SVM. They achieved the best results with an F1-score of 90.51% by ensembling SVM and DNN.

3 Task and Dataset Description

In the Shared Task on Sarcasm and Sentiment Detection in Arabic from WANLP 2021(Abu Farha et al., 2021) challenge, all tasks have different requirements. The shared task includes two subtasks: subtask 1, Sarcasm Detection, which aims to detect if the tweet is sarcastic or not. Subtask 2, Sentiment Analysis, focused on analyzing tweets then identifying their sentiments. Table1 shows a sample of the training dataset. It is worth mentioning that we have participated in subtask 1.

#	Example	Sarcastic
290	#عرب_ولكن عربي :قهوته برازيلية بدلته ايطالية ساعته سويسرية وعطره فرنسي سيارته المانية.الخ ويذهب لالقاء محاضرته بعنوان #قاطعوا_الغرب	True
9029	من احتفالات المولد النبوي الشريف	False

Table 1: sample for subtask1 Sarcasm Detection from the training dataset

In our solution system, we have used the ArSarcasm-v2 dataset provided by (Abu Farha et al., 2021). The data is separated into two parts: a training dataset containing 12,548 tweets and four features labeled as follows: tweet, sarcasm, sentiment, and dialect. The second is the test dataset containing 3,000 tweets and two features labeled as a tweet and dialect. Table1 shows a description of the 15,548 rows of data. One of the challenges in this task is the imbalanced dataset that contains 2,168 sarcastic tweets and 10,380 nonsarcastic tweets. Figure 1 shows the distribution of classes in the training set. Data preprocessing used

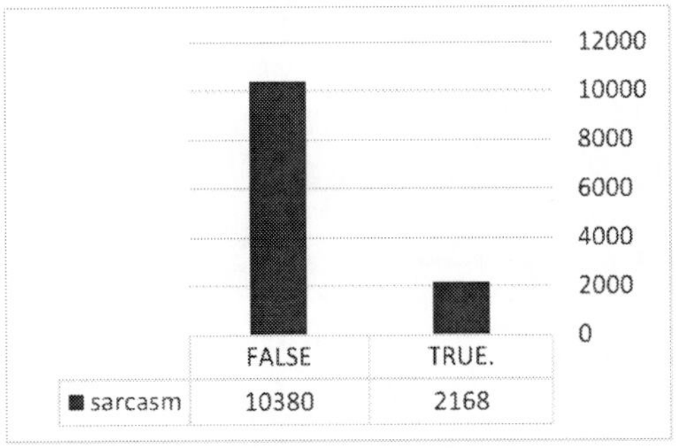

Figure 1: Classes Distribution in the training set for the sarcastic tweet labels.

are from the NLTK library (Bird, 2006), such as normalized duplicated characters and cleaning data from emojis, links, and Html tags.

Dataset	Size	sarcastic	non-sarcastic
Train	12548	2168	10380
Test	3000	821	2179
Total	**15548**	**2989**	**12559**

Table 2: The total size of the training and testing dataset, and an indication of the number if it's sarcastic tweets or not.

4 SarcasmDet Description

In our approach, we have used the Arabic pre-trained model called AraBERT (Antoun et al.). AraBert is a pre-trained model that focuses directly on the Arabic language, and it is based on the BERT architecture (Devlin et al., 2018). The AraBERT model's strength is being one of the best language models for NLP and sentiment analysis for the Arabic language. There are two versions of AraBERT(v01 and v02). The first version, AraBERT-v01, was trained on 77M sentences, with a size of 23GB and 2.7B of words. The second version, AraBERT-v02, was trained on 200M sentences with a size of 77GB and 8.6B words. In our approach, we have used both versions that are located in HuggingFace library(Wolf et al., 2019). We have experimented with several hyperparameters and the best result achieved from AraBERT-v02 is 0.5650 f1-score for the sarcastic class (f1-sarcastic), with learning_rate= 1e-5, manual_seed= 17, train_batch_size= 16 and num_train_epochs= 5. To enhance our results, we have used the ensemble technique, hard-voting (Chou et al., 2009). The best-ensembled model, SarcasmDet, achieved an f1-sarcastic (f1-score for sarcastic class) with 0.5989 in the testing phase. SarcasmDet has ensembled the AraBERT-v01 and AraBERT-v02 models. Figure 2 shows the architecture of SarcasmDet in detail.

5 Experiments

We have experimented with several deep learning models to detect sarcastic Arabic tweets through our training and testing phases. One of the experimented models is XLM-RoBERTa(XLM-R) (Liu et al., 2019), which performed less than other models in this task. The multilingual BERT (mBERT) model obtained one of the best results in our experiments because of multilingual support. The AraBERT was the one that captured the highest score with the v02 model. Table 3 shows the hyper-parameters we have used in our experiments for the tested models.

All of the models have been implemented using the HuggingFace library and SimpleTransforner pre-trained package. Some models, such as XLM-R, have default learning_rate=6e, but we changed it to 1e-5, which increased the results.

6 Results and Discussion

Our solution was separated into two phases. The first phase was the development phase. We have experienced several deep learning models XLM-R, AraBERT(v01,v02), mBERT(cased/uncased) by implementing them into the dataset to make the solution that suits the next phase, which is the test phase. In the test phase, our model performed great by using the ensemble technique and was ranking in the top 5 models. We believe that The AraBERT-v02 model has an excellent understanding of the Arabic language and sentence analysis. We have noticed that, with or without data preprocessing and hard-voting ensemble techniques, the model outperformed other models remarkably. We expect the exceeding of the AraBERT-v02 since it is already trained and tested on a massive amount of Arabic data. In the test phase section, we showed our experiments and the results that we achieved. Figure3 shows a plot chart for the best results.

6.1 Test Phase

We run multiple experiments on the ArSarcasm-v2 dataset in the test phase using AraBERT, XLM-R, and mBERT models. We chose AraBERT-v02 because this model scored the best F1-score with

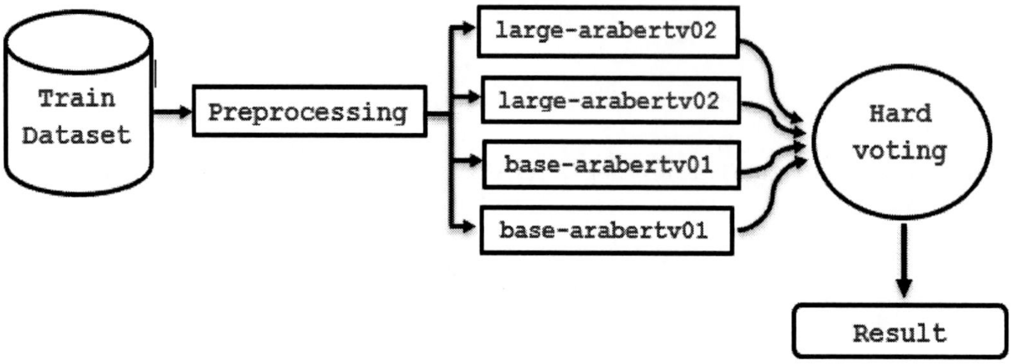

Figure 2: The architecture of our model.

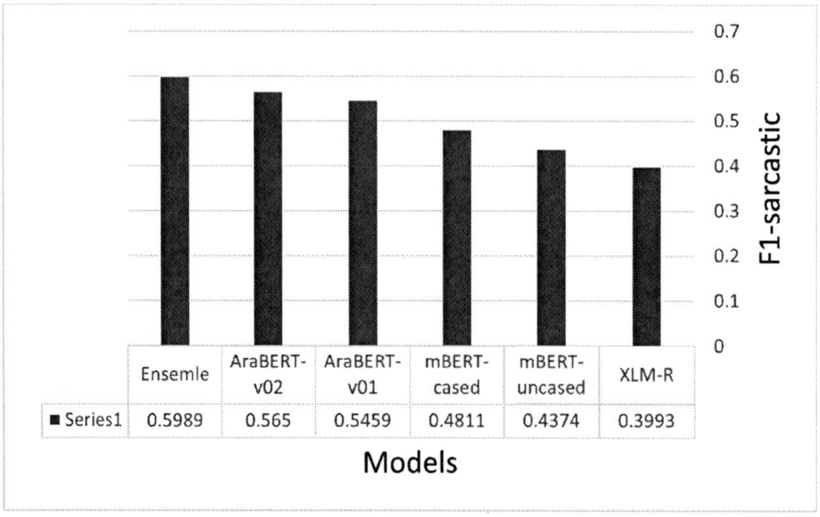

Figure 3: Compresion between result of all models.

#	Model	Epoch	Batch Size	LR	F1-sarcastic
1	AraBERTv01	5	16	1e-5	0.5459
2	AraBERTv02	5	16	1e-5	0.5650
3	XLM-R	5	16	1e-5	0.3993
4	mBERT-cased	5	16	1e-5	0.4811
5	mBERT-uncased	5	16	1e-5	0.4374

Table 3: all the hyper-parameter that we used in our experiments

Rank	F1-sarcastic	Accuracy	Macro F1	Precision	Recall
5th	0.5989	0.7830	0.7251	0.7268	0.7235

Table 4: Official results on subtask 1 (sarcasm Detection) test set.

0.5650 on the development phase. Table 4 shows the organizers' final result and table 5 shows all experiments that we have implemented, and table 6 shows all ensemble results. Finally, we noticed that AraBERT-v02 has strong performance on most complex implementations with the dataset, especially with the hard-voting ensemble technique on imbalanced data classes.

#	Preprocessing	F1-sarcastic
(1)	with	0.3993
(2)	without	0.4374
(3)	with	0.4650
(4)	with	0.4811
(5)	without	0.5419
(6)	with	0.5459
(7)	without	0.5560
(8)	with	0.5650

Table 5: Result for all experiment.

Ensemble	F1-sarcastic
(6)(7)(8)	0.5682
(5)(6)(7)(8)	0.5989

Table 6: All Ensemble result.

7 Conclusion

Our paper showed and described our approach that achieved the best accuracy score model in the Shared Task on Sarcasm and Sentiment Detection in Arabic (Sub-task 1 - Sarcasm Detection). We have implemented and experimented with several NLP-based language models, such as XLM-R, mBERT, and AraBERT, with hard-voting ensemble techniques to detect and solve the sarcasm in Arabic tweets. Our last and best solution is to ensemble the four models scoring F1-sarcastic 0.5650, 0.5459, 0.5560, 0.5419 by applying hard-voting ensemble technique. The SarcasmDet model achieved 0.5989 F1-sarcastic score, which outperformed the baseline model (0.3993 F1-sarcastic). Our proposed model has earned 5th place among 27 teams.

References

Nawaf A Abdulla, Nizar A Ahmed, Mohammed A Shehab, and Mahmoud Al-Ayyoub. 2013. Arabic sentiment analysis: Lexicon-based and corpus-based. In *2013 IEEE Jordan conference on applied electrical engineering and computing technologies (AEECT)*, pages 1–6. IEEE.

Malak Abdullah and Mirsad Hadzikadic. 2017. Sentiment analysis on arabic tweets: Challenges to dissecting the language. In *International Conference on Social Computing and Social Media*, pages 191–202. Springer.

Malak Abdullah, Mirsad Hadzikadicy, and Samira Shaikhz. 2018. Sedat: Sentiment and emotion detection in arabic text using cnn-lstm deep learning. In *2018 17th IEEE International Conference on Machine Learning and Applications (ICMLA)*, pages 835–840. IEEE.

Ibrahim Abu Farha, Wajdi Zaghouani, and Walid Magdy. 2021. Overview of the wanlp 2021 shared task on sarcasm and sentiment detection in arabic. In *Proceedings of the Sixth Arabic Natural Language Processing Workshop*.

Mahmoud Al-Ayyoub, Abed Allah Khamaiseh, Yaser Jararweh, and Mohammed N Al-Kabi. 2019. A comprehensive survey of arabic sentiment analysis.

Information processing & management, 56(2):320–342.

Dana Al-Ghadhban, Eman Alnkhilan, Lamma Tatwany, and Muna Alrazgan. 2017. Arabic sarcasm detection in twitter. In *2017 International Conference on Engineering & MIS (ICEMIS)*, pages 1–7. IEEE.

Wissam Antoun, Fady Baly, and Hazem Hajj. Arabert: Transformer-based model for arabic language understanding. In *LREC 2020 Workshop Language Resources and Evaluation Conference 11–16 May 2020*, page 9.

Steven Bird. 2006. Nltk: the natural language toolkit. In *Proceedings of the COLING/ACL 2006 Interactive Presentation Sessions*, pages 69–72.

Li-Chen Cheng and Song-Lin Tsai. 2019. Deep learning for automated sentiment analysis of social media. In *Proceedings of the 2019 IEEE/ACM International Conference on Advances in Social Networks Analysis and Mining*, pages 1001–1004.

Te-Shun Chou, Jeffrey Fan, Sharon Fan, and Kia Makki. 2009. Ensemble of machine learning algorithms for intrusion detection. In *2009 IEEE International Conference on Systems, Man and Cybernetics*, pages 3976–3980. IEEE.

Jacob Devlin, Ming-Wei Chang, Kenton Lee, and Kristina Toutanova. 2018. Bert: Pre-training of deep bidirectional transformers for language understanding. *arXiv preprint arXiv:1810.04805*.

Rehab Duwairi and Mahmoud El-Orfali. 2014. A study of the effects of preprocessing strategies on sentiment analysis for arabic text. *Journal of Information Science*, 40(4):501–513.

Ibrahim Abu Farha and Walid Magdy. 2020. From arabic sentiment analysis to sarcasm detection: The arsarcasm dataset. In *Proceedings of the 4th Workshop on Open-Source Arabic Corpora and Processing Tools, with a Shared Task on Offensive Language Detection*, pages 32–39.

Ronen Feldman. 2013. Techniques and applications for sentiment analysis. *Communications of the ACM*, 56(4):82–89.

Roberto González-Ibánez, Smaranda Muresan, and Nina Wacholder. 2011. Identifying sarcasm in twitter: a closer look. In *Proceedings of the 49th Annual Meeting of the Association for Computational Linguistics: Human Language Technologies*, pages 581–586.

Sabit Hassan, Younes Samih, Hamdy Mubarak, Ahmed Abdelali, Ammar Rashed, and Shammur Absar Chowdhury. 2020. Alt submission for osact shared task on offensive language detection. In *Proceedings of the 4th Workshop on Open-Source Arabic Corpora and Processing Tools, with a Shared Task on Offensive Language Detection*, pages 61–65.

Jihen Karoui, Farah Banamara Zitoune, and Veronique Moriceau. 2017. Soukhria: Towards an irony detection system for arabic in social media. *Procedia Computer Science*, 117:161–168.

Yinhan Liu, Myle Ott, Naman Goyal, Jingfei Du, Mandar Joshi, Danqi Chen, Omer Levy, Mike Lewis, Luke Zettlemoyer, and Veselin Stoyanov. 2019. Roberta: A robustly optimized bert pretraining approach. *arXiv preprint arXiv:1907.11692*.

Kingsley A Ogudo and Dahj Muwawa Jean Nestor. 2019. Sentiment analysis application and natural language processing for mobile network operators' support on social media. In *2019 International Conference on Advances in Big Data, Computing and Data Communication Systems (icABCD)*, pages 1–10. IEEE.

Thomas Wolf, Lysandre Debut, Victor Sanh, Julien Chaumond, Clement Delangue, Anthony Moi, Pierric Cistac, Tim Rault, Rémi Louf, Morgan Funtowicz, et al. 2019. Huggingface's transformers: State-of-the-art natural language processing. *arXiv preprint arXiv:1910.03771*.

Sarcasm and sentiment detection in Arabic language: A hybrid approach combining embeddings and rule-based features

Kamel Gaanoun[1]
[1]SI2M Lab
National Institute of Statistics
and Applied Economics

Rabat, Morocco
kamel.gaanoun@gmail.com

Imade Benelallam[1,2]
[1]SI2M Lab
National Institute of Statistics
and Applied Economics
[2]AIOX Labs
Rabat, Morocco
i.benelallam@insea.ac.ma

Abstract

This paper presents the ArabicProcessors team's system designed for sarcasm (subtask 1) and sentiment (subtask 2) detection shared task. We created a hybrid system by combining rule-based features and both static and dynamic embeddings using transformers and deep learning. The system's architecture is an ensemble of Gaussian Naive Bayes, MarBERT and Mazajak embedding. This process scored an F1-sarcastic score of 51% on sarcasm and an F1-PN of 71% for sentiment detection.

1 Introduction

Automatic sarcasm detection is a sub-discipline of sentiment analysis. This process, however, presents specific challenges (Nigam and Hurst, 2006; Pang and Lee, 2008) related to the fact that sarcasm can present opposite polarities between surface and intended sentiment. Macmillan English dictionary show the complexity of this phenomenon by defining it as *"the activity of saying or writing the opposite of what you mean, or of speaking in a way intended to make someone else feel stupid or show them that you are angry"*. This imposes additional layers to go beyond the methods used so far for sentiment analysis; since in addition to the sentimental polarity of the text, it will also be necessary to consider, among others, pragmatic factors (Kreuz and Caucci, 2007), based on context and background knowledge (Hazarika et al., 2018), behavior modelling (Rajadesingan et al., 2015; Agrawal et al., 2020) and the linguistic theory of incongruity (Joshi et al., 2015).

This observation is even more accentuated when it comes to the treatment of Arabic sources. Undoubtedly, the scarcity of data available in Arabic relative to English and the different Arabic dialects, for example, makes the detection of sarcasm even more complicated. Should sarcasm in the Arabic language be treated the same way it is treated in the English language? (Karoui et al., 2017) is sarcasm also present in Arabic the same way in its different dialects? This complexity is reflected in the scarcity of studies on automatic Arabic sarcasm detection, such that first works Karoui et al. (2017) and Ghanem et al. (2019) dealing with this problem, were recently published in 2017 and 2019.

Shared task on sarcasm and sentiment detection in Arabic (Abu Farha et al., 2021) is a new step in exploring this problem, aimed at both sarcasm detection (Subtask 1) and the analysis of sentimental polarity (Subtask 2). In this paper, we present our contribution to this challenge, by illustrating a novel approach based on a hybrid system that combines rule-based features and both static and dynamic embeddings using transformers and deep learning.

In the next sections, we describe used data in Section 2, describe our system in Section 3, present and discuss our results in Section 4, and finally summarize our work in Section 5.

2 Data

To train our models, we were provided with the same dataset for both subtasks; ArSarcasm-v2 (Abu Farha et al., 2021). It comprises of four variables, namely; the text of the tweet, a boolean label for sarcasm, sentimental polarity label (Positive, neutral and negative) as well as a dialect label.

In the cause of this shared task, a total of 12,548 tweets were made available to us, of which 2168 are labeled as sarcastic tweets, representing 17.3% of all tweets (Figure 1). Therefore, it is an unbalanced dataset, as is the case for the majority of sarcasm and irony datasets (Joshi et al., 2017).

With regards to sentiment distribution, approximately half were neutral, while 37% were negative and 17% positive (Figure 1). It is noteworthy, how-

Proceedings of the Sixth Arabic Natural Language Processing Workshop, pages 351–356
Kyiv, Ukraine (Virtual), April 19, 2021.

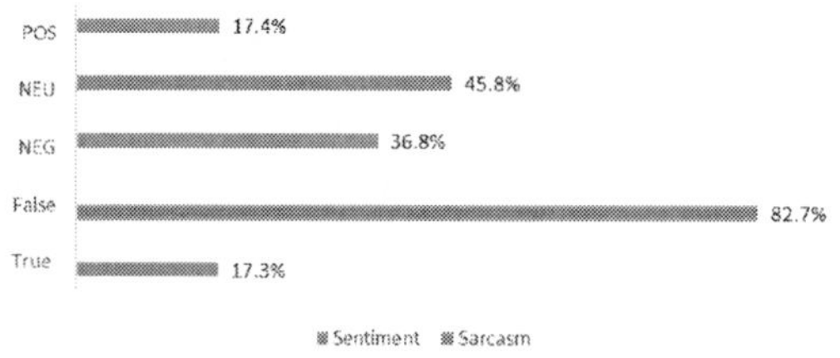

Figure 1: Sarcasm and Sentiment distribution.

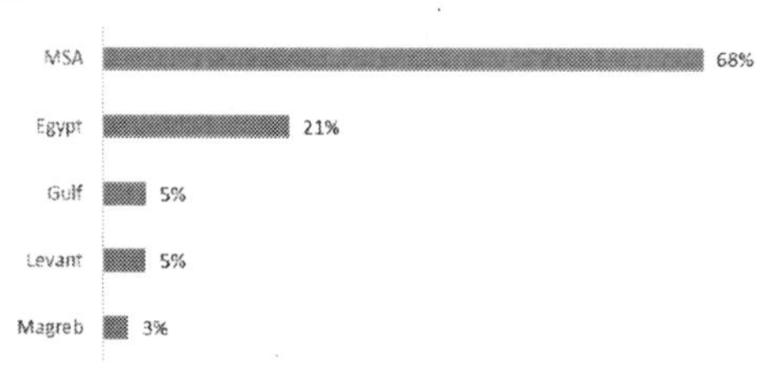

Figure 2: MSA and dialects distribution.

ever, that the vast majority of tweets were written in MSA (68%) and dominantly in Egyptian dialect (Figure2).

With respect to the sentimental polarity label, we established overriding amount of negative sentiments among sarcastic tweets (Figure 3). Moreover, it was noted that the Egyptian dialect, which has the same provided dataset general distribution with non-sarcastic tweets, it represents the same share as MSA among sarcastic tweets.

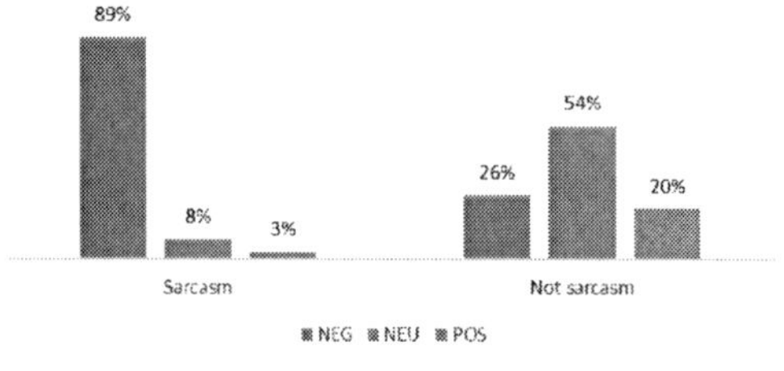

Figure 3: Sarcasm per sentiment polarity.

In analysing the most common words among sarcastic tweets, we noted two main groups, political personalities, or entities or events (Sissi, Trump, Morsi,«انقلاب»-coup d'etat-, Hilary, etc.) and punctuation dominated by quotation marks, colons, replies (@) and exclamation mark.

We further observed that averagely, there are more words in sarcastic tweets (18 words) than in the non-sarcastic ones (15 words). Sarcastic tweets are, however, on an average, shorter with 5.6 characters as against 6.6 characters for other tweets. The same applies to stopwords, which are more frequent among sarcastic tweets, reaching an average of 2.1 stopwords as against 1.7 for the rest of the tweets.

The most common emoticons in sarcastic and non-sarcastic tweets include the "face with tears of joy", the "new moon face", and the "pensive face". The emoticon showing a "face with tears of joy" sums up to 32% of sarcastic tweets, far ahead of the rest of the emoticons, while it sums up to only 7% of non-sarcastic tweets.

Regarding the interjection «ههه» with n repetition of the letter «ـهـ», equivalent to «haha», we found out that it is more present in sarcastic tweets with 4% compared to other tweets not exceeding 0.5%.

These findings are a strong indication of the potential efficiency of the use of features extracted from tweets. Indeed, this would be a factor for sarcasm detection. In that regard, we analyzed the features presented in the following section.

2.1 Features set

In addition to features extraction, the only preprocessing step was the removal of urls. We took inspiration from, and extended the features used by Karoui et al. (2017) to create features that have been classified into three groups:

(1) Surface features:

- Punctuation marks
- Quotation mark
- Sequence of exclamation or question marks
- Combination of question and exclamation marks
- Hashtags : presence and count
- Emoticons: total count and count of "face with tears of joy"
- Replies (@)
- Number of repeated words (stopwords excluded)
- Word count, char count, char per word, number of stopwords
- Diacritics percentage and boolean diacritics more than 45% to detect Quranic texts
- Url existence
- Interjections : «ههه ،هههه»
- Sarcasm words, see the list in Appendix A
- Opposition words, see the list in Appendix A

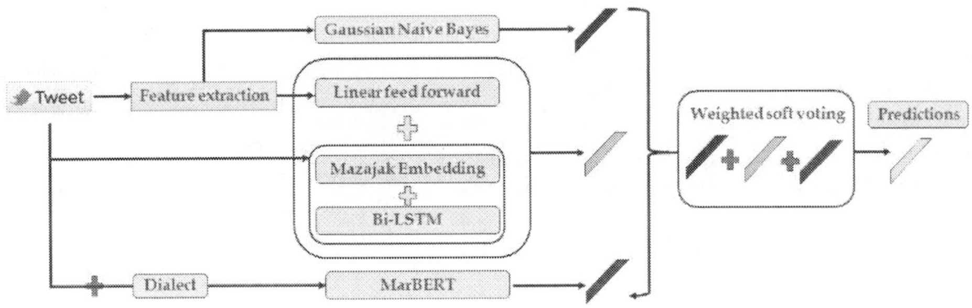

Figure 4: System architecture
Illustration inspired from Kang and Gwak (2020).

- Politic entities, see the list in Appendix A

(2) Sentiment features:

In order to get word sentiment scores, we combined two publicly available Arabic sentiment lexicons, namely *The Arabic Emoticon Lexicon* and *The Arabic Hashtag Lexicon (dialectal)*[1]. We also used *Emoji Sentiment Ranking 1.0* (Kralj Novak et al., 2015) to extract emoticons sentiment

- Total sentiment score and average sentiment score
- Positive/negative sentiment words count and percent
- Reversed sentiment score between the beginning and end of the tweet (Boolean), i.e. is the sentiment of the first part of the tweet the opposite of the last part's sentiment?
- Emoticons sentiment: total sentiment score, average sentiment score, positive/negative (Boolean)
- Emoticons count

(3) Intensifiers: As «إطلاقا، دهشة، مذهل», complete list is available in Appendix A

3 System

We adopted an ensemble hybrid system (Figure 4) combining extracted features and embeddings. The final prediction is the result of a weighted soft voting of the following models:

- Gaussian Naïve Bayes, with scaled features.
- MarBERT *"a large-scale pre-trained masked language model focused on both Dialectal Arabic (DA) and MSA"* (Abdul-Mageed et al., 2020). We first concatenated the tweets' text with their dialect label before feeding them to the model.
  - MarBERT, AraBERT (Antoun et al., 2020),and Arabic-BERT (Safaya et al., 2020) were compared. The former presented better results.
- Bidirectional long short term memory (Bi-LSTM) using Mazajak embeddings (Abu Farha and Magdy, 2019), concatenated with a fully connected layer with extracted features as input.

A 5-fold stratified cross-validation was used to evaluate and compare models. Also, the weights for the soft voting step were obtained by Bayesian optimization.

We used the hyper-paremeters as shown in Table 1.

GPU	Tesla P100-PCIE-16GB
Language	Python 3.6.9
Main librairies	Hugging Face Transformers 4.4.2, Torch 1.7.0, Sklearn 0.22.2, bayesian-optimization-1.2.0
Bert Hyperparameters	Learning rate: 2e-5, Epochs: 4, Batch size: 64, Embedding maximum length: 125
Bi-LSTM - Mazajak-	Hidden units: 64, Dropout: 0.2, Activation: ReLU, Spatial dropout: 0.3, Epochs: 20, Batch size: 64

Table 1: Used infrastructure and hyperparameters

[1] http://saifmohammad.com/WebPages/ArabicSA.html

4 Results and discussion

We oriented the development of our system towards the use of an ensemble model including MarBERT, Bi-LSTM with Mazajak embedding and Gaussian Naive Bayes. Gaussian Naive Bayes was chosen after comparison with Logistic regression, SVM, XGBoost, LightGBM, and Random forest was done.

Results obtained for individual models on the 5-fold cross validation, and ensembled one are reported in Table 2.

Model	Sarcasm	Sentiment
Gaussian Naive Bayes	43	46
MarBERT	57	71
Bi-LSTM -Mazajak-	46	58
Weighted ensemble	59	73

Table 2: 5-fold cross validation scores (%)
Sarcasm: F1-score for sarcastic class, Sentiment: Macro average of the F-score of the positive and negative classes

We draw attention to the fact that among the ensembled models, MarBERT accounts for the largest share. This confirms the effectiveness of dynamic embeddings and BERT based models.

Results obtained on the official evaluation set are reported in the next subsection.

4.1 Official results

The organizers provided us with an unlabeled TEST dataset, intended for the final evaluation of the system, composed of 3000 tweets as well as their respective dialects. The scores obtained on this dataset was used for system ranking (see Table 3).

Model	Sarcasm	Sentiment
Gaussian Naive Bayes	39.34	32.33
MarBERT	54.17	73.32
Bi-LSTM -Mazajak-	23.15	51.32
Final official results	**50.86**	**71.45**

Table 3: Scores obtained on final evaluation set (%)
Sarcasm: F1-score for sarcastic class, Sentiment: Macro average of the F-score of the positive and negative classes

These scores reflect the complexity of the sarcasm detection when compared to sentiment analysis. Furthermore, our model shows better generalization capacity on sentiments, by loosing only 1.5 points between cross-validation and the final evaluation results. Exploring the evaluation set distribution, we note that 27% of the tweets are labeled as sarcastic compared to only 17% among Train set tweets. Covariate shift is then one possible reason for the generalization issue raised regarding sarcastic tweets.

We also note that the Bi-LSTM is the model suffering the most from this generalization issue by loosing 34 points. This leads us to conclude that this model could be enhanced adopting a better regularization strategy, or even not considering it in the final ensemble model.

Finally the results are confirming the higher accuracy of Bert based model upon other models, and thus going deeper in this direction can lead to better results, by adopting some eventual improvement methods as mentioned in the next subsection.

4.2 Discussion

This shared task presents three main challenges: the few amount of data, the unbalanced labels, and the complexity of the sarcasm detection even for humans. Indeed, with no information about the text context nor the writer profile, this indicates a lack of primordial clues for sarcasm detection. Adding this information could enhance the system's performance. Furthermore, balancing the data is a possible way of improvement by upsampling the minority label.

We could also use a hierarchical system by taking advantage of the efficiency of the sentiment prediction model. Indeed, a first step would be to predict the tweets' sentiment, then use this prediction as a feature for sarcasm prediction, since we have seen that sarcasm is strongly linked to the polarity of the tweet.

Finally, we can still explore other ways to improve BERT-based models by concatenating more information in addition to the dialect.

5 Conclusion

In this paper, we have described our contribution to the WANLP'21 sarcasm and sentiment detection in Arabic subtasks. The system's architecture is an ensemble of Gaussian Naive Bayes, MarBERT and Mazajak embedding. By recording an F1-score of 51% at subtask 1, and 71% at subtask 2, this approach demonstrates the efficiency of our hybrid system in the challenging field of sarcasm and sentiment detection for Arabic texts.

References

Muhammad Abdul-Mageed, AbdelRahim Elmadany, and El Moatez Billah Nagoudi. 2020. Arbert & marbert: Deep bidirectional transformers for arabic. *arXiv preprint arXiv:2101.01785.*

Ibrahim Abu Farha and Walid Magdy. 2019. Mazajak: An online Arabic sentiment analyser. In *Proceedings of the Fourth Arabic Natural Language Processing Workshop*, pages 192–198, Florence, Italy. Association for Computational Linguistics.

Ibrahim Abu Farha and Walid Magdy. 2020. From Arabic sentiment analysis to sarcasm detection: The ArSarcasm dataset. In *Proceedings of the 4th Workshop on Open-Source Arabic Corpora and Processing Tools, with a Shared Task on Offensive Language Detection*, pages 32–39, Marseille, France. European Language Resource Association.

Ibrahim Abu Farha, Wajdi Zaghouani, and Walid Magdy. 2021. Overview of the wanlp 2021 shared task on sarcasm and sentiment detection in arabic. In *Proceedings of the Sixth Arabic Natural Language Processing Workshop*.

Ameeta Agrawal, Aijun An, and Manos Papagelis. 2020. Leveraging transitions of emotions for sarcasm detection. pages 1505–1508.

Wissam Antoun, Fady Baly, and Hazem Hajj. 2020. Arabert: Transformer-based model for arabic language understanding. In *LREC 2020 Workshop Language Resources and Evaluation Conference 11–16 May 2020*, page 9.

Bilal Ghanem, Jihen Karoui, Farah Benamara, Véronique Moriceau, and Paolo Rosso. 2019. Idat at fire2019: Overview of the track on irony detection in arabic tweets. In *Proceedings of the 11th Forum for Information Retrieval Evaluation*, FIRE '19, page 10–13, New York, NY, USA. Association for Computing Machinery.

Devamanyu Hazarika, Soujanya Poria, Sruthi Gorantla, Erik Cambria, Roger Zimmermann, and Rada Mihalcea. 2018. CASCADE: Contextual sarcasm detection in online discussion forums. In *Proceedings of the 27th International Conference on Computational Linguistics*, pages 1837–1848, Santa Fe, New Mexico, USA. Association for Computational Linguistics.

Aditya Joshi, Pushpak Bhattacharyya, and Mark J Carman. 2017. Automatic sarcasm detection: A survey. *ACM Computing Surveys (CSUR)*, 50(5):1–22.

Aditya Joshi, Vinita Sharma, and Pushpak Bhattacharyya. 2015. Harnessing context incongruity for sarcasm detection. In *Proceedings of the 53rd Annual Meeting of the Association for Computational Linguistics and the 7th International Joint Conference on Natural Language Processing (Volume 2: Short Papers)*, pages 757–762, Beijing, China. Association for Computational Linguistics.

Jaeyong Kang and Jeonghwan Gwak. 2020. Ensemble learning of lightweight deep learning models using knowledge distillation for image classification. *Mathematics*, 8(10).

Jihen Karoui, Farah Banamara Zitoune, and Veronique Moriceau. 2017. Soukhria: Towards an irony detection system for arabic in social media. *Procedia Computer Science*, 117:161–168.

Petra Kralj Novak, Jasmina Smailović, Borut Sluban, and Igor Mozetič. 2015. Sentiment of emojis. *PLoS ONE*, 10(12):e0144296.

Roger Kreuz and Gina Caucci. 2007. Lexical influences on the perception of sarcasm. In *Proceedings of the Workshop on Computational Approaches to Figurative Language*, pages 1–4, Rochester, New York. Association for Computational Linguistics.

Kamal Nigam and Matthew Hurst. 2006. Towards a robust metric of polarity. In *Computing Attitude and Affect in Text: Theory and Applications*, pages 265–279. Springer.

Bo Pang and Lillian Lee. 2008. Opinion mining and sentiment analysis. *Foundations and Trends in Information Retrieval*, 2:1–135.

Ashwin Rajadesingan, Reza Zafarani, and Huan Liu. 2015. Sarcasm detection on twitter: A behavioral modeling approach. *WSDM 2015 - Proceedings of the 8th ACM International Conference on Web Search and Data Mining*, pages 97–106.

Ali Safaya, Moutasem Abdullatif, and Deniz Yuret. 2020. Kuisail at semeval-2020 task 12: Bert-cnn for offensive speech identification in social media. In *Proceedings of the International Workshop on Semantic Evaluation (SemEval)*.

A Appendices

- Sarcasm words: استهبال ، إستهبال، إستهبل، استهبل، مسخرة، سخر، إستهزاء، اِستهزاء ، تهكم، طنز، طنز
- Opposition words: لكن ،مع أنه ، مع ان ، مع انه ، مع ذلك ،في حين أن،في حين ان، من ناحية ثانية،من ناحية تانية،من ناحيه ثانية،من ناحيه تانية،من ناحية ثانيه،من ناحية تانيه، مع إنو،بالرغم،غير أن، غير أنه،فيما أن،فيما ان،غير ان، غير انه،بينما،بيد ان،بيد أن،إلا أن،الا ان،إلا ان،الا أن،بخلاف،
- Politic entities: مرسي، سيسي، سوريا، ترامب، ، مصر، الانقلاب، انقلاب، داعش، الاخوان ، هيلاري، الشعب، حزب، كلنتون، السعودية ، بوتن، انتخاب، انتخب، حرب، بشار، ثورة،سياسة

- Intensifiers list: اطلاق، مذهل، دهشة، إطلاقا، مخيف، ميت، جنون، تماما، دموي، مرارة، ابعد حد، إفراط، استثنائي، خصوصا، هائل، لا يصدق، للغاية مخيف، خيالي، غير عادي، كبير، ثمين، شائن، غاضب،بقوة، حرفيا، قليلا، وبالتالي، لافت للنظر، حقيقة، جذريا، لا جدا، رائع، رهيب، بدرجة عليا، ممتاز، يصدق،حقيقي

Combining Context-Free and Contextualized Representations for Arabic Sarcasm Detection and Sentiment Identification

Amey Hengle[1], **Atharva Kshirsagar**[1], **Shaily Desai**[1], and **Manisha Marathe**[2]

[1,2]Department of Computer Engineering, PVG's College of Engineering and Technology, affiliated to Savitribai Phule Pune University, India.

[1]{ameyhengle22, atharvakshirsagar145, shailysd02} @gmail.com

[2]mvm_comp@pvgcoet.ac.in

Abstract

Since their inception, transformer-based language models have led to impressive performance gains across multiple natural language processing tasks. For Arabic, the current state-of-the-art results on most datasets are achieved by the AraBERT language model. Notwithstanding these recent advancements, sarcasm and sentiment detection persist to be challenging tasks in Arabic, given the language's rich morphology, linguistic disparity and dialectal variations. This paper proffers team SPPU-AASM's submission for the WANLP ArSarcasm shared-task 2021, which centers around the sarcasm and sentiment polarity detection of Arabic tweets. The study proposes a hybrid model, combining sentence representations from AraBERT with static word vectors trained on Arabic social media corpora. The proposed system achieves a F1-sarcastic score of 0.62 and a F-PN score of 0.715 for the sarcasm and sentiment detection tasks, respectively. Simulation results show that the proposed system outperforms multiple existing approaches for both the tasks, suggesting that the amalgamation of context-free and context-dependent text representations can help capture complementary facets of word meaning in Arabic. The system ranked second and tenth in the respective sub-tasks of sarcasm detection and sentiment identification.

1 Introduction

With the advent of social media platforms as a valuable source of opinion-rich information, work on subjectivity language analysis has continued to receive increasing interest from the Arabic NLP community. Sentiment Analysis (SA) has been the dominant theme in this area, with notable works ranging from the creation of lexical resources and sentiment datasets (El-Beltagy, 2016; Badaro et al., 2014; AbdelRahim Elmadany and Magdy, 2018; Kiritchenko et al., 2016) to the contrivance of neural network-based classification models (Alayba et al., 2018; Heikal et al., 2018; Kaibi et al., 2020). In comparison, the literature in Arabic sarcasm detection is still in its nascent stage, limited to a few notable works (Karoui et al., 2017; Ghanem et al., 2019; Abbes et al., 2020).

Recently, transformer-based language models have proved highly efficient at language understanding, achieving promising results across multiple NLP tasks and benchmark datasets. The language modeling capability of these models is aiding in capturing the literal meaning of context-heavy texts. For Arabic NLP in particular, the best results for sentiment analysis are currently achieved by AraBERT, a language model proposed by Antoun et al. (2020).

Despite this recent progress, sarcasm detection remains a challenging task, primarily due to the use of implicit, indirect phrasing and the figurative nature of language (Abu Farha et al., 2021). The task becomes even more challenging when working with Twitter data, as the social media posts tend to be short and often contain sources of noise, code-switching, and the use of nonstandard dialectal variations (Baly et al., 2017). Furthermore, BERT-based models are found to struggle with rare words (Schick and Schütze, 2019), which can be encountered more in social media texts due to their informal nature and the prevalent use of slang words. For language models like AraBERT, this can pose a challenge, primarily since it has been trained on structured corpora from Wikipedia.

Building on the capabilities of language models, some recent studies have shown that incorporating entity vectors can benefit the BERT-based language models, especially for domain-specific tasks or datasets (Poerner et al., 2020; Lin et al., 2019; Peinelt et al., 2020). An interesting approach followed by Alghanmi et al. (2020) suggests that the

Proceedings of the Sixth Arabic Natural Language Processing Workshop, pages 357–363
Kyiv, Ukraine (Virtual), April 19, 2021.

performance of language models can be boosted by incorporating static word embeddings trained on specific social media corpora.

In this study, we posit a solution for subtask-1 and subtask-2 of the WANLP ArSarcasm shared task 2021 (Abu Farha et al., 2021). While subtask-1 focuses on identifying sarcasm, subtask-2 deals with classifying the sentiment polarity in Arabic tweets. Inspired by the works of Peinelt et al. (2020) and Alghanmi et al. (2020), we propose a hybrid model, combining the sentence representations learned from AraBERT with pre-trained Arabic word vectors proposed by Abu Farha and Magdy (2019). Results attest that the proposed methodology can provide a competent way of subsuming the advantages of both the contextualized and context-free word representations, outperforming all the baseline models for both tasks.

The rest of the paper is organized as follows: In Section 2, we provide a concise literature review of previous works in Arabic sentiment and sarcasm detection. Section 3 provides a descriptive analysis of the dataset at hand. In Section 4, we present the proposed system, and in Section 5, we describe the experimental setup details. Section 6 interprets the results. Finally, Section 7 concludes the study and points to possible directions for future work.

2 Related Work

Early works in Arabic subjectivity analysis focused on using conventional machine learning approaches and lexical methods (Al-Ayyoub et al., 2019). With the emergence of deep learning techniques, research in Arabic NLP has shifted from the traditional statistical standpoint to designing complex neural network models and learning word representations. Al Sallab et al. (2015) experimented with various deep learning models such as a recursive autoencoder (RAE), deep belief networks (DBN), and a deep auto-encoder (DAE). Alayba et al. (2018) built an Arabic SA system based on a combination of CNNs and LSTMs. In (Al-Smadi et al., 2018), the authors proposed an aspect-based sentiment analysis system based on a hybrid architecture of BiLSTM and conditional random field (CRF).

The success of the English word2vec (Mikolov et al., 2013) and fast-Text (Bojanowski et al., 2016) motivated other works to achieve the same feat by creating language-specific word embeddings. For Arabic NLP, some early attempts include word2vec-based AraVec (Soliman et al., 2017), followed by fast-Text (Bojanowski et al., 2016). Recently, Abu Farha and Magdy (2019) proposed the Mazajak embeddings, trained exclusively on a large Arabic twitter corpus for handling the varied Arabic dialects. Multiple studies leveraged this advancement in word representations for both the sarcasm and sentiment detection tasks. For instance, Heikal et al. (2018) developed a CNN and LSTM ensemble model for Arabic SA. The authors employed pre-trained AraVec word embeddings for the text representation. Kaibi et al. (2020) proposed a hybrid model for Arabic SA, concatenating pre-trained AraVec and fast-Text vectors. Abu Farha and Magdy (2019) used the pre-trained Mazajak vectors on a CNN-BiLSTM ensemble model, achieving state-of-the-art results on three benchmark datasets. For sarcasm detection, a similar approach was followed by Abu Farha et al. (2021), where the authors used the Mazajak vectors in combination with a BiLSTM model.

The best results for multiple datasets is currently achieved by fine-tuning the AraBERT model (Antoun et al., 2020), eliminating the need to use the static word vectors in standard settings. Despite this fact, we believe that AraBERT and Mazajak have complementary strengths and can lead to improved results if used in coalescence. In this study, we investigate the effectiveness of combining the word representations obtained from these two models on the sarcasm detection and sentiment identification tasks.

3 Dataset

The WANLP ArSarcasm shared-task 2021 follows the ArSarcasm v2 dataset (Abu Farha et al., 2021). The dataset contains sarcasm, sentiment and dialect labels of 12,549 Arabic tweets. The tweets span across five Arabic dialects including MSA, Gulf, Egyptian, Levantine, and Maghrebi, with MSA and Egyptian dialects having the highest percentage of tweets. For development, we follow a standard 80-20 stratified split on the ArSarcasm v2 dataset. This leaves us with a validation set of 2510 tweets, which are used for the primary evaluation of the proposed system along with the baseline models. The organizers provide a separate dataset for testing, consisting of 3,000 tweets. Table 1 and Table 2 provide a descriptive analysis of the final training, validation and test sets for the tasks of sentiment identification and sarcasm detection respectively.

Set	Positive	Negative	Neutral	Total
Training	1744	3697	4598	10039
Validation	436	925	1149	2510
Testing	575	1677	748	3000
Total	2755	6298	6495	15548

Table 1: Label wise distribution for sentiment analysis.

Set	True	False	Total
Training	1734	8305	10039
Validation	434	2076	2510
Testing	821	2179	3000
Total	2989	12559	15548

Table 2: Label wise distribution for sarcasm detection.

4 Proposed System

Unlike the static word models such as word2vec or fast-Text, language models like AraBERT follow a different tokenization strategy; wherein each word is split into one or more wordpiece tokens (Antoun et al., 2020). Thus, we cannot simply concatenate the pre-trained Mazajak embeddings with the contextualized representations predicted by AraBERT at the word level. We instead combine these word representations at the sentence level, following an approach similar to the one used by Peinelt et al. (2020). The final sentence representation is passed to the dropout layer, followed by a dense layer with Softmax activation for classification. Fig 1 gives an overview of the proposed system's architecture. The following section describes each system component in detail.

4.1 CNN-BiLSTM emsemble

In order to get a sentence representation from the static word embeddings, we employ a CNN-BiLSTM ensemble model. The model learns a 128-dimensional feature vector from the pre-trained Mazajak embeddings. While CNN excels at extracting features from the input data, BiLSTM supports better modeling of sequential dependencies. Thus, using an ensemble helps us subsume the advantages of both these techniques.

4.1.1 Static Embedding Input

The proposed system makes use of the Skip-Gram model variant of the Mazajak word embeddings, pre-trained on 250 million Arabic tweets [1]. During training, the embedding layer maps each word in a

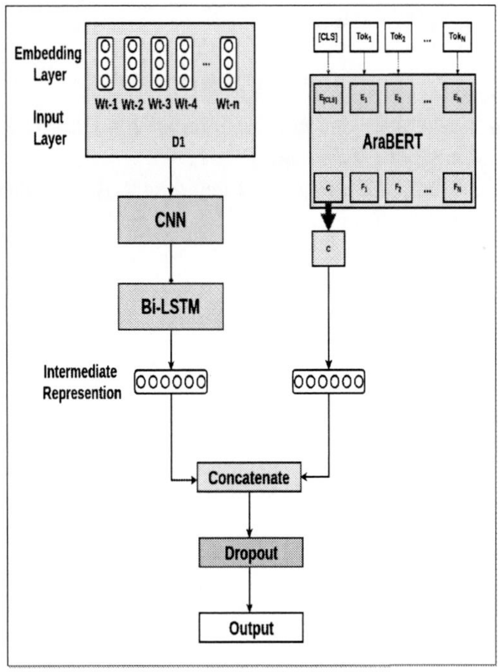

Figure 1: Architecture diagram of the proposed model.

tweet to its corresponding embedding, converting the tweet into a real valued dense vector.

4.1.2 CNN Layer

The word vectors generated by the embedding layer are fed to a CNN layer. The discrete convolutions performed by the CNN layer help to extract the most influential n-grams in the tweet. This is followed by a max-pooling layer.

4.1.3 BiLSTM Layer

The bidirectional short term memory (BiLSTM) layer is just a combination of two LSTMs running in opposite direction (Graves and Schmidhuber, 2005), allowing the network to simultaneously encode the forward and backward information of a sequence at each time step. The intermediate sentence representation generated by the CNN layer is passed to the BiLSTM layer, which encodes it into a 128-dimensional feature vector $D \in \mathbb{R}^{d_1}$.

4.2 AraBERT

The contextualized tweet representations are obtained using the pre-trained AraBERT model (Antoun et al., 2020). In particular, each tweet t is encoded using the C vector from AraBERT's final hidden state layer corresponding to the special

[1] http://mazajak.inf.ed.ac.uk:8000/

classification token [CLS]:

$$C = AraBERT(t) \in \mathbb{R}^{d_2} \quad (1)$$

where d_2 denotes the internal hidden size of AraBERT (768 for AraBERT v0.2).

Computed using self-attention, the [CLS] token vector is designed to collect information from the rest of the hidden states and be used as a unique representation of the entire sequence (Devlin et al., 2019). We find that this method is more robust than averaging the hidden states, mainly since it avoids every state to be averaged with the same weight, including stopwords and tokens not relevant to the classification task.

4.3 Combined Classification Layer

The final sentence representation F is obtained by simply concatenating the C vector predicted by the AraBERT model with the feature vector D obtained from the CNN-BiLSTM ensemble.

$$F = [D; C] \in \mathbb{R}^{d1+d2} \quad (2)$$

After applying a dropout, the resultant concatenated vector is passed to a dense layer with Softmax activation for classification.

5 Experimental Setup

5.1 Data Preparation

For each tweet in the corpus, we apply standard text cleaning steps including the removal of hashtags, mentions, urls, punctuations and arabic diacritics (Said et al., 2009). For stopword removal, we used a publicly available resource [2]. To replace emojis and emoticons with their corresponding Arabic translations, we created a custom dictionary mapping. Arabic text normalization and lemmatization is done using the AraBERT preprocessor [3]. Each tweet is padded to a maximum length of 100 for both the AraBERT and the CNN-BiLSTM model. Longer tweets are truncated.

5.2 Parameters and Training Environment

For the CNN-BiLSTM ensemble part of the proposed system, we employ a CNN layer with 256 filters and relu activation. For the BiLSTM layer, we use 128 dimensional units (64 for each LSTM), and apply a recurrent dropout rate of 0.2. All layers are implemented using Keras [4]. For using the pre-trained AraBERT model, we follow the Tensorflow implementation of Hugging Face [5]. We make use of the AraBERT v0.2 version, which is officially available under the name bert-base-arabertv02. The same model is used for text tokenization. After predicting the [CLS] token vector from the AraBERT model, we freeze the model weights. We then jointly train the CNN-BiLSTM ensemble with the combined classification layer. The model is trained using the Adam optimizer (Kingma and Ba, 2017), a learning rate of 5e-5, epsilon value of 1e-08, clipnorm equal to 1.0, a batch size of 16, and sparse categorical crossentropy loss, with the usage of early stopping for a callback.

5.3 Baseline Models

As a baseline, we compare the performance of the proposed system against the results of the pre-trained AraBERT model (Antoun et al., 2020), for both the sarcasm and sentiment detection tasks. Furthermore, we show the performance of the previous systems proposed by Abu Farha and Magdy (2020) and Abu Farha and Magdy (2019) for the tasks of sarcasm detection and sentiment identification respectively.

6 Results and Discussion

The official evaluation metric for the sarcasm detection subtask is the F-score of the sarcastic class, while that for the sentiment identification subtask is the F-PN score (macro average of the F-score of the positive and negative classes). For each model, the validation set results are averaged over five runs to ensure a fair comparison.

Table 3 shows the results for the sarcasm detection subtask. The proposed model shows a 10-percent improvement in the F1-sarcasm score over the baseline AraBERT model in identifying sarcastic tweets. This indicates that the proposed system offers a more nuanced ability to capture the figurative meaning of tweets and identify implicit negative sentiments. Table 4 lists the baseline models' performances and the proposed system for sentiment identification subtask. It is observed that both the proposed and AraBERT baseline model perform well on the neutral class. However, a better F-PN score indicates that the proposed model can more efficiently distinguish the positive and negative sentiment polarities from the neutral class. Furthermore, the proposed system seems to

[2]https://github.com/mohataher/arabic-stop-words

[3]https://github.com/aub-mind/arabert

[4]https://keras.io/about/

[5]https://github.com/huggingface/transformers

Model	Accuracy	Precision	Recall	F1-Macro	F1-Sarcastic
(Abu Farha and Magdy, 2020)	-	0.62	0.38	0.46	0.44
AraBERT	0.85	0.75	0.70	0.72	0.52
AraBERT + CNN-BiLSTM	**0.86**	**0.76**	**0.78**	**0.77**	**0.62**
AraBERT + CNN-BiLSTM (Official results on test set)	**0.7410**	**0.7031**	**0.7447**	**0.7096**	**0.6140**

Table 3: Performance comparison of models for subtask-1 : sarcasm detection. All metrics correspond to the results on the sarcastic class.

Model	Accuracy	Precision	Recall	F1-Macro	F-PN
(Abu Farha and Magdy, 2019)	0.67	0.64	0.66	0.64	0.60
AraBERT	0.73	0.71	0.68	0.70	0.67
AraBERT + CNN-BiLSTM	**0.75**	**0.72**	**0.73**	**0.72**	**0.71**
AraBERT + CNN-BiLSTM (Official results on test set)	**0.6840**	**0.6421**	**0.6388**	**0.6232**	**0.7073**

Table 4: Performance comparison of models for subtask-2: sentiment identification.

better handle the data-imbalance for both the tasks and is more robust to overfitting on the minority classes, showing a significant lead in the recall scores.

Overall, the proposed method shows improved results across all the metrics for both the sarcasm and sentiment detection tasks. The performance improvements can be attributed to the fact that unlike the Mazajak word embeddings, which are exclusively trained on a Twitter corpus, the AraBERT model is trained on the Arabic Wikipedia and news corpora, preventing it from witnessing the varied dialects in which social media posts are written. It is reasonable to postulate that while language models like AraBERT capture rich contextual information, the Mazajak word vectors can provide valuable complementary information for rare words, which can be found abundantly in social media texts. Hence, using them in combination can only help a system capture complementary facets of word meaning, thereby enhancing its performance on the downstream sentiment and sarcasm detection tasks.

7 Conclusion

In this study, we proposed a hybrid model to combine the contextualized sentence representations obtained from AraBERT with pre-trained Mazajak word vectors. We show that the proposed model outperforms the standalone AraBERT model for both the sarcasm and sentiment detection tasks. Our findings suggest that incorporating static word vectors might help language models like AraBERT to deal with rare words and the constantly updating language of social media. An alternative strategy would be to pre-train AraBERT on specific social media corpora like Twitter. However this can prove to be extremely expensive and is not feasible in practice. It is also important to note that, while the proposed model leads in performance, it is more complex, and has a greater number of trainable parameters. Hence, it would be essential to test its feasibility on datasets larger than the ArSarcasm v2 dataset.

References

Ines Abbes, Wajdi Zaghouani, Omaima El-Hardlo, and Faten Ashour. 2020. Daict: A dialectal arabic irony corpus extracted from twitter. In *Proceedings of The 12th Language Resources and Evaluation Conference*, pages 6265–6271.

Hamdy Mubarak AbdelRahim Elmadany and Walid Magdy. 2018. Arsas: An arabic speech-act and sentiment corpus of tweets. In *Proceedings of the Eleventh International Conference on Language*

Resources and Evaluation (LREC 2018), Paris, France. European Language Resources Association (ELRA).

Ibrahim Abu Farha and Walid Magdy. 2019. Mazajak: An online Arabic sentiment analyser. In *Proceedings of the Fourth Arabic Natural Language Processing Workshop*, pages 192–198, Florence, Italy. Association for Computational Linguistics.

Ibrahim Abu Farha and Walid Magdy. 2020. From Arabic sentiment analysis to sarcasm detection: The ArSarcasm dataset. In *Proceedings of the 4th Workshop on Open-Source Arabic Corpora and Processing Tools, with a Shared Task on Offensive Language Detection*, pages 32–39, Marseille, France. European Language Resource Association.

Ibrahim Abu Farha, Wajdi Zaghouani, and Walid Magdy. 2021. Overview of the wanlp 2021 shared task on sarcasm and sentiment detection in arabic. In *Proceedings of the Sixth Arabic Natural Language Processing Workshop*.

Mahmoud Al-Ayyoub, Abed Allah Khamaiseh, Yaser Jararweh, and Mohammed N Al-Kabi. 2019. A comprehensive survey of arabic sentiment analysis. *Information processing & management*, 56(2):320–342.

Ahmad Al Sallab, Hazem Hajj, Gilbert Badaro, Ramy Baly, Wassim El Hajj, and Khaled Bashir Shaban. 2015. Deep learning models for sentiment analysis in Arabic. In *Proceedings of the Second Workshop on Arabic Natural Language Processing*, pages 9–17, Beijing, China. Association for Computational Linguistics.

Mohammad Al-Smadi, Omar Qawasmeh, Mahmoud Al-Ayyoub, Y. Jararweh, and Brij Gupta. 2018. Deep recurrent neural network vs. support vector machine for aspect-based sentiment analysis of arabic hotels' reviews. *J. Comput. Sci.*, 27:386–393.

Abdulaziz M. Alayba, Vasile Palade, Matthew England, and Rahat Iqbal. 2018. A combined cnn and lstm model for arabic sentiment analysis. *Machine Learning and Knowledge Extraction*, page 179–191.

Israa Alghanmi, Luis Espinosa Anke, and Steven Schockaert. 2020. Combining BERT with static word embeddings for categorizing social media. In *Proceedings of the Sixth Workshop on Noisy User-generated Text (W-NUT 2020)*, pages 28–33, Online. Association for Computational Linguistics.

Wissam Antoun, Fady Baly, and Hazem Hajj. 2020. Arabert: Transformer-based model for arabic language understanding. *arXiv preprint arXiv:2003.00104*.

Gilbert Badaro, Ramy Baly, Hazem Hajj, Nizar Habash, and Wassim El-Hajj. 2014. A large scale Arabic sentiment lexicon for Arabic opinion mining. In *Proceedings of the EMNLP 2014 Workshop on Arabic Natural Language Processing (ANLP)*, pages 165–173, Doha, Qatar. Association for Computational Linguistics.

Ramy Baly, Gilbert Badaro, Georges El-Khoury, Rawan Moukalled, Rita Aoun, Hazem Hajj, Wassim El-Hajj, Nizar Habash, and Khaled Shaban. 2017. A characterization study of Arabic Twitter data with a benchmarking for state-of-the-art opinion mining models. In *Proceedings of the Third Arabic Natural Language Processing Workshop*, pages 110–118, Valencia, Spain. Association for Computational Linguistics.

Piotr Bojanowski, Edouard Grave, Armand Joulin, and Tomas Mikolov. 2016. Enriching word vectors with subword information. *arXiv preprint arXiv:1607.04606*.

Jacob Devlin, Ming-Wei Chang, Kenton Lee, and Kristina Toutanova. 2019. Bert: Pre-training of deep bidirectional transformers for language understanding.

Samhaa R. El-Beltagy. 2016. NileULex: A phrase and word level sentiment lexicon for Egyptian and Modern Standard Arabic. In *Proceedings of the Tenth International Conference on Language Resources and Evaluation (LREC'16)*, pages 2900–2905, Portorož, Slovenia. European Language Resources Association (ELRA).

Bilal Ghanem, Jihen Karoui, Farah Benamara, Véronique Moriceau, and Paolo Rosso. 2019. Idat at fire2019: Overview of the track on irony detection in arabic tweets. In *Proceedings of the 11th Forum for Information Retrieval Evaluation*, pages 10–13.

Alex Graves and Jürgen Schmidhuber. 2005. Framewise phoneme classification with bidirectional lstm and other neural network architectures. *Neural networks*, 18(5-6):602–610.

M. Heikal, Marwan Torki, and N. El-Makky. 2018. Sentiment analysis of arabic tweets using deep learning. In *ACLING*.

Ibrahim Kaibi, Hassan Satori, et al. 2020. Sentiment analysis approach based on combination of word embedding techniques. In *Embedded Systems and Artificial Intelligence*, pages 805–813. Springer.

Jihen Karoui, Farah Banamara Zitoune, and Veronique Moriceau. 2017. Soukhria: Towards an irony detection system for arabic in social media. *Procedia Computer Science*, 117:161–168.

Diederik P. Kingma and Jimmy Ba. 2017. Adam: A method for stochastic optimization.

Svetlana Kiritchenko, Saif Mohammad, and Mohammad Salameh. 2016. SemEval-2016 task 7: Determining sentiment intensity of English and Arabic phrases. In *Proceedings of the 10th International Workshop on Semantic Evaluation (SemEval-2016)*, pages 42–51, San Diego, California. Association for Computational Linguistics.

Bill Yuchen Lin, Xinyue Chen, Jamin Chen, and Xiang Ren. 2019. Kagnet: Knowledge-aware graph networks for commonsense reasoning.

Tomas Mikolov, Kai Chen, Greg Corrado, and Jeffrey Dean. 2013. Efficient estimation of word representations in vector space.

Nicole Peinelt, Dong Nguyen, and Maria Liakata. 2020. tBERT: Topic models and BERT joining forces for semantic similarity detection. In *Proceedings of the 58th Annual Meeting of the Association for Computational Linguistics*, pages 7047–7055, Online. Association for Computational Linguistics.

Nina Poerner, Ulli Waltinger, and Hinrich Schütze. 2020. E-BERT: Efficient-yet-effective entity embeddings for BERT. In *Findings of the Association for Computational Linguistics: EMNLP 2020*, pages 803–818, Online. Association for Computational Linguistics.

Dina Said, Nayer M Wanas, Nevin M Darwish, and Nadia Hegazy. 2009. A study of text preprocessing tools for arabic text categorization. In *The second international conference on Arabic language*, pages 230–236.

Timo Schick and Hinrich Schütze. 2019. Rare words: A major problem for contextualized embeddings and how to fix it by attentive mimicking.

Abu Bakr Soliman, Kareem Eissa, and Samhaa R. El-Beltagy. 2017. Aravec: A set of arabic word embedding models for use in arabic nlp. *Procedia Computer Science*, 117:256–265. Arabic Computational Linguistics.

Leveraging Offensive Language for Sarcasm and Sentiment Detection in Arabic

Fatemah Husain
Kuwait University / State of Kuwait
f.husain@ku.edu.kw

Ozlem Uzuner
George Mason University / USA
ouzuner@gmu.edu

Abstract

Sarcasm detection is one of the top challenging tasks in text classification, particularly for informal Arabic with high syntactic and semantic ambiguity. We propose two systems that harness knowledge from multiple tasks to improve the performance of the classifier. This paper presents the systems used in our participation to the two sub-tasks of the Sixth Arabic Natural Language Processing Workshop (WANLP); Sarcasm Detection and Sentiment Analysis. Our methodology is driven by the hypothesis that tweets with negative sentiment and tweets with sarcasm content are more likely to have offensive content, thus, fine-tuning the classification model using large corpus of offensive language, supports the learning process of the model to effectively detect sentiment and sarcasm contents. Results demonstrate the effectiveness of our approach for sarcasm detection sub-task over sentiment analysis sub-task.

1 Introduction

Current trend in sentiment analysis research is moving toward the special sub-field of sarcasm detection. It is becoming one of the most challenging and relevant task for the sentiment analysis community. The complexity of detecting sarcastic content is attributed to multiple factors including context understanding, cultural aspects, and personal traits (Oprea and Magdy, 2019).

This paper describes two systems that have been submitted to the shared sub-tasks of Sarcasm Detection and Sentiment Analysis at the Sixth Arabic Natural Language Processing Workshop (WANLP 2021)(Abu Farha et al., 2021). The approach adopted in developing the systems is inspired by the findings from offensive language studies. Previous researchers highlight sarcastic content as one of the main causes of confusion for offensive language detection systems (Djandji et al., 2020; Keleg et al., 2020). Additionally, multiple studies applied sentiment features into the task of offensive language detection and report significant gain in performance (Haidar et al., 2017; Elmadany et al., 2020; Abu Farha and Magdy, 2020b). All of these findings demonstrate the relationship among sentiment analysis, sarcasm detection, and offensive language detection tasks.

Our main methodology is based on transfer learning that is performed by joint fine-tuning over the concatenated tasks; offensive language, sarcasm detection, sentiment analysis, and transfer corpora. Thus, the contextualized word embedding is learned based on the entire fine-tuning corpus. The main goal from applying this system pipeline is to examine the impact of offensive language linguistic features on sarcastic language and sentiment content.

2 Related Work

Abu Farha and Magdy (2020a) introduce the first version of ArSarcasm dataset, which includes labels for sentiment analysis, dialect identification, and sarcasm detection tasks with a total of 10,547 tweets, of which only 1,682 (16%) are sarcastic tweets. The ArSarcasm dataset is still a relatively new dataset and few researchers apply it in their studies. In (Abu Farha and Magdy, 2020a), the authors use Mazajak word embedding (Farha and Magdy, 2019) and develop a Bi-LSTM model. The results record very low performance; 62% precision, 38% recall, and F1-score of 0.46. Authors highlight the challenging in developing high performance system for detecting sarcasm because of the contextual and cultural aspects of sarcasm content. Abdul-Mageed et al. (2021) explore multiple BERT models for multiple text classification tasks in Arabic. Results for sentiment analysis task using

Proceedings of the Sixth Arabic Natural Language Processing Workshop, pages 364–369
Kyiv, Ukraine (Virtual), April 19, 2021.

the ArSarcasm dataset record the highest F1 score of 71.50 when applied with MARBERT model (Abdul-Mageed et al., 2021). The same study also reports results for Sarcasm detection task using the ArSarcasm dataset. The highest achieved F1 score is 76.30 by MARBERT.

Multiple researchers from offensive language detection studies report findings from their experiments that highlight the relationship between sarcasm detection and offensive language detection. For example in (Djandji et al., 2020), the authors applied a multitask learning and multilabel classification approach with AraBERT model (Antoun et al., 2020), for hate speech detection and offensive language detection. The findings from their error analysis showed some mislabeled hate speech tweets that are mostly related to mockery, sarcasm, or mentioning other offensive and hateful statements within tweets. Keleg et al. (2020) also report similar findings. In (Keleg et al., 2020), multiple classification models for offensive language detection were explored, and the results from the error analysis highlight some issues that confused the classifiers including the use of sarcastic speech to quote scenes from popular movies.

Furthermore, various offensive language detection studies apply sentiment features in their models and report positive effects in system performance. For instance, Haidar et al. (2017) deploy a cyberbullying detection system that consists of SentiStrength[1] features related to sentiment polarity of Twitter users to train a classifier. Results report higher performance when using the system with SentiStrength features from the model that does not apply sentiment features. Elmadany et al. (2020) develop an offensive language detection system based on assuming a correlation between negative sentiment and offensive language. They use AraNet(Abdul-Mageed et al., 2020) to augment the imbalanced dataset by adding negative tweets and develop M-BERT[2]-based classifiers. Results show higher performance of the model that applies negative sentiment augmented dataset over the others that do not consider the sentiment augmentation approach. Additionally, Abu Farha and Magdy (2020b) explored various classifiers using different multitask learning settings across offensive language, hate speech, and sentiment analysis. Result demonstrates higher performance for the model that is trained on offensive language, hate speech, and sentiment, assuming all offensive and hate speech tweets are negative sentiment and others are positive sentiment.

[1] http://sentistrength.wlv.ac.uk/

[2] https://github.com/google-research/bert/blob/master/multilingual.md

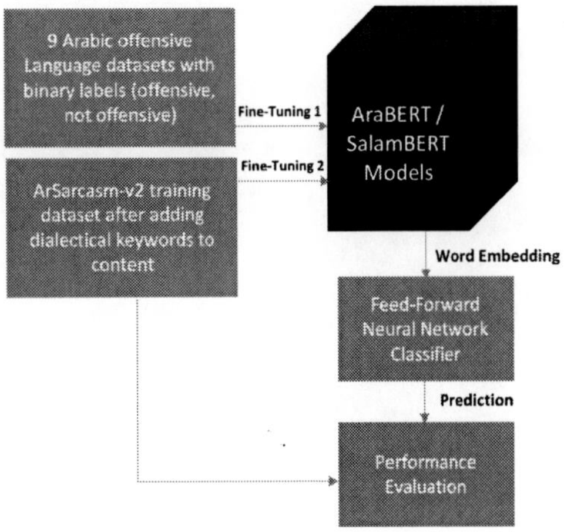

Figure 1: System Pipeline

3 Methodology

Transfer learning is performed by joint training over the concatenated task and transfer corpora, and subwords are learned over the concatenation of both corpora; offensive language and sarcasm detection or sentiment analysis. The overall proposed system architecture is described in Fig.1. We submitted two separate submissions that were independently trained and tested for each sub-task.

3.1 Tasks and Datasets

The main dataset of our study is the ArSarcasm-v2 dataset (Abu Farha et al., 2021), which includes 15,548 tweets with three labels assigned to each tweet; sentiment, sarcasm, and dialect, and consists of two parts; 12,548 tweets in training dataset and 5,000 tweets in testing dataset. During our experimental studies, the ArSarcasm-v2 dataset (Abu Farha et al., 2021) is randomly classified into 80% training dataset and 20% development dataset to evaluate our model. The training part of the dataset consists of the following sentiment tweets: 4,623 neutral, 3,672 negative, and 1,743 positive, and the following sarcasm tweets: 1,749 sarcasm and 8,289 not sarcasm. While the development part of the dataset consists of 1,124 neutral, 949 negative, and 437 positive sentiment tweets, and 419 sarcasm and 2,091 not sarcasm tweets. Labels for the testing dataset are not available during the

Model	Class	Precision	Recall	Macro-F1
Baseline	Not Sarcasm	0.91	0.94	0.92
AraBERT	Sarcasm	0.63	0.52	0.57
	Average	**0.77**	0.73	**0.75**
Main	Not Sarcasm	0.90	0.92	0.91
AraBERT	Sarcasm	0.56	0.54	0.54
	Average	0.73	0.72	0.73
Baseline	Not Sarcasm	0.91	0.93	0.92
SalamBERT	Sarcasm	0.59	0.52	0.56
	Average	0.75	0.72	0.74
Main	Not Sarcasm	0.91	0.92	0.92
SalamBERT	Sarcasm	0.59	0.57	0.58
	Average	0.75	**0.74**	**0.75**

Table 1: Performance Evaluation Results of the Development Dataset for the Sarcasm Detection Sub-Task.

time of writing this paper, however, results are announced by the shared task organizers and included in the results section of this paper. The full details of the dataset are available in the task guidelines (Abu Farha et al., 2021).

We also use 9 Arabic offensive language datasets in developing the proposed classification system. The datasets consist of Aljazeera.net Deleted Comments (Mubarak et al., 2017), Egyptian Tweets (Mubarak et al., 2017), YouTube Comments (Alakrot et al., 2018a), Religious Hate Speech (Albadi et al., 2018), L-HSAB (Mulki et al., 2019), T-HSAB (Haddad et al., 2019), MPOLD (Chowdhury et al., 2020), OSACT4 (Mubarak et al., 2020), and the Multi-Platform Hate Speech Dataset (Omar et al., 2020). All datasets were used without any changes in content, no filtering or preprocessing were performed. However, to maintain consistency among all datasets, the labels were changed for some datasets. Only binary classes are applied; offensive or not offensive. Thus, we convert different types of offensive languages to offensive class. For example, the L-HSAB and T-HSAB datasets differentiate between hate and abusive languages classes; which were both converted to offensive class.

3.2 Preprocessing

Only one preprocessing procedure is conducted over ArSarcasm-v2 dataset (Abu Farha et al., 2021), which consists of adding a keyword token to the end of the tweet to refer to the dialect of the tweet. Thus, if the record in ArSarcasm-v2 Dataset (Abu Farha et al., 2021) shows a label for the dialect as "gulf", then the keyword 'خليجي/ Gulfian' is added as the last token in the tweet corresponding to that record. Similarly to the other dialects; 'msa', 'egypt', 'levant', and 'magreb', which were assigned the following keyword tokens respectively, 'عربي/ Arabic', 'مصري/ Egyptian', 'شامي/ Levantine', and 'مغربي/ Moroccan'.This preprocessing procedures is based on the assumptions that adding a word of similar meaning to the dialect to create a semantic relationship with the dialect of the tweet can enrich the process of contextual understanding for the classification model.

3.3 Classification Model

The experiment depends mainly on AraBERT model (aubmindlab/bert-base-arabert)(Antoun et al., 2020). The architecture of AraBERT model is adopted from HuggingFace[3] library with AutoModelForSequenceClassification module. The pooled output from AraBERT encoder is used with a simple Feed Forward Neural Network layer to build the classification model. Experimental settings include maximum sample length of 256, patch size of 8, 4 epochs, 1e-8 epsilon, and 3e-5 learning rate. All experiments are created in Python using PyTorch-Transformers library, and evaluation metrics were developed using Scikit-Learn Python library. The implementation environment is based on Google Colab Pro for all experiments. We develop two classifications models using exactly the same system pipeline. Firstly, AraBERT model is used with fine-tuning on the 9 offensive language datasets as mentioned earlier, then, the same model is further fine-tuned using the training dataset from ArSarcasm-v2

[3]https://huggingface.co/

Model	Class	Precision	Recall	Macro-F1
	Positive	0.66	0.58	0.62
Baseline	Neutral	0.74	0.78	0.76
AraBERT	Negative	0.76	0.75	0.76
	Average	**0.72**	**0.71**	**0.71**
	Positive	0.62	0.52	0.56
Main	Neutral	0.73	0.79	0.76
AraBERT	Negative	0.74	0.74	0.74
	Average	0.70	0.68	0.69
	Positive	0.54	0.66	0.60
Baseline	Neutral	0.73	0.79	0.76
SalamBERT	Negative	0.76	0.73	0.74
	Average	0.71	0.69	0.70
	Positive	0.67	0.56	0.61
Main	Neutral	0.73	0.80	0.77
SalamBERT	Negative	0.75	0.73	0.74
	Average	**0.72**	0.70	0.70

Table 2: Performance Evaluation Results of the Development Dataset for the Sentiment Analysis Sub-Task.

Dataset for the target task. The second system deploy a customized version of AraBERT, called SalamBERT[4], which adds more tokens to the vocabulary of AraBERT and continue pre-training the model using the MADAR corpus (Salameh et al., 2018; Bouamor et al., 2019), which consists of multiple Arabic dialects to ensure the coverage of dialectical Arabic in word embeddings.

3.4 Results

Training and Development datasets experiments were evaluated with 5-fold cross validation for all performance metrics. Baseline models do not consider transfer learning across tasks, and are used as benchmarks for the evaluation process. Thus, baseline models in each sub-task are trained using the training dataset and evaluated using the development dataset. Results for the sarcasm detection sub-task are shown in Table 1 and for the sentiment analysis sub-task are shown in Table 2 from the development dataset. Main models refer to the model that consider transfer learning from offensive language detection task to the targeted task. As can be noticed from the tables, the variation among the performance of all models is insignificant for the development dataset.

The official results from the shared task organizers from the testing dataset are presented in Table 3 for the sarcasm detection sub-task and Table 4 for the sentiment analysis sub-task. Overall, SalamBERT-based system reports higher performance in sarcasm detection sub-task, while AraBERT-based system demonstrates higher performance in sentiment analysis sub-task. Among the 27 teams who participated in sarcasm detection sub-task, SalamBERT-based system ranked the 12th (0.5348 F1-sarcastic) and AraBERT-based system the 18th (0.5041 F1-sarcastic) based on F1-sarcastic metric. For the sentiment analysis sub-task, a total of 22 participants were included in the competition from which the AraBERT-based system ranked the 12th (0.6877 F-PN) and the

Metric	AraBERT	SalamBERT
F1-Sarcasm	0.5041	**0.5348**
Precision	0.6950	**0.7128**
Recall	0.6622	**0.6807**
Macro-F1	0.6732	**0.6922**
Accuracy	0.7607	**0.7727**

Table 3: Official Shared Task Results for the Testing Dataset from Sarcasm Detection Sub-Task.

Metric	AraBERT	SalamBERT
F-PN	**0.6877**	0.6259
Precision	**0.6136**	0.5580
Recall	**0.6318**	0.5813
Macro-F1	**0.6210**	0.5635
Accuracy	**0.6630**	0.6073

Table 4: Official Shared Task Results for the Testing Dataset from Sentiment Analysis Sub-Task.

[4] `https://huggingface.co/Fatemah`

SalamBERT-based system the 16th (0.6259 F-PN) according to the F-PN metric.

4 Error Analysis and Discussion

We manually investigate samples of the misclassified samples for each sub-task from both models. Among the common errors for sarcasm detection sub-task is offensive tweets that were classified as sarcasm, while it is not sarcasm. For example the following tweet is misclassified as sarcasm by all experiments using both models: ‘ميسي قليل أدب المدربين يحطون خطين دفاع وهو يضربهم بتمريره وحده/ Messi is impolite, the coaches draw two lines of defense and he hits them alone’. For the sentiment analysis sub-task, most of the common errors are from the neutral class, such as ‘اخبار الدوري الاسباني - الإصابة تضرب حارس مرمى برشلونةالإسبانى/ La Liga news - The injury hits Barcelona’s Spanish goalkeeper’, which has some offensive terms ‘تضرب/ hit’ but it is not negative, while all models classify it as a negative sentiment tweet. Further analysis is required to examine the extent of the overlap among the three tasks and the forms of content that are shared across them.

5 Conclusions

This paper represents the system used in submissions for Sarcasm Detection and Sentiment Analysis sub-tasks at the Sixth Arabic Natural Language Processing Workshop (WANLP)(Abu Farha et al., 2021). Our approach examines transfer learning across offensive language, saracsm detection, and sentiment analysis. The results highlight valuable impact of our approach for sarcasm detection task over sentiment analysis task.

References

Muhammad Abdul-Mageed, AbdelRahim Elmadany, and El Moatez Billah Nagoudi. 2021. Arbert & marbert: Deep bidirectional transformers for arabic. *ArXiv*, abs/2101.01785.

Muhammad Abdul-Mageed, Chiyu Zhang, Azadeh Hashemi, and El Moatez Billah Nagoudi. 2020. AraNet: A deep learning toolkit for Arabic social media. In *Proceedings of the 4th Workshop on Open-Source Arabic Corpora and Processing Tools, with a Shared Task on Offensive Language Detection*, pages 16–23, Marseille, France. European Language Resource Association.

Ibrahim Abu Farha and Walid Magdy. 2020a. From Arabic sentiment analysis to sarcasm detection: The ArSarcasm dataset. In *Proceedings of the 4th Workshop on Open-Source Arabic Corpora and Processing Tools, with a Shared Task on Offensive Language Detection*, pages 32–39, Marseille, France. European Language Resource Association.

Ibrahim Abu Farha and Walid Magdy. 2020b. Multitask learning for Arabic offensive language and hate-speech detection. In *Proceedings of the 4th Workshop on Open-Source Arabic Corpora and Processing Tools, with a Shared Task on Offensive Language Detection*, pages 86–90, Marseille, France. European Language Resource Association.

Ibrahim Abu Farha, Wajdi Zaghouani, and Walid Magdy. 2021. Overview of the wanlp 2021 shared task on sarcasm and sentiment detection in arabic. In *Proceedings of the Sixth Arabic Natural Language Processing Workshop*.

Azalden Alakrot, Liam Murray, and Nikola S. Nikolov. 2018a. Dataset construction for the detection of anti-social behaviour in online communication in arabic. *Procedia Computer Science*, 142:174–181.

Nuha Albadi, Maram Kurdi, and Shivakant Mishra. 2018. Are they our brothers? analysis and detection of religious hate speech in the arabic twittersphere. In *2018 IEEE/ACM International Conference on Advances in Social Networks Analysis and Mining (ASONAM)*, pages 69–76.

Wissam Antoun, Fady Baly, and Hazem Hajj. 2020. AraBERT: Transformer-based model for Arabic language understanding. In *Proceedings of the 4th Workshop on Open-Source Arabic Corpora and Processing Tools, with a Shared Task on Offensive Language Detection*, pages 9–15, Marseille, France. European Language Resource Association.

Houda Bouamor, Sabit Hassan, and Nizar Habash. 2019. The MADAR shared task on Arabic fine-grained dialect identification. In *Proceedings of the Fourth Arabic Natural Language Processing Workshop*, pages 199–207, Florence, Italy. Association for Computational Linguistics.

Shammur Absar Chowdhury, Hamdy Mubarak, Ahmed Abdelali, Soon-gyo Jung, Bernard J Jansen, and Joni Salminen. 2020. A multi-platform Arabic news comment dataset for offensive language detection. In *Proceedings of The 12th Language Resources and Evaluation Conference*, pages 6203–6212, Marseille, France. European Language Resources Association.

Marc Djandji, Fady Baly, Wissam Antoun, and Hazem M. Hajj. 2020. Multi-task learning using arabert for offensive language detection. In *OSACT*.

AbdelRahim Elmadany, Chiyu Zhang, Muhammad Abdul-Mageed, and Azadeh Hashemi. 2020. Leveraging affective bidirectional transformers for offensive language detection.

Ibrahim Abu Farha and Walid Magdy. 2019. Mazajak: An online arabic sentiment analyser. In *Proceedings of the Fourth Arabic Natural Language Processing Workshop*, pages 192–198.

Hatem Haddad, Hala Mulki, and Asma Oueslati. 2019. T-hsab: A tunisian hate speech and abusive dataset. In *Arabic Language Processing: From Theory to Practice*, pages 251–263, Cham. Springer International Publishing.

Batoul Haidar, Maroun Chamoun, and Ahmed Serhrouchni. 2017. Multilingual cyberbullying detection system: Detecting cyberbullying in arabic content. In *2017 1st Cyber Security in Networking Conference (CSNet)*, pages 1–8.

Amr Keleg, Samhaa R. El-Beltagy, and Mahmoud Khalil. 2020. ASU_OPTO at OSACT4 - offensive language detection for Arabic text. In *Proceedings of the 4th Workshop on Open-Source Arabic Corpora and Processing Tools, with a Shared Task on Offensive Language Detection*, pages 66–70, Marseille, France. European Language Resource Association.

Hamdy Mubarak, Kareem Darwish, and Walid Magdy. 2017. Abusive language detection on Arabic social media. In *Proceedings of the First Workshop on Abusive Language Online*, pages 52–56, Vancouver, BC, Canada. Association for Computational Linguistics.

Hamdy Mubarak, Kareem Darwish, Walid Magdy, Tamer Elsayed, and Hend Al-Khalifa. 2020. Overview of osact4 arabic offensive language detection shared task. 4.

Hala Mulki, Hatem Haddad, Chedi Bechikh Ali, and Halima Alshabani. 2019. L-HSAB: A Levantine twitter dataset for hate speech and abusive language. In *Proceedings of the Third Workshop on Abusive Language Online*, pages 111–118, Florence, Italy. Association for Computational Linguistics.

Ahmed Omar, Tarek M. Mahmoud, and Tarek Abd-El-Hafeez. 2020. Comparative performance of machine learning and deep learning algorithms for arabic hate speech detection in osns. In *Proceedings of the International Conference on Artificial Intelligence and Computer Vision (AICV2020)*, pages 247–257, Cham. Springer International Publishing.

Silviu Oprea and Walid Magdy. 2019. Exploring author context for detecting intended vs perceived sarcasm. In *Proceedings of the 57th Annual Meeting of the Association for Computational Linguistics*, pages 2854–2859, Florence, Italy. Association for Computational Linguistics.

Mohammad Salameh, Houda Bouamor, and Nizar Habash. 2018. Fine-grained Arabic dialect identification. In *Proceedings of the 27th International Conference on Computational Linguistics*, pages 1332–1344, Santa Fe, New Mexico, USA. Association for Computational Linguistics.

The IDC System for Sentiment Classification and Sarcasm Detection in Arabic

Abraham Israeli,[1,2] Yotam Nahum,[1] Shai Fine[1], Kfir Bar[1]
[1]The Data Science Institute, Interdisciplinary Center, Herzliya, Israel
[2]Department of Software and Information System Engineering
Ben-Gurion University of the Negev, Beer-Sheva, Israel

{abraham.israeli,yotam.nahum,kfir.bar}@post.idc.ac.il,
shai.fine@idc.ac.il

Abstract

Sentiment classification and sarcasm detection attract a lot of attention by the NLP research community. However, solving these two problems in Arabic and on the basis of social-network data (i.e., Twitter) is still of lower interest. In this paper we present designated solutions for sentiment classification and sarcasm detection tasks that were introduced as part of a shared task by Abu Farha et al. (2021). We adjust the existing state-of-the-art transformer pretrained models for our needs. In addition, we use a variety of machine-learning techniques such as down-sampling, augmentation, bagging, and usage of meta-features to improve the models performance. We achieve an F1-score of 0.75 over the sentiment classification problem where the F1-score is calculated over the positive and negative classes (the neutral class is not taken into account). We achieve an F1-score of 0.66 over the sarcasm detection problem where the F1-score is calculated over the sarcastic class only. In both cases, the above reported results are evaluated over the *ArSarcasm-v2*–an extended dataset of the ArSarcasm (Farha and Magdy, 2020) that was introduced as part of the shared task. This reflects an improvement to the state-of-the-art results in both tasks.

1 Introduction

Sarcasm and sentiment detection are two central tasks in the research field of natural language processing (NLP). Sentiment classification can be defined as the process of estimating emotion polarity of a given piece of text (Liu, 2012). Sarcasm detection is usually treated as the process of determining whether a piece of text was sarcastically written or not. The Free Dictionary[1] defines sarcasm as a form of verbal irony that is intended to express contempt or ridicule. According to Wilson (2006), sarcasm is correlated with expressing the author's opinion in an indirect form, where the intended meaning is different from the literal one.

Although these two tasks are highly related to each other and are usually solved by using a classification model, they differ in significant nuances. Sarcasm heavily dependent on *context* – in most of the cases, a given sentence can be interpreted as sarcastic only if it is written (or said) in a specific context. Moreover, a speaker will use sarcastic language in cases where she thinks that her words will be interpreted as so (Joshi et al., 2017). In many cases, sarcasm detection is treated as a sub-task of the broader problem of sentiment anlaysis. It does not mean that sarcasm detection becomes redundant if the sentiment classification problem is solved accurately enough, since sarcastic language remains the biggest challenge for sentiment-analysis models. The reason behind this is the fact that a sarcastic language usually carries a negative implicit sentiment, while it is expressed using positive expressions (Bouazizi and Ohtsuki, 2016). The nuanced differences between the two tasks motivated us to take the approach of building two distinct solutions.

There is an active research area on sarcasm and sentiment analysis, but it is mostly done on English (Joshi et al., 2017; Bharti et al., 2016; Zhang et al., 2018). The research efforts that focus on sarcasm and sentiment classification in Arabic is limited. However, with the recent growing interest in non-English NLP, processing Arabic becomes one of

[1]https://www.thefreedictionary.com/

Proceedings of the Sixth Arabic Natural Language Processing Workshop, pages 370–375
Kyiv, Ukraine (Virtual), April 19, 2021.

Dataset	Dialect (%) MSA	Egypt	Levant	Gulf	Magreb	Sentiment (%) Pos	Neu	Neg	Sarcasm (%) True	False	Total
$train_{arsar}$	67.0	22.5	5.2	4.9	0.3	15.9	50.6	33.5	15.9	84.1	10587
$train_{\overline{arsar}}$	75.0	14.6	3.6	6.2	0.5	25.1	20.3	54.6	24.3	75.7	2001
$test$	77.4	10.2	1.6	10.7	0.1	-	-	-	-	-	3000

Table 1: Data statistics. *ArSarcasm-v2* (15587 tweets) is the complete corpus published by Abu Farha et al. (2021). It consists of three parts as demonstrated in the table. $train_{arsar}$ denotes $train$ data that is taken from the ArSarcasm dataset (Farha and Magdy, 2020) while $train_{\overline{arsar}}$ is the complementary part of the $train$ set. All numbers besides the last column are percentages. Last column is the actual number of instances in each dataset. The $test$ dataset sentiment and sarcasm annotation was unknown while building the models and was revealed after the shared task ended.

the most active research topics (Bouamor et al., 2018; Farha and Magdy, 2019; Obeid et al., 2020).

For the last two decades, social networks (e.g., Twitter,Reddit) became a central communication tool for humans. These data sources enable the usage of textual data for sarcasm detection and sentiment classification models building.

In this paper, we present our solution to the shared task of sarcasm and sentiment detection in Arabic, organized as part of the the sixth workshop for Arabic NLP (Abu Farha et al., 2021). We implemented two distinct algorithms for each task (sentiment and sarcasm). Both algorithms use some of the recent advanced transfer-learning models followed by traditional machine-learning techniques (e.g., usage of meta-feature, down-sampling).

2 Data

As part of the shared task, the *ArSarcasm-v2* dataset is introduced (Abu Farha et al., 2021). The dataset consists of two separate datasets–$train$ and $test$. We note that the ArSarcasm (Farha and Magdy, 2020) dataset (10587 tweets) is a *subset* of the $train$ dataset. We denote the two parts of the $train$ dataset as $train_{arsar}$ and $train_{\overline{arsar}}$ throughout the paper. Each tweet in the $train$ dataset is additionally tagged with a dialect value (five Arabic dialects), a sentiment value (three classes), and whether the tweet is sarcastic or not (two classes). The $test$ dataset contains 3K tweets for which only the dialect value is available. Dataset statistics are provided in Table 1. As observed in the table, $train_{arsar}$ and $train_{\overline{arsar}}$ distribute differently. For both tasks, a subset of the train dataset was used as an evaluation set (i.e, $eval$). However, the $train$ and $eval$ datasets were differently created for each of the tasks.

2.1 Sentiment Classification Data

For the sentiment classification task, we randomly split the original $train$ dataset into a 83%-17% $train$-$eval$ parts. We used stratified sampling to ensure an equal distribution of the label (i.e., sentiment) over the two datasets.

2.2 Sarcasm Detection Data

Due to the unique challenges of the sarcasm-detection task, we process the data in two steps: (i) Down-Sampling, and (ii) Augmentation.

Down-Sampling We build a topic model (Grootendorst, 2020) for each of the five dialects, to detect the different topics in the $train$ dataset. We found that topics are distributed significantly different over $train_{arsar}$ and $train_{\overline{arsar}}$. Therfore, we down-sample the majority class (not sarcastic) and keep only tweets, which their major topic is broadly represented in $train_{\overline{arsar}}$. This way, we ensure that irrelevant topics (assuming that $train_{\overline{arsar}}$ is the more relevant corpus) are removed. Overall, we remove 32% of the $train$ data in the down-sampling process. The majority (92%) of the removed data were selected from the MSA dialect.

Augmentation We use the suggested algorithms by Qiu et al. (2020), which allow usage of transformer models. We utilize the transformer model that is used for the actual classification (see Section 4) for the generation of augmented instances. Since most transformer models are trained using 'Mask-LM' (MLM) and 'Next Sentence Prediction' (NSP) (Devlin et al., 2018) they are capable of augmenting new sentences out of existing ones. We allow the augmentation algorithm to replace text within existing tweets, as well as to fill in "missing" words–injecting new words by the model to existing tweets. An example of the augmentation

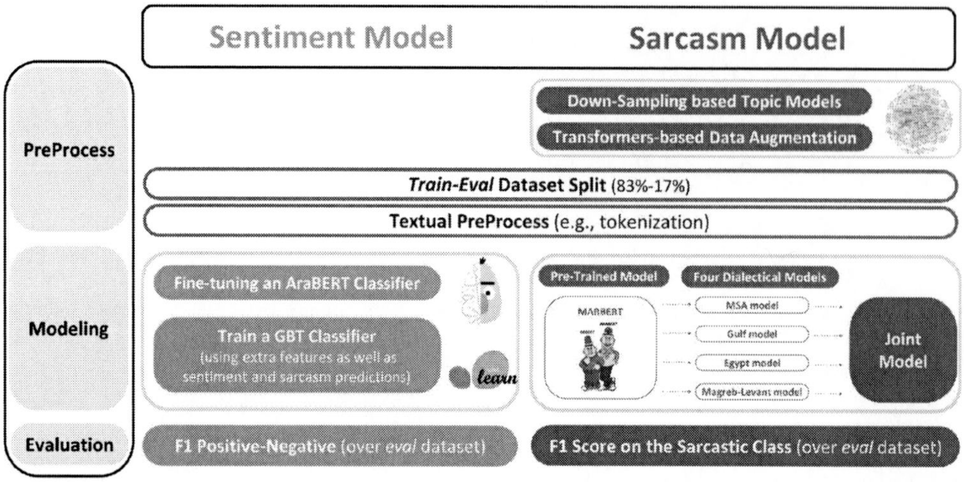

Figure 1: System pipelines. Both algorithms rely on transformer models followed by a tailor-made modeling layer as part of the prediction pipeline.

process over a single tweet is presented in Table 2. Using this novel approach, we reduplicate the corpus (after the down-sampling step).

3 System Description

For both tasks, we use a transformer architecture as a major part of the system. For sentiment classification we use AraBERT (Antoun et al., 2020) while for the sarcasm detection we use MARBERT (Abdul-Mageed et al., 2020). Both are recent pre-trained autoregressive models in Arabic. In both systems, we preprocess the data prior to training. The preprocessing steps include tokenization, removal of redundant text and punctuation marks (e.g., 'RT'), and replacement of links and mentions with placeholders. Figure 1 provides a high-level overview of both systems.

3.1 Sentiment Classifier System

The sentiment classifier uses two-steps modeling. In the first step, we fine-tune an AraBERT (Antoun et al., 2020) transformer model. We do the following adjustments for the particular task we face: (i) Since data are imbalanced (see Table 1), we re-weight the instances according to the inverse proportion of their class weight. (ii) We use the FocalLoss (Lin et al., 2017) as our loss function while training, as it has been shown to work well for imbalanced datasets. (iii) We set the $F1$ score over the positive and negative classes ($F1^{PN}$) as the evaluation criteria of the classifier (tested over the $eval$ dataset) as this is the target evaluation measure of the task. In the second step, we train a Gradient Boosting Trees (GBT) classifier as the final predictor (Friedman, 2002). The GBT model uses the transformer model predictions in addition to some other extra features (e.g., text length, number of emojis, number of hashtags). Another useful feature that we add to the GBT model is the prediction output of the sarcasm classifier (trained over *the same* $train$ dataset as used for the sentiment task). We train the GBT model using 30 iterations (i.e., number of trees) and limit the maximum tree depth to three.

3.2 Sarcasm Detection System

The sarcasm classifier fine-tunes MARBERT (Abdul-Mageed et al., 2020) for each dialect. The training process is composed of two stages of fine-tuning. For every dialect, the first training epoch is performed on the full, multi-dialect training set, and from the second epoch onwards, the training data includes only the relevant examples (referring to the specific dialect). One exception is that we join together the the Levantine and Maghrebi dialects due to their relative small support. Following this way, four distinct classifiers are trained. We set the maximum epoch size to five, batch size to 16 and a relative low learning rate, which ranges ($4e^{-6}$ to $4e^{-7}$).

4 Results

The results of the sentiment classification and the sarcasm detection tasks are reported in Table 3

	Tweet (Arabic)	Tweet (English)
Original	ما اسخف مطاردة الارهاب و هو في مجلس الأمن!	What a ridiculous chase of terrorism in the Security Council!
Replacement	ما اسرع مطاردة الارهاب و العدالة في مجلس الامن!	What a quick chase of terrorism and justice in the Security Council!
Addition	ما اسخف تهمة مطاردة الارهاب للبنان و هو في مجلس الامن!	What a ridiculous charge to chase terrorism for Lebanon while it is in the Security Council!
Both	ما اسخف مطاردة الارهاب والعالم هو يتراس اليوم مجلس لمجلس الامن!	What a ridiculous chase of terrorism and the world now chairs the Security Council!

Table 2: Augmentation example. Replacement and addition of tokens is possible. We use both options in the preprocess steps of the sarcasm model. The augmentation allows us to enlarge the corpus and to add context.

	Acc.	Prec.	Recall	F1	$F1^{PN}$
GigaBERT	0.708	0.687	0.7	0.692	0.674
AraBERT	0.735	0.714	0.729	0.72	0.699
Mod. AraBERT	0.761	0.741	0.762	0.749	0.741
Mod. AraBERT +GBT	**0.77**	**0.757**	**0.763**	**0.758**	**0.75**

Table 3: Sentiment classification results. 'Acc.' and 'Prec.' stand for accuracy and precision respectively. Precision, recall and F1 are calculated using the 'macro' average. $F1^{PN}$ is calculated over the positive and negative classes only. 'Mod'. stands for Modified and it includes the adjustments we applied to the standard AraBERT model.

	Acc.	Prec.	Recall	F1	$F1^{P}$
MARBERT	0.832	0.724	0.771	0.74	0.583
MSA (56%)	0.852	0.747	0.791	0.762	0.61
Egypt (30%)	0.772	0.778	0.787	0.772	0.742
Gulf (7%)	0.771	0.733	0.732	0.731	0.634
Magreb - Levant (7%)	0.8	0.766	0.791	0.775	0.701
All	0.831	0.764	0.80	0.774	0.661

Table 4: Sarcasm detection results. 'Acc.' and 'Prec.' stand for accuracy and precision respectively. Precision, recall and $F1^P$ are calculated over the positive class only (sarcastic tweets). The MARBERT model (first row) is a standard run using default parameters. Last row are the results over all dialects.

and Table 4, respectively. All reported results are measured on the *eval* dataset. It is important to note that we use a different *eval* dataset for each task (see Section 2). Therefore, it is impossible to compare the results of the two models. Table 3 includes the results of a GigaBERT classifier (Lan et al., 2020) as an additional baseline. Although we did not expand about the experiment done using the GigaBERT model, it is important to note that the model achieves impressive results and almost equivalent to the AraBERT classifier. As observed, in both algorithms we improve the state-of-the-art results (Lan et al., 2020; Abdul-Mageed et al., 2020). In Table 5 we present the confusion matrix of the best model we trained for the sentiment classification problem. As observed, the distinction between 'Negative' and 'Neutral' instances is the vulnerable point of the model.

Actual Classes \ Predicted Classes	NEG	NEU	POS	Total
NEG	667	100	29	796
NEU	174	697	94	965
POS	48	53	272	373
Total	889	850	395	2134

Table 5: Sentiment classification confusion matrix. Results are recorded over the *eval* dataset – 17% of the full *train* dataset.

4.1 Official Submission Results

As explained in the Section 2, the *test* dataset (3000 tweets) true annotations were unknown by the time the predictive models were created. Our two suggested algorithms (as well as other teams' solutions) were evaluated according to the *test* dataset by the deadline time of the shared task[2].

The results of the sentiment classification and the sarcasm detection tasks over the *test* dataset are reported in Table 6. We were ranked in the 5'th place (out of 22 participation teams) in the sentiment classification task and 9'th place (out of 27 participation teams) in the sarcasm detection task. As observed, there is a significant detraction of both models' performance when evaluated over the *test* set. Based on the to the decisive evaluation metrics ($F1^{PN}$ in the sentiment classification and $F1^P$ in the sarcasm detection) there is a performance drop of 4% and 13.6% in both problems respectively.

[2]A single submission per team was allowed

	Acc.	Prec.	Recall	F1	$F1^*$
Sentiment Classification	0.692	0.643	0.658	0.645	0.719
Sarcasm Detection	0.767	0.706	0.702	0.704	0.568

Table 6: Official submission results. The reported results are over the $test$ dataset (see the third row in Table 1). F^* is the F-Score decisive metric. In the sentiment classification it is the $F1^{PN}$ while in the sarcasm detection it is the F-Score over the sarcastic class. The sentiment classification algorithm is ranked 5'th (out of 22 participants). The sarcasm detection algorithm is ranked 9'th (out of 27 participants).

5 Discussion

One of the challenges we were facing in both tasks is overfitting. We assume that the root cause of the problem is the relative small corpus size and label imbalance. To handle the challenge, We control the learning process in different ways (e.g., small number of training epochs, relative low learning rate). Another challenge we identified and dealt with is the significant difference between $train_{arsar}$ and $train_{\overline{arsar}}$. The difference is reflected through the dialect distribution as well as the label distribution (see Table 1). We assume that the root cause of this difference is either in the way that the data were collected or the way the data were annotated. In both cases, such a "data-mixture" situation raises modeling challenges that we had to handle, mainly in the sarcasm detection algorithm.

6 Conclusion

As observed in previous works as well as in this one, sarcasm detection is a "harder" task to solve than sentiment classification. In this work we introduced two different approaches for solving each of the tasks. Both approaches rely on transformer architectures. However, in both algorithms we adjust the transformer model by using machine-learning techniques (e.g., instance weighting, a more suitable loss function). In addition, in both solutions we add machine-learning components to the pipeline prior or subsequent to the transformer model (e.g., down-sampling, data augmentation). We showed that these techniques improve the existing baselines in both tasks when we evaluate results over the dataset provided as part of the shared task.

References

Muhammad Abdul-Mageed, AbdelRahim Elmadany, and El Moatez Billah Nagoudi. 2020. Arbert & marbert: Deep bidirectional transformers for arabic. *arXiv preprint arXiv:2101.01785.*

Ibrahim Abu Farha, Wajdi Zaghouani, and Walid Magdy. 2021. Overview of the wanlp 2021 shared task on sarcasm and sentiment detection in arabic. In *Proceedings of the Sixth Arabic Natural Language Processing Workshop.*

Wissam Antoun, Fady Baly, and Hazem Hajj. 2020. Arabert: Transformer-based model for arabic language understanding. *arXiv preprint arXiv:2003.00104.*

Santosh Kumar Bharti, Bakhtyar Vachha, RK Pradhan, Korra Sathya Babu, and Sanjay Kumar Jena. 2016. Sarcastic sentiment detection in tweets streamed in real time: a big data approach. *Digital Communications and Networks*, 2(3):108–121.

Houda Bouamor, Nizar Habash, Mohammad Salameh, Wajdi Zaghouani, Owen Rambow, Dana Abdulrahim, Ossama Obeid, Salam Khalifa, Fadhl Eryani, Alexander Erdmann, et al. 2018. The madar arabic dialect corpus and lexicon. In *Proceedings of the Eleventh International Conference on Language Resources and Evaluation (LREC 2018).*

Mondher Bouazizi and Tomoaki Otsuki Ohtsuki. 2016. A pattern-based approach for sarcasm detection on twitter. *IEEE Access*, 4:5477–5488.

Jacob Devlin, Ming-Wei Chang, Kenton Lee, and Kristina Toutanova. 2018. Bert: Pre-training of deep bidirectional transformers for language understanding. *arXiv preprint arXiv:1810.04805.*

Ibrahim Abu Farha and Walid Magdy. 2019. Mazajak: An online arabic sentiment analyser. In *Proceedings of the Fourth Arabic Natural Language Processing Workshop*, pages 192–198.

Ibrahim Abu Farha and Walid Magdy. 2020. From arabic sentiment analysis to sarcasm detection: The arsarcasm dataset. In *Proceedings of the 4th Workshop on Open-Source Arabic Corpora and Processing Tools, with a Shared Task on Offensive Language Detection*, pages 32–39.

Jerome H Friedman. 2002. Stochastic gradient boosting. *Computational statistics & data analysis*, 38(4):367–378.

Maarten Grootendorst. 2020. Bertopic: Leveraging bert and c-tf-idf to create easily interpretable topics.

Aditya Joshi, Pushpak Bhattacharyya, and Mark J Carman. 2017. Automatic sarcasm detection: A survey. *ACM Computing Surveys (CSUR)*, 50(5):1–22.

Wuwei Lan, Yang Chen, Wei Xu, and Alan Ritter. 2020. Gigabert: Zero-shot transfer learning from english to arabic. In *Proceedings of The 2020 Conference on Empirical Methods on Natural Language Processing (EMNLP)*.

Tsung-Yi Lin, Priya Goyal, Ross Girshick, Kaiming He, and Piotr Dollár. 2017. Focal loss for dense object detection. In *Proceedings of the IEEE international conference on computer vision*, pages 2980–2988.

Bing Liu. 2012. Sentiment analysis and opinion mining. *Synthesis lectures on human language technologies*, 5(1):1–167.

Ossama Obeid, Nasser Zalmout, Salam Khalifa, Dima Taji, Mai Oudah, Bashar Alhafni, Go Inoue, Fadhl Eryani, Alexander Erdmann, and Nizar Habash. 2020. Camel tools: An open source python toolkit for arabic natural language processing. In *Proceedings of the 12th language resources and evaluation conference*, pages 7022–7032.

Siyuan Qiu, Binxia Xu, Jie Zhang, Yafang Wang, Xiaoyu Shen, Gerard de Melo, Chong Long, and Xiaolong Li. 2020. Easyaug: An automatic textual data augmentation platform for classification tasks. In *Companion Proceedings of the Web Conference 2020*, pages 249–252.

Deirdre Wilson. 2006. The pragmatics of verbal irony: Echo or pretence? *Lingua*, 116(10):1722–1743.

Lei Zhang, Shuai Wang, and Bing Liu. 2018. Deep learning for sentiment analysis: A survey. *Wiley Interdisciplinary Reviews: Data Mining and Knowledge Discovery*, 8(4):e1253.

Preprocessing Solutions for Detection of Sarcasm and Sentiment for Arabic

Mohamed Lichouri, Mourad Abbas, Besma Benaziz, Aicha Zitouni, Khaled Lounnas
Computational Linguistics Department / CRSTDLA, Algiers, Algeria
{m.lichouri, m.abbas, b.benaziz}@crstdla.dz
{a.zitouni, k.lounnas}@crstdla.dz

Abstract

This paper describes our approach to detecting Sentiment and Sarcasm for Arabic in the ArSarcasm 2021 shared task. Data preprocessing is a crucial task for a successful learning, that is why we applied a set of preprocessing steps to the dataset before training two classifiers, namely Linear Support Vector Classifier (LSVC) and Bidirectional Long Short Term Memory (BiLSTM). The findings show that despite the simplicity of the proposed approach, using the LSVC model with a normalizing Arabic (NA) preprocessing and the BiLSTM architecture with an Embedding layer as input have yielded an encouraging F1score of 33.71% and 57.80% for sarcasm and sentiment detection, respectively.

1 Introduction

Sentiment Analysis (SA) is a natural language processing field that aims to detect people's opinions and emotions (Nassif et al., 2020). Recently, SA becomes a big challenge in which several works were realized using different methods. Considering works that investigate twitter/tweets as data source, we can cite (Abdul-Mageed et al., 2019) who describe a collection of deep learning Arabic social media processing tools (AraNet) to analyze 15 datasets related to sentiment analysis of Arabic including MSA and its dialects by the way of a Bidirectional Encoder Representations from Transformers (BERT). (Farha and Magdy, 2020) presented ArSarcasm dataset to train a deep learning model for sarcasm detection based on SA using Bidirectional Long Short Term Memory (BiLSTM). In (Beseiso and Elmousalami, 2020), authors have carried out a comparative study by applying three deep learning techniques: Convolutional Neural Network (CNN), Bidirectional Gated Recurrent Unit (BiGRU), and Attention on two datasets (ASTD and LABR). In the case of a single dialect, we find the work done for the Algerian ALGED dataset by (Moudjari et al., 2020), who used classical and deep learning classification to tackle the problem of sentiment analysis.

One of the main challenges of SA is the Sarcasm detection which could be beneficial in many areas. Sarcasm can be defined as a special form of verbal irony that is intended to express contempt or ridicule (Joshi et al., 2017), where people convey the opposite of what they mean, using implicit indirect phrasing, where the intended meaning is different from the literal one (Wilson, 2006). In recent years, we have noticed that Arabic corpora are diversifying more and more according to the task at hand, for instance, one can mention those built by (Bouamor et al., 2018; Zaghouani and Charfi, 2018; Maamouri et al., 2010; Zaghouani et al., 2014; Bouamor et al., 2015). In addition, irony and sarcasm detection has recently drawn a significant attention in computational linguistics (Joshi et al., 2017). Fewer studies considered in detail irony detection in Arabic. The only and earliest corpus on Arabic sarcasm/irony detection is SOUKHRIA corpus in (Karoui et al., 2017), where the authors created a corpus of Arabic tweets, by collecting a set of political keywords. They used the Arabic equivalent of sarcasm # , # #. However, this corpus has not been released to public yet. There is also the work done by (Al-Ghadhban et al., 2017) who proposed a classification model that detects Arabic-sarcasm tweets by using some data mining algorithms. In the first shared task on irony detection for the Arabic language organized by (Ghanem et al., 2019), where they collected their data using distant supervision and used similar Arabic hashtags. The task consists of a binary classification of tweets as ironic or not using a dataset composed of 5,030 Arabic tweets about different political issues and events related to the Middle East and the Maghreb. Another contribution to the creation of

Proceedings of the Sixth Arabic Natural Language Processing Workshop, pages 376–380
Kyiv, Ukraine (Virtual), April 19, 2021.

	Train (ArSarcasm-v2)	Dev	Test (ArSarcasm-v2)
# sentences	12,548	2,110	3,000
# words	275,854	46,456	64,347
Max # word per sentence	148	52	92
Min # word per sentence	1	1	1
Max # char per sentence	298	52	92
Min # char per sentence	2	1	1

Table 1: ArSarcasm-v2 dataset statistics

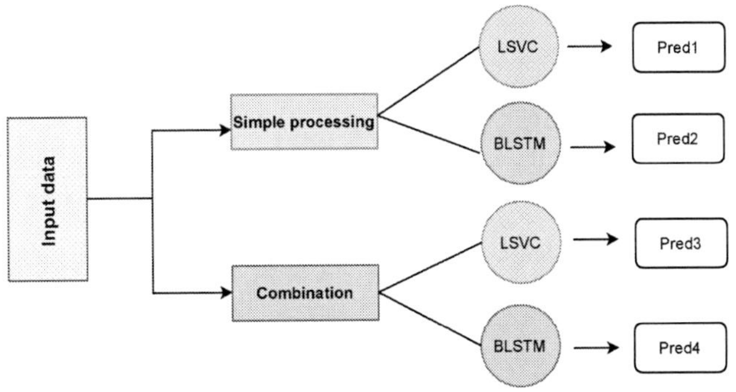

Figure 1: Sarcasm and sentiment detection system.

new corpus, (Abbes et al., 2020) proposed a new open domain Arabic corpus annotated for irony detection, which was also collected from Twitter. The rest of the paper is organized as follows: In section 2, a description of the used dataset is presented. The applied cleaning steps and preprocessing are explained in section 3. In section 4, we expose the proposed approach and experiments. Finally, the findings and discussion are presented in section 5. We conclude the paper in section 6.

2 Description of the Dataset

ArSarcasm-v2 dataset (Abu Farha et al., 2021) has been built using previously available Arabic sentiment analysis datasets (SemEval 2017 (Rosenthal et al., 2017) and ASTD (Nabil et al., 2015)) for which sarcasm and dialect labels have been assigned to them. More details about this dataset is addressed, in Table 1. Note that these statistics are related to the dataset after removal of punctuation and emojis.

3 Data Cleaning and Preprocessing

The cleaning process is the first step to apply with Arabic tweets. We define it as a surface preprocessing which includes one or many of the following steps: punctuation removal, emojis removal, stop words removal, Arabic diacritics removal, Arabic Letter normalization, Latin letter and words removal, repeating words and chars removal. The second step is morphological preprocessing: lemmatization (WorADRetLemmatizer (Lem)), stemming (ISRI Arabic Stemmer (Stem)) and part of speech tagging (PosTagger (PosTag) of NLTK)[1] (Lichouri and Abbas, 2020; Lichouri et al., 2020).

4 Experiments

As our focus is on detecting sentiment and sarcasm, we present, in this section, our contribution which is preprocessing as a solution to improve detection, in order to build LSVC and BiLSTM classification models (see figure 1). After performing this preprocessing step, features are calculated using the TFIDF vectorizer. These features are used to learn the LSVC model, where default parameters defined in the sklearn library are used (Pedregosa et al., 2011).

For BiLSTM, we adopted RNN model which uses an embedding layer with an input of 20k words which will be converted to vector with size 50. We fixed the max length of the input sequences (tweets) to 70 words (Table 1, max token length in train is 148 and test 92). After that we added a Bidirectional LSTM layer with 512 units, followed by a max pooling layer. We then added a dense layer

[1]https://www.nltk.org/index.html

	Sentiment		Sarcasm	
Params\Models	BiLSTM	LSVC	BiLSTM	LSVC
Default (Without Pre-processing)	88.23	98.21	**86.05**	98.83
Arabic Diacretics Removal (ADR)	86.66	98.23	57.76	98.68
normalizeArabic (NA)	88.29	**98.46**	83.87	98.83
remove_emoji (RE)	86.04	98.32	75.61	98.83
remove_repeating_char (RRC)	86.83	98.23	85.98	98.83
removeLatinLetter (RLL)	87.20	98.26	79.72	98.68
removeOneLetterWord (ROLW)	86.25	98.21	84.51	98.83
removePunctuation (RP)	87.34	98.35	84.67	98.68
removeStopWord (RSW)	86.81	98.11	84.89	98.83
removeWordRepetition (RWR)	86.64	98.33	81.47	98.83
applyLemme (Lemme)	86.31	98.21	81.63	98.83
applyPosTag (PosTag)	52.77	73.39	32.38	98.83
applyStem (Stem)	87.61	98.32	82.1	98.83

Table 2: Obtained score in the development phase in both sarcasm (F1-sarcastic) and sentiment (F1-PN) detection using a combination of processing steps.

	Sentiment		Sarcasm	
Params\Models	BiLSTM	LSVC	BiLSTM	LSVC
RP+RE	85.95	98.33	85.76	98.68
RP+RE+RSW	85.53	98.14	70.73	98.53
RP+RE+RSW+RRC	86.77	98.26	85.14	98.53
RP+RE+RSW+RRC+NA	87.08	98.22	85.22	98.68
RP+RE+RSW+RRC+NA +ADR	86.79	98.22	81.32	98.53
RP+RE+RSW+RRC+NA +ADR+RWR	87.74	98.23	84.58	98.53
RP+RE+RSW+RRC+NA +ADR+RWR+ROLW	87.44	98.23	75.56	98.53
RP+RE+RSW+RRC+NA +ADR+RWR+ROLW+RLL	87.17	97.62	84.62	97.94
RP+RE+RSW+RRC+NA +ADR+RWR+ROLW+RLL+Stem	86.80	97.08	82.57	97.03
RP+RE+RSW+RRC+NA +ADR+RWR+ROLW+RLL +Stem+Lemme	87.25	97.46	80.88	98.09
RP+RE+RSW+RRC+NA +ADR+RWR+ROLW+RLL +Stem+Lemme+PosTag	66.63	95.42	56.47	91.22

Table 3: Obtained score in the development phase in both sarcasm (F1-sarcastic) and sentiment (F1-PN) detection using a combination of processing steps with LSVC and BiLSTM.

of 256 units followed by a dropout layer of 0.4, and a second dense layer with 2 units (Sentiment: 2 classes) or 3 units (Sarcasm: 3 classes). The BiLSTM model is compiled using the binary and categorical cross entropy and the RMSprop for optimization. For training, we used a batch size of 128, 5 epochs, and a validation split of 0.2. For development, we used the test set from the ArSarcasm corpus [2]. The results are reported in Tables 2 and 3.

[2]https://github.com/iabufarha/ArSarcasm

	Sarcasme Task		Sentiment Task	
	F1-sarcastic	Accuracy	F1-PN	Accuracy
Our proposed system	33.71%	72.87%	57.87%	59.23%
Average for all system	52.52%	80.48%	65.43%	64.61%

Table 4: Obtained results of our submitted system vs the average for all the participant for sarcasm and sentiment detection in the test phase.

5 Results and Discussion

In Table 2, we summarize the results obtained using the development set from Abu Farha GitHub. All the preprocessing and morphological processing steps are applied independently.

The reported results shows that in the case of sentiment detection, the best performance is obtained using the Arabic normalizer with an F-PN score of 88.29% and 98.46% with BiLSTM and LSVC, respectively. In the case of sarcasm detection, the best performance is achieved without applying any preprocessing step with an F1-sarcastic score of 86.05% and 98.83% with BiLSTM and LSVC, respectively. We should note that the combination of preprocessing steps didn't improve the performance of the system (Table 3).

Results on the test set

Our submitted prediction during the test phase is based on the models that use preprocessing and morphological processing steps independently. The performance we achieved for the test phase was F1-sarcastic = 33.71% and F-PN = 57.87% which is less than the average values of all submitted systems by around (+8%) and (+7%) for sarcasm and sentiment detection, respectively (see Table 4).

6 Conclusion

In this work, we presented a simple but intuitive detection system based on the investigation of a number of preprocessing steps and their combinations. A comparison between LSVC and BiLSTM classfiers was conducted where we tried to find the best combination of "preprocessing + classifiers". After conducting more than 200 experiments, we found that feeding BiLSTM (used for sarcasm detection) with raw text without preprocessing is better and allowed to achieve a score of 33.71%. In the case of LSVC (used to detect the sentiment of tweets), we found that the better preprocessing step, in our case, is the Arabic Letter Normalizer with an achieved score of 57.87%.

References

Ines Abbes, Wajdi Zaghouani, Omaima El-Hardlo, and Faten Ashour. 2020. Daict: A dialectal arabic irony corpus extracted from twitter. In *Proceedings of The 12th Language Resources and Evaluation Conference*, pages 6265–6271.

Muhammad Abdul-Mageed, Chiyu Zhang, Azadeh Hashemi, and El Moatez Billah Nagoudi. 2019. Aranet: A deep learning toolkit for arabic social media. *arXiv preprint arXiv:1912.13072*.

Ibrahim Abu Farha, Wajdi Zaghouani, and Walid Magdy. 2021. Overview of the wanlp 2021 shared task on sarcasm and sentiment detection in arabic. In *Proceedings of the Sixth Arabic Natural Language Processing Workshop*.

Dana Al-Ghadhban, Eman Alnkhilan, Lamma Tatwany, and Muna Alrazgan. 2017. Arabic sarcasm detection in twitter. In *2017 International Conference on Engineering & MIS (ICEMIS)*, pages 1–7. IEEE.

Majdi Beseiso and Haytham Elmousalami. 2020. Subword attentive model for arabic sentiment analysis: A deep learning approach. *ACM Transactions on Asian and Low-Resource Language Information Processing (TALLIP)*, 19(2):1–17.

Houda Bouamor, Nizar Habash, Mohammad Salameh, Wajdi Zaghouani, Owen Rambow, Dana Abdulrahim, Ossama Obeid, Salam Khalifa, Fadhl Eryani, Alexander Erdmann, et al. 2018. The madar arabic dialect corpus and lexicon. In *Proceedings of the Eleventh International Conference on Language Resources and Evaluation (LREC 2018)*.

Houda Bouamor, Wajdi Zaghouani, Mona Diab, Ossama Obeid, Kemal Oflazer, Mahmoud Ghoneim, and Abdelati Hawwari. 2015. A pilot study on arabic multi-genre corpus diacritization. In *Proceedings of the Second Workshop on Arabic Natural Language Processing*, pages 80–88.

Ibrahim Abu Farha and Walid Magdy. 2020. From arabic sentiment analysis to sarcasm detection: The arsarcasm dataset. In *Proceedings of the 4th Workshop on Open-Source Arabic Corpora and Processing Tools, with a Shared Task on Offensive Language Detection*, pages 32–39.

Bilal Ghanem, Jihen Karoui, Farah Benamara, Véronique Moriceau, and Paolo Rosso. 2019. Idat at fire2019: Overview of the track on irony detection in arabic tweets. In *Proceedings of the 11th Forum for Information Retrieval Evaluation*, pages 10–13.

Aditya Joshi, Pushpak Bhattacharyya, and Mark J Carman. 2017. Automatic sarcasm detection: A survey. *ACM Computing Surveys (CSUR)*, 50(5):1–22.

Jihen Karoui, Farah Banamara Zitoune, and Veronique Moriceau. 2017. Soukhria: Towards an irony detection system for arabic in social media. *Procedia Computer Science*, 117:161–168.

Mohamed Lichouri and Mourad Abbas. 2020. Speechtrans@ smm4h'20: Impact of preprocessing and n-grams on automatic classification of tweets that mention medications. In *Proceedings of the Fifth Social Media Mining for Health Applications Workshop & Shared Task*, pages 118–120.

Mohamed Lichouri, Mourad Abbas, and Besma Benaziz. 2020. Profiling fake news spreaders on twitter based on tfidf features and morphological process.

Mohamed Maamouri, Ann Bies, Seth Kulick, Wajdi Zaghouani, David Graff, and Michael Ciul. 2010. From speech to trees: Applying treebank annotation to arabic broadcast news. In *LREC*. Citeseer.

Leila Moudjari, Karima Akli-Astouati, and Farah Benamara. 2020. An algerian corpus and an annotation platform for opinion and emotion analysis. In *Proceedings of The 12th Language Resources and Evaluation Conference*, pages 1202–1210.

Mahmoud Nabil, Mohamed Aly, and Amir Atiya. 2015. Astd: Arabic sentiment tweets dataset. In *Proceedings of the 2015 conference on empirical methods in natural language processing*, pages 2515–2519.

Ali Bou Nassif, Ashraf Elnagar, Ismail Shahin, and Safaa Henno. 2020. Deep learning for arabic subjective sentiment analysis: Challenges and research opportunities. *Applied Soft Computing*, page 106836.

F. Pedregosa, G. Varoquaux, A. Gramfort, V. Michel, B. Thirion, O. Grisel, M. Blondel, P. Prettenhofer, R. Weiss, V. Dubourg, J. Vanderplas, A. Passos, D. Cournapeau, M. Brucher, M. Perrot, and E. Duchesnay. 2011. Scikit-learn: Machine learning in Python. *Journal of Machine Learning Research*, 12:2825–2830.

Sara Rosenthal, Noura Farra, and Preslav Nakov. 2017. Semeval-2017 task 4: Sentiment analysis in twitter. In *Proceedings of the 11th international workshop on semantic evaluation (SemEval-2017)*, pages 502–518.

Deirdre Wilson. 2006. The pragmatics of verbal irony: Echo or pretence? *Lingua*, 116(10):1722–1743.

Wajdi Zaghouani and Anis Charfi. 2018. Arap-tweet: A large multi-dialect twitter corpus for gender, age and language variety identification. *arXiv preprint arXiv:1808.07674*.

Wajdi Zaghouani, Behrang Mohit, Nizar Habash, Ossama Obeid, Nadi Tomeh, Alla Rozovskaya, Noura Farra, Sarah Alkuhlani, and Kemal Oflazer. 2014. Large scale arabic error annotation: Guidelines and framework.

iCompass at Shared Task on Sarcasm and Sentiment Detection in Arabic

Malek Naski **Abir Messaoudi** **Hatem Haddad**
Moez Ben HajHmida **Chayma Fourati** **Aymen Ben Elhaj Mabrouk**
iCompass, Tunisia
{malek,abir,hatem,moez,chayma,aymen}@icompass.digital

Abstract

We describe our submitted system to the 2021 Shared Task on Sarcasm and Sentiment Detection in Arabic (Abu Farha et al., 2021). We tackled both subtasks, namely Sarcasm Detection (Subtask 1) and Sentiment Analysis (Subtask 2). We used state-of-the-art pretrained contextualized text representation models and fine-tuned them according to the downstream task in hand. As a first approach, we used Google's multilingual BERT and then other Arabic variants: AraBERT, ARBERT and MARBERT. The results found show that MARBERT outperforms all of the previously mentioned models overall, either on Subtask 1 or Subtask 2.

1 Introduction

Sentiment Analysis and especially Sarcasm Detection in Arabic are challenging tasks, not only because of the labelled data scarcity, but also because of the complexity of sarcasm detection for models. Sarcasm is highly dependent on the culture, gender and other aspects like dialects. Indeed, the Arabic language has many variants and dialects, other than the Modern Standard Arabic (MSA). Even if some dialects share some vocabulary, they still differ according to countries, where each dialect has its own specifications which makes an impact on the task. For example, the sentence "ما فيه إمكانيه تقربون المذيع والمذيعه بالأخبار اكثر من بعض!! مرره بعيدين بشكل يشتت الانتباه" represents a sarcastic text from the gulf region (Abu Farha et al., 2021) and reflects conservatism. The following example in gulf Arabic means "Where can I find dresses for Ramadan and elegant cloaks?": "وين احصل جلبيات لرمضان وعبايات كشخة؟". For a Tunisian speaker for example, this can be very confusing as "كشخة" means "ugly" in the Tunisian dialect! This can be used to express sarcasm if a Tunisian speaker addresses a gulf Arabic speaker using this word to express something negative while knowing that it means something positive in the gulf region.

Similarly, some words or concepts in dialects can be interpreted differently from one to another. As an example, the sentence " فضيعين فضيعين " presents a positive sentiment for some local dialects and a negative one for others.

In the sarcasm detection task, it is difficult to extract the information needed to detect if the sentence is sarcastic or not. A sarcastic one is defined by the shared task as the following: "a sarcastic sentence usually carries a negative implicit sentiment, while it is expressed using positive expressions". However, in some cases, sentences may contain contradictory sentiments expressed at the beginning and at the end. As examples:

- حلو أوي شعور الإهانة لما أقول لسواق التاكس قصر يقوم مشوحلي بإيده وسايق كإني خدت لطشة على وشي كده فعلا أبدعتي
- نفاق من الدرجة الأولئ ممتاز استمري ولكي كرسي في أسفل الدرك من النار

In other examples like "كلها بقت احمد الشيخ اهو" , the task becomes even harder since the sentence is extracted from its context. For instance, people usually use positive words to express negative sentiments.

Working on Arabic sentiment analysis was first initiated by (Abdul-Mageed et al., 2011), and afterwards many contributions took place (Mulki et al., 2018), such as the open dataset on sentiment analysis and sarcasm by (Abu Farha and Magdy, 2020), followed by the dataset of this competition, ArSarcasm-v2 (Abu Farha et al., 2021).

The paper is structured as follows: Section 2 provides a concise description of the used dataset.

Proceedings of the Sixth Arabic Natural Language Processing Workshop, pages 381–385
Kyiv, Ukraine (Virtual), April 19, 2021.

Section 3 describes the used systems and the experimental setup to build models for Sentiment Analysis and Sarcasm Detection. Section 4 presents the obtained results. Section 5 presents a general discussion. Finally, section 6 concludes and points to possible directions for future work.

2 Data

The provided training dataset of the competition, ArSarcasm-v2 (Abu Farha et al., 2021), consists of **12548 tweets**, labelled with the tweet's sentiment class (POS: positive, NEG: negative and NEU: neutral), its sarcasm class (TRUE: sarcastic, FALSE: non-sarcastic), and its dialect (namely "msa", "gulf", "egypt", "levant" and "magreb"). The initial released training data was provided without the validation dataset. For this reason, we had to split the data to be able to validate our models. We chose a 80:20 split given the size of the dataset. We chose to have a balanced validation set. The distributions for the two subtasks are as shown in Table 1 and Table 2 respectively.
To preprocess the data, we removed emojis, URLs, diacritics, punctuation and any non-UTF characters.

Class	Train	Validation	Total
Sarcastic	913	1255	2168
Non-sarcastic	9125	1255	10380
Total	10038	2510	12548

Table 1: The dataset description for Subtask 1 - Sarcasm Detection.

Class	Train	Validation	Total
POS	1343	837	2180
NEG	3784	837	4621
NEU	4911	836	5747
Total	10038	2510	12548

Table 2: The dataset description for Subtask 2 - Sentiment Analysis.

3 System description

Pretrained contextualized text representation models have shown to perform effectively in order to make a natural language understandable by machines. Bidirectional Encoder Representations from Transformers (BERT) (Devlin et al., 2019) is, nowadays, the state-of-the-art model for language understanding, outperforming previous models and opening new perspectives in the Natural Language Processing (NLP) field. As a first approach, we used multilingual cased BERT model (hereafter mBERT) (Pires et al., 2019). Recent similar work have been conducted for Arabic which is increasingly gaining attention. As a second approach, we used three BERT Arabic variants: AraBERT (Antoun et al., 2020), ARBERT (Abdul-Mageed et al., 2021) and MARBERT (Abdul-Mageed et al., 2021).

3.1 mBERT

Following BERT's success, large pretrained language models were extended to the multilingual setting such as mBERT (Pires et al., 2019). mBERT was trained on 104 languages and has been used for fine-tuning on languages other than English.

3.2 AraBERT

AraBERT (Antoun et al., 2020), was trained on 70 million sentences, equivalent to 24 GB of text, covering news in Arabic from different media sources. It achieved state-of-the-art performances on three Arabic tasks including Sentiment Analysis. Yet, the pre-training dataset was mostly in MSA and therefore can't handle dialectal Arabic as much as official Arabic. A while afterwards, GigaBERT (Wuwei et al., 2020), a bilingual language model for English and Arabic, outperformed AraBERT on several tasks.

3.3 ARBERT

ARBERT (Abdul-Mageed et al., 2021) is a large-scale pretrained language model using BERT base's architecture and focusing on MSA. It was trained on 61 GB of text gathered from books, news articles, crawled data and the Arabic Wikipedia. The vocabulary size was equal to 100k WordPieces which is the largest compared to AraBERT (60k for Arabic out of 64k) and mBERT (5k for Arabic out of 110k).

3.4 MARBERT

MARBERT, also by (Abdul-Mageed et al., 2021) is a large-scale pretrained language model using BERT base's architecture and focusing on the various Arabic dialects. It was trained on 128 GB of Arabic Tweets. The authors chose to keep the Tweets that have at least 3 Arabic words. Therefore, Tweets that have 3 or more Arabic words and some other non-Arabic words are kept. This is because dialects are often times mixed with other foreign languages. Hence, the vocabulary size is equal to 100k WordPieces. MARBERT enhances the language variety as it focuses on representing the previously underrepresented dialects and Arabic variants.

3.5 System submission

We use these pretrained language models and build upon them to obtain our final models. Other than outperforming previous techniques, huge amounts of unlabelled text have been used to train general purpose models. Fine-tuning them on much smaller annotated datasets gives good results thanks to the knowledge gained during the pretraining phase, which is expensive especially in computational power. This is why, given our relatively small dataset, we chose to fine-tune BERT pretrained models. The fine-tuning actually consists of adding an untrained layer of neurons on top of the pre-trained model and only tweaking the weights of the last layers to adjust them to the new labelled dataset.

We chose to train our models on a Google Cloud TPU of 8 cores using Google Colaboratory. The average training time of one model is around 5 minutes. We experimented with mBERT, AraBERT, ARBERT and MARBERT with different hyperparameters.

The final models that we used to make the submissions were:

- For Sarcasm Detection: a model based on MARBERT, trained for 8 epochs with a learning rate of 2e-5, a batch size of 128 and max sequence length of 128
- For Sentiment Analysis: a model based on MARBERT, trained for 3 epochs with a learning rate of 2e-5, a batch size of 128 and max sequence length of 128

4 Results

We have validated our models through balanced validation sets as mentioned in the data section, after splitting the training dataset into training and validation sets with a 80:20 ratio. The models based on MARBERT achieved the best results. We believe this is because MARBERT was trained mostly on dialectal Arabic which was underrepresented in previous pretrained models. Since this task's data is multi-dialectal, this model is expected to achieve the best performances.

4.1 Subtask 1 - Sarcasm Detection

The best results that we obtained for sarcasm detection on the sarcastic and non-sarcastic class are shown in Table 3. The accuracy achieved was **68.8%** and the F1-sarcastic was **57.7%**.

For reference, and to compare with other models,

Class	Precision	Recall
Sarcastic	89.7 %	42.5 %
Non-sarcastic	62.3 %	95.1 %

Table 3: The best results using MARBERT for Subtask 1 - Sarcasm Detection.

we also showcase the results obtained with mBERT and AraBERT. For AraBERT, the best results were found using a learning rate of 2e-5 and training for 3 epochs. The accuracy achieved was **64.1%** and the F1-sarcastic was **47%**. The results are shown in Table 4.

Class	Precision	Recall
Sarcastic	89.9 %	31.8 %
Non-sarcastic	58.6 %	96.4 %

Table 4: The results using AraBERT for Subtask 1 - Sarcasm Detection.

For mBERT, the best results were performed using a learning rate of 2e-5 and training for 5 epochs. The accuracy achieved was **58.2%** and the F1-sarcastic was **31.2%**. Results are presented in Table 5.

Class	Precision	Recall
Sarcastic	88.5 %	19.0 %
Non-sarcastic	54.6 %	97.5 %

Table 5: The results using mBERT for Subtask 1 - Sarcasm Detection.

4.2 Subtask 2 - Sentiment Analysis

The best results that we obtained for sarcasm detection on the sarcastic and non-sarcastic class are shown in Table 6. The accuracy achieved was **72%** and the F-PN was **72.95%** .

For reference, and to compare with other models, we also showcase the results obtained with mBERT and AraBERT.

For AraBERT, the best results were found using a learning rate of 2e-5 and training for 3 epochs. The accuracy achieved was **69%** and the F-PN was **68.7%**. The results are shown in Table 7.

Class	Precision	Recall
POS	85.0 %	58.3 %
NEG	76.1 %	77.3 %
NEU	61.8 %	80.3 %

Table 6: The best results using MARBERT for Subtask 2 - Sentiment Analysis.

Class	Precision	Recall
POS	82.2 %	54.1 %
NEG	69.9 %	74.6 %
NEU	61.4 %	78.2 %

Table 7: The best results using AraBERT for Subtask 2 - Sentiment Analysis.

For mBERT, the best results were also found using a learning rate of 2e-5 and training for 3 epochs. The accuracy was **63.4%** and the F-PN was **60.15%**. The results are shown in Table 8.

Class	Precision	Recall
POS	74.6 %	42.4 %
NEG	63.9 %	68.6 %
NEU	58.4 %	79.3 %

Table 8: The best results using mBERT for Subtask 2 - Sentiment Analysis.

4.3 Official submission results

The final results that we achieved on the test set of the 2021 Shared Task on Sarcasm and Sentiment Detection in Arabic were:

- Sarcasm Detection: F1-sarcastic equal to **48.6%**
- Sentiment Analysis: F-PN equal to **70.85%**

5 Discussion

Table 9 shows the results obtained over development data for the Sarcasm Detection task (True being sarcastic and False being non-sarcastic) and Table 10 shows the results obtained over development data for the Sentiment Analysis task. The development sets are as described in the data section. The results shown in Table 9 are clearly due to the training data being very unbalanced. The provided dataset has 2168 sarcastic examples and 10380 non-sarcastic ones. After the 80:20 split, the training set is left with 913 sarcastic examples and 9125 non-sarcastic ones.

It's also important to emphasise the difference between MARBERT's results and the other models' results. MARBERT was pretrained on various Arabic dialects and therefore works better with dialectal data.

	Predicted	
	False	**True**
False	1194	61
True	722	533

Table 9: Confusion matrix over development data - Sarcasm Detection

	Predicted		
	NEG	**NEU**	**POS**
NEG	647	162	28
NEU	107	671	58
POS	96	253	488

Table 10: Confusion matrix over development data - Sentiment Analysis

Table 11 and Table 12 review the official results of iCompass system for Sentiment Analysis and Sarcasm Detection against the top three ranked systems.

Team	Rank	F-PN
CS-UM6P	1	0,7480
DeepBlueAI	2	0,7392
rematchka	3	0,7321
iCompass	8	0,7085

Table 11: Ranking and results on the Sentiment Analysis Test set.

Team	Rank	F1-sarcastic
BhamNLP	1	0,6225
SPPU-AASM	2	0,6140
DeepBlueAI	3	0,6127
iCompass	21	0,4860

Table 12: Ranking and results on the Sarcasm Detection Test set.

6 Conclusion

Four language models were used to classify sentiment and to detect sarcasm (mBERT, AraBERT, ARBERT and MARBERT). The best results were obtained by MARBERT for both tasks with different hyperparameters, which was selected for the final submission. Future work would involve working on bigger contextualized pretrained models and enriching the existing Sarcasm Detection and Sentiment Analysis datasets.

References

Muhammad Abdul-Mageed, Mona Diab, and Mohammed Korayem. 2011. Subjectivity and sentiment analysis of modern standard Arabic. In *Proceedings of the 49th Annual Meeting of the Association for Computational Linguistics: Human Language Technologies*, pages 587–591, Portland, Oregon, USA. Association for Computational Linguistics.

Muhammad Abdul-Mageed, AbdelRahim Elmadany, and El Moatez Billah Nagoudi. 2021. Arbert marbert: Deep bidirectional transformers for arabic. *ArXiv*, abs/2101.01785.

Ibrahim Abu Farha and Walid Magdy. 2020. From Arabic sentiment analysis to sarcasm detection: The ArSarcasm dataset. In *Proceedings of the 4th Workshop on Open-Source Arabic Corpora and Processing Tools, with a Shared Task on Offensive Language Detection*, pages 32–39, Marseille, France. European Language Resource Association.

Ibrahim Abu Farha, Wajdi Zaghouani, and Walid Magdy. 2021. Overview of the wanlp 2021 shared task on sarcasm and sentiment detection in arabic. In *Proceedings of the Sixth Arabic Natural Language Processing Workshop*.

Wissam Antoun, Fady Baly, and Hazem Hajj. 2020. AraBERT: Transformer-based model for Arabic language understanding. In *Proceedings of the 4th Workshop on Open-Source Arabic Corpora and Processing Tools, with a Shared Task on Offensive Language Detection*, pages 9–15.

Jacob Devlin, Ming-Wei Chang, Kenton Lee, and Kristina Toutanova. 2019. BERT: Pre-training of deep bidirectional transformers for language understanding. In *Proceedings of the 2019 Conference of the North American Chapter of the Association for Computational Linguistics: Human Language Technologies, Volume 1 (Long and Short Papers)*, pages 4171–4186.

Hala Mulki, Hatem Haddad, and İsmail Babaoğlu. 2018. Modern trends in arabic sentiment analysis: A survey. *TAL Traitement Automatique des Langues*, 58(3):15–39.

Telmo Pires, Eva Schlinger, and Dan Garrette. 2019. How multilingual is multilingual BERT? In *Proceedings of the 57th Annual Meeting of the Association for Computational Linguistics*, pages 4996–5001, Florence, Italy. Association for Computational Linguistics.

Lan Wuwei, Chen Yang, Xu Wei, and Ritter Alan. 2020. Gigabert: Zero-shot transfer learning from english to arabic. In *Proceedings of The 2020 Conference on Empirical Methods on Natural Language Processing (EMNLP)*.

Machine Learning-Based Model for Sentiment and Sarcasm Detection

Aya H. Allam[1], Hanya M. Abdallah[1], Eslam Amer[2], Hamada A. Nayel[1]
[1]Department of Computer Science
Faculty of Computers and Artificial Intelligence, Benha University
[2]Faculty of Computer Science, Misr International University

{aya.allam,hanya.abdelhak,hamada.ali}@fci.bu.edu.eg,
eslam.amer@miuegypt.edu.eg

Abstract

Within the last few years, the number of Arabic internet users and Arabic online content is in exponential growth. Dealing with Arabic datasets and the usage of non-explicit sentences to express an opinion are considered to be the major challenges in the field of natural language processing. Hence, sarcasm and sentiment analysis has gained a major interest from the research community, especially in this language. Automatic sarcasm detection and sentiment analysis can be applied using three approaches, namely supervised, unsupervised and hybrid approach. In this paper, a model based on a supervised machine learning algorithm called Support Vector Machine (SVM) has been used for this process. The proposed model has been evaluated using ArSarcasm-v2 dataset. The performance of the proposed model has been compared with other models submitted to sentiment analysis and sarcasm detection shared task.

1 Introduction

Today, social networks such as Facebook and Twitter are considered new forms of social interaction, knowledge exchange, and collaboration. Social networking sites allow users to exchange ideas, post updates, reviews, and comments while sharing their broader interests. Du to the extreme usage of social networks, it is crucial to apply related analysis tasks automatically. These tasks ranges over sarcasm detection, offensive language detection(Nayel and L, 2019; Nayel, 2020), author profiling (Nayel, 2019), irony detection (Nayel et al., 2019) and sentiment analysis. Sentiment analysis is precious as it allows us to capture an overview of social network users' opinions towards specific topics, products, or services. Sentiment analysis refers to the use of Natural Language Processing (NLP) and Machine Learning (ML) to identify and extract subjective information in a piece of writing. Sarcasm is defined as an indirect way to express an opinion as the written is literally not the intended meaning (Wilson, 2006). It is considered a widespread phenomenon in social media, which is difficult to analyse, not just automatically but also for humans (Maynard and Greenwood, 2014). Although It has a significant effect on sentiment, it is ignored in social media analysis because it is considered too difficult to handle. So, sarcasm is still considered a challenge in sentiment analysis.

Due to the importance of sentiment analysis, many research works have been developed in this research field. However, most of these studies have focused on English and other Indo-European languages (Lunando and Purwarianti, 2013). Actually, few studies have been conducted on sarcasm and sentiment analysis in morphologically rich languages such as Arabic (Boudad et al., 2018). Three main variations of the Arabic language exist classical Arabic, which is the language of the Qur'an (Islam's Holy Book); Modern Standard Arabic (MSA), and dialectical Arabic. MSA is an Arabic language form used greatly in formal speeches and writings. Dialectical Arabic refers to all oral varieties spoken in daily communication. These vary from one Arab country to another and from one region of the same country to another.

The work in Arabic Sarcasm Sentiment analysis using a variety of Arabic dialects started in 2008. Besides, a set of research work has been rapidly conducted such as (Abdul-Mageed et al., 2011; Al-Ghadhban et al., 2017; Alsayat and Elmitwally, 2020; Karoui et al., 2017). The authors use different ML approaches such as supervised, unsupervised, and hybrid approaches to detect sarcasm and sentiment. These approaches carry out the classification task as it classifies text into either sarcasm or not. However, more work is still needed to achieve better accuracy.

Proceedings of the Sixth Arabic Natural Language Processing Workshop, pages 386–389
Kyiv, Ukraine (Virtual), April 19, 2021.

In this paper, we present a model to detect sarcastic and sentiment Arabic tweets from real ones using SVM. The model is developed in the framework of the shared task on sarcasm and sentiment detection in Arabic (Abu Farha et al., 2021). The rest of this paper is organized as follows. Section 2 reviews the dataset, section 3 gives a detailed description of how the systems were built and trained. In Section 4, the system is evaluated, and the results are discussed. The paper is concluded in Section 6 after a general discussion is introduced in section 5.

2 Dataset

For both tasks, ArSarcasm-v2 (Abu Farha et al., 2021) a dataset has been distributed to all participants. It contains a labeled training set with 12,548 tweets and a blind test set contains 3,000 unlabelled tweets. Table 1 contains a statistics of the training set for both tasks. In addition to the two labels for both tasks, dialect information about a tweet is also given.

3 System

The proposed system, as described in Figure 1, combines three main phases: preprocessing phase, the feature extraction phase, and the classification phase.

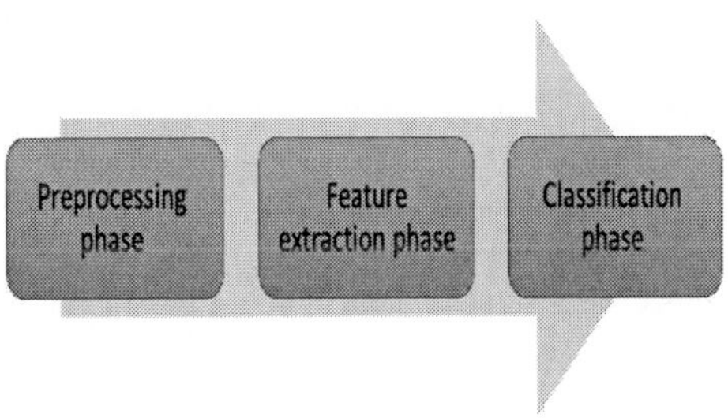

Figure 1: Proposed system structure

3.1 Preprocessing Phase

In social media communications, users use slang words instead of formal words such as emojis, numbers, etc. Hence, it is a must to clean and prepare data for the feature extraction process. At first, We changed the encoding of the dataset file to UTF-8 to recognize Arabic characters. Then, We preprocessed the tweets by removing the hashtags, emojis, numbers, and URLs. This process reduces the dimensionality of the problem low. Hence, it speeds up the classification process and makes it more accessible.

3.2 Feature Extraction Phase

In this phase, unigram or bigram can be used as features for the Arabic tweets. Several methods can be used to determine the significance of each feature in the whole text, such as Term Frequency (TF) or and Term Frequency Inverse Document Frequency (TF/IDF).

For term weights, we used TF/IDF calculated as follows:-

$$t_j = tf_j * \log\left(\frac{N+1}{df_j+1}\right)$$

where tf_j is the total number of occurrences of term t_j in the given tweet, df_j is the number of tweets in which the token/term t_j occurs and N is the total number of tweets.

3.3 Classification Phase

Sentiment Analysis can be classified into three levels: document level, sentence level and aspect level. In this phase, the document level is adopted where the whole piece of writing is dealt with as one unit and is assigned to a particular class label. SVM is a linear classifier that have been designed binary classification problem (Theodoridis and Koutroumbas, 2009). It can be adjusted for multi class classification problems using one-vs-one or one-vs-many strategies. SVM is one of the strongest and accurate algorithms used with Arabic text (Nayel, 2020, 2019; Nayel et al., 2019).

4 Experiments and Results

4.1 Evaluation Metric

The performance evaluation of sarcasm and sentiment detection shared task is measured as the accuracy of the system in addition to class-wise accuracy which is calculated using Precision (**P**), Recall (**R**) and **F1** measure [1]. For each class, **P** is the number of tweets correctly classified over the total number of tweets that system classified as same class. **R** is the number of tweets correctly classified over the actual number of tweets of the class. **F1** measure is the harmonic mean of **P** and **R**, which can be calculate as follow:-

$$F1 = \frac{2 * P * R}{P + R}$$

[1] http://www.nltk.org/_modules/nltk/metrics/scores.html

Task	Class	No. of Tweets	Percentage (%)
Sarcasm Detection	TRUE	2,168	17.28%
	FALSE	10,380	82.72%
Sentiment Analysis	POS	2,180	17.37%
	NEG	4,621	36.83%
	NEU	5,747	45.80%

Table 1: Statistics of training set for both tasks

The official metric of the sarcasm detection task is F1-score of the sarcastic class (F1-sarcastic), while macro average of the F-score of the positive and negative classes (F-PN) will be the official metric of the sentiment detection task.

4.2 Results

In developing phase, cross-validation approach with five folds has been used to train different classification algorithms for each subtask. These algorithms are: SVM, Linear Regression (LR), Naïve Bayes (NB), Complementary Naïve Bayes (CNB) and Stochastic Gradient Descent (SGD). The performance of all classifiers during development phase are given in Table 2.

	Sentiment	Sarcasm
SVM	**85.55%**	**84.22%**
CNB	83.47%	82.97%
NB	78.92%	78.10%
LR	65.89%	64.03%

Table 2: 5-fold Cross-Validation performance of different classifiers for both tasks

From Table 2 it is clear that SVM outperforms all other algorithms in both tasks.

4.2.1 Official Submission Results

The proposed model has been applied to the blind test set and the output of both tasks have been submitted to the shared task. Table 3 shows the detailed results of the proposed model for both subtasks.

	Sarcasm	Sentiment
Accuracy	0.7460	0.5980
Macro-F1	0.5457	0.5291
Precision	0.7048	0.5434
Recall	0.5602	0.5207
Oficial Metric	F1-sarcastic	F-PN
	0.5936	0.2440

Table 3: The official results of our submissions

5 Discussion

Sarcasm and sentiment detection in Arabic is a widely NLP studied problem. The supervised learning approach outperforms unsupervised and semi-supervised methods in this detection process. Note also that some supervised classifiers such as SVM have repeatedly been applied. The effectiveness of this classifier is the reason behind this choice. The same thing can be said about the used feature; n-grams are frequently chosen as features.

6 Conclusion

Sarcasm and sentiment detection is one of the most useful and challenging tasks. In this paper, we proposed SVM based classifier model to detect Arabic sarcasm and sentiment in Twitter. The results are produced from training the model using SVM classifier, one of the accurate classification algorithms. The model achieves moderate accuracies, which are relatively high, especially regarding Arabic text. The performance can be improved using different weighting scores such as word embeddings. Deep learning based models also can be used for the training purpose.

References

Muhammad Abdul-Mageed, Mona Diab, and Mohammed Korayem. 2011. Subjectivity and sentiment analysis of Modern Standard Arabic. In *Proceedings of the 49th Annual Meeting of the Association for Computational Linguistics: Human Language Technologies*, pages 587–591, Portland, Oregon, USA. Association for Computational Linguistics.

Ibrahim Abu Farha, Wajdi Zaghouani, and Walid Magdy. 2021. Overview of the WANLP 2021 Shared Task on Sarcasm and Sentiment Detection in Arabic. In *Proceedings of the Sixth Arabic Natural Language Processing Workshop*.

D. Al-Ghadhban, E. Alnkhilan, L. Tatwany, and M. Alrazgan. 2017. Arabic sarcasm detection in twitter. In *2017 International Conference on Engineering MIS (ICEMIS)*, pages 1–7.

Ahmed Alsayat and Nouh Elmitwally. 2020. A comprehensive study for arabic sentiment analysis (challenges and applications). *Egyptian Informatics Journal*, 21(1):7–12.

Naaima Boudad, Rdouan Faizi, Rachid Oulad Haj Thami, and Raddouane Chiheb. 2018. Sentiment analysis in arabic: A review of the literature. *Ain Shams Engineering Journal*, 9(4):2479–2490.

Jihen Karoui, Farah Banamara Zitoune, and Véronique Moriceau. 2017. Soukhria: Towards an irony detection system for arabic in social media. *Procedia Computer Science*, 117:161–168. Arabic Computational Linguistics.

E. Lunando and A. Purwarianti. 2013. Indonesian social media sentiment analysis with sarcasm detection. In *2013 International Conference on Advanced Computer Science and Information Systems (ICACSIS)*, pages 195–198.

Diana Maynard and Mark Greenwood. 2014. Who cares about sarcastic tweets? investigating the impact of sarcasm on sentiment analysis. In *Proceedings of the Ninth International Conference on Language Resources and Evaluation (LREC'14)*, pages 4238–4243, Reykjavik, Iceland. European Language Resources Association (ELRA).

Hamada Nayel. 2020. NAYEL at SemEval-2020 task 12: TF/IDF-based approach for automatic offensive language detection in Arabic tweets. In *Proceedings of the Fourteenth Workshop on Semantic Evaluation*, pages 2086–2089, Barcelona (online). International Committee for Computational Linguistics.

Hamada A. Nayel. 2019. NAYEL@APDA: Machine Learning Approach for Author Profiling and Deception Detection in Arabic Texts. In *Working Notes of FIRE 2019 - Forum for Information Retrieval Evaluation, Kolkata, India, December 12-15, 2019*, volume 2517 of *CEUR Workshop Proceedings*, pages 92–99. CEUR-WS.org.

Hamada A. Nayel and Shashirekha H. L. 2019. DEEP at HASOC2019: A machine learning framework for hate speech and offensive language detection. In *Working Notes of FIRE 2019 - Forum for Information Retrieval Evaluation, Kolkata, India, December 12-15, 2019*, volume 2517 of *CEUR Workshop Proceedings*, pages 336–343. CEUR-WS.org.

Hamada A. Nayel, Walaa Medhat, and Metwally Rashad. 2019. BENHA@IDAT: Improving Irony Detection in Arabic Tweets using Ensemble Approach. In *Working Notes of FIRE 2019 - Forum for Information Retrieval Evaluation, Kolkata, India, December 12-15, 2019*, volume 2517 of *CEUR Workshop Proceedings*, pages 401–408. CEUR-WS.org.

Sergios Theodoridis and Konstantinos Koutroumbas. 2009. Chapter 3 - Linear Classifiers. In *Pattern Recognition (Fourth Edition)*, fourth edition edition, pages 91 – 150. Academic Press, Boston.

Deirdre Wilson. 2006. The pragmatics of verbal irony: Echo or pretence? *Lingua*, 116(10):1722–1743. Language in Mind: A Tribute to Neil Smith on the Occasion of his Retirement.

DeepBlueAI at WANLP-EACL2021 task 2: A Deep Ensemble-based Method for Sarcasm and Sentiment Detection in Arabic

Bingyan Song **Chunguang Pan** **Shengguang Wang** **Zhipeng Luo**
DeepBlue Technology (Shanghai) Co., Ltd
{songby,panchg,wangshg,luozhp}@deepblueai.com

Abstract

Sarcasm is one of the main challenges for sentiment analysis systems due to using implicit indirect phrasing for expressing opinions, especially in Arabic. This paper presents the system we submitted to the Sarcasm and Sentiment Detection task of WANLP-2021 that is capable of dealing with both two subtasks. We first perform fine-tuning on two kinds of pre-trained language models (PLMs) with different training strategies. Then an effective stacking mechanism is applied on top of the fine-tuned PLMs to obtain the final prediction. Experimental results on ArSarcasm-v2 dataset show the effectiveness of our method and we rank third and second for subtask 1 and 2.

1 Introduction

Social media is growing as a communication medium where people can express online their feelings and opinions on a variety of topics in ways they rarely do in person. Detecting sarcasm and sentiment in text have become a crucial element for decision-makers and business leaders as well as for common users to understand public opinion. The significant role of the Arab region in international politics and in the global economy have led to the investigation on the task of detecting sarcasm and sentiment in Arabic. The task involves detecting whether a piece of text expresses a **positive**, a **negative**, or a **neutral** sentiment; and whether it is **sarcasm** or **non-sarcasm**.

Sarcasm or Irony is a form of speech that, in the context of sentiment analysis, mostly takes place when the speaker expresses a positive opinion but actually aims to complain about the opinion target (Majumder et al., 2019). Sarcasm is particularly hard to detect in Arabic language due to the use of positive indicators to express negative emotions. Sentiment detection is also challenging because the same sentiment word may have different polarity according to the domain (Oraby et al., 2013).

There are two main approaches for the monolingual approach of Sarcasm and Sentiment Detection in Arabic: corpus-based and lexicon-based (Oueslati et al., 2020). Then combination of these two can be referred to as the hybrid approach. The corpus-based method, typically trains sentiment classifiers. Several supervised learning algorithms (e.g. SVM) (Duwairi and El-Orfali, 2014) have been used to classify the sentiment label into positive or negative. These algorithms require handcrafted features including part-of-speech (POS) tags and social media-driven features. Recently, deep learning techniques such as recurrent neural network (RNN) (Al-Sallab et al., 2017; Al-Smadi et al., 2019) and convolutional neural network (CNN) (Alayba et al., 2017) emancipate researchers from feature engineering. The lexicon-based method commonly determines the sentiment or polarity of opinion by evaluating the sentiment words in the document or the sentence which is used when the data is unlabelled. It often uses predefined dictionaries of annotated sentiment terms to label each word in the document by its sentiment (Al-Ayyoub et al., 2015). Then lexicon scores are used as input features to the classifier and thus plays an important role in the hybrid approach (Elshakankery and Ahmed, 2019).

However, more recent word embedding techniques, such as fastText, ELMo, BERT, are yet to be fully explored for Sarcasm and Sentiment Detection in Arabic despite having pretrained Arabic vesrions of them publicly available like EMLoForManyLangs (Zeman et al., 2018), AraBERT (Antoun et al., 2020). Therefore, in this paper, we introduce our system for Sarcasm and Sentiment detection in Arabic, which leverages multiple PLMs with several training strategies. There are two main steps for our system, **(i)** fine-tuning two kinds of

Proceedings of the Sixth Arabic Natural Language Processing Workshop, pages 390–394
Kyiv, Ukraine (Virtual), April 19, 2021.

Dialect	Non-Sarcastic	Sarcastic	Negative	Neutral	Positive	Total
Egyptian	1,745	930	1,376	793	506	2,675
Gulf	487	157	264	259	121	644
Levantine	486	138	285	197	142	624
Maghrebi	28	15	25	12	6	43
MSA	7,634	928	2,671	4,486	1,405	8,562
Total	10,380	2,168	4,621	5,747	2,180	12,548

Table 1: Dataset statistics for sarcasm and sentiment over the dialects

PLMs, including XLM-R (Conneau et al., 2020) and AraBERT (Antoun et al., 2020), with various hyperparameters and training strategies, obtaining diverse models; **(ii)** applying an effective stacking mechanism on top of these PLMs to predict the final complexity scores.

Our experiments, merging PLMs in total, indicate that our method successfully utilizes weaker PLMs as well as high-performing PLMs. As a result, our system ranks third and second for the Subtask 1 and 2 of Sarcasm and Sentiment Detection in Arabic, WANLP-2021 (Abu Farha et al., 2021).

2 Data

In this paper, we use the dataset called **ArSarcasm-v2** (Abu Farha et al., 2021). This is an Arabic sarcasm detection dataset based on several other Arabic sentiment analysis datasets including ArSarcasm (Abu Farha and Magdy, 2020), SemEval's 2017 (Rosenthal et al., 2017) and ASTD (Nabil et al., 2015). For the annotation process, the annotators were asked to provide three labels for each tweet including **Sarcasm** (sarcastic or non-sarcastic), **Sentiment** (positive, negative or neutral) and **Dialect** (Egyptian, Gulf, Levantine, Maghrebi or Modern Standard Arabic). Each tweet was annotated by at least three different annotators.

ArSarcasm-v2 contains 12,548 training samples with annotations and 3,000 testing samples without annotations. Table 1 shows statistics of training set, where we can find that 17.28% of the data is sarcastic (2,168 tweets). Most of the data is either in MSA or the Egyptian dialect, while there are few examples of the Maghrebi dialect. Figure 1 shows the sentiment distribution over the sarcastic tweets. It illustrates that most of the sarcastic tweets have negative sentiment, and this agrees with the definition, which implies that sarcasm includes making ridicule of someone or something.

Since there is no official validation set, we use 7-fold cross-validation on the training dataset for performance estimation of our model.

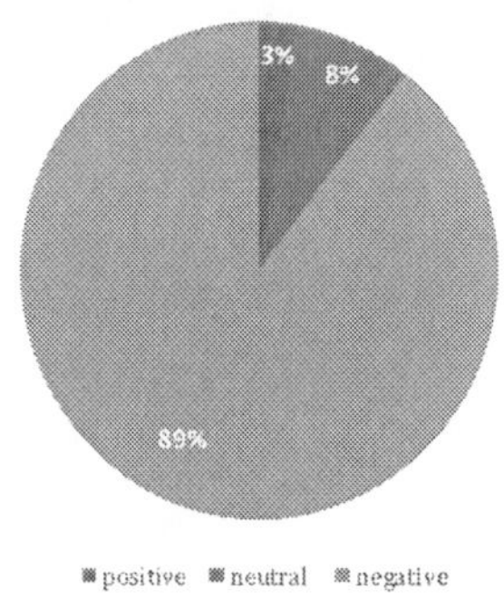

Figure 1: Sentiment distribution over sarcastic tweets.

3 System

3.1 Model

Architecture Figure 2 shows the architecture of our model that is capable of dealing with both subtask 1 and 2. We add dialect information before the tweet to construct the input segment. Since we utilize a BERT-like model as the encoder, we segment them with special tokens `[CLS]` and `[SEP]`. Then the embedding of `[CLS]`, which can stand for the whole input context, can be obtained. We feed it into a dense layer and get the final prediction through the Multi-Sample Dropout (Inoue, 2019). The output of dense layer x is depicted as below,

$$x = ReLU(W_0 dropout(x_{[CLS]})) \quad (1)$$

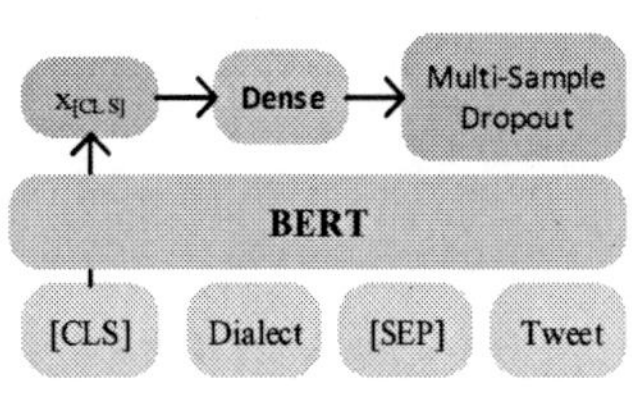

Figure 2: The overall architecture for sarcasm and sentiment detection.

where $W_0 \in R^{d \times k}$ is the learning weight, k is the dimension of $x_{[CLS]}$ and d is the hyperparameter which we set as 256.

Multi-Sample Dropout Dropout is a simple but efficient regularization technique for achieving better generalization of deep neural networks. During training, dropout randomly discards a portion of the neurons to avoid overfitting. The original dropout creates a randomly selected subset (called a dropout sample) from the input in each training iteration while the multi-sample dropout creates multiple dropout samples. The loss is calculated for each sample, and the sample losses are averaged to obtain the final loss.

Thus, the final prediction of subtask 1 and 2 can be calculated as following,

$$\hat{y}_{sub1} = \frac{1}{N}\sum_{i=1}^{N} Sigmoid(W_i dropout_i(x))$$
$$\hat{y}_{sub2} = \frac{1}{N}\sum_{j=1}^{N} W_j dropout_j(x)) \quad (2)$$

where $W_i \in R^{1 \times d}$ and $W_j \in R^{3 \times d}$ are the learning weights, N is the number of dropout values which we set as 5. By using this training mechanism, we can accelerate training and achieve lower error rates as well.

Loss Function Since subtask 1 is a binary classification task and subtask 2 is a multiclass classification task, we choose the Binary Cross Entropy Loss and Cross Entropy Loss for the two subtasks respectively.

3.2 Training strategies

In order to further improve the performance of our model, we adopt two training strategies and are introduced below.

Task-Adaptive Pre-training Task-adaptive pre-training (TAPT) can effectively improve model performance (Gururangan et al., 2020). The data used in general pre-training usually does not contain task-specific data. Thus we do task-adaptive pre-training by pre-training the masked language model task on the given Arabic dataset.

Knowledge Distillation Inspired by Hinton et al. (2015), we adopt the knowledge distillation mechanism into our system. The whole procedure consists of three steps. First, we train the original big model using a hard target, which is the true label (e.g. [0,1,0]). Then, we use the trained model to predict the soft target, which is the probability of each class. After this, we train a small model by minimizing the loss between the scores predicted by the small model and the soft target. We choose MSE or Smoothl as the loss function. Finally, we utilize the small model to predict the final results.

3.3 Stacking Trained Models

Model stacking is commonly used in competitions to improve mode accuracy. The main procedure of stacking trained models in our method including five steps. First, since the dataset we use is in Arabic, we choose XLM-R (Conneau et al., 2020) which is a new state-of-the-art multilingual masked language model and AraBERT (Antoun et al., 2020) which is a transformer-based model for Arabic as base models. Second, we do TAPT on these PLMs to achieve new PLM models. Third, we perform 7-fold cross-validation during the whole training process to avoid overfitting or selection bias. Fourth, we train multiple models with different hyperparameters (e.g. learning rate) and different training strategies to improve the model diversity. Ultimately, we train a simple Linear Regression (LR) model and a Support Vector Machine (SVM) model as the final estimator for subtask 1 and 2 respectively.

4 Results and Discussion

Evaluation Metrics As mentioned in the evaluation procedure of WANLP-2021 Sarcasm task, the F-score of the sarcastic class is the official metric for subtask 1 and F-PN (Marco average of the F-score of the positive and negative classes) is the official one for subtask 2.

PLMs with Training Strategies As shown in Table 2, for both subtask 1 and 2, we use two kinds of PLMs which are XLM-R and AraBERT. The results are the average scores of 7-fold cross-validation on the training dataset. XLM-R performs better on this task.

We evaluate the performance of adding different training strategies as well. By adding TAPT, F1 scores of both XLM-R and AraBERT in subtask 1 and 2 increase. It demonstrates that further pre-train the language model with task-specific data will improve the performance. We then add knowledge distillation to the models after TAPT and achieves the best F1 scores on the cross-validation

	Subtask 1		Subtask 2	
Tpye	**Model**	**F1-sarcastic**	**Model**	**F1-PN**
XLM-R	XLM-R$_{LARGE}$	0.5725	XLM-R$_{LARGE}$	0.7348
	XLM-R$_{LARGE}$+TAPT	0.6027	XLM-R$_{LARGE}$+TAPT	0.7460
	XLM-R$_{LARGE}$+TAPT+Distillation	**0.6687**	**XLM-R$_{LARGE}$+TAPT+Distillation**	**0.7919**
AraBERT	AraBERT$_{LARGE}$	0.5724	AraBERT$_{LARGE}$	0.7413
	AraBERT$_{LARGE}$+TAPT	0.6079	AraBERT$_{LARGE}$+TAPT	0.7451
	AraBERT$_{LARGE}$+TAPT+Distillation	0.6538	AraBERT$_{LARGE}$+TAPT+Distillation	0.7790
Ensemble	mean	0.5964	mean	0.7782
	LR	0.6627	-	-
	LR+ Threshold	**0.6899**	**SVM**	**0.8024**

Table 2: Comparison of F1 scores for stacking different models of subtask 1 and 2.

Subtask 1			Subtask 2		
Team	**F1-sarcastic**	**Macro-F1**	**Team**	**F-PN**	**Macro-F1**
BhamNLP	0.6225	0.7268	CS-UM6P	0.7480	0.6625
SPPU-AASM	0.6140	0.7096	**DeepBlueAI**	**0.7392**	**0.6570**
DeepBlueAI	**0.6127**	**0.7310**	rematchka	0.7321	0.6587
CS-UM6P	0.6000	0.7183	Phonemer	0.7255	0.6531
dalya	0.5989	0.7251	IDC	0.7190	0.6446

Table 3: Leaderboard

of training data. It indicates that the soft target predicted by the original big model contains useful information that needs to be learned.

Stacking trained models For subtask 1, we adopt a linear regression (LR) model as the final estimator to stack all the trained models with different training strategies. We train the weights of each model in LR on the training set and then use the learning weights to predict final scores of test set. We compare the result of LR model and the result of averaging all the trained models, the former one is much more better which proves the necessity of using LR estimator. Due to the imbalanced of positive and negative samples, we adjust the threshold as 0.41. Samples with predicted scores higher than 0.41 are sarcastic. For subtask 2, we train a SVM model as the final predictor to stack all the different trained models. The score of SVM is also better than the score obtained by averaging the trained models. The scores of all the ensemble methods are higher than the scores predicted by one model, this shows that stacking trained models is an effect way to further improve the system performance.

5 Official Submission

We submitted the scores predicted by the ensemble method introduced above. The official ranking have been released and the top five teams are presented in Table 3. We rank third in subtask 1 and second in subtask 2, which demonstrates the effectiveness of our system.

6 Conclusion

In this paper, we propose a top performing model for the task of Sarcasm and Sentiment Detection. We fine-tune two kinds of pre-trained language models including XLM-R and AraBERT with different training strategies contains task-adaptive pretraining and knowledge distillation. Then we stack them with a simple linear regression model in subtask 1 and a SVM model in subtask 2. Experimental results show the validity of this ensemble method and we rank third and second for subtask 1 and 2.

References

Ibrahim Abu Farha and Walid Magdy. 2020. From Arabic sentiment analysis to sarcasm detection: The ArSarcasm dataset. In *Proceedings of the 4th Workshop on Open-Source Arabic Corpora and Processing Tools, with a Shared Task on Offensive Language Detection*, pages 32–39, Marseille, France. European Language Resource Association.

Ibrahim Abu Farha, Wajdi Zaghouani, and Walid Magdy. 2021. Overview of the wanlp 2021 shared task on sarcasm and sentiment detection in arabic.

In *Proceedings of the Sixth Arabic Natural Language Processing Workshop*.

Mahmoud Al-Ayyoub, Safa Bani Essa, and Izzat Alsmadi. 2015. Lexicon-based sentiment analysis of arabic tweets. *International Journal of Social Network Mining*, 2(2):101–114.

Ahmad Al-Sallab, Ramy Baly, Hazem Hajj, Khaled Bashir Shaban, Wassim El-Hajj, and Gilbert Badaro. 2017. Aroma: A recursive deep learning model for opinion mining in arabic as a low resource language. *ACM Transactions on Asian and Low-Resource Language Information Processing (TALLIP)*, 16(4):1–20.

Mohammad Al-Smadi, Bashar Talafha, Mahmoud Al-Ayyoub, and Yaser Jararweh. 2019. Using long short-term memory deep neural networks for aspect-based sentiment analysis of arabic reviews. *International Journal of Machine Learning and Cybernetics*, 10(8):2163–2175.

Abdulaziz M Alayba, Vasile Palade, Matthew England, and Rahat Iqbal. 2017. Arabic language sentiment analysis on health services. In *2017 1st international workshop on arabic script analysis and recognition (asar)*, pages 114–118. IEEE.

Wissam Antoun, Fady Baly, and Hazem Hajj. 2020. Arabert: Transformer-based model for arabic language understanding. In *Proceedings of the 4th Workshop on Open-Source Arabic Corpora and Processing Tools, with a Shared Task on Offensive Language Detection*, pages 9–15.

Alexis Conneau, Kartikay Khandelwal, Naman Goyal, Vishrav Chaudhary, Guillaume Wenzek, Francisco Guzmán, Édouard Grave, Myle Ott, Luke Zettlemoyer, and Veselin Stoyanov. 2020. Unsupervised cross-lingual representation learning at scale. In *Proceedings of the 58th Annual Meeting of the Association for Computational Linguistics*, pages 8440–8451.

Rehab Duwairi and Mahmoud El-Orfali. 2014. A study of the effects of preprocessing strategies on sentiment analysis for arabic text. *Journal of Information Science*, 40(4):501–513.

Kariman Elshakankery and Mona F Ahmed. 2019. Hilatsa: A hybrid incremental learning approach for arabic tweets sentiment analysis. *Egyptian Informatics Journal*, 20(3):163–171.

Suchin Gururangan, Ana Marasović, Swabha Swayamdipta, Kyle Lo, Iz Beltagy, Doug Downey, and Noah A Smith. 2020. Don't stop pretraining: Adapt language models to domains and tasks. *arXiv preprint arXiv:2004.10964*.

Geoffrey Hinton, Oriol Vinyals, and Jeff Dean. 2015. Distilling the knowledge in a neural network. *arXiv preprint arXiv:1503.02531*.

Hiroshi Inoue. 2019. Multi-sample dropout for accelerated training and better generalization. *arXiv preprint arXiv:1905.09788*.

Navonil Majumder, Soujanya Poria, Haiyun Peng, Niyati Chhaya, Erik Cambria, and Alexander Gelbukh. 2019. Sentiment and sarcasm classification with multitask learning. *IEEE Intelligent Systems*, 34(3):38–43.

Mahmoud Nabil, Mohamed Aly, and Amir Atiya. 2015. Astd: Arabic sentiment tweets dataset. In *Proceedings of the 2015 conference on empirical methods in natural language processing*, pages 2515–2519.

Shereen Oraby, Yasser El-Sonbaty, and Mohamad Abou El-Nasr. 2013. Finding opinion strength using rule-based parsing for arabic sentiment analysis. In *Mexican International Conference on Artificial Intelligence*, pages 509–520. Springer.

Oumaima Oueslati, Erik Cambria, Moez Ben HajHmida, and Habib Ounelli. 2020. A review of sentiment analysis research in arabic language. *Future Generation Computer Systems*, 112:408–430.

Sara Rosenthal, Noura Farra, and Preslav Nakov. 2017. Semeval-2017 task 4: Sentiment analysis in twitter. In *Proceedings of the 11th international workshop on semantic evaluation (SemEval-2017)*, pages 502–518.

Daniel Zeman, Jan Hajic, Martin Popel, Martin Potthast, Milan Straka, Filip Ginter, Joakim Nivre, and Slav Petrov. 2018. Conll 2018 shared task: Multilingual parsing from raw text to universal dependencies. In *Proceedings of the CoNLL 2018 Shared Task: Multilingual parsing from raw text to universal dependencies*, pages 1–21.

AraBERT and Farasa Segmentation Based Approach For Sarcasm and Sentiment Detection in Arabic Tweets

Anshul Wadhawan
Flipkart Private Limited
anshul.wadhwan@flipkart.com

Abstract

This paper presents our strategy to tackle the EACL WANLP-2021 Shared Task 2: Sarcasm and Sentiment Detection. One of the subtasks aims at developing a system that identifies whether a given Arabic tweet is sarcastic in nature or not, while the other aims to identify the sentiment of the Arabic tweet. We approach the task in two steps. The first step involves pre processing the provided ArSarcasm-v2 dataset by performing insertions, deletions and segmentation operations on various parts of the text. The second step involves experimenting with multiple variants of two transformer based models, AraELECTRA and AraBERT. Our final approach was ranked seventh and fourth in the Sarcasm and Sentiment Detection subtasks respectively.

1 Introduction

During the last two decades, work on subjective language processing has been very common in literature. The work on sentiment analysis was a major theme that was pursued during this time. Sentiment Analysis is a process, according to (Liu, 2012), in which we extract out and examine the emotional stance in a particular piece of text. With the introduction of user-driven networks such as websites for social media, the work on Sentiment Analysis flourished. Most of this work was based on English, while not much attention was gathered by the Arabic language. The work on Arabic Sentiment Analysis was initiated by (Abdul-Mageed et al., 2011), but as compared to English it still needs development. This can be due to the many complexities pertaining to the language, including the broad range of dialects (Shaalan, 2010; Darwish, 2014) and the complicated language morphology (Abdul-Mageed et al., 2011). Some of the prominent problems while tackling the task of Sentiment Analysis are domain dependency, negation handling, lack of sarcasm and knowledge (Hussein, 2018). Sarcasm is described as a form of verbal irony designed to convey disdain or ridicule (Joshi et al., 2017). There has been a lot of work on the identification of English sarcasm, including datasets, like the works of (Barbieri et al., 2014b; Ghosh et al., 2015; Abercrombie and Hovy, 2016; Filatova, 2012; Joshi et al., 2016; Barbieri et al., 2014a) and detection systems like (Joshi et al., 2015; Rajadesingan et al., 2015; Amir et al., 2016). Work on Arabic sarcasm is, to our knowledge, restricted to the work of (Karoui et al., 2017), an irony detection task (Ghanem et al., 2019), and sarcasm datasets by (Abbes et al., 2020; Abu Farha and Magdy, 2020).

This paper puts forth the approach we applied to handle the WANLP-2021 Shared Task 2. The paper is ordered in the following manner: The problem statement, along with details of the ArSarcasm-v2 dataset are presented in Section 2. The methodology that we propose as our solution is described in Section 3. The experiments which were carried out, dataset statistics, system settings and results of the experiments are provided in Section 4. The paper ends with a brief section that talks about the conclusion and future directions of our research, in section 5.

2 Task Definition

The WANLP-2021 Shared Task 2 (Abu Farha et al., 2021) is based on a text classification problem, based on identifying sentiment and sarcasm in Arabic tweets. The provided training and test datasets have a total of 12,548 and 3,000 tweets respectively.

The shared task is divided into two subtasks:

Subtask 1 (Sarcasm Detection): The aim is to identify whether a tweet is sarcastic or not. Given a tweet, the task is to return TRUE if there is sarcasm present in the tweet and FALSE otherwise. This is

Proceedings of the Sixth Arabic Natural Language Processing Workshop, pages 395–400
Kyiv, Ukraine (Virtual), April 19, 2021.

a binary classification problem. Precision/Recall/F-score/Accuracy are the evaluation metrics, where F-score of the sarcastic class is the official metric of evaluation.

Subtask 2 (Sentiment Analysis): The aim is to identify the sentiment of a tweet by assigning one of three labels (Positive, Negative, Neutral). Given a tweet, the task is to return POS if the tweet has a positive sentiment, NEG if the tweet has a negative sentiment or NEU if the tweet has a neutral sentiment. This is a multiclass classification problem. Precision/Recall/F-score/Accuracy are the evaluation metrics, where macro average of the F-score of the positive and negative classes (F-PN) is the official metric of evaluation.

3 Methodology

This section describes the process we employed to tackle the task. The process is divided into two steps: data preprocessing and transformer based models application. The first step involves processing the provided ArSarcasm-v2 dataset to convert it into a format better processed by the models. The second step involves experimenting with different models to decide which model performs the best for the ArSarcasm-v2 dataset. Details about these steps have been provided in the following sub-sections.

3.1 Data Pre-Processing

The data that is used for pre training the transformer based models is processed to create a better representation of the data. Thus, for the models to perform at their best ability, the data has to be processed in the same manner in the fine tuning process also. Raw data that is fetched from social media websites is diverse due to vast differences in expressions of opinions among users from different parts of the world. ArSarcasm-v2 dataset has these variations in different forms, evident from manual analysis. Social media users often make use of slang words, and non ascii characters such as emojis. URLs, user mentions and spelling errors are prominent in many posts on social media platforms. These attributes do not qualify as discerning features for classification tasks like Sarcasm and Sentiment Detection, and contribute to noise within the dataset. Therefore, we employ different pre processing techniques to clear this noise, so that the transformer based models only receive the relevant features. These techniques are as follows:

1. Remove HTML line breaks and markup, unwanted characters like emoticons, repeated characters (> 2) and extra spaces.
2. Perform Farasa segmentation (for select models only) (Abdelali et al., 2016).
3. Insert whitespace before and after all non Arabic digits or English Digits and Alphabet and the 2 brackets, and between words and numbers or numbers and words.
4. Replace all URLs with [رابط], emails with [بريد], mentions with [مستخدم].

3.2 Transformer Based Models

Deep learning methods have shown promising results in different machine learning domains such as Computer Vision (Krizhevsky et al., 2012) and Speech Recognition (Graves et al., 2013). The traditional machine learning methods have been over taken by deep learning techniques in the recent past, because of their superior performance owing to architectures inspired by the human brain. On the lines of Natural Language Processing, most deep learning techniques have been making use of word vector representations (Yih et al., 2011; Bengio et al., 2003; Mikolov et al., 2013) mainly as a way of representing the textual inputs. These techniques are further being replaced by transformer based techniques (Vaswani et al., 2017) due to significant improvements on most NLP tasks like text classification (Chang et al., 2020), which is the task at hand. Transformer based techniques have the ability to produce efficient embeddings as an output of the pre training process, which makes them proficient language models.

3.2.1 AraBERT

(Antoun et al.) Pre trained to handle Arabic text, AraBERT is a language model that is inspired from the Google's BERT architecture. Six variants of the same model are available for esxperimentation: AraBERTv0.2-base, AraBERTv1-base, AraBERTv0.1-base, AraBERTv2-large, AraBERTv0.2-large, and AraBERTv2-base. The architectural attributes of each of these models have been highlighted in Table 1.

3.2.2 AraELECTRA

(Antoun et al., 2020) With reduced computations for pre training the transformers, ELECTRA is a method aimed towards the task of self-supervised

Model	Size		Pre-Segmentation	Dataset		
	MB	Params		#Sentences	Size	#Words
AraBERTv0.1-base	543MB	136M	No	77M	23GB	2.7B
AraBERTv1-base	543MB	136M	Yes	77M	23GB	2.7B
AraBERTv0.2-base	543MB	136M	No	200M	77GB	8.6B
AraBERTv0.2-large	1.38G	371M	No	200M	77GB	8.6B
AraBERTv2-base	543MB	136M	Yes	200M	77GB	8.6B
AraBERTv2-large	1.38G	371M	Yes	200M	77GB	8.6B

Table 1: Architectural Attributes of Models

language representation learning. ELECTRA models are inspired from the two primary components of Generative Adversarial Networks: generator and discriminator. They aim at distinguishing between real input tokens and the fake ones. These models have shown convincing state-of-the art results on Arabic QA data.

For the pretraining process of all new AraBERT and AraELECTRA models, the same data is used, which has a size of 77GB. It has in total 8,655,948,860 words or 82,232,988,358 characters or 200,095,961 lines, before Farasa segmentation. For an initial pre training dataset, several websites were crawled, which are: Assafir news articles, OSCAR unshuffled and filtered, The OSIAN Corpus, Arabic Wikipedia dump from 2020/09/01, and The 1.5B words Arabic Corpus. For newer models, a fresh dataset was developed for the pre training process, which did not include the data crawled from the above websites, but had unshuffled and properly filtered OSCAR corpus in addition to the dataset used in AraBERTv1.

4 Experiments

We split the provided training dataset in a 90:10 ratio to create our training and validation splits. This is followed by experimenting with eight transformer based models, for which performance on the validation split is compared. The pre trained models are fine tuned on the training split and metrics for the validation split are calculated. The final test set predictions are made from the model that performs the best on the validation split, among the eight models. This section includes the dataset distribution, system settings, results and a brief analysis of the system, for both the subtasks: sarcasm and sentiment detection.

	Sarcasm		Total
	FALSE	TRUE	
Train	9356	1937	11293
Dev	1024	231	1255
Total	10380	2168	12548

Table 2: Data Distribution w.r.t Sarcasm

	Sentiment			Total
	NEG	NEU	POS	
Train	4139	5197	1957	11293
Dev	482	550	223	1255
Total	4621	5747	2180	12548

Table 3: Data Distribution w.r.t Sentiment

4.1 Dataset

Tables 2 and 3 show the class wise distribution of the 90:10 training-validation splits created from the provided ArSarcasm-v2 dataset, for the tasks of sarcasm detection which has class labels TRUE and FALSE and sentiment detection which has class labels NEG, NEU and POS, respectively.

4.2 System Settings

We make use of hugging-face[1] API to fetch the pre-trained AraBERT and AraELECTRA models. The API provides the six variants of AraBERT

[1] `https://huggingface.co/transformers/`

Parameter	Value
Epsilon (Adam optimizer)	1e-8
Learning Rate	1e-5
Batch Size (for base models)	40
Batch Size (for large models)	4
Maximum Sequence Length	256
#Epochs	10

Table 4: Parameter Values

Model	Subtask 1				Subtask 2			
	P	R	F1	A	P	R	F1	A
AraBERTv0.1-base	84.15	84.62	84.36	84.62	72.38	72.43	72.40	72.43
AraBERTv0.2-base	84.31	85.42	84.62	85.42	74.90	74.98	74.90	74.98
AraBERTv0.2-large	84.57	85.90	84.63	85.90	76.25	76.41	76.20	76.41
AraBERTv1-base	84.73	85.02	84.86	85.02	73.27	73.55	73.17	73.55
AraBERTv2-base	85.39	85.74	85.55	85.74	75.93	75.86	75.89	75.86
AraBERTv2-large	85.16	86.37	85.07	86.37	74.28	74.50	74.31	74.50
AraELECTRA-base-generator	82.72	83.19	82.94	83.19	72.45	72.03	71.99	72.03
AraELECTRA-base-discriminator	84.75	85.34	84.99	85.34	74.70	74.82	74.57	74.82

Table 5: Results on Validation Set

models by the names of bert-base-arabertv02, bert-base-arabert, bert-base-arabertv2, bert-base-arabertv01, bert-large-arabertv2, and bert-large-arabertv02, and the two variants of AraELECTRA models by the names of araelectra-base-discriminator and araelectra-base-generator. We fine tune these models on the training split with hyper parameter values specified in Table 4.

4.3 Results and Analysis

This section provides the detailed results obtained on the created validation and provided test sets.

4.3.1 Validation Set Results

The experimental results in terms of weighted Precision(P), weighted F1 scores(F1), weighted Recall(R) and Accuracy(A) on the created validation split have been depicted in Table 5, for both subtasks: Sarcasm Detection (Subtask 1) and Sentiment Detection (Subtask 2).

Our observations from Table 5 are as follows:

1. When comparing all the models, AraELECTRA generator model has the worst performance in terms of both F1 scores and Accuracy, for both the subtasks. This is possibly due to its forte of handling GAN related tasks rather than general classification tasks.

2. When comparing all AraBERT models, one of the large models seem to perform the best in terms of accuracy for both the subtasks. This is possibly due to superior architectures and heavier models.

3. For Subtask 1, AraBERTv2-base has the highest weighted F1-score and for Subtask 2, AraBERTv0.2-large has the highest weighted F1-score.

	C_E	A	P	R	M-F1
$T_S{}^1$	58.72	78.30	72.64	71.47	72.00
$T_S{}^2$	72.55	69.83	65.15	66.23	65.31

Table 6: Official Results on Test Set

4.3.2 Test Set Results

From the above observations, we select AraBERTv2-base for Subtask 1 and AraBERTv0.2-large for Subtask 2 as final models to formulate our officially submitted predictions. Table 6 presents the final test set results, with $T_S{}^1$ denoting Subtask 1, $T_S{}^2$ denoting Subtask 2, P denoting Precision, R denoting Recall, A denoting Accuracy, M-F1 denoting Macro-F1 score, and C_E denoting the criteria of evaluation for the two subtasks (F-score of the sarcastic class for $T_S{}^1$, and Macro averaged F score of positive and negative classes for $T_S{}^2$).

5 Conclusion and Future Work

In this paper, we present our strategy to approach the EACL WANLP-2021 Shared Task 2. We tackle the task in two steps. In the first step, the ArSarcasm-v2 dataset is pre-processed by altering different parts of text. This is followed by running experiments with multiple variants of two transformer based models pre-trained on Arabic text, AraELECTRA and AraBERT. The final submissions for the tasks of Sarcasm and Sentiment Detection are based on that variant of model which performs the best. Our approach fetches a private leaderboard rank 7 and 4 in the Sarcasm and Sentiment Detection tasks respectively. As future scope, we plan to explore other features which may be relevant for this task, and inculcate ensemble learning taking into consideration both word vector based and transformer based embeddings.

References

Ines Abbes, Wajdi Zaghouani, Omaima El-Hardlo, and Faten Ashour. 2020. DAICT: A dialectal Arabic irony corpus extracted from Twitter. In *Proceedings of the 12th Language Resources and Evaluation Conference*, pages 6265–6271, Marseille, France. European Language Resources Association.

Ahmed Abdelali, Kareem Darwish, Nadir Durrani, and Hamdy Mubarak. 2016. Farasa: A fast and furious segmenter for Arabic. In *Proceedings of the 2016 Conference of the North American Chapter of the Association for Computational Linguistics: Demonstrations*, pages 11–16, San Diego, California. Association for Computational Linguistics.

Muhammad Abdul-Mageed, Mona Diab, and Mohammed Korayem. 2011. Subjectivity and sentiment analysis of Modern Standard Arabic. In *Proceedings of the 49th Annual Meeting of the Association for Computational Linguistics: Human Language Technologies*, pages 587–591, Portland, Oregon, USA. Association for Computational Linguistics.

Gavin Abercrombie and Dirk Hovy. 2016. Putting sarcasm detection into context: The effects of class imbalance and manual labelling on supervised machine classification of Twitter conversations. In *Proceedings of the ACL 2016 Student Research Workshop*, pages 107–113, Berlin, Germany. Association for Computational Linguistics.

Ibrahim Abu Farha and Walid Magdy. 2020. From Arabic sentiment analysis to sarcasm detection: The ArSarcasm dataset. In *Proceedings of the 4th Workshop on Open-Source Arabic Corpora and Processing Tools, with a Shared Task on Offensive Language Detection*, pages 32–39, Marseille, France. European Language Resource Association.

Ibrahim Abu Farha, Wajdi Zaghouani, and Walid Magdy. 2021. Overview of the wanlp 2021 shared task on sarcasm and sentiment detection in arabic. In *Proceedings of the Sixth Arabic Natural Language Processing Workshop*.

Silvio Amir, Byron C. Wallace, Hao Lyu, Paula Carvalho, and Mário J. Silva. 2016. Modelling context with user embeddings for sarcasm detection in social media. In *Proceedings of The 20th SIGNLL Conference on Computational Natural Language Learning*, pages 167–177, Berlin, Germany. Association for Computational Linguistics.

Wissam Antoun, Fady Baly, and Hazem Hajj. Arabert: Transformer-based model for arabic language understanding. In *LREC 2020 Workshop Language Resources and Evaluation Conference 11–16 May 2020*, page 9.

Wissam Antoun, Fady Baly, and Hazem Hajj. 2020. Araelectra: Pre-training text discriminators for arabic language understanding.

Francesco Barbieri, Francesco Ronzano, and Horacio Saggion. 2014a. Italian irony detection in twitter: a first approach.

Francesco Barbieri, Horacio Saggion, and Francesco Ronzano. 2014b. Modelling sarcasm in Twitter, a novel approach. In *Proceedings of the 5th Workshop on Computational Approaches to Subjectivity, Sentiment and Social Media Analysis*, pages 50–58, Baltimore, Maryland. Association for Computational Linguistics.

Yoshua Bengio, Réjean Ducharme, Pascal Vincent, and Christian Janvin. 2003. A neural probabilistic language model. *J. Mach. Learn. Res.*, 3(null):1137–1155.

Wei-Cheng Chang, Hsiang-Fu Yu, Kai Zhong, Yiming Yang, and Inderjit Dhillon. 2020. Taming pretrained transformers for extreme multi-label text classification.

Kareem Darwish. 2014. Arabic information retrieval. *Foundations and Trends® in Information Retrieval*, 7:239–342.

Elena Filatova. 2012. Irony and sarcasm: Corpus generation and analysis using crowdsourcing. In *Proceedings of the Eighth International Conference on Language Resources and Evaluation (LREC'12)*, pages 392–398, Istanbul, Turkey. European Language Resources Association (ELRA).

Bilal Ghanem, Jihen Karoui, Farah Benamara, Véronique Moriceau, and Paolo Rosso. 2019. Idat at fire2019: Overview of the track on irony detection in arabic tweets. In *Proceedings of the 11th Forum for Information Retrieval Evaluation*, FIRE '19, page 10–13, New York, NY, USA. Association for Computing Machinery.

Debanjan Ghosh, Weiwei Guo, and Smaranda Muresan. 2015. Sarcastic or not: Word embeddings to predict the literal or sarcastic meaning of words. In *Proceedings of the 2015 Conference on Empirical Methods in Natural Language Processing*, pages 1003–1012, Lisbon, Portugal. Association for Computational Linguistics.

Alex Graves, Abdel rahman Mohamed, and Geoffrey Hinton. 2013. Speech recognition with deep recurrent neural networks.

Doaa Mohey El-Din Mohamed Hussein. 2018. A survey on sentiment analysis challenges. *Journal of King Saud University - Engineering Sciences*, 30(4):330–338.

Aditya Joshi, Pushpak Bhattacharyya, and Mark J. Carman. 2017. Automatic sarcasm detection: A survey. *ACM Comput. Surv.*, 50(5).

Aditya Joshi, Vinita Sharma, and Pushpak Bhattacharyya. 2015. Harnessing context incongruity for sarcasm detection. In *Proceedings of the 53rd Annual Meeting of the Association for Computational*

Linguistics and the 7th International Joint Conference on Natural Language Processing (Volume 2: Short Papers), pages 757–762, Beijing, China. Association for Computational Linguistics.

Aditya Joshi, Vaibhav Tripathi, Pushpak Bhattacharyya, and Mark J. Carman. 2016. Harnessing sequence labeling for sarcasm detection in dialogue from TV series 'Friends'. In *Proceedings of The 20th SIGNLL Conference on Computational Natural Language Learning*, pages 146–155, Berlin, Germany. Association for Computational Linguistics.

Jihen Karoui, Farah Banamara Zitoune, and Véronique Moriceau. 2017. Soukhria: Towards an irony detection system for arabic in social media. *Procedia Computer Science*, 117:161–168. Arabic Computational Linguistics.

Alex Krizhevsky, Ilya Sutskever, and Geoffrey E. Hinton. 2012. Imagenet classification with deep convolutional neural networks. In *Proceedings of the 25th International Conference on Neural Information Processing Systems - Volume 1*, NIPS'12, page 1097–1105, Red Hook, NY, USA. Curran Associates Inc.

Bing Liu. 2012. Sentiment analysis and opinion mining. volume 5.

Tomas Mikolov, Ilya Sutskever, Kai Chen, Greg Corrado, and Jeffrey Dean. 2013. Distributed representations of words and phrases and their compositionality. In *Proceedings of the 26th International Conference on Neural Information Processing Systems - Volume 2*, NIPS'13, page 3111–3119, Red Hook, NY, USA. Curran Associates Inc.

Ashwin Rajadesingan, Reza Zafarani, and Huan Liu. 2015. Sarcasm detection on twitter: A behavioral modeling approach. In *Proceedings of the Eighth ACM International Conference on Web Search and Data Mining*, WSDM '15, page 97–106, New York, NY, USA. Association for Computing Machinery.

Khaled Shaalan. 2010. Nizar y. habash, introduction to arabic natural language processing (synthesis lectures on human language technologies). *Machine Translation*, 24(3–4):285–289.

Ashish Vaswani, Noam Shazeer, Niki Parmar, Jakob Uszkoreit, Llion Jones, Aidan N. Gomez, Lukasz Kaiser, and Illia Polosukhin. 2017. Attention is all you need.

Wen-tau Yih, Kristina Toutanova, John C. Platt, and Christopher Meek. 2011. Learning discriminative projections for text similarity measures. In *Proceedings of the Fifteenth Conference on Computational Natural Language Learning*, pages 247–256, Portland, Oregon, USA. Association for Computational Linguistics.